# Global Derivatives

Visit the *Global Derivatives: A Strategic Risk Management Perspective* Companion Website at **www.pearsoned.co.uk/andersen** to find valuable **student** learning material including:

- Downloadable statistical tables for use in the practical application of models described in the book
- An online glossary to explain key terms

**PEARSON**
Education

We work with leading authors to develop the
strongest educational materials in finance and
management, bringing cutting-edge thinking and
best learning practice to a global market.

Under a range of well-known imprints, including
Financial Times Prentice Hall, we craft high quality print and
electronic publications which help readers to understand
and apply their content, whether studying or at work.

To find out more about the complete range of our
publishing, please visit us on the World Wide Web at:
www.pearsoned.co.uk

# Global Derivatives

## A Strategic Risk Management Perspective

Torben Juul Andersen

FINANCIAL TIMES

An imprint of **Pearson Education**

Harlow, England • London • New York • Boston • San Francisco • Toronto • Sydney • Singapore • Hong Kong
Tokyo • Seoul • Taipei • New Delhi • Cape Town • Madrid • Mexico City • Amsterdam • Munich • Paris • Milan

**Pearson Education Limited**

Edinburgh Gate
Harlow
Essex CM20 2JE
England

and Associated Companies throughout the world

*Visit us on the World Wide Web at:*
www.pearsoned.co.uk

First published 2006

© Pearson Education Limited 2006

ISBN 978-0-273-68854-9

**British Library Cataloguing-in-Publication Data**
A catalogue record for this book is available from the British Library

**Library of Congress Cataloging-in-Publication Data**
A catalog record for this book is available from the Library of Congress

10  9  8  7  6  5  4  3
10  09

Typeset in 10/12pt ITC Century Book by 35
Printed and bound in Malaysia, KHL (CTP)

*The publisher's policy is to use paper manufactured from sustainable forests.*

# Contents

## Part 1 Global markets and strategic risk exposures

### 1 International flow of funds, interest rate structure, and default spreads

## Supporting resources

Visit **www.pearsoned.co.uk/andersen** to find valuable online resources

### Companion Website for students

- Downloadable statistical tables for use in the practical application of models described in the book
- An online glossary to explain key terms

### For instructors

- Complete, downloadable Instructor's Manual containing solutions to end of chapter questions and exercises found in the book
- PowerPoint slides that can be downloaded and used as OHTs

For more information please contact your local Pearson Education sales representative or visit **www.pearsoned.co.uk/andersen**

# List of figures

# List of tables

# Preface

Derivatives in different shades and forms constitute an increasingly important element of the global business environment. A recent survey indicated that more than 90% of the world's largest companies headquartered in different countries around the globe use derivatives to manage their manifold risk exposures.[1] These findings illustrate the significance of derivatives as an integral part of corporate risk management practices among leading international companies that operate across national boundaries and industrial sectors. A majority of companies use derivatives to hedge the risks that expose their ordinary lines of business, such as, interest rate, currency, and commodity risks but the scope of derivatives extend far beyond the common use of traded derivative instruments. Periodic assessments of the development in international markets for derivative instruments indicate an exponential growth across different types of derivatives leaving the notional amount of outstanding derivatives at impressive levels comparable to the aggregate credit extension in the global capital market.[2] The growth patterns also indicate that the emergence of derivatives associated with credit and related business exposures, that are harder to quantify, has been expanding at particularly high growth rates underscoring the potential use of derivatives in business related and strategic contexts.

In view of the increasing global use of derivative instruments, opinions about their potential benefits have been surprisingly varied. Some see derivatives as 'time bombs . . . financial weapons of mass destruction, carrying dangers that, while now latent, are potentially lethal'.[3] Granted, many companies have failed their risk management obligations over the past decades and mismanaged the use of traded derivatives while ignoring underlying corporate exposures. These examples remind us that there is a need to understand the concrete underpinnings of derivative structures and their practical applications in institutional settings. However, when handled appropriately, derivatives can be effective tools to manage the residual risk exposures assumed by both financial intermediaries and multinational corporations emphasizing why risk management constitutes an essential element of the strategic management process. Hence, other people find that 'derivative instruments provide significant benefits to corporations, financial institutions, and institutional investors by allowing them to isolate and manage risks associated with their business activities'[4] and see the emergence of more complex financial derivatives as essential 'to the development of a far more flexible, efficient and resilient financial system'.[5] These views point toward a fundamental need to better understand the potential use of derivatives and expanding the scope of derivative instruments to reap the positive economic effects from strategic risk management approaches.

The emergence of derivative instruments and associated risk management techniques has its origin in the financial industry among credit intermediaries in the global capital market. Many such initiatives developed as means to circumvent market imperfections and achieve more favorable funding arrangements and have frequently evolved into markets trading generic contractual arrangements that allow market participants to modify exposures and hedge risk positions. Exchange traded derivatives have attracted natural counterparts, such as borrowers and lenders, and thereby established marketplaces for the exchange of countervailing financial positions. With an emphasis on lending and depositor protection in the regulated banking sector, the conventional risk management approaches have typically focused on downside risk avoidance. However, given the importance of investors as providers of market liquidity, the essence of risk management arguably has to do with the ability to gain upside potential within reasonable downside risk parameters. As the risk management perspective is extended beyond price volatility effects to comprise, e.g. operational and technology exposures, the relationship between risk management and upside potential becomes more apparent. For example, creating general risk awareness and imposing total quality management approaches to deal with operational exposures may contribute to the development of continuous improvement initiatives that enhance internal efficiencies and circumvent extreme loss situations. The imposition of new technology is an essential strategic issue across the data intensive financial industry but also constitutes an exposure that affects participants in most other industries. These types of high-risk irreversible investment scenarios may be dealt with by adopting an options perspective and reason around real option structures that identify the resource committing decisions. This way of conceiving specific institutional derivatives constitutes a promising risk management approach to deal with strategic risk exposures.

The continued globalization of the business environment has expanded commercial and financial cross-border interactions and has intensified the related commodity, interest rate, and currency exposures. All the while the establishment of globally networked organizational structures has introduced new significant risk factors. For example, the ability to outsource essential business processes to business partners located in cost efficient national markets reduces fixed asset commitments and increases flexibility. However, it also introduces new operational and strategic counter-party risks that must be taken into consideration. With the emergence of globally intertwined market activities, potential adverse effects associated with operational disruptions, political risk, negative publicity and reputation risk increases. Locating productive assets in low cost emerging market environments may also increase exposures to extreme natural hazards as well as terrorist events can hit essential resources of multinational companies in different locations around the globe. A common characteristic of many of these new risk factors deriving from the global competitive setting is that they are harder to quantify and yet represent highly significant exposures that must be dealt with. Hence, it seems like some of the most important risk exposures often are of a less quantifiable nature. One aspect of 'hypercompetitive' conditions where change may be frequent and abrupt is that many risk events cannot be foreseen in advance. These situations require a different type of strategic responsiveness based on risk awareness, information processing capabilities, effective communication systems, fast decision structures, and general event preparedness.

In view of the global nature of commercial and financial market activities, the analysis of financial derivatives as well as overall risk management approaches cannot be confined to a national market perspective. Various derivatives are related through an intricate web of global cross-border transactions. As a consequence, management students, financial managers, and corporate executives can benefit from a better understanding of the role played by global derivatives in this context. This book aims to satisfy the need to understand the basic mechanics of different derivative instruments while extending the scope to a strategic risk management perspective. Hence, the book introduces derivatives in an international setting while considering competitive and institutional market developments. However, the book goes well beyond a mere description of derivative instruments and the markets that trade them. There is an equal emphasis on the practical application of derivatives and their actual uses in business transactions and corporate risk management situations.

## Audience

The content and structure of the book has been inspired by developments in the international financial markets observed over the past two decades and various finance and strategy courses taught to diverse audiences of undergraduate, graduate, and executive MBA students. Hence, the topical framing adopted in the book should be relevant for anybody aspiring to work in a managerial capacity in the contemporary global business environment whether as a manager in a financial institution, in a finance department, or in an international business unit. The content should be relevant whether the management challenge resides within the financial sector or a multinational business faced with global economic exposures. Hence, the book applies to most business students that have a finance and managerial focus and to general managers in need of an update on current risk management issues. The book can be used in courses on derivative instruments for students in a finance concentration. It may also serve as a complementary textbook in courses like global capital markets, international financial management, multinational business management, and strategic risk management as a source on global derivatives markets and their applications in corporate risk management. Furthermore, the book should cater to a wider audience of practicing managers and executives that feel a need to understand current developments in the global derivatives markets and assume state-of-the-art insights on strategic risk management issues.

Throughout the book chapters there are inserts covering areas for readers that want to obtain a higher degree of specialization. However, the inserts can be skipped without loss of continuity and understanding. Hence, executives that initially have an interest in gaining a general overview of the topic may skip inserts during a first reading and revert to them later for more thorough studies on an as-need basis. Different sections of the book may also serve classes with a different focus on derivative instruments. For example, one course may emphasize the mechanics of the derivatives markets while another is more focused on corporate risk management. These classes could also be organized as sequential course offerings, e.g. to undergraduate students, based on different parts of the same book. For graduate-level classes the book with its inserts can serve as a comprehensive source on global derivatives markets, the underlying pricing mechanisms, and the practical utilization of derivative instruments.

## Distinguishing features

The book presents derivative instruments in the context of developments in the international financial markets and discusses their use on the basis of current risk-transfer techniques. The text describes the dynamics of international trade and financial flows that affect the pricing of derivatives and explains the inner workings of the derivatives markets. The book illustrates how derivatives are applied in practice based on modern strategic risk management approaches. The book provides an overview of various derivative instruments to business students and managers that want to acquire a more holistic view of derivatives in a global market context and develop hands-on techniques for managerial applications.

The book covers all essential aspects of global derivatives and their actual applications in risk management but the coverage is unique in a number of ways:

- There is a focus on exchange traded as well as over-the-counter derivatives.
- The development of derivative instruments is seen in a global market perspective.
- There is a discussion of current market developments and competitive trends.
- The text offers a comprehensive overview of alternative instruments and markets.
- There is an emphasis on the practical applications of derivative instruments.
- The use of derivatives in corporate risk management is rich on illustrations and examples.
- There is a discussion of strategic risk factors and applications of real option structures.
- The derivatives perspective is extended to contemporary strategic management issues.

These distinct features of the text make the book very suitable for students aspiring to work in the dynamic global business environment whether this will take place within a financial institution or a multinational corporation. The book also provides a good platform for practicing managers faced with the complexities of global competition and who want to gain insights into contemporary strategic risk management approaches.

The book is structured around specific themes organized into four parts:

Part 1   Global markets and strategic risk exposures
Part 2   Exchange traded and OTC derivatives
Part 3   Hedging with financial derivatives
Part 4   Strategic risk management.

Part 1 provides an overview of essential parameters in the global economy that impose strategic risk exposures on institutions operating internationally and affect the fundamental pricing relationships of the derivatives. Part 2 describes the different types of derivative instruments and the mechanics of the markets that trade them. Part 3 looks at the practical application of derivative instruments to hedge financial risk exposures and support corporate risk management processes. Part 4 focuses attention on the harder to quantify competitive and strategic risk factors and introduces approaches to deal with these types of exposures.

The different parts of the book may be studied independently, for example, an undergraduate introductory course may use Parts 1 and 2 to lay the foundations for a deeper understanding of the derivatives markets whereas Parts 3 and 4 may be used in a subsequent course focused on practical applications of different derivatives and developing the strategic risk management perspective further. In graduate courses certain chapters may be skipped to adapt the readings to a specific course format. If the class requires completion of prior foundation courses, e.g. international finance, global capital markets, etc., elements of the first part may be skipped using these chapters only on an as-needed basis, so the course can be focused more on corporate risk issues and strategic risk management practices. Conversely, if the students lack some of the fundamental prerequisite skills, the book can serve as a good entry point where Part 1 provides a thorough treatment of fundamental market relationships while skipping the last chapters, so the course puts less emphasis on the strategic risk management perspectives. In short, the different parts of the book may be used flexibly to underpin the specific course being planned. The book provides a cohesive overview of the important aspects of global derivatives and their role in contemporary risk management practices and, therefore, may serve as a comprehensive guide to students after course completion. The book may also serve executives that are looking for a single accessible source on global derivatives and strategic risk management.

The flexible structure of the book content contained within eleven chapters makes the text suitable for courses organized around ten double class sessions (corresponding more or less to one chapter per session) or courses with twenty single class sessions (one chapter for every two sessions). However, the coverage in each of the chapters is sufficiently detailed and comprehensive to cover two double class sessions at undergraduate level foundation courses possibly complemented by other selective readings. In other words, there are many ways in which the book can support different course formats. For the course instructor, and the self-motivated reader, the study of the book should develop insights and skills that allow the student to master the following areas:

- Understand the relationships between international financial market conditions and the prices on different financial derivatives
- Determine international interest rate structures, forward money market, forward foreign exchange rates, interest rate and currency swap spreads
- Gain a comprehensive overview of the wide diversity of financial derivatives being offered in the global market environment
- Appreciate the mechanics and interrelationships between exchange traded contracts and derivative instruments offered over-the-counter
- See derivatives as an element of the global capital market and understand the role of the implied risk-transfer in the international credit intermediation process
- Identify and discuss major competitive market developments and regulatory issues relating to derivatives and their utilization
- Price and analyze different plain-vanilla instruments as well as more exotic derivatives including firm specific real option structures
- Use derivative instruments to hedge and manage basic commercial transactions and underlying financial exposures
- Use derivatives to manage institutional risk exposures, e.g. institutional investors, financial institutions, multinational corporations, etc.
- Identify essential strategic risk exposures and use the derivatives perspective in strategic risk management

Hence, the book should provide its readers with a thorough understanding of instruments and practices in the global derivatives markets and develop an ability to apply a diversity of derivative instruments in contemporary investment, funding, and economic exposure situations.

# Acknowledgements

I would like to thank Justinia Seaman, acquisition editor at Pearson Education, for her challenge to develop this book and carrying it to its final completion. I am also indebted to Stephanie Poulter and Sarah Wild who provided invaluable support in the editing and proofreading of the manuscript. I owe thanks to many individuals who over time have ignited my professional interests and inspired my personal development. I was fortunate to work in the encouraging international environment of the Citicorp organization through the formative years of the over-the-counter derivatives markets and had the opportunity to operate in the Euromarket in its heyday. In my academic studies I remain indebted to Hugh O'Neill for his unabated support, Richard Bettis for contributing his valuable insights into finance and strategic management issues, and to David Ravenscraft and Robert Connolly who enlisted me in a one-man class in real options at UNC Chapel Hill. I also appreciate the fruitful discussions with Clas Wihlborg and Nicolai Foss here at the Copenhagen Business School as work on this book progressed. Frances Maloy at the University of Washington and three anonymous reviewers acting on behalf of Pearson Education provided useful feedback to initial drafts of the book for which I am thankful. Finally, I wish to thank the numerous students at George Mason University, Johns Hopkins University, and the Copenhagen Business School who bore the burden of testing different parts of the current text in various classes and provided feedback in those teaching situations. However, any discrepancies that may remain in the text are all of my own doing.

## Notes

[1] A survey conducted by the International Swaps and Derivatives Association (ISDA) and released at its annual general meeting (2003).
[2] The Bank for International Settlements, Central Bank Survey of Foreign Exchange and Derivatives Market Activity in 2004.
[3] The quotes are from Warren Buffet, Chairman of Berkshire Hathaway, in his critique of the markets for financial derivatives (2003).
[4] The quotes derive from Annette L. Nazareth, Director, Division of Market Regulation of The US Securities and Exchange Commission, in her comments regarding risk management (2000).
[5] The quotes refer to Alan Greenspan, Chairman of the US Federal Reserve Bank, in his comments about the derivatives markets (2002).

# About the author

Torben Juul Andersen is Associate Professor at the Copenhagen Business School. He has been visiting professor of Strategic Management and Financial Economics at George Mason University and adjunct professor at the School of Professional Studies, Johns Hopkins University. He has acted as consultant to various multilateral institutions including the World Bank, the International Finance Corporation, the Inter-American Development Bank, and the OECD. Dr. Andersen has previously held executive positions at Citibank, N.A., Citicorp Investment Bank Ltd., SDS Securities a/s, and Unibank A/S. He was also a senior consultant with PHB Hagler Bailly Inc. He has written numerous articles in professional journals and books on corporate strategy and international financial management issues. He holds an economics degree (cand. polit.) from the University of Copenhagen, an MBA from McGill University, and a PhD from the Kenan-Flagler Business School, the University of North Carolina at Chapel Hill.

## Author's dedication

This book is dedicated to Mette, Christine, and Christian, without whose love, care, and support this book would never have materialized.

# Publisher's acknowledgments

We are grateful to the Financial Times Limited for permission to reprint the following material:

Figure 4.3 Currency futures quotes, © *Financial Times*, 18 June 2004; Figure 4.4 Interest rate futures quotes, © *Financial Times*, 18 June 2004; Figure 4.5 Bond futures quotes, © *Financial Times*, 18 June 2004; Figure 4.13 Currency options quotes, © *Financial Times*, 18 June 2004; Figure 4.14 Interest rate options quotes, © *Financial Times*, 18 June 2004; Figure 4.15 Bond options quotes, © *Financial Times*, 18 June 2004; Figure 6.5 Interest rate swaps quotes, © *Financial Times*, 18 June 2004.

# Global markets and
# strategic risk exposures

# International flow of funds, interest rate structure, and default spreads

## Objectives

- Set the context for derivative instruments in the global economy
- Outline the major cash flow patterns in international trade and investment activities
- Determine fundamental interest rate and foreign exchange rate relationships
- Derive forward–forward rates and forward foreign exchange rates
- Derive spot and forward credit spreads

## 1.1 The globalization of markets

The rapid development of international communication capabilities and increased effectiveness in transportation of commodities and people has intensified commercial interaction around the world. The ease of physical transportation and coordination of corporate activities through telecommunications has fuelled the emergence of a new type of global network economy where companies organize within truly international structures around a global network of vendors and partners.

As commercial transactions and international trade in goods and services have expanded over the past decades, so has the underlying exchange of money between participants in the global economy. Financial institutions are actively engaged in the execution of the associated monetary transactions. Economists define money by its capacity to measure and store value, and its ability to facilitate commercial interactions. Formally, money is constituted by the amount of coins and notes that circulate in an economy, the deposit balances maintained in the banking system, which to a large part is made up of transactional accounts and other types of marketable financial assets. Hence, the monetary stock is primarily made up of bank deposits, which constitute the prime vehicle for payments associated with commercial transactions. The physical attributes of money are therefore to a large extent found in the bank ledgers as electronic bits that register cash balances and changes in them as a result of commercial transactions. The banks debit and credit the deposit accounts to facilitate the exchange of cash among account holders. Accordingly, modern money is arguably the most international of all 'goods' because the electronic bits that underpin the bulk of the money supply can be transferred around the globe almost instantaneously, restricted solely by the possible imposition of regulatory restrictions. However, as international trade transactions and monetary transfers via the financial markets have been exposed to considerable liberalizations over the past decades, there has been a steady increase in cross-border commercial interactions and associated exchanges of cash flows.

This global environment has opened new ways to exploit scale and scope economies in multinational commercial structures and created new opportunities for financial institutions involved in the international payment flows and credit intermediation processes. Institutional investors now consider engagements on a global scale that expand the scope of possible investments and improve the risk–return profile of invested portfolios. Conversely, corporations consider alternative financing opportunities in the international financial markets to establish the most opportune funding structure. However, the increased volume in cross-border interactions has also imposed new financial and economic exposures to the involved parties that must be addressed. A wide range of financial instruments, commonly referred to as *derivatives*, have been developed over the past 25 years to help institutions manage these inherent risk exposures, while at the same time constituting an investment opportunity for astute investors.

## 1.2 International trade and balance of payment

Engagement in international trade transactions has a direct influence on cross-border cash flows, e.g. a seller (exporter) of goods and services requires some form of pecuniary compensation for the delivery, while the buyer (importer) somehow must honour the financial claims imposed by the seller. So, many cross-border payment transactions relate to compensation for export and import of goods and services. Obviously it is more complicated than that, because commercial entities can obtain various types of credit, e.g. short-term trade facilities or longer-term loan transactions, if they are short of cash needed for immediate payment. Some of these credit arrangements are retained in the banks' loan portfolios, while other credit instruments may be sold in the money and capital markets to institutional investors. Hence, the cross-border cash flows also stem from various financial transactions arranged between corporations and financial institutions located in different national economies and payments associated with the subsequent servicing of such credit instruments.

To the extent that a country's cross-border transactions are liberalized, economic entities in that country can freely seek commercial transactions in other national markets, and investment transactions can be carried out in different overseas markets. Liquidity surpluses may be placed in currencies that seem to provide the most promising returns while borrowing can be obtained in currencies that seem to offer the most advantageous financing costs. This environmental setting results in an intricate web of global commercial and financial transactions. Various financial intermediaries provide prices on investment and funding opportunities in different

**Figure 1.1** The balance of payment accounts

| | | Cash flow impact |
|---|---|:---:|
| Current accounts: | Export of goods | + |
| | Import of goods | − |
| | **Trade balance** | |
| | Export of services | + |
| | Import of services | − |
| | **Service balance** | |
| | Interest and dividends from foreign assets | + |
| | Interest and dividends to foreign investors | − |
| | **Income balance** | |
| | **Balance of payment current accounts** | CUR |
| Financial accounts: | Loans and investment in financial assets from overseas entities | + |
| | Foreign direct investment from abroad | + |
| | Loans and investment in financial assets to overseas' entities | − |
| | Foreign direct investment made abroad | − |
| | **Balance of payment financial accounts** | FAC |
| | Official sale of foreign exchange | + |
| | Official purchase of foreign exchange | − |
| Reserves: | **International reserve position** | RES |

currency areas and foreign exchange rates between currencies to facilitate the associated cross-border interactions. In this market-making process, financial intermediaries and other institutional participants often assume interest rate and currency positions in their attempts to take advantage of ongoing price adjustments. This combination of speculative and arbitrage transactions constitutes the larger part of the short-term cross-border cash flows.

All commercial and financial cross-border transactions to and from a specific country are recorded in the national balance of payments accounts (Figure 1.1). The balance of payments consists of **current accounts** (trade in goods and services, income, and transfers), **financial accounts** (deposit, loan, and investment transactions), and the **reserve position** made up by the country's official holdings of foreign currency assets and gold.[1] For every cross-border sale there will be a payment claim in the other direction and all trade transactions will somehow have cash payments or supporting credit arrangements attached to them. Therefore, a trade imbalance will be associated with a financial imbalance in the opposite direction. Similarly, official transactions in foreign currencies will have an opposite effect on the financial balance. As a consequence of this double entry bookkeeping system,[2] the net changes on the trade balance, financial balance, and official reserve position will all be zero.

$$\Delta CUR + \Delta FAC + \Delta RES = 0$$

or

$$\Delta CUR = -(\Delta FAC + \Delta RES)$$

Furthermore, if a country maintains a relatively stable level of official reserves ($\Delta RES = 0$), then changes in the current accounts and the financial balance will more or less be of equal size and opposite direction ($\Delta CUR = -\Delta FAC$).

The transactions registered on the balance of payment have implications for the amount of local and foreign currency that is available to the country. When economic entities in a country export goods and services they receive payments from overseas entities in the country's own currency or in foreign currencies. If the payments are made in their own currency it reduces foreign claims on the country because the foreign entities reduce their cash balances in the currency, and if the payments are made in foreign currencies it increases the country's claims on other countries because their foreign currency balances increase. In either case, the country's financial balance will register an inverse movement, i.e. as the current account will show a surplus, the financial balance will show a deficit as foreign claims on the country go down or domestic claims on foreign countries go up. Conversely, when agents in a country import goods and services they make payments to overseas entities in their own currency or in foreign currencies. If the payment is made in own currency foreign claims on the country increase, and if the payment is made in other currencies the country's claims on foreign countries will fall. Again, the financial balance will register an inverse movement, i.e. as the current accounts indicate a deficit, the financial balance will show a surplus as foreign claims on the country increase or the country's overseas claims go down (Figure 1.2). Whereas the current accounts post real economic transactions, i.e. trade and income transactions, the corresponding monetary transactions are registered on the financial accounts. Whenever overseas entities make loans or investments in the country it increases its claims on that country, and when domestic entities make loans and investments overseas it

**Figure 1.2** Current accounts and financial balance in Japan and the USA (1985–2003)

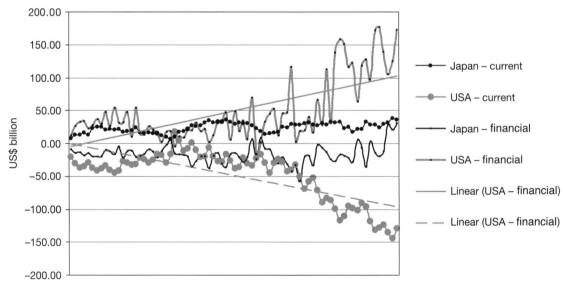

*Source*: International Monetary Fund

decreases the country's claims on foreign countries. It is common to distinguish between cross-border investment in financial assets, e.g. deposits, loans, and securities, and foreign direct investment (FDI), which constitutes the acquisition of productive assets in some form of managerial ownership capacity.[3]

The reserve accounts for the country's official reserve position in foreign currencies are usually held by the country's central bank. If the central bank increases its foreign currency balance it either buys domestic claims on foreign countries (if the foreign currencies are bought from domestic entities) or sells claims on the domestic economy to foreign countries (if the foreign currencies are bought from overseas entities against the local currency). In either case, the transaction will cause a drop in the financial balance. Conversely, if the central bank reduces its foreign currency balance it either sells claims on foreign countries (if the foreign currencies are sold to domestic entities) or buys claims on the domestic economy from foreign countries (if the foreign currencies are sold to foreign entities against the domestic currency). In either case, the transaction causes an increase in the financial balance. As a consequence, if a country's current balance deficit exceeds the financial balance surplus, it will encounter a drain on its international reserves. Conversely, a country that has a current account surplus that exceeds its financial balance deficit will accumulate international reserves.

---

### Box 1.1 Macroeconomic perspectives on the balance of payment

The international commercial and financial interactions can be expressed in terms of fundamental macroeconomic relationships. In a closed economy with no international trade, total income ($Y$) created over a certain period can be expressed as its total uses on private consumption ($C$), investment ($I$), and government spending ($G$) during that period. This is reflected in the national income identity where the total output produced corresponds to the different ways in which the output is used.

$$Y = C + I + G$$

However, in an open economy where international trade and financial transactions take place, part of the production is used overseas as goods and services are exported ($X$) while some of the goods and services consumed in the country are imported ($M$) and, therefore, produced overseas. The national income equation must reflect these cross-border trade transactions.

$$Y = C + I + G + (X - M)$$

In addition to the trade transactions, we should also account for net income payments and transfers from abroad ($R$), which similarly constitute sources of production and represent current consumption opportunities. Consequently, the national income equation would be extended as follows.

$$Y = C + I + G + (X + R - M)$$

The net amount ($X + R - M$) reflects the country's surplus on the balance of payments' current accounts.

If the current account shows a surplus, the country will accumulate more overseas financial receivables and productive resources that support future income generation, than other countries accumulate within the country. Accordingly, the country's current account surplus represents the excess of savings over investment in the economy.[4]

$$(X + R - M) = (S - I)$$

A savings surplus is generally considered a positive thing although the dynamics of the real economy exert significant influence on the relationship and distort simple conclusions. For example, a very productive economy with prospects of high future returns may attract significant overseas investment in financial and productive assets, which will cause a savings deficit. Hence, a country can have a deficit on the current accounts for long periods of time if the financial balance is supported by ingoing capital flows motivated by genuine investment prospects. This requires that overseas investors perceive the economic climate in the country as favorable.

## 1.3 Capital flows in the global economic system

In completely liberalized foreign exchange, money, and capital markets, where there are no restrictions applied to exchanges between different currency areas, financial assets and liabilities are easily switched from one currency denomination to another. In this global market setting, financial agents can engage in short-term cash transactions to take advantage of periodic changes in international financial returns and movements in foreign exchange rates. These sometimes voluminous financial flows can be further enhanced by the leading and lagging of trade- and debt-related currency payments. The foreign exchange rate movements are influenced by views on the country's fundamental economic strength and competitiveness as reflected in trade and corporate earnings developments, the country's debt burden and international reserve position, the investment outlook in the country's capital markets, inflationary expectations, etc.

The global trade pattern has assumed some persistent trends over the past decades. The United States and the United Kingdom have posted trade balance deficits whereas continental European countries, including Germany and France, have posted trade surpluses in recent years. Japan has continued to enjoy a surplus on the current accounts. Several Asian countries, e.g. China, Malaysia, and Indonesia, have posted sizeable trade balance surpluses over the past decade (Figure 1.3). Since all trade transactions are accomplished among countries within the global network, the global economy as a whole has neither trade surplus nor deficit – it is in balance. Every export from one country is matched by an import in another country and, therefore, the sum of imports and exports are the same in the global trade system. That is, if some countries have trade deficits, other countries necessarily have trade surpluses. Due to the inverse relationship between the current account and financial balance, the countries with trade deficits have surpluses on their financial accounts, and countries with trade surpluses have deficits on their financial accounts. In other words, countries with trade surpluses are financing the countries with trade deficits.

While there may be sizeable discrepancies in the trade balances between countries, the international money and capital markets, and the financial intermediaries that operate within them, serve to channel cash flows between surplus and deficit countries.

**Figure 1.3** The trade balance for selected countries (1985–2003)

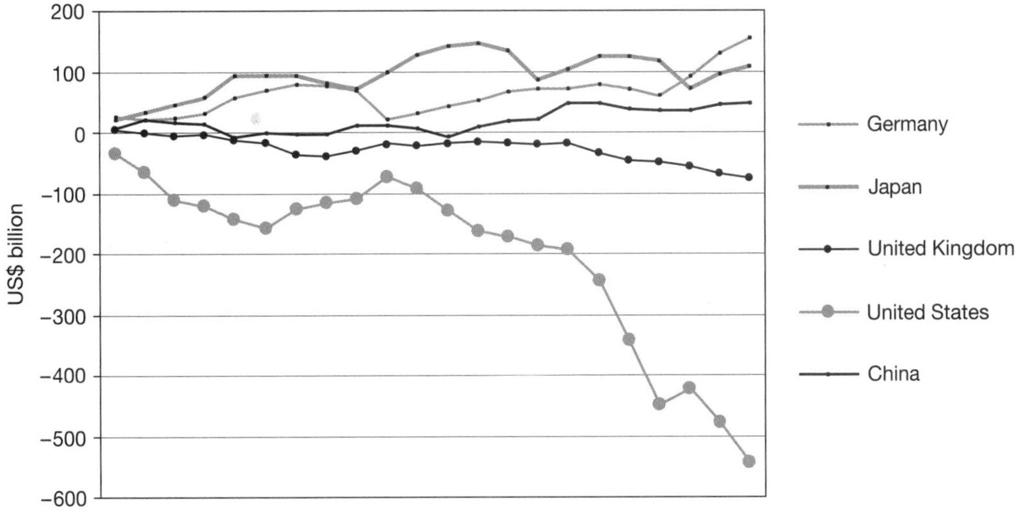

Source: International Monetary Fund

## 1.4 The international financial system

Several initiatives have served to further international economic integration and gradually abolish restrictions imposed on international trade and foreign exchange transactions. Discussions after the Second World War to facilitate international trade established the General Agreement on Tariffs and Trade (GATT) as an important vehicle to reduce inhibiting tariff barriers. The GATT ratified initial agreements on tariff cuts that subsequently has been extended through a series of negotiated 'trade rounds' committing global participants to eliminate tariff barriers on an increasing number of manufactured goods. Whereas the GATT initially was seen as a set of agreements to be administered by an international trade organization, this administrative structure was never established.[5] However, in 1995 the World Trade Organization (WTO), with a central administration based in Geneva, took over this function. The WTO can engage in potential dispute settlements but has no formal jurisdiction and, therefore, cannot enforce the GATT, which is solely promoted by mutual acceptance among member states. The GATT has been renegotiated and revised several times to increase the number of participating countries and expand the scope of the agreements to increasingly consider services, intellectual property rights, and foreign direct investment in addition to manufactured goods. The ongoing discussions to liberalize trade in agricultural products are hampered by the fact that dominant members, including the United States, the European Union, and Japan, provide significant subsidies to their agricultural sectors. Other concerns in the trade discussions relate to workers' rights and general working conditions across participating countries to counter global trade advantages based on human exploitation and poor working conditions. Environmental concerns also affect negotiations around genetically engineered agricultural products and manufacturing based on polluting technologies.

An international monetary system to guide the global financial flows was outlined in the Bretton Woods Agreement of 1944 aimed at the rebuilding of the world economic system after the Second World War. The underlying vision was to impose a global financial order in support of international trade and economic development. It required a stable international currency system and facilities to accommodate periodic international trade imbalances. The agreement established a credit intermediation centre where countries with severe balance of payment deficits could get temporary funding until necessary stabilizing economic policy measures were imposed. Temporary credit facilities would be made available by member countries maintaining balance of payment surpluses. This credit intermediation arrangement was instituted through the establishment of the International Monetary Fund (IMF) located in Washington, DC. In the same vein the World Bank was founded with the purpose of extending longer-term credits to support economic development in needy countries. Member countries would hold reserves with the IMF as a combination of gold and national currency quotas. In principle, deficit countries could draw on credit facilities equal to their gold quota while further borrowings would be conditioned and negotiated with the IMF. In the initial quota system the countries were obliged to maintain a fixed currency exchange rate against a gold standard price of US$ 35/ounce. This gold standard was subsequently abandoned and a system of **special drawing rights** (SDRs) implemented to create sufficient international liquidity and reduce the dependency on gold. For some time the gold standard was replaced by a fixed-rate system whereby currencies were allowed to vary within a $2^{1}/_{4}$% band around the US dollar exchange rate, but eventually the system gave way to freely floating foreign exchange rates in 1973.

The Organization for Economic Cooperation and Development (OECD) was established in 1961 on the basis of the Organization for European Economic Cooperation, which was formed under the Marshall Plan to furnish reconstruction of the European economy after the Second World War. The OECD currently has 29 industrialized countries as members that together account for around two-thirds of the world's goods and services. The underlying premises of the OECD are to facilitate open market economies with democratic political governance and respect for human rights. The organization works on behalf of its members to coordinate economic policies and establish binding codes, e.g. for the free flow of goods, services, and capital.

The Bank for International Settlements (BIS), headquartered in Basel, Switzerland, was created in 1930 as an international central banking institution. The BIS is owned by central banks in major industrialized countries and provides a variety of specialized services to them to promote international regulatory cooperation and foster international financial market stability. One of the major contributions of the BIS has been the imposition of common regulatory standards for the banking industry expressed in the so-called Basel I and Basel II agreements. As is the case with many other international institutions, the BIS does not have the means to enforce the agreements but purely functions through the principle of mutual acceptance among regulatory authorities in the member countries.

The European Union (EU) evolved from the European Economic Community and the European Coal and Steel Community (ECSC) established in 1951 to furnish economic and political cooperation. The EU has continued to expand its member countries, which now also include economies from the former Eastern European block. The European Union constitutes a common economic area where capital, labour, services, manufactured, and agricultural products in principle can move freely across national borders within the union. Similarly, corporations and financial institutions have wide latitude to establish commercial operations in other member countries provided they fulfill common standards established by community directives. The European Currency Unit (ECU) was introduced as a common currency reference for the member countries. The European Monetary System (EMS) established a foreign exchange rate mechanism to keep exchange rates between member country currencies within reasonable limits. This eventually resulted in the creation of a European Monetary Union in 2000 and the conversion to a common currency, the euro, among a majority of member countries.

Other economic regions have established similar cooperative initiatives typically to create international free trade areas with more limited scope for political co-ordination. The North American Free Trade Agreement (NAFTA) established such a regional free trade area comprising the United States, Canada, and Mexico. The Andean Community promotes economic development among a number of countries in South America through trade liberalization and economic and social harmonization among the member countries.[6] The Asean economic cooperation among countries in South-East Asia has imposed trade liberalizations and promoted cross-border investments among member countries.[7]

The heads of state of the major industrial democracies have met annually since 1975 to discuss global economic and political issues. The so-called group of eight (G8) provides a potential forum for international economic coordination. Whereas this has been far from a perfect mechanism of international policy coordination it does reflect attempts to increase global understanding and political interaction.[8]

International trade and foreign exchange transactions have frequently been restricted to reduce feared vulnerabilities associated with international competition and cross-border financial flows. An underlying rationale for these policies has been to enforce domestic monetary policies and prevent obstructive pressures from the foreign exchange market. These regulatory concerns were particularly relevant under the fixed exchange rate regimes, where large financial flows could undermine the ability of central banks to maintain currency parities and manage rate adjustments in an orderly manner. The general experience with foreign exchange regulation has been that it is very difficult to restrict financial flows from adjusting to expected economic developments. A potential side effect of protective foreign exchange rate regulations is that domestic companies may tend to become complacent in the absence of international competition and hence less efficient. At the same time, the credit intermediation process in restricted economies tends to confront inefficiencies due to the added complexity of regulatory peculiarities. The increased awareness of global interdependencies and the importance of international commercial interactions have contributed to a gradual move toward more liberal views on regulation of financial flows and foreign exchange transactions.

## 1.5 Global credit intermediation

Individuals and institutions in countries with trade balance surpluses make their funds available to financial intermediaries that channel the funds on to economic entities in deficit countries in the form of deposits, loans, securities portfolios, and direct investments. This complex exchange of cash between economic entities in countries with a current account surplus and countries with a current account deficit constitutes the **global capital market**. The implied credit transmission process can take place in various ways. International banks may receive deposits from economic entities located in the surplus countries and pass these funds on to economic entities located in the deficit countries, e.g. in the form of syndicated credit facilities to corporations, public institutions, etc. Investment banks may arrange global securities issues for entities in the deficit countries and place the debt instruments among investors residing in surplus countries. Securities firms may receive money from their clients with cash surplus to invest in international pension schemes, mutual funds, etc. Firms in surplus countries may engage in corporate acquisitions and foreign direct investments in deficit countries and so forth. Conversely, economic entities in the deficit countries may engage securities firms and investment banks to arrange global securities issues that place debt instruments on their behalf among institutional investors that receive funds from agents in surplus countries. In sum, there will be a variety of financial institutions engaged in the credit intermediation process that employ a diversity of financial instruments to accomplish this. Activities within different sub-classes of financial instruments are often considered distinct financial markets even though they all constitute a part of the international credit intermediation process. The associated cash transfers are obviously highly complex as funds are exchanged between economic entities in deficit and surplus countries through different credit intermediation processes. When significant amounts of money pass across national boundaries, they will affect liquidity and credit conditions and influence developments in the interest rates and foreign exchange rates of the implied countries. The global credit intermediation process is further complicated by the fact that there also can be surplus entities in deficit countries and deficit entities in surplus countries. Hence, the underlying cash transactions do not represent simple one-way flows, they go both in and out of every country, but the net effect will reflect the country's current account position.

**Figure 1.4 Cross-border credit intermediation – institutions, instruments, and markets**

Financial intermediation between economic entities in surplus and deficit countries:
- Financial institutions
  - International banks
  - Investment banks and securities firms
  - Insurance companies, mutual funds, etc.
  - Stock and futures exchanges
- Financial instruments
  - Bankers' acceptances, commercial paper, etc.
  - Syndicated credit facilities
  - Global securities issues
  - Derivative securities
- Financial markets
  - Money markets
  - Bank markets
  - Securities markets
  - Derivatives markets

**Figure 1.5** The credit intermediation process

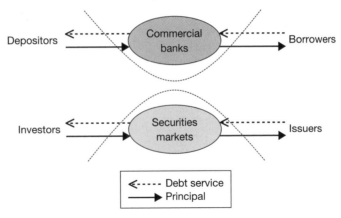

As foreign exchange regulations have been relaxed among OECD member countries and beyond, the volume of financial flows between different currency jurisdictions has increased correspondingly. As a consequence, financial managers of internationally oriented institutions consider both domestic and international money, banking, and securities markets as possible sources of funding and investment and these credit intermediation markets will subsequently be referred to as the global capital market. There are two principal ways of intermediating credit in the global capital market (Figure 1.5).[9] One is intermediation through the banking system, where commercial banks accept deposit instruments and use the funding to extend loans while retaining a large part of the commitments on their books.[10] Credit extension through the banking system is influenced by the credit multiplier process and is therefore exposed to regulatory interference, e.g. reserve ratios, capital requirements, etc. Another way to intermediate credit is through the securities markets where borrowers issue debt instruments, place them among institutional investors, and subsequently provide debt service payments to the investors that hold the financial assets. The extension of credit in the securities market is not directly subjected to the credit multiplier process but the securities can typically be traded in liquid secondary markets.

The domestic and international capital markets are interrelated as deregulated cash flows can drift freely across national borders and currency jurisdictions. The link between the national credit intermediation processes is established through the foreign exchange market, where funds in one currency are transferred into other currencies (Figure 1.6).[11] Activities in the international capital market can be formally separated into **foreign market** transactions, where non-residents obtain funding within the country of the currency, and **Euro market** transactions, where borrowers obtain foreign currency denominated funding outside the country of the currency. Foreign capital market transactions are subjected to national regulatory requirements. This is not the case with Euro transactions, although market discipline is influenced indirectly by prudent risk management approaches, self-imposed industry practices, the requirements of rating agencies, etc. With increasing deregulation, practices in the foreign and Euro markets have become more homogeneous thus making the distinction between the two markets less meaningful than has been the case before.

**Figure 1.6** The global capital market in different currencies

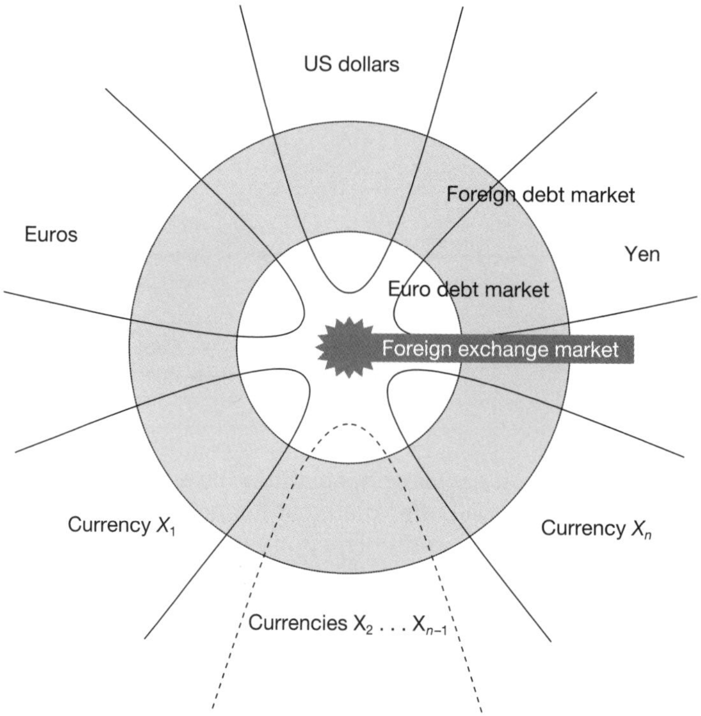

The Euro market in different currencies emerged in response to regulatory constraints imposed on the domestic capital markets of those currencies.[12] However, the national monetary authorities had no direct influence on transactions in their currencies once they took place outside the country. Therefore, Euro market transactions were not constrained by restrictive rules that could make domestic credit intermediation relatively uncompetitive. Hence, transactions in the Euro market could typically be achieved at interest rates below domestic lending rates while deposits could offer higher returns. With fewer regulatory restrictions in the Euro market, the credit multiplier among banks in the Euro market could be substantially higher than in the comparable domestic capital market of the currency, thus making the credit intermediation process less costly.

## 1.6 Credit intermediation, interest rates and the role of financial institutions

The existence of surplus and deficit entities can arise for a variety of reasons. For example, individuals may have different preferences for current and future consumption. Some economic entities operate in mature industries and generate surplus cash flows, whereas start-up companies in evolving industries need cash to fund new activities. It can be demonstrated that the capital market facilitates the exchange of cash with the interest rate serving as a pricing mechanism to ensure that resources made available for savings correspond to the amount of borrowings needed in the economy.[13]

### Box 1.2 Interest rates as balancing mechanism between surplus and deficit entities

Assume a simple economy with just two agents (they could be individuals, firms, or public institutions). The agents can choose between consumption in the current period $(C_1)$ or in the next period $(C_2)$. The two agents have similar endowments of resources, skills, and capabilities reflected in the same **investment opportunity set**. The investment opportunity set provides the agents with the means to produce for consumption now or in the next period shown by the 'fat' concave curve (Figure 1.7). The agents can choose to consume $A_1$ this period and nothing the next period, nothing this period and $A_2$ the next period, or any combination of consumption between the periods along the concave production frontier $A_1 - A_2$. The concavity of the curve reflects the principle of diminishing marginal returns. When the agents make their consumption decisions, they are influenced by their specific preferences expressed in different **utility curves**, or indifference curves, shown by the 'fat' convex curves. The utility curves can be conceived as topographical contours on a map, where utility increases as we move in a north-easterly direction. The agents are assumed to be materialists that want to consume as much as possible at any time. Hence, the agents get the highest utility at the points where the utility curves are tangential to the investment opportunity set.

With an efficient capital market agents can exchange resources, i.e. means of consumption, between them. This is reflected in the straight **capital market line** that cuts off the axes at points $E_1$ and $E_2$ respectively. The slope of the line reflects the return lenders require from borrowers as compensation for providing consumption opportunities in current period. This compensation is the market's interest rate $(i)$ expressed as: $i = E_2/E_1 - 1$. Hence, the agents can choose a different point on the investment opportunity set and move along the capital market line by saving or borrowing to achieve higher levels of utility than would otherwise be possible. In the absence of a capital market the two agents would chose $(X_1', Y_1')$ and $(X_2', Y_2')$ on the investment opportunity set as the optimal choices (Figure 1.8). However, when there is a capital market, agent 1 could choose the consumption combination $(X_1'', Y_1'')$ and then borrow funds in the capital market and thereby move along the capital market line to the consumption point $(X_1''', Y_1''')$, which reaches a higher-level utility curve. Similarly, agent 2 could choose consumption combination $(X_2'', Y_2'')$ and save funds, i.e. invest

**Figure 1.7** Investment opportunities and consumption choice

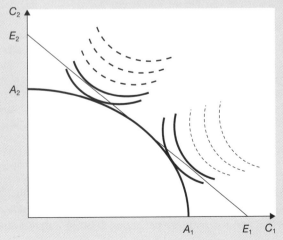

**Figure 1.8 Consumption choice with common investment opportunities**

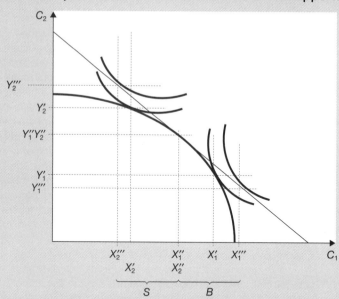

them in the capital market by moving along the capital market line until consumption point $(X_2''', Y_2''')$, which reaches a higher-level utility curve. So, when the agents have different preferences, the existence of a capital market allows both agents to achieve higher utility levels. There is only one market constraint, namely that savings must equal borrowings. In this example agent 1 borrowed $B$ $(= X_1''' - X_1'')$ while agent 2 saved $S$ $(= X_2''' - X_2'')$. Hence, the capital market is in equilibrium when $S = B$. This can be achieved by tilting the capital market line until the two are equal in size. Since the slope of the capital market line reflects the interest rate, the market interest rate is determined, so savings equal borrowings in the market.

We could pursue the same argument in another simple situation of two agents where they differ in terms of their resource endowments as opposed to their preferences (Figure 1.9). The different resource endowments of the agents are expressed in two different investment opportunity sets. On the other hand, both agents share the same consumption preferences, i.e. there is only one set of indifference curves. In this situation, the first agent would initially choose consumption point $(X_1', Y_1')$. However, higher utility could be achieved by choosing consumption point $(X_1'', Y_1'')$ and then saving funds in the capital market and moving along the capital market line to point $(X_1''', Y_1''')$. Similarly, the second agent could achieve higher utility by choosing consumption combination $(X_2'', Y_2'')$, and then borrow funds by moving along the capital market line to point $(X_2''', Y_2''')$. Again, the market condition is that $S = B$, which can be achieved by a capital market line with an interest rate that clears the sources and uses of funds in the capital market.

It has been shown how different preferences and resource endowments among agents can create advantages through the exchange of funds in the capital market between two time periods. If this analysis is extended from a specific two-period situation, e.g. between year 1 and 2, to exchanges between year 1 and 3, 1 and 4, etc., say up to 1 and 25 and beyond, then we get a sense of the highly complex cash flow exchanges that may be considered in the implied credit intermediation processes. Each of the maturity scenarios reflects different investment opportunity sets, where

**Figure 1.9** Consumption choice with common utility function

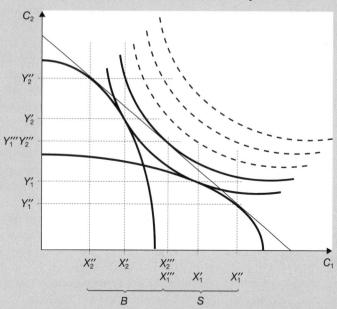

longer-term exchanges typically reflect prospects for higher future consumption opportunities compared to short term exchanges (Figure 1.10). Hence, interest rates can be determined for different maturities typically showing higher rates for longer maturities. Agents do have different time horizons, e.g. a household may have a two-year budget horizon while an inventor working on a good opportunity may have a ten-year horizon, etc. Similarly, a consumer bank usually has a shorter time horizon than a venture capital investor. This illustrates the many intricate credit transmission mechanisms at play in the capital market.

**Figure 1.10** Consumption choice across different time horizons

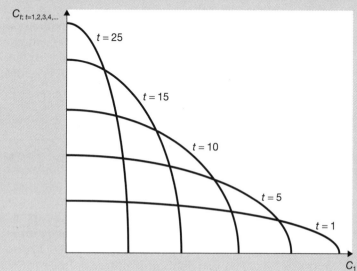

The capital market provides intermediating mechanisms between entities with cash surpluses and deficits. Economic entities, including households and institutions, with different resource endowments, consumption preferences, and business profiles are given the opportunity to rearrange the timing of their consumption and investment patterns by engaging in capital market transactions. Different types of financial institutions facilitate the intermediation of cash and provide associated asset and liability management services. Banks accept deposits and on-lend the proceeds, investment banks organize debt and equity issues and intermediate between borrowers and investors in the process. They also provide advisory services in support of acquisitions and other kinds of direct corporate investments, venture funds make longer-term entrepreneurial capital available, etc. In other words, there is a wide set of specialized financial institutions focused on specific types of credit intermediation characterized by different maturities, repayment profiles, etc. One implication is the existence of interest rates determined for different debt maturities, credit structures, and future time periods.

The global capital market is further complicated by open-economy settings where cross-border interactions bind national credit markets together via the market for foreign exchange. Credit intermediation takes place in many different currencies that are closely intertwined. Therefore, when economic entities make investment and borrowing decisions, they not only consider domestic market conditions, but also investigate opportunities in overseas markets. This implies a simultaneous analysis of both interest rate and foreign exchange rate conditions. As a consequence, the structure of interest rates across different currencies is aligned to rate developments in national markets and sentiments in the foreign exchange market. The outlook for interest and foreign exchange rates is constantly evolving and may vary significantly from time to time as market conditions change. A number of derivative instruments have been developed that trade financial assets at their expected future values. These instruments allow institutions to modify and hedge their financial risk exposures while providing alternative opportunities for astute investors. Money, securities, and foreign exchange market instruments are traded in secondary markets comprising dealer markets and formal exchanges. Dealer markets are made up by professional market participants committed to make price quotes on different financial instruments. These over-the-counter markets set prices as the professional participants commit to post tradable prices on a continuous basis. Formal exchanges usually establish a common pricing platform, e.g. in the form of an auction system with market specialists, open outcry of prices by floor dealers, or common electronic quotation and trading systems.

## 1.7 Term structure of interest rates (yields, zero-coupon, and forward rates)

There is more than one interest rate in the global capital market. Generally speaking, there is one interest rate for every traded cash maturity in a given currency area. These rates tend to co-vary across different types of financial instruments and markets. The distribution of interest rates for low risk issuers across the maturity spectrum is referred to as the **term structure of interest rates**. It is often developed on the basis of the returns on risk-free government securities by calculating the **yield-to-maturity** (YTM), e.g. of treasuries with different final maturities.

The yield calculation is based on the assumption that all the future cash flows in the financial asset earn the same internal rate of return. The calculation of **zero-coupon rates** is based on the assumption that cash flows with different maturities receive different returns specific to the maturity. Finally, **forward rates** refer to future interest rates over shorter time periods, e.g. the one-year rate in one year's time, the one-year rate in two years' time, etc. Let us illustrate the calculations of yield, zero-coupon rates, and forward rates through a simple example of a treasury market that trades T-Notes with three different maturities of one, two, and three years:

| Coupon (rate) | Maturity (years) (t) | Market Price (bond value) ($P_t$) | Annual cash flows (year) 1 | 2 | 3 | Yield (YTM_t) ($y_t$) | Zero-coupon ($z_t$) | Forward ($f_t$) |
|---|---|---|---|---|---|---|---|---|
| 5.00 | 1 | 99.90 | 105 | | | | | |
| 5.00 | 2 | 99.54 | 5 | 105 | | | | |
| 5.00 | 3 | 99.06 | 5 | 5 | 105 | | | |

The market price of a security ($P$), is found by discounting the future cash flows (outlined in the bond indenture) by the market's **required rate of return**, i.e. the return investors on average require to invest in the financial asset. The market's required rate of return is also referred to as the yield to maturity (YTM). Here we denote the yield for a financial asset with a maturity of $t$ years as $y_t$.

For the one-year bond, the future payment of 105 due by the end of year one discounted for one year at the one-year yield should correspond to the going market price of 99.90,

$$99.90 \qquad\qquad\qquad P_1 = 105/(1 + y_1)$$

That is,

$$99.90 = \frac{105}{(1 + y_1)}$$

We can find the one-year yield by solving the equation for $y_1$, i.e.

$$y_1 = \frac{105}{99.90} - 1 = 0.0510 = 5.10\%$$

Hence, the one-year yield is determined numerically as 5.10%.

For the two-year bond the aggregate present value of the two future payments of 5 and 105, due by the end of years one and two and discounted for one and two years respectively at the two-year yield should correspond to the going market price of 99.54.

$$P_2 = 5/(1 + y_2) + 105/(1 + y_2)^2$$

That is,

$$99.54 = \frac{5}{(1 + y_2)} + \frac{105}{(1 + y_2)^2}$$

We can find the two-year yield by solving the equation for $y_2$. However, this cannot be done numerically. Therefore, we must interpolate, i.e. try out various rates for $y_2$ until we find the one that satisfies the equation. This rate will correspond to $y_2$.

Let us first try out $y_2 = 5.2\%$, i.e.

$$P = \frac{5}{(1.052)} + \frac{105}{(1.052)^2} = 99.63$$

This bond value is slightly higher than the current market price. Therefore, we should try to discount with a slightly higher interest rate, e.g. 5.25%:

$$P = \frac{5}{(1.0525)} + \frac{105}{(1.0525)^2} = 99.5363$$

Since this is very close to the current market price, the two-year yield must correspond to 5.25%.

For the three-year bond the aggregate present value of the three future payments of 5, 5, and 105, due by the end of years one, two, and three and discounted for one, two, and three years respectively at the three-year yield should correspond to the going market price of 99.06.

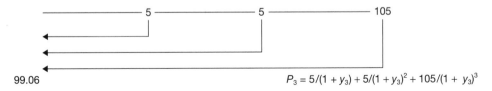

$$P_3 = 5/(1 + y_3) + 5/(1 + y_3)^2 + 105/(1 + y_3)^3$$

That is,

$$99.06 = \frac{5}{(1 + y_3)} + \frac{5}{(1 + y_3)^2} + \frac{105}{(1 + y_3)^3}$$

We can find the three-year yield by solving the equation for $y_3$. Again, we must interpolate until we find the one rate that makes the equation hold. This rate will correspond to $y_3$. Let us first try out $y_3 = 5.3\%$:

$$P = \frac{5}{(1.053)} + \frac{5}{(1.053)^2} + \frac{105}{(1.053)^3} = 99.1975$$

This bond value is higher than the market price. Therefore, we should try a slightly higher rate, e.g. 5.35%:

$$P = \frac{5}{(1.0535)} + \frac{5}{(1.0535)^2} + \frac{105}{(1.0535)^3} = 99.0531$$

Since this is very close to the current market price, the three-year yield must be 5.35%.

To determine the zero-coupon rates we employ different rates to each of the three maturities of one, two and three years. We denote the zero-coupon rates by $z_t$ to indicate that they differ across maturities. Although we discount the future cash flows by different zero-coupon rates in each period, the aggregate present value of the cash flows should still correspond to the market price of the bond.

For the one-year bond, there is only one future payment of 105 due by the end of year one. Discounting that payment for one year at the one-year zero-coupon rate should correspond to the market price 99.90.

That is,

$$99.90 = \frac{105}{(1 + z_1)}$$

We can find the one-year zero-coupon rate by solving the equation for $z_1$, i.e. it must correspond to the one-year yield ($y_1$) determined before as 5.10%.

For the two-year bond the aggregate present value of the two future payments of 5 and 105, due by the end of years one and two and discounted for one and two years by the respective zero-coupon rates should equal the market price 99.54.

That is,

$$99.54 = \frac{5}{(1 + z_1)} + \frac{105}{(1 + z_2)^2}$$

Since we just determined that $z_1 = 5.10\%$, we can enter that into the equation and find the two-year zero coupon rate by solving the equation for $z_2$. Hence,

$$99.54 = \frac{5}{(1.051)} + \frac{105}{(1 + z_2)^2}$$

$$(1 + z_2)^2 = \frac{105}{\left[ 99.54 - \dfrac{5}{(1.051)} \right]}$$

$$z_2 = \left\{ \frac{105}{\left[ 99.54 - \dfrac{5}{(1.051)} \right]} \right\}^{1/2} - 1$$

$$= 0.052515$$

So, the two-year zero-coupon rate corresponds to 5.2515%.

For the three-year bond the sum of present values of the three future payments of 5, 5, and 105, due by the end of years one, two, and three and discounted by the one-, two-, and three-year zero-coupon rates respectively should equal the market price 99.06.

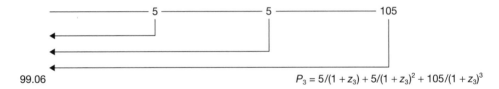

$$P_3 = 5/(1 + z_3) + 5/(1 + z_3)^2 + 105/(1 + z_3)^3$$

99.06

So,

$$99.06 = \frac{5}{(1 + z_1)} + \frac{5}{(1 + z_2)^2} + \frac{105}{(1 + z_3)^3}$$

As we already found the one-year and two-year zero-coupon rates $(z_1, z_2)$, we can derive the three-year zero-coupon rate by solving the equation for $z_3$. Hence,

$$99.06 = \frac{5}{(1.051)} + \frac{5}{(1.052515)^2} + \frac{105}{(1 + z_3)^3}$$

$$(1 + z_3)^3 = \left\{ \frac{105}{99.06 - \left[ \frac{5}{(1.051)} + \frac{5}{(1.052515)^2} \right]} \right\}$$

$$z_3 = \left( \frac{105}{99.06 - \left[ \frac{5}{(1.051)} + \frac{5}{(1.052515)^2} \right]} \right)^{1/3} - 1$$

$$= 0.053525$$

So, the three-year zero-coupon rate is 5.3525%.

The one-year forward rate for the coming year $(f_1)$ is the same as the current one-year yield and the one-year zero-coupon rate, which indicates the required rate of return for one-year money today. Hence, $f_1 = 5.10\%$.

The one-year forward rate in year two is derived from the fact that the return should be the same whether we invest for the two-year period by placing funds at the two-year zero-coupon (spot) rate, or receive the one-year yield, which is equal to the one-year zero-coupon rate, from investment in the first year, and receive the one-year forward rate as we reinvest principal and interest for the second year period:

$$(1 + z_2)^2 = (1 + z_1)(1 + f_2)$$

The first part of the equation indicates that we receive interest-on-interest by investing at the two-year zero-coupon rate. The other side of the equation indicates that we earn the one-year zero-coupon rate from the initial one-year investment, and then receive a return equal to the forward rate during the second year. Since we have already determined the one- and two-year zero-coupon rates, we can find the second-year forward rate $(f_2)$ by solving the equation. Hence,

**Figure 1.11 Different paths to a three-year investment**

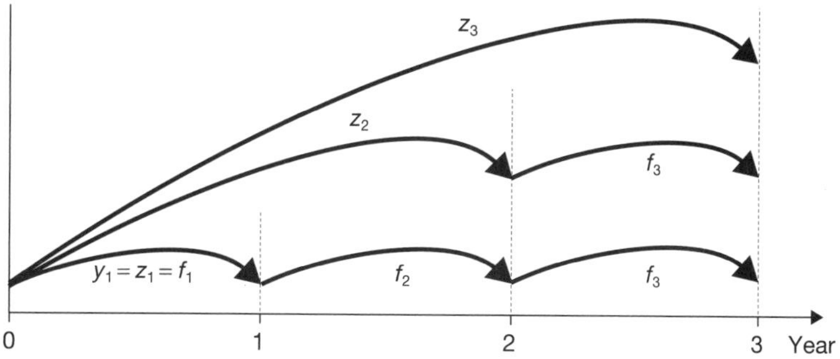

$$(1.052515)^2 = (1.051)(1 + f_2)$$

$$\left\{ \frac{(1.052515)^2}{(1.051)} \right\} - 1 = f_2$$

$$= 0.0540$$

Therefore, the one-year forward rate one year from now is 5.40%.

To determine the one-year forward rate in year three, we use the underlying rationale that return must be the same whether we (1) invest for three years at the three-year zero-coupon rate, or (2) receive the one-year zero-coupon rate the first year, then receive the one-year forward rate as we invest principal and interest for the second year period, and then receive the one-year forward rate as we reinvest for the third year, or (3) invest for two years at the two-year zero-coupon rate and then invest at the one-year forward rate over the third year (Figure 1.11).

Hence,

$$(1 + z_3)^3 = (1 + z_2)^2(1 + f_3)$$

Since we have already determined the two-year and three-year yields, we can find the third-year forward rate ($f_3$) from the following equation:

$$(1.053525)^3 = (1.052515)^2(1 + f_3)$$

$$\left\{ \frac{(1.053525)^3}{(1.052515)^2} \right\} - 1 = f_3$$

$$= 0.05555$$

Therefore, the one-year forward rate two years from now is 5.55%.

**Box 1.3 Calculating the zero-coupon rates**

When we calculate the zero-coupon rate for a given period $n$ (i.e. $t = n$), the following general formula applies:

$$z_n = \left\{ \left[ \frac{(PR + C)}{P - \left( \frac{C}{(1 + z_1)} + \frac{C}{(1 + z_2)^2} + \ldots + \frac{C}{(1 + z_{n-1})^{n-1}} \right)} \right]^{1/n} \right\} - 1$$

where

$PR$ = principal (= 100 if the market price is quoted in %);
$C$ = coupon (the indicated coupon paid at the end of each period $t = 1, 2, 3, \ldots, n$);
$P$ = bond value (current market price quoted for bond with maturity $n$).

When we calculate the forward rate for a given period $n$ the following general formula applies:

$$f_n = \frac{(1 + z_n)^n}{(1 + z_{n-1})^{n-1}} - 1$$

where

$z_n$ = the spot rate (zero-coupon rate on the $n$-year bond).

We can now fill in the blanks in our table and draw the corresponding interest rate structures (Figure 1.12):

| Coupon (rate) | Maturity (years) (t) | Market price (bond value) ($P_t$) | Annual cash flows (year) 1 | 2 | 3 | Yield (YTM_t) ($y_t$) | Zero-coupon ($z_t$) | Forward ($f_t$) |
|---|---|---|---|---|---|---|---|---|
| 5.00 | 1 | 99.90 | 105 | | | 5.1000 | 5.1000 | 5.1000 |
| 5.00 | 2 | 99.54 | 5 | 105 | | 5.2500 | 5.2515 | 5.4000 |
| 5.00 | 3 | 99.06 | 5 | 5 | 105 | 5.3500 | 5.3525 | 5.5555 |

**Figure 1.12** The interest rate structure

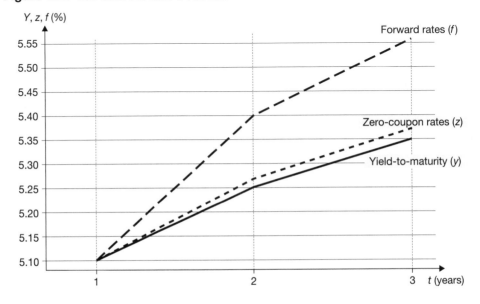

The yield curve can have different shapes, e.g. a flat line, an upward-sloping line, a downward-sloping line, etc. Each of these market characteristics may be explained by different theories. The **liquidity hypothesis** argues that the prices of more distant cash flows are more sensitive to changes in the interest rate, and therefore investors will require a higher return on financial assets with longer maturities. Accordingly, there should be a natural tendency toward an upward-sloping yield curve. The **expectations theory** argues that if investors expect future market rates to go up, they will require a higher return on financial assets with longer maturities, because they forego the higher future returns associated with reinvestment of the proceeds from shorter-term financial assets. Conversely, if the market expects future rates to go down, investors in longer-term assets are content with a lower return, because it is locked-in for the period, and they suffer no loss from a lower reinvestment rate in the interim. The **market segmentation theory** argues that different investor groups display varying maturity preferences dependent on their relative emphasis on short-term liquidity needs and cover for longer-term liabilities. Accordingly, different maturity segments of the securities market would be influenced by the investment behaviour of the dominant investor groups within that maturity range.[14] The expectations theory suggests that sentiments of interest rate increases should be reflected in an upward-sloping yield curve and sentiments of falling interest rates should be reflected in a downward-sloping yield curve – everything else equal. Combining the theories makes conclusions slightly more ambiguous. A downward-sloping yield curve should indicate lower-rate expectations, because the expectations element 'overrules' the liquidity incentive for an upward-sloping yield curve. On the other hand, we cannot be sure that an upward-sloping yield curve reflects expectations of higher rates, because the liquidity preference already should induce a positive slope. Outcomes from market segmentation depend on specific institutional conditions and, therefore, do not contribute general insights to the expectations debate. Since different currency areas represent different market conditions, the yield curve structures of different currencies can differ in accordance with the foreign exchange outlooks (Figure 1.13).

Interest rates can change in different ways, e.g. parallel shifts where all the interest rates across the maturity spectrum increase or decrease by the same absolute

**Figure 1.13** Yield curves in different currency areas

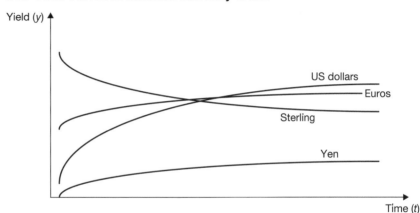

**Figure 1.14** Changes in the structure of interest rates

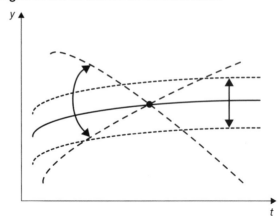

amount (Figure 1.14). However, we can also construe other more complicated scenarios, such as shifts from an upward-sloping yield curve to a downward-sloping yield curve, and vice versa, changes in curvature, etc.

It is common practice to analyze interest rate structures on the basis of risk-free market rate indicators, e.g. government bonds, treasuries, etc. The yield measures the internal rate of return (IRR) on the future cash flow stream of a financial asset given its current market price. In other words, the yield reflects the return investors on average require to buy that particular financial asset. Since the yield is calculated on a string of future cash flows many of which are paid out before the final maturity date, the yield calculation implies that these initial cash payments can be reinvested at the indicated yield until the asset matures. Of course this assumption is rarely fulfilled, as future market rates can turn out to be both higher and lower than the yield throughout the remainder of an asset's lifetime. This obviously influences the realized return on investment calculated on an *ex post* basis, i.e. the realized return will most likely vary from the yield calculated at the time of the initial investment. The yield is an *ex ante* return measure that provides a reasonable basis to compare the return potential of different financial assets. The yields calculated on treasuries with different maturities constitute the basis to determine the prevailing term structure of interest rates.

The zero-coupon (spot) rate measures the implied return on a single payment at a certain future date, i.e. there are no coupon payments and only a principal amount is repaid at maturity. The zero-coupon rates measured on the basis of treasuries, and treasury strips, constitute the zero-coupon term structure of interest rates. The zero-coupon structure has no implied reinvestment of payments, because there is only one future cash flow, namely the payment at final maturity. Therefore, the zero-coupon rate has no implied assumptions about the interim reinvestment rates, as is the case with yield calculations, i.e. there is no reinvestment risk in a zero-coupon structure.

The forward rates indicate the implied interest rates over future time periods, as determined by the zero-coupon term structure of interest rates. Banks can create forward rates by transacting in the interbank money market for loans and placements, commonly referred to as the **spot** market. Hence, banks can use the implied zero-coupon spot rates to determine future rates for any period, e.g. one year one

**Figure 1.15** Forward and zero-coupon rates

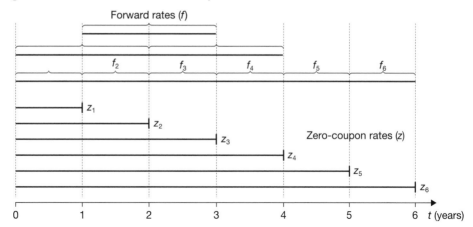

**Figure 1.16** Establishing a one-year forward–forward rate in one year

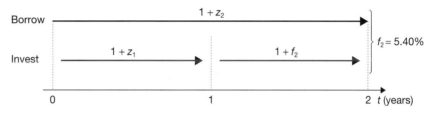

year from now, one year two years from now, two years one year from now, six months eighteen months from now, 45 days six months from now, etc. (Figure 1.15).

A financial institution can create a 'synthetic' forward rate on a committed loan arrangement by engaging in spot money market transactions, e.g. borrow funds for two years at the two-year spot rate, and place the proceeds at the one-year spot rate (Figure 1.16). When the one-year placement is repaid at the end of year one, there is liquidity to provide the funding over the coming year until the two-year loan falls due at the end of year two. The one-year forward rate has effectively been locked-in at a rate of $f_2 = 5.40\%$ (derived just like the previous example).[15]

## 1.8 Liquidity

A corporate bank loan typically provides a higher return than a corresponding corporate bond. So why do banks charge higher spreads than institutional buyers of corporate bonds? That is because corporate bonds everything else equal have higher liquidity. Since they are traded in the market and can be sold at quoted prices, an investor has higher flexibility in managing the associated cash flows and financial risk exposures. This is worth something, which is reflected in the return requirements, i.e. banks charge slightly more for the less liquid financial assets. How much less an investor will charge for a more liquid financial asset is difficult to determine exactly, but it has value. Liquidity is often measured by the size of the market makers' bid–ask spread on financial assets, where a low spread reflects higher liquidity. It may also be measured by the daily trading volume of the security compared to the size of the total issue (market turnover), etc. However, none of these measures have proven particularly precise and only serve as imperfect indicators of liquidity. Suffice it to say that the market normally provides a liquidity premium to financial assets with high liquidity.[16]

## 1.9 Credit risk and required return

Another important determinant of the return on a financial asset is the implied credit risk. Any lender and investor would like to receive all the promised future cash flows as stipulated in the loan agreement or bond indentures. If there is any reason to doubt the future receipt of the promised cash flows, the financial asset must offer some compensation in the form of a higher prospective return. If a financial asset provides a higher return than the return on a risk-free treasury, it must reflect the market's implied evaluation of the borrower's risk of default before maturity:

$$(1-p)(1+c) = (1+i)$$

where

$p$ = probability of default before final maturity;
$c$ = period return on corporate loan/bond;
$i$ = period return on risk-free asset/treasury.

Conversely, if the lender has a way to assess what the probability of default is, which is often the case, it can be used to determine an appropriate return on a loan or corporate bond:

$$c = \frac{(1+i)}{(1-p)} - 1$$

These return relationships can be transposed to multiple periods, where $p$ then denotes the likelihood that the borrower defaults at any time before the final maturity $n$:

$$(1-p)(1+c)^n = (1+i)^n$$

$$c = \left\{ \frac{(1+i)^n}{(1-p)} \right\}^{1/n} - 1$$

Similarly, the corporate rates required by investors on average should reflect the market's assessment of the corporate default risk. Hence, we can use the market determined risk-free treasury rate and corporate rate to derive the implied corporate default risk:

$$p = 1 - \frac{(1+i)}{(1-c)}$$

*Example*: Simple one-period case. The one-year treasury rate (i) is 5%, and the one-year default risk is determined to be 1%, i.e. there is a 1% chance that the corporate borrower will be unable to redeem the loan at maturity, then the appropriate corporate rate is 6.1%.

$P_{.05} = 95.24$  5.0%
$P_{.061} = 94.29$  6.1%

$$c = \frac{(1 + 0.05)}{(1 - 0.01)} - 1 = 0.061 \ (6.1\%) \qquad \text{credit-risk spread: } 6.1 - 5.0 = 1.1\%$$

*Example*: Multiple-period case. The five-year treasury rate (i) is 5%, and the five-year default risk is determined to be 5%, i.e. there is a 5% chance that the corporate borrower will be unable to redeem the loan at maturity in five years, then the appropriate corporate rate is 6.1%.

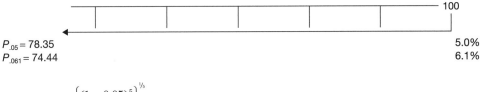

$P_{.05} = 78.35$  5.0%
$P_{.061} = 74.44$  6.1%

$$c = \left\{ \frac{(1 + 0.05)^5}{(1 - 0.05)} \right\}^{1/5} - 1 = 0.061 \ (6.1\%) \qquad \text{credit-risk spread: } 6.1 - 5.0 = 1.1\%$$

There is no reason why credit risk should remain constant over longer periods of time, rather it may increase or decrease over time, depending on the particular circumstances of the borrower. If credit risk differs from one period to the next the forward rate structure of financial assets in that particular risk class should reflect the market's assessment of those borrowers' default risk in future periods. By comparing the risk-free treasury forward rates and the corporate forward rates, the implied default risk for future periods can be determined.

By identifying corporate bonds with similar payment structures as the T-Notes, it is possible to calculate comparable corporate forward rates, e.g.

| Maturity (years) (t) | Market price (bond value) ($P_t$) | Annual cash flows (year) 1 | 2 | 3 | Corporate yield ($YTM_t$) | Corporate spot rate ($s_t$) | Corporate forward ($c_t$) | Treasury forward ($f_t$)* |
|---|---|---|---|---|---|---|---|---|
| 1 | 96.69 | 105 | – | – | 8.60 | 8.60 | 8.60 | 5.10 |
| 2 | 93.13 | 5 | 105 | – | 8.90 | 8.91 | 9.22 | 5.40 |
| 3 | 89.06 | 5 | 5 | 105 | 9.35 | 9.38 | 10.33 | 5.55 |

* Determined in previous example of the treasury forward rate structure.

Determining the corporate bond yield adopts the same procedure as followed earlier in the case of treasuries. That is, for the one-year bond, the future payment of 105 due by the end of year one discounted for one year at the one-year yield should correspond to the going market price of 96.69.

$$\begin{array}{ll} & 105 \\ 96.69 & P_1 = 105/(1 + y_1) \end{array}$$

That is,

$$96.69 = \frac{105}{(1 + y_1)}$$

We can find the one-year yield by solving the equation for $y_1$, i.e. it is determined as 8.60%.

For the two-year bond the present value of the two future payments of 5 and 105, due by the end of years one and two and discounted for one and two years respectively at the two-year yield should correspond to the going market price of 93.13.

That is,

$$93.13 = \frac{5}{(1 + y_2)} + \frac{105}{(1 + y_2)^2}$$

We can find the two-year yield by solving the equation for $y_2$, and so forth.

To determine the corporate zero-coupon rates, or spot rates $(s_t)$, we employ different rates to each of the three maturities of one, two and three years. For the one-year corporate bond, there is only one future payment of 105 due by the end of year one. Discounting that payment for one year at the one-year spot rate should correspond to the market price 96.69.

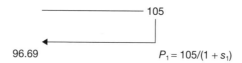

That is,

$$96.69 = \frac{105}{(1 + s_1)}$$

Hence, the one-year corporate spot rate corresponds to the one-year corporate yield of 8.60%.

For the two-year bond the present value of the two future payments of 5 and 105, due by the end of years one and two and discounted for one and two years by the respective spot rates should equal the market price 93.13.

That is,

$$93.13 = \frac{5}{(1 + s_1)} + \frac{105}{(1 + s_2)^2}$$

Since $s_1 = c_1 = 8.60\%$, we can enter that into the equation and find the two-year spot rate by solving the equation for $c_2$, and so forth.

The one-year corporate forward rate for the coming year ($c_1$) is the same as the current one-year corporate yield ($YTM_1$) and one-year corporate zero-coupon rate ($s_1$), i.e. $YTM_1 = s_1 = c_1 = 8.60\%$.

The one-year corporate forward rate in year two is determined by the one- and two-year corporate spot rates, i.e. $c_2 = (1 + s_2)^2/(1 + s_1) - 1 = 1.0891^2/1.086 - 1 = 0.0922$ (9.22%), and so forth.

The calculated interest rates are included in bold numbers in the table above.

Based on the one-year risk-free treasury forward rates and the corporate forward rates that we have just calculated, we can determine the implied default rates for years one, two, and three as follows:

$$\text{1st year's default rate:} \quad p_1 = 1 - \frac{1.0510}{1.086} = 0.0322 \ (3.22\%)$$

$$\text{2nd year's default rate:} \quad p_2 = 1 - \frac{1.0540}{1.0922} = 0.0350 \ (3.50\%)$$

$$\text{3rd year's default rate:} \quad p_3 = 1 - \frac{1.0555}{1.1033} = 0.0447 \ (4.47\%)$$

These default rates reflect the implied likelihood that the borrower will default during that year, given that no default occurred during the preceding years, i.e. they represent conditional probabilities. If we want to determine the likelihood of default at any time during the first two-year period, we use the two-year zero-coupon rates of treasuries and corporate bonds, i.e. $p_{1,2} = 1 - 1.054^2/1.0922^2 = 6.87\%$. If we want to determine the like-lihood of default during the first three-year period, we use the three-year zero-coupon rates of treasuries and corporate bonds, i.e. $p_{1,2,3} = 1 - 1.0555^3/1.1033^3 = 12.86\%$.

The credit risk of various institutional borrowers and their debt instruments is monitored by professional rating agencies, such as Standard & Poor's and Moody's Investor Services. The long-term ratings of the rating agencies classify the borrowers by credit quality, where the highest quality has the lowest probability of default. Investment grade bonds comprise ratings between AAA and BBB (or Aaa and Baa in the case of Moody's), whereas lower ratings represent speculative investment with high probabilities of default (Figure 1.17). The credit rating agencies also monitor the historical default risks of different types of corporate risk classes.

So far we have discussed the different interest rate structures (yield, zero-coupon, and forward rates) that prevail in the debt market of a given currency. We have also discussed how global capital flows relate to commercial trade transactions and investment considerations between different countries and how cross-border cash flows incorporate foreign exchange market transactions. The interest rate structure, which incidentally is monitored by the central bank, is deemed to impact business conditions and investment activities in the economy that in turn affect global capital flows and foreign exchange markets. In other words, interest rate conditions in different currency areas are intertwined with conditions in the foreign exchange markets. Due to the global linkage of financial markets, major international events can influence credit and interest rate conditions across international markets. For example, incidents like the Asian crisis in the fall of 1997, and the Russian debt crisis in late 1998 influenced the risk premiums charged on corporate bonds issued in the domestic US market (Figure 1.18).

## Figure 1.17 Long-term corporate bond ratings

| Moody's | Standard & Poor's | Fitch Ratings |
|---------|-------------------|---------------|
| *Investment grade* | | |
| Aaa | AAA | AAA |
| Aa1 | AA+ | AA+ |
| Aa2 | AA | AA |
| Aa3 | AA– | AA– |
| A1 | A+ | A+ |
| A2 | A | A |
| A3 | A– | A– |
| Baa1 | BBB+ | BBB+ |
| Baa2 | BBB | BBB |
| Baa3 | BBB– | BBB– |
| *Speculative/high yield bonds* | | |
| Ba1 | BB+ | BB+ |
| Ba2 | BB | BB |
| Ba3 | BB– | BB– |
| B1 | B+ | B+ |
| B2 | B | B |
| B3 | B– | B– |
| Caa | CCC+ | CCC |
| Ca | CCC | CC |
| C | CCC– | C |
| | CC | DDD |
| | C | DD |
| | D | D |

## Figure 1.18 Credit risk spread over corporate bonds

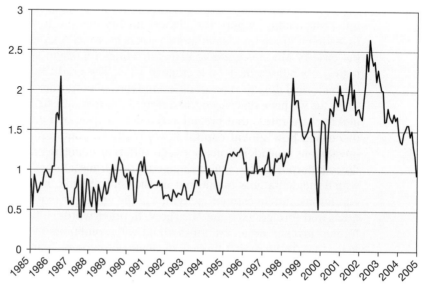

*Source*: Datastream

# 1.10 The foreign exchange market

As balance of payment transactions typically relate to the cash flows effectuated between entities located in different currency areas, international commerce may also influence the development in foreign exchange rates. The markets for foreign currencies constitute so-called over-the-counter (OTC) markets, i.e. there is no formal stock exchange to auction foreign currencies. Instead the currencies are traded in dealer markets, where the market participants quote two-way prices (bid–ask or bid–offer). A market participant that quotes two-way prices is obliged to buy the foreign currency at the quoted bid price, and sell the foreign currency at the quoted offer price. Professional market participants typically comprise international banks, securities firms, insurance companies, and the treasury departments of large multinational corporations. The two-way market prices quoted by the professional market participants on an ongoing basis are often referred to as the **interbank market**. A market price as we read it in the daily newspaper would be indicated by an average of representative market quotes at a given point in time, e.g. 12:00 a.m. every day. Market makers in the professional interbank market earn a profit from the small margin provided by the difference in the quoted buying and selling prices, and by taking short-term positions in the markets in an attempt to take advantage of prevailing market trends.

*Example*: Euro/US dollar foreign exchange quote

$$1.1286 - 1.1290 \text{ €/\$}$$

When individuals and institutions engage in international commercial transactions they normally contact a professional market participant (a bank or securities firm) to buy or sell the foreign currencies.

The professional market participants will then trade the currencies at the best available interbank rate and add a margin to the offer price if they are selling currency to the customer, or deduct a margin from the bid price if they are buying currency from the customer. The activities of professional interbank traders ensure that there is very high liquidity in the foreign exchange markets, and that market prices always are available on the major currencies.

Like any other commodity, the price of a currency for spot delivery, i.e. settled within the next two business days, is determined by supply and demand conditions. For example, a US-based exporter to Germany could receive foreign currency (euros) as payment. To convert the foreign currency into the local currency of accounting, the exporter would sell the euros against dollars, i.e. the demand for US dollars would increase, which will result in an appreciation of the US$ foreign exchange rate against the euro. Conversely, a US-based importer of goods from Germany may make payments in dollars. However, the German supplier will try to convert the dollar receivables into euros, i.e. there will be a higher supply of dollars that tend to depreciate the foreign exchange rate of US dollars against the euro. We can make similar arguments for all transactions posted on the balance of payments account in different foreign currencies, and show their foreign exchange rate effects.

**Figure 1.19** Supply and demand in the foreign exchange market

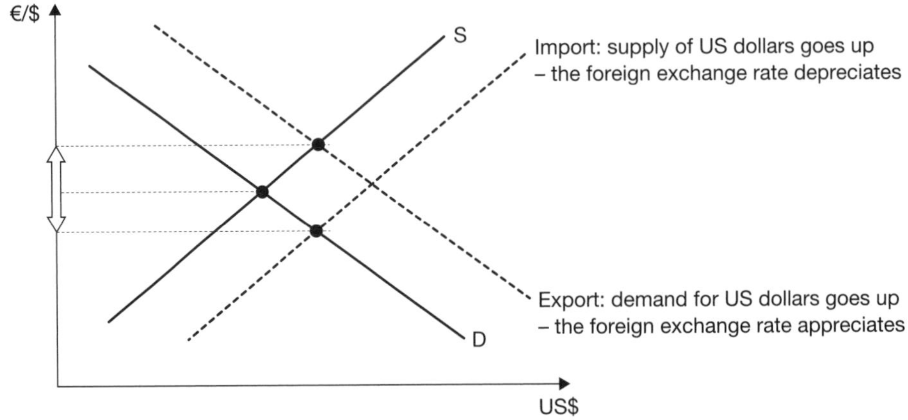

## 1.11 Foreign exchange rates

Foreign exchange rates indicate the conversion price of one currency for another. The purchase of a currency is the simultaneous sale of another currency, and vice versa. Hence, exchange rates indicate bilateral exchanges of currencies. Currencies are usually quoted as amount of currency per US dollar, with the exception of pound sterling, which is quoted as dollars per sterling. In the USA it is common to publish quotes in terms of dollar per foreign currency unit as well, often referred to as direct quotes. A **direct quote** indicates how much domestic currency is needed to buy a foreign currency unit. The direct quote is simply the inverse of the indirect quote and vice versa, e.g. 0.9533 $/€ corresponds to 1.1490 €/$ (= 1/0.9533), it reflects the same rate. This also means that a direct quote on the euro in the US is an indirect quote in Germany, and vice versa. Foreign exchange dealers active in the interbank markets for currencies quote foreign exchange rates as two-way prices, **bid** and **offer**, to indicate the prices at which the bank is willing to buy and sell a given currency. Consider the following quotes for the US dollar in Swiss franc and euro terms in the professional foreign exchange market:

| Bid | Offer | (Denomination) | Market |
|-----|-------|----------------|--------|
| 1.7001 | 1.7030 | (Swiss francs/US dollars) | Zurich |
| 1.1488 | 1.1511 | (euros/US dollars) | Frankfurt |

The indirect bid–offer quotes for US dollars against Swiss francs correspond to direct offer–bid quotes for Swiss francs against US dollars:

| 1.7001 | 1.7030 | (Swiss francs/US dollars) |
| 0.5872 | 0.5882 | (US dollars/Swiss francs) |

The indirect bid–offer quotes for US dollars against euros, correspond to direct offer–bid quotes for euros against US dollars:

| 1.1488 | 1.1511 | (euros/US dollars) |
| 0.8687 | 0.8705 | (US dollars/euros) |

If Zurich and Frankfurt are the only accessible markets, how can we determine the implied **cross rates** quoted as Swiss francs per euro? To get the euro bid rate in Swiss franc terms, a bank would first buy euros against dollars at the offer rate in Frankfurt (1.1511 €/$) because the €/$ offer rate corresponds to the $/€ bid rate, and then sell Swiss francs against dollars at the bid rate in Zurich (1.7001 SFr/$), because the SFr/$ bid rate corresponds to the $/SFr offer rate. The resulting cross rate is 1.4769 SFr/€ (= 1.7001/1.1511) – see below.

To get the euro offer rate in Swiss franc terms, a bank would sell euros against dollars at the bid rate in Frankfurt (1.1488 €/$), because the €/$ bid rate corresponds to the $/€ offer rate, and then buy Swiss francs against dollars at the offer rate in Zurich (1.7030 SFr/$), because the SFr/US$ offer rate corresponds to the $/SFr bid rate. The resulting cross rate is 1.4824 SFr/€ (= 1.7030/1.1488) – see below.

| Bid | Offer | (Denomination) | Market |
|-----|-------|----------------|--------|
| 1.7001 | 1.7030 | (Swiss francs/US dollars) | Zurich |
| 1.1488 | 1.1511 | (euros/US dollars) | Frankfurt |
| 1.4769 | 1.4824 | (Swiss francs/euros) | cross rates |

Notice that the bid–offer spread on the cross rates is higher than the market spreads in the €/$ and SFr/$ markets, because we engage in two markets to create the cross rate and therefore incur spreads from both market transactions. However, a major currency like the Swiss franc is also traded directly against the euro. Since this is an active currency market, the direct cross rates will have a narrower spread than the one indicated by the cross rates created through the €/$ and SFr/$ markets. If the Swiss franc against euro market gets out of line compared to the cross rates derived from the €/$ and SFr/$ markets there are opportunities for **three-way arbitrage**, which will force the direct Swiss franc/euro quotes back within the calculated bid–offer cross rates.

## 1.12 Purchasing power parity

If we accept the idea of completely open and unrestricted international markets for goods, services, and capital, there must be one universal set of commodities and services prices and interest rates. If this is true, then all goods should cost the same anywhere around the globe, i.e. they should carry the same price tags no matter which currency is chosen as the basis for comparison. This underlying condition can be expressed in the absolute purchasing power parity equation, which indicates that the foreign exchange rate (e) reflects the general price levels in two currency areas:

$$\frac{\text{Price level}_{\text{domestic}}}{\text{Price level}_{\text{foreign}}} = e \ (domestic/foreign \ currency)$$

Since the interest rate in principle provides compensating consumption to the lenders in future periods in exchange for giving up consumption in the current

**Figure 1.20** The purchasing power relationships

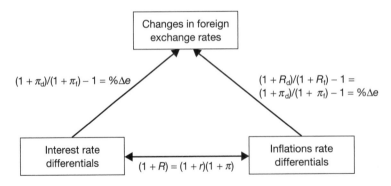

period, it is the real interest rate rather than the nominal interest rate that matters when the market between borrowers and lenders is cleared. In other words, the nominal interest rate $(R)$ must reflect the real interest rate $(r)$ as well as the rate of inflation $(\pi)$ in any given economy whatever its currency denomination:

$$(1 + R) = (1 + r)(1 + \pi) \Rightarrow$$

$$R = r + \pi + r\pi$$

Since absolute price levels are difficult to determine exactly, it may be useful to use a more relaxed version of the purchasing power parity equation, expressing that the percentage change in the foreign exchange rate reflects the relative size of inflation rates in each of the two currency areas:

$$\frac{(1 + \pi_d)}{(1 + \pi_f)} - 1 = \% \, \Delta e \; (domestic/foreign \; currency)$$

Combining the arguments that the nominal interest rate and foreign exchange rate are determined by the level of inflation within the currency areas, we can deduce that percentage changes in the foreign exchange rates relate to the relative size of the nominal interest rates in the two currency areas (Figure 1.20):

$$\frac{(1 + R_d)}{(1 + R_f)} - 1 = \frac{(1 + \pi_d)}{(1 + \pi_f)} - 1 = \% \, \Delta e \; (domestic/foreign \; currency)$$

In practice, the **purchasing power parity** (PPP) relationships seem to hold rather well over longer periods of time, that is, multiple years rather than months and quarters. Hence, these theoretical relationships may be useful for long-term currency predictions, but are not relevant as predictors for short-term foreign exchange rate changes.

## 1.13 Interest rate parity

A corporation with significant foreign currency denominated cash flows may want to lock-in the foreign exchange rates relating to future currency payments. This can be accomplished by creating 'synthetic' forward foreign exchange transactions.

*Example*: €10 000 000 receivable due in three months. Borrow euros in the spot money market for three months so that €10 million are due at maturity. Convert the up-front loan proceeds into US dollars at the current spot rate, and place the amount for three months in the spot money market. Use the €10 million receivable to repay the loan after three months, and you have the corresponding dollar amount as the three-month placement is paid out. *Voilà tout –* we have created a bid-forward foreign exchange rate (Figure 1.21).

## Figure 1.21 Determining the forward foreign exchange rate

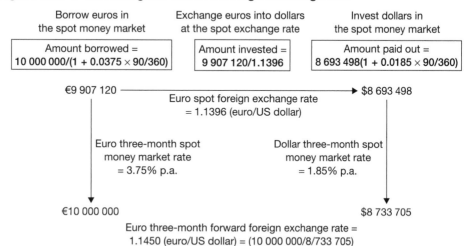

*Example*: €10 000 000 payable due in three months. Borrow dollars in the spot money market for three months, convert the amount into euros at the current spot rate, and place the euros for three months in spot money market. Arrange the dollar borrowing so there will be €10 million due after three months. Use the €10 millions from the placement to make the euro payment, and repay the dollar loan at maturity. *Voilà tout –* we have created an offer forward foreign exchange rate (Figure 1.22).

## Figure 1.22 Determining the forward foreign exchange rate

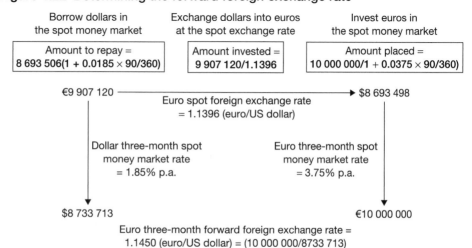

Since we disregarded the bid–offer rates prevailing in the spot money markets and used presumed mid-rates to derive the synthetic forward rates, the bid–offer forward foreign exchange rates are the same in the two examples. If we take into account that we must borrow at a slightly higher rate than we place funds, the euro bid and offer forward foreign exchange rates will differ slightly. Consequently, just as in the spot foreign exchange market, forward foreign exchange rates are quoted as bid–offer rates by professional market participants.

The **forward foreign exchange rates** can be calculated using the interest rate parity equations derived from the two examples above:

$$F_{\$/€,t} = \frac{S_{\$/€}(1 + i_\$ \times t/360)}{(1 + i_€ \times t/360)}$$

$$F_{€/\$,t} = \frac{S_{€/\$}(1 + i_€ \times t/360)}{(1 + i_\$ \times t/360)}$$

where

$t$ = the actual number of days until maturity (forward date); 1 year = 360 days.

*Example*: $F_{€/\$,90} = 1.1396(1 + 0.0375 \times 90/360)/(1 + 0.0185 \times 90/360)$
$= 1.1396 \times 1.009375/1.004625 = 1.1450.$

Professional market participants normally use the outright rate to calculate the forward foreign exchange rates. The **outright rate** is derived directly from the interest rate differentials between the two currency areas. This is a simplification of the interest rate parity conditions, but it reaches quite comparable results that for all practical purposes are sufficiently precise at four decimal points:

$$\text{Outright}_{\$/€,t} = S_{\$/€}\left\{1 + \frac{(i_\$ - i_€)t}{360}\right\}$$

$$\text{Outright}_{€/\$,t} = S_{€/\$}\left\{1 + \frac{(i_€ - i_\$)t}{360}\right\}$$

*Example*: $\text{Outright}_{€/\$,90} = 1.1396\{1 + (0.0375 - 0.0185)90/360\} = 1.1396 \times 1.00\,475 = 1.1450.$

Hence, forward foreign exchange rates maturing at different future dates are determined by the prevailing interest rate differentials between the two currency areas at those maturities. The span of interest rate differentials that influence the forward foreign exchange rates at different maturities can be assessed by comparing the prevailing zero-coupon yield curves in the two currency areas (Figure 1.23).

**Figure 1.23** Interest rate structure

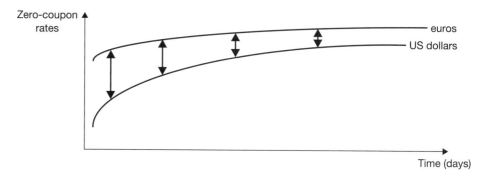

## Conclusion

Continued trade liberalizations have expanded the volume of cross-border commercial interaction dramatically and created an active global capital market to intermediate the underlying financial flows. In the contemporary economic environment the financial markets and their actors in different currency jurisdictions are intertwined through transactions in the global capital market and bound together through the foreign exchange markets. This establishes a set of intricate price relationships between instruments traded in these markets expressed in structures of interest rates and foreign exchange rates.

## Summary

- As international trade and capital transactions have become increasingly unrestricted, multinational corporations exploit new opportunities in the global economy and financial institutions engage in associated international payments and credit intermediation processes.

- The internationalization process has not evolved by itself, but has been induced by conscious political efforts to furnish global cooperation and economic development and has in many cases been institutionalized, e.g. the IMF, World Bank, OECD, BIS, EU, NAFTA, etc.

- An integrated global market by necessity comprises countries that register periodic current account deficits and surpluses where the countries with surpluses on the current accounts provide funding to countries with deficits on the current accounts.

- Interest rates are determined to balance the availability of savings and the need for funding among economic entities located in different currency jurisdictions for different purposes and maturities as reflected in yield curves, zero-coupon and forward rate structures.

- The foreign exchange market trades currencies against each other and forward foreign exchange rates are determined by the interest rate differentials between the different currencies across the zero-coupon rate structure.

## Questions

1.1 Explain how a country can finance a trade balance deficit.

1.2 Explain the relationship between a country's trade balance, current accounts, and capital accounts.

1.3 Explain the relationship between a country's current accounts, the capital accounts, and the reserve position.

1.4 Briefly outline and explain the relationships between monetary flows in the domestic economy and the international financial markets.

1.5 Briefly outline the macro economic relationship in an open economy.

1.6 What is the role of credit markets and financial institutions in the global economy.

1.7 Explain the difference between yield-to-maturity, zero-coupon rates, and forward rates.

1.8 Explain how to calculate yield, zero-coupon, and forward rates.

1.9 Briefly discuss how we may determine the appropriate credit-risk spread (compared to the risk-free T-Note rate) on a corporate financial asset.

1.10 Explain how the foreign exchange market works.

1.11 Explain how the forward foreign exchange rates are determined.

## Exercises

1.1 Given the following annual yield-to-maturity (yields) on government bonds with annual coupons of 5%, calculate the zero-coupon rates for the corresponding maturities.

| Maturity (years) | Yield | Bond Value | Zero-coupon rate |
|---|---|---|---|
| 1 | 5.65 | 99.38 | |
| 2 | 5.87 | 98.40 | |
| 3 | 6.14 | 96.96 | |

1.2 Given the following annual zero-coupon rates (spot rates) on government bonds with annual coupons of 5%, calculate the annual forward rates for the coming year and for years one to two, two to three, and three to four.

| Maturity (years) | Spot rates | Forward rate |
|---|---|---|
| 1 | 5.81 | |
| 2 | 6.06 | |
| 3 | 6.38 | |
| 4 | 6.53 | |

1.3 On the basis of the quotes below, please determine the following:

(a) five-year yield curve;
(b) five-year zero-coupon structure;
(c) the one-year forward-forward rates for years 2 to 5.

Govt. Notes (Wednesday, August 2, 2001)
Over-the-counter quotes as of mid-afternoon based on transactions of $1 million and above.
Colons in bid–ask quotes represent 32nds. Change in 32nds.

| Rate | Maturity(Mo/Yr) | Bid | Ask | Change | Ask yield* |
|------|-----------------|-----|-----|--------|-----------|
| 6.250 | Aug. 02 | 101:30 | 102:00 | −1 | 4.14 |
| 5.250 | Aug. 03 | 101:19 | 101:21 | −2 | 4.36 |
| 6.000 | Aug. 04 | 103:20 | 103:22 |  | 4.66 |
| 6.500 | Aug. 05 | 105:28 | 105:30 | −1 | 4.83 |
| 7.000 | Aug. 06 | 108:23 | 108:25 |  | 4.97 |

* The ask yield measures the annualized rate of return to an investor who buys the bond and holds it to maturity. For bonds with semi-annual coupons, it is calculated by determining the semi-annual yield and doubling it, i.e. it is not compounded over two semi-annual periods.

1.4 Calculate the appropriate market value of a five-year corporate zero-coupon bond when the expected default risk is 10% for the five-year period. The comparable Treasury strip is currently trading at 78.35.

> *Hint*: Use the relationship $(1 - p)(1 + c)^n = (1 + i)^n$ to determine $c$, and then calculate the implied corporate bond value. $p$ = likelihood of default during period; $c$ = corporate rate of return; $i$ = return on risk-free treasury.

1.5 Determine the market's implied forward credit risk spreads based on the following market quotes.

Govt. Notes (Wednesday, August 2, 2001)
Over-the-counter quotes as of mid-afternoon based on transactions of $1 million and above.
Colons in bid–ask quotes represent 32nds. Change in 32nds.

| Rate | Maturity(Mo/Yr) | Bid | Ask | Change | Ask yield | Forward rate |
|------|-----------------|-----|-----|--------|-----------|--------------|
| 6.250 | Aug. 02 | 101:30 | 102.00 | −1 | 4.14 | 4.14 |
| 5.250 | Aug. 03 | 101:19 | 101:21 | −2 | 4.36 | 4.61 |
| 6.000 | Aug. 04 | 103:20 | 103:22 |  | 4.66 | 5.29 |
| 6.500 | Aug. 05 | 105:28 | 105:30 | −1 | 4.83 | 5.44 |
| 7.000 | Aug. 06 | 108:23 | 108:25 |  | 4.97 | 5.65 |

Corp. Bonds (Wednesday, August 2, 2001)
Official quotes of corporate bonds traded on the New York Stock Exchange.
Volume in million dollars.

| Volume | Coupon – Maturity | Close | Change | Current yield | Corporate forward rate |
|---|---|---|---|---|---|
| 25 | $6^1/_4$–02 | 99.95 | $-^1/_4$ | 6.3 | |
| 30 | 7 –03 | 100.18 | $-^1/_2$ | 6.9 | |
| 35 | $6^1/_4$–04 | 97.52 | $-^1/_4$ | 7.2 | |
| 40 | 7 –05 | 98.66 | | 7.4 | |
| 35 | $5^3/_4$–06 | 90.64 | $+^1/_4$ | 8.1 | |

*Hint*: Determine the implied corporate forward rates and calculate the corresponding default probabilities for each of the one-year forward periods, i.e. year one, two, three, four, and five.

1.6 Calculate the forward foreign exchange rates for one to six months when the current spot foreign exchange rate is 1.1195 €/$.
Current money market (spot) rates (%):

| Maturity | US dollars | Euros |
|---|---|---|
| 1 month | 4.30 | 4.50 |
| 2 months | 4.20 | 4.45 |
| 3 months | 4.15 | 4.40 |
| 4 months | 4.10 | 4.30 |
| 5 months | 4.25 | 4.35 |
| 6 months | 4.50 | 4.55 |

1.7 A US-based corporation expects receivables of €2 million due in three months' time. At which exchange rate (using the calculations completed in Exercise 1.6) can the company lock-in these proceeds in the forward market and how many dollars does that correspond to?

## Notes

[1] The official reserves are typically held by the country's Central Bank and official transactions in the foreign exchange market are similarly carried out or fronted by the Central Bank.

[2] For a more detailed account of book entries see, for example, Shapiro, A. P. (2003), *Multinational Financial Management*, 7th edn, Wiley.

[3] The net flows of these types of cross-border transactions are sometimes referred to as the capital balance and the financial balance respectively.

[4] For further foundational work on macroeconomic analysis see, for example, Dornbusch, R. (1980), *Open Economy Macroeconomics*, Basic Books.

[5] See, for example, Rugman, A. (2000), *The End of Globalization*, Random House.

[6] Member countries in the Andean Community include Bolivia, Columbia, Ecuador, Peru, and Venezuela.

[7] The Asean member countries include Indonesia, Malaysia, the Philippines, Singapore, Thailand, Brunei, Vietnam, Cambodia, Laos, and Mayanmar.

[8] The group of eight consists of Britain, Canada, France, Germany, Italy, Japan, and the United States, and has also included Russia since 1994.

[9] See Andersen, T. J. (1990), *Euromarket Instruments*, Simon & Schuster.

[10] Many banks have consciously worked to make their loan portfolios more liquid, e.g. through loan sales and various asset securitization efforts.

[11] See Andersen, op. cit.

[12] The origins of credit intermediation in the euro market has nothing to do with the introduction of the common European currency. The euro (€) was introduced much later and simply constitutes another currency denomination. Euro market credit intermediation can take place in many different currencies, e.g. US$, £, ¥, and euro (€).

[13] This analysis draws on Fisher's two-period analytical framework. See Fisher, I. (1961), *Theory of Interest as Determined by Impatience to Spend and Opportunity to Invest it*, London (first published in 1930).

[14] See, for example, Santomero, A. and Babbell, D. (2001), *Financial Markets, Instruments, and Institutions*, 2nd edn, McGraw-Hill.

[15] Here we assume that the financial institutions can borrow and place money in the spot market at the same rate. In reality, professional money brokers quote two-way prices with a small Bid–Ask spread. However, we ignore the effect of the spread in these calculations.

[16] Even this is a truth with modification, because many high quality small company stocks that are illiquid reflect very high market values due to their scarcity and limited availability. However, for most fixed-income securities the liquidity hypothesis prevails on a *ceteris paribus* basis.

## Chapter 2

# Interest rate, foreign exchange, and other commercial risk exposures

**Objectives**

- Define different types of risk exposure
- Derive measures of interest rate and currency exposures
- Outline how major risk exposures can be monitored and managed
- Discuss the interrelationship between different economic risk factors
- Develop an integrative risk management framework
- Relate to financial and commercial risk issues

With the ongoing efforts to reduce international trade barriers and liberalize cross-border investment, institutions are increasingly exposed to global commercial activities and financial transactions as they operate across the globe. These exposures are generally bound in unexpected changes in economic conditions across key markets in different nation states and are influenced by technological innovations, competitive developments, national policy initiatives, etc. Whereas global commercial exposures are driven by uncertainties in overall macroeconomic and business conditions, they often pan out in the form of foreign exchange and interest rate exposures in different currency areas as economic conditions in national markets affect the global capital market. In accordance with conventional financial market perspectives, this chapter will discuss risk management in the context of volatility in financial prices. However, the discussion extends these perspectives to consider the interaction between financial markets and general economic conditions and the implications for managing the commercial cash flows of international enterprises.

Before turning to the relevant discussion of financial market and macroeconomic interrelationships and their practical application in multinational corporate management, we will familiarize ourselves with the conventional ways in which we analyze financial and commercial assets and the risks associated with changes in the value of the firm's assets and liabilities.

## 2.1 Valuing financial assets and commercial cash flow streams

The value of assets and liabilities, whether they constitute contractual financial obligations or relate to future commercial transactions are in principle determined by their
**net present value**. Chapter 1 provided examples of how to calculate the yield-to-
maturity of a given security. The yield to maturity is determined as the 'internal rate
of return' that, when applied to discount the future cash payments constituted by the
coupon and principal payments, would result in a net present value of those cash flows
that corresponds exactly to the quoted market price of the security. Arguably, the
pricing exercise is performed the other way around as investors, brokers, and other
market participants determine what they consider to be an appropriate value of the
financial assets and act accordingly. This so-called **intrinsic value** of the security is
determined by discounting the future payments by the return required by investors
to hold this type of financial asset on their books. All market participants are supposed to go through this fundamental valuation exercise and trade in the securities
market in accordance with their valuations, i.e. buy the securities if the intrinsic
value is above the current market price and sell if it is below the quoted price. Since
market participants, after all, are likely to have different valuation criteria reflected
in different required rates of return, the market price will be determined at any point
in time by the securities price that settles the amount of bonds that market participants want to dispose of with the amount of bonds there is a willingness to acquire.
It is this price quotation that is used to determine the yield-to-maturity corresponding to the quoted market price. The yield-to-maturity provides a comparative metric
for investors when they evaluate the potential return of different financial assets.

For reasons of compatibility with the discussion in Chapter 1, the following provides an example on the basis of 5% annual coupon bonds with maturities of one,
two, and three years. For simplicity, the example uses a situation with a flat yield
curve where the bonds of different maturities provide investors with a constant
yield-to-maturity of 5.10%, compared to a positively sloping yield curve in Chapter 1.
The corresponding bond prices $(P_t)$, which obviously will differ from those given in
the example in the previous chapter, are shown in the table below.

| Coupon (rate) | Maturity (years) (t) | Market Value (bond price) $(P_t)$ | Annual cash flows (year) 1 | 2 | 3 | Yield $(YTM_t)$ $(y_t)$ | AVG (bond price) $(P_{t,avg})$ | Implied yield $(y_t^*)$ |
|---|---|---|---|---|---|---|---|---|
| 5.00 | 1 | 99.90 | 105 | | | **5.1000** | | |
| 5.00 | 2 | 99.81 | 5 | 105 | | **5.1000** | | |
| 5.00 | 3 | 99.73 | 5 | 5 | 105 | **5.1000** | | |

The bond prices $(P_t)$ are calculated as the present value of the bond's future cash
flows discounted at the required rate of return of 5.10% (see the three-year bond
example below).

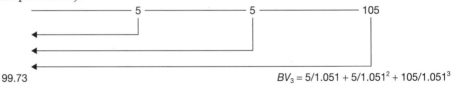

$$BV_3 = 5/1.051 + 5/1.051^2 + 105/1.051^3$$

The value of a financial asset is also influenced by the relative uncertainty that surrounds the realization of the stipulated future cash flows. As discussed in Chapter 1, the required rate of return should reflect the implied risk of default associated with each of the cash flows falling due at different points in time until final maturity. Consequently, a risk bearing financial assets should have a lower market price than a risk free asset to compensate for the implied default risk. Similarly, a 'thinly' traded security with a lower market liquidity represents a potential liquidity risk associated with a reduced ability to realize the 'fair' value of the security in the market and, therefore, should be priced at some discount. Furthermore, changes in general economic conditions may affect the level of interest rates in the market, i.e. given the complexities of contemporary international markets, there are real uncertainties associated with the future structure of interest rates that in turn affect the market prices of financial assets at any given time. The higher the level of uncertainty associated with future interest rate structures, the more uncertain will be the ability to determine market values of the financial assets in the future and hence the realized return associated with those assets when they are sold in the market. The higher the level of uncertainty about interest rate developments then the lower must be the current market valuation, as a compensation for the potential future shortfall associated with a sale of the securities in the market.

An example may help illustrate the potential price effects that can derive from the uncertainties associated with future interest rates. The example assumes a binomial outcome structure with a fifty–fifty chance of an increase and a decrease in the interest rate level during the first year of the security's lifetime. The example considers two scenarios, i.e. a situation of moderate uncertainty where the interest rate level can change by plus or minus 0.5 percentage points, and another situation of high uncertainty where the interest rate level can change by plus or minus 1.0 percentage points. Given the new interest rate level, the future cash flows are discounted for each of the two outcomes in each of the two uncertainty scenarios for the 5% annual coupon one-, two-, and three-year securities. This exercise will result in two new bond values $(P_t)$ for each scenario, corresponding to the two future interest rate levels. The simple average of these bond values $(P_{t,avg})$ provides the basis for a calculation of the implied yield-to-maturity $(y_t^*)$ corresponding to the expected future bond value (see below).

| | Change (±) | | | Bond price $(P_t)$ | Average $(P_{t,avg})$ | Implied YTM $(y_t^*)$ |
|---|---|---|---|---|---|---|
| $P_{1,a}$ | +0.5%: | $105/1.056$ | = | 99.4318 | 99.9071 | 5.0975 |
| | −0.5%: | $105/1.046$ | = | 100.3824 | | |
| $P_{1,b}$ | +1.0%: | $105/1.061$ | = | 98.9632 | 99.9139 | 5.0905 |
| | −1.0%: | $105/1.041$ | = | 100.8646 | | |
| $P_{2,a}$ | +0.5%: | $5/1.056 + 105/1.056^2$ | = | 98.9632 | 99.8209 | 5.0965 |
| | −0.5%: | $5/1.046 + 105/1.046^2$ | = | 100.8646 | | |
| $P_{2,b}$ | +1.0%: | $5/1.061 + 105/1.061^2$ | = | 97.9861 | 99.8406 | 5.0860 |
| | −1.0%: | $5/1.041 + 105/1.041^2$ | = | 101.6951 | | |
| $P_{3,a}$ | +0.5%: | $5/1.056 + 5/1.056^2 + 105/1.056^3$ | = | 98.3841 | 99.7408 | 5.0955 |
| | −0.5%: | $5/1.046 + 5/1.046^2 + 105/1.046^3$ | = | 101.0975 | | |
| $P_{3,b}$ | +1.0%: | $5/1.061 + 5/1.061^2 + 105/1.061^3$ | = | 97.0657 | 99.7785 | 5.0815 |
| | −1.0%: | $5/1.046 + 5/1.046^2 + 105/1.046^3$ | = | 101.0975 | | |

These calculations allow us to complete the table by inserting the numbers for average bond prices ($P_{t,\text{avg}}$) and the corresponding implied yields ($y_t^*$).

| pct.pt change (yield) | Maturity (years) (t) | Market Value (bond price) ($P_t$) | annual cash flows (year) 1 | 2 | 3 | Yield (YTM$_t$) ($y_t$) | AVG (bond price) ($P_{t,avg}$) | Implied yield ($y_t^*$) |
|---|---|---|---|---|---|---|---|---|
| 0.0% | 1 | 99.90 | 105 | | | 5.1000 | 99.904 | 5.1000 |
| ±0.5% | 1 | | | | | | 99.907 | 5.0975 |
| ±1.0% | 1 | | | | | | 99.914 | 5.0905 |
| 0.0% | 2 | 99.81 | 5 | 105 | | 5.1000 | 99.814 | 5.1000 |
| ±0.5% | 2 | | | | | | 99.821 | 5.0965 |
| ±1.0% | 2 | | | | | | 99.841 | 5.0860 |
| 0.0% | 3 | 99.73 | 5 | 5 | 105 | 5.1000 | 99.728 | 5.1000 |
| ±0.5% | 3 | | | | | | 99.741 | 5.0955 |
| ±1.0% | 3 | | | | | | 99.778 | 5.0815 |

What we notice from this exercise is that the implied yield ($y_t^*$) associated with the expected future bond price ($P_{t,\text{avg}}$) is reduced exponentially with higher levels of uncertainty as reflected in the variability in the future interest rate levels (Figure 2.1). The reason for this is that the price sensitivity of a future cash flow stream is higher when the interest rate drops by an absolute amount compared to an absolute increase in the interest rate of the same size, a phenomenon sometimes referred to as the asymmetry in value change.[1] In other words, the level of uncertainty surrounding economic conditions as reflected in changes in the interest rate structure can have a profound impact on the realized returns from financial assets and cash flows from commercial enterprise in general.

**Figure 2.1  Implied yield-to-maturity as a function of interest rate uncertainty**

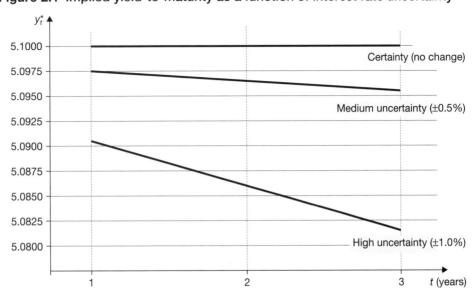

**Figure 2.2** Developments in interest rates (1985–2005)

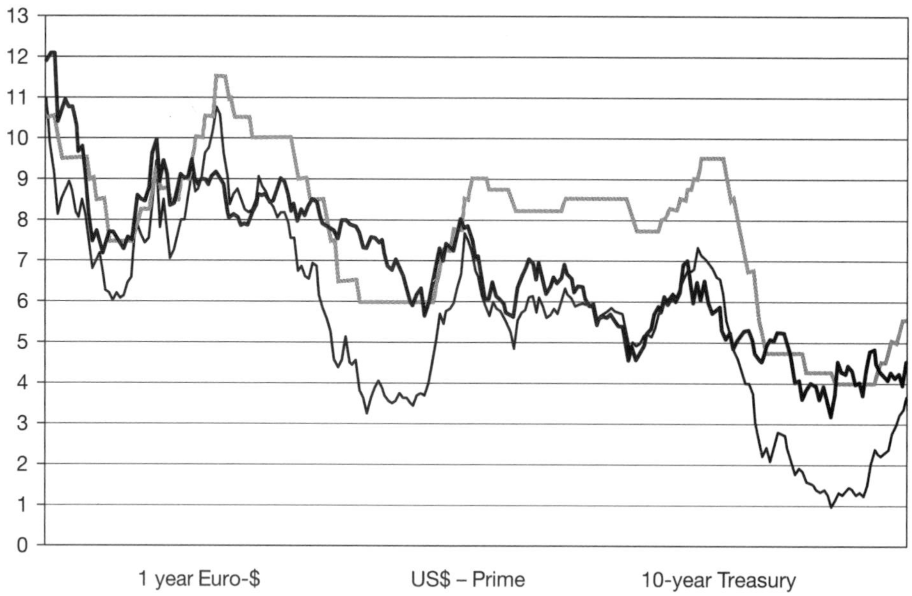

1 year Euro-$          US$ – Prime          10-year Treasury

*Source*: Datastream

The example developed above is obviously a gross simplification of the many possible ways in which the interest rate level may change over time. We assumed a single change in the interest rate level at the beginning of the security's life once and for all and remaining until final maturity, whereas interest rates actually might change in both upward and downward direction many times during the lifetime of a given security. One way to assess the effects of particular rate development scenarios would be to apply simulation techniques to determine the market prices under alternative future market scenarios and thereby through many iterations provide a profile of returns under particular simulated market conditions. Such approaches could be useful as a way to assess the price sensitivity of financial assets, particularly in view of a situation where market rates and the differentials between them are volatile (Figure 2.2).

As discussed in the previous chapter, there is a relationship between interest rates determined in the debt markets of different currency areas and price developments in the market for foreign exchange. The forward foreign exchange rate is determined directly by the interest rate differentials between the two currency areas at the forward maturity date. Hence, the forward foreign exchange rates will correspond to the prevailing interest rate structures in the two currency areas. The example below illustrates the relationship in an environment of upward-sloping yield curves with US interest rates exceeding the level of European rates. In this case the dollar will trade forward at a discount against the euro, i.e. more dollars must be paid forward for euros compared to the spot foreign exchange rate. However, other interest rate scenarios have prevailed over recent years resulting in vastly different forward rates between the two currencies. Interest rates in different currencies are settled in the markets based on ongoing events often spurred by the expressed views and actions taken by the central banks in the respective currency areas. The Federal Reserve

**Figure 2.3** Interest rate differentials determine forward foreign exchange rates

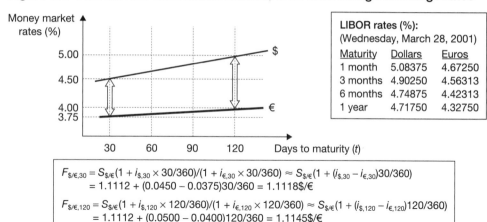

$$F_{\$/€,30} = S_{\$/€}(1 + i_{\$,30} \times 30/360)/(1 + i_{€,30} \times 30/360) \approx S_{\$/€}(1 + (i_{\$,30} - i_{€,30})30/360)$$
$$= 1.1112 + (0.0450 - 0.0375)30/360 = 1.1118\$/€$$

$$F_{\$/€,120} = S_{\$/€}(1 + i_{\$,120} \times 120/360)/(1 + i_{€,120} \times 120/360) \approx S_{\$/€}(1 + (i_{\$,120} - i_{€,120})120/360)$$
$$= 1.1112 + (0.0500 - 0.0400)120/360 = 1.1145\$/€$$

Bank (FED) gradually reduced short-term interest rates to historical lows at the beginning of the millennium, so the interest rate structure became downward sloping. As the European Central Bank (ECB) was reluctant to follow suit, the interest rate level in the euro-zone soon exceeded the level of US interest rates, which reversed the interest rate differentials so that the euro eventually traded forward at a discount. Hence, the forward foreign exchange rates are determined at any point in time by the prevailing interest rate structures of the two currencies, and as market conditions develop dynamically, the interest rate scenarios may change considerably over time.

The orderly nature of the forward foreign exchange rate determination through the interest rate parity equation should not be mistaken for stability in forward rates as interest rates for different maturities constantly change and adapt to views on future market conditions. Furthermore, it is apparent that the forward foreign exchange rates are heavily influenced by the current spot foreign exchange rate and hence the forward rates do not constitute good predictors of future spot rates (Figure 2.4).

In principle interest rates are settled so they balance the supply of funds (savings) from entities with excess cash and the demand for funds (borrowings) from entities with a shortage of cash (Figure 2.5). The interest rates at different maturities are influenced by the aggregate resource endowments of agents in the economy that determine the opportunity for exchange between consumption now and consumption at the future maturity date and the interest rate reflects this required exchange of value from consumption. Hence, an economy that is relatively well endowed should be able to gain a certain amount of future consumption against a lower compensation today compared to an economy with a lesser endowment because agents in that economy are more effective. The interest rate for different future maturities must also be influenced by potential changes in the resource endowment of agents operating in the economy. The determination of changes in resource endowment is a highly complex affair that entails an evaluation of subtle economic policy influences and entrepreneurship among economic agents, as well as the management capabilities of the organizations that are conducive of the economic activity. Furthermore, leading monetary authorities, and notably the FED, have focused their policy initiatives around managing the short-term interest rate. In the case of the USA this usually

**Figure 2.4** Developments in spot and forward foreign exchange rates (2000–5)
(The rates are quoted as US$/€)

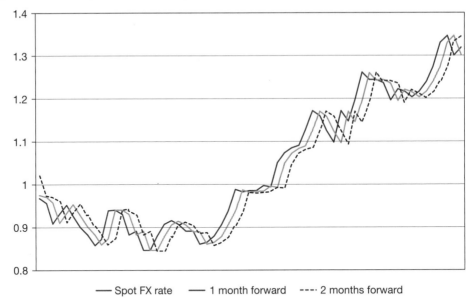

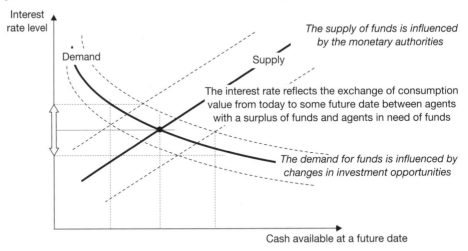

*Source*: Datastream

Note: The spot FX rate is lagged two months and the one-month forward rate is lagged one month.

**Figure 2.5** The interest rate determined by supply and demand of funds

takes place through interventions in the market for overnight funds, the so-called Fed-funds market. The perspective is that a reduction of short-term interest rates through an increase in the supply of money eventually will induce economic activity whereas an increase in the short-term rates will have the inverse effect. Hence, updated information about economic and managerial conditions as well as the potential for new interventions will influence the evaluations made by participants in the debt markets and affect the expectations that drive their actions. Market participants act in accordance with their expectations about the future and thereby affect supply and demand conditions. Hence, interest rates change all the time and the structure of interest rates is modified according to the changed expectations.

One of the assumptions behind the purchasing power parity theorem discussed in the previous chapter argues that what matters in the exchange between current and future consumption value is the real rate of exchange, i.e. the real interest rate after extracting the inflation effects from the nominal interest rates. If this is true in its stringent form then the market interventions by monetary authorities should arguably not have any effects. Yet, they do seem to have significant short-term effects, which might indicate that the monetary authorities have become effective at reversing policy initiatives on a timely basis before major inflationary effects materialize or alternatively that it takes some time for market participants to recognize potential inflationary effects and compensate for them. We will revert to a discussion of the applicability and consequences of the purchasing power parity later.

As argued, the frequent changes in the interest rate structure affect the forward foreign exchange rates and render any stability in the forward rates themselves unlikely. As a consequence the forward foreign exchange rates are typically poor predictors of the future spot foreign exchange rate. Another reason is that the spot foreign exchange rate is determined by supply and demand conditions one currency against another (Figure 2.6). The previous chapter discussed how supply and demand against two currencies can be influenced by the bilateral trade patterns as well as cross-border financial transactions between the two currency areas. A very substantial part of all foreign exchange transactions, estimated around 85%, relate to 'speculative' financial transactions, e.g. as traders and other market participants actively manage short-term currency positions without the backing of underlying trade or debt servicing transactions.[2] Monetary authorities may also intervene directly into the foreign exchange markets to enforce a preferable foreign exchange rate development. However, the experience from massive market interventions over past decades has been rather negative due to the sheer size of the foreign exchange market where speculative positions in the long run seem to outweigh the capacity of

**Figure 2.6 The foreign exchange rate determined by supply and demand**

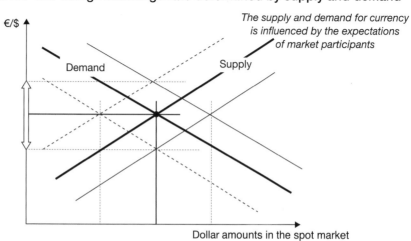

even coordinated intervention by major monetary authorities. Hence, supply and demand conditions are to a large extent influenced by the expectations of major market participants and developments in the spot foreign exchange rate are determined by a wealth of information furnished to market participants during the trading day and may be used to direct their buying and selling behaviours in the currency markets. Whereas the fundamental elements of the balance of payments trade and capital transactions continue to form the basis for long-term trends in foreign exchange rates, short- to medium-term price developments may be affected by a variety of interim factors driven by expectations and speculation.

The purchasing power parity theorem introduced in the previous chapter implies that only real prices matter, i.e. nominal interest rates will merely reflect the level of inflation and consequently changes in spot foreign exchange rates will reflect the relative level of inflation in the two currency areas. In other words, there is no free lunch to an economy purely driven by expansion of the monetary base because such an 'artificial' increase in demand will be reflected in higher inflation, higher nominal interest rates, and a corresponding reduction of the foreign exchange rate so the purchasing power of the currency remains unchanged. Whereas there is much appeal in these arguments, empirical research seems to show that the effects predicted by the purchasing power parity only can be expected to hold over longer periods of time, e.g. over 5–10 year time spans, and therefore constitute a poor explanation for short-term movements in interest rates and foreign exchange rates.

The purchasing power parity conditions hold other implications, namely that real economic conditions are fundamental determinants of commercial performance. More specifically, the better endowed the agents in the economy are with productive assets, relevant competencies, technological know how, entrepreneurial spirit, effective management capabilities, etc., the higher the potential for wealth creation and the better off should be the economy. It is hard to determine what the resulting effects on interest rates will be in a well-endowed economy. A high endowment should reduce the current compensation for future consumption corresponding to a lower interest rate level but there might also be a higher demand for debt deriving from new ventures and business innovations driven by qualified entrepreneurs. In such a scenario there would be a positive effect on the foreign exchange rate possibly for two reasons. First, the development of new innovative and effective products and services should increase overseas demand for domestic output. Secondly, foreign investors would be very willing to buy and establish productive assets in the economy. In the first case a positive demand effect will derive from trade related activities and in the latter case the currency would be in demand on the basis of capital investment activities. A major consequence of this is that interest rate and foreign exchange rate developments to a large extent can be influenced by a variety of real economic factors over time.

> ### Box 2.1 Measuring risk as variation in prices and volatility
>
> Risk measures should somehow capture the potential downside effects on investor returns and firm profits. In practice, the variance in financial prices as they affect asset values or financial returns over a certain time period is commonly used as practical risk indicators. It is relatively easy to derive based on standard statistical methods and is typically expressed in terms of variance and standard deviation. This provides the

advantage of being able to quantify the size of the risk exposures, which is considered a major advance in financial risk management. However, price variability depends on the frequency with which the market prices are observed, e.g. hourly, daily, weekly, monthly, etc. The variance in price development can also change over time and, there-fore, the calculation of standard deviation as a risk indicator depends on the time period chosen for its calculation. In the example below, which might show stock price developments over fifty trading days or reflect the trend in foreign exchange quotes, the variance and hence the standard deviation in daily prices is higher when calculated on the full period compared to, e.g. the last ten days. In other words, standard devia-tion as a risk indicator depends on the choice of period.

$$\text{Standard deviation } (\sigma) = \sqrt{\sigma^2} = \sqrt{\sum\left\{\frac{(x - \mu)^2}{N}\right\}} = \sqrt{\sum\left\{\frac{(x)^2}{N}\right\}} - \mu$$

where

$\mu$ = the mean value of prices during the period;
$N$ = the number of daily observations.

**Figure 2.7 Price development and distribution of prices**

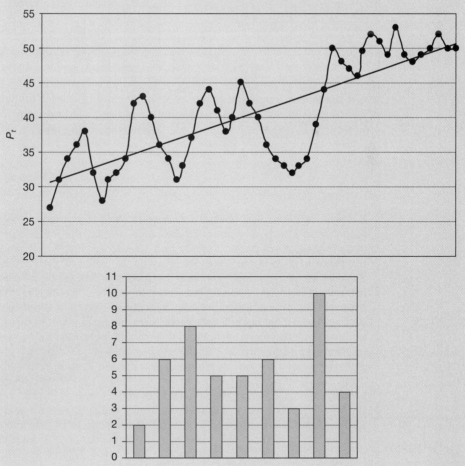

**Figure 2.8** Development and distribution of price returns

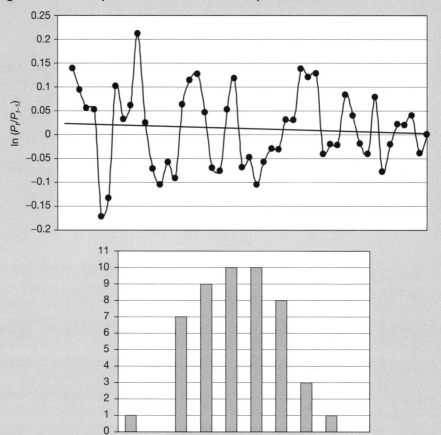

Since stock prices and foreign exchange rates for that matter often are exposed to longer-term trends, the standard deviation around the mean can be a somewhat skewed measure of price variability and, therefore, daily returns are used rather than the absolute price quote. Financial return is calculated as the increase in value of the financial assets plus cash payments accrued over the period as a percentage of the initial value invested. However, the natural logarithm of the daily price quote divided by the price the previous day, $\ln(P_t/P_{t-1})$, is often used as a practical return measure. Since $\ln(1) = 0$ a flat price development corresponds to a zero-return situation. Another advantage of this approach is that the distribution of daily returns may become closer to a normal distribution, i.e. it displays log-normality.

If we for example had used weekly as opposed to daily return measures the variability would most likely be higher, i.e. the longer the return periods, the higher the variance in return. Hence, the standard deviation in returns is an increasing function of the time intervals used to calculate the return but is increasing at a decreasing rate. Consequently, there is a need to streamline the measure of standard deviation to provide a basis for comparison. Volatility is a transformation of the standard deviation to reflect an annualized return measure:

$$\text{Volatility} = \text{Standard deviation } (\sigma) \times \sqrt{\frac{252}{n}}$$

where

　252 = the number of trading days in a year;
　$n$ = the number of days in the return interval.

Hence, a typical process in determining volatility follows three steps:

1. Estimate the daily return from a time series of financial prices.
2. Calculate the standard deviation of the daily returns in the time series.
3. Annualize the standard deviation of daily returns.

| Observations | Standard deviation | | Volatility |
| --- | --- | --- | --- |
| | $P_t$ | $In(P_t/P_{t-1})$ | $sd \times (252)^{1/2}$ |
| Past 50 days | 7.47 | 0.0828 | 1.314 |
| Past 30 days | 6.73 | 0.0673 | 1.068 |
| Past 20 days | 5.62 | 0.0613 | 0.972 |
| Past 10 days | 1.52 | 0.0453 | 0.719 |

*Example*: The standard deviation of daily returns has been determined as 0.1112 based on data from all trading days over the past year. This risk measure is converted into the standardized annual volatility measure as follows:

$$\text{Volatility} = 0.1112 \times (252)^{1/2} = 0.1112 \times 15.8745 = 1.765$$

*Example*: The standard deviation of weekly returns has been determined as 0.0910 based on data from the past 30 weeks. This risk measure is converted into the standardized annual volatility measure as follows:

$$\text{Volatility} = 0.0910 \times (252/5)^{1/2} = 0.0910 \times 7.0993 = 0.646$$

*Example*: The standard deviation of hourly returns has been determined as 0.0220 based on data from the ten-hour trading days over the past month, i.e. ten observations per day. This risk measure is converted into the standardized annual volatility measure as follows:

$$\text{Volatility} = 0.0220 \times (2520)^{1/2} = 0.0220 \times 50.1996 = 1.104$$

## 2.2 Financial and commercial cash flow exposures

The classical textbooks on multinational financial management typically confine the discussion of risk exposures to the earnings effects associated with future changes in the foreign exchange rates. In broad terms, the field distinguishes between accounting exposures that deal with the translation of foreign currency denominated assets and liabilities into the financial statements and the future net cash flow effects of financial and commercial activities denominated in foreign currencies. The former risk perspective is often referred to as **translation exposure** because it deals with the conversion of foreign currency denominated assets and liabilities into the domestic currency of accounting with its implications for the income statement. Whereas the application of different accounting principles can result in significant differences in the firm's pro forma reporting of earnings,[3] the differences do not reflect comparable cash flow effects. Hence, provided markets are efficient and market participants are acting rationally these risk exposures should be of little real economic effect. Conversely, the eventual conversion of foreign currency denominated financial and commercial activities will have real influences on the eventual size of the cash flows that are realized in the future and hence constitute exposures with true potential economic effects. True risk exposures reflect the potential adverse effects on future net cash inflows, no matter what the pro forma accounts look like, i.e. cash flows matter, not the bookkeeping.[4]

The risks associated with payments relating to financial and commercial activities are usually classified as **transaction exposure** that derives from existing contractual obligations denominated in foreign currencies, and **operating exposure** that derives from future effects on cash flows as changing foreign exchanges rates affect demand conditions, relative price developments, etc. Hence, transaction exposures relate to activities that are already contracted for whereas operating exposures have not yet been recorded in the books and, therefore, constitute unrealized future projections. Consequently, transaction exposures are relatively shorter-term in nature, whereas operating exposures may comprise stipulations of the longer-term effects of the institutions' strategic and competitive position in a global market context. Together transaction and operating exposures are referred to as **economic exposures** comprising all potential future cash flow implications deriving from changes in the foreign exchange rates.[5]

The recorded and projected cash flow effects from changes in foreign exchange rates deriving from financial and commercial activities will be effectuated at different points in time in the future and may include activities in many different currencies. Hence, there is a need to develop a reasonable overview of the corporation's economic exposures for different future time intervals, e.g. quarterly periods, per currency, e.g. US dollars, euros, yen, etc. (Figure 2.9). The choice of time intervals may vary, e.g. it could be of interest to divide the near term into shorter time intervals to create a more precise overview of the immediate exposures, whereas more distant periods could be divided into annual aggregates and maybe a final long-term aggregate exposure beyond say a five-year horizon.

Given the distinction between recorded transaction exposures and projected operating exposures, it may be worthwhile to develop a more detailed analysis for each of the major currency areas in which the corporation is active (Figure 2.10). Most registered transactions are relatively short-term in nature, such as already booked trade transactions, but could also be medium-term in the case of financial payments associated with debt obligations, etc. The operational exposures, on the other hand typically relate to longer-term estimates of commercial activities although not exclusively so, i.e. operational exposures can also exist to some extent in the immediate future.

The distinction between transaction and operational exposures is potentially important because there is a tendency to focus more on the former because they appear more real once they have been recorded in the books and thereby reflect the

**Figure 2.9** Periodic cash flow projections per currency

| Period | Currency | Inflows | Outflows | Net flows |
|---|---|---|---|---|
| 1. | US dollars | 130 000 | 210 000 | −80 000 |
| | Euros | 295 000 | 105 000 | 190 000 |
| | Yen | 25 000 | 75 000 | −50 000 |
| | Currency$_x$ | – | – | – |
| | . . . | | | |
| | Currency$_n$ | – | – | – |
| 2. | US dollars | – | – | – |
| | Euros | – | – | – |
| | Yen | – | – | – |
| | Currency$_x$ | – | – | – |
| | . . . | | | |
| | Currency$_n$ | – | – | – |
| 3. | US dollars | – | – | – |
| | Euros | – | – | – |
| | Yen | – | – | – |
| | Currency$_x$ | – | – | – |
| | . . . | | | |
| | Currency$_n$ | – | – | – |
| – | | | | |
| – | | | | |

**Figure 2.10** Periodic cash flow projections (US dollar book)

| Period | Activity | Inflows | Outflows | Net flows |
|---|---|---|---|---|
| 1. | Booked transactions | 40 000 | 65 000 | −25 000 |
| | Financial payments | 35 000 | 55 000 | −20 000 |
| | Transaction exposure | 75 000 | 120 000 | −45 000 |
| | Commercial activities | 55 000 | 90 000 | −35 000 |
| | Sub-total | 130 000 | 210 000 | −80 000 |
| 2. | Booked transactions | – | – | – |
| | Financial payments | – | – | – |
| | Transaction exposure | – | – | – |
| | Commercial activities | – | – | – |
| | Sub-total | – | – | – |
| 3. | Booked transactions | – | – | – |
| | Financial payments | – | – | – |
| | Transaction exposure | – | – | – |
| | Commercial activities | – | – | – |
| | Sub-total | – | – | – |
| – | | | | |
| – | | | | |

exposures that are most likely to materialize.[6] One approach is to consider the transaction exposures on a regular basis and possibly cover them as they arise. However, there may still be significant short-term operational exposures, e.g. associated with business transactions solicited within the current accounting period and that consequently should be considered to the extent they counterweigh effects from transaction exposures. The characteristics of these exposure issues depend on the industrial environment in which the firm operates. For example, capital-intensive primary industries and construction businesses are typically based on longer-term contractual arrangements and hence tend to have longer lead times on the recording of future transactions. In contrast, different service industries such as engineering consultancies and other professional businesses may be more dependent on shorter-term customer relationships with relatively short lead times on transaction recording.

Financial assets are typically included in the transaction exposure calculations whether they constitute short- or long-term instruments because the structure of their future cash flows is well defined and constitute contractual obligations. Since all asset values in principle are determined as the present value found by discounting the future cash flows accruing from the assets, any changes in the interest rate level will have a direct impact on their valuation, i.e. an increase in the interest rate will lead to a reduction of asset values, whereas a drop in the interest rate will increase the asset values. As a consequence, the interest rate level is often considered a central risk factor, and a factor characterized by its frequent measurement and reporting, which facilitates the quantification of the interest rate exposures. The longer the discount period, the higher the impact on the present value from possible changes in the interest rate level and, therefore, the determination of market values through the discounting principle is particularly relevant when considering the potential effects on assets of a longer-term nature. In contrast, short-term interest rate exposures are often considered on a cash basis as discussed in the following.

## 2.3 Measuring interest rate gaps

**Interest rate exposures** typically arise when there is a mismatch between the maturity and interest rate basis of assets and liabilities (Figure 2.11).[7] Financial institutions often fund themselves by the balances maintained on short-term transaction accounts while they on-lend the proceeds in the form of longer-term fixed rate commitments. Insurance companies and pension funds invest in financial assets of medium- to longer-term maturities as a reserve against expected fulfillment of future financial obligations materializing at different points in time. A corporation may generate cash from its current operations and obtain additional financing through bank

**Figure 2.11** Interest rate exposure

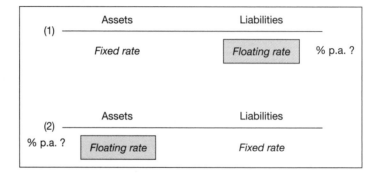

loans and securities issuance to fund different investment opportunities identified around the world. In all of these cases the expected timing of future cash flows and the rate bases associated with assets and liabilities differ and hence constitute potential interest rate exposures.

For financial institutions and corporate finance departments that are actively engaged as deposit takers and placement agents in the money market a major concern relates to the mismatch between assets and liabilities at different maturity intervals and the potential income effects from changes in the interest rate level. Placements in the money market are often characterized by two payments, namely the initial deposit and the repayment at maturity, which is often referred to as a zero-coupon structure. Money market placements are usually not traded in the market as liquid instruments, but are kept on the books until maturity. In this situation the interest rate exposure is typically considered on the basis of the book values of the deposits received (liabilities) and the placements made (assets). The interest rate exposure can be assessed in different time intervals to consider the potential future effects on income, e.g. over the coming day, week, month, etc., from changes in the interest rate level. The exposure is measured by **re-pricing gaps** calculated for each of the relevant time intervals (Figure 2.12). To the extent this type of gap analysis is extended to general portfolios of financial assets and liabilities it is important to keep in mind that the criteria is the re-pricing date of the asset and liability and not the final maturity date.[8] For example, a ten-year floating rate note with semi-annual rate setting dates would figure under the 3–12 months interval in the table.

> **Re-pricing gap**: the difference between rate sensitive assets and liabilities measured at book value.

For each of these intervals it is possible to calculate the net interest income effect from a one-percentage point change in the interest rate level. For example, there is a negative cumulative gap of $120 million overnight, that is, a one percent increase in the interest rate will result in a next-day decrease in net interest income of $3333 (= 120 000 000 × 0.01/360) as this gap is refinanced. If the current funding structure is maintained this will correspond to a drop in annual net interest income of $1 200 000. These types of calculations can be made for different re-pricing dates using the cumulative gap, e.g. for three months, six months, twelve months, etc., to assess the potential effect on net income from changes in the interest rate level over different time horizons. However, it is also possible to calculate the effect on

**Figure 2.12 Interest rate re-pricing profile (US dollar book)**

| Re-pricing date | Assets | Liabilities | Interest rate gap | Cumulative gap |
|---|---|---|---|---|
| Overnight | 150 | 270 | −120 | −120 |
| < 3 months | 170 | 210 | −40 | −160 |
| 3–12 months | 120 | 240 | −120 | −280 |
| 1–3 years | 280 | 150 | 130 | −150 |
| 3–5 years | 370 | 230 | 140 | −10 |
| > 5 years | 20 | 10 | 10 | – |
| Total | 1110 | 1110 | – | – |

net interest income if the structure of interest rates changes where the interest rates for different maturities change in different order, e.g. reflecting a move from a downward-to an upward-sloping yield curve, etc.

$$\Delta NII = \sum_{x=0,1,\ldots\, m} (A_x - L_x)\Delta R_x$$

where

$\Delta NII$ = aggregate change in net interest income for the time intervals 1, 2, ... $m$;
$A_x$ = assets (placements) made in time interval $x$;
$L_x$ = liabilities (deposits) received in time interval $x$;
$\Delta R_x$ = change in the interest rate level applicable to time interval $x$;
$m$ = number of time intervals considered.

To determine whether these interest rate gaps are reasonable or represent excessive exposures they must be considered in relation to a meaningful base. For example, the interest rate gaps could be compared to total assets to provide a comparative measure or the potential effect on net interest income could be compared to total equity to determine whether the exposure is too large in relation to the current equity buffer.

$$\text{Gap ratio} = \frac{\text{Gap}_x}{A}$$
$$x = 0,1,\ldots\, m$$

where

$\text{Gap}_x$ = the interest rate gap for time interval $x$;
$A$ = total assets.

$$\text{Exposure ratio}_x = \frac{\Delta NII_x}{E}$$
$$x = 0,1,\ldots\, m$$

where

$\Delta NII_x$ = change in net interest income for time interval $x$;
$E$ = total equity.

Once the appropriate levels of the interest rate gaps have been determined, a simple way of managing these risk exposures is to impose maximum acceptable gap levels within which organizational units can operate (Figure 2.13). These limits can be

**Figure 2.13 Interest rate re-pricing profile and gap limits**

| Re-pricing date | Assets | Liabilities | Interest rate gap | Cumulative gap | Limit 1 | Limit 2 |
|---|---|---|---|---|---|---|
| Overnight | 150 | 270 | −120 | −120 | 150 | 300 |
| < 3 months | 170 | 210 | −40 | −160 | 150 | 300 |
| 3–12 months | 120 | 240 | −120 | −280 | 150 | 300 |
| 1–3 years | 280 | 150 | 130 | −150 | 150 | 300 |
| 3–5 years | 370 | 230 | 140 | −10 | 150 | 300 |
| > 5 years | 20 | 10 | 10 | – | 150 | 300 |

**Figure 2.14** Interest rate gapping limits per currency

| Currency | < 3 months | < 12 months | < 3 years | Cumulative gap limit |
|---|---|---|---|---|
| US Dollars | 150 | 150 | 120 | 200 |
| Euros | 170 | 120 | 100 | 180 |
| Yen | 120 | 120 | 100 | 180 |
| Currency$_1$ | – | – | – | – |
| . . . | | | | |
| . . . | | | | |
| Currency$_n$ | – | – | – | – |

applied to the interest rate gaps for each applicable time interval (limit 1) and also imposed on the cumulative gap (limit 2).

In principle the interest rate gaps exist within each of the currency areas in which the organization is engaged. Consequently, the gap analysis should be performed for each of the currency areas in which there are major activities (Figure 2.14).

## 2.4 Interest rate sensitivity and the concept of duration

As discussed previously, the market value of financial assets is sensitive to changes in the interest rate level as it affects the discounted value of the future cash flows accruing from the asset. To the extent the asset and liability position relates to cash flow streams of a longer-term nature, it is more important to consider the interest rate effects on market value, because the assets and liabilities may be considered for liquidation in the interim to restructure the balance sheet and modify the implied risk exposures. For this purpose, the duration construct is often used as a measure of the sensitivity of asset values to changes in the interest rate level.

**Duration** (D) is defined by the following formula, also referred to as Macaulay's formula:

$$D = \Sigma t \times \frac{CF_t(1 + y)^{-t}}{P}$$

where

$t$ = point in time;
$CF_t$ = size of cash flow accruing at time $t$;
$y$ = yield-to-maturity;
$P$ = market price of asset (bond value).

The duration measure indicates an average weighted maturity of the cash flows in the financial or commercial assets under consideration, where the weights are based on the relative size of the period's cash flows indicated by the present value discounted at the yield. To calculate the duration we can use the following neat layout applied to the previous example of the three-year annual coupon bearing T-Note with a 5.35% yield.

| $t$ | $CF_t$ | $PV_{CF}$ | $w_t$ | $t \times w_t$ |
|---|---|---|---|---|
| 1 | 5 | $5/1.0535 = 4.75$ | $4.75/99.06 = 0.0480$ | $1 \times 0.0480 = 0.0480$ |
| 2 | 5 | $5/1.0535^2 = 4.51$ | $4.51/99.06 = 0.0455$ | $2 \times 0.0455 = 0.0910$ |
| 3 | 105 | $105/1.0535^3 = 89.80$ | $89.80/99.06 = 0.9065$ | $3 \times 0.9065 = 2.7195$ |
| | | $\Sigma = 99.06 = P$ | $\Sigma = 1.0000$ | $\Sigma = 2.8600 = D$ |

As discussed in the previous chapter, the yield is an *ex ante* comparative indicator of the internal rate-of return accruing from a future cash flow stream, e.g. embedded in a coupon bearing security. However, the calculation assumes that any coupon payments received prior to the final maturity date can be reinvested for the remainder of the period at the yield. However, this is obviously not always possible in reality, i.e. either the market rate may increase above the yield or decrease below the yield in the interim. If the interest rate level increases, the reinvestment return is higher than assumed and therefore the realized return at maturity will exceed the *ex ante* yield. Conversely, if the interest rate level drops, the realized return will be lower than the yield. This phenomenon is often referred to as the **reinvestment risk**. Now, it is interesting to note that the interest rate effect on the market value of the cash flow stream counteracts the reinvestment risk. If interest rates go up and the reinvestment return increases, the market value of the asset will fall, and conversely, if interest rates go down and the reinvestment return decreases, the market value of the asset will go up. This indicates that there must be a certain time period within which these two counteracting effects equal out. In this context, the duration indicates exactly the holding period for which the price risk counterweighs the reinvestment risk. In the example the duration of the cash flow stream (T-Note) was determined to be 2.86. Therefore, if the proceeds from this asset are needed in approximately 2.86 years, this investment is relatively safe in providing the promised yield whether or not there are marginal changes in the interest rate level.

*Example*: The duration of a five-year cash flow with annual coupon payments of 9% at a yield-to-maturity of 9.0%

| $t$ | $CF_t$ | $PV_{CF}$ | $w_t$ | $t \times w_t$ |
|---|---|---|---|---|
| 1 | 90 | 82.57 | 0.083 | 0.083 |
| 2 | 90 | 75.75 | 0.076 | 0.152 |
| 3 | 90 | 69.50 | 0.069 | 0.207 |
| 4 | 90 | 63.76 | 0.064 | 0.256 |
| 5 | 1090 | 708.42 | 0.708 | 3.540 |
| | | 1000.00 | 1.000 | **4.238** |

*Example*: The duration of a five-year cash flow with annual coupon payments of 9.0% at a yield-to-maturity of 7.0%

| $t$ | $CF_t$ | $PV_{CF}$ | $w_t$ | $t \times w_t$ |
|---|---|---|---|---|
| 1 | 90 | 84.11 | 0.078 | 0.078 |
| 2 | 90 | 78.61 | 0.073 | 0.146 |
| 3 | 90 | 73.47 | 0.068 | 0.204 |
| 4 | 90 | 68.66 | 0.063 | 0.252 |
| 5 | 1090 | 777.15 | 0.718 | 3.590 |
| | | 1082.00 | 1.000 | **4.270** |

*Example*: The duration of a five-year zero-coupon cash flow at a yield-to-maturity of 8.5%

| $t$ | $CF_t$ | $PV_{CF}$ | $w_t$ | $t \times w_t$ |
|---|---|---|---|---|
| 1 | 0 | 0.00 | 0.00 | 0.000 |
| 2 | 0 | 0.00 | 0.00 | 0.000 |
| 3 | 0 | 0.00 | 0.00 | 0.000 |
| 4 | 0 | 0.00 | 0.00 | 0.000 |
| 5 | 1000 | 712.99 | 1.000 | 5.000 |
| | | 712.99 | 1.000 | **5.000** |

These examples illustrate the potential shortcoming of duration, namely that it depends on the prevailing interest rate level. In this case the duration increases from 4.24 to 4.27 for the same cash flows when the yield-to-maturity drops from 9% to 7%, and this effect would be more pronounced for longer-term assets. However, the duration of zero-coupon structures is insensitive to interest rate changes and remains equal to the final maturity, which makes them particularly interesting for interest rate risk management purposes.

The duration also indicates how sensitive a financial cash flow stream is to changes in the interest rate level.

$$\frac{\Delta P}{P} = -D \left[ \frac{\Delta(1 + y)}{(1 + y)} \right]$$

$$\Delta P = \frac{-D}{(1 + y)} \times \Delta y \times P$$

where

$$D^* = \frac{D}{(1 + y)}$$

$D^*$ indicates the **modified duration**, which can be used to determine the absolute change in financial asset prices for a given change in the interest rate level. For example, if the interest rate increases by 0.25%-points then the price of the three-year T-Note would drop by 0.67 from its current price of 99.06 given the yield of 5.35%, i.e.

$$\Delta P = \frac{-2.86}{(1 + 0.0535)} \times 0.0025 \times 99.06 = 0.67$$

**Figure 2.15** The interest rate sensitivity of the bond price

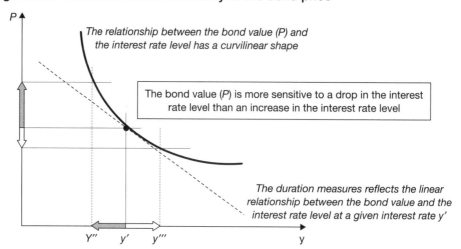

However, the price sensitivity from changes in the interest rate level of a financial cash flow stream is not linear, it follows a convex curvilinear relationship, so the duration measure is strictly speaking only accurate for marginal changes in the yield (Figure 2.15). The curvilinear price-yield relationship also illustrates the asymmetric value change as a drop in the interest rate level from y′ to y″ results in a much higher change in the bond value compared to an increase in the interest rate of an equal size from y′ to y‴. Furthermore, the duration measure depends on the interest rate level (yield), so the duration measures should be adjusted regularly to reflect changing market conditions.

## 2.5 Duration and interest rate risk

The duration of a financial asset indicates how much the market value of the under-lying future cash flows will be affected by a marginal change in the interest rate level. The duration effect is always negative, that is, if the interest rate level goes up the present value of the discounted future cash flows will go down, and if the interest rate level goes down the present value will go up. The duration of financial liabilities can be calculated in the same manner, which can be equally interesting and relevant. For example, if the interest rates go up, the market value of liabilities, e.g. issued corporate bonds, goes down, and the issuer can buy them back in the market at a price that is lower than the initial issuance price. In other words, an institution is affected both on its assets and liabilities from changes in interest rates.

The duration of asset and liability portfolios can be derived as the weighted aver-age of the durations of the individual assets and liabilities, weighted by the market values of each of the assets and liabilities that constitute the portfolios. This approach is consistent with the definition of duration, which is the weighted average maturity of the future cash flows, weighted by the present value of each of the cash flows against the sum of the present value of all the cash flows corresponding to market value or bond price.

$$D_P = \frac{\sum_{n=1}^{m} (D_n \times MV_n)}{\sum_{n=1}^{m} MV_n}$$

where

$D_P$ = duration of asset or liability portfolio;
$D_n$ = duration of asset or liability $n$;
$MV_n$ = market value of asset or liability $n$;
$n$ = the number of assets in the asset or liability portfolio; $n = 1, 2, 3, \ldots, m$.

*Example*: An institution has two assets with current market values of $30 and 20 million, and durations of 2 and 3 respectively. The institution also has two liabilities with current market values of $20 and 20 million, and durations of 1 and 2 respectively. The duration of the asset portfolio is 2.4, and the duration of the total liabilities is 1.5.

| *Two assets:* | | MV | D | $D_n \times MV_n$ |
|---|---|---|---|---|
| | | 30 | 2 | 60 |
| | | 20 | 3 | 60 |
| Σ | | 50 | | 120 |

$$D_P = \frac{120}{50} = 2.4$$

| *Two liabilities:* | | MV | D | $D_n \times MV_n$ |
|---|---|---|---|---|
| | | 20 | 1 | 20 |
| | | 20 | 2 | 40 |
| Σ | | 40 | | 60 |

$$D_P = \frac{60}{40} = 1.5$$

The net exposure to changes in the interest rate level is indicated by the difference between the duration of assets and the duration of liabilities. In this case the duration of assets exceeds the duration of liabilities, i.e. the institution has a positive duration gap of 0.9 ($= 2.4 - 1.5$). In other words, if the interest rate level goes up, the institution will be exposed to a net loss in value, that is, a loss in equity (equity = assets − liabilities). Conversely, if interest rates go down the institution will register a gain.

The duration concept provides any institution with the means to determine its overall sensitivity to changes in the interest rate level as the duration of the equity position equals the duration of assets minus the duration of liabilities:

$$D_{equity} = D_{assets} - D_{liabilities}$$

To the extent the institution operates with major business engagements in several currency areas, the equity duration gaps should be considered for each of the respective currency areas. Each of these duration gaps indicate how changes in the interest rate levels in the respective currencies would impact the corporation's equity position in that currency. Hence, to consolidate the currency denominated interest rate exposures there would have to be some conversion of the value effects in the foreign currencies to the local currency of accounting. Such an analysis can quickly become rather complex if it takes a variety of possible interest rate and foreign exchange rate scenarios into consideration. Whereas this might be a worthwhile exercise, it is sufficient to say that the 'simple' duration gap calculations in the major currencies do provide some indication of the risk exposures the corporation is assuming.

The conventional approach to transaction exposures is to consider the potential cash flow effect on foreign currency denominated receivables and payables from changes in the foreign exchange rates. This approach is distinct from and unrelated to the analyses of interest rate exposures in the different currency areas, which more often than not is ignored in corporate risk management. The currency risk exposures simply reflect the potential effects on the net cash flows calculated in the local currency as the foreign currency denominated payments are converted at the foreign exchange rates that might exist at the future payment dates.

## 2.6 Measuring foreign exchange rate gaps

**Currency exposures** typically arise when there is a mismatch between foreign exchange rate denominated receivables and payables over time because the future conversion of value into the local currency of accounting is unknown (Figure 2.16).[8]

The payments in foreign exchange that constitute the currency exposures can derive from commercial trade transactions in the global market, international financial investments, overseas direct investments, financing and debt servicing transactions in global debt markets, and short-term transactions in the foreign exchange market to assume speculative positions and take advantage of ongoing foreign exchange rate movements. Foreign currency receivables are registered as assets and foreign currency payables are registered as liabilities and hence the currency exposure for a given time period, e.g. overnight or three months, would correspond to the liquidity gap calculated as assets minus liabilities in that currency (Figure 2.17). Hence, a negative overnight liquidity gap of $120 million, for example, expresses that more payables are due in US dollars tomorrow than there are receivables, and hence there is a need to acquire this amount of foreign currency at the going market price,

**Figure 2.16** Currency exposure

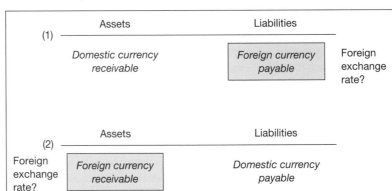

**Figure 2.17** Cash maturity profile (US dollar book)

| Maturity | Assets | Liabilities | Liquidity gap | Cumulative outflow |
|----------|--------|-------------|---------------|--------------------|
| Overnight | 150 | 270 | −120 | −120 |
| < 3 months | 170 | 210 | −40 | −160 |
| 3−12 months | 120 | 240 | −120 | −280 |
| 1−3 years | 280 | 150 | 130 | −150 |
| 3−5 years | 370 | 230 | 140 | −10 |
| > 5 years | 20 | 10 | 10 | − |
| Total | 1110 | 1110 | − | − |

**Figure 2.18** Cash maturity profile and gap limits

| Maturity | Assets | Liabilities | Liquidity gap | Cumulative outflow | Limit 1 | Limit 2 |
|----------|--------|-------------|---------------|--------------------|---------|---------|
| Overnight | 150 | 270 | −120 | −120 | ±150 | −300 |
| < 3 months | 170 | 210 | −40 | −160 | ±150 | −300 |
| 3−12 months | 120 | 240 | −120 | −280 | ±150 | −300 |
| 1−3 years | 280 | 150 | 130 | −150 | ±150 | −300 |
| 3−5 years | 370 | 230 | 140 | −10 | ±150 | −300 |
| > 5 years | 20 | 10 | 10 | − | − | − |

which remains unknown until the market opens tomorrow.[9] The uncertainty about the future foreign exchange rate from this mismatch between payments and receivables in US dollars constitutes a currency exposure. To get a better sense of the development of currency exposures over time, the liquidity gaps can be calculated for suitable future time intervals. Hence, the gap can be measured within each time period and as a cumulative outflow expressing the total exposure until the end of the period.

A simple way to manage the foreign exchange rate risks is first to provide a good overview of the currency exposures associated with transactions in all the major currencies, secondly to determine what constitutes reasonable currency exposures, e.g. by comparison to reported net income, total assets, and total equity, and on that basis set limits for maximum acceptable exposures (Figure 2.18). The limits can be set both in terms of the within period liquidity gaps (Limit 1) and in terms of cumulative outflows for the entire period (Limit 2).

Since the institution is likely to engage in transactions in many foreign currencies, it may be worthwhile to outline the cash maturity profile for each of the currency areas in which the corporation has major engagements and set appropriate exposure limits for each of the currencies (Figure 2.19).

The distinction between transaction exposures and translation exposures is often a question of managerial judgment. Once overseas investments or acquisitions are made they are subjected to specific accounting practices that in some cases may allow immediate write downs of goodwill or allow for protracted periods of depreciation in case of long-term assets of perceived durability. However, that does not necessarily mean that these assets are associated with translation exposures only. The criteria should rather be to which extent these assets remain part of the corporation's operating asset base that in the name of strategic flexibility sooner or later

**Figure 2.19** Cumulative outflow limits per currency

| Currency | < 3 months | < 12 months | < 3 years | Cumulative outflow limit |
|---|---|---|---|---|
| US Dollars | 150 | 150 | 120 | 200 |
| Euros | 170 | 120 | 100 | 180 |
| Yen | 120 | 120 | 100 | 180 |
| Currency$_1$ | – | – | – | – |
| ... | | | | |
| ... | | | | |
| Currency$_n$ | – | – | – | – |

might be subjected to divestment at prevailing market prices. Hence, it is important for risk management purposes to include all relevant assets and liabilities of any substance at their assessed market values in the analysis of both interest rate and currency gaps.

The corporate history is replete with examples of firms that were forced to restructure, i.e. liquidate, divest, and acquire other productive assets to reach a more appropriate competitive position. Hence, if these exposures are ignored in the gapping analyses they remain invisible for risk management purposes and cannot be taken into consideration when the corporation's true exposures are evaluated. For example, the restructurings pursued by Royal Ahold, the Dutch-based global retailing outfit, resulted in reported losses of around half a billion US dollars during the first quarter of 2004 as they divested business assets in Brazil and other places.[10] In other words, these assets did not constitute 'sunk cost' to be hidden under a heading of translation exposures, but constituted marketable real assets that should be assessed at their presumed market value at any time to fully capture the interest rate and currency risks exposing the global enterprise.

## 2.7 Portfolio optimization

The interest rate and currency exposure puzzle in the choice of investing on a global scale can be facilitated by applications of modern portfolio theoretical considerations. The different combinations of all possible assets with different cash flow structures and different currency denominations can be arranged so as to determine the expected return and standard deviation in returns measured in the local currency of accounting. These calculations are derived on the basis of historical time series data and thus project previous market conditions into the assessment of the future risk-return conditions. If these hold true, the border area of the resulting investment feasibility space depicts the contours of what must be considered an optimal choice of portfolio combinations. Hence, any investment portfolio combining different financial and commercial assets should be chosen along this **efficient frontier** because any point along this line represents a better choice compared to all points below the line within the investment feasibility space. In practice, the final choice must be determined by managerial considerations, balancing the leadership's preferences for economic returns and exposures to risk. A number of economic constraints will also frame these decisions including various resource limitations that reduce the scope of organizational activities (Figure 2.20).

**Figure 2.20** Optimizing the corporate asset portfolio

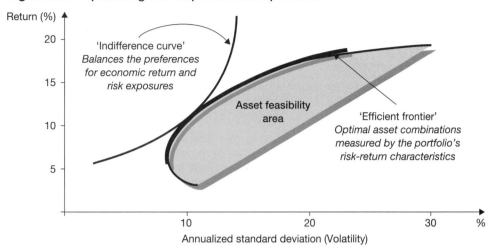

---

**Box 2.2 Aspects of modern portfolio theory and associated risk measures**

The analytical framework underlying modern portfolio theory as developed by Markowitz and others utilizes the relatively simple but useful concept of risk diversification.[11] Hence, when risk is defined as the variability in market prices or financial returns, it is possible to reduce this risk by including more assets into the portfolio. If the returns of two financial assets always move in completely opposite directions, there must be one combination of these assets that makes return fluctuations even out in the portfolio. However, this is not the criterion for diversification. It is sufficient that returns are not developing in complete unison for diversification to happen because this will reduce the relative variability of returns on the overall portfolio consisting of combinations of those assets.

Since financial risk usually is measured by the standard deviation in market returns it is important to be able to calculate this in the context of a portfolio consisting of various assets. Assuming a portfolio of say $n$ different assets then the returns of these assets move in concert to some extent over time two-by-two as expressed by their covariance $(\sigma_{ij})$. The correlation coefficient is the covariance standardized by the standard deviations of returns on the two securities $(\rho_{ij} = \sigma_{ij}/\sigma_i\sigma_j)$ and thus falls within a range between $-1$ and $+1$ (see a textbook on statistics if further elaboration is needed). A correlation coefficient of $-1$ indicates that returns move in completely opposite directions, whereas a correlation coefficient of $+1$ indicates complete co-variation of returns. The bilateral relationships between assets can be represented in a so-called variance/covariance matrix:

$n$ assets $(1, 2, 3, \ldots n)$
$n^2$ return-relationships

|  | 1 | 2 | 3 |  | $j$ |  | $n$ |
|---|---|---|---|---|---|---|---|
| 1 | $\sigma_1^2$ | $\sigma_{12}$ | $\sigma_{13}$ | $\cdots$ | $\sigma_{1j}$ | $\cdots$ | $\sigma_{1n}$ |
| 2 | $\sigma_{21}$ | $\sigma_2^2$ | $\sigma_{23}$ | $\cdots$ | $\sigma_{2j}$ | $\cdots$ | $\sigma_{2n}$ |
| 3 | $\sigma_{31}$ | $\sigma_{32}$ | $\sigma_3^2$ | $\cdots$ | $\sigma_{3j}$ | $\cdots$ | $\sigma_{3n}$ |
| $j$ | $\sigma_{j1}$ | $\sigma_{j2}$ | $\sigma_{j3}$ | $\cdots$ | $\sigma_{ij}$ | $\cdots$ | $\sigma_{jn}$ |
| $n$ | $\sigma_{n1}$ | $\sigma_{n2}$ | $\sigma_{n3}$ | $\cdots$ | $\sigma_{nj}$ | $\cdots$ | $\sigma_n^2$ |

▶

These measures of bilateral return-relationships are used to calculate the standard deviation of the portfolio returns as expressed in the following general formula:

$$\text{Standard deviation of portfolio } (\sigma_p) = (\Sigma \Sigma \, w_i \, w_j \, \rho_{ij} \, \sigma_i \, \sigma_j)^{1/2}$$

where

$w_i$ = the weight by market value by which asset $i$ is included in the portfolio;
$\rho_{ij}$ = the correlation coefficient between the returns of asset $i$ and asset $j$;
$\sigma_i$ = the standard deviation of the returns of asset $i$.

The standard deviation in market returns of a given portfolio as derived then is the relevant risk measure for a specific combined asset portfolio. Given sufficient historical data on, e.g. daily price developments and associated return measures for a series of assets, it is possible to calculate the expected returns of different portfolio combinations, by weighting the returns of the assets included in the portfolio, and the associated risk (standard deviation in return) based on the formula given above. What derives from this exercise is that different portfolio combinations can lead to vastly different risk-return characteristics of the overall portfolio (Figure 2.21).

The most interesting portfolio choices are the ones that fall along the edge of the fat line (the efficient frontier) because they all represent portfolio combinations that provide the highest returns for a given level of risk or the lowest risk for a given level of return. Whereas these portfolio perspectives are developed for investment in financial assets, they could be applied as well to combinations of financial and commercial investment alternatives alike. In conventional portfolio theory, the argument claims that portfolios with the optimal risk-return characteristics should reflect combinations that fall along the straight line determined by the risk free rate ($r_f$) on the vertical scale and the tangential point of the efficient frontier (the capital allocation line). This line represents different combinations of the optimal portfolio of risky assets (OP) and the risk free asset, i.e. short-term government bonds.[12]

Due to the portfolio diversification effects the more extensive the portfolio, the higher the likelihood that the efficient frontier can be pushed further in a north-westerly direction. This will be the case until the situation where all possible financial

**Figure 2.21  Risk-return characteristics of different portfolios**

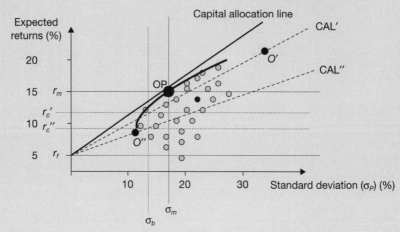

and commercial assets in the global economy are considered in the portfolio composition, and hence the optimal portfolio of risky assets in this case would correspond to the total market portfolio. At this point no more diversification gains are possible and hence the diversified portfolio would only be exposed to the overall movements in market returns (systematic risk) whereas risk elements peculiar to the individual invested assets (unsystematic risk) have been diversified away. As a consequence, any asset should be priced in accordance with its expected covariance with market returns as expressed in the asset's β-value, which, in practice, is determined as the correlation coefficient between asset and market returns. This is the premise of the capital asset pricing model (CAPM) as developed and modified by Sharpe (1966) and others:[13]

$$r_a = r_f + \beta_a(r_m - r_f)$$

This relationship expresses that the return of a given asset (a) is proportional to the β-value of the asset in question, i.e. the compensation above the risk-free rate should reflect the systematic risk element of the asset. The risk-return relationship captured in the capital allocation line reflects the risk-adjusted return that must prevail for assets with different levels of risk in an efficient debt market where portfolios can be easily adjusted and restructured to improve on return conditions. This relationship is expressed in the so-called **Sharpe ratio**, which is equal to the slope of the capital allocation line:

$$\text{Sharpe ratio} = \frac{(r_o - r_f)}{\sigma_o}$$

The Sharpe ratio indicates the expected excess return above the risk-free rate that should be achieved per unit of risk for any asset portfolio (O) given that it is optimally priced and hence lies on the capital allocation line. The same relationship can be expressed in terms of the portfolio's β-value, the so-called **Traynor ratio**, where the expected excess return is indicated in terms of systematic risk (β) as opposed to percentage variance (volatility):

$$\text{Traynor ratio} = \frac{(r_o - r_f)}{\beta}$$

An alternative risk-adjusted risk-return measure is suggested by the so-called Modigliani–Modigliani (M-squared) model. Since optimal portfolio combinations lie on the capital asset line, we can determine what the expected excess return should be for any risk level by combining the optimal risky portfolio (OP) with risk-free cash instruments. This 'trick' provides for the possibility of adjusting the return of any portfolio to a common standard risk level serving as a benchmark to compare the risk-adjusted returns:

$$\text{M-squared return} = r_f + \frac{(r_o - r_f)\sigma_b}{\sigma_o}$$

For example, a portfolio (O′) that lies on the capital asset line (CAP′) could be adjusted to a common benchmark risk level ($\sigma_b$) by including more risk-free assets into the portfolio and at this risk level has a comparable return of ($r'_c$), while a portfolio (O″) that lies on the capital asset line (CAP″) could be adjusted to the same benchmark risk level ($\sigma_b$) by including less risk-free assets into the portfolio and at this risk level has a comparable return of ($r''_c$). Hence, this ratio allows different portfolios to be compared to a common benchmark.

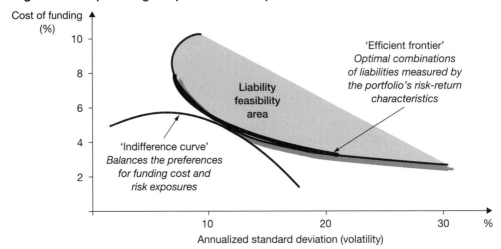

**Figure 2.22** Optimizing the portfolio of corporate liabilities

The portfolio theoretical perspectives can be adapted to liabilities as well as to assets and thus the same approach can be applied to determine the most optimal combinations of different funding alternatives from the global capital market. By analyzing the expected risk-return characteristics of all possible combinations of available financing alternatives, the institution can outline the contours of its financing feasibility space. The optimal choices will then lie along the south-western edge of this space because all the portfolio combinations on this efficient frontier will have lower financing cost for a given level of risk or lower risk for a given level of funding cost. The final choice of financing structure is determined by managerial considerations balancing the preferences for funding costs and risk exposures, while these decisions are constrained by a number of limiting factors such as credit rating, access to financial markets, supplier relationships, etc. (Figure 2.22).

The application of portfolio optimization models must be based on historical market information because recorded price data are needed to determine prevailing variance and covariance patterns between different assets and liabilities. This dependency on past market behaviour constitutes a potential shortcoming of this approach. Market conditions are constantly changing and results in ongoing modifications to the efficient frontiers for both assets and liabilities as data on market price developments are updated. Furthermore, the riskiest of all situations are made up by events where exogenous risk factors develop in unusual and hitherto unexpected ways. Under these circumstances the models are likely to misrepresent the true situation and, therefore, portfolio theory should be applied with caution as one of several informative sources. Hence, the model results should not be perceived as final truths but should constitute part of the analytical support used for decision-making purposes.

## 2.8 An integrative risk management perspective

The portfolio optimization approach in effect considers the potential influence of a variety of risk factors on the expected return on financial and commercial assets invested on a global scale and the expected cost of a collection of global funding alternatives. The variance–covariance relationship between returns of different international assets as measured in the local currency of accounting incorporates both the interest rate fluctuations in each of the currency areas as well as concurrent changes in the foreign exchange rates. Hence, the resulting local currency based risk measures incorporate both interest rate and currency risks simultaneously as they evolve and affect exposures over time. Price developments in the debt and currency markets are a consequence of attempts by market participants to forestall and position themselves in view of foreseeable changes in many other elements, including monetary intervention, policy initiatives, political risk, default risk, etc. As such, the resulting conjoint effects of interest rate and foreign exchange rate movements arguably capture the influences of many relevant risk factors that interact in highly complex ways. Hence, despite the potential shortcomings of the portfolio optimization approach, it does provide for a relatively simple way to capture the potential effects of different risk factors at the same time.

Many of the risk management perspectives have evolved among financial institutions that operate in environments circumscribed by volatile price developments in financial markets. Hence, the major risk factors considered in the financial industry include interest rate risk, foreign exchange rate risk, and credit risk. In a financial context, credit risk is related to the viability of commercial enterprises to service and repay their debt commitments, including bank loans, corporate bonds, trade receivables, etc. Part of this risk exposure relates to general macroeconomic and industrial conditions, while another part relates to firm specific circumstances as some organizations are better at responding to the environmental challenges and exploiting emerging opportunities than others. To some extent this division corresponds to the distinction between systematic and unsystematic risk in the capital asset pricing model. While credit risk can be systematized to some degree through analysis of historical default records and development of credit scoring models, etc., there are still major influences deriving from competitive market dynamics and the heterogeneity of strategic management capabilities. Other risk exposures caused by the failure of human and technological interactions in organizations, including mistakes, fraud, computer breakdowns, etc., have received increased recognition in recent years.[14] Country, sovereign, and political risk factors are related to default risk, but constitute additional concerns associated with cross-border transactions and global operations as the corporation gets exposed to political, economic, and legal systems outside the jurisdiction of the home country. Many insurance products and derivative instruments are developed to provide coverage for these diverse types of risks on a stand-alone basis, i.e. interest rate, foreign exchange rate, and credit risks are often considered as exposures that are independent of each other.

It is straightforward to see the relationship between earnings sensitivity and fluctuations in the value of assets and liabilities. These can comprise financial investments and obligations as well as commercial payables and receivables, the net value of which can be affected by a variety of exogenous factors, i.e. events in the environment that are outside managerial control. Such events include changes in the interest rates of foreign currency areas and changes in the foreign exchange rates. The sensitivity to these types of financial events is relatively easy to quantify because the assets are actively traded and price developments in the quoted markets serve as the basis for the risk measures, and the associated earnings effect can be readily calculated on the basis of identified exposures. However, other important risk factors relating to socio-political, macroeconomic, systemic, and behavioural events are much more difficult to quantify even though they may represent highly significant exposures. Furthermore, the earnings effects of these events may be interrelated in very complex ways, such as demand, inflation, default, and human behavioural events that usually are disregarded in the risk exposure considerations.

One way to cope with the potential relatedness of several risk factors at the same time is captured by the notion of **value-at-risk** (VaR), which was developed to reach a single risk measure capturing the aggregate exposure of many different risk factors. The need for a single risk measure arose out of the expanding activities of large globally engaged financial conglomerates with trading activities in many different types of assets and financial instruments, taking place in many different entities located around the world. The sheer complexity of all these trading activities required some simplification in the assessment of the institutions' overall exposures that also took into account the interaction between price developments of instruments traded in different markets.

The conventional calculation of value-at-risk relates to financial market risks and hence is based on analyses of historical trading prices, e.g. in the form of daily price quotes, for all assets and financial instruments in which the institution is engaged. To the extent the analysis also includes commercial assets, it requires data developed on a daily mark-to-market basis, where asset values are formally assessed over time across regular time intervals, e.g. using a discounted cash flow methodology. The resulting data time-series provide the basis for a variance–covariance matrix containing statistical measures of the price variation for each individual asset and the price co-variation of all the assets two-by-two. This information provides the foundation for calculating the standard deviation of the overall portfolio of all assets and financial instruments the institution regularly engages in (see insert on aspects of modern portfolio theory for a more detailed discussion of these calculations). Given the historical price patterns, the distribution of daily profits on the portfolio of traded assets and financial instruments over a certain time period can be described as a normal distribution. In a portfolio of more than ten assets and financial instruments the normality of profit distribution will usually hold, and the more diversified the portfolio, the higher the likelihood that the profit development is normally distributed. This is rather important because it provides us with a relatively simple way of assessing the overall market risk imposed by this portfolio of many different assets and financial instruments (Figure 2.23).

The value-at-risk indicates the size of loss, i.e. change in portfolio value, the institution can expect to incur over a certain time period with a specific likelihood or probability ($\alpha$) under the assumption that past price relationships remain unchanged, i.e. there is an $\alpha$ chance that the loss will exceed VaR during the period:

$$\text{Prob}(\Delta \text{Profit} \leq \text{VaR}) = \alpha$$

In many cases the variance–covariance measures relate to daily price quotes and hence the loss or change in profit calculation corresponds to potential daily losses although other time periods might be relevant as well. However, the risk measures based on the standard deviation in the daily returns of an asset portfolio can easily be adapted to other applicable time periods.

*Example*: The standard deviation of daily returns on a portfolio of financial and commercial assets has been determined as 0.0283 ($\sigma_{\text{daily}} = 2.83\%$) based on market valuation data collected over some time.

**Figure 2.23** Value-at-risk of traded portfolio

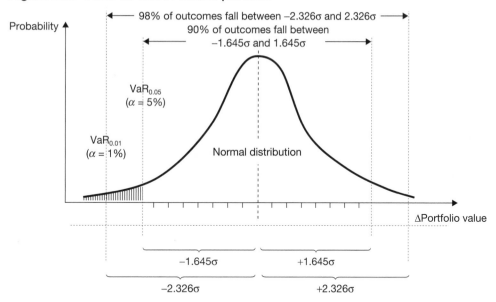

- The daily risk measure is converted to a weekly risk measure as follows:

$$\sigma_{\text{weekly}} = \sigma_{\text{daily}} \times (5)^{1/2} = 0.0283 \times 2.236 = 0.06328 = 6.32\%$$

- The daily risk measure is converted to a biweekly risk measure as follows:

$$\sigma_{\text{biweekly}} = \sigma_{\text{daily}} \times (10)^{1/2} = 0.0283 \times 3.162 = 0.08949 = 8.95\%$$

- The daily risk measure is converted to a monthly risk measure as follows:

$$\sigma_{\text{monthly}} = \sigma_{\text{daily}} \times (21)^{1/2} = 0.0283 \times 4.5826 = 0.12969 = 12.97\%$$

- The daily risk measure is converted to a semi-annual risk measure as follows:

$$\sigma_{\text{semiannual}} = \sigma_{\text{daily}} \times (126)^{1/2} = 0.0283 \times 11.225 = 0.31767 = 31.77\%$$

- The daily risk measure is converted to an annual risk measure as follows:

$$\sigma_{\text{annual}} = \sigma_{\text{daily}} \times (252)^{1/2} = 0.0283 \times 15.8745 = 0.44925 = 44.95\%$$

In other situations the variance-covariance measures may out of necessity be developed less frequently, for example, as monthly mark-to-market calculations applied to a commercial asset. The risk measures based on the standard deviation in monthly returns of an asset portfolio can also be adapted to other time periods.

*Example*: The standard deviation of monthly returns on a portfolio of financial and commercial assets has been determined to approximate 0.20 ($\sigma_{\text{monthly}} = 20.0\%$) based on regular mark-to-market valuations in the past.

- The monthly risk measure is converted to a weekly risk measure as follows:

$$\sigma_{\text{weekly}} = \sigma_{\text{monthly}} \times (5/21)^{1/2} = 0.20 \times 0.4880 = 0.0976 = 9.76\%$$

- The daily risk measure is converted to a semi-annual risk measure as follows:

$$\sigma_{\text{semiannual}} = \sigma_{\text{monthly}} \times (126/21)^{1/2} = 0.20 \times 2.4495 = 0.4898 = 48.98\%$$

- The daily risk measure is converted to an annual risk measure as follows:

$$\sigma_{\text{annual}} = \sigma_{\text{monthly}} \times (252/21)^{1/2} = 0.20 \times 3.4641 = 0.6928 = 69.28\%$$

The value-at-risk concept depends on the chosen level of statistical significance where a lower level of significance will correspond to a higher value-at-risk, i.e. a lower confidence level reflects a more conservative risk perception. Hence, to assess the aggregate risk exposure assumed by the institution, we might use a probability level of 5%, where the associated value-at-risk then would indicate the size of loss that might be assumed with a 5% likelihood of occurrence. Whether this level of significance is representative for the institution's risk-return profile is a subjective question to be determined by senior management on behalf of the owners and other important stakeholders. The lower the level of significance, the higher the calculated potential risk exposure, and consequently the more conservative will be the value-at-risk measure as an indicator of risk exposure. Among financial institutions that use the value-at-risk concept to measure overall trading exposures in financial assets and instruments, a normal cut-off level is 1% rather than 5%.

Provided the profit development of the portfolio follows a normal distribution, we can use the derived standard deviation ($\sigma$) in portfolio profits to determine the loss associated with 5% or 1% levels of confidence. Since 90% of all observations in a normal distribution fall within a range spanning from $-1.645\sigma$ to $+1.645\sigma$, the lower range indicator determines the loss reflecting a 5% likelihood of occurrence. Conversely 98% of all observations in a normal distribution fall within $-2.326\sigma$ and $+2.326\sigma$, where the lower indicator then determines the loss reflecting a 1% probability. Once the standard deviation of the profitability of the asset portfolio is determined and the level of significance is chosen, the value-at-risk of the portfolio can be determined.

$$VaR = MV \times \text{Factor} \times \text{Standard deviation of portfolio}$$

where

$MV$ = the market value of the asset portfolio;
Factor = 1.645 (5% confidence level) or 2.326 (1% confidence level).

*Example*: Assume a financial institution with an equally weighted three-asset portfolio consisting of a security ($s$), a currency position ($c$), and an equity investment ($e$) with a total current market value of $100 million. This situation could also be interpreted as a commercial enterprise that holds liquid assets (traded securities), has foreign exchange receivables (currency assets), and runs a business in the form of an equity position (direct investment).

The standard deviations on the daily returns of each of the assets have been determined as: $\sigma_s = 0.06\%$, $\sigma_c = 0.55\%$, $\sigma_e = 1.85\%$, and the correlation coefficients between returns of the assets have been determined as: $\rho_{sc} = -0.2$, $\rho_{ce} = 0.1$, $\rho_{se} = 0.4$ then, the standard deviation of the portfolio returns can be determined as follows (the three-portfolio case):

$$\begin{aligned}
\sigma_{\text{portfolio}} &= [(w_s\sigma_s)^2 + (w_c\sigma_c)^2 + (w_e\sigma_e)^2 + 2(\rho_{sc}w_sw_c\sigma_s\sigma_c) + 2(\rho_{ce}w_cw_e\sigma_c\sigma_e) + 2(\rho_{se}w_sw_e\sigma_s\sigma_e)]^{\frac{1}{2}} \\
&= [(0.33 \times 0.0006)^2 + (0.33 \times 0.0055)^2 + (0.33 \times 0.0185)^2 + 2(-0.2 \times 0.33^2 \times 0.0006 \times 0.0055) \\
&\quad + 2(0.10 \times 0.33^2 \times 0.0055 \times 0.0185) + 2(0.4 \times 0.33^2 \times 0.0006 \times 0.0185)]^{\frac{1}{2}} \\
&= [0.00000004 + 0.00000329 + 0.00003727 - 0.00000014 + 0.00000222 \\
&\quad + 0.00000097]^{\frac{1}{2}} \\
&= 0.00004365^{\frac{1}{2}} = 0.006607
\end{aligned}$$

Hence, the standard deviation in daily returns on the portfolio is around 0.66%. This is less than the weighted average of the three standard deviations of 0.82% (={0.06 + 0.55 + 1.85}/3) due to diversification effects as the co-variations in returns of all the assets are less than perfect ($\rho < 1$).

From this we can calculate the daily value-at-risk associated with this portfolio at the 5% level of confidence:

$$VaR = \$100\ 000\ 000 \times 1.645 \times 0.006607 = \$1\ 086\ 852$$

That is, there is a 5% probability that this asset portfolio can cause a daily loss of around $1.1 million.

If we instead want to determine the daily value-at-risk at the 1% level of confidence:

$$VaR = \$100\ 000\ 000 \times 2.326 \times 0.006607 = \$1\ 536\ 788$$

So, there is a 1% probability that this asset portfolio can cause a daily loss of around $1.5 million.

For highly liquid portfolios of financial assets where the portfolio composition can be readily changed, it may be appropriate to consider the daily VaR. However, to the extent we are dealing with relatively illiquid commercial assets the annual VaR might be a more appropriate risk indicator.

To do this we must first convert the standard deviation of daily returns to an annual return basis:

$$\sigma_{portfolio,annual} = \sigma_{portfolio,daily} \times 252^{1/2} = 0.006607 \times 15.8745 = 0.10488\ (10.5\%)$$

From this we can calculate the annual value-at-risk associated with a 5% level of confidence:

$$VaR = \$100\ 000\ 000 \times 1.645 \times 0.10488 = \$17\ 252\ 760$$

That is, there is a 5% probability that this asset portfolio can lead to an annual loss of around $17.2 million.

If we instead want to determine the annual value-at-risk at the 1% level of confidence:

$$VaR = \$100\ 000\ 000 \times 2.326 \times 0.10488 = \$24\ 395\ 088$$

So, there is a 1% probability that this asset portfolio can lead to an annual loss of around $24.4 million.

The example illustrates how it may be possible to quantify an aggregate risk exposure and develop a measure of the potential downside loss associated with a given asset portfolio. It should be noted here that variation in returns and profit reflects an upside potential for extraordinary gains as well, but in a risk exposure context only the downside loss potential is recognized because it relates to default risk in the institutions and, therefore, has elemental importance to the management of a going concern. Just as in the case of the volatility and risk-return calculations, the VaR calculations are very dependent on the choice of time period used for the underlying data time-series. In other words, the VaR calculations can result in more than one absolute value and therefore the methodology has its limitations and should be used with healthy scepticism.

Whereas the previous discussion of the value-at-risk describes the **variance–covariance approach** to the derivation of the VaR measures, there are alternative methodologies. One alternative approach is to perform **historical simulations** based on market and valuation data collected over a previous time period. According to this approach, the daily values of the total asset portfolio could be calculated in accordance with the registered prices and values, say over the past 500 days. Hence, the daily VaR at a 5% confidence limit would correspond to the performance (loss) associated with the 25th worst day. Another alternative is to perform so-called **Monte Carlo simulations** where random numbers are drawn to generate many possible value-scenarios in accordance with assumed distributions about the variance–covariance relationships. Hence, computers can be used to generate, e.g.

10 000 simulated daily value scenarios, in which case the VaR with a 5% confidence limit would correspond to the 500th worst daily portfolio value.

The value-at-risk methodology, as well as the portfolio optimization perspectives, provides the means to assess the overall effects of an elaborate set of exogenous risk factors that are likely to interact in highly complex manners without necessarily engaging in a very detailed and complicated analysis. This could be a very practical approach to measure, monitor, and manage the general risk exposure because the relationships between the individual risk factors that can be identified as important to the institution are less than clear-cut. For example, we realize that there are some intricate relationships between the interest rate structures in different currency areas and developments in foreign exchange rates. The final effects of these relationships in turn are potentially counteracted by macroeconomic developments, such as demand and price developments.[15] If the purchasing power parity paradigm prevails, changes in foreign exchange rates should reflect inflationary developments in the respective currency areas. So, if foreign currency receivables are exposed to a potential weakening of the foreign exchange rates then it could be associated with demand driven inflationary pressures in the foreign economies, which over time should compensate for the immediate downside risk on short-term recorded transactions. Furthermore, the interest rate and currency relationships reflect highly complex influences from short-term financial speculation, medium- to long-term investment inducements, monetary interventions, policy initiatives, economic endowments, entrepreneurial opportunities, etc., all of which matter to some extent. Rather than trying to detail each of these complex relationships one approach could be to identify the major risk exposures and assess the potential impact these factors may have on the stability of profitability over time and make sure that the downside risk exposures are not excessive to the extent that they may jeopardize the continued operations of the institution. Risk identification and exposure measurement constitute necessary first steps to evaluate the potential risks that affect the institution and determine the appropriate risk–return trade-offs in the institution's policies.

## 2.9 Modern risk management perspectives

Risk relates to potentially adverse economic impacts caused by uncertainty and unexpected events beyond managerial control. However, the risk concept is somewhat subjective, because the level of uncertainty and the degree of unexpectedness depend on how risk is approached. An institution that ignores its environment and what possibly might evolve around it will be taken by surprise when adverse things happen and as a consequence will be more exposed. Conversely, an institution that conceives of potentially adverse events and tries to take precautions against them will not be taken by surprise to the same extent and might even with some ingenuity reduce the potential downside effects. In other words, the more effort devoted to identify, measure, monitor, and mitigate the causes of potentially adverse events, the more the element of surprise is reduced and the better the risk exposures can be managed.

The risk management perspective suggests that risk exposures should be managed in an explicit process following distinct steps.[16] According to this perspective, the relevant risk factors should first be identified. It is necessary to know what the potential risks are in order to cope with their potential adverse effects. Once identified, the risk exposures should be analyzed, measured, and incorporated into a formal reporting system to assess the significant risk exposures. This overview of the relevant risk landscape eventually allows decision makers to consider whether and how to reduce risk exposures and establish prudent precautionary measures. One outcome of the risk management process could be a framework for acceptable over-all risk limits as well as limits applied to key risk factors as discussed above. However, the real challenge relates to the issues of covering, hedging, or managing the residual risks that an enterprise decides is part-and-parcel of its business activities. Some of these risks may be covered by engagement in conventional insurance contracts, committed credit facilities from banks, risk-linked securities and contingent capital arrangements in the debt markets, as well as a wide variety of derivative instruments furnished through exchanges and direct over-the-counter distribution.

## Box 2.3 Risk management and economic efficiency

Companies manage risk and obtain financial cover for extreme developments that may jeopardize the firm's survival due to events beyond their control. Excessive economic exposures increase the insolvency risk of exposed entities and make it more difficult to obtain funding at economical rates. If funding gets scarce and the financial cost prohibitive due to increased **bankruptcy risk**, investment activities are curtailed, economic activity will drop, and partnerships will suffer and affect long-term business development adversely. An environment with a defunct insurance market will tend to have lower long-term economic growth. In the absence of appropriate risk-transfer arrangements, corporate investment considerations and financing decisions by financial institutions may be affected by extreme risks and cause financial resources to be channelled more cautiously towards less exposed uses.

Insurance contracts and derivative securities constitute risk transfer where payments are made in exchange for a commitment to reimburse for specific types of losses emanating from developments in asset prices and other economic events. Insurance markets pool funds from multiple entities and diversify the risks due to the law of large numbers. The trading of derivative securities between issuers and buyers allows multiple entities to exchange elements of risk exposures and thereby diversify exposures across many participants. Hence, risk transfer through insurance and derivatives allows individual institutions to smooth extreme impacts on future income streams and thereby protect their existing stocks of corporate wealth. However, insurance and derivatives also create incremental value for the economy as a whole as the availability of such risk transfer mechanisms encourages **firms** to behave in ways that induce investment and hence improve economic growth.

Insurance and derivatives can compensate corporations for large losses associated with extreme events that otherwise would have adverse implications for income creation and economic wealth. When future income is uncertain corporate decision makers tend to avoid tying economic resources into long-term commercial investments. Instead, savings are kept in short-term liquid financial assets so funds are available when the income falls. This propensity to self-insure may result in short-term low-risk investments and reduce funding for longer-term entrepreneurial investment opportunities. Risk transfer opportunities help smooth extreme volatilities in corporate earnings and thereby reduce bankruptcy and general relationship risk. Hence, shielding against extreme earnings impacts will improve the corporation's stakeholder relationships and provide for the establishment of long-term beneficial economic relationships to employees, customers, suppliers, partners, etc.

It seems reasonable to hedge against the extreme effects of identified risk exposures to shield against situations that might jeopardize the very survival of the firm, i.e. to reduce the potential bankruptcy costs. It is argued that financial hedging should be pursued to such an extent that it ensures cash availability for sound investment propositions.[17] If an institution with a given funding base is exposed to excessive risks, there is not sufficient cash available for positive net present value projects, because the inherent bankruptcy risk requires a larger level of liquidity. This so-called **under investment problem** reduces the ability to optimize the economic potential of the institution in the absence of risk management. To the extent that earnings volatility of the firm is reduced it will arguably lead to lower average cost of capital, which should expand the number of viable business opportunities available to the firm. It is further argued that hedging should be pursued to the extent that it stabilizes relationships to all the essential stakeholders.[18] A number of stakeholder groups such as employees, customers, and partners establish idiosyncratic structural relationships to work more closely with the firm and may not be able to readily trade and restructure this position as might investors in the firm's debt and equity instruments. Hence, the firm may have a vested interest not to jeopardize these intricate relationships by a highly erratic earnings development. This means that hedging should be pursued to ensure that financial resources remain available at reasonable costs and that important commercial relationships are retained even when the firm is exposed to unexpected and unforeseeable events.

A formal risk management process starts with the identification of significant risk factors. Once the important risk factors are identified the vulnerability to the risks are analyzed and the implied economic exposures measured and reported. This risk measurement framework is used to monitor developments in economic exposures and assess changes in the risk environment that may require responsive actions. The monitoring process helps determine excess exposures that should be covered through different risk transfer arrangements to shield against excessive earnings disruptions. The entire risk management approach should be conceived as a dynamic and ongoing process.[19] Since the environmental conditions continue to change, the profile of the institution's risk exposures may also change, and hence should be updated to reflect trends in political and regulatory initiatives, macroeconomic conditions, financial market prices, competitive developments, etc. The ongoing efforts to monitor the changing contours of the risk exposure should also comprise continuous evaluations of derivative solutions that provide new risk-transfer opportunities. The dynamic character of the risk management process implies that the identification of significant risk factors is an ongoing exercise (Figure 2.24). Simple environmental awareness, updating of existing exposure models and possibly using advanced simulation methodologies can help assess the changing profile of the risk

**Figure 2.24 The dynamics of risk management**

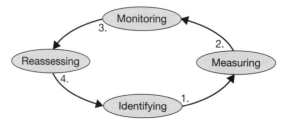

exposure and support the ongoing assessment of risk factors and their potential economic impacts.

The ongoing monitoring of the institution's key risk factors provides the means to assess the aggregate effects of the identified risk exposures. This makes it possible to determine whether the institution is moving towards an excessive level of risk and identify needs to modify existing risk-transfer arrangements, for example through use of different derivative instruments. By monitoring and maintaining risk exposures within acceptable limits, the firm can ensure that beneficial investment programs are shielded from unwarranted disruptions to the benefit of the future business growth.

## Conclusion

The internationalization of markets and commercial interactions exposes institutions to the volatility of business conditions and price developments in the global capital market. International financial institutions and multinational corporations with operational facilities in multiple currency areas typically incur interest rate gaps in each of these currencies and assume currency gaps in connection with the exchanges between the currency areas. These financial exposures should be continuously monitored and managed actively. Various techniques provide ample opportunity to account for potential exposure effects as well as the growing market for financial derivatives provide opportunities to modify and transfer excessive exposures.

## Summary

- Organizations are exposed to a variety of risk factors characterized by their potential adverse effects on return and profitability and comprise interest rate, foreign exchange rate, and other types of financial price risks as well as exposures associated with changes in socio-political, macroeconomic, and competitive conditions.

- Corporate risk exposures generally distinguish between translation and economic exposures constituting potential effects on future cash flow streams, which in turn are comprised by short-term transaction exposures and longer-term operational exposures.

- General measures of interest rate sensitivity on asset value and retained earnings can be derived on the basis of the duration concept in each of the major currency areas as well as gapping positions in the currencies capturing the associated foreign exchange rate exposures.

- Modern portfolio theory can be applied to optimize the asset and liability combinations based on the historical development in the asset value relationships and through scenario testing in advanced computer-based simulation models.

- The concept of value-at-risk (VaR) provides the means for an overall measure of the aggregate effects of all exogenous risk factors that affect the development in the total value of an institutional portfolio combining financial and commercial assets.

## Questions

2.1 Explain how interest rate exposures can arise and how they can be monitored and managed.

2.2 Explain why currency exposures can arise and how they can be monitored and managed.

2.3 Explain the concept of duration and what it can be used for.

2.4 What is the difference between duration and modified duration and what is its significance?

2.5 What are some essential limitations of the duration measure?

2.6 Explain the relationship between interest rate and currency risk.

2.7 Outline major types of risk and discuss the relationships between them.

2.8 How is the concept of risk conceived in:

   (a) financial theory?
   (b) financial institutions?
   (c) multinational corporations?

2.9 Explain the concept of volatility and how it may be used.

2.10 How can portfolio theory be applied in risk management?

2.11 Explain the concept value-at-risk (VaR) and its potential usefulness.

2.12 How can value-at-risk (VaR) be determined?

2.13 What are some essential limitations of value-at-risk (VaR)?

2.14 Explain how the risk management process should be structured.

## Exercises

2.1 Calculate the market value of the following financial and commercial assets:

   (a) Fixed-income security: a five-year $100 million nominal bond with annual coupon payments. The coupon rate is 5%, and the yield on comparable bonds is 7.5%

   (b) Zero-coupon bond: a seven-year $100 million bond with one bullet payments at final maturity. The current yield on bonds of comparable credit risk is 9.25%

   (c) Fixed-income security: a seven-year $100 million nominal bond with semi-annual coupons. The annual coupon rate is 6%, and the current yield on seven-year bonds of comparable credit risk is 9.25%

   (d) Commercial loan: a five-year $100 million corporate term loan with quarterly interest payments at prime plus 2.5% payable in four equal instalments at the end of year two, three, four, and five. Prime rate is currently 8.65% and the yield on a corresponding corporate bond is 9.56%

(e) Commercial project: a project with an initial investment of $100 million is expected to pay $20 million at the end of the first year, and then amounts increasing incrementally by $5 million annually each year until the project is terminated after ten years. A stock of comparable risk has a yield of 17.5%

2.2 Calculate the duration of each of the five financial and commercial assets described in 2.1(a)–(e) – Hint: use the table outline suggested in the text to perform the calculations.

2.3 Calculate the modified duration of the five financial and commercial assets described in 2.1(a)–(e).

2.4 Determine how the market values of the five financial and commercial assets described in 2.1 will change if the interest rate level increases by 0.50%-points.

2.5 An institution has two assets and two liabilities with current market values and durations as indicated in the following balance sheet:

| Assets ($ million) | (duration) | Liabilities ($ million) | (duration) |
|---|---|---|---|
| 5000 | 2.2 | 6000 | 1.9 |
| 3800 | 3.4 | 1200 | 4.7 |

Determine the interest rate sensitivity of the institution's equity position given a current interest rate level of 2.5%.

2.6 An institution has a portfolio consisting of the five financial and commercial assets described in 2.1. Calculate the duration of the portfolio before the interest rate level increases.

2.7 Determine how the market value of the portfolio consisting of the five financial and commercial assets described in 2.1 will change if the general interest rate level increases by 0.50%-points.

2.8 Access the website of the Federal Reserve Bank (www.federalreserve.gov) and derive the daily dollar/euro foreign exchange rates for the past 50 days and determine the volatility of the price development.

2.9 Calculate the daily value-at-risk (VaR) for the portfolio consisting of the five financial and commercial assets described in 2.1 given the following variance–covariance matrix (expressed in percentage terms):

$$
\begin{bmatrix}
\sigma_1^2 & \sigma_{12} & \sigma_{13} & \sigma_{1i} & \sigma_{1n} \\
\sigma_{21} & \sigma_2^2 & \sigma_{23} & \sigma_{2i} & \sigma_{2n} \\
\sigma_{31} & \sigma_{32} & \sigma_3^2 & \sigma_{3i} & \sigma_{3n} \\
\sigma_{j1} & \sigma_{j2} & \sigma_{j3} & \sigma_{ji} & \sigma_{jn} \\
\sigma_{n1} & \sigma_{n2} & \sigma_{n3} & \sigma_{ni} & \sigma_n^2
\end{bmatrix}
=
\begin{bmatrix}
0.11 & 0.34 & 0.24 & 0.09 & 0.13 \\
- & 0.15 & 0.28 & 0.05 & 0.11 \\
- & - & 0.16 & 0.16 & 0.08 \\
- & - & - & 0.21 & 0.32 \\
- & - & - & - & 0.25
\end{bmatrix}
$$

What would be the corresponding annual value-at-risk?

### Notes

[1] See, for example, Santomero, A. and Babbell, D. (2001), *Financial Markets, Instruments, and Institution*, 2nd edn, McGraw-Hill.

[2] The share of the total transaction volume effectuated between foreign exchange dealers and non-financial institutions has dropped from 17% to 13% from 1998 to 2001. See *Triennial Central Bank Survey of Foreign Exchange and Derivatives Market Activity 2001*, Bank for International Settlement, March 18, 2002

[3] The major accounting principles on currency translation comprise the current/non-current method, the monetary/non-monetary method, the temporal method, and the current rate method. In the current/non-current method all the current assets and liabilities of foreign affiliates are translated into the local currency of accounting at the current foreign exchange rates. In the monetary/non-monetary method all monetary assets and liabilities of foreign affiliates are translated into the local currency of accounting at the current foreign exchange rates. By monetary is understood balance sheet items relating to actual cash flows, such as cash balances, receivables, etc., while non-monetary items are items posted from historical payments, e.g. inventory, fixed assets, etc. The temporal method combines elements of the two former approaches, i.e. inventory can be reported at current rates if it is recorded at market value, even though it is considered a non-monetary method. The current rate method, which has been adopted by US multinationals since 1981 in accordance with *Statement of Financial Accounting Standards No. 52* (FASB 52), uses the current foreign exchange rates at the time of recording to translate all the assets and liabilities of foreign affiliates. However, a major portion of the associated translation gains and losses are posted directly into the equity account and thereby avoid direct influences on reported earnings on the income statement. See, for example, Shapiro, A. C. (2003), *Multinational Financial Management*, 7th edn, Wiley.

[4] Many companies have learned this the hard way, Enron being a recent example of monumental proportions.

[5] See, for example, Eiteman, D. K., Stonehill, A. I. and Moffett, M. H. (2004). *Multinational Business Finance*, 10th edn, Pearson Education.

[6] One should keep in mind that even though transactions are registered in the books it does not necessarily mean that they will be effectuated in all cases. For example, all foreign currency payments, whether they relate to commercial transactions or financial contracts, can be exposed to credit risk, counter-party risk, political risk, operational risk, etc., and, therefore, to the extent these risks occur the currency payments may not materialize as expected.

[7] See Andersen, T. J. (1993), *Currency and Interest Rate Hedging*, Prentice-Hall.

[8] This approach is arguably less applicable and relevant if the exposures comprise traded financial assets where changes in their market values probably ought to be included to provide a better picture of the 'true' interest rate exposure.

[9] In this context 'overnight' means foreign exchange transactions that must be closed the following business day, i.e. for cash settlement in three days since spot foreign exchange transactions are settled with two days' value.

[10] Shelley, T., 'Year of transition puts Ahold into red', *Financial Times*, June 14, 2004.

[11] See, for example, Markowitz, H. (1956), *Portfolio Selection: Efficient Diversification of Investments*, Wiley.

[12] See, for example, standard textbooks like Alexander, G. J., Sharpe, W. F. and Bailey, J. V. (2001), *Fundamentals of Investments*, 3rd edn, Prentice-Hall, and Bodie, Z., Kane, A. and Marcus, A. J. (2001), *Essentials of Investments*, 4th edn, McGraw-Hill.

[13] See, for example, Sharpe, W. F. (1964), 'Capital asset prices: a theory of market equilibrium under conditions of risk', *Journal of Finance*, **19**, pp. 425–42.

[14] The new Basel accord, Basel II, as something new considers operational risk. Although this type of risk is difficult to quantify, it is important to take into consideration.

[15] For a good discussion of these issues, see Oxelheim, L. and Wihlborg, C. (2003), *Managing in a Turbulent World Economy: Corporate Performance and Risk Exposure*, Wiley.

[16] Doherty, N. A. (2000), *Integrated Risk Management: Techniques and Strategies for Managing Corporate Risk*, McGraw-Hill.

[17] Froot, K. A., Scharfstein, D. S. and Stein, J. C. (1994), 'A framework for risk management', *Harvard Business Review*, **72**(6), pp. 91–102.

[18] Miller, K. D. (1998), 'Economic exposure and integrated risk management', *Strategic Management Journal*, **19**, 497–514.

[19] See, for example, Culp, C. L. (2002), *The Art of Risk Management*, Wiley.

# Chapter 3

# International financial markets and competitive developments

## Objectives

- Identify drivers of market innovation
- Introduce the arguments for economic risk-transfer effects
- Provide an overview of alternative risk-transfer markets and instruments
- Outline the financial market environments that fostered the wider use of derivatives
- Describe how risk-transfer markets support trends toward convergence and specialization
- Consider regulatory and accounting issues

Financial institutions increasingly operate under conditions of global competition where national, international, and Euro markets interact within a larger pool of exchangeable liquidity and buying power managed and allocated throughout the globe. Different types of credit intermediation and risk-transfer markets are linked through the specialized functions provided by financial institutions and spurred by various regulatory, competitive, and technological developments. This chapter outlines the contours of these interacting forces that provide a backdrop for the dramatic growth in financial derivatives and addresses some of the issues and concerns that circumscribe this trend.

## 3.1 Credit intermediation and risk-transfer

One of the major roles of financial institutions is to interact between economic entities with liquidity surplus and entities with a shortage of liquidity at different maturities. As such they play a major role in the credit intermediation process whereby agents in the economy are able to exchange immediate consumption, or buying power, for consumption at future points in time. Different types of financial institutions specialize in the exchange of funds across different maturity spectrums and provide buying power for different economic purposes. Commercial banks typically offer short- to medium-term commercial and consumer credits and obtain funding through balances on transactional demand deposits. Savings and loan institutions provide long-term mortgage credits funded by savings accounts. Casualty insurance companies receive regular premium payments and invest in short- to medium-term securities as financial reserves for future insurance claims. Life insurance companies and pension funds receive premiums on an ongoing basis and place the proceeds in medium- and long-term financial assets to cover their future commitments. Mutual funds exist in many shades, e.g. money market mutual funds invest in liquid short-term financial instruments, income funds invest in coupon-bearing securities and stocks with regular dividend payments, growth funds excel in small- to medium-sized companies, many of which represent innovative entrepreneurial outfits, etc. Different venture funds specialize in seed funding and provide financial and managerial support to start-up companies with a promising future potential. So-called hedge funds invest in many different financial assets including foreign exchange, commodities, derivative securities, etc., and frequently engage in arbitrage transactions between different types of credit intermediation and across capital markets located in different currency areas. Finance companies provide financing for a variety of specialized purposes, such as consumer credits, credit card receivables, commercial leasing contracts, etc., funded through issuance of various debt instruments. In other words, the financial industry represents a complex amalgam of institutions specializing in different types of credit intermediation and catering to specific types of funding and investment needs. In this process, the financial institutions make important decisions as they allocate funds across different types of debt obligations and thereby have significant influence on the resource allocation process in the economy. As borrowers receive loan proceeds from the banking system they obtain buying power that allows them to acquire durable consumer goods and organize productive assets in support of commercial activities and business projects. Consequently, there is a strong and direct relationship between the placement of funds in financial assets among financial institutions and investments in real assets made by commercial enterprises. These investments are made by enterprises in accordance with business plans that project future positive net cash flows and generate profits to the owners as well as providing income to employees and business partners. The cash flows generated from the corporate income streams, in turn, provide the basis for debt service payments in the form of interest and loan reimbursements to creditors and dividends to equity owners. In this way, there is an intricate link between the ability to generate profits in commercial markets and the financial returns provided in the capital market (Figure 3.1).[1]

**Figure 3.1** Relationship between capital and commercial markets

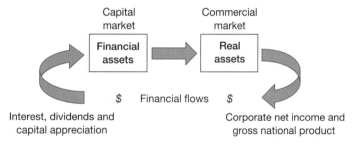

**Figure 3.2** The credit transformation process

Large uncertainties associated with the generation of future net income from commercial activities will have an adverse effect on the decisions made by financial institutions to fund these activities. Similarly, uncertainties associated with investment in financial assets will affect the ability of corporations to access the capital market. If the level of uncertainty is high, financial institutions in possession of current consumption capacity will require a higher future compensation to make it available today, which will reduce credit transformation, and hence the level of investment. In other words, there are positive economic outcome effects associated with efforts to reduce uncertainties arising from risk exposures in commercial and capital markets alike as more funding is made available for commercial investment. These positive economic outcomes have induced the development of various risk-transfer markets providing economic entities with opportunities to hedge against adverse effects from excessive levels of environmental uncertainty.

### 3.1.1 The role of financial institutions

The credit transformation process takes place via the banking system and through the securities market. In the first instance, funding is provided in the form of loan commitments that typically are held on the books of the financial institutions until repayment. In the latter case, loan proceeds are derived through issuance of securities that subsequently are placed with and traded among investors (Figure 3.2).

Whereas this is a convenient simplification of the way the credit intermediation process functions at large, the reality is considerably more complex. A wide range of financial institutions are involved that operate in rather distinct ways (Figure 3.3). Hence, credit intermediation through loaning of funds in different ways is typically carried out by commercial banks, savings and loan institutions, credit unions, and

**Figure 3.3** Financial institutions in the credit intermediation process

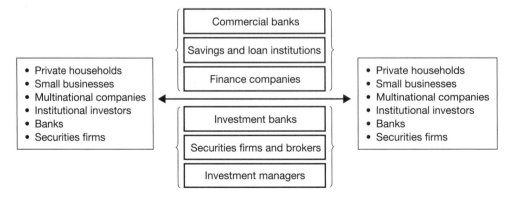

finance companies. The securities issuance route is typically managed by investment banks and securities firms as organizers and underwriters of new issues and placement of securities among institutional investors, such as life insurance companies, pension funds, and mutual funds. The institutional investors in turn take the advice of investment managers as they invest and divest funds in their asset portfolios while securities firms and brokers provide price information, and trade the securities in the market. The commercial banks, savings and loan institutions, and investment companies that originate borrowers and extend loans, as well as the investment banks, securities firms, and investment managers that arrange the new issuance and placement activities can all be considered financial intermediaries involved in the direct interactions between entities with excess cash and shortage of cash. In addition to this the securities firms and investment managers are involved in ongoing portfolio assessments and dispositions of financial assets in the secondary market, where previously issued securities are priced and traded. Private households, small businesses, and multinational corporations constitute the major groups of borrowers while institutional investors like insurance companies and mutual and pension funds make up the bulk of investors in securities. However, the entire picture is blurred by the fact that all financial intermediaries also act as borrowers and investors to some extent. At the same time, individuals and firms typically invest and borrow simultaneously, just like institutional investors not only invest but also may draw on bank lines and issue securities.

The financial intermediaries provide a series of rather distinct services that constitute different value propositions to their customers (Figure 3.4). Deposit taking institutions, such as commercial banks and savings and loan institutions are the sole suppliers of money on transactional deposit accounts and usually complement this capacity with various payment services. In addition, many banks offer a variety of medium-term savings and investment opportunities combined with a range of depository and fiduciary services. As lenders that typically keep the loans until maturity, banks maintain core skills in areas such as loan structuring, credit evaluation, and default risk assessment. In contrast, investment banks maintain close ties to institutional issuers and try to structure new issues by balancing the demand for specific financial assets among institutional investors with the funding needs of the issuers. Investment banks act as managers of the new issues including stock exchange listing, syndication, underwriting, and placement of securities. The investment banks often provide complementary advisory services on financial strategies and corporate

**Figure 3.4** Financial institutions engaged in credit intermediation and risk transfer

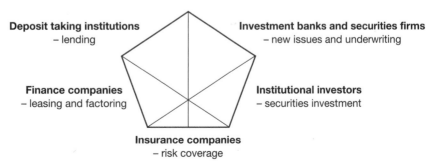

restructurings. Securities firms operate as market makers on securities by providing two-way prices in dealer markets, functioning as brokers on securities trades, and providing analyst services to institutional investors for whom they act as securities broker.

Among the institutional investors, life insurance companies, pension funds, and mutual funds cater much to the same market constituents and offer quite comparable opportunities for long-term savings and investment purposes. Whereas these financial institutions arose out of different business traditions many of their core product offerings compete with each other. Life insurance companies have traditionally received premium payments to provide financial cover for future events of death but have also sold more standardized savings products like annuities with guaranteed returns. Many of the actuarially based products have been supplemented with more flexible term-based investment propositions where policyholders can receive the investment proceeds after a certain holding period. Pension plans are commonly structured as defined contribution plans where the pension holder has some discretion over investment decisions as opposed to defined benefits plans where the pension fund manages and guarantees the future payments. Mutual funds are relatively flexible investment vehicles in the sense that they are funded through issuance of redeemable stock certificates that allow investors to increase and decrease their investment as they see fit. This may provide added benefits to investors as they have flexibility to restructure, adjust, and scale portfolio investments over time, while longer-term life insurance policies and pension plans sometimes are favoured by special tax incentives that can make them more interesting. Investment and asset management skills are the common prerequisites for these types of financial institutions to ensure investment returns, but they also provide straightforward services by monitoring the portfolio investments on behalf of their clients.

Insurance companies, and, notably, casualty insurance companies, sell protection to individuals and institutions for risk exposures that have a potential to jeopardize the economic well being of the customers caused by events beyond their direct control. The insurance companies manage the casualty risk exposures through diversification and charge actuarially determined insurance premiums often differentiated on the basis of essential customer characteristics. Many of the aggregate risk exposures are reinsured either in the form of mutual industry arrangements or through specialized reinsurance companies. Hence, participants in the insurance industry have distinctive skills in actuarial techniques and risk underwriting practices.

Whereas these main types of financial institutions retain distinctive features there is also some convergence between the products and services offered by them. Money market mutual funds can easily be liquidated and converted into cash overnight and are often combined with cheque writing capabilities, which makes them hard to distinguish from checking accounts offered by commercial banks. Securities firms that offer money market mutual funds often provide a range of payment services, which enforce the direct competition with conventional banking institutions. Many securities firms have established name-associated mutual funds to complement their investment advisory and securities brokerage activities. Many commercial banks have engaged in similar types of asset management activities to complement their conventional savings products. Securities firms are unaffected if customers reduce balances on their money market mutual funds, but the liquidity of commercial banks is affected directly by withdrawals from transactional deposit accounts. To circumvent this, deposit-taking institutions commenced the issuance of certificates of deposit, which provide investors with tradable savings instruments while the banks obtain secured funding until final maturity. This way the banks made inroads to the issuance of securities type funding instruments. Commercial banks have shown increasing interest in the securities issuance and underwriting business as potential sources of fee based earnings and maintain strong positions as arrangers and dealers in markets for commercial paper and bankers acceptances. Furthermore, there has been some experimentation with bank assurance products whereby conventional insurance products are distributed through the branch networks of retail banks. The combination of deposit taking, bank lending, securities issuance, and other cross-selling initiatives has been facilitated in the US market subsequent to the approval of the Gramm–Leach–Bliley Financial Modernization Act of 1999, which allowed the combination of banking, underwriting, and insurance activities under a holding structure. This effectively abolished the restrictions imposed by the Glass–Steagal Act of 1933 whereby deposit-taking institutions were refrained from engagement in securities underwriting. In contrast, the national banking systems in Europe have generally not faced any such restrictions and, therefore, have fostered universal banks with simultaneous engagements in deposit taking, loan extension, securities issuance, and brokerage activities although insurance activities typically have been contained in separate legal entities operating as a part of larger financial conglomer-ates. At the same time, there have been moves among insurance and reinsurance companies to experiment with alternative risk-transfer instruments distributed via the global capital market and placed among professional institutional investors. As these and other examples illustrate, many of the conventional distinctions between financial products and services offered by the major types of financial institutions are being blurred in many ways and this trend is likely to continue as the competitive market forces intensify.

As a general trend, the relative importance of bank facilitated credit intermediation has given way to securities issuance and placement among institutional investors. It is symptomatic for this development that the share of assets in deposit-taking institu-tions in the USA has dropped from 60% in 1980 to around 30% today.[2] In contrast the asset share of pension funds has increased over the same time period from around 18% to 25% and mutual funds from 4% to around 23%. Hence, it is clear that the credit intermediation process has moved in favour of the securities issuance route. This trend is universal but it covers over relatively large discrepancies between different national market environments where some countries have a stronger banking tradi-tion than others. For example, in many European countries and Japan, the asset share of deposit-taking institutions is currently closer to 50% compared to around 30% in the USA as a consequence of the historical restrictions imposed on banking activities in the US market.[3] The asset share of insurance companies has remained relatively stable in the USA hovering around 15% throughout the period partly reflecting the specificity of insurance based risk-transfer services that provide rather unique market solutions and the fact that the life insurers have been part of a shift towards secur-ities intermediation through longer-term investment schemes. There has been a significant convergence towards the investment business as insurance companies acquired investment managers with complementary skills in this area. Banks have also taken a keen interest in this market and have in many cases engaged in comple-mentary efforts distributing life insurance and pension products through bank branches. With the absence of regulatory restrictions, a large portion of life insurance policies are distributed through bank branches in some European countries, e.g.

more than 80% in Portugal and well over 50% in Spain, Italy, and France.[4] However, the cross selling of casualty insurance products within a wider portfolio of financial services does not seem to have gained any momentum in the banking industry.

Financial institutions engage in a variety of functions as credit intermediaries facilitating the distribution of buying power among diverse economic entities and as providers of liquidity and payment services that are essential for the exchange of commercial activities in the economy. In this process, financial institutions provide the means for savings and longer-term financial investments as well as funding on-going commercial activities and new business projects and thereby influencing resource allocation decisions that affect economic growth. Depository accounts, money market mutual funds, as well as short- to medium-term liquid securities con-stitute the elements of various definitions of the economy's monetary base that serve as reservoirs for current and future cash payments. As such the financial institutions are important constituents in the transmission of monetary policy initiatives that often are carried out through open market operations where the central bank trades financial assets with the financial institutions and thereby regulates the availability of money and hence the associated interest rates. Securities firms act as price setters on financial assets and trade them on behalf of investors at prevailing market prices. As part of these activities they also offer asset valuation services and dissem-inate essential market information to investors. The trading of financial assets requires a number of transactional services to clear the trades and settle the associated exchange of money for assets. Specialized clearing agents, liquidity providers, and depositories are the principal players in these activities. Banks sell demand deposit accounts and securities firms may offer money market mutual funds both of which can be used as the basis for transacting essential cash payments. The depositories keep track of all the outstanding securities and often register the holdings of investors and note changes in individual holdings as trades are made. The clearing process deter-mines who owes what after the trades are made, while the settlement process executes the switch between cash and financial assets that results from the trades.

Credit extension through bank intermediation entails a credit evaluation and approval process as the loans often remain on the books of the financial institutions until maturity. Banks are funded by balances on short-term deposit accounts and extend commercial credits with longer maturities, i.e. they typically act as maturity converters and engage in positive maturity gapping.[5] This process is sometimes referred to as an inter-temporal wealth transfer whereby excess cash received on deposits from, say, middle-aged households and well-established firms, is on-lent to, e.g. young families and company start-ups, who invest in real assets for the future. Funding for credit extension through securities issuance is provided by the end-investors that eventually acquire the securities and hold them in their invested port-folios. This engagement requires active asset management skills that also take the potential adverse effects of default and market risks into account. In short, financial institutions are exposed to a variety of risks when they engage in the credit inter-mediation processes, e.g. transaction failures, credit defaults, interest rate gaps, currency gaps, and country exposures, to the extent they engage in cross-border activities (Figure 3.5).[6]

The risk factors that financial institutions are exposed to can be addressed within the formal risk management framework discussed in the previous chapter where a first step entails the identification of essential risks and registration of the resulting exposures. The awareness of risk exposures may allow for some mitigating efforts

**Figure 3.5** Common risk exposures in financial institutions

| | |
|---|---|
| Credit risk: | Defaults and delays in debt service payments |
| Liquidity risk: | Inability to pay due to shortage of cash |
| Market risk: | Effects of price volatility on asset values |
| | Effects of price volatility on liability values |
| Interest rate risk: | Refinancing gap |
| | Reinvestment gap |
| Foreign exchange risk: | Net long foreign exchange positions |
| | Net short foreign exchange positions |
| Country and sovereign risk: | Economic exposures |
| | Legal jurisdiction and regulatory change |
| | Expropriation of property |
| Operational risk: | Human errors and mistakes |
| | Technology breakdown |

aimed at limiting the potential effects of the exposures, e.g. decreased reaction time, effective contingency plans, alternative actions, etc. However, due to the very nature of activities in the financial industry some risk exposures that constitute essential elements of the business will inevitably be retained. The very risks that expose financial institutions also affect commercial enterprises in different degrees and, therefore, the risk management approaches that were initially developed with a particular emphasis on the financial industry can have wide applications for the management of corporate exposure as well. Whenever high levels of uncertainty circumscribe commercial opportunities and financial returns, they will obscure the trade-offs between current and future buying power that underpin the credit intermediation processes and cause the credit extension to become less efficient. This constitutes an essential rationale for the emergence of different risk-transfer markets that allow financial institutions and commercial enterprises to obtain financial cover for excessive risk exposures. Conventional risk-transfer takes place in the insurance market where insurance providers charge a premium that reflects the average expected loss and diversify the aggregate risk exposure across large portfolios of insurance takers. Other initiatives have been taken by financial institutions to transform the structure of their assets and liabilities and thereby reduce some of the inherent risk exposures. This is the case, for instance when commercial banks engage in loan syndication, asset trading, securitization of loan receivables, etc. Securities may be structured to incorporate features of specific exposures and link the cash flows of the security to the valuation of underlying risk factors. Recent moves by large insurance companies to restructure catastrophe risk exposures and distribute them in securitized form in the debt market exemplify this phenomenon. As in the case of conventional insurance, the underlying idea is to spread the risk and diversify excessive exposures among a large number of professional institutional investors. Another alternative risk diversification channel has been the creation of derivative instruments in the form of exchange traded futures and options contracts. These instruments have allowed market participants to exchange different types of exposures among themselves with the aim of smoothing the effects of inherent exposures over time for the individual counterparts. Some natural counterparts in these transactions could for example include a corn farmer, who has a long exposure on future corn prices, and Kellogg's the producer of cornflakes, who has a short position on future corn prices. Many other derivative instruments have been developed through interbank trading and are commonly referred to as over-the-counter products. The forward rate agreements and forward foreign exchange contracts described earlier belong to this class of derivative products, but they also span various option structures and swap arrangements.

The scale of the global credit intermediation and risk-transfer markets is significant. The total value of the global securities market exceeds $60 trillion and consists more or less equally of equities and bonds. Almost half of this market is based in the USA and 25–30% in Europe reflecting the higher emphasis on securities issuance in the American market and the fact that many overseas institutions are net investors in the US market. The global bank intermediated market for credit extension is of a comparable size to the securities market but has continued to contract in importance over the past decade. Global insurance premiums including both life and casualty insurance policies amount to around $2.5 trillion annually[7] with the USA and Europe accounting each for around one third of the market and Japan around one fifth. The global market for open exchange traded derivatives contracts amounted to around $25 trillion by 2001 with North American exchanges accounting for more than half and Europe around 30% of the total market size. The total nominal outstanding of contracts in the over-the-counter markets for derivatives is substantially higher than exchange traded contracts and amounted to around $120 trillion by 2001,[8] i.e. more or less comparable to the aggregate size of the global credit intermediation markets. Of this the market for securitized credit exposures has been estimated at around $4 trillion. These figures provide stark evidence of the significant role played by derivative instruments in the contemporary market environment.

Considering the involvement of different types of financial institutions in the global credit intermediation and risk-transfer markets, it may be useful to provide a snapshot overview of how various parts of the financial markets fit together. Whereas the market structure is highly complex it may be worthwhile to try to illustrate the intricate relationships across different financial institutions that frame the conjoint developments toward converging service areas and specialization around core competencies that seem to characterize the current market environment (Figure 3.6).

From a credit intermediation perspective the central financial institutions are the commercial banks as lenders and the investment banks/securities firms as managers

**Figure 3.6 Institutional relationships across financial markets**

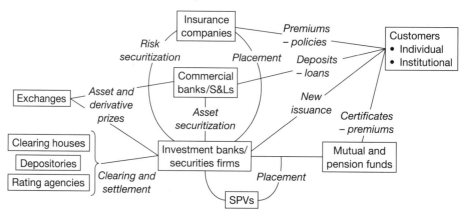

of new issues where institutional investors comprising insurance companies, mutual funds, and pension funds are essential takers of new securities. In new securities issues, investment banks are involved in the pricing decisions in connection with the **underwriting** together with the securities firms included in the **sales consortium** and possibly seconded by recognized rating agencies. Once the securities have been issued and placed, the securities firms may engage as market makers in the secondary market and act as brokers that execute trades on behalf of investors. Hence, market prices are determined by dealers quoting firm two-way prices and who thereby provide liquidity in the securities to the benefit of investors who may wish to trade and restructure asset portfolios from time to time. Formal stock exchanges provide comparable market based pricing platforms.[9] Financial analysts in the securities firms may offer different valuation services to their investor customers. The rating agencies monitor individual issuers or particular securities and provide regular evaluations of the associated default risk. New securities issues in the primary market and subsequent trades in the secondary market require the involvement of clearing houses and depositories as well as payment execution on transactional accounts to effectuate the deals. Many stock exchanges and specialized futures and options exchanges quote current market prices for a wide range of standardized derivatives contracts. Commercial banks, investment banks, and securities firms similarly provide dealer quotes for a wide range of over-the-counter derivatives. Despite these intricate interactions between different parts of the financial market, there is increased competition between banks, securities firms, and insurance companies in certain business areas as new product developments obscure the distinctiveness of the services offered by the particular type of financial institution. This has caused some convergence within areas like transactional accounts, payment services, depository services, investment management, securities underwriting, etc. In other areas, asset trading activities and new asset securitization techniques, that often use **special purpose vehicles** (SPVs) as issuing entities, have been adopted to increase the liquidity of conventional bank loans and insurance portfolios. These developments have converged conventional banking and insurance products towards the credit intermediation practices associated with securities issuance. The cash flows of securitized financial assets have increasingly been tailored to match specific investor requirements by incorporating various derivative positions in structured finance transactions. A paradoxical outcome of the securitization processes spearheaded by investment banks is that while they increase credit intermediation through securities issuance and transfer risk exposures to the capital market they also allow the banks and insurance companies to concentrate activities around their areas of expertise, i.e. loan origination and insurance underwriting. Hence, we seem to observe conjoint market forces towards convergence where different industry segments interact by employing various derivative instruments and increased specialization around core financial skills.

## 3.2 Financial innovation and the effects of risk-transfer

The ongoing developments in the financial markets are arguably related to demand and supply driven influences as well as regulatory effects many of which are unintended. The demand driven influences relate to the increasing needs for economic entities to protect themselves from various market related risk exposures. Market risks derive from volatilities in asset values, e.g. caused by ongoing changes in interest rate structures and foreign exchange rates. Change in the interest rate level has a direct effect on the present value of future cash generated by financial assets as well as commercial activities, and changes in foreign exchange rates affect the value of the cash flows to the extent they are denominated in foreign currencies. Hence, both financial institutions and commercial enterprises are affected by these exposures and have a demand for protection against these market risks. After the collapse of the fixed exchange rate regime that existed until the 1970s, the determination of foreign exchanges rates has largely been left to market forces. Monetary policy initiatives have increasingly focused on achieving targeted levels for key interest rates in response to the general level of economic activity thus leaving much of the monetary transmission mechanisms that shape the interest rate structure to market forces. With the significant increase in cross-border investment and borrowing activities, the supply and demand conditions for debt at different maturities are influenced by positions taken across debt markets in different currency areas. As a consequence, the increased volatility in currency markets affects the variability in the interest rate structures across currencies.

The supply driven influences relate to the refined competencies in financial institutions enabled by new technological enhancements and spurred by intensified market competition. The ability to separate different cash flow and risk elements embedded in financial and commercial assets has provided new opportunities to isolate these elements and trade them as independent strips and derivatives as well as repackage them into new structured financial assets tailored to serve specific market needs. Hence, many financial institutions ranging from banks and securities firms to insurance companies and hedge funds have excelled in the development of new financial products often marketed using fancy and idiosyncratic acronyms to gain differentiation advantages in a highly competitive marketplace.[10] As some of the traditional regulatory barriers have been eased between banking, securities underwriting, and insurance, the competition across certain types of financial services has intensified. In this situation, structured finance transactions provide new opportunities to excel against the competition and create new value-added products. The emergence of derivative instruments has enhanced this development. Finally, regulatory restrictions may stimulate the development of derivatives as a way to minimize the cost impact of imposed limitations. For example, the imposition of minimum capital ratios and reserve requirement arguably constitute indirect taxation of financial institutions as the optimal utilization of financial resources is limited while central banks in some cases may compensate reserve balances well below prevailing market rates. To the extent capital requirements are differentiated across different types of financial assets it may be beneficial to restructure certain asset classes from one type to another. For example, if commercial loans have relatively higher capital requirement, it may be worthwhile to sell the direct loan and acquire a credit swap with comparable risk-return characteristics, which will encourage the creation of these types of derivatives. Engagement in derivative instruments, e.g. futures on stock indices, equity call options, etc. can be used to create comparable risk-return characteristics and thus opens for arbitrage opportunities between different types of derivatives. Differential tax treatment across asset classes can provide similar incentives to engage in different derivatives. To the extent capital requirements and other debt market restrictions differ across currency jurisdictions, there will be

**Figure 3.7** External factors affecting the financial industry

opportunities for arbitrage between different national markets where advantages can be exchanged through engagement in interest rate and currency swaps. In short, uncoordinated regulatory restrictions can provide strong incentives for the introduction of different derivative instruments. It is even argued that governments have encouraged financial innovation and spurred the development of the derivatives markets through unintended regulatory and legal frameworks.[11]

A number of environmental factors affect the financial industry and influence innovation and product development in the financial markets (Figure 3.7). Regulation and taxation constitute influences that can be categorized under the broader heading of political and legal developments. Many regulatory issues should be considered in an international perspective. General bank supervision is discussed under the umbrella of the Bank for International Settlements, and securities market regulation is dealt with by the International Association of Securities Regulators, while the European Union is making strides to streamline regulation and market conditions in a European context. Whereas these efforts may coordinate regulatory initiatives there is a long way to go in achieving common international rules. Furthermore, tax rules for financial instruments remain highly diverse as taxation continues to be a national political priority. Hence, significant regulatory and tax rule differentiation may remain well into the foreseeable future. Nonetheless, the trend towards increased globalization of financial markets has been achieved in a political context as governments around the world have liberalized international trade and abolished many restrictions that imposed limitations on both financial and commercial cross-border transactions. The macroeconomic conditions also influence the financial industry. As wealth has continued to increase over the past decades, the demand for investment products and services has increased and spurred the development of securitized financial assets.

Demographic and social trends have similarly affected industry conditions, e.g. as the ageing populations in the industrialized countries cause sizeable funding gaps in the public pay-as-you-go pension schemes and contribute to the need for private investment arrangements. Technological innovations in the areas of telecommunications and integrative information systems have improved the ability to handle large amounts of financial data, such as customer transactions, asset positions, market prices, etc., that serve as important input in financial calculations on risk-return profiles, derivatives pricing, etc. The associated computational capacity has been instrumental in the ability to un-bundle and price different risk-return elements and

**Figure 3.8** Relative positions of different financial institutions

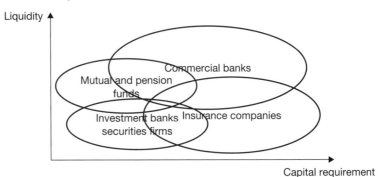

repackage them into more suitable financial instruments for redistribution to various investors. The development of financial derivatives is a basic outcome of this innovation process.

We have argued that activities in financial markets are carried out by four major types of financial institutions, namely commercial banks, investment banks and securities firms, mutual and pension funds, and insurance companies that represent relatively distinct segments of the financial market. The commercial banks are engaged in direct lending whereas investment banks and securities firms arrange and distribute new securities issues among mutual and pensions funds and insurance companies as major institutional investors. Direct loan engagements impose significant capital requirements on commercial banks as well as they need liquidity to fund the loan portfolios. In contrast, the investment banks and securities firms act as intermediaries and only keep trading portfolios of securities, which limits their capital requirements and liquidity needs (Figure 3.8). Mutual funds have low formal capital requirements as the certificate holders carry the entire investment risk but they are exposed to liquidity risk because they must honor potential withdrawals that require redemption of the stock certificates. Insurance companies maintain liquid reserves against future claims forecasted by actuarial techniques but are also required to maintain significant capital reserves as a guarantee for future solvency.

The four types of financial institutions are characterized by certain competencies that are distinct to their areas of expertise. Commercial banks are rather unique in their contacts with potential borrowers and provide advice on loan structures and base eventual loan extension on professional credit evaluation. Investment banks and securities firms are primarily engaged in new issues and securities trading, areas under competitive threat by the increasingly liberal banking laws in the USA and universal banking practices across Europe. However, their major role in this process is to balance corporate funding needs with investor requirements a process that engages them as providers of advice on financial strategies, corporate restructuring issues, and merger and acquisitions. Mutual and pension funds provide investors with wide choices of investment strategies and use their asset management skills to accomplish this task. However, the market for investment services is of increasing interest to banks, securities firms, and insurance companies and these institutions take strides to enter this area. Insurance companies represent the conventional risk-transfer market based on actuarial capabilities and experience in risk underwriting. Despite the trends towards market convergence in areas of asset securitization and

**Figure 3.9** The resource requirements of different financial services

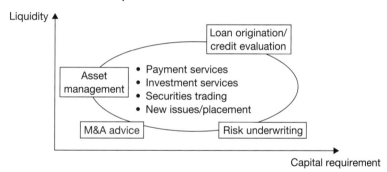

structured finance solutions, the central areas of expertise remain in these industry segments and constitute core competencies to be exploited in future financial service offerings. In contrast, areas like payment services, investment advice, depository services, securities trading, and new issuance seem to be up for grabs to financial conglomerates that want to offer a wider range of financial services (Figure 3.9). From this analysis, we may deduce that there is a trend towards conglomeration within a range of central financial services and some convergence in areas like asset securitization and structured finance, while specialized contributions are retained within each of the financial groups.

The emergence of financial derivatives of different shades and colors has enabled the integration of activities across different types of financial institutions where many product offerings converge across conventional industry segments. Derivative instruments provide the means to restructure assets and liabilities and thereby modify the risk-return characteristics of invested portfolios as well as the equity position of financial institutions and commercial enterprises. The availability of a range of financial derivatives provides many alternative ways to achieve specific asset or liability structures. This ability to reach specific risk-return characteristics in more than one way through several market channels is a source of increased market efficiencies. For example, if an equity position can be established through direct investment in a stock portfolio, stock index futures contracts, call options on a stock index, or debt-equity swaps, the cheapest alternative route will be chosen. Derivatives can also facilitate specialization as a financial institution with core competencies in one area of expertise can restructure financial solutions to incorporate other areas of expertise. For example, a securities firm with expertise in debt issues may lever this expertise to equity investors by incorporating **debt-equity swaps** that convert standard debt returns to standard equity returns. Thereby any extraordinary returns obtained in the debt market can be converted into comparably favourable equity returns. Hence, financial innovations based on derivative instruments can increase economic efficiencies as risk sharing is extended across investors in the capital market and by reducing the transaction cost associated with active asset management.[12]

The **unbundling** of specific cash flows and risk elements in financial assets and the trading of these securities strips and derivatives can help increase market transparency and reduce asymmetric information that often exist between corporate managers, stockowners, bank lenders, and bondholders. Thereby potential adverse effects associated with agency problems where some interests are given preferential treatment at the expense of other stakeholders may be eliminated or at least reduced. The emergence of different risk-transfer solutions and financial derivatives also emphasizes the role of hedging as an alternative to equity maintained as a general buffer against unforeseen economic events. The range of risk-transfer opportunities comprises committed credit facilities from banks, insurance contracts, and contingent capital structures offered as alternative means to transfer risk in the financial markets. Whereas equity serves as a general buffer for adverse effects of unexpected events, the use of insurance contracts and financial derivatives for hedging purposes requires more insight and knowledge about corporate risk exposures. However, to the extent these alternative risk-transfer opportunities are used to hedge identified risk exposures it will also lead to a more efficient use of the debt and equity markets as the reduced volatility in commercial cash flows lowers the average cost of capital to the firm and creates a higher debt capacity for new profitable business opportunities. Some argue for this phenomenon as a reduction in the firm's potential bankruptcy cost that will ease the financial costs of the firm. In this way, the use of derivatives can furnish economic growth as capital allocation is improved through better market insight and risk profiling that reduce the adverse impact of uncertainty and increase overall investment capacity.

Derivative securities comprise a range of tradable financial instruments whose values are based on, or derived from, the price development of underlying assets or commodities. There are three main types of financial derivatives (Figure 3.10). First, the trend towards increased securitization of different credit exposures and other types of risk has created a somewhat heterogeneous market for securitized risks. Second, markets for exchange traded futures and options contracts have emerged in all the major currency areas linked to a wide range financial assets and commodities. Third, commercial banks, investment banks, and securities firms have developed dealer markets for a variety of derivative products traded over-the-counter. However, before further indulging in a discussion of practices in these markets, we will first enhance our insights into the conventional risk transfer and financing techniques.

**Figure 3.10** Three types of derivative securities

**Over-the-counter derivatives:**
- forward rate agreements
- interest rate caps
- forward foreign exchange
- currency options
- interest rate swaps
- currency swaps
- credit swaps
- risk swaps

**Exchange-traded derivatives:**
- interest rate futures
- currency futures
- stock index futures
- commodity futures
- options on futures
- currency options

**Securitized risks:**
- mortgage backed securities
- collateralized debt obligations
- structured securities issues
- risk-linked securities

## 3.3 Risk-transfer and financing mechanisms

When banks provide committed credit facilities they ensure that the recipient can draw on funds at any time on predetermined conditions, e.g. after unexpected events have occurred or any adverse situations that give rise to incremental liquidity needs. Different financial institutions, including deposit-taking institutions and finance companies may offer different types of committed revolving term facilities that provide funding by rolling over short-term credits at a fixed spread over a variable rate indicator like LIBOR. Term committed facilities typically require payment of an up-front **commitment fee** to compensate for the implied liquidity, interest rate, and credit risks. More advanced forms of committed funding arrangements may constitute syndicated facilities shared among banks and other financial institutions in larger consortia. The committed credit facilities might also take hybrid forms somewhere between pure bank lines and capital market instruments. The funding arrangement could, for example, be construed as **short-term commercial paper** or **medium-term note issuance facilities** where debt instruments are placed directly in the market or are offered to a prearranged panel of institutional investors. These credit facilities would typically be supported by **committed backstop facilities** offered by commercial banks to ensure future funding availability in case the debt market dries up or offers funding at uncompetitive rates. Committed **revolving term facilities** are usually not conditioned around specific funding needs, but constitute general buffers that serve as reservoirs for unexpected financing requirements. As such, committed credit facilities can be used to make short–medium term financing available as a cover for immediate liquidity needs that arise in the aftermath of unforeseeable economic events.

The common **capital requirements** for the banking sector were outlined in the **Basel accords** sponsored by the Bank for International Settlements and the initial implementation in the late 1980s forced some banks to contain their credit expansion. This development in conjunction with the build up of large loan exposures to emerging markets during the 1980s urged the launch of different loan sales and asset trading initiatives. Loan sales build on the basic principle of loan syndications where large loan commitments traditionally have been shared between a select group of managers and a wider syndicate group typically ranging from five and up to 50 participants in the case of very large credit facilities. The **management group**, and notably the **lead-manager**, would maintain contacts to the borrowers and monitor the fulfillment of the terms and conditions outlined in the loan agreement. The syndication implies the sale of loan participations by the lead-manager to the managers and participants, which provides participants with the right to debt service payments from the borrower accorded to the lead-manager, also if the lead-manager should become insolvent. These types of loan sales do not provide the participants with the right of setoff against the borrower, e.g. against deposits maintained with the bank, but remain an agreement between the lead-manager and the participants. The participation agreement can provide recourse to the participant whereby the lead-manager retains the credit risk. It may also be structured as assignment whereby the participant is party to the loan agreement and hence have direct claims on the borrower. **Loan participations** can be traded among banks after the initial credit extension has been made and can even be sold to institutional investors who may find the higher returns on bank loans attractive. Such asset sales provide commercial

## Figure 3.11 Loans sales and asset trading

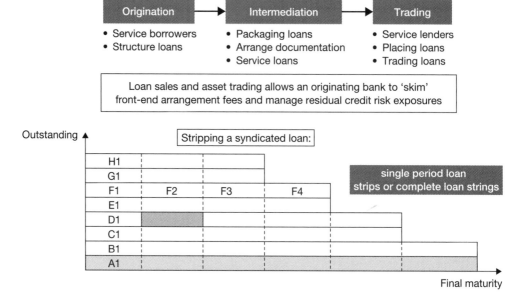

banks with increased flexibility to manage the inherent liquidity and credit risk exposure of conventional loan assets. These techniques have been refined further in asset trading techniques whereby the bank loans may be divided into different zero-coupon structures and single period and forward strips that are sold to investors with these specific maturity needs (Figure 3.11). Some banks provide two-way prices in the loan strips in an over-the-counter dealer market to increase the liquidity of the loan participations.

The loan sales and asset trading techniques have been employed by the largest commercial banks that maintain a broad customer network, often with a global reach, and possess strong loan management capabilities. These banks often have loan origination capabilities that exceed their funding capacity, therefore, loan sales and asset trading technique allow them to excel in areas where they maintain strong core competencies even though they are unable to keep all the loans on their own books. The eventual takers of loan participations are smaller regional banks with limited loan origination capabilities, and other types of financial institutions such as mutual funds, pension funds, and insurance companies that enjoy the excess returns afforded on bank loans compared to plain vanilla securities traded in the market.

The savings and loan institutions in the USA were under strain in the early 1980s as sizeable interest rate gaps between long-term mortgage loans and short-term deposit balances caused problems in an environment with increasing interest rates. This situation caused a major restructuring of the S&L industry but also spurred the introduction of asset securitization techniques that allowed the banks to take large mortgage portfolios off their balance sheets and thereby reduce the inherent liquidity, interest rate, and credit risk exposures. Asset securitization has grown in importance since the 1980s as an attractive funding alternative for banks and finance companies. The asset securitization technique uses the cash flows generated from

**Figure 3.12 Asset securitization through special purpose vehicles**

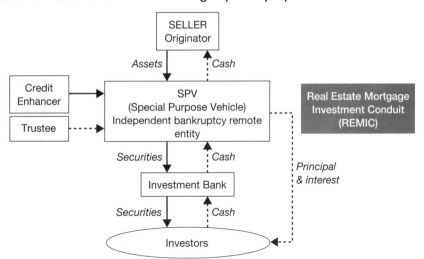

an indigenous financial asset portfolio to support the issuance of securities that often can be of higher credit quality than the originator of the financial assets. The improved credit rating provides this financing alternative with lower cost of funding and offers the issuer an opportunity to obtain favourable off-balance-sheet financing. For many financial institutions, e.g. commercial banks, stringent capital require-ments have restricted the ability to put new loans on the books. Hence, for banks that are active loan originators, asset securitization provides an attractive financing opportunity (Figure 3.12). The asset securitization technique can be applied to many different types of receivables but works best on financial assets with relatively stable and predictable cash flows, such as mortgage loans, automobile loans, credit card debt, etc.

The largest securitization market in the USA is the market for mortgage pass-through securities, where the cash flow from portfolios of mortgage loans is used to service the issuance of securities. The financial assets are placed in an independent legal entity, a special purpose vehicle (SPV), which will apply all the incoming cash flows from the financial assets to service the payment obligations of the securities issued by the SPV (see Figure 3.12). Before the advent of asset securitization, the banks kept all the mortgage loans on their own balance sheets, which limited their ability to arrange new loans. After the three government supported agencies, Federal National Mortgage Association (Fannie Mae), Federal Home Loan Mortgage Corporation (Freddie Mac) and Government National Mortgage Association (Ginnie Mac), started to buy the mortgage loans from banks and issue **mortgage-backed securities** (MBS), the market has become more efficient through specialization. This development has allowed banks to concentrate on loan origination and advisory services to individual and institutional borrowers, while the mortgage facilitating agencies have specialized in the securitization process and tailoring securities to the investor markets.

The development of the market for mortgage backed securities has become more sophisticated with the introduction of new derivative mortgage instruments, such

**Figure 3.13** Collateralized mortgage obligations

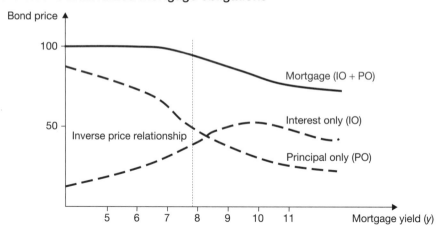

as **collateralized mortgage obligations** (CMO) with different tranches, e.g. fixed rate, floating rate, reverse floaters, etc., and stripped mortgage-backed securities with different classes of **principal-only** (PO) and **interest-only** (IO) payment struc- tures (Figure 3.13).[13] The PO and IO pass-through securities have some interesting properties in terms of inverse price sensitivities to changes in the interest rate level. The market value of the PO cash flows has an inverse relationship to movements in the interest rate level because the size of principal repayments is unaffected by changes in the interest rates. Conversely, the market value of the IO cash flows will show a positive relationship to movements in the interest rate level because the size of the interest payments is affected directly by changes in the interest rate. The inverse rate sensitivity features can, for example, be used to hedge interest rate exposures of assets and liabilities that have inverse effects on the firm's equity posi- tion. The successful development of the mortgage-backed securities market in the USA was enhanced by favourable regulatory and federal tax regimes. With the Tax Reform Act in 1986, the special purpose vehicle, referred to as a **real estate mort- gage investment conduit** (REMIC), avoided double taxation of interest income as the residual holders of the mortgage payments became liable to pay income tax, whereas the REMIC was held free of any tax obligations. Without this favourable tax ruling, the market for mortgage-backed securities probably would not have been as successful as has actually been the case.

The securitization approach provides an effective technique to restructure large pools of financial assets into different tranches with specific cash flow features, such as floating rate, and inverse floating rate payments, etc., that subsequently can be distributed and traded as independent securities. Similarly, it is possible to incor- porate various exposures, such as interest rate, currency, and market risks into structured debt issues and distribute them among institutional investors in securit- ized form.

*Example*: Consider a $200 million pool of mortgage loans with an average yield of 8%. We want to create three distinct tranches: A fixed rate tranche (F), a floating rate tranche (FL), and an inverse floating rate tranche (IFL).

| | Par amount (m) | Coupon rate | Coupon rate | Interest amount (LIBOR = 5%) |
|---|---|---|---|---|
| F tranche: | $m_F$ = 100 000 000 | 8.00 | 8.00 | $8 000 000 |
| FL tranche: | $m_{FL}$ = 75 000 000 | LIBOR + 0.50 | LIBOR + 0.50 | $4 125 000 |
| IFL tranche: | $m_{IFL}$ = 25 000 000 | $\delta - \lambda \times$ LIBOR | $30.5 - 3 \times$ LIBOR | $3 875 000 |
| Total | 200 000 000 | 8.00 | 8.00 | $16 000 000 |

Then determine the values of $\delta$ and $\lambda$:

$$
\begin{aligned}
(1) \quad \lambda &= m_{FL}/m_{IFL} = 75/25 &&= 3 \\
(2) \quad & 75(\text{LIBOR} + 0.50) + 25(\delta - 3 \times \text{LIBOR}) &&= 100 \times 8.00 \Rightarrow \\
\delta &= (800 - 37.5)/25 &&= 30.5
\end{aligned}
$$

*Example*: The introduction of participating hybrid option note exchangeable securities (PHONEs) constitutes a financial innovation pursued to monetize long-term strategic equity holdings in a specific company X and thereby obtain funding at favourable rates while at the same time optimizing existing tax and accounting rules. The securities could have the following characteristics:

**Final maturity:** 30 years (extendable to 60 years if the share price of company X exceeds 150% of its value at issuance).

**Interest payments:** 1.75% plus any dividends paid on the stock of company X.

**Exchangeability:** After one year, the notes can be changed for cash equal to 95% of the value of the shares in company X (the percentage increases to 100% in case dividend payments are deferred).

**Redemption amount:** At final maturity, the notes are redeemed by the nominal amount or the value of the shares in company X, whichever is highest.

From a tax perspective, the notes are considered debt instruments with contingent payments, and the interest payments are, therefore, accounted on the basis of a comparable yield. Whereas the actual interest payment is 1.75% the comparable yield may be considerably higher, e.g. 9.25% because it is an equity-linked security. This feature results in significantly higher tax deductions for interest expenses. This is clearly interesting to the issuer who obtains tax efficient funding at low rates but it can also be interesting to investors that want to obtain an equity play that imposes lower formal requirements on capital reserves and provides a minimum coupon payment.

## 3.4 Insurance and reinsurance

The **direct insurance** and the reinsurance markets remain a major reservoir for the transfer of casualty risks. Primary insurers provide cover to homeowners and commercial entities and act as financial intermediaries that aggregate the major exposures associated with underlying risk events across large portfolios of individual customers. As primary insurers often assume regional risk profiles they may want to reinsure part of the portfolio to obtain geographical diversification. **Reinsurance** may take place on a proportional basis or excess exposures can be ceded to the reinsurance market on a facultative basis, e.g. to shield against effects

### Figure 3.14 The primary and reinsurance markets

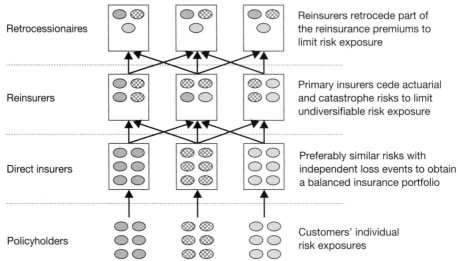

Unbalanced insurance portfolios and catastrophe risks cannot be diversified
and are therefore typically ceded in the reinsurance market

Retrocessionaires — Reinsurers retrocede part of the reinsurance premiums to limit risk exposure

Reinsurers — Primary insurers cede actuarial and catastrophe risks to limit undiversifiable risk exposure

Direct insurers — Preferably similar risks with independent loss events to obtain a balanced insurance portfolio

Policyholders — Customers' individual risk exposures

from specific catastrophic events. In turn, the reinsurance companies trade reinsurance treaties among themselves to obtain risk diversification on a global scale.

The primary insurance companies may insure homeowners' properties, automobiles, industrial facilities, agricultural crops, etc. Insurance policies can combine exposures to a variety of events within comprehensive policies although they may exclude certain risks. As long as the risk events that expose the insurance portfolio happen independently of each other, the exposures can be diversified and an insurance premium determined probabilistically based on actuarial techniques. If primary insurers have accumulated large exposures within similar types of insurance they may trade part of the portfolio among themselves to diversify the risk exposures further. This basic diversification principle is refined in the reinsurance market. Primary insurance companies cede part of their exposures to global reinsurance companies and the reinsurance companies may in turn retrocede part of their exposures to other reinsurance companies and thereby diversify the risk exposures across the international insurance community (Figure 3.14).

In a balanced insurance portfolio, loss ratios are reasonably predictable although there can be some discrepancies between expected and realized losses. In the case of man-made or natural catastrophe exposures, individual policy risks are not independent of each other, e.g. property exposures to catastrophes will cluster within certain regions. So, when disaster strikes, aggregate losses tend to be large. Catastrophe risk exposures are special in the sense that their occurrences are highly uncertain and they represent extreme loss potentials. Since catastrophic events are highly correlated within geographical areas it is impossible to diversify them through portfolio aggregation. Economic losses from man-made and natural disasters occur relatively infrequently over short time intervals that are depicted statistically as event spikes rather than evenly distributed loss events. Hence, for these types of events there is a need to cede excess exposures directly in the reinsurance market because it is the only viable way to obtain wider geographical diversification. In some cases the risk exposures can be covered through insurance pools where larger groups of insurance companies share the un-diversifiable risk exposures. Insurance portfolios with a good balance between different types of exposures and insurance takers are typically covered through obligatory proportional reinsurance treaties where the direct insurer cedes a share of all the written insurance policies to the reinsurance market. Large unbalanced risk exposures, such as catastrophe risks, are often covered through facultative non-proportional treaties where specific defined loss exposures are ceded in the reinsurance market (see Box 3.1). The reinsurance industry has for many years operated on a highly collegial manner based on mutual trust and long-standing business relationships. This rather informal approach carries low legal and administrative costs and provides a high degree of contract flexibility. However, as global catastrophe risk exposures have increased this operational mode has come under some pressure.

---

### Box 3.1 Transfer of extreme risk exposures in the reinsurance market

Facultative insurance treaties provide cover for individual risk factors such as windstorm, flood, and earthquake, while in the case of man-made disasters they deal with accidents, industrial explosions, terrorist attacks, etc. Reinsurance treaties can be either proportional or non-proportional. In proportional reinsurance treaties, the direct insurer and the re-insurer divide all premiums and losses between them in accordance with a contractually determined ratio. In non-proportional reinsurance treaties there is no pre-determined division of premiums and losses. A non-proportional treaty typically defines a deductible, net retention or attachment point, up to which the direct insurer will cover all losses. The reinsurance company is obliged to cover all losses in excess of the deductible up to a certain maximum amount, sometimes referred to as the exhaustion point. Coverage provided within the loss range determined by the attachment point and the exhaustion point is usually called a **layer**. A given insurance exposure can be divided into different layers, each of which may be covered by different insurance treaties and risk transfer mechanisms.

**Figure 3.15 Insurance layer**

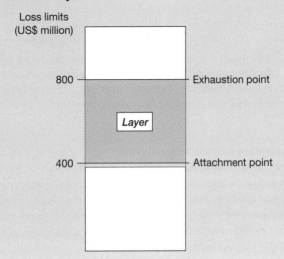

Facultative risk exposures are usually covered in non-proportional excess-of-loss insurance treaties (contracts), where the cedant obtains insurance cover from the reinsurance companies in case a catastrophe event leads to a loss in excess of the deductible, **attachment point**, and, up to a maximum amount, **exhaustion point**. The reinsurance cover can be structured in layers, where a ceded insurance exposure, for example, may cover a certain percentage of the total losses incurred between the deductible and the contractual maximum.

**Figure 3.16 Layered insurance program**

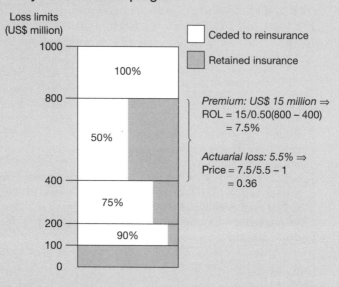

The cost of reinsurance coverage is typically indicated by the rate-on-line (ROL) derived as the premium divided by the covered insurance limit:[14]

$$ROL = Premium/Cover\ limit$$

The price of the reinsurance cover in turn can be indicated in relation to the actuarial probability that the full loss within the covered limit will occur:

$$Price = ROL/Actuarial\ probability - 1$$
$$= Premium/(Actuarial\ probability \times Cover\ limit) - 1$$

This means that, when the price indication is zero, the insurance cover can be obtained at a premium equal to the expected loss. A positive price indicates that the re-insurer receives a return in excess of the expected loss, whereas a negative price indicates that the re-insurer gets a premium below the expected loss of the contract.

Catastrophe risks can threaten the solvency of individual insurance companies, due to the at times extreme agglomeration of loss events and may even strain the stability of the entire insurance industry. Hence, in some cases these types of risk cannot obtain insurance coverage and constitute so-called uninsurable risk, because reinsurance companies are unwilling to commit their capital to cover these extreme exposures, even though the event probability is very low. With an estimated size of the catastrophe reinsurance market at around $75 billion,[15] it appears evident that upper reinsurance layers representing extreme loss exposures, potentially ranging

**Figure 3.17** Global reinsurance prices 1990–2003

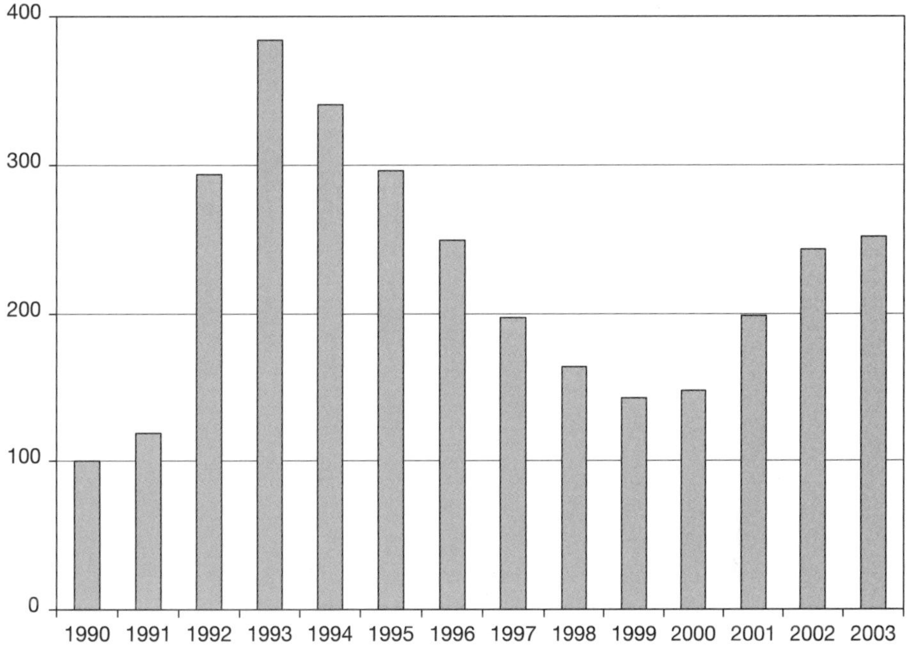

*Source*: Guy Carpenter

World rate-on-line (1990 = 100)

between $50–75 billion,[16] can be very difficult to cover through conventional reinsurance contracts. Furthermore, reinsurance prices are influenced by the immediate loss experiences from significant catastrophic events and are highly cyclical (Figure 3.17).[17] When severe catastrophe losses occur, the solvency of marginal reinsurance companies is threatened, and the accumulated reserves of well-capitalized reinsurance companies are significantly drained. Conversely, during longer periods with relatively low loss frequencies, the reinsurance companies accumulate large reserve positions that allow them to pursue a more aggressive price behaviour. A number of regulatory constraints can enforce this behaviour, e.g. when accounting rules prohibit insurance companies from assigning the accumulated surplus into irreversible reserves dedicated to cover specific future catastrophe losses.

The tightened conditions for reinsurance of catastrophe exposures during the early 1990s induced a search for alternative financial structures to transfer catastrophe risk. Since institutional investors are used to sizeable swings in day-to-day changes in invested market values they should be able to absorb large potential losses associated with catastrophe risk.[18] Several studies indicate that losses associated with catastrophes are uncorrelated with the return on different types of securities traded in the capital market.[19] This should make it attractive for institutional investors to include catastrophe risk-linked financial assets into their portfolio because it can diversify the invested portfolio further and thereby furnish a marginally higher return for a given level of portfolio risk (Figure 3.18).

The first capital market instrument linked to catastrophe risk was placed in 1994 and since then many other risk-linked securities have been issued raising a total insurance coverage of around $6 billion. Given the size of the global capital market

**Figure 3.18** Incorporating risk-linked securities in invested portfolio

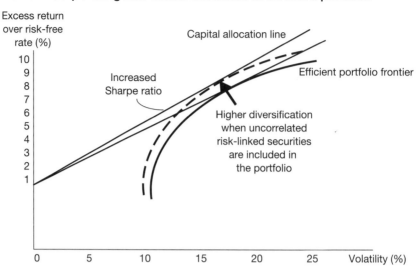

there should be a good potential for the issuance of risk-linked securities such as cat-bonds, contingent securities and cat-put equity instruments. As the returns from catastrophe risk exposures are fundamentally unrelated to the return on commercial and market risks of conventional debt instruments, well diversified investors can benefit from investment in risk-linked securities. In many ways the market for risk-linked securities can be compared to the mortgage-backed securities market, which took off in the USA during the 1980s partially induced by a favourable tax regime and adherence to a market standard. Mortgage pass-through securities, where the cash flow from portfolios of mortgage loans is used to service the issuance of securities, constitutes the largest securitization market. The market for mortgage-backed securities has become more sophisticated with the introduction of derivative mortgage instruments, such as collateralized mortgage obligations (CMOs). Similarly, the asset securitization technique was applied to the reinsurance market. Through issuance of catastrophe risk-linked bonds, cat-bonds for short, the issuer, typically an insurance or reinsurance company obtained cover for specified catastrophic events. The catastrophe risk-transfer opportunities have primarily been exploited by insurance and reinsurance companies to obtain complementary coverage in the capital market but have also been adopted by corporate entities.

A cat-bond is typically structured around a special purpose vehicle established in a tax-favourable jurisdiction.[20] The SPV issues the cat-bonds and receives up-front payments from the investors buying the securities. The SPV engages in an insurance contract with the ceding entity, that in turn pays an insurance premium for the entire insurance period up front or on a pro-rata basis. The insurance contract typically provides the cedant with insurance coverage on an excess-of-loss basis corresponding to practice in the catastrophe reinsurance market. Hence, the ceded risk exposure may cover losses associated with particular insurance layers between specified attachment and exhaustion points. The SPV uses the up-front proceeds from the bond issue less the expenses accrued in connection with the placement to buy a liquid securities portfolio of high credit quality and low interest rate sensitivity. The securities portfolio is placed in a trust account as collateral for the debt service

**Figure 3.19** Securitization of risk exposures

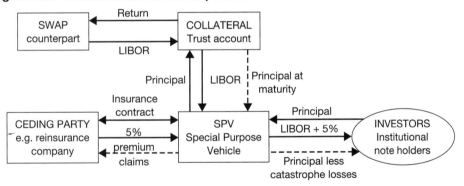

payments due on the cat-bonds (Figure 3.19). The SPV is rated by one of the leading credit agencies. The SPV often engages into a fixed–floating interest rate swap agreement that converts the interest returns from the invested securities portfolio into monthly LIBOR-based floating rate payments. The investors receive a relatively high spread above the LIBOR rate to compensate for the catastrophe risk exposure. The investors only receive the full principal back at maturity if no catastrophe losses materialize in the interim. Hence, the major risk consideration for cat-bond investors is the inherent catastrophe risk exposure.

A critical element of the credit evaluation process is an assessment of the validity and integrity of the supporting catastrophe risk analysis. Such analysis is usually performed by specialized consulting firms on the basis of simulation models that estimate the probabilities of catastrophic events of different magnitudes and the associated losses. The cat-bonds can use different bases to trigger compensation under the reinsurance contract. Compensation can be triggered as a loss indemnity of the actual insurance losses incurred by the ceding party. For the cedant, this solution provides close to perfect coverage of losses. However, for the cat-bond investors the solution is wrought with the issues of moral hazard and adverse selection, because there is no guarantee that the cedant will try to mitigate losses once the cat-bonds are placed, and as an insider, the cedant may actually know more about the catastrophe risk exposure than the investors buying the cat-bonds. The trigger could also be based on a loss index, which eliminates the risks associated with moral hazard and adverse selection, because the index is well defined and cannot be manipulated. However, a standardized index will expose the cedant to basis risk as the index may differ from the actual losses incurred. A final methodology is to adopt a parametric formula as a trigger. This hybrid approach can develop triggers that are closely associated with the cedant's exposure, but at the same time are well defined, objectively measurable, and analyzable.

## 3.5 Financial derivatives markets

We can now look at the emergence of organized markets for derivatives in the context of conventional risk transfer and financing mechanisms and the increased emphasis on securitizing risk exposures. It constitutes a process driven by a combination of policy approaches, regulatory pressures, tax and accounting incentives, and competitive forces that circumscribe institutions in the financial markets comprising insurance companies, commercial banks, investment banks, securities firms, mutual and pension funds and other institutional investors. The formation of markets where derivative instruments are actively traded reflects the underlying business conditions and needs of the financial institutions and their institutional and corporate customers. The increased globalization of business activities has created new institutional exposures, e.g. to interest rate, currency, and sovereign risks, while pursuit of market-based policies has caused the volatility of financial prices to go up all of which require more attention. Under these circumstances, the financial industry has refined techniques to manage essential risk exposures and awareness about these strategic risk management techniques is also spreading to other multinational enterprises.

The financial derivatives can be broadly divided according to the structure of the contracts. Forward contracts establish a basis for determining the future price of different financial assets and commodities, e.g. in the form of interest rate agreements and forward foreign exchange contracts as discussed in the previous chapter. Hence, forward contracts lock-in the future price, which can be an advantage to both buyers and sellers of assets. Options contracts provide a choice of execution, i.e. the option structure allows the contract holder to decide whether or not they want to use the locked-in price implied by the agreed purchase or sale in a forward contract. This obviously increases the flexibility of option holders since they will want to exercise the forward agreement if conditions are favourable but not if conditions are unfavourable. Option buyers pay a certain premium to acquire the potential advantage associated with this flexibility. Furthermore, the forward and options type contracts are traded in two distinct forms. In one market environment the derivatives are quoted and traded on formal exchanges where all transactions are cleared through affiliated clearing organizations that become the counterpart to all contract holders. In another environment the derivatives are traded in dealer markets with prices quoted by individual market participants and where subsequent deals are cleared as bilateral transactions and settled through common agreement (Figure 3.20).

Exchange-traded derivatives take the form of futures contracts and options on the futures. These futures and options contracts are offered for essential commodities that characterize commercial activities in the region surrounding the exchange, for example, corn, wheat, and cattle feeder in Chicago, wool in Sydney, and so forth

**Figure 3.20** Overview of financial derivatives markets

|  | Forward agreements | Options contracts |
|---|---|---|
| Over-the-counter markets | • Rate agreements<br>• Currency forwards<br>• Swap agreements | • Caps, collars<br>• Currency options<br>• Swaptions<br>• Hybrids |
| Exchange-traded markets | Futures contracts:<br>• stocks, bonds, CDs, deposits, indexes<br>• currencies | Options contracts:<br>• stocks, bonds, CDs, deposits, indexes<br>• currencies |

**Figure 3.21** Some derivatives exchanges and representative contracts

| Exchanges | Derivative Contracts |
|---|---|
| Chicago Board of Trade (CBOT): | Corn, oats, soybeans, wheat<br>T-bonds, T-notes, Fed funds<br>DJ industrial average |
| Chicago Mercantile Exchange (CME): | Cattle-feeder, hogs-lean, pork bellies<br>T-bills, Libor-1mo, eurodollar, euroyen<br>S&P 500, S&P Midcap, Nikkei 225, Nasdaq 100,<br>Russell 2000 |
| New York Board of Trade (NYBOT): | Cocoa, coffee, sugar, cotton, orange juice |
| New York Mercantile Exchange (NYMEX): | Copper, gold, platinum, silver<br>Crude oil, heating oil, gasoline, natural gas<br>Palo Verde Electricity, Cal/Oregon Border |
| Montreal Exchange (ME): | Canadian BAs, Canadian Gov. Bonds |
| International Petroleum Exchange (IPE): | Brent crude, gas oil |
| London International Financial Futures Exchange (LIFFE): | Short sterling, long gilt, Euribor, Euroswiss<br>FT-SE 100 index |
| Marche à Terme (MATIF): | Euro Notional Bond, Euribor, CAC-40 index |
| European Exchange (Eurex): | Euro German Gov. Bond<br>Dax-30 German stock, DJ euro stock |
| Johannesburg Securities Exchange (JSE): | FTSE/JSE Top-40 index |
| Hong Kong Futures Exchange (HKFE): | Hang Seng index |
| Tokyo International Financial Futures Exchange (TIFFE): | Euroyen, Euroyen Libor |
| Sydney Futures Exchange (SFE): | Australian Gov. Bonds, All Ordinaries index, wool, wheat |

(Figure 3.21). Other exchanges specialize in international commodities, such as cocoa, coffee, copper, and gold in New York, oil in London, etc. Similarly, the financial futures and options contracts typically relate to national benchmarks, e.g. T-Notes, Fed Funds, and S&P 500 in Chicago, the long gilt and FTSE 100 Index in London, euro Government bonds in Paris and Frankfurt, etc. However, there is increased competition between large exchanges on major international currency and interest rate indicators, such as contracts on Eurodollar, $-LIBOR, and Euribor, that are traded on both sides of the Atlantic.

Over-the-counter markets for financial derivatives developed from innovations among international financial institutions in response to increasing needs for hedging services among their institutional clients and take advantage of potential arbitrage opportunities across national debt markets. The forward foreign exchange agreements have existed for many years as an essential service provided in the interbank currency markets where price volatilities increased after the gradual collapse during 1970s of the fixed-rate system outlined in the Bretton Woods agreement. Similarly, the abolition of Regulation Q in the USA in the early 1980s and similar liberalizations in other national markets in conjunction with a regime of floating currencies led to higher interest rate volatilities and spurred the development of forward rate agreements in the major currencies. As part of the continued evolution

**Figure 3.22** Some representative derivatives contracts in the OTC-markets

Over-the-counter products:

- Forward foreign exchange agreements
- Forward rate agreements
- Interest rate caps and collars
- Currency options and collars
- Interest rate and currency swaps
- Swaptions

of the forward markets, other options-related services were developed including currency options, interest rate caps, and collar agreements to ensure that currency and interest payments are retained within certain ranges. Swap agreements on currency and interest payments were developed during the early 1980s first as bilateral arrangements with financial institutions acting as intermediaries but later established as a liquid interbank quotation system much like the foreign exchange and forwards markets (Figure 3.22).

The markets for exchange-traded and over-the-counter derivatives constitute different market structures and have retained their distinctive features. Each of the futures and options exchanges offer unique contracts with standardized amounts and maturities since meaningful price quotations must be based on specified standard units, and they use their own designated clearinghouses as sole counter-parties to all transactions. This approach is associated with both advantages and disadvantages. The advantages relate to the high liquidity of the futures and options contracts and the transparency of public price quotations. Hence, it is easy for market participants to create futures and options positions and subsequently to modify and reverse them. Furthermore, since the designated clearinghouse guarantees transactions, the exchange-traded contracts entail very limited counter-party risk. The disadvantages relate to the relative inflexibility of the contract amounts and maturities that sometimes makes it difficult to match futures and options positions to underlying exposures for hedging purposes. Most financial futures are relatively short-term, e.g. go three, six, and nine months into the future, which limits their use as a tool to hedge long-dated exposures. In contrast, the over-the-counter products are offered in dealer markets on the basis of unofficial two-way price quotes by financial institutions that are expected to honour the posted quotes as part of their professional market conduct. The advantage of this type of market is the greater flexibility in determining the amount and maturity of the contracts and sometimes even the asset basis for the contract. Forward and options contracts in the OTC-market can often have longer maturities than corresponding exchange-traded products. The potential downsides to the over-the-counter products relate exactly to their un-standardized nature, which reduces liquidity and in some cases makes it difficult to unwind and reverse a derivatives position once it is established. Since these products are traded in dealer markets, they are arranged as bilateral transactions with the quoting financial institution and therefore are associated with direct credit exposures to the contract providers (Figure 3.23). Although the two types of derivatives markets are distinct there is a relationship between them. Financial institutions that are active market makers in over-the-counter products use exchange-traded contracts to cover some of the residual risk exposures arising from these activities. Professional traders

**Figure 3.23** Characteristics of derivatives traded on exchanges and OTC-markets

| Exchange-traded products: | Over-the-counter products: |
|---|---|
| • Standardized contract specifications | • Tailored contract specifications |
| • Major financial assets and commodities | • Specified assets and risk exposures |
| • Fixed expiry dates | • Flexible expiry dates |
| • Relatively short maturities | • Short to medium-term maturities |
| • Public price development | • Bilateral non-public transactions |
| • High liquidity of contracts | • Low liquidity in hybrid instruments |
| • Little counter-party risk | • Potential credit exposures |

monitor both types of markets and take arbitrage positions when unreasonable price discrepancies seem to occur and thereby facilitate price alignments between market segments that trade comparable instruments. In a sense, financial institutions act as intermediaries when they engage as professional traders in the futures markets to cover residual risk exposures and use this hedging opportunity to offer tailored over-the-counter products that fit the specific needs of their institutional clients.

The total trading volume of futures and options contracts on exchanges around the globe has continued to increase over the past decade with annual growth rates during 2000–4 in excess of 30% (Figure 3.24). The large US and European exchanges top the list of the most active exchanges but other exchanges in emerging markets including the Korea Futures Exchange, the Shanghai Futures Exchange, Dalian

**Figure 3.24** The top twenty derivatives exchanges by volume (1st quarter, 2004)

| Exchange | No. contracts traded | Increase 2003/04 (%) |
|---|---|---|
| Korea Futures Exchange | 621 510 636 | −8.3 |
| Eurex | 289 641 405 | 9.3 |
| Euronext | 234 077 525 | 29.8 |
| Chicago Mercantile Exchange | 182 690 652 | 24.8 |
| Chicago Board of Trade | 136 573 117 | 43.5 |
| Chicago Board Options Exchange | 94 591 726 | 48.4 |
| International Securities Exchange | 91 991 254 | 99.1 |
| Bovespa | 55 428 925 | 84.0 |
| American Stock Exchange | 55 380 996 | 33.8 |
| Bolsa de Mercadorias & Futuros | 45 284 528 | 89.4 |
| Mexican Derivatives Exchange | 45 197 104 | 15.6 |
| Philadelphia Stock Exchange | 42 919 326 | 90.7 |
| New York Mercantile Exchange | 37 536 236 | −1.1 |
| Pacific Exchange | 28 837 665 | 48.3 |
| Shanghai Futures Exchange | 22 625 978 | 206.5 |
| OM Stockholm | 20 514 224 | 19.3 |
| London Metal Exchange | 18 780 879 | 9.7 |
| Dalian Commodity Exchange | 17 289 816 | −13.0 |
| Taiwan Futures Exchange | 16 433 992 | 786.2 |
| Sydney Futures Exchange | 13 350 353 | 32.7 |

*Source*: Futures Industry Association

Commodity Exchange (China), Bovespa (Brazil), and Bolsa de Mercadorias & Futures (Brazil) also rank high. The dominant contracts remain the benchmarks for government debt, such as US treasuries and euro bunds, and the major growth has emerged from interest rate related contracts while selective stock indices and commodities also have created interest.[21]

The presence of futures and options exchanges around the globe with distinct contract denominations and clearing arrangements makes international competition and cross-border integration an interesting aspect of these markets. In Europe over twenty national futures and options exchanges trading in local currency interest rate instruments emerged during the 1990s. When exchange-traded contracts cater primarily to national market participants, the issue of market integration is less relevant, but in the case of contracts that have international interest, transnational links between exchanges may serve to integrate cross-border transactions. Hence, the Chicago Mercantile Exchange (CME) and Singapore International Monetary Exchange (SIMEX) have allowed members to trade on both exchanges through CME's Globex trading system. With the introduction of a common currency within the European Union since 2000, the national interest rate contracts will lose their relevance and the issue of integrating cross-border trading and clearing practices intensifies. As a consequence, a consolidation process has started across European derivatives markets and there have been some inroads to intensified transatlantic competition. The futures exchanges have been characterized by two major trading approaches, namely open outcry where brokers quote the prices through physical interaction on an exchange floor, and electronic trading where brokers interact via screen based quotation systems. The Chicago exchanges that inspired the global development of futures exchanges have always been devoted to the open outcry system whereas the exchanges established on the European continent typically adopted electronic trading platforms. Another distinction is the degree to which exchanges integrate the clearing process through wholly owned outfits or instead adhere to independent clearing services. In the USA, the Depository Trust Clearing Corp. (DTCC) is an example of an independent clearing service for equity and debt instruments. DTCC is owned by its users and is run as a not-for profit organization. Similarly, the Options Clearing Corporation (OCC) clears US exchange-listed securities options on, e.g. the American Stock Exchange, Chicago Board Options Exchange, Philadelphia Stock Exchange, etc. In Europe, the London Clearing House (LCH) clears derivatives contracts for London International Financial Futures Exchange (LIFFE), International Petroleum Exchange (IPE), London Metal Exchange (LME), and London Stock Exchange (LSE).

Contrasting and competing approaches are emerging across the exchange-traded derivatives markets. Euronext is an example of an exchange moving towards a common electronic trading platform with an open clearing system. This confederation of exchanges in Paris, Amsterdam, and Brussels was established in 2000 after the French operators including MATIF and MONEP had merged into the Paris Bourse during 1999. It acquired LIFFE in 2002 and also incorporated Portugal's stock and derivatives exchange (BVLP). Euronext adopted LIFFE's Connect trading platform, a system developed to move LIFFE from the initial open outcry system towards electronic trading.[22] Euronext uses a common clearing system, Clearing 21®, licensed from the Chicago Mercantile Exchange (CME) and the New York Mercantile Exchange (NYMEX) and aims to achieve technical integration with Euroclear, a major securities settlement system in the Euromarket. Eurex is an example of a pure electronic derivatives exchange with a wholly owned and fully integrated clearing system. Eurex arose from a merger in 1998 between Deutsche Terminsbörse (DTB) and the Swiss Options and Futures Exchange and is now owned by Deutsche Börse and the Swiss Exchange. Eurex has acquired full control of Clearstream, a European depository and settlement house and major competitor to Euroclear. The exchange offers a fully electronic trading platform with an integrated clearing system, and claims to possess efficiency advantages from technology enhancements and automated clearing processes.[23]

The Chicago based derivatives exchanges, including the Chicago Board of Trade (CBOT) have insisted on a continuation of the traditional open outcry trading pits. Nonetheless, CBOT decided in early 2003 to opt for LIFFE's Connect order-matching and trading technology to introduce an effective complementary electronic market alternative and link up with CME's clearing house rather than adopting the electronic trading platform intended for a five-year alliance with Eurex. Eurex then announced its direct establishment in the US market through a global partnership with the Clearing Corporation (CCorp), formerly the Board of Trade Clearing Corp., where CCorp customers also have direct access to Eurex's European products. Hence, a somewhat complex confrontation between global electronic trading platforms with integrated clearing systems and combined open outcry and electronic order matching platforms with more open clearing systems has become symptomatic of the competitive setting in the exchange-traded derivatives markets.

The total notional amount of outstanding derivatives contracts on the over-the-counter markets had increased to around $200 trillion by year end 2003 against a total contract volume of exchange-traded contracts around $40 trillion (Figure 3.25). The largest share of the OTC-market is made up by interest rate contracts accounting for almost three quarters of the total amount outstanding. In turn, interest rate swap agreements count for more than two thirds of the interest rate contracts. Around 40% of the interest rate derivatives have maturities between one and five years and around 25% of the contracts mature beyond five years. Approximately one eighth of the total market volume is made up by foreign exchange contracts of which half constitutes outright forward foreign exchange agreements. Credit derivatives represent the fastest growing segment with annual growth rates above 50% and total amounts outstanding of close to $8 trillion. The share of euro-denominated derivatives has been increasing and exceeds the notional amounts in US dollars with the euro counting for around 40% of the interest rate derivatives.[24]

**Figure 3.25** The global OTC derivatives markets by amounts outstanding (US$ billions by year end, 2003)

| Derivatives contracts | Notional amounts | Increase 2002/03 |
|---|---|---|
| Foreign exchange contracts | 24 483 | 32.6% |
| Interest rate contracts | 141 991 | 39.7% |
| Equity-linked contracts | 3 787 | 64.0% |
| Commodity contracts | 1 406 | 52.3% |
| Other | 25 510 | 39.2% |
| Total | 197 177 | 39.2% |
| Exchange-traded contracts | 36 750 | 54.3% |

*Source*: Bank for International Settlements

**Figure 3.26** The trends in derivatives markets (notional amounts outstanding)

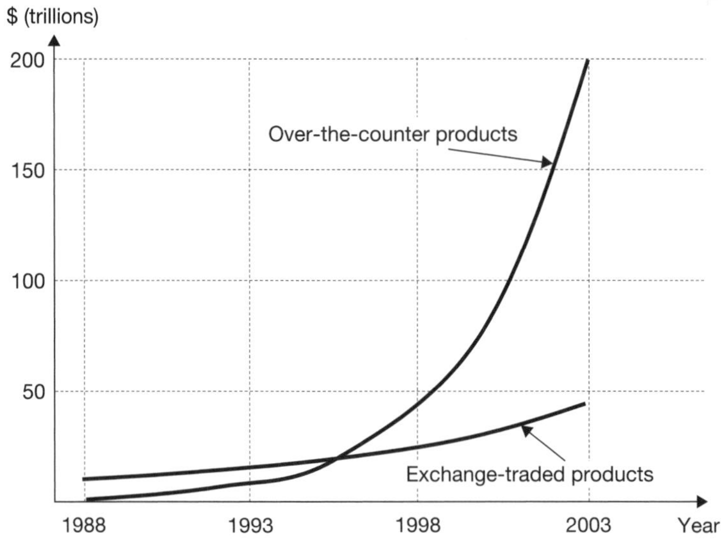

Source: Bank for International Settlements

The exchange-traded derivatives markets can count their early history back several decades whereas the over-the-counter markets have evolved since the mid-1980s. The markets for exchange-traded contracts have continued to expand through the establishment of global exchanges and the addition of new futures and options contracts although with some variation in annual growth rates across different product types (Figure 3.26). The over-the-counter markets have shown impressive growth over the past decade reflecting extensive use of derivatives for strategic risk management purposes. In terms of total amounts outstanding, the OTC-markets now appear more important that the exchange-traded markets. However, it should be kept in mind that the OTC-contracts generally have longer maturities and the data reflect gross notional amounts that ignore the effect of netting agreements. Furthermore, the financial institutions that act as derivatives dealers and offer tailored to specific institutional needs often use the standardized exchange-traded contracts to hedge net positions they assume in the OTC-markets. Hence, the market trends to a large extent reflect complementary rather than competitive developments.

## 3.6 Regulatory and accounting issues

The global regulatory environment is made up of a highly complex patchwork of national legislations, legal frameworks, tax rules, and supervisory authorities. The common denominator of national regulations is to maintain a safe financial system with high levels of integrity, fairness, and efficiency in the execution of derivatives transactions. The Commodity Futures Trading Commission (CFTC) regulates the commodity and futures and options markets in the USA while options on stock indexes and options on individual stocks fall under the jurisdiction of the Securities and Exchange Commission (SEC) and most swap transactions are exempted from direct supervision. In principle, the Federal Reserve Bank (FED) monitors all factors that potentially expose the US financial system and the Bank for International Settlements, of which the FED is a member together with other national financial regulators, has been following developments in the global derivatives markets closely in recent years. In the absence of direct supervision, the International Swaps and Derivatives Association (ISDA) has evolved into a trend setting global association for participants in the derivatives industry across all asset classes including interest rate, currency, commodity, credit, and equity contracts. The ISDA has developed a master agreement and related documents that are widely accepted as the standard in the global swaps markets. Within the European Union (EU) harmonization of national financial markets has been based on the principle of mutual recognition whereby national rule sets must fulfil the requirements of common directives while authorization in one member country provides a passport to business operations in the other member countries. The ongoing revisions of the Investment and Services Directive (ISD), which is central to this framework, aim to integrate the securities and derivatives markets across the EU. The long-term perspectives of these efforts are to create integrated platforms for payment systems and transactions clearing across the EU and eliminate tax obstacles to the integration of financial markets across member states. Efforts to harmonize global regulatory principles and rule sets are facilitated by work in the International Organization of Securities Commissions (IOSCO), an international cooperative forum for securities regulatory agencies that count over 180 members regulating more than 90% of the world's securities markets.

Financial reporting may be important to the way financial institutions and commercial enterprises are perceived by the public and their close stakeholders. In the context of financial derivatives, a major consideration has been to achieve a fair representation of the true derivatives positions and thereby eliminate the possible ignorance for off-balance-sheet exposures. One way to achieve this is by registering all derivatives positions on the balance sheet at their proper market values, the so-called **mark-to-market** principle. However, this approach is not as straightforward as it may seem because it can defeat one of the very purposes for engaging in derivatives in the first place, namely to reduce the variance in cash flows and accounting income. The applicable accounting rules are under current scrutiny by specialized accounting standard setters. The Financial Accounting Standards Board (FASB) is a private organization designated to establish standards for accounting practices and is recognized by the Securities and Exchange Commission, which has statutory authority to establish reporting standards for public companies, and the American Institute of Certified Public Accountants. The International Accounting Standards Board (IASB) is a London-based private organization committed to develop global accounting standards in cooperation with national standard setters and is considered as a potential global benchmark in conjunction with the FASB and a common EU standard.

Both the FASB and the IASB are considering the importance of accounting rules for financial derivatives. FAS 133 as imposed by the FASB requires corporations to mark all derivatives positions to market but permits hedge accounting for qualifying positions where the derivative contracts serve as a hedge for other assets or liabilities included on the balance sheet. As a consequence, all derivatives are registered at their true market value and all gains and losses are accounted for whether they are realized or not. **Hedge accounting** allows gains and losses of matching derivatives to be offset by the losses and gains incurred on the hedged positions thus reducing the volatility in accounted earnings. IAS 39 as imposed by the IASB applies to all types of financial instruments and derivatives except insurance contracts, investments in affiliates, and employee commitments. A derivative is considered a financial instrument whose value changes in response to an underlying variable, requires a smaller investment, and is settled at a future date. A financial instrument creates financial assets in one entity and financial liabilities in another entity and these assets and liabilities should be accounted for at their fair value through profit or loss unless they constitute a hedged item or a hedging instrument. The hedges can be fair value hedges of a specific asset investment or cash flow hedges associated with recognized assets or liabilities or constituting probable forecasted transactions. The key issue with the possibilities for hedge accounting is to what extent the hedged items must be minutely specified and matched piece by piece which clearly might jeopardize some of the general approaches to risk management. For example, **macro hedging** used by institutions to manage their overall interest rate exposures in different currencies may impose excessive and administrative accounting burdens and might be associated with an increased volatility in periodic accounting earnings. Here it seems appropriate to reiterate that while accounting is important, the true earnings effects relate to the actual cash flows generated by the institution. However, the accounting rules should obviously not be construed so they obscure the potential benefits to be gained from risk management processes and effective financial hedging practices.

## Conclusion

The global markets for financial derivatives have grown within a highly complex industrial environment comprising alternative credit intermediation and transaction facilitating practices. As international commercial and financial interactions have expanded the general demand for hedging of financial risk exposures has increased exponentially. The competitive playing field among different financial institutions has become more even and barriers between conventional industry segments have diminished. The development of new derivative instruments has facilitated this emergent integration across financial sectors.

The following three chapters (4–6) describe instruments and trading practices in different derivatives markets including futures contracts traded on international exchanges, options contracts and options on futures, and instruments offered in the over-the-counter markets.

## Summary

● The basic role of financial institutions, including deposit-taking institutions, investment banks, securities firms, investment companies, and insurance companies, is to facilitate the credit transformation process through direct lending and securities issuance.

● Credit intermediation constitutes the interaction between financial and commercial assets, and excessive uncertainties associated with this process will have an adverse effect on resource allocation and economic growth potentials.

● Volatile market prices and complex global exposures increase the need for risk management and hedging instruments while improved analytical and technological capabilities support new products. Financial innovation often seeks to avoid unintended restrictive regulations and take advantage of disparate accounting and tax rules.

● A number of risk-transfer techniques have emerged to complement conventional insurance products, e.g. loan sales, asset securitization, structured finance, risk-linked securities, and contingent capital, and use untapped diversification opportunities among institutional investors.

● Financial derivatives are traded on the basis of broker quotes on formal futures exchanges or in informal dealer-based over-the-counter markets, and the derivative products are made up by trades for future settlement or constitute options on such settlements.

● The key competitive concerns in the global derivatives markets include the introduction of electronic trading and the efficiencies of associated clearing systems all the while demand for derivative products is affected by regulation, tax rules, and accounting standards.

## Questions

3.1 Explain the relationship between the creation of financial assets and investment in commercial assets in the credit intermediation process.

3.2 Explain how uncertainties around the creation of financial assets and investment in commercial assets may affect economic growth.

3.3 Outline three major types of derivative instruments that are commonly observed in financial markets.

3.4 Explain the rationales behind the introduction of the loan sales, asset trading, and asset securitization techniques. Who benefits from these techniques?

3.5 Explain how risk exposures are managed through conventional risk-transfer arrangements in the insurance and reinsurance markets.

3.6 Explain the rationale behind the introduction of risk-linked securities and contingent capital instruments. Who benefits from these techniques?

3.7 Outline different motivations for financial innovation in the form of derivative instruments.

3.8 Explain the major difference between exchange-traded contracts and over-the-counter derivatives.

3.9 Explain the rationale behind current accounting rules applied to financial derivatives.

## Exercises

3.1 Consider a $1 billion pool of car loans with an average maturity of 4.5 years and a 5% yield. Determine how this loan portfolio can be securitized and divided into three distinct tranches:

(a) a fixed rate tranche;
(b) a floating rate tranche;
(c) an inverse floating rate tranche.

3.2 Consider the same $1 billion pool of car loans with an average maturity of 4.5 years and a 5% yield. Now determine how this loan portfolio can be securitized and instead divided into four distinct tranches:

(a) a $100 million zero-coupon tranche;
(b) a fixed rate tranche;
(c) a floating rate tranche;
(d) an inverse floating rate tranche.

## Notes

[1] See, for example, Bodie, Z., Kane, A. and Marcus, A. J. (2000), *Essentials of Investments*, 4th edn, McGraw-Hill.

[2] Federal Reserve Bank – flow of funds accounts.

[3] The restrictions imposed on banks in the US market relate notably to the Banking Act of 1933 (Glass–Steagal), which prohibited engagements in securities underwriting, but also to the Bank Holding Company Act of 1956, which enforced restrictions on interstate banking while many US states retained limitations on intrastate branching activities. These restrictions were not abolished until 1994 with the passage of the Riegle–Neal Interstate Banking and Branching Efficiency Act, which furnished a trend toward interstate consolidation of the banking industry.

[4] Swiss Re, Sigma 7/2001.

[5] A positive maturity gap means that the average maturity of assets exceeds the average maturity of liabilities. This can also be expressed as a positive duration gap where the weighted average duration of assets exceeds the weighted average duration of liabilities, i.e. the duration of the equity position is positive. The latter is arguably a more precise measure of the implied interest rate risk exposure.

[6] See, for example, Sounders, A. and Cornett, M. M. (2003), *Financial Institutions Management: A Risk Management Approach*, 4th edn, McGraw-Hill.

[7] This figure is not directly comparable to the total outstanding in the capital market. However, assuming average net premiums of say 3.5% and administrative expenses of 30% of gross premiums the indicated premium amount would correspond to a total insurance cover of around US$50 trilllion.

[8] Bank for International Settlement and Swiss Re.

[9] In dealer markets prices emerge through two-way quotes (bid–ask) provided by market participants who are committed to buy in the market at the bid price and sell in the market at the ask price, i.e. if you approach a dealer you can sell to him at his bid price and buy from him at his ask price. Stock exchanges can use different quotation systems, e.g. the New York Stock Exchange uses an auction system where market specialists provide current prices for all buy and sell transactions on a limited number of securities. Other exchanges, e.g. LSE, use electronic quotation systems that are comparable to a dealer market.

[10] For example, TIGRs, CATs, LIONs, and COUGARs were all comparable zero-coupon strips sold by different investment banks and securities firms during the 1980s.

[11] See, for example, Miller, M. (1986), 'Financial innovation: the last twenty years and the next', *Journal of Financial and Quantitative Economics*, **21**, 459–71.

[12] See, for example, Merton, R. C. (1995), 'Financial innovation and the management and regulation of financial Institutions', *Journal of Banking & Finance*, **19**, 461–81.

[13] See, for example, Fabosi, F. J. (1998), *Valuation of Fixed Income Securities and Derivatives*, 3rd edn, FJF.

[14] See, for example, Froot, K. A. (1999), 'The market for catastrophe risk: a clinical examination', *The National Bureau of Economic Research*, NBER working papers 10184.

[15] The estimate refers to the purchase of catastrophe reinsurance contracts from global reinsurance companies, and the number may underestimate the aggregate reinsurance capacity somewhat, because a portion of ceded insurance contracts are distributed among other primary insurance companies, which are not included in the estimate (Guy Carpenter (2000), *The World Catastrophe Reinsurance Market*, Guy Carpenter, New York). Additional coverage for catastrophe risk exposures may also be obtained through alternative proportional and facultative property insurance treaties that normally would be excluded from the reinsurance figures.

[16] Total insured property losses associated with the attacks on the World Trade Center in September 2001 amounted to around US$50 billion (Sigma No. 2 (2003), *Natural Catastrophes and Man-made Disasters*).

[17] See, for example, Guy Carpenter (2003), *The World Catastrophe Reinsurance Market*, Guy Carpenter, New York.

[18] The historical volatility of the stock market corresponds to a daily change in market value of approximately 1%, whereas the daily fluctuation in bond returns is closer to 0.7%. Hence, the expected daily change in the market value of all liquid securities can have a magnitude of around $125 billion. In addition, the default risk of corporate bonds has ranged from 0 to 6% of the principal depending on the issuers' credit quality, e.g. speculative corporate bonds rated 'Ba' and lower by Moody's, have experienced default rates in the range of 2–6% over recent years.

[19] See, for example, Sigma 5/1996; Goldman Sachs (2000), *Investing in Risk-linked Securities*.

[20] There are a number of tax issues related to the establishment of SPVs for catastrophe risk transfer. Therefore, most SPVs have been established in Bermuda, the Cayman Islands, or Ireland, which allow reinsurance companies to establish the SPVs as separate cells with zero or favourable tax status and without this tax treatment the securitzation technique would not be economical.

[21] Futures Industry Association, Annual Volume Survey, March/April 2004.

[22] The other exchanges, e.g. MATIF, had also moved to adopt electronic trading alongside the floor trading of their contracts.

[23] The London Clearing House (LCH) also merged with Clearnet and considered expanding the clearing services to a wider range of products, including foreign exchange forwards, options, and swap agreements, thus offering some interesting prospects for the management of counter-party risks in the areas of conventional OTC products. The increased emphasis on counter-party and derivative risks Basel II accord proposed by the Bank for International Settlements makes it more relevant to use independent clearing houses as a means to reduce counter-party risk associated with derivatives trading and optimise the use of capital.

[24] Bank for International Settlement, OTC Derivatives Market Activity in the Second Half of 2003, Monetary and Economic Department, May 2004. The credit derivative contracts take a variety of forms, including credit default and total return swaps, but are not included in the BIS semi-annual survey data.

# Part 2

# Exchange traded and OTC derivatives

# Chapter 4

# Financial futures contracts and options on futures

**Objectives**

- Describe the markets for financial futures
- Provide an overview of different futures and options contracts
- Explain the mechanics of futures contracts and options on futures
- Develop basic pricing relationships and principles for valuation
- Outline market practices for standardized contracts
- Consider newer contract developments

Futures and options on futures are important elements of modern financial markets. Shaped initially around agricultural commodity markets in Chicago, the trading of futures contracts has expanded to other exchanges around the globe with Asia and Europe emerging as increasingly important regions. The futures contracts have also expanded well beyond the initial focus on commodities to include all sorts of financial assets and indexes relating to relevant commercial uncertainties. The standardization of contracts and market practices combined with limited requirements for up-front investment has invited professional participants to these markets and created the liquidity needed to price the underlying assets effectively. Hence, the financial futures exchanges play an important role in the international financial markets as professional reservoirs for commercial risks and price setters for essential financial assets.

## 4.1 The futures contract

Futures contracts have their roots in the markets for raw materials, such as agricultural products (corn, soybeans, wheat, sugar, cocoa) and metals (copper, tin, silver, gold, platinum). As opposed to making forward dealings in commodities, where the goods are exchanged physically at a future date at an agreed price between two

**Table 4.1 Standardized futures contract – gold**

| | |
|---|---|
| Commodity: | Gold |
| Exchange: | New York Mercantile Exchange (NYMEX)[1] |
| Contract size: | 100 troy ounces |
| Delivery months: | Current calendar month, the next two months, and Feb./Apr./June/Aug./Oct./Dec. |

- First Friday of the delivery month is the first day on which delivery may be made.
- Two business days before the first delivery date is the last day on which a seller may issue notice of intention to deliver.
- Second Friday before delivery of the futures contract is the last day on which an option on the future may be exercised.
- Minimum price fluctuation $0.10 per ounce and constitutes the smallest change allowable in the price movement of a contract.

counterparts, the idea of the futures contract is to create standard instruments to be traded by many participants on formal exchanges. An exchange-traded futures contract for a given commodity is interchangeable with other contracts on the same commodity traded on that exchange, that have common specifications on size of contract, commodity grade, delivery months, and so on (Table 4.1). Contract standardization introduced by the exchanges makes the futures easy to trade but the contracts can normally not be traded between the different exchanges. A **futures contract** is a legal commitment for the seller to make delivery and for the buyer to take delivery of a standard quantity and quality of an underlying asset at a specified point in time, the **expiration date**. The value of a futures contract relates to the market price of the underlying commodity in the **spot** or **cash** market but fundamentally reflects the market participants' expectation about the future price development. Hence, the futures price reflects the spot price expected by the market at the expiration date. To determine the value of a futures contract at expiration one should multiply the quoted futures price by the size of the contract.

*Example*: If gold is quoted at $305 per ounce on NYMEX, then a gold futures contract is worth $30 500 ($305 per ounce times 100). A minimum price movement of $0.10 in the price of gold is therefore equal to a $10 change in the price of the contract ($0.10 per ounce times 100 ounces in a contract).

## 4.2 Opening and closing transactions

A transaction in futures contracts is identified either as an 'opening' or a 'closing' of a position. The initial buying and selling of a futures contract results in an **open position** for the buyer and seller, respectively. The seller's position is open because it is considered **short**, i.e. the seller has sold a commodity that he or she does not own. The buyer's position is considered **long** because the contract is for a future purchase of the commodity. As a result, the buyer's position is also open.

A **closing** transaction offsets an open position and the embedded commitment of the futures contract can be closed in two ways:

- By an **offsetting** (liquidating) **transaction**. To close, or offset, a short position, a seller buys a comparable contract (a closing purchase transaction). A buyer closes a long position by selling a comparable contract (a closing sale transaction). All but a small percentage of positions are closed this way.
- By **delivering** or **receiving** the commodity at expiration. A seller may also close a position by delivering the underlying commodity as specified, and a buyer by receiving the commodity.

## 4.3 Role of the exchange

The futures exchange provides a trading arena for the standardized futures contracts. As in the case of stock exchanges, only de facto members may trade on futures exchanges. Eligibility for membership depends on creditworthiness, business history, character, and integrity.

## 4.4 Role of the clearinghouse

The clearinghouse is an agency, sometimes affiliated with the exchange, that clears the trades performed between exchange members, guarantees contract performance until expiry, and handles contract fulfilment through delivery.

### 4.4.1 Clearing

For every trade, the member firms of the buyers and sellers submit the trading data to the clearinghouse. At the clearinghouse, data from the buyer and seller firms are compared. If the data match, the trade is cleared. If not, the data are sent back to the firms for correction. Should the trade data still not match, the trade is handled as an 'out trade', that is, as a special case.

### 4.4.2 Performance guarantee

The clearinghouse thus acts as a third party to all trades. During the course of a trading day, Smith may sell a contract to Jones, Jones to Doe, and Doe to someone else. Once the trade is made, however, the contract no longer exists between the last buyer and seller. Rather, the clearinghouse becomes the counterpart to each transaction, a buyer to every seller and a seller to every buyer. The buyers and sellers of the futures contracts create financial obligations not to one another but to the clearing corporation or to the exchange through its member firms.

### 4.4.3 Delivery

Although only a small fraction of all futures contracts result in physical delivery, clearing corporations usually provide the mechanism for delivery of the underlying asset with the exception of certain European exchanges where exchange of cash is the only mode of settlement.

### 4.4.4 Margin

To ensure that member firms have enough funds to cover their positions in the market, the clearinghouse requires members to deposit and maintain margin against their positions. All futures trades require margin payments. The margin is typically less than 10% for a futures trade depending on the types of futures contract and varies somewhat from one exchange to the other. In futures transactions the margin is a performance bond, or 'earnest' money, which ensures that buyers and sellers will be able to honour their contractual obligations. There are two kinds of margin in futures trading: initial margin and maintenance margin.

### 4.4.5 Initial margin

The **initial margin** is the money deposited when the contract is purchased or sold and usually makes up around 10% of the total worth of the contract. The exchanges determine the initial margin, depending on the price volatility of the contract's underlying asset and the futures market itself. Brokerage houses usually ask their customers for a slightly higher margin than that set by the exchange.

*Example*: If an exchange requires initial margin of 10% on its orange juice contracts, a member brokerage firm might require 15%. If the cash price of orange juice is $0.9500 per pound and a contract consists of 15 000 pounds, then the value of the contract is $14 250 (15 000 pounds times $0.95). The brokerage firm will then require an initial margin deposit of $2187.50 (15% of $14 250).

The initial margin may typically be posted in any of the following ways, or combinations of them:

● cash (possibly in the form of bank-issued margin certificates);
● stock in the clearing corporation;
● high-quality securities (e.g. government bonds, T-Bills, T-Notes, T-Bonds, etc.);
● letters of credit from an approved commercial bank.

### 4.4.6 Maintenance margin

The **maintenance margin** is additional margin required on an established position as a result of a decline in the value of the contract bought or sold position. It is calculated by the clearinghouse at the end of each trading day. Retail clients are asked by their broker to put up more margin or have their positions liquidated. The exchanges determine the total amount of margin required at any time in relation to the net short or long position each member holds in the futures contracts.

*Example*: A member holds a long position (the bought side) of fifteen silver contracts and a short position (the sold side) in ten silver contracts, and delivery for all the contracts is in the same month. The total margin required is then calculated for the net long position of five silver contracts.

However, some exchanges and independent clearing corporations may seek additional protection by requiring maintenance margin on all long and short positions even if they can be offset by other contracts with the same delivery date.

## 4.4.7 Normal and inverted markets

When the futures prices for the near months are lower than the months farther out, the market is said to be a **carrying charge** market, i.e. the distant months trade at a premium over near months. Hence, most commodity futures are traded higher than the spot prices, a situation also referred to as **contango**, because they save on storage cost by not holding the physical asset. The premium is attributed to a carrying charge that is added to the value of the contract, which represents insurance, warehousing, and financing cost of holding the asset. The more distant months cost more when they entail positive carrying charges. In a **normal market**, the maximum that a distant month is traded over a near month reflects the total carrying charges. If a price premium exceeds these charges, arbitrageurs would sell the distant contracts and take delivery in the nearer contracts, to lock-in a profit whether or not the distant price rises or falls.

An **inverted market** is the opposite of a carrying market, i.e. the distant months sell at lower prices than near months. The implication of an inverted market is that the underlying asset is in short supply. Buyers are bidding up the price of the near months to the extent that these prices more than offset the carrying charges included in the prices of contracts for the distant months. In an inverted, or **discount**, market, each contract that is further out in time trades at a lower price than contracts closer in. Situations where a futures contract is traded below the spot price, are also referred to as **backwardation**, and can occur, e.g. when future supply is expected to exceed current supply due to improved crop conditions. Whereas in a normal market the prices of the more distant contracts are limited by the carrying charges, there is no limit to the amount that a near contract can trade over a more distant contract in an inverted market. Inverted markets may often occur in spurts of extreme market bullishness.

### Box 4.1  Basic futures price relationships

When a hedger or investor buys a futures contract they establish an open position at the bought futures price, which indicates the expected spot price for the underlying asset at the contract's expiration date. The value of this open long futures position is proportional to changes in the futures price. When expectations about the spot price at the expiration date changes so does the quoted futures price. Since the open long futures position is closed by selling back the contract at the prevailing futures price any returns from this investment will follow movements in the futures price. For example, if the spot price at the expiration date is expected to increase, then the futures contract can be sold at a higher price than it was bought and is thereby closed out at a profit.

As time goes by, the futures price will slowly converge towards the market price of the underlying asset, and, by the time the contract expires, the futures price will be the same as the market price of the underlying asset (Figure 4.1). Since the futures contract can provide physical delivery of the underlying asset, the futures price and cash market price must be equivalent at expiry. If not, arbitrageurs will engage in the market to make a risk-free profit from the price discrepancy and this will move prices back into line.

At the expiration date a long futures position will, therefore, generate a profit if the market price of the underlying asset exceeds the price at which the future was initially

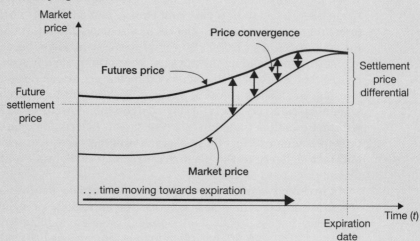

**Figure 4.1** Convergence between the futures price and the spot price of the underlying asset

bought, i.e. the future settlement price, whether it is closed out by selling back the futures contract or by taking delivery and selling the asset in the cash market. Conversely, a long futures position will result in a loss if the market price of the underlying asset is below the future settlement price at the contract expiration date (Figure 4.2).

A short futures position will result in a loss if the market price of the underlying asset exceeds the price at which the future was initially sold, i.e. the future settlement price, whether it is closed out by buying back the futures contract or the asset is bought in the cash market and delivery made under the terms of the contract. Conversely, a short futures position will generate a profit if the market price of the underlying asset has fallen below the future settlement price by the contract expiration date (Figure 4.2).

> The value of a long futures position is positively related to the market price of the underlying asset ($dFP/dMP > 0$).

> The value of a short futures position is inversely related to the market price of the underlying asset ($dFP/dMP < 0$).

Futures prices quoted on the exchanges reflect the market participants' general assessment of the development in the future spot price of the underlying asset in the cash market as it is expected to materialize around the contract expiration date. Consequently, any profits made by investors and speculators from open futures positions, whether long or short, will derive from an ability to outguess or outsmart the market through astute position management over the period until the contract expires. Hedgers trading in the futures market use the profit and losses incurred on a futures position to counter changes in the value of the underlying position they are trying to cover.

## Figure 4.2 The price relationship of long (a) and short (b) futures positions

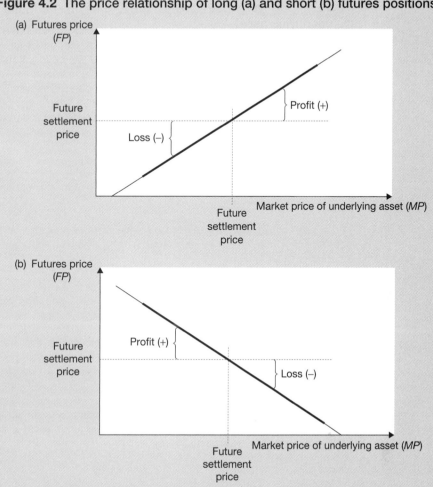

*The relationship between future (forward) and spot prices*

Given the nature of the futures contract as the means to obtain or make future delivery of a certain asset at a given price, at a given point in time, the futures price must reflect the expected price at which this asset can be exchanged in the underlying cash market at that future time. The relationship between the futures price and the expected future cash market price of the underlying asset is also influenced by differences in direct cost and opportunity costs between advance acquisition of the asset in the cash market and purchase of a futures contract that entails future delivery of the asset. For example, by buying at a future date, the holder of the futures contract avoids financing cost associated with a long cash market position. For certain commodities, e.g. orange juice, copper, crude oil, etc., the holder of the futures contract will also save associated transportation, storage, and insurance costs, while in the case of certain financial assets, e.g. long-term securities, the holder of the financial futures contract may forego fixed income payments.

In the case of commodities without storage cost, such as electricity, the futures price would exceed the expected future spot price by an amount equivalent to the saved financing cost. This can be expressed in terms of compound interest, where interest is accrued on a continuous basis as opposed to over regular time intervals. Hence, the futures price would equal the expected spot price in the cash market at the contract expiration date multiplied by one plus the accrued interest. This is normally expressed as $(1 + r)$, where $r$ is the interest rate for the period. If the period is split into $n$ smaller sub-periods, the accrued interest can be expressed as $(1 + r/n)^n$. Dividing the interest period into an increasing number of sub-periods, where $n \to \infty$, corresponds to a situation of compounded interest calculations, which can be expressed as $e^{rt}$, where $e = 2.71828$, $r$ = interest rate for period $t$ expressed as percent per annum, and $t$ = time period until expiration expressed as share of the year.

*Example*: Principal plus accrued interest over a three month period is calculated as 1.015 (= 1 + 0.06/4), where $r = 6\%$ p.a. Using compound interest calculations we get 1.01511 (= $e^{0.06 \times 0.25}$ = $2.71828^{0.015}$). For small time intervals there is hardly any noticeable difference between the two approaches to interest calculation.

In the case of physical assets that require storage cost, the accrued interest and saved storage cost would be expressed as $e^{(r+s)t}$, where $s$ = storage cost expressed as a percentage per annum.

*Example*: Assume that the annual storage cost of crude oil on average amounts to 6% of the initial purchase price then the principal plus accrued interest and storage cost over a three month time interval can be expressed as 1.03045 (= $e^{(0.06+0.06)/4}$ = $2.71828^{0.03}$), where $r = 6\%$ p.a. and $s = 6\%$ p.a.

In the case of a bought foreign currency the holder 'saves' the interest rate differential between the two currency areas, i.e. the accrued interest could be expressed as $e^{(r-f)t}$, where $f$ = interest rate of the foreign currency for period $t$ expressed as percentage per annum.

*Example*: Buying euros against US dollars three months from now implies euro-denominated interest expenses and US dollar-denominated interest income, i.e. one plus accrued net interest on the long euro futures position can be calculated as 1.0050 (= $e^{((0.06-0.04)0.25)}$ = $2.71828^{0.005}$), where $r = 6\%$ p.a. (three-month euro interest rate) and $f = 4\%$ p.a. (three-month US dollar interest rate).

In the case of a fixed income security the holder of the futures contract may forego coupon payments on the bonds in which case the quoted futures price would be reduced by the paid coupons expressed as $P_t - C$, where $C$ = coupon payment expressed as percentage of bond price and assuming coupon payment at the expiration date. If the bond carries a storage cost, e.g. payable to a depository bank, this should be taken into consideration as well. Individual stocks represent comparable financial assets to be treated in a similar manner by deducting any dividend payments paid.

*Example*: By buying a three-month bond future the holder foregoes a 5% coupon payment, in which case the futures price would be expressed as 99.0 (= $(102.3 - 5.0)e^{((0.06+0.01)0.25)}$ = 97.3 × $2.71828^{0.0175}$), where $P_t = 102.3$ (the expected bond price in three months), $r = 6\%$ p.a., and $s = 1\%$ p.a. (depository fees).

In the case of a stock index, the dividend payments may be more effectively expressed as an average dividend yield for the underlying stock portfolio as opposed to exact dividend amounts, i.e. the accrued interest would take the foregone dividend into account and be expressed as $e^{(r-q)t}$, where $q$ = average dividend yield expressed as a percentage per annum.

*Example*: A holder of a three-month stock index future on average foregoes a dividend yield of 2.5% p.a. on the underlying stock portfolio, i.e. one plus accrued interest on the index can be calculated as 1.008788 ($= e^{((0.06-0.025)0.25)} = 2.71828^{0.00875}$), where $q = 2.5\%$ p.a.

The futures prices ($F$) for different types of assets expressed in relation to the expected spot market price ($P$) of the underlying asset at the expiration date ($t$) are summarized below:

$$\text{Commodity (no storage cost): } F = P_t\, e^{rt}$$

$$\text{Commodity (with storage cost): } F = P_t\, e^{(r+s)t}$$

$$\text{Foreign currency: } F = P_t\, e^{(r-f)t}$$

$$\text{Fixed income bond (no storage cost): } F = (P_t - C)\, e^{rt}$$

$$\text{Fixed income bond (with storage cost): } F = (P_t - C)\, e^{(r+s)t}$$

$$\text{Individual stock (with dividend): } F = (P_t - D)e^{rt}$$

$$\text{Stock index (with dividend): } F = P_t\, e^{(r-q)t}$$

where

$P_t$ = expected future spot price at time $t$;
$t$ = contract expiration date;
$F$ = forward or futures price;
$r$ = compound interest rate for period $t$;
$s$ = storage cost;
$f$ = foreign compound interest rate;
$C$ = coupon payments;
$D$ = dividend payments;
$q$ = dividend yield.

## 4.5 Market participants

Futures traders can be categorized as **hedgers**, **investors**, and **arbitrageurs**. For example, General Mills as a major food processor is exposed to the future price of its grain supplies, while the grain farmers have similar price exposures on their grain production. Hence, the food processors can fix the commodity costs by hedging, i.e. buying a number of grain contracts equal to its planned consumption. The processor is thereby covered against an unexpected rise in the price. Conversely, the farmers can fix the commodity revenues by selling a number of grain contracts equal to their expected production and are thereby covered against an unexpected drop in the price. The food processors and farmers constitute natural counterparts with opposing positions and thereby constitute natural hedgers whose main interest is to protect their business against adverse price fluctuations. The investors trade futures contracts and assume futures positions to earn a profit from expected changes in the market prices of the underlying assets. Hence, the investors speculate in future price developments to profit through the astute buying and selling of contracts prior to expiration. We can distinguish between different types of speculators. **Position**

**traders** speculate in short-term developments in the price of the underlying asset and may take long and short positions over a couple of days before they are liquidated. **Day traders** speculate in short-term price fluctuations and take positions in accordance with immediate price movements during the day and close out the position by the end of the trading day. **Scalpers** are exchange members that take short-term positions of only minutes to balance bid and offer contracts as they make market prices in the futures contract. These market makers make money from small differences between the bid–ask spread.

The futures exchanges are interesting in this context because the contracts require margin payments of around 10% of the amounts that would be required to speculate by buying the underlying asset directly in the cash market. The distinction between the role of hedger and investor is not always hard and fast. Futures contracts bought or sold to hedge an underlying position may be lifted, or offset, by buying or selling other futures contracts to dodge the initial futures trades. The hedgers can benefit from the futures marketplace by reducing business uncertainty, which allows them to lower prices. Without hedging, both producers and processors would have to add an extra amount to the price to counterbalance the risk of adverse price change. The investors are important participants in the futures markets as providers of liquidity and a willingness to take positions in the price risk already inherent in futures markets and that would otherwise be borne solely by natural hedging parties of producers and consumers.

Arbitrageurs eliminate price differentials between compatible contracts with similar expiration dates and hence serve to maintain market discipline whereby prices are determined effectively over contract maturities, for example, by maintaining carrying charges within reasonable ranges in normal markets. Arbitrageurs are typically members of the exchange and as professional market participants know the insides of the market very well but they may also include external investors who through particular market insights are able to take advantage of small periodic price discrepancies. In practice, it can be difficult to distinguish between arbitrageurs and investors. The main characteristic of an arbitrageur, as opposed to an investor, is that the arbitrageur in principle does not assume a risk position but makes risk-free profits by taking advantage of short-term market inefficiencies, which in itself serves to eliminate market discrepancies.

### 4.5.1 Limits

Trading on futures exchanges is usually conducted within the restraints of several types of limit:

- position limits;
- reportable positions;
- trading limits.

### 4.5.2 Position limit

A **position limit** is the maximum number of contracts a given trader may hold as a net uncovered position in a given commodity or financial asset. The position limits for different contracts are set by the exchanges for each broker individually, depending on the broker's capital reserves and general credit standing. In the USA, the Commodity Futures Trading Commission (CFTC) approves the limits set by exchanges. In Europe, the operations of futures exchanges are monitored by the national financial regulators.

### 4.5.3　Reportable limit

A **reportable limit** is the number of contracts at which traders must report their total positions by delivery month to the authorized exchange. In the USA the reportable limit is usually 25 contracts, a criterion set by the CFTC. Traders who hold 25 or more contracts, either long or short, are considered large traders.

Both position and reportable limits apply only to large traders. Because of their economic needs, hedgers are not limited in the number of contracts that they may hold at any time. Notice, however, that position limits are considerably higher than reportable positions. If a reportable position is 40 contracts, the position limit may be 400 or even 600, depending on the nature of the specific contract.

### 4.5.4　Trading limit

A **trading limit** is the maximum price movement an exchange will allow for a futures contract in a trading session.

*Example*: The NYMEX gold futures contract can move 2500 points above or below the prior day's settlement.

In a trading session, the market can be limit up or limit down. When the market is **limit up**, or **bid limit**, all participants want to buy and no one wants to sell. In such a situation, the bids to buy are at the top of the daily allowable limit, with no offers to sell at that price. In a **limit down** market participants are looking to sell, and no one wants to buy.

The trading limit is established to prevent market panics. On stock exchanges, trading may be suspended until extreme news and catastrophic events have had sufficient time to be assessed and consummated. The futures exchanges may experience a series of limit up or limit down days, but losses are generally curtailed.

## 4.6 Types of futures contracts

For many years futures contracts were primarily traded on commodities. The Chicago-based futures exchanges and other Midwestern stock exchanges traded agricultural commodity futures, such as corn, wheat, pork bellies, soybeans, etc. The New York and London-based exchanges excelled in world commodities and precious metals, including sugar, oil, copper, gold, silver, etc. In the early 1980s futures contracts became available on a range of financial assets, such as currencies, debt instruments, and different stock indexes (Table 4.2). Over the years a variety of futures contracts have been introduced including yield curve spreads, inflation rates, bankruptcy indexes, etc., on exchanges around the world.

**Table 4.2** Different futures contracts

| Underlying asset | Delivery months | Contract size | Futures exchange |
|---|---|---|---|
| **Commodities** | | | |
| Wheat (hard red winter)[2] | Mar./May/July/Sep./Dec. | 5000 bushels | Kansas City Board of Trade (KCBT) |
| Live cattle | Feb./Apr./June/Aug./Oct./Dec. | 40 000 pounds | Chicago Mercantile Exchange (CME) |
| **Energy** | | | |
| PJM Interconnection monthly peak | Jan./Feb./Mar./Apr./May/June/ July/Aug./Sep./Oct./Nov./Dec. | 40 MW h per peak day | New York Mercantile Exchange (NYMEX) |
| **Financials** | | | |
| Three-month Eurodollar deposit (LIBOR) | Mar./June/Sept./Dec. | $1 000 000 | Singapore Exchange (SGX)[3] |
| German government bond (Bund) | Mar./June/Sep./Dec. | €100 000 | Euronext. liffe |
| US Treasury bonds | Mar./June/Sept./Dec. | $100 000 | Chicago Board of Trade (CBOT) |
| **Stock indexes** | | | |
| TOPIX (Tokyo price index) | Mar./June/Sept./Dec. | ¥10 000 × index | Tokyo Stock Exchang (TSE) |
| DAX (Deutsche Aktienindex) | Mar./June/Sept./ | €25 × index | Eurex |

## 4.7 Commodity futures

Commodity futures contracts deserve a mention because these contracts represent the birth of futures trading in the Chicago markets. The commodity futures markets were created initially to reduce the impact of price fluctuations on agricultural produce the availability of which often can be seasonal. However, the futures contracts cover a wide range of commodities that constitute important ingredients and raw materials in commercial activities (Table 4.3).

Futures contracts on essential commodities continue to be actively traded on various exchanges around the world where the underlying products are essential commercial inputs and outputs. Agricultural futures have emerged in many regional markets where contract specifications are adapted to local product peculiarities and qualities. Other contracts on commodities and metals traded in the world market, such as cocoa, coffee, copper, and zinc are typically traded on international exchanges with members from different parts of the world. The futures contracts for precious metals are special due to the durability and scarcity value of the underlying asset. Gold in particular can serve as a safe keeper in times of economic distress and may be included in diversified investment portfolios. The commodity futures exchanges are the forerunners for the markets in financial futures contracts.

### Table 4.3 Some commodities traded in futures markets

**Agricultural contracts**
- *Grain* – barley, corn, oats, rice, rye, wheat
- *Oilseed products* – coconut oil, cottonseed, palm oil, soybeans, sunflower seeds
- *Fiber products* – cotton, wool,
- *Dairy products* – butter, cheddar cheese, milk
- *Foodstuffs* – eggs, orange juice, corn syrup, potatoes, shrimp
- *World commodities* – cocoa, coffee, sugar
- *Livestock* – Boneless beef, broilers, cattle, hogs, pork bellies, skinned ham, turkeys

**Fertilizer futures**
- *Fertilizer* – anhydrous ammonia, diammonium phosphate

**Wood futures**
- *Wood products* – Oriented strand board, plywood, lumber

**Metals**
- *Industrial* – aluminium, copper, ferrous scrap, zinc
- *Precious* – gold, palladium, platinum, silver

## 4.8 Energy futures

A variety of energy futures have emerged as an active, albeit specialized, element of the international futures markets. Different types of crude oil have formed the basis for the initial energy commodity contracts but the futures contracts have been extended in recent years to comprise contracts based on refined oil products, natural gas, and electricity. A number of representative energy futures contracts are shown in Table 4.4.

Crude oil and refined oil products constitute an important factor cost in the modern economy and hence there is a need to use the futures market as a reservoir for hedging purposes. Crude oil has different quality grades dependent on the place of origin, i.e. prices are quoted for each of these major types of oil. As natural gas has become an increasingly important energy source gas prices have become equally important. In recent years the markets for electricity in the USA and Europe have

### Table 4.4 Some energy contracts traded in futures markets

**Oil products**
- Crude oil, Brent, Arab light, North Sea
- Refined gasoline, diesel
- Propane

**Natural gas**
- Henry Hub, North Sea natural gas

**Electricity**
- Palo Verde, California–Oregon Border
- Spark spreads

been exposed to increased market liberalization, which has tended to increase price volatility thus emphasizing the need to hedge inherent price risks associated with this essential energy source. There is little difference in electricity in different regions or parts of the world, but the availability of electricity depends on the transmission networks that link up the different power sources. Therefore, contracts are specified around the power sources available at specific transmission nodes, such as the California–Oregon Border, etc.

## 4.9 Financial futures

Financial futures contracts can be differentiated into the three categories of currency futures, interest rate futures, and stock index futures (Table 4.5). Just like commodity futures, financial futures contracts are traded by hedgers, investors, and arbitrageurs. Hedging is conducted primarily by commercial enterprises, such as large corporations and financial institutions seeking protection against unexpected changes in foreign exchange rates, interest rates, and other financial prices. Speculators can be specialized financial intermediaries and institutional investors that try to take advantage of opportunities for general investment in the financial futures market. Due to the relatively low margin payments, maintaining positions in the futures market requires less liquidity than positions established in the cash market. Arbitrageurs are typically brokers and intermediaries who are members of the futures exchange, and who consistently trade large volumes with both buyers

**Table 4.5** Some financial assets traded in futures markets

Currencies
- Australian dollar, Australian dollar/Canadian dollar, Australian dollar/Japanese yen
- British pound spot-forward, British pound/euro, British pound/Japanese yen, British pound/Swiss franc
- Canadian dollar spot-forward, Canadian dollar/Japanese yen
- Euro spot-forward, euro/British pound, euro/Japanese yen, euro/Australian dollar, euro/Canadian dollar, euro/Swiss franc, euro/Swedish krone
- Brazilian real, Malaysian ringgit, Mexican peso, Russian ruble, South African rand

Interest rates
- Thirty-day commercial paper loans, 90-day domestic CDs, three-month eurodollar time deposit rates
- Three-month Euribor deposit rates, three-month euroyen deposit rates, Federal funds rate
- US treasury bonds, UK gilts, German government bonds, French government bonds
- Japanese government bonds, Mexican treasury bills, Brazilian par Brady bond
- Mortgage-backed securities, Emerging market debt index

Stock indexes
- CBT stock market index, COMEX 500 stock index, Nasdaq 100 index, NYSE composite index
- Dow Jones composite average, Eurotop 100 stock index, S&P 100 stock price index
- FT-SE 100 share index, Mexico 30 index, Nikkei 225 stock index, Tokyo stock price index
- Russell 1000 index, Wilshire small cap index, Morgan Stanley Int'l index

and sellers in the market, and who often use specific market knowledge to maintain advisory capacities to external investors. The natural hedgers in financial futures are large corporations and financial institutions acting in the different capacities of borrowers, lenders, and investors.

The financial futures exchanges consist of members dealing on the trading floor with prices determined by supply and demand. The member dealers trade either for own account or for third parties against a commission fee. Memberships are purchased from the exchange. The exchange carries out the clearing function or engages an affiliated agency to settle all transactions completed by exchange members during the trading day. Hence, the direct counterpart in traded financial futures contracts is usually the clearing-house and not the member dealer that closed the trade.

As the financial futures are developed to suit the conditions of the specific exchange on which they are traded, the characteristics of futures contracts on the same underlying assets, e.g. euros traded against US dollars, might differ slightly from one exchange to the other in terms of contracts size, maturity dates, and other characteristics. In other words, the same type of financial futures contract available on different futures exchanges might not be completely compatible.

### 4.9.1 Benefits

The development of markets for financial futures contracts not only provides an efficient way of matching economic entities with differing financial exposures, but also enables them to ameliorate the financial exposure through trading of financial futures contracts. The involvement of many active dealers in the financial futures markets provides the necessary liquidity to ensure continuous and effective pricing of contracts. The financial futures markets provide the means for institutions to neutralize price risks whether the exposure is brought about by interest rate gaps, a mismatch in currency flows, or the price sensitivity of invested portfolios. Furthermore, the price determination in financial futures markets provides the actors in the underlying cash markets with a valuable source of information on market expectations and trends. Current price developments on major financial futures contracts are available daily in the international newspapers and these exchange statistics constitute essential financial market information.

## 4.10 Currency futures

A **currency future** is a standard contract that provides the buyer with a certain amount of foreign currency, as determined by the contract size, against another currency at a predetermined foreign exchange rate at a certain future time, as determined by the contract expiration date. Conversely, the seller is obliged to make the currency available according to the terms specified under the contract. However, most of these open trading positions are closed out before the final maturity date as buyers sell the contracts again and the sellers buy them back. The contracts are standardized so each contract specifies the same amount of foreign currency settled at specified maturity dates, say the third Wednesday in March, June, September, and December.

**Table 4.6** Currency futures

---

**Currencies**
- US dollar/Australian dollar, Australian dollar/Canadian dollar, Australian dollar/Japanese yen
- British pound/US dollar, British pound/euro, British pound/Japanese yen, British pound/Swiss franc
- US dollar/euro, British pound/euro, euro/Japanese yen, euro/Australian dollar, euro/Canadian dollar, euro/Swiss franc, euro/Swedish krone

---

| International Monetary Market (IMM)[4,9] | London International Financial Futures Exchange (LIFFE)[5] |
|---|---|
| Euros (€125 000)[6] | US dollars (US$20 000)[7] |
| British pounds (£62 500)[6] | Euros (€20 000)[8] |
| Canadian dollars (C$100 000)[6] | |
| Japanese yen (¥12 500 000)[6] | |

---

### 4.10.1 Pricing

Financial futures contracts on currencies are typically quoted as the amount of local currency against the foreign currency being traded. Hence, on US-based futures exchanges currency futures contracts are usually quoted as US dollars and cents per unit of the foreign currency. Heavily traded currencies are often quoted in terms of the foreign exchange cross-rate (Table 4.6).

*Example*: A financial futures contract on euros against US dollars, with a contract denomination of €100 000, might be quoted as 1.0185. This means that the price for the specific euro contract on the futures exchange amounts to US$101 850 = (€100 000 × 1.0185 US$/€).

### 4.10.2 Quotations

Figure 4.3 presents quotations for different currency futures contracts listed on the respective futures exchanges. The exchange is typically indicated by an abbreviation of the name, for instance, the Chicago Mercantile Exchange is listed as CME, the Chicago Board of Trade as CBOT, the London International Financial Futures Exchange as LIFFE, Tokyo Stock Exchange as TSE, etc. Some of the European exchanges are indicated by their short names, such as Eurex and Euronext.

The top of the columns for the currency futures quotations has the following headings:

- *Open*: The price at which trading in each contract opened for the day.
- *Latest*: The price at which trading in each contract closed for the day.
- *High*: The highest price quoted during the trading day.
- *Low*: The lowest price quoted during the trading day.
- *Estimated volume*: The total number of futures contracts traded during the day.
- *Open Interest*: The total number of futures contracts (purchases or sales) that have not been offset by an opposite transaction or fulfilled by delivery at the end of the trading day.

The quotation listings provide figures for total volume and open interests in each of the futures contracts. The volume indicates the number of contracts that were

**Figure 4.3** Currency futures quotes

## Currency futures

**FT**

| Jun 17 | | Open | Latest | Change | High | Low | Est. vol | Open int |
|---|---|---|---|---|---|---|---|---|
| €-Sterling* | Sep | 0.6610 | 0.6595 | −0.0016 | – | 0.0000 | 486 | 7 773 |
| €-Dollar* | Sep | 1.1965 | 1.2029 | −0.0116 | 1.2029 | 1.2029 | 327 | 333 |
| €-Yen* | Sep | 131.40 | 131.34 | −0.07 | 131.34 | 131.10 | 184 | 12 676 |
| $-Can $ † | Sep | 0.7270 | 0.7253 | −0.0036 | 0.7297 | 0.7250 | 4 678 | 52 287 |
| $-Euro € † | Sep | 1.1990 | 1.2032 | −0.0006 | 1.2051 | 1.1976 | 29 163 | 90 805 |
| $-Euro € † | Dec | 1.1989 | 1.2027 | −0.0005 | 1.2044 | 1.1979 | 12 | 763 |
| $-Sw Franc † | Sep | 0.7910 | 0.7973 | +0.0032 | 0.7988 | 0.7903 | 4 504 | 40 048 |
| $-Yen † | Sep | 0.9118 | 0.9154 | +0.0027 | 0.9215 | 0.9104 | 9 942 | 80 676 |
| $-Yen † | Dec | 0.9214 | 0.9214 | +0.0044 | 0.9249 | 0.9214 | 0 | 10 397 |
| $-Sterling † | Sep | 1.8128 | 1.8216 | +0.0035 | 1.8244 | 1.8103 | 4 786 | 48 334 |
| $-Aust $ † | Sep | 0.6824 | 0.6793 | −0.0127 | 0.6850 | 0.6752 | 3 919 | 8 412 |
| $-Mex Peso † | Sep | 86 850 | 86 900 | +475 | 87 100 | 86 400 | 1 484 | 12 563 |

Sources: * FINEX; Sterling €100 000, Dollar: €200 000 and Yen: €100 000. †CME: Australian $: A$100 000, Canadian $: C$100 000, Euro: €125 000; Mexican Peso: 500 000, Swiss Franc: SFr125 000; Yen: Y12.5m ($ per Y100); Sterling: £62 500. CME volume, high & low for pit & electronic trading at settlement. Contracts shown are based on the volumes traded in 2003.

Source: Financial Times, Friday, June 18, 2004.

traded during the day, whether the transactions constituted opening or closing positions. The **open interest** is the total number of open contracts outstanding, whether buys or sells or different expiry dates, as of the close of trading. The volume and open interest do not necessarily increase or decrease in relationship to each other. Heavy volume during a trading day, for example, could leave open interest almost unchanged from the previous day if the opening and closing transactions are roughly equal in number. Volume could also increase from one day to the next while the open interest decreases if most of the trades were made to close positions.

In the international foreign exchange markets, the exchange rate is normally quoted against the US dollar as the amount of foreign currency per unit of the US dollar, except Commonwealth currencies, which are quoted as the amount of US dollars against the foreign currency. However, based on these basic quotes, it is fairly straightforward to calculate cross-rates between any pair of currencies.

*Example*: The spot rate for the euro against the US dollar is quoted at 0.9250 €/US$. The spot rate for the Swiss franc is quoted at 2.7500 SFr/US$. Hence, the €/SFr cross-rate is 0.3364 (= 0.9250/2.7500).

In the international foreign exchanges markets, currencies are sometimes traded on the basis of the foreign exchange cross-rates. For certain cross-rates (X-rates) with particularly high trading activities, it can be worthwhile to establish financial futures contracts on the cross rates.

The currency futures contracts trade the foreign currency amounts for delivery at future dates and therefore correspond to the prices quoted on the forward foreign exchange market. The calculation of forward foreign exchange rates was discussed in detail in Chapter 2, where forward foreign exchange rates were determined on the basis of the spot foreign exchange rate and the interest rate differential between the two currencies until the final maturity date of the futures contract. Hence, the prices on currency futures contracts tie into the relative interest rate levels of the two currencies exchanged. If not, arbitrageurs will drive prices toward the futures price determined by the interest parity theorem expressed in the following formula:

$$F_{\$/f,t} = S_{\$/f} \frac{(1 + i_{\$,t} \times t/360)}{1 + i_{f,t} \times t/360}$$

where

$F_{\$/f,t}$ = the forward foreign exchange rate (US dollars/foreign currency (f));
$S_{\$/f}$ = the spot foreign exchange rate (US dollars/foreign currency (f));
$i_{\$,t}$ = the $t$ days money market rate for US dollars;
$i_{f,t}$ = the $t$ days money market rate for the foreign currency (f);
$t$ = the actual number of days until maturity (forward date).

and

$$O_{\$/f,t} = S_{\$/f}(1 + (i_{\$,t} - i_{f,t})t/360)$$

where

$O_{\$/f,t}$ = the outright foreign exchange rate (US dollars/foreign currency (f)).

From these relationships, we deduce the following basic rules of thumb:

> The currency of the lower interest rate area will sell at a forward premium in terms of the higher interest currency.

> The currency of the higher interest rate area will sell at a forward discount in terms of the lower interest currency.

This assumes that cash payments can flow freely between the two currency areas in unrestricted capital and foreign exchange markets. This also implies that the interest rate parity theorem is valid for liberalized and economically stable currency areas.

## 4.11 Interest rate and bond futures

An **interest rate future** is a standard contract that provides the buyer with a short-term interest-bearing financial asset at a predetermined price at a future point in time. The contracts are standardized so that each type of financial asset is well

**Table 4.7** Interest rate and bond futures

---

**Interest-bearing financial assets**
- Thirty-day commercial paper, one-month Canadian dollar bankers' acceptance, three-month sterling deposit
- Three-month US treasury bills, three-month eurodollar deposit, six-month German government bonds
- Five-year US treasury notes, ten-year Canadian government bonds, twenty-year UK gilts
- Five-year eurobonds, ten-year mortgage-backed securities

---

| International Monetary Market (IMM) | London International Financial Futures Exchange (LIFFE) |
|---|---|
| | |
| O/N Fed Funds deposit (US$45 000 000) | One-month EUNIA[10] (€3 000 000) |
| One-month eurodollar deposit (US$3 000 000) | Three-month Euribor[11] (€1 000 000) |
| Three-month eurodollar deposit (US$1 000 000) | Three-month eurodollar deposit ($1 000 000) |
| Three-month US T-bills (US$1 000 000) | Three-month sterling short (£500 000) |
| Five/ten-year agency notes (US$100 000) | Long-term gilt (£100 000) |
| Three-month euroyen (¥100 000 000) | Long-term bund (€100 000) |
| Japanese government bond (¥10 000 000) | Japanese government bond (¥100 000 000) |

---

defined and offered in standard trading units on the exchange. The contracts are usually delivered at predetermined dates in specific delivery months, e.g. March, June, September, and December (Table 4.7).

### 4.11.1 Pricing

The prices on short-term financial futures, such as three-month Eurodollar deposits and three-month US T-Bills, are quoted on an index basis. That is, the par value of 100.00 minus the annual discount rate of, say, 2.25% provides a quoted price of 97.75. With this pricing approach, changes in the interest rate lead to a comparable converse change in the contract price.

*Example*: If the interest rate increases by ten basis points (0.1%), the price quoted on the three-month eurodollar deposit contract will drop by ten basis points (0.1%) to 97.65 (= 97.75 − 0.10).

### 4.11.2 Quotations

Figure 4.4 presents quotations for different interest rate futures listed on the respective futures exchanges. The quotes include short-term Euribor, sterling, and Swiss franc rates quoted on the London International Financial Futures Exchange (LIFFE), short-term eurodollar rates quoted on the Chicago Mercantile Exchange (CME), and short-term euroyen rates quoted on the Chicago Board of Trade (CBOT) and the Tokyo International Financial Futures Exchange (TIFFE).

A **bond futures** contract refers to a standard agreement that provides the buyer with a long-term interest bearing financial asset at a predetermined price at a future point in time. The futures prices quoted correspond to the actual market price (bond price) of the underlying long-term security. Since securities such as US Treasury

**Figure 4.4** Interest rate futures quotes

## Interest rate futures  FT

| Jun 17 | | Open | Sett | Change | High | Low | Est. vol | Open int. |
|---|---|---|---|---|---|---|---|---|
| Euribor 3m* | Sep | 97.76 | 97.75 | −0.01 | 97.77 | 97.73 | 100 654 | 569 113 |
| Euribor 3m* | Dec | 97.52 | 97.48 | −0.03 | 97.52 | 97.46 | 144 161 | 585 498 |
| Euribor 3m* | Mar | 97.25 | 97.20 | −0.04 | 97.26 | 97.17 | 238 528 | 405 638 |
| Euribor 3m* | Jun | 96.98 | 96.93 | −0.04 | 96.98 | 96.90 | 172 606 | 313 787 |
| Euribor 3m* | Sep | 96.74 | 96.69 | −0.04 | 96.74 | 96.66 | 83 169 | 239 028 |
| Euroswiss 3m* | Sep | 99.18 | 99.08 | −0.09 | 99.22 | 99.04 | 30 110 | 92 478 |
| Euroswiss 3m* | Dec | 98.82 | 98.71 | −0.09 | 98.85 | 98.67 | 14 379 | 99 975 |
| Sterling 3m* | Sep | 94.80 | 94.78 | −0.03 | 94.81 | 94.76 | 32 283 | 197 397 |
| Sterling 3m* | Dec | 94.59 | 94.54 | −0.05 | 94.59 | 94.52 | 55 909 | 251 920 |
| Sterling 3m* | Mar | 94.45 | 94.39 | −0.05 | 94.46 | 94.37 | 53 996 | 191 393 |
| Sterling 3m* | Jun | 94.37 | 94.31 | −0.06 | 94.38 | 94.29 | 34 816 | 135 124 |
| Sterling 3m* | Sep | 94.33 | 94.27 | −0.05 | 94.33 | 94.25 | 16 298 | 133 702 |
| Eurodollar 3m† | Sep | 97.87 | 97.84 | −0.02 | 97.87 | 97.82 | 54 728 | 968 723 |
| Eurodollar 3m† | Dec | 97.35 | 97.28 | −0.05 | 97.35 | 97.27 | 58 921 | 899 559 |
| Eurodollar 3m† | Mar | 96.87 | 96.80 | −0.07 | 96.88 | 96.79 | 68 950 | 759 439 |
| Eurodollar 3m† | Jun | 96.47 | 96.38 | −0.08 | 96.47 | 96.37 | 67 458 | 626 636 |
| Eurodollar 3m† | Sep | 96.12 | 96.03 | −0.08 | 96.13 | 96.02 | 31 240 | 490 442 |
| Eurodollar 3m† | Dec | 95.83 | 95.74 | −0.07 | 95.83 | 95.73 | 5 968 | 391 995 |
| Eurodollar 3m† | Mar | 95.58 | 95.51 | −0.06 | 95.60 | 95.50 | 3 069 | 326 291 |
| Fed Fnds 30d‡ | Jun | 98.990 | 98.990 | – | 98.990 | 98.990 | 1 077 | 108 139 |
| Fed Fnds 30d‡ | Jul | 98.725 | 98.725 | – | 98.730 | 98.725 | 23 887 | 167 864 |
| Fed Fnds 30d‡ | Aug | 98.470 | 98.455 | – | 98.470 | 98.450 | 38 681 | 142 203 |
| Euroyen 3m‡‡ | Sep | 99.885 | 99.890 | +0.005 | 99.890 | 99.885 | 4 527 | 185 495 |
| Euroyen 3m‡‡ | Dec | 99.840 | 99.840 | – | 99.850 | 99.830 | 13 709 | 271 320 |
| Euroyen 3m‡‡ | Mar | 99.760 | 99.740 | −0.005 | 99.760 | 99.730 | 27 742 | 254 250 |

Contracts are based on volumes traded in 2001.  Sources: * LIFFE. † CME. ‡ CBOT. ‡‡ TIFFE

Source: *Financial Times*, Friday, June 18, 2004.

bonds are issued over time with different coupons, the bond futures contract specifies a standardized coupon and maturity structure to identify the underlying financial asset of the contract. The market price of the underlying bond is determined in accordance with normal yield-to-maturity calculations, e.g. the price of a five-year 5% annual coupon bond with a yield of 5% p.a. would trade at par (100), while a yield above 5% would cause the bond to trade below par, and a yield below 5% would correspond to a price above par.

*Example*: A yield of 5.5% p.a. would require a market price quoted at 97.86 ($= 5/1.055 + 5/1.055^2 + 5/1.055^3 + 5/1.055^4 + 105/1.055^5$). A yield of 4.5% p.a. would correspond to a market price of 102.17 ($= 5/1.045 + 5/1.045^2 + 5/1.045^3 + 5/1.045^4 + 105/1.045^5$).

**Figure 4.5** Bond futures quotes

**Bond futures** **FT**

| Jun 17 | | Open | Sett | Change | High | Low | Est. vol | Open int. |
|---|---|---|---|---|---|---|---|---|
| Euro-Eurex | Sep | 112.50 | 112.46 | −0.09 | 112.55 | 112.25 | 889 093 | 928 075 |
| | Dec | 111.43 | 111.54 | −0.09 | 111.48 | 111.43 | 54 | 1 501 |
| Japan 10yr-TSE | Sep | 133.49 | 133.43 | −0.47 | 133.57 | 133.09 | 45 308 | 115 990 |
| | Dec | 132.37 | 132.75 | −1.10 | 132.37 | 132.15 | 110 | 3 773 |
| US Tr long-CBOT | Jun | 106–02 | 105–30 | −0–01 | 106–06 | 105–30 | 4 958 | 35 840 |
| | Sep | 104–24 | 104–20 | −0–01 | 104–28 | 104–12 | 104 209 | 473 744 |
| US Tr 10yr-CBOT | Jun | 109–205 | 109–135 | −0–040 | 109–205 | 109–085 | 12 391 | 86 691 |
| | Sep | 108.050 | 107–315 | −0–030 | 108–090 | 107–275 | 330 111 | 1 217 581 |
| Euro-Bobl-Eurex | Sep | 109.80 | 109.75 | −0.10 | 109.83 | 109.58 | 743 657 | 814 226 |
| | Dec | 108.88 | 108.89 | −0.06 | 108.89 | 108.88 | 1 220 | 155 |
| Euro-Schatz-Eurex | Sep | 105.335 | 105.315 | −0.045 | 105.350 | 105.230 | 650 289 | 703 096 |
| | Dec | – | 104.965 | −0.045 | – | – | 5 469 | 0 |
| US Tr 5 yr-CBOT | Jun | 109–000 | 108–315 | – | 109–015 | 108–290 | 13 602 | 59 536 |
| | Sep | 107–275 | 107–195 | −0–035 | 107–275 | 107–175 | 176 343 | 1 075 466 |
| Long gilt-Liffe | Jun | 105.24 | 105.20 | −0.18 | 105.29 | 105.12 | 1 338 | 23 706 |
| | Sep | 104.95 | 104.89 | −0.16 | 105.02 | 104.73 | 62 053 | 211 690 |
| SFE 3 yr | Sep | 94.51 | 94.51 | – | 94.51 | 94.48 | 8 846 | 274 738 |
| Kofex 3 yr | Sep | 109.62 | 109.34 | −0.34 | 109.63 | 109.28 | 60 853 | 76 723 |

Contracts shown are the most heavily traded in 2003. Open interest figures and are for the previous day. CBOT volume, high & low for pit & electronic trading at settlement. For more contract details see: www.eurexchange.com,cbot.com, tse.or.jp, liffe.com. Changes based on prev sett price. US data in 32nds. US latest prices                               Source: Reuters.

*Source: Financial Times*, Friday, June 18, 2004.

Figure 4.5 presents quotations for different bond futures contracts listed on various futures exchanges. The contracts include euro-denominated government bonds quoted on Eurex, five- and ten-year US treasury notes traded on the Chicago Board of Trade (CBOT), long-term UK gilts quoted on the London International Financial Futures Exchange (LIFFE), and ten-year Japanese government bonds traded on the Tokyo Stock Exchange (TSE).

Figure 4.5 shows that the government bond contracts trading in euros, US dollars, and Japanese yen were all quoted above par in June 2004, indicating a market environment where the general interest rate level had continued to fall over some time. Hence, the required market yield was considerably lower than the implied coupon rates of the underlying bonds that specify the futures contracts.

### 4.11.3 Price limit

During the course of a trading day prices might fluctuate widely or show a strong trend. To prevent extreme volatility and to stabilize the quotation of contract prices, the futures exchanges have introduced **price limits** on the financial futures quotes indicating the maximum allowable change in trading prices during any one day. When the limit is reached, the market will be suspended for a period, in some instances until the following business day until trading is resumed.

### 4.11.4 Margin

Any change in value position caused by price changes will be settled in cash on a day-to-day basis. When a trade is completed on the financial futures exchange, the dealer will pay an **initial margin** to the exchange, which eventually will be funded by the client if the dealer is trading on behalf of third party.

The size of the margin varies across contracts and from exchange to exchange but usually ranges between 2 to 3%. The rationale behind the initial margin is that the sum total of all cash margins will reduce the immediate risk of default in the exchange's clearing operation if a counterpart is unable to fulfil the contract obligations.

The change in value of a trader's position is calculated on a daily basis and is settled in cash through a **variation margin**, which represents the profit or loss for the day on the futures position. The current cash settlement procedure practically eliminates potential impacts from inherent counter-party risks. For traders in the financial futures market, the daily settlement procedure has cash flow implications that should be considered before engaging in any trading activities.

### 4.11.5 Conversion factor

The US treasury bond futures contract has been traded actively on the Chicago Board of Trade (CBOT) for many years. However, one problem with the US treasury bond futures contract, as well as other long-term bond contracts is that the underlying cash markets trade these securities with different maturity profiles and coupons. Therefore no single security acts as a 'natural' standard trading unit for a financial futures contract to be offered on the exchange. To circumvent this problem, the exchanges have introduced the concept of a conversion factor whose function is to bring any eligible security into a standard tradable value.

For the US treasury note futures contract traded on CBOT the unit of trading is the par value of a US$100 000 notional ten-year US treasury with a 6% coupon. The contract standard determines that an eligible security for delivery under the futures contract should mature for at least 6.5 years, but not more than ten years, from the first day of the delivery month. The invoice price equals the futures settlement price times a conversion factor plus accrued interest. The conversion factor corresponds to the price of the delivered note at a yield-to-maturity of 6% p.a. The same principle of eligible securities is applied to bond contracts traded on other exchanges as well, e.g. Euronext–Liffe uses a £100 000 notional thirteen-year 6% UK gilt as the trading unit for the long gilt futures contract and Eurex uses a €100 000 notional ten-year 6% German government bond as the trading unit for the euro bund futures contract.

### 4.11.6 Settlement price

When bond futures contracts are settled between buyers and sellers on the exchange, the contract amount is made up by the principal amount plus accrued interest comparable to practice in the underlying cash securities market. The principal amount is calculated by multiplying the exchange delivery settlement price by the applicable conversion factor:

Principal amount = Exchange delivery settlement price × Conversion factor

The **exchange delivery settlement price** (EDSP) is determined by the current market price of the bond futures contract. The **conversion factor** (CF) is the par value multiplier, which determines the discount or premium applying to a security whose maturity date or coupons differ from the standard trading unit that defines the specific bond futures contract.

*Example*: A fifteen-year security with a 7% coupon will be traded at a discount value of 91.44% to provide a yield of 8% p.a. Hence, for this type of security the conversion factor is 0.9144. Similarly, a twenty-year security with a 7% coupon will be traded at a discount value of 90.18% to give a yield of 8% p.a. Hence, for this type of security the conversion factor is 0.9018.

As indicated by these examples, the conversion factor decreases when the coupon $(C)$ decreases and when the maturity $(M)$ increases, whereas the conversion factor increases when the coupon increases and when the maturity decreases $(\delta CF/\delta C > 0, \delta CF/\delta M < 0)$.

The application of the par value multiplier as the conversion factor ensures that all securities eligible for the contract standard will obtain a comparable evaluation. Thus it provides for an efficient way of dealing with contracts on securities with non-homogenous characteristics.

## 4.12 Stock index futures

A **stock index future** is a standard contract that provides the holder with a given index at a predetermined price at a future point in time corresponding to the specific settlement days determined by the individual exchanges trading the contracts (Table 4.7). Trading in stock index futures is important to many of the financial futures exchanges.

**Table 4.8** Stock index futures

Underlying stock indexes
● Standard & Poor's 100, FT-SE 100 index, Nikkei 225 stock index
● Standard & Poor's midcap 400 index, Standard & Poor's 500
● Russell 1000 index, Wilshire composite market index

| International Monetary Market (IMM) | London International Financial Futures Exchange (LIFFE) |
|---|---|
| S&P 500 (US$250 × index) | AEX-Index (€200 × index) |
| Nasdaq–100 (US$100 × index) | BEL 20 (€20 × index) |
| Russell 2000 (US$500 × index) | CAC 40 (€10 × index) |
| Nikkei 225 (US$5 × index) | FTSE 100 (€20 × index) |
| GSCI[12] (US$250 × index) | MSCI[13] (€20 × index) |

### (4.12.1) Pricing

The stock indexes are typically calculated as the average or weighted price movements of a predefined portfolio of stocks. The price of the index contract at a given point in time is determined as the value of an index point, the **multiplier**, multiplied by the index value that defines the contract on the specific futures exchange. Hence, to arrive at the dollar value of the underlying index value, the index should be multiplied by the multiplier.

*Example*: The OEX Index has a multiplier of 100. Then an OEX June Future trading at index 95 has an underlying index value of $9500 ($95 times the multiplier of 100).

### (4.12.2) Settlement value

The settlement value of different stock index contracts is sensitive to the way the underlying index is calculated, which again is a function of the underlying composition of the stock portfolio. Hence, there is no guarantee that the various indexes will follow each other over time as different segments of the stock market may react differently to changing economic conditions. In general, the more diversified and comprehensive the underlying stock portfolio, the more the index will reflect the general trend of the stock market. Since there is no directly related cash market for the stock indexes, the futures exchanges have developed a procedure of cash settlement at the final maturity date. Hence, buyers and sellers of specific contracts exchange cash through the clearing house at delivery equal to the difference between the settlement value, representing the actual price of the contract on that day, and the price at which the futures contract were traded initially.

## 4.13 Insurance futures

A number of exchange-traded derivatives linked to catastrophe risk were introduced during the 1990s. The contracts were specified to address the associated direct economic losses in certain predefined geographical regions. The direct losses reflect the size of insurance claims on private property, which constitutes an important loss factor after major natural disasters. Hence, the disaster futures contracts constitute a type of index futures contract indicating the development of insurance claims over time, much like the stock indexes. A number of insurance contracts related to catastrophe losses as well as weather-related contracts have been introduced (Table 4.9).

**Table 4.9 Catastrophe- and weather-related futures contracts**

**Insurance losses**
● Guy Carpenter Catastrophe Index (GCCI), Property Claims Service (PCS) Catastrophe Index

**Temperatures**
● Heating Degree Days (HDD), Cooling Degree Days (CDD)

The Bermuda Commodity Exchange introduced catastrophe futures contracts based on the Guy Carpenter Catastrophe Index (GCCI) indicating insured property losses in different US regions caused by hurricanes, winter storms, thunderstorms, tornadoes and other 'atmospheric perils'. The Chicago Board of Trade (CBOT) introduced catastrophe futures based on quarterly property losses of 22 insurers caused by windstorms, hail, floods, earthquakes, and riots reported by the Insurance Services Office (ISO). In addition, the CBOT introduced futures contracts based on regional indexes for catastrophe losses established by the Property Claims Service (PCS). However, the Bermuda Commodities Exchange suspended trading of its catastrophe futures and options contracts in 1999 due to sluggish trading volume. CBOT experienced a similar decline in interest for their contracts and has closed trading of its catastrophe futures.

Insurance companies are the natural hedgers in the derivatives market, whereas there are few natural investors to counter this interest. For example, construction companies could arguably be considered natural investors in catastrophe derivatives because they experience a boom in demand subsequent to severe property damages. However, there are no good reasons why they should counter this potential windfall by investing in a market environment that needs highly specialized trading and risk management skills. Acting as an investor in catastrophe risk derivatives requires deep insights into the reinsurance market and specific catastrophe risk exposures that few outside investors possess, and without active investors there will be no successful markets in traded derivatives.

In contrast, trading in the weather derivatives, e.g. as offered by the Chicago Mercantile Exchange (CME), has continued to show high market interest. These contracts involve a large number of natural counterparts including different types of energy producers and energy consumers and allow them to hedge against volumetric risk effects associated with changes in weather conditions. Financial institutions, energy traders, and energy companies have developed an active dealer-market in a number of over-the-counter weather futures based on Heating Degree Days (HDD) and Cooling Degree Days (CDD) temperature indexes.[14] The buyers of the futures contract are compensated when the index value exceeds the agreed index value while the sellers of the futures contract make the payout. The sellers of the futures contract receive compensation when the index value falls below the agreed strike price while the futures buyers make the payout. These futures are sometimes referred to as swap contracts.

## 4.14 Option contracts and options on futures

Options were first introduced on the international stock exchanges and stock options have been quoted for many years. By comparison, currency, interest rate, and index options are relatively new inventions introduced on the futures and options exchanges during the 1980s. Hence, as a starting point we look at the market for stock options as representative for the principles of traded options markets in general.

## 4.15 Stock options

The **stock option** has been a common feature of stock exchanges in North America and Europe for decades. However, an organized trading floor for standardized stock options was first introduced in the United States in 1973 with the establishment of the Chicago Board of Options Exchange (CBOE). Many other futures and options exchanges have since introduced standardized options contracts or options on futures.

An option is the right, but not the obligation, to buy or sell a stated number of shares at a specified price, the **strike** or **exercise price**, at a certain point in time, the **expiration date** or within a predetermined time interval, the exercise period. The option to purchase stock is known as a **call option** and gives the holder the right to buy the underlying asset. A **put option** entails the right to sell the underlying asset. Either type of option contract can be traded on the market and exercised by the holder throughout the exercise period or at the expiration date. Stock options are usually exercisable into 100 shares of the underlying stock, the normal round lot unit of trading.

*Example*: An 'MP Feb 40 call' is a call option that gives the owner the right to *buy* one hundred shares of MetPath Lines (MP) stock (the underlying and, in this case, fictitious asset). An 'MP Feb 40 put' is a put option that entitles the owner to *sell* 100 shares of MetPath stock at $40 per share.

If the put option or call options are not exercised (that is, the underlying asset bought or sold) by the expiration date, then they expire worthless.

### 4.15.1 Options clearinghouse

After the option buyer has paid the price of the option, referred to as the **option premium**, to the original seller, the options clearinghouse assumes both sides of the options transaction. That is, the clearinghouse issues and guarantees each and every option contract, clears all trades in listed options, and assigns exercise notices to the option holders.

By acting as the issuer of the option contracts, the clearinghouse ultimately steps between the original seller and the buyer. Once the trade is executed, the option clearinghouse clears the transaction. At that point, the original buyer and seller have no further responsibility to each other. Their relationships are now with the clearinghouse. If the buyers choose to exercise the option, they rely on the clearinghouse, not on the sellers, for contract performance. Thus, the clearinghouse guarantees the performance to all market participants. The clearinghouse also handles the assignment of options exercise notices submitted by the option holders. Although most option writers and option holders close their positions with offsetting purchases and sales, a writer should not be surprised to be notified that some holder has exercised his or her option and that the writer has been assigned the obligation of delivering stock (call option) or purchasing it (put option). Holders of call options may elect to buy the stock at the strike price, and put holders may choose to sell it at the strike price. In either case, option holders will simply notify their brokerage firm about their intent to exercise the options. The brokerage firm in turn notifies the clearinghouse, which then assigns an exercise notice to a member brokerage firm that has options writers identical to the one exercised. The exercise obligation is then assigned to one of those option writers, usually to the oldest options first (first in, first out).

The clearinghouse takes it from there. For every buyer of an option contract, there must be an option writer on its books. The clearinghouse finds a member firm in its records that has written an option and assigns it as the firm against which the option is to be exercised. The selection is usually made at random. Upon receipt of the exercise notice, the firm must assign the exercise notice to one of its customers who has written such an option. That customer then has to honour the exercise notice and deliver or purchase the stock depending on whether it is a call or a put option, as the case may be.

## (4.15.2) Trading options

Option investors are said to 'open' or 'close' their positions. Buying an option is an opening transaction by which the holder takes a long open position. Writing an option is also an opening transaction in which the seller is considered to create an open short option position. A closing transaction reduces, or closes, an open option position. A closing buyer reduces, or closes, a prior opening sale, and a closing sale closes a previous opening purchase.

Going long or short is an indicator of investors' expectations. Those who buy calls or sell puts are generally regarded as bullish because they will profit if the underlying stock price rises. By instead writing calls or buying puts, the investors present themselves as bearish, i.e. they expect the stock value to decline and will profit if it does so.

## (4.15.3) Call writers

Option writers have one basic aim, namely to earn a profit. A writer may be classified as 'covered' or 'uncovered' (naked). A call option is **covered** when the writer owns enough of the underlying stock to meet the requirements if the contract is exercised. In such a case, a covered **call writer** is not required to pay any initial margin costs. A call option writer is also covered if he or she owns another call option of the same maturity that has a lower strike price.

*Example*: Investor Smith writes an MP May 35 call, which represents 100 shares of MetPath. Because Smith owns 100 shares of MP, the call is covered.

The covered call writer, by pocketing the option premium paid by the buyer, gives up the right to any future increase in the value of the stock beyond the strike price. Hence, the call writers are usually neutral to bearish on the stock. At the same time, they retain the risk that their stock might decline in price.

*Example*: If MetPath is trading at $30 a share when Smith writes his Mar 30 call as a covered writer, the contract is at parity. If the MetPath stock declines to a price below $30, the option holder will not exercise. The premium income Smith receives for selling the call will offset, or cushion, Smith's stock portfolio up to the amount received. If the MetPath stock increases in value to $35 per share before expiration, then Smith has limited his share of this increase to the premium.

When the option writer does not own shares of the underlying stock to meet the requirements of the exercise notice, the contract is said to be **uncovered** or **naked**.

*Example*: Smith writes an MP 30 call, but he does not own 100 shares of MetPath. The call is naked, or uncovered. Since this is equivalent to a short sale, Smith must pay initial margin as collateral.

Writers of naked calls face the possibility of a theoretically unlimited loss. As the market price of the underlying stock increases beyond the options strike price, the writer's loss grows.

*Example*: MetPath's stock price increases above $30 (to $34 per share, for example) just before expiration, and Smith receives an exercise notice from his broker. He is forced to buy 100 shares of MetPath in the open market at its current price of $34 and deliver it to the option exercising holder at $30, for a loss of $4 per share, which is only partially offset by the premium income.

## 4.15.4 Put writers

The risk to a **put writer** is that the price of the underlying stock will decline. Put writers are generally bullish on the security because they will benefit if the stock price increases above the strike price.

*Example*: Smith sells an MP Mar 40 put for 2 ($200) when MetPath stock is trading at $40. Over the next few weeks, MetPath declines to $32, and Smith gets an exercise notice. He must buy the stock from the holder at $40 per share even though its market value is only $32. The $2 premium only eases some of the $8 loss ($40 less $32).

These examples illustrate events that make option writing unprofitable. Needless to say, whenever the market price moves in the direction that writers expect, they see their contracts expire worthless to the holders, and they keep the premiums.

## 4.15.5 Buyers

People and institutions buy options for a number of reasons. Some need to hedge a position or otherwise manage their risk exposure by locking in a capital gain from a stock investment or protecting an investment position in some other way. Others are speculators who are trading and taking positions simply in the pursuit of profit.

The potential loss faced by an option holder is limited to the premium paid. If the underlying stock does not move as expected, the holder simply lets the contract expire and tries again. Perhaps a greater benefit is **leverage**. By buying options that require relatively modest initial margin payment, option investors can control a great deal more stock than by buying the stock outright.

## 4.15.6 Margin

In some markets investors may borrow money, referred to as 'margin', from their brokerage firms to purchase stock. Options, however, cannot be purchased on margin. With options, margin is the money or stock that the naked (uncovered) call writer must deliver to the brokerage firm to assure performance as a writer. Since option holders pay the option premiums in full, they do not come under any margin requirements. The minimum collateral a writer is required to put up is set by

Regulation T in the United States, but the brokerage firms often require more than the exchanges do. Outside the USA, margin requirements are typically fixed by the exchanges whose practices, in turn, are under the scrutiny of the regulatory authorities of the host country.

---

### Box 4.2 Basic options price relationships

The price of call and put options (premium) is a function of (1) the market price of the underlying asset, (2) the strike price of the option, (3) the time remaining to the final expiration date, (4) the price volatility of the underlying asset, and (5) the interest rate level:

$$OP = f(MP, SP, t, v, r)$$

where

  $OP$ = quoted option premium;
  $MP$ = market price of underlying asset;
  $SP$ = strike price of option;
  $t$ = time to expiration date;
  $v$ = volatility of the asset price;
  $r$ = risk-free rate.

*Intrinsic value*

The relationship between the stock's current market price and the option's strike price determines whether or not the option has an actual value if exercised, referred to as the option's **intrinsic value**. This relationship also establishes whether the option is in-the-money or out-of-the-money.

Options are said to be **in-the-money** if they can be exercised at a profit. A call option is in-the-money if the stock is selling at a price higher than the strike price.

*Example*: An MP 40 call is in-the-money because MetPath stock is trading at $41. The call holder may exercise the option, buy 100 shares of MetPath at $40, and sell it profitably at $41. An MP 45 call with the stock trading at $41 has no intrinsic value and is out-of-the-money. No holder of MP 45 would exercise and pay $45 per share for a stock currently at $41.

A put is in-the-money if the stock is trading below the strike price.

*Example*: An MP 45 put is in-the-money because the stock is at $41. The holder of the put may exercise the option and sell the 100 shares of MP stock at $45 per share. At the same time, an MP 40 put is out-of-the-money. With the stock at $41, no holder of MP 40 would exercise, which would require the holder to sell 100 MetPath shares at $40 per share.

An option is said to be **at-the-money** if the market price of the stock is equal to the strike price.

*Example*: Assume that MetPath stock currently is trading at $40 per share. Any MP option-put or call with a strike price of 40 is at-the-money.

An at-the-money option has no intrinsic value and were it to be exercised, it would yield no profit.

An option is **out-of-the-money** if exercising it would result in a loss.

A call is out-of-the-money when the stock price is lower than the strike price.

*Example*: Assume that MetPath is trading at $39 An MP 40 call is out-of-the-money by $50 ($40 less $39.50 equals $0.50 times 100).

For a put to be out-of-the-money, the strike has to be lower than the stock price.

*Example*: An MP 40 put is out-of-the-money when MetPath stock is trading at $41. The out-of-the-money amount is $100 ($41 less $40 equals $1 times 100).

Out-of-the-money options have zero intrinsic value, but cannot have a negative value. An options premium is said to be at parity when it is trading at a dollar amount equal to its intrinsic value without any additional charge.

*Example*: An MP Mar 40 call option is at parity when the market price of MetPath stock is $43 and the option premium is quoted at $3.

*Time value*

An option contract has a limited and relatively short life span. If it is not exercised, liquidated, or covered by the expiration date, it ceases to exist and becomes worthless. As a result, an option is considered a wasting asset. As the expiration date gets nearer, the contract is worth less and less because of the diminishing time of its life span. **Time value** is reflected in the current price of an option, or the premium, as an amount in excess of the option's intrinsic value. The **intrinsic value** indicates the benefits a holder of the option position gains, if it is exercised at the current market price of the underlying asset.

*Example*: An MP Feb 40 call, with MetPath trading at 43, is in-the-money by three points ($300). That is, its intrinsic value is $3. Yet in early December the premium is quoted in the market at $5. The difference of $2 between the call's intrinsic value ($3) and the actual trading price ($5) is the call's time value. By mid-January, with MetPath still trading at 43, the February call is selling for $4. Its premium is lower, even though the intrinsic value is unchanged. The time value has decreased as the expiration date has approached.

Time value plays more of a role in American options, as opposed to European options. An **American option** can be exercised at any time up to expiration. A **European option** can be exercised only at the expiration date. Time value theoretically follows a fairly predictable pattern during the life of an option, decreasing as time passes. Investors are always willing to pay more than the intrinsic value for an option because the option represents a right and not an obligation and, therefore, can never have a value below zero.

For a call option, the following price relationships hold (Figure 4.6):

**Call premium > Intrinsic value + Time value ≥ 0**

Intrinsic value of Call = (Stock price − Exercise price) × Number of shares

Time value of Call = Call premium − Intrinsic value ≥ 0

The time value of the option is at its optimal level when the strike price of the options is close to the market price of the underlying asset, i.e. when the option is closer to being at-the-money (Figure 4.7).

For a put option, the following price relationships hold (Figure 4.8):

**Put premium > Intrinsic value + Time value ≥ 0**

Intrinsic value of Put = (Exercise price − Stock price) × Number of shares

Time value of Put = Put premium − Intrinsic value ≥ 0

Why is an investor willing to pay more for an option than its intrinsic value? The reason has to do with the nature of an option as it provides the holder with a chance to make money by exercising the contract under favourable conditions some time before or at

**Figure 4.6** The premium of a call option as a function of the market price

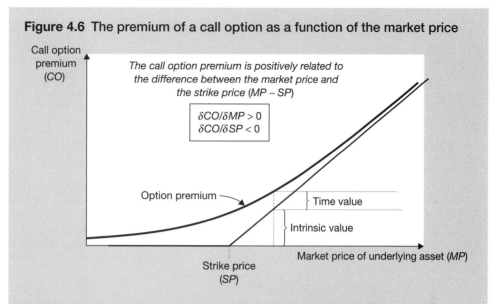

**Figure 4.7** The value components of the call option premium

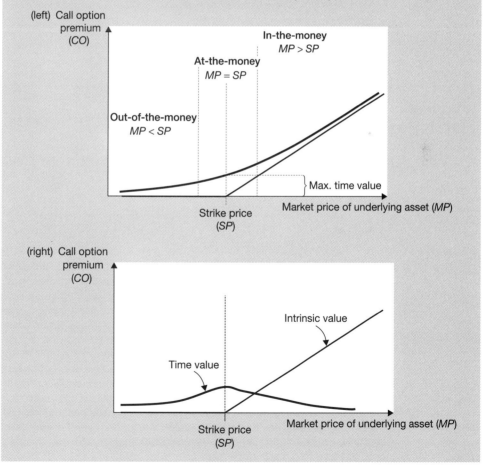

**Figure 4.8** The premium of a put option as a function of the stock price

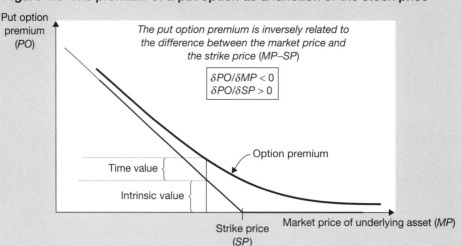

**Figure 4.9** The historical price development and option premiums

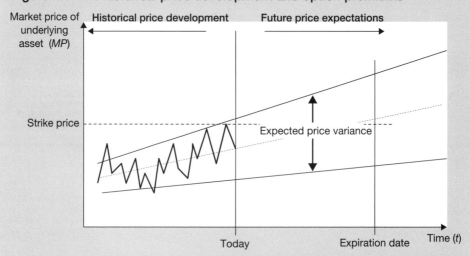

the maturity date (Figure 4.9). If the price development of the underlying stock histor-ically has shown a positive trend line, then the likelihood of making a future profit is increased. Similarly, if the price movements of the underlying stock have been volatile, then the chance of finding an opportune moment to make money through exercise is enhanced. Hence the price a buyer would be willing to pay for an option is higher the higher the expected future variation in the price of the underlying stock.

The longer the time remaining to the final maturity, the higher the option premium because the holder has more opportunity to exercise the option at a profit in the interim, i.e. the option retains a high time value component. As time goes by and the expiration date of the option gets nearer, the opportunity to profit from the option is gradually reduced. The time value decays to eventually become zero by the expiration date, i.e. there is no time left to exploit the option. Hence, as the option contract expires, the premium is equal to the option's intrinsic value only (Figure 4.10).

**Figure 4.10** The relationship between the time to maturity and option premiums (a) Call option (b) Put option

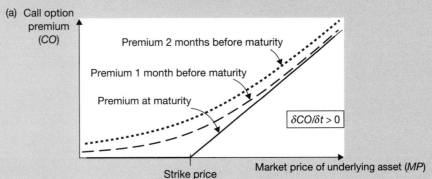

(a) Call option premium (CO)

Premium 2 months before maturity

Premium 1 month before maturity

Premium at maturity

$\delta CO/\delta t > 0$

Strike price

Market price of underlying asset (MP)

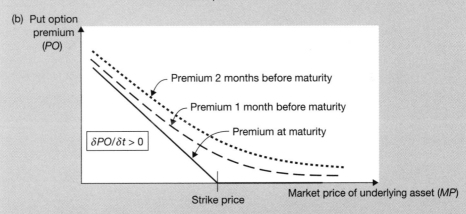

(b) Put option premium (PO)

Premium 2 months before maturity

Premium 1 month before maturity

Premium at maturity

$\delta PO/\delta t > 0$

Strike price

Market price of underlying asset (MP)

High volatility reflects a very erratic price development, which vastly increases the chance that the option holder can exercise the option at a sizeable profit some time before the final maturity or at the expiration date (Figure 4.11). Hence, the price volatility, a comparative measure of the variability in the price development of the underlying asset, constitutes an essential determinant of the option premium.

**Figure 4.11** The relationship between price volatility and option premiums (a) Call option

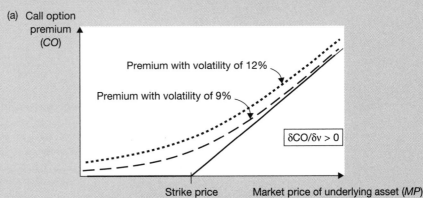

(a) Call option premium (CO)

Premium with volatility of 12%

Premium with volatility of 9%

$\delta CO/\delta v > 0$

Strike price

Market price of underlying asset (MP)

**Figure 4.11 (b) Put option**

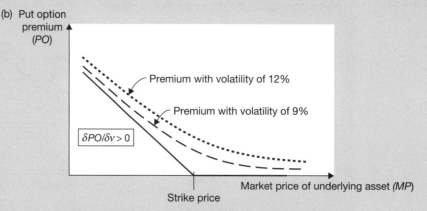

(b) Put option premium (*PO*)

Premium with volatility of 12%

Premium with volatility of 9%

$\delta PO/\delta v > 0$

Strike price

Market price of underlying asset (*MP*)

The option premium will follow changes in the market price of the underlying asset. So, an investor can establish a risk-free position by buying the asset and writing call options where the premium then reflects the risk-free return. Accordingly, the option premium will change in proportion to changes in the interest rate (Figure 4.12).

**Figure 4.12 The relationship between the interest rate and option premiums (a) Call option (b) Put option**

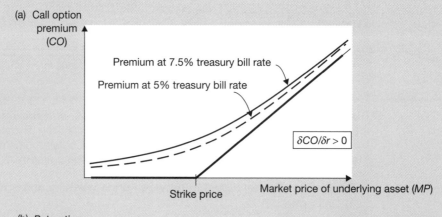

(a) Call option premium (*CO*)

Premium at 7.5% treasury bill rate

Premium at 5% treasury bill rate

$\delta CO/\delta r > 0$

Strike price

Market price of underlying asset (*MP*)

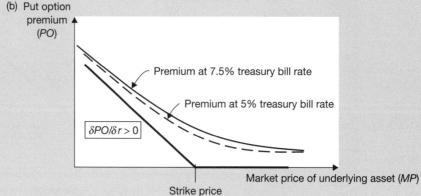

(b) Put option premium (*PO*)

Premium at 7.5% treasury bill rate

Premium at 5% treasury bill rate

$\delta PO/\delta r > 0$

Strike price

Market price of underlying asset (*MP*)

## 4.16 Options on futures contracts

Most futures and options exchanges trade options contracts on the basis of the futures contracts rather than using the cash market directly as the underlying asset. A few exchanges trade options directly on the underlying currencies, e.g. the Philadelphia Stock Exchange (PHLX), but most exchanges trade options contracts as calls and puts on the futures contracts quoted on the exchange.

*Example*: The fifteen-year US treasury bond futures contract traded on the Chicago Board of Trade (CBOT) is based on an actively traded US treasury bond futures contract.

This means that the relationship to the underlying cash market prices so to speak operates indirectly through the pricing of the futures contract rather than the direct cash market price. In practice this has limited consequence, but one should keep in mind that price sensitivities could differ somewhat as, e.g. carrying cost and financial costs change and thereby affect the relationship between the cash market prices and the futures prices. To the extent that option holders may want to take delivery at maturity, it also implies that the access to physical delivery goes through the underlying futures contracts.

### 4.16.1 Quotations

Figure 4.13 presents quotations for different currency options contracts listed on the respective futures exchanges. The exchange is typically indicated by an abbreviation

**Figure 4.13** Currency options quotes

## Currency options FT

■ US $/€ OPTIONS (CME)

| Strike price | CALLS | | | PUTS | | |
|---|---|---|---|---|---|---|
| Jun 17 | Sep | Dec | Mar | Sep | Dec | Mar |
| 11900 | 2.82 | 3.85 | 4.70 | 1.97 | 3.04 | 3.84 |
| 12000 | 2.30 | 3.41 | 4.21 | 2.45 | 3.59 | 4.34 |
| 12100 | 1.86 | 2.96 | 3.76 | 3.01 | 4.13 | 4.88 |
| 12200 | 1.49 | 2.55 | 3.35 | 3.63 | 4.71 | 5.46 |

Previous day's data: volume, 3357; calls, 1162 puts, 4519; open interest, 49 561.

Source: Reuters/CME.

■ US $/YEN OPTIONS (CME)

| Strike price | CALLS | | | PUTS | | |
|---|---|---|---|---|---|---|
| Jun 17 | Sep | Dec | Mar | Sep | Dec | Mar |
| 8900 | 3.07 | 4.03 | 4.87 | 0.89 | 1.39 | 1.69 |
| 9000 | 2.44 | 3.42 | 4.25 | 1.25 | 1.77 | 2.06 |
| 9100 | 1.92 | 2.89 | 3.72 | 1.73 | 2.24 | 2.51 |
| 9200 | 1.49 | 2.44 | 3.24 | 2.30 | 2.78 | 3.02 |

Previous day's data: volume, 135; calls, 195 puts, 330; open interest, 41 087. Source: Reuters/CME.

*Source*: *Financial Times*, Friday, June 18, 2004.

of the name, for instance, the Chicago Mercantile Exchange is listed as CME, the Chicago Board of Trade as CBOT, the London International Financial Futures Exchange as LIFFE, Tokyo Stock Exchange as TSE, etc. Some of the European exchanges are indicated by their short names, such as, Euronext and Eurex.

The top of the columns for the currency futures quotations has the following headings:

- *Open*: The price at which trading in each contract opened for the day.
- *Latest*: The price at which trading in each contract closed for the day.
- *High*: The highest price quoted during the trading day.
- *Low*: The lowest price quoted during the trading day.
- *Estimated volume*: The total number of futures contracts traded during the day.
- *Open Interest*: The total number of futures contracts (purchases or sales) that have not been offset by an opposite transaction or fulfilled by delivery at the end of the trading day.

## 4.17 Options on interest rate and bond futures

Options on interest rate and bond futures respond directly to changes in the interest rate level. When interest rates are on the rise, new issues of debt generally have increased yields. Old debt issues with lower yields lose value in this market situation, as bond prices drop. In other words, the value of a debt instruments varies inversely with interest rates. That is, bond prices generally go down when interest rates are up, and rise when interest rates are down. Interest rates also affect, of course, the prices of debt options. Specifically when rates increase, the market prices of the lower-yielding underlying debt instruments drop, and so the call option premiums will go down, and put option premiums will go up. Conversely, when rates decrease, the underlying prices advance, call premiums rise, and put premiums drop.

Interest rate and bond options have become common features of modern futures and options exchanges. Interest rate contracts exist on many benchmark government bonds and corresponding options contracts are available in the major currency areas, such as US dollars, euros, and Japanese yen. A variety of options contracts on domestic market interest rate instruments, including pound sterling, Swiss francs, Canadian dollars, Australian dollars, etc. For example, the Montreal Exchange has concentrated its options trading around Canadian dollar denominated debt instruments.

### 4.17.1 Quotations

Figure 4.14 presents quotations for different interest rate options contracts listed on the respective futures exchanges. Where the exchange typically is indicated by an abbreviation of the name.

Figure 4.15 presents quotations for different bond options contracts on benchmark government securities listed on the respective futures exchanges.

**Figure 4.14** Interest rate options quotes

## Interest rate options  FT

■ **THREE MONTH EURODOLLAR OPTIONS $1m** (CME)

| Strike price | ············· CALLS ················ | | | ·············· PUTS ················ | | |
|---|---|---|---|---|---|---|
| Jun 17 | Jun | Jul | Aug | Jun | Jul | Aug |
| **98** | 0.46 | 0.03 | 0.05 | – | 0.18 | 0.20 |
| **98.125** | 0.33 | 0.02 | 0.03 | – | 0.28 | 0.29 |
| **98.25** | 0.21 | 0.01 | 0.01 | – | 0.40 | – |
| **98.375** | 0.08 | – | 0.01 | – | 0.52 | – |

Prev day's data: volume, 334 315; calls, 251 509 puts, 585 814; open interest, 10 501 012.

Source: Reuters/CME.

■ **EURIBOR OPTIONS** (Euronext.liffe) £1m 100 – rate

| Strike price | ··············· CALLS ················ | | | | ··············· PUTS ················ | | | |
|---|---|---|---|---|---|---|---|---|
| Jun 17 | Jul | Aug | Sep | Dec | Jul | Aug | Sep | Dec |
| **97625** | 0.130 | 0.135 | 0.145 | 0.075 | 0.005 | 0.010 | 0.020 | 0.220 |
| **97750** | 0.030 | 0.045 | 0.055 | 0.035 | 0.030 | 0.045 | 0.055 | 0.305 |
| **97875** | – | 0.005 | 0.010 | 0.015 | 0.125 | 0.130 | 0.135 | 0.410 |
| **98000** | – | – | – | 0.005 | 0.250 | 0.250 | 0.250 | 0.525 |

Est. vol. total, Calls 49 601 Puts 58 256. Previous day's open interest, Calls 5 955 015 Puts 2 052 404.

■ **SHORT STERLING OPTIONS** (Euronext.liffe) E500 000 100 – rate

*Source: Financial Times*, Friday, June 18, 2004.

## 4.18 Options on stock index futures

The introduction of the Standard & Poor's 500 Stock Index future on the Chicago Mercantile Exchange and the introduction of the NYSE Composite Index future on the New York Futures Exchange during the 1980s led both the exchanges to introduce option contracts on the two stock index futures. Several other index options are traded on exchanges around the world including options on other stock index futures like the NYSE Double Index contract, the AMEX Major Market Index contract, and the Value Line Index option of the Kansas City Board. In conjunction with the introduction of the FT-SE 100 index futures contract, the London International Financial Futures Exchange also offered an option on the index future. This initial success has led to the introduction of other option contracts including the Euro FT-SE Stock Index and the FT-SE Eurotrack 100 Stock Index.

The maturity of the index option contracts has been extended on some exchanges, and these contracts are commonly referred to as LEAPS. These

**Figure 4.15** Bond options quotes

## BOND OPTIONS

**FT**

### ■ US TREASURY 10 YEAR OPTIONS $100 000 (CBOT)

| Strike price | CALLS | | | PUTS | | |
|---|---|---|---|---|---|---|
| Jun 17 | Jul | Aug | Sep | Jul | Aug | Sep |
| **108** | 0–29 | 0–58 | 1–29 | 0–26 | 0–57 | 1–17 |
| **109** | 0–05 | 0–31 | 0–59 | 0–61 | 1–26 | 1–50 |
| **110** | 0–01 | 0–14 | 0–34 | 1–54 | 2–07 | 2–27 |
| **111** | 0–01 | 0–06 | 0–23 | 2–53 | 2–60 | 3–11 |

Prev day's data: volume: 63 236; calls: 92 663 puts: 155 899; open interest, 2 235 833.

Source: Reuters/CBOT.

### ■ 10 YEAR JAPANESE GOVT BOND OPTIONS (TSE)

| Strike price | CALLS | | | PUTS | | |
|---|---|---|---|---|---|---|
| Jun 17 | Jun | Jul | Sep | Jun | Jul | Sep |
| **1330** | – | – | – | 0.01 | 0.58 | 1.25 |
| **1335** | – | 0.93 | – | – | 0.72 | – |
| **1340** | – | 0.50 | 1.39 | 0.01 | 0.85 | 1.42 |
| **1345** | 4.06 | 0.33 | – | 0.01 | 1.07 | – |

Calls: na Puts: na. Volume: na. Previous day's Open Interest: na.

Source: Reuters/TSE.

### ■ EURO BUND OPTIONS €100 000 (Eurex)

| Strike price | CALLS | | | PUTS | | |
|---|---|---|---|---|---|---|
| Jun 17 | Jul | Aug | Sep | Jul | Aug | Sep |
| **112** | 0.49 | 0.95 | – | 0.15 | 0.50 | – |
| **112.5** | 0.22 | 0.63 | 0.95 | 0.30 | 0.70 | 0.99 |
| **113** | 0.07 | 0.43 | 0.68 | 0.60 | – | – |
| **113.5** | 0.02 | 0.27 | – | – | – | – |

Calls: 25 513 Puts: 22 535. Volume: 48 048. Previous day's Open Interest: 867 353.

Source: Reuters/Eurex.

Source: *Financial Times*, Friday, June 18, 2004.

contracts are traded on the Chicago Board Options Exchange based on the S&P 500 Index and the S&P 100 Index contracts. The LEAP contracts extend the expiry date of the option contracts up to two years, hence widening the applicability of the contracts.

The Chicago Board Options Exchange also trades the so-called CAPS on the S&P 100 and the S&P 500 Index contracts. The CAP contracts have limited upside potential (for call options) or limited downside potential (for put options), and consequently the contract premiums are somewhat lower. The CAP contracts resemble the limited bull and bear spreads that can be pursued in a double option strategy based on standard option contracts. The difference is that the CAP contracts are standardized, while the double option strategy is more flexible.

An index contract has no underlying physical asset but is benchmarked to a specific index through the multiplier. Hence, the link between the index value and the option's value is the multiplier. To arrive at the dollar value of the option contract's settlement value, the underlying index should be multiplied by the multiplier.

*Example*: The OEX Index has a multiplier of 100. Then, an OEX June 95 call has a contract value of $9500 ($95 strike price times the multiplier of 100).

### (4.18.1) Settlement

Index options are unusual in that settlement consists solely of a cash payment due to the lack of an underlying physical asset. Hence, no exchange of securities is involved. For either a put or a call, the writer is obligated to pay the holder the intrinsic value, which is the cash difference between the strike price and the index value.

*Example*: With the OEX index at 80, Barnes exercises his OEX Mar 89 put, which is nine points in-the-money (strike price of $89 less index value of $80 equals intrinsic value of $9). The assigned writer must pay Barnes $900 (intrinsic value of $9 times the OEX multiplier of 100).

*Example*: With the OEX index at 95, Barnes exercises his OEX June 90 call, which is five points in-the-money ($95 index value less $90 strike price). The assigned writer must pay Barnes $500 ($5 intrinsic value times the multiplier of 100).

### Conclusion

Agricultural commodity futures have traded actively for more than a hundred years and many other types of commodity related futures have emerged in the interim. Over the past 25 years a wide range of financial futures based on foreign currencies, interest rates, benchmark bonds, and stock indices have been introduced on exchanges around the world. The variety and depth of available futures contracts provide astute investors with new investment opportunities and offer alternative means to manage underlying financial exposures.

### Summary

● Exchange traded futures contracts in commodities, energy, financials, and different indices provide ample possibilities for investment and hedging.

● Options on traded futures contracts provide additional investment opportunities in various assets and indices and give alternative risk management choices.

- The initial cash outlay is limited to deposits on margin accounts giving an added incentive to use futures and options contracts for investment and hedging purposes.

- Trading in standardized futures and options contracts forms an efficient basis to price financial assets at future settlement dates.

- Trading in standardized contracts on formal exchanges creates high liquidity in the instruments and increases the flexibility of opening and closing transactions.

- The most commonly traded financial futures and options are based on interest rates, bonds, foreign exchange rates, and stock indices as underlying assets.

## Questions

4.1 Please access the Internet (world wide web) and try to investigate the following:

   (a) the number of futures and options exchanges around the world;
   (b) the number of financial futures and options contracts offered on the exchanges.

4.2 What is the underlying idea behind the creation of financial futures?

4.3 Outline the major types of financial futures contracts.

4.4 What are the roles of the futures exchange and the clearinghouse?

4.5 Explain what distinguishes forward agreements from futures contracts.

4.6 Explain the major participants in the futures markets and what their roles are.

4.7 Explain the difference between a call option and a put option.

4.8 Explain the factors that determine the price of an option.

4.9 Explain how an option on a futures contract works.

4.10 Why is it potentially interesting to invest in futures and options contracts?

## Exercises

4.1 A futures contract was bought at price 225 and the current futures price is quoted at 223. If the long open futures position is closed out in today's market, does it results in a profit or a loss?

4.2 A futures contract was sold at price 76 and the current futures price is quoted at 72. If the short open futures position is closed out in today's market, does it lead to a profit or a loss?

4.3 A financial futures contract on euros against US dollars, with a contract denomination of €100 000, is quoted at 1.1150. Please calculate the value of eight euro contracts.

4.4 The current one-month eurodollar LIBOR rate is 3.25%. Please indicate the price quoted on a one-month eurodollar deposit futures contract.

4.5 A fifteen-year 8% notional bond future is currently trading at 99.95. An eligible (cheapest-to-deliver) security has a conversion factor of 0.9176. Please calculate the principal amount of the futures contract.

4.6 The OEX Sep. future is trading at index 101 (The OEX future has a multiplier of 100). Please calculate the underlying index value of the contract.

4.7 Determine the intrinsic value of a call option with a strike price of 32 when the current market price of the underlying asset is 36.

4.8 Determine the intrinsic value of a call option with a strike price of 32 when the current market price of the underlying asset is 29.

4.9 Determine the intrinsic value of a put option with a strike price of 32 when the current market price of the underlying asset is 36.

4.10 Determine the intrinsic value of a put option with a strike price of 32 when the current market price of the underlying asset is 29.

( Notes )

[1] This gold contract was one of the primary futures contracts traded on the Commodity Exchange (COMEX) in New York. The New York Mercantile Exchange (NYMEX) and the Commodity Exchange in New York (COMEX) merged in 1994 to form the world's largest commodity exchange.

[2] The Hard Red Winter Wheat Future is one of the longest-trading derivative contracts in the USA, and was introduced on the Kansas City Board of Trade in 1876.

[3] SGX was formed through a merger of the Stock Exchange of Singapore (SES) and the Singapore International Monetary Exchange (SIMEX) in 1999.

[4] The International Monetary Market was founded in 1972 and constitutes a division of the Chicago Mercantile Exchange (CME) specializing in currency, interest rate, and stock index futures.

[5] The London International Financial Futures Exchange (LIFFE) merged with the continental European exchanges to form the pan-European exchange Euronext.liffe. Euronext is a Dutch-registered holding company operating local subsidiaries formed through the merger between exchanges in Amsterdam, Brussels, and Paris in 2000. Euronext subsequently merged with LIFFE and the Portuguese exchange BVLP.

[6] This contract is quoted in US$.

[7] This contract is quoted as €/$.

[8] This contract is quoted as $/€.

[9] CME trades many other currencies, including the Australian dollar, Brazilian real, Czech koruna, Hungarian forint, Mexican peso, New Zealand dollar, Norwegian kroner, Polish zloty, Russian ruble, South African rand, Swedish kroner, and Swiss franc.

[10] Euro overnight index average.

[11] Euro interbank offered rate.

[12] Goldman Sachs Commodity Index.

[13] Morgan Stanley Capital International is a provider of global and regional equity indices.

[14] A heating degree day (HDD) is derived from the average daily temperature corresponding to the level of energy consumption used to heat buildings. The HDD index increases by one point for every degree by which the daily temperature is below 65 °F. A cooling degree day (CDD) is derived from the average daily temperature corresponding the level of energy consumption used to cool buildings. The CDD index increases by one point for every degree by which the daily temperature is above 65 °F.

# Chapter 5

# Forward agreements and option contracts

## Objectives

- Introduce basic forward agreements
- Present interest rate ceiling, floors, and collar agreements
- Introduce basic currency options and second-generation instruments
- Outline different option pricing methodologies
- Discuss newer market developments

In the previous chapter we familiarized ourselves with a variety of standardized futures and options contracts traded on futures and stock exchanges around the world. This chapter focuses on contracts traded in over-the-counter (OTC) markets by which we refer to financial derivatives offered and traded by individual dealers. The way the OTC derivatives are structured and traded can operate in a rather structured manner as dealers adhere to an unwritten market codex, much like the foreign exchange market, the spot money market, and the market for forward rates. However, these trading practices are distinct from the standardization of contracts on futures exchanges where quotations are obtained through formalized auction systems, such as open outcry or screen-based platforms. A number of derivatives offered in the OTC market are specifically designed to take advantage of temporary market imperfections and customer needs and therefore at times assume rather esoteric forms. Hence, the OTC market for derivatives covers a wide range of products from fairly standard forward agreements to more tailored contracts incorporating exotic structures and more complex combinations of underlying options.

## 5.1 Forward agreements

As a complementary development and partially in response to the continued expansion of exchange traded futures and options contracts, international commercial banks and investment banks have introduced a wide spectrum of financial services delivered directly to their clients over-the-counter as an alternative to dealings on the formal exchanges. Usually these OTC products and services are tailored to the specific situation and needs of the client and thereby break free of some of the restrictions imposed by standardization of exchange-traded contracts. However, the financial institutions that are active in the OTC derivatives markets in turn engage in the financial futures markets to hedge part of their net positions deriving from the tailored derivatives they offer. Therefore, the emergence of exchange traded futures and options contracts has arguably been an encouragement and even a necessary element of a complete financial market environment required for the development of the OTC derivatives.

Active forward markets exist for all the major commodities and similar markets have evolved for financial assets. The most well established of these markets is the trading in forward foreign exchange agreements and forward rate agreements used to hedge against changes in the interest rate level. The international forward foreign exchange market has existed for many years and today represents a major trading arena, together with spot foreign exchange dealings in the treasury departments of banks and corporations around the world. Interest rate forwards, on the other hand, have developed in the wake of expanded trading in interest rate contracts on the futures exchanges over the past decades.

### 5.1.1 Currency forwards

A financial institution can create a **synthetic forward foreign exchange** rate by engaging in the spot foreign exchange market and the spot money markets of the two currency areas (see Chapter 1 for a more detailed discussion). Hence, a foreign currency can be created at a future date by borrowing money in the local currency, converting the local currency into the foreign currency in the spot foreign exchange market and then investing the proceeds in the money market until the future date. Hence, the forward foreign exchange rate is determined by the current spot foreign exchange rate and the difference in the money market interest rates until the future date between the two currency areas. This price relationship was expressed in the interest rate parity theorem and in practice the forward foreign exchange rate is calculated by the outright rate.

The difference between the spot foreign exchange rate and the forward foreign exchange is often popularly referred to as the **swap**. Hence, the swap value is a direct function of the interest rate differential between the two currencies as indicated in the following formula:

$$\text{Swap} = \text{Spot foreign exchange rate} \times \text{Interest rate differential} \times \frac{\text{Number of days}}{360}$$

The calculation of the interest rate differential depends on the denomination of the foreign exchange rate. Since the foreign exchange rate is quoted as the amount of one currency per unit of another currency, the interest differential would be indicated as the interest rate of the numerator currency minus the interest rate of the denominator currency.

*Example*: The spot foreign exchange rate is currently 1.1000 €/US$, and the three-month spot money market rate in the euro area is quoted at 4% p.a. whereas the three-month eurodollar rate is quoted at 6% p.a. Hence, the swap on the three-month €/US$ forward foreign exchange rate is calculated as: Swap = $1.1000 \times (0.04 - 0.06) \times 90/360 = -0.0055$. Consequently, the three-month forward foreign exchange rate is quoted as: $1.1000 - 0.0055 = 1.0945$ (€/US$).

The agents operating in the foreign exchange market will manage their net forward foreign exchange positions in accordance with the interest rate parity theorem (discussed in Chapter 1), otherwise there would be opportunities for arbitrageurs in the market to establish synthetic forward foreign exchange positions in the spot money markets of the two currency areas and earn a risk-free return until the rates are aligned again. So the swap calculation in the forward market generally will be in accordance with the interest rate differential approach indicated in the swap.

However, the preceding example was slightly simplified because it did not take into consideration that foreign exchange and interest rates in the spot money market are quoted as two-way bid and offer prices.

| (Bid and offer quotes) | Bid | Offer |
|---|---|---|
| Spot foreign exchange rate (€/US$) | 1.0995 | 1.1005 |
| Three-month euro rate (% p.a.) | 3.95 | 4.05 |
| Three-month US dollar rate (% p.a.) | 5.95 | 6.05 |

In the case of a forward purchase (bid) of US dollars against euros, the dollars are sold spot at the bid rate of 1.0995 €/US$. The euros are deposited at the bid rate of 3.95% and the US dollar amount is borrowed at the offer rate of 6.05%. Hence, the US dollar swap bid against euros is calculated as follows:

$$\text{Swap (bid)} = 1.0995 \times (0.0395 - 0.0605) \times 90/360 = -0.0058$$

Conversely, in the case of a forward sale (offer) of US dollars against euros, dollars are bought spot at the offer rate of 1.1005 €/US$. Euros are borrowed at the offer rate of 4.05% and the corresponding dollar amount is deposited at the bid rate of 5.95%. Hence, the US dollar swap offer against euros is calculated as follows:

$$\text{Swap (offer)} = 1.1005 \times (0.0405 - 0.0595) \times 90/360 = -0.0052$$

As a consequence, the two-way forward swaps should be quoted as 0.0058/0.0052 (€/US$). By convention the negative sign is omitted, but we can see that the US dollar is traded forward at a discount because the bid quote is higher than the offer quote. Hence the outright rate is found as follows:

| (Bid and offer quotes) | Bid | Offer |
|---|---|---|
| Spot foreign exchange rate (€/US$) | 1.0995 | 1.1005 |
| Three-month swap (€/US$) | 0.0058 | 0.0052 |
| Three-month outright rate (€/US$) | 1.0937 | 1.0953 |

If the three-month forward foreign exchange rates are not quoted within the price range of 1.0937/1.0953 (€/US$) there will be risk free arbitrage opportunities. These bid–offer rates correspond to the quotes prevailing in the interbank market among professional currency traders. When an institutional client asks for a forward quote at a commercial bank acting as a foreign exchange dealer in the market, they will usually charge a spread, which will be subtracted from the bid quote and added to the offer quote. These commercial spreads compensate the financial institution for the transaction costs and the counter-party risk it assumes when it closes the forward foreign exchange agreement.

Like the financial futures contracts in foreign currencies, the forward foreign exchange agreements lock-in the future price of the currency. Since markets in currency forwards exist in a variety of cross currencies and many different maturities they have wider applications than do currency futures contracts.

### 5.1.2 Par forward

A **par forward** is the typical term for a **flat rate forward** currency agreement. The par forward puts together a series of traditional forward foreign exchange agreements at different future dates and settles these forward agreements at the same forward foreign exchange rate. Hence, a flat rate forward enables a company to cover a series of exposures in the same currency at different future dates at the same forward rate.

*Example*: A French corporation has regular receivables in US dollars over a two-year period. The forward foreign exchange rates that convert the US dollars into euros are gradually lower at longer maturity dates reflecting euro interest rates that are lower than the corresponding dollar interest rates (Figure 5.1).

Hence, the French corporation will increasingly get fewer euros for the US dollar receivables at the six, twelve, eighteen, and 24-month forward dates. By incurring a flat rate forward, the exporter books the receivables at the same forward rate for the entire two-year period. In this instance, the par forward defers part of the foreign exchange earnings to later time-periods, because the initial dollar receivables are converted at lower foreign exchange rates than would otherwise prevail. Conversely, in the case of an American corporation with euro receivables, a par forward could represent a cash flow advantage because the receivables initially are converted at a relatively higher forward foreign exchange rate.

**Figure 5.1** Flat rate forward currency agreement

> When selling a higher interest rate currency or when buying a lower interest rate currency a flat rate forward provides an initial cash flow disadvantage.

> When selling a lower interest rate currency or when buying a higher interest rate currency a flat rate forward provides an initial cash flow advantage.

These types of modifying features on a forward foreign exchange contract can partially move earnings from export receivables and import payables between different accounting periods.

### 5.1.3 Forward rate agreements

Many national markets have an active market in domestic currency denominated forward rate agreements (FRAs) and international banks offer FRAs in the major currencies. Through the use of FRAs, an institutional borrower or lender can fix the future interest rate on loans and deposits for periods of up to several years with the varying maturities depending on the depth of the FRA market.

A **forward rate agreement** (FRA) is an agreement between two counterparts to exchange interest rate differentials periodically according to an agreed interest rate basis (the **reference rate**) on a predetermined notional amount over a given period of time. The FRAs are often quoted as two-way bid and offer prices in the interbank market.

| (Bid and offer quotes) | *Bid* | *Offer* |
|---|---|---|
| Three-month rate in three months' time | 2.56 | 2.70 |

When the FRAs are sold to counterparts outside the interbank market, the bank will typically add a margin or charge an up-front fee to cover handling cost and management of the implied credit risk. The reference rate of an FRA is usually a dominant money market rate for the period of the agreement. If the market rate moves above the agreed forward rate, the seller will compensate the buyer with the interest rate differential calculated on the notional contract amount. If the market rate moves below the agreed forward rate, the buyer will compensate the seller with the interest rate differential on the contract amount. It is an advantage of the FRA that only the interest rate differential changes hands whereas nothing happens to the principal amount. Hence, the FRA can be considered an off-balance-sheet instrument as opposed to the corresponding forward forward transactions in the money market, which require full disclosure on the balance sheet. FRAs can in principle cover any broken amount and any future time period. However, standard market practice often confines the use of FRAs to multiples of full millions and full monthly periods:

| *Interest period* | *Settlement dates (from today)* |
|---|---|
| 1 month | 1 month, 2 months, 3 months, 4 months, 5 months, 6 months |
| 3 months | 1 month, 2 months, 3 months, 4 months, 5 months, 6 months |
| 6 months | 1 month, 2 months, 3 months, 4 months, 5 months, 6 months |

The FRA is settled between the two counterparts, the buyer and the seller, who thereby are able to hedge underlying cash positions against interest rate movements. A bank active in the interbank market will typically act either as buyer or seller to institutional clients. A buyer obtains protection against an increase in the interest rate level above the agreed forward rate, and thus can secure maximum level of interest expenses on loans. A seller obtains protection from a drop in the interest rate below the agreed forward rate, and thus can secure a minimum return on a loan or investment.

> The buyer of an FRA agrees to a future borrowing rate.

> The seller of an FRA agrees to a future lending rate.

The forward rate agreement is settled on the first day of the interest period. The **settlement amount** is determined as the difference between the market rate (the reference rate of the agreement) and the agreed forward rate for the interest period. The buyer will receive the difference in interest amounts from the seller if the reference rate exceeds the agreed forward rate. The seller will receive the difference in the interest amount from the buyer if the reference rate is below the agreed forward rate. These characteristics make forward rate agreements distinct from interest rate futures in several respects (Table 5.1).

The settlement amount (SA) is calculated as follows:[1]

$$SA = \frac{(MR - FR) \times T \times A}{(360 \times 100) + (MR \times T)}$$

**Table 5.1** Comparing interest rate futures contracts and forward rate agreements

| Interest rate futures contracts | Forward rate agreements |
| --- | --- |
| Trading takes place on organized trading floor or screens where buyers and sellers make price quotes | Banks provide two-way quotes and transactions are closed over the phone |
| Brokers who are members of the exchange trade for own account and on behalf of third parties | Transactions are closed directly between counterparts |
| Market participants and contract counterparts are unknown to each other | Counterparts are well known to each other |
| Clearing and settlement takes place through a clearinghouse acting as counterpart to all transactions | All transactions entail counter-party risk |
| Contract denominations and specifications are standardized | Agreements are relatively flexible on amounts, settlement periods and maturity dates |

where

$MR$ = market rate (reference rate);
$FR$ = agreed forward rate;
$T$ = number of days in the interest period;
$A$ = contract amount of the agreement.

A positive settlement amount ($MR > FR$) denotes that the seller pays the buyer. A negative settlement amount ($MR < FR$) denotes that the buyer pays the seller. If the FRA is covering periods exceeding one year, the formula for calculating the settlement rate is extended as follows:

$$SA_1 = \frac{(MR - FR) \times T_1 \times A}{36\ 000 + (MR \times T_1)}$$

$$SA_2 = \frac{(MR - FR) \times T_2 \times A}{36\ 000 + (MR \times T_2)}$$

$$\ldots$$

$$SA_n = \frac{(MR - FR) \times T_n \times A}{36\ 000 + (MR \times T_n)}$$

where

$SA_n$ = settlement amount in year $n$;
$T_n$ = number of days in year $n$.

It follows that

$$SA = \frac{\sum\limits_{x=1,2,\ldots n} SA_x}{\dfrac{1 + T_{x-1}}{36\ 000 \times MR} \dfrac{1 + T_{x-2}}{36\ 000 \times MR} \cdots \dfrac{1 + T_1}{36\ 000 \times MR}}$$

The applicable forward rate is determined by the discounted forward break-even rate, which makes up the alternative hedge or arbitrage opportunity to the FRA market.

*Example*: A three-month deposit in three months' time is created as a forward forward transaction by placing the amount for six months at the six-month money market bid rate of 2.50% p.a. and borrowing the amount for three months at the three-month money market offer rate of 2.90% p.a. Conversely, a three-month loan in three months' time is created by borrowing the amount for six months at the six-month money market offer rate of 2.65% p.a. and placing the amount for three months at the three-month money market bid rate of 2.75% p.a. (Figure 5.2).

| *Money market rates* | *Bid* | *Offer* |
|---|---|---|
| ● Three months | 2.75 | 2.90 |
| ● Six months | 2.50 | 2.65 |

The FRA bid and offer rates are then approximated in the following manner:

$$\text{FRA bid rate:} \left( 2.50 \times \frac{180}{36\ 000} - 2.90 \times \frac{90}{36\ 000} \right) \frac{36\ 000}{90} \times \frac{1}{90} = 2.10\% \text{ p.a.}$$

$$\text{FRA offer rate:} \left( 2.65 \times \frac{180}{36\ 000} - 2.75 \times \frac{90}{36\ 000} \right) \frac{36\ 000}{90} \times \frac{1}{90} = 2.55\% \text{ p.a.}$$

**Figure 5.2 Creating synthetic FRAs through forward–forward transactions**

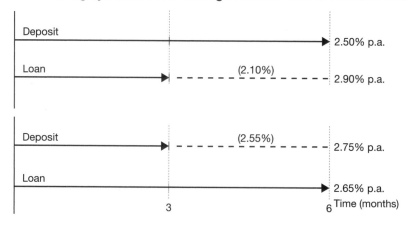

The general formula for calculating the forward rate can be expressed in generalized form:

$$FR = \frac{(RL \times TL) - (RS \times TS)}{(TL - TS)}$$

where

$FR$ = forward rate;
$RL$ = interest rate of the longer period;
$RS$ = interest rate of the shorter period;
$TL$ = number of days in the longer period;
$TS$ = number of days in the shorter period.

Since the difference in interest amounts for the whole interest period normally is paid in the beginning of the interest period, the settlement rate is the forward rate discounted back to the first day of the interest period:

$$\text{Discounted settlement rate } (DSR) = \frac{FR}{\left(1 + \dfrac{(RS \times TS)}{36\,000}\right)}$$

$$\text{DSR (bid): } \frac{2.10}{\left(1 + \left(2.90 \times \dfrac{90}{36\,000}\right)\right)} = 2.08\% \text{ p.a.}$$

$$\text{DSR (offer): } \frac{2.55}{\left(1 + \left(2.75 \times \dfrac{90}{36\,000}\right)\right)} = 2.53\% \text{ p.a.}$$

## 5.2 Currency options

In the forward foreign exchange market, a pseudo-option has existed for many years. This traditional 'option' in the forward market gives the buyer of a forward foreign exchange agreement the right to choose the time to exercise the forward agreement before the maturity date. However, because the 'option' must be exercised before or on the maturity date, it does not constitute a true option. A true option provides the holder with the right but not the obligation to exercise before maturity. In principle it is similar to a forward agreement, but it does not oblige the holder of the option to exercise the forward transaction. Parallel to the development of exchange-traded option contracts, an over-the-counter (OTC) market has been established by major international banks, merchant banks, and brokerage houses, providing tailor-made currency options to institutional clients.

True options in the OTC market take many shapes adapted to the specific hedging requirements of institutional clients. Option quotes can usually be obtained for all major currencies against US dollars and they are available in most international currencies. In addition, cross-currency options are quoted on request, which can be an advantage compared to exchange-traded options contracts.

## 5.2.1 Expiration dates

OTC currency options normally have maturities of up to one year but maturities can be considerably longer. The final maturity date is flexible and can be fixed on broken (irregular) dates as opposed to the standard dates imposed on exchange-traded options. The expiration date of a currency option agreement is the last day on which it can be exercised and usually corresponds to the spot date of the underlying currency. In spot foreign exchange deals, settlement takes place two days after the spot transaction has been closed, except transactions in US dollars against Canadian dollars and Mexican pesos, which settle the following day.

*Example*: A Swiss franc call option, written for value on May 17, has expiration date on May 15. Most banks require to be informed by the option holder before a certain deadline on the expiration date in order to execute the option.

## 5.2.2 Contract size

Usually the size of a currency option agreement entails a minimum requirement, often around US$1 000 000. For smaller contract sizes, the transaction costs may be too high to make it worthwhile. Above the minimum requirement the amount is flexible. It can be set at broken amounts at the buyer's choice to match a specific hedging position.

## 5.2.3 Strike price

The strike price is chosen by the option buyer and quotes are provided by the banks to match the request of the client. The exchange-traded option terminology also pertains to the OTC market. Although the holder of a European option can exercise only at the expiration date, he can lock-in profits prior to expiration by engaging in an offsetting forward or options agreement. Hence it can be argued that the strike price of a European option should be based on the outright rate. The holder of an American option can exercise the option at any time up to the expiration date, and profit can be locked-in prior to expiration either by engaging in an offsetting forward agreement or a foreign exchange spot transaction. So, it can be argued that the strike price of an American option should be based on the foreign exchange spot rate.

Whether one or the other principle is used does not matter as long as the market participants agree among themselves on the practice and terminology of the deal. This is especially true of an at-the-money strike price. Whether it is defined as the current spot price or as the forward rate, be sure to obtain agreement on the definition of the at-the-money strike price when requesting option quotes to avoid confusion and misinterpretation of competitive bids.

### 5.2.4　Premium

Quotes are usually given for both American-type and European-type options. Since the American option is slightly more expensive than the European, it usually pays to clarify whether the flexibility of the American option brings additional benefits to the option buyer in a given hedging situation. Usually the option premium is paid up front and is quoted as a percentage of the currency amount of the option agreement, with the calculation of the currency amount based on the current spot exchange rate. However, under special circumstances the premium can be paid in arrears. For example, the premium for the **limited option** is not paid until the contract's expiration date (Table 5.2). In this case the option holder must act on the option on the expiration date. If the option is profitable, the option holder will exercise the option and pay the premium as the percentage calculated on the currency amount. The currency amount is determined by using the strike price of the option agreement. If the option is unprofitable, the option holder will not exercise the option but will pay the premium on the currency amount calculated from the current spot price prevailing at the expiration date. The feature of the delayed payment of premium has cash implications for the option buyer, who will pay the premium at the time where, for example, a foreign currency receivable will materialize.

Often financial managers have an aversion against paying a front-end premium for something where the outcome is unknown. For this reason traditional forward contracts are often used because they provide the contract buyer with full certainty about the future foreign exchange rate, even though this might not be an optimal

### Table 5.2　Different types of currency option contracts

**True option**
- A right to buy or sell a currency before a future date at a predetermined price
- No obligation to exercise
- Contract amounts in excess of $1 000 000 are flexible
- The maturity date is flexible
- The strike price is determined at the buyer's choice
- The option premium is payable up front

**Limited option**
- Same as true option, but premium is payable on maturity date

**Option-on-option**
- A right to buy an option contract before a future date at a predetermined premium
- The buyer determines the terms of the future option
- The bank quotes the option premium, which is payable up front

hedging solution for a given situation. Most users of forward contracts do not make comparative calculations between the forward contract and the comparable option contract at the maturity date to analyze whether the hedging decision was optimal. Although previous decisions represent 'sunk cost', that cannot be reversed, such analysis might bring about more knowledge so as to determine the optimal hedging technique to pursue in similar future situations. Paying the option premium at the expiration date, as is the case in the limited option, makes it easier for the option buyer to see the advantage of the option purchase. The profitability of the option is then straightforward to calculate.

*Example*: An American company is expecting a receivable of €1 100 000 in three months and has bought a euro limited put option against US dollars with an at-the-money strike price of 1.1000 €/US$ at a premium of 2.75%. After the three-month period, the spot rate has gone to 1.0450 €/US$ so the option is not exercised. If the put option nonetheless is exercised at the strike price, the euro receivables would bring the company US$1 000 000. Conversely, if the euro receivables were sold in the spot foreign exchange market at the current exchange rate, they would bring the company US$1 052 632. Because the option puts no limitation on the upside potential for price gains, the company earns $52 632 more than if it had engaged in a forward agreement at a forward rate of 1.1000 €/US$. On expiration date, the company pays a 2.75% premium of US$28 947 (0.0275 × $1 052 632). The net gain from the favourable exchange rate development amounts to US$23 685 ($52 632 – $28 947) compared to a situation where the euro receivables were covered by a forward foreign exchange contract at the same future rate.

## 5.2.5 Option-on-option agreement

A further development on the OTC option market is the creation of the **option-on-option** or **compound option** agreement. The holder of the option on an option has the right to purchase a given option contract at or before a certain future date at a predetermined premium. The buyer determines the characteristics of the option to purchase in the future, and the bank will quote a premium to be paid up front or in arrears. The option-on-option agreement can be advantageous, for example, to a construction company negotiating a future contract that might require hedging of foreign currency flows.

## 5.2.6 Option writer's risk

When writing options, financial institutions have to hedge considerable open positions day-by-day. The option writer has two inherent risks to cover: an unfavourable development in the forward foreign exchange rate and an unfavourable development in the spot foreign exchange rate.

*Example*: Assume the forward foreign exchange rate on Swiss francs against US dollars is determined as 1.2000 SFr/US$. Assume further that a three-month Swiss franc European call option has been written at a strike price of 1.2000 SFr/US$ (0.8333 US$/SFr). If the US dollar interest rate increases by 1% and the Swiss franc interest rate decreases by 1%, then the swap is changing by −0.0200 and the new outright rate amounts to 1.1800 SFr/US$ (0.8475 US$/SFr). In this situation a holder of a European option could sell Swiss francs forward at 0.8475 US$/SFr and exercise the call option at 0.8333 US$/SFr thereby realizing a gain of 142 points, or **pips**, in the foreign exchange jargon (0.0142 = 0.8475 – 0.8333).

The chance of exercise would also increase in the case of a continued strengthening of the Swiss franc spot foreign exchange rate toward the expiration date. The option position could be closed by the option writer through the purchase of Swiss francs forward and selling them spot against the US dollar.

*Example*: A three-month Swiss franc American call option has been written at a strike price of 1.2000 SFr/US$ (0.8333 US$/SFr). If the Swiss franc spot foreign exchange rate starts to strengthen against the US dollar, the chance that the option holder will exercise increases. This open position can be closed by the option writer by buying Swiss franc spot against the US dollar.

The decisions on when to close the call option gap, how to close it (either through the spot purchase of the currency or through the purchase of the currency forward), and the timing of the transactions is very much based on subjective evaluations of the future foreign exchange rate as a part of the overall foreign exchange position management of the financial institution. Similar exposure management applies to the put options written by the institution. Consider that hedged options that are out-of-the-money also represent a position to the option writer. Hence the option position must be hedged and un-hedged in response to current changes in the foreign exchange rate.

## 5.3 Option pricing

From the preceding discussion, we deduce that the call option premium on an in-the-money American option must exceed the difference between the spot rate and the exercise price. Otherwise the option holder can exercise the option at a profit right after purchase. Similarly, the call option premium on a European or an American option must exceed the difference between the forward exchange rate and the exercise price. If not, the option holder can lock-in a future profit right after purchase by selling the currency forward and exercising the option at expiration date (Table 5.3).

In accordance with the option pricing discussion (conducted in Chapter 4), the premium on (currency) options (O) depends on the following factors:

● The underlying asset price (spot or forward foreign exchange rate) ($P$).
● The option strike or exercise price ($S$).
● The time to expiration date ($t$) (days/365).
● The volatility of asset returns or foreign exchange rate ($v$).
● The risk-free rate ($r$).

In the case of dividend bearing stock options a sixth factor would also influence the option premium:

**Table 5.3** The price relationship of currency call options

| | |
|---|---|
| European option: | Call option premium ≥ (Forward foreign exchange rate – Exercise price)* ≥ 0 |
| American option: | Call option premium ≥ (Spot foreign exchange rate – Exercise price) ≥ 0 |

* Discounted to present value at the current money market spot rate.

● The present value of dividend payments ($D$) ($(\text{div})e^{-rt}$)

$$O = g(P, S, t, v, r) - D$$

The option price relationship to these factors was formalized by Black and Scholes as they developed a formula to approximate the option premium.[2]

## 5.3.1 Covered call

The option pricing relationship is derived from the establishment of a long position in the underlying asset, e.g. a stock, a foreign currency, etc., and the simultaneous sale of call options on that same asset. This position is commonly referred to as a **covered call** because the investor physically holds the underlying asset of the options contract. If the market price is below the strike price at maturity, the call options will not be exercised and the investor may incur some loss on the long asset position, which is compensated by the call premium received from the sale of call options. Conversely, if the market price increases above the strike price, the call option will be exercised and the investor must sell (deliver) the asset to the option holder at the strike price and possibly earns a small return if the acquisition price was lower than the exercise price. If the call option is appropriately priced in relation to the expected price development of the underlying asset, and an appropriate number of call options are written, the covered call position should earn a risk free return to the investor, which then becomes the basis for determining the theoretical call option premium. Therefore, if the risk free rate increases, the investor should also charge a higher call option premium to ensure a return on the covered call position in line with the general market. Whereas this may not be intuitively clear since an increase in the interest rate level would normally cause asset prices to drop, thus reducing the value of call option, the following theoretical example might clarify the argument.[3]

An investor makes an initial investment in a certain asset, e.g. a non-dividend paying stock at an acquisition value of 100 local currency units. In terms of the future price development, assume that only two events are possible in a simple one-period world:

● The market price can increase to 105.
● The market price can decrease to 95.

Probabilities can be attached to these events to reflect the return characteristics of the underlying asset. For example, in the case of a foreign currency without any long-term trend line in the foreign exchange development, the events may represent outcomes with a 50:50 chance of occurring. In the case of a zero-dividend stock where the investment return relates solely to an increase in the stock price, the high price event may be assigned a higher likelihood than the low price event to reflect the expected positive return characteristics of the stock. Hence, assume that there is a likelihood of 60% that the price will increase to 105 and only a 40% chance that the price will decrease to 95 (Figure 5.3).

The expected value of the investment at the end of the period is $(0.6 \times 105) + (0.4 \times 95) = 101$, which corresponds to a 1% return on the investment for the period. To hedge this investment, a certain number of at-the-money call options can be written on the same asset. The number of options to issue can be found by dividing the maximum fluctuation of the asset price by the comparable fluctuation in the call

**Figure 5.3** Price development of the underlying asset

option premium over the period. The price of the underlying asset varies between 95 and 105 whereas the option premium varies between 0, if the call is out-of-the-money at maturity, and 5, if the call is in-the-money at maturity. The option premium can never assume a negative value. Hence,

$$\text{Number of option contracts} = \frac{105 - 95}{5 - 0} = \frac{10}{5} = 2$$

So two call option contracts are issued with an exercise price of 100. If the asset price goes up, the investor will incur a gain of 5 on the asset portfolio. On the other hand, the two options will be exercised at a total cost of 10 ($2 \times 5$), leaving the investor with an end-of-period net worth position of 95 ($105 - 10$).

If the risk free rate in this period amounts to 0.50%, the call option premium that secures a risk free return on the covered call position can be determined. The net investment at the beginning of the period equals the capital outlay for the asset minus the premium received from the sale of the option contracts. The net worth position at end of the period should then amount to the initial net investment plus the risk free return earned on this investment. Hence, the corresponding call option premium ($O_c$) can be derived:

$$\text{Return condition: } (100 - 2O_c) \times 1.0050 = 95 \Rightarrow$$

$$O_c = \frac{100.50 - 95}{2 \times 1.0050} = 2.7363$$

Hence, the initial net investment is 94.5274 ($= 100 - 2 \times 2.7363$), and the return on the investment equals the risk free return of 0.50% ($= 100 \times (95 - 94.5274)/94.5274$). If the market price of the option differs from the equilibrium price, investors would be able to increase the return above the risk free rate by going long or short on the covered call position, which would force the option premium back towards the equilibrium price.

If the risk free rate increases to 0.75%, the call option premium can be determined under the new market conditions using the same principle:

$$(100 - 2O_c) \times 1.0075 = 95 \Rightarrow$$

$$O_c = \frac{100.75 - 95}{2 \times 1.0075} = 2.8536$$

The initial net investment would be 94.2928 ($= 100 - 2 \times 2.8536$), and the return on the investment equals the new risk free return of 0.75% ($= 100 \times (95 - 94.2829)/94.2829$). As appears, an increase in the risk free rate from 0.50% to 0.75% per period results in an increase in the call option premium from \$2.7363 to \$2.8536, if the options are efficiently priced.

## Box 5.1 Indulging in the Black–Scholes framework

The determination of a theoretical call option price is based on a description of the price development of the underlying asset as a so-called *Wiener process* or **Brownian motion with drift**, generally expressed as:

$$\delta x = a\delta t + b \ \epsilon\sqrt{\delta t}$$

That is, the incremental change in variable $x$ ($\delta x$) is a function of time ($t$) captured as drift or a general trend ($a\delta t$) and a noise term ($b \ \epsilon\sqrt{\delta t}$) introducing variability around the trend. The coefficient 'a' is a **drift rate** indicating change per unit of time ($\delta x/\delta t$), and the coefficient 'b' is multiplied with a random drawing from a standardized normal distribution ($\epsilon$) to constitute the *noise* element. Hence, mean ($\delta x$) = $a\delta t$, variance ($\delta x$) = $b^2\delta t$, and standard deviation ($\delta x$) = $b\sqrt{\delta t}$ .

An *Itô process* can refer to a certain specification of a Brownian motion with drift:

$$\delta x = a(x, t)\delta t + b(x, t) \ \epsilon\sqrt{\delta t}$$

where the drift rate (a) and the variance rate (b$^2$) can change as x changes over time.

Itô's lemma shows that a variable $g$, where $\delta g = f(\delta t, \epsilon\sqrt{\delta t})$ and assuming the same Wiener process as variable $x$, follows a comparable Itô process expressed as:

$$\delta g = (a\delta g/\delta x + \delta g/\delta t + \tfrac{1}{2}b^2 \ \delta^2 g/\delta x^2)\delta t + b\delta g/\delta x \ \epsilon\sqrt{\delta t}$$

with drift rate ($a\delta g/\delta x + \delta g/\delta t + \tfrac{1}{2}b^2 \ \delta^2 g/\delta x^2$) and variance rate ($b\delta g/\delta x$)$^2$.

The development of an asset price (P), e.g. a stock price, commodity price, interest rate, foreign exchange rate, etc., can be characterized as a special Itô process, sometimes referred to as a geometric Brownian motion with drift, in which the price is influenced by expected return and variability of the asset price:

$$\delta P = \mu P\delta t + \sigma P \ \epsilon\sqrt{\delta t} \quad \text{or} \quad \delta P/P = \mu\delta t + \sigma \ \epsilon\sqrt{\delta t}$$

where $\mu$, the expected rate of return on the asset, and $\sigma$, the volatility of the asset price, are assumed constant.

If $g = \ln P$ and P follows a lognormal distribution, then $\delta g = \delta\ln P = (\mu - \sigma^2/2)\delta t + \sigma \ \epsilon\sqrt{\delta t}$ with mean $(\mu - \sigma^2/2) \ t$ and standard deviation $\sigma\sqrt{t}$ for period t. Further, the continuous compound rate of return, e.g. determined as $\ln(P_t/P_{t-i})$ for short intervals $i$, has mean $(\mu - \sigma^2/2)$ and standard deviation $\sigma/\sqrt{t}$ and P has volatility equal to the standard deviation of the continuously compounded return in one year (See Figure 5.4).

The call option premium moves in tandem with changes in the price of the underlying asset and Itô's lemma suggests that the prices will follow comparable Itô processes. This provides the means to solve the conditions of a covered call position. Hence, the derivative, e.g. a call option, and an inverse position in the underlying asset can eliminate the Brownian motion, and this position must earn a risk-free return. For each short derivative contract, the risk-free position should include a long position in the underlying asset, so the price effect is inversely related to the change in the call option premium:

$$-1 \quad \text{derivative (short)}$$

$$\delta O_c/\delta P \quad \text{securities (long)}$$

The term $\delta O_c/\delta P$ is often referred to as the *delta* or *hedge ratio*.

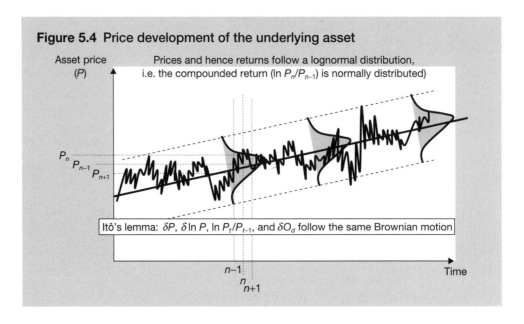

**Figure 5.4 Price development of the underlying asset**

The relationship between the option premium and its characterizing variables has been approximated by Black and Scholes under simplifying assumptions. The following expresses the formula for the premium derived on a European-type option, which today is used both by professional option traders and finance scholars to explore developments in market prices of call options. The call option premium is determined as follows:

$$O_c = P(N(d_1)) - S(N(d_2))e^{-rt}$$

where

$$(d_1) = \frac{\ln\left(\dfrac{P}{S}\right) + \left(r + \dfrac{v^2}{2}\right)t}{v\sqrt{t}}$$

$$(d_2) = \ln\left(\frac{P}{S}\right) + \frac{\left(r - \dfrac{v^2}{2}\right)t}{v\sqrt{t}}$$

$$= d_1 - v\sqrt{t}$$

and

$O_c$ = call option price;
$P$ = asset price (stock, commodity, foreign exchange rate, etc.);
$N(\bullet)$ = cumulative normal density function;
$S$ = strike or exercise price;
$e = 2.71828$;
$r$ = risk free rate;
$t$ = time to maturity (days/360);
$v$ = volatility – annualized standard deviation of returns.

*Example*: (Refer to Table 1 on website www.pearsoned.co.uk/andersen.) Assume the following market conditions; the market price of the asset is currently 41, the volatility of the price development is determined as 0.20 (20%), and the risk-free rate is 5%. Then we can determine the theoretical option premium of a call option contract ($O_c$) on the underlying asset with strike price of 42, i.e. an option slightly out-of-the-money, and with 90 days to final maturity, i.e. $t = 0.25$. To determine the premium of the call option, we first calculate $d_1 = (\ln(41/42) + (0.05 + 0.2^2/2)0.25)/(0.2\sqrt{0.25}) = (-0.0241 + 0.07 \times 0.25)/0.1 = -0.066$, and then determine $d_2 = -0.066 - 0.1 = -0.166$. Thereafter, we find $N(d_1) = N(-0.066) = 0.4745$ and $N(d_2) = N(-0.166) = 0.4351$. Then $O_c = P(N(d_1)) - S(N(d_2))e^{-rt} = 41 \times 0.4745 - 42 \times 0.4351 \times e^{-0.05(0.25)} = 19.45 - 18.05 = \$1.40$.

As Black and Scholes developed the options pricing framework they depended on a number of assumptions:

● there are no transaction costs or taxes;
● the price development of the underlying asset follows a log normal distribution, i.e. the compounded rate of return is normally distributed;
● the volatility on the price movements is constant;
● the interest rate level is unchanged;
● there is continuous trading in the underlying asset;
● in the case of stock options, no dividends are paid out before the maturity date.

In most cases, all of these assumptions will not be fulfilled. However, the theoretical option premium still provides a useful benchmark for the assessment of option premiums. Whenever the model is used to determine the theoretical option premiums, the analyst will have to consider all the underlying preconditions and make assessments about the future volatility of the underlying asset price.

*Example*: An institution is about to write call options on an asset and considers at which minimum price (premium) they should issue the options. A statistical analysis shows a volatility of 9% over the past six months. However, the minimum premium required in the offering is adjusted upwards because the market volatility is expected to increase.

The Black and Scholes formula assumes that no dividend payments take place during the period until the option's expiration date. However, this is not always the case and therefore the option premium should be adjusted accordingly. This is usually done by subtracting the present value of the expected dividend payment from the theoretical option premium.

*Example*: An institution issues European call options on MetPath's stock in January at a strike price of \$40 per share with expiration in May ('MP May 40 calls'). The theoretical value of the call option, which allows the holder to buy 100 MP shares at \$40 per share, is calculated to be \$410. Since a dividend of \$1.50 a share has been announced for payment at the end of April, the actual call premium is fixed at \$261.8 (= $410 - (100 \times 1.50)/1.05^{0.25} = 410 - 148.2$).

Conversely, the theoretical Black and Scholes model is often used to indicate the **implied volatility** of a given option premium being quoted in the market. This can often help an investor decide whether an option premium is set too high or too low in the market according to their own assessment of future developments in the price volatility.

*Example*: The AT&T Sept. 23 call option is quoted at a premium of 1.21 corresponding to an implied volatility of around 10%. However, an investor expects the volatility to increase to 19%

**Figure 5.5** 'Smile' curves or volatility spreads

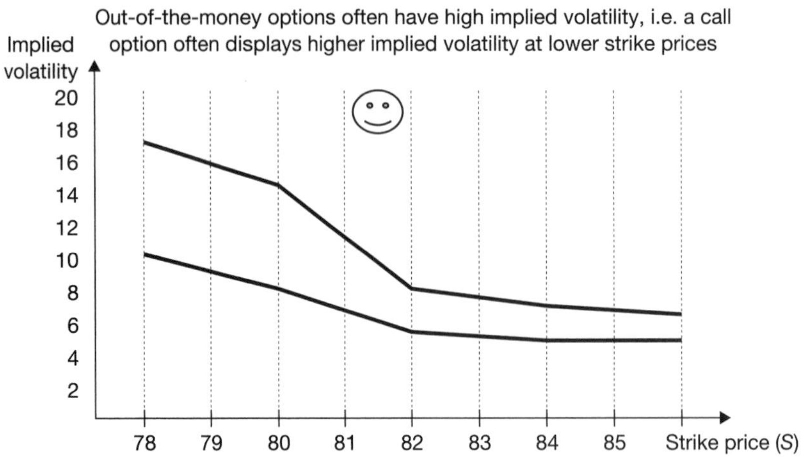

over the coming month. She is therefore willing to buy the AT&T call options at the going price, because she considers the contracts to be cheap and because she expects the premiums on that contract to increase in the near future.

The Black and Scholes formula assumes that the periodic returns on the underlying asset are normally distributed. This assumption is violated specifically when the price movements include a few extreme jumps. The other model assumptions can also become critical such as the assumption of constant volatility throughout the life of the option and the assumption of a constant interest rate level. We know that by the very nature of the financial market interest rates and price variability change constantly. Also, it often turns out, for example, that out-of-the-money options have higher implied volatility than at-the-money options. Therefore, option contracts with the same maturity but with different strike prices can have different implied volatilities. This phenomenon is illustrated graphically in the so-called **smile curve**, which sets out the implied volatility for similar contracts with different strike prices (Figure 5.5). The differences in implied volatility can from time to time provide an opportunity to establish **volatility spreads**, in which the investor will buy contracts with a relatively low implied volatility and sell similar option contracts with a relatively high implied volatility.

The preceding price discussion relates to the European type of option, but all the arguments apply as well to the American type of option. In general an American option is worth more than a European option because it provides the holder with more flexibility of exercising the option at the opportune moment. Consequently, an American option will trade at a higher price than the equivalent European option.

### 5.3.2 Pricing puts

Similarly the price of a put option on the asset can be determined. The intrinsic value of the put is equal to the difference between the current market price and the exercise price of the underlying asset times the number of asset units the put entitles the holder to sell. The put holder will make a profit if the going market price of the asset is lower than the exercise price. Because the put represents a right and not an obligation, it

**Figure 5.6** A zero-risk position

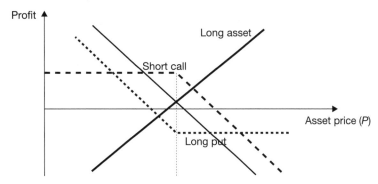

cannot have a negative value. The Black–Scholes option-pricing model can be adapted to the put option case through the relationship between call and put options.

A risk free position can be created by buying the asset, buying a put option on that asset, and simultaneously selling or writing a call option on the asset with the same exercise price as the put option. This transaction is sometimes referred to as **conversion** (Figure 5.6).

If the asset price increases, the capital gain on the asset portfolio outweighs the loss from the holder's exercise of the call option. If the asset price decreases, the gain from exercising the put option will outweigh the loss incurred on the asset portfolio. Hence, it describes a risk free position. What is interesting in this context is that the conversion process also describes the relationship between the call and put option premiums in an efficient option market. The cost equation of the zero-risk position can be established in the following way:

| Establish zero-risk position: | *Action* | *Cash flows* |
|---|---|---|
| | Buy asset | Pay asset price (−) |
| | Buy put option | Pay put premium (−) |
| | Write call option | Receive call premium (+) |
| Unwind zero-risk position: | *Action* | *Cash flows* |
| | Sell asset | Receive exercise price (+) |
| | | Funding cost of position (−) |

Cash flow equation: Asset price + Put premium − Call premium
= Exercise price − funding cost of position

That is,   Call premium = Put premium + (Asset price − Exercise price)
+ funding cost of position

or,   Put premium = Call premium − (Asset price − Exercise price)
− funding cost of position

Furthermore,   Put premium = Call premium − funding cost of position

when   Exercise price = Initial asset price

A comparable logic can be applied to the price relationship between currency options. Buying a call option and writing a put option on a currency at the same strike price (conversion) corresponds to buying a forward foreign exchange agreement for the purchase of the currency in question, i.e. it's a synthetic forward created through a combination of two option contracts. In an efficient market the cost of establishing a future long position in the currency in either of the two ways must be the same. Otherwise financial intermediaries could engage in arbitrage transactions and generate risk free profits until the appropriate pricing relationship are reinstated. The cost of the currency acquired through the combined option position, or through a forward agreement, is calculated as follows:

$$\text{Forward rate* = Exercise price* + Call premium - Put premium + interest on net premium}$$

that is,

$$\text{Call premium = Put premium + (Forward rate* - Exercise price*) - interest on net premium}$$

and

$$\text{Put premium = Call premium - (Forward rate* - Exercise price*) + interest on net premium}$$

* the 'forward rate' and 'exercise price' are discounted to present value at the current money market rate

The put option premium can also be derived from the Black–Scholes framework. Hence, the put option premium is determined as follows:

$$O_p = S(N(-d_2))e^{-rt} - P(N(-d_1))$$

where

$$(d_1) = \frac{\ln\left(\frac{P}{S}\right) + \left(r + \frac{v^2}{2}\right)t}{v\sqrt{t}}$$

$$(d_2) = d_1 - v\sqrt{t}$$

and

$O_p$ = put option premium;
$P$ = asset price;
$N(\bullet)$ = cumulative normal density function;
$S$ = strike or exercise price;
e = 2.71828;
$r$ = risk free rate;
$t$ = time to maturity (days/360);
$v$ = volatility – annualized standard deviation of returns.

*Example*: (Refer to Table 1 on website www.pearsoned.co.uk/andersen.) Assume a market price of the asset is 41, the price volatility is 0.20 (20%), and the risk-free rate is 5%. Then we can determine the theoretical premium of a put option ($O_p$) with strike price of 40, that is, the option is slightly out-of-the-money, and with 90 days to final maturity, i.e. $t = 0.25$. We first calculate $d_1 = (\ln(41/40) + (0.05 + 0.2^2/2)0.25)/(0.2\sqrt{0.25}) = (0.0247 + 0.07 \times 0.25)/0.1 = 0.422$, and then determine $d_2 = 0.422 - 0.1 = 0.322$. Thereafter, we calculate $N(-d_1) = N(-0.422) = 0.3367$ and $N(-d_2) = N(-0.322) = 0.3741$. Then $O_p = S(N(-d_2))e^{-rt} - P_s(N(-d_1)) = 40 \times 0.3741 \times e^{-0.05(0.25)} - 41 \times 0.3367 = 14.78 - 13.80 = \$0.98$.

## The role of volatility

In view of the inherent risk associated with the management of an option position, another approach has been to look at the option agreement as an 'insurance policy' that protects the option holder against adverse changes in asset prices, such as foreign exchange rates. Seen in this perspective, the option premium becomes an insurance premium covering the cost of a probable future loss on the option position. To analyze the future loss structure and to assess the potential risk associated with a given option agreement we can adopt statistical simulation analysis. In this analysis the price of the underlying asset, e.g. the foreign exchange rate volatility plays an important role. The volatility calculation can be based on changes in the foreign exchange rate within regular intervals during a given time period. There is no general agreement on which time intervals to use or what time periods are most appropriate in the analysis. The fact of the matter is that all statistical analyses are based on historical data. However updated these might be, what matters is rather the expected price volatility over the coming period until the option's expiration date. So, judgement is called for when determining the appropriate volatility measure for a given option agreement.

*Example*: To calculate the foreign exchange rate volatility of the euro foreign exchange rate against the US dollar, we might use prices over monthly intervals covering the past twelve months (Table 5.4). Notice an increase in the exchange rate volatility towards the latter half of the year. If the expectation is that the price pattern will be repeated over the coming months, we would use the annualized monthly change of 15.76% for our calculations.

**Table 5.4** Foreign exchange rates and volatility calculations

| Date | FX rate (€/US$) | Return $ln(P_t/P_{t-1})$ | Return $ln(P_t/P_{t-1})$ | Return $ln(P_t/P_{t-1})$ |
|---|---|---|---|---|
| September 28 | 1.1200 | | | |
| October 30 | 1.0825 | −0.0341 | . | . |
| November 30 | 1.0575 | −0.0234 | . | . |
| December 31 | 1.1330 | 0.0690 | . | . |
| January 31 | 1.1005 | −0.0291 | −0.0291 | . |
| February 28 | 1.0945 | −0.0055 | −0.0055 | . |
| March 29 | 1.0905 | −0.0037 | −0.0037 | . |
| April 30 | 1.0857 | −0.0044 | −0.0044 | −0.0044 |
| May 30 | 1.1675 | 0.0726 | 0.0726 | 0.0726 |
| June 28 | 1.1455 | −0.0190 | −0.0190 | −0.0190 |
| July 31 | 1.2235 | 0.0659 | . | 0.0659 |
| August 30 | 1.1475 | −0.0641 | . | −0.0641 |
| September 30 | 1.1950 | 0.0406 | . | 0.0406 |
| Standard deviation | | 0.0455 | 0.0361 | 0.0536 |
| Annualized s.d. | sqrt(12) × | 0.1576 | 0.1252 | 0.1856 |
| Volatility (%) | | 15.76% | 12.52% | 18.56% |

*Example*: The *spot* foreign exchange rate is 1.1675 €/US$ and we are about to quote a three-month European call option with a strike price of 1.1500 €/US$. Assuming a future annual change of 15.76% in the foreign exchange rate, we expect that the exchange rate might increase or decrease by 7.88% (15.76/$\sqrt{4}$) over the coming three-month period.

If the foreign exchange rate develops randomly, we can assign a 50% likelihood that the foreign exchange rate will increase and a 50% likelihood that it will drop given that there is no clear trend in the foreign exchange rate development (Figure 5.7). Let us consider a call option on euros against US dollars. Here the option holder will only exercise the call option if the foreign exchange rate drops below the strike price. The option writer's potential payout on the call option can then be calculated as 0.50 (0.0000) + 0.50 (1.1500 − 1.0755) = 0.03725. Given that the three-month interest rate presently is 4% p.a., the present value of the potential payout is 0.0369 (0.03725/1.01), which as a percentage of the spot price amounts to 3.16% (= 100 × 0.0369/1.1675). This then corresponds to the up-front premium required to cover the future potential payouts of the call option (Figure 5.7).

This binomial approach to option pricing analysis based on dual outcomes of currency values over a time interval and hence periodic returns on currency positions can be made more precise by splitting the time interval into shorter sequences, e.g. months instead of quarters.[4] For example, in the first month there could be a 50% likelihood that the foreign exchange rate increases to say 1.2206 and a 50% likelihood that the foreign exchange rate decreases to 1.1144, and so forth. That is, for the entire three-month period, each of the dual foreign exchange rate outcomes each month has assigned a 50% likelihood of occurrence. Given unchanged price volatility, the monthly change in the foreign exchange rate is 4.55% (= 15.76/$\sqrt{12}$). Therefore there is a 50% likelihood that the foreign exchange rate increases to 1.2206 (= 1.1675 × 1.0455) in the first month and a 50% likelihood that the foreign exchange rate will decrease to 1.1144 (= 1.1675 × (1 − 0.0455)). In the second month, the outer range for the price development is 1.2762 (= 1.2206 × 1.0455) and 1.0636 (= 1.1144 × (1 − 0.0455)), and so on (Figure 5.8).

As appears, the future rate of 1.3342 can only occur in one way, namely with three successive monthly outcomes of foreign exchange rate increases. The likelihood of the rate being 1.3342 after three months is therefore 12.5% (= 0.50 × 0.50 × 0.50). The foreign exchange rate of 1.2206 can arise in three ways over the three-month period.

**Figure 5.7** Capturing the foreign exchange rate volatility in the option price

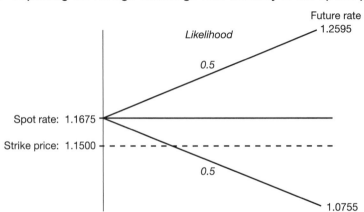

## Figure 5.8 Determining the currency option premium over consecutive time periods

| | Future rate | Likelihood |
|---|---|---|
| | 1.3342 | 0.125 |
| | 1.2206 | 0.375 |
| | 1.1144 | 0.375 |
| | 1.0152 | 0.125 |

Spot rate: 1.1675
Strike price: 1.1500

Tree values: 0.5 everywhere; 1.2762, 1.2206, 1.1144, 1.0636.

Time (months): 1, 2, 3

The foreign exchange rate can increase to 1.2206 in the first month, increase again to 1.2762 in the second month, and then drop to 1.2206 in the third month. Or, it can rise to 1.2206, drop to 1.1675, and then increase to 1.2206 again. Or, it can drop to 1.1144 and then increase to 1.1675 and then again to 1.2206. The likelihood of the rate being 1.2206 after the three-month time interval is therefore calculated as 37.5% (= 3 × 12.5%). Similarly, the likelihood of the rate being 1.1144 after three months is found to be 37.5% and for the rate to be 1.0152 the likelihood is determined to be 12.5%.

### Box 5.2 Determining the parameters in the binomial tree

The probability ($p_u$) of an increase in the asset price is chosen to match the underlying 'drift' (return) and noise (volatility) of the asset price development. Since there are only two possible outcomes in each period in the binomial model, the probability ($p_d$) of a decrease in the asset price is determined by default as $(1 - p_u)$. In the risk neutral setup of a covered call discussed earlier, the drift, i.e. the return on the investment position must correspond to the risk free rate ($r$). Then the probabilities can be determined as follows:[5]

$$\text{Probability up} = p_u = \frac{(a - d)}{(u - d)}$$

$$\text{Probability down} = p_d = (1 - p_u)$$

where

$a = e^{r \times dt}$
$u = e^{v \times dt \times 0.5}$
$d = e^{-v \times dt \times 0.5}$
$dt$ = time intervals as % of year.

*Example*: The current asset price $(P) = 20$, volatility $(v) = 0.33$ (33%), the risk free rate $(r) = 12\%$, and there are 90 days until final maturity, i.e. $t = 90/365$ and we apply the binomial framework to monthly price intervals $(dt) = 30/365$. On this basis we can determine the associated probabilities:

$$a = e^{r \times dt} = e^{0.00986} = 1.00991$$
$$u = e^{v \times dt \times 0.5} = e^{0.0946} = 1.09922$$
$$d = e^{-v \times dt \times 0.5} = e^{-0.0946} = 0.90974$$

$$p_u = \frac{1.00991 - 0.90974}{1.09922 - 0.90974} = 0.5287$$

$$p_d = 1 - 0.5287 = 0.4713$$

If the spot foreign exchange rate ends up above 1.1500 €/US$, the currency option will not be exercised. This will happen only if the foreign exchange rate falls below the strike price indicated as euros per US dollar. Hence, the potential payout on the call option is calculated as:

| | | |
|---|---|---|
| +0.125 (0.000) | = | 0.00000 |
| +0.375 (0.000) | = | 0.00000 |
| +0.375 (1.1500 − 1.1144) | = | 0.00225 |
| +0.125 (1.1500 − 1.0152) | = | 0.01685 |
| | | 0.01910 |

The present value of the potential payout amounts to 0.01891 $(= 0.01910/1.01)$, which as a percentage of the spot price makes up 1.62% $(= 100 \times 0.01891/1.1675)$. The smaller we make the time intervals, the more interactions will be performed and the closer we will get to determining an option premium that adequately reflects the risk associated with the writing of an option. The more interactions we perform, the closer the statistical distribution of resulting future foreign exchange rates will approximate a normal distribution (Figure 5.9). The mean value, in this situation, will then be

**Figure 5.9** Foreign exchange rate development following a log-normal distribution

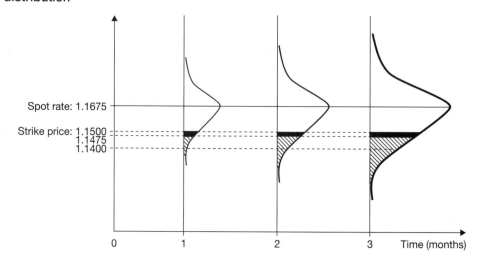

equal to the initial spot exchange rate and a standard deviation corresponding to the assumed future volatility of the foreign exchange rate development.

This value can be used in further analysis of the call option. The probability ($p$) that the foreign exchange rate will fall within a certain interval, say between 1.1475 and 1.1500 €/US$ (the dark area in Figure 5.9), can be found by applying a tabularized cumulative normal distribution. This likelihood is then multiplied by the cost of exercise to find the expected cost of the exchange rate falling inside this interval. This can be performed for all similar intervals ($n$) below the strike price say between 1.1450 and 1.1475, 1.1425 and 1.1450, 1.1400 and 1.1425, and so forth. If the costs of falling within each of these intervals are added together it will correspond to the total expected cost of the call option with strike price 1.1500 €/US$ for different time intervals (the shaded areas in Figure 5.9):

$$\text{Cost of call option} = \Sigma p\{((s - 0.0025 \times n) < FX < (s - 0.0025 \, (n - 1))) \times (0.0025 \times n)\},$$
$$\text{for all } n$$

where

$p$ = Probability of falling within price interval;
$FX$ = the foreign exchange rate (€/US$);
$y$ = strike price of 1.1500 €/US$;
$n$ = 1, 2, 3, 4, 5, . . . , sufficiently large number;
0.0025 = determined here as an appropriate price interval;
$(0.0025 \times n)$ = cost of exercise in specific price interval.

The situation discussed above relates to a European call option. To analyze an American call option we have to monitor the development of the spot foreign exchange rate through each of the sequential iterations. By determining the intrinsic value of the call option at each time period, we can assess the potential value of the option if it is exercised at different times before final maturity. This present value of the intrinsic value at different points in time is compared to the option value determined at expiration. Whichever of these values is the highest represents the potential cost of an option that can be exercised at any time before final maturity, which then becomes the option premium to charge by the writer of an American call option. After the first month there is a 50% chance that the call option will be in-the-money, which represents a present value of 0.02629 (= 0.5(1.1675 – 1.1144)/1.01) corresponding to 2.25% of the spot foreign exchange rate (= 100 × 0.02629/1.1675). By the second month there is a 25% chance (= 0.5 × 0.5) that the call option will be in-the-money with a present value of 0.025466 (= 0.25(1.1675 – 1.0636)/1.02) corresponding to 2.18% of the spot foreign exchange rate (= 100 × 0.025466/1.1675). Since the highest option price over the three-month period corresponds to 2.25% potentially achieved after 1 month, this becomes the option premium charged for the American currency call option.

## 5.4 Profitability patterns

In Chapter 4, it was discussed how future financial prices, such as foreign exchange rates and interest rates, can be locked-in through engagement in forward contracts and financial futures contracts. This means that the prices are fixed and the future

**Figure 5.10** Profitability pattern of a call option contract

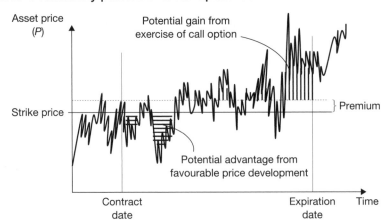

price uncertainty for specific exposures eliminated barring potential basis risk. The benefit of lock-in is obvious when prices have moved in an unfavourable direction. However, it is more difficult to defend when market prices have developed favourably after the contract was closed because the upside potential of the gain is eliminated and hence entails *ex post* opportunity cost. Options, as opposed to futures contracts, close the downside price risk while leaving the upside potential for gains from favourable price movements open. This is the significant benefit of the options contract that may explain the increasing use of options contracts for hedging applications. In an uncertain business environment, the decision makers often do not know with exactitude whether the future commercial transactions will actually occur or not. However, in some situations it may still be desirable to cover potential financial risk exposures before committing to large business propositions. Under these circumstances options may constitute highly applicable hedging solutions because the option holders exercise the option at their choice but with no obligation to do so.

A call option will be profitable for the holder if the market price of the underlying asset increases above the strike price including the premium quote. If the market price drops below the strike price, the option holder will not exercise the option but will take full advantage of the favourable development in the commodity price (Figure 5.10).

A put option will be profitable if the market price of the underlying asset falls below the strike price minus the premium quote. If the market price increases above the strike price, the option holder will not exercise the option but will take full advantage of the favourable price development (Figure 5.11).

### 5.4.1 Profit and loss profiles

The call option buyer pays a premium up front for the right, with no obligation, to acquire an asset at a specified price, the strike price, during a specified period of time. Conversely, the seller, or writer, of the call option is obliged to make the asset available to the option holder against receipt of the premium. The put option buyer pays a premium up front for the right, with no obligation, to dispose of an asset at a specified price, the strike price, during a specified period of time. Conversely, the

**Figure 5.11 Profitability pattern of a put option contract**

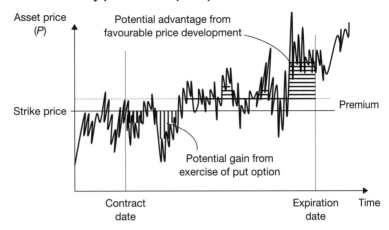

seller, or writer, of the put option is obliged to acquire the asset from the option holder against receipt of the premium. The profit and loss profiles of option buyers and sellers are inversely related (Figure 5.12).

Whether an option is in-, at-, or out-of-the-money at the time of purchase influences the profit and loss profile of the option. If the strike price of a call is lower than the current market price of the underlying asset, the contract is in-the-money and the option premium will be high. It is beneficial to exercise the option right away because the intrinsic value is positive or to sell it in the market. If the strike price is higher than the current market price, the call is out-of-the-money, the intrinsic value is zero, and the option premium is relatively low. Variations in the size of the option premium will have a corresponding impact on the option holder's break-even points. The higher the call option premium, the higher the market price (break-even price) must be before the option will be beneficial to the holder (Figure 5.13).

**Figure 5.12 Profit and loss profile of option buyers and sellers**

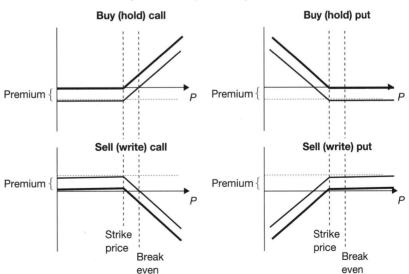

**Figure 5.13** Profit and loss profile of a call option

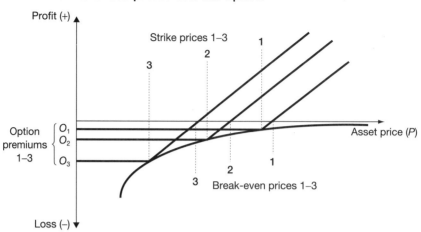

The higher the strike price on a call option, the lower the option premium. The lower the strike price on a call option, the higher the option premium. In the case of a put option, the inverse relationship holds, i.e. the higher the strike price the higher the option premium, and the lower the strike price the lower the option premium. Assuming that the future market price moves randomly, we can conclude that choosing too low a strike price on a call option will become way too expensive while choosing too high a strike price hardly has any benefits even if the premium is low. Similarly, choosing too high a strike price on a put option can become prohibitively expensive while a very low strike price has limited benefits. As a general rule, the optimum strike price to choose for an option buyer is a slightly out-of-the-money option, because the premium is relatively low and the upside potential for gain is relatively high. If a highly in-the-money option is chosen, the premium will be relatively high, due to the high intrinsic value of the option with a relatively limited upside potential for a gain.

The investor who has to choose the appropriate strike price of a given call or put option should take into consideration several factors, such as, the expected price change of the underlying asset, the probability that an expected price trend will materialize, the size of the premium, either the premium income for the option writer or the maximum loss for the option buyer, and the maturity of the option, e.g. compared to the time horizon of the expected price development. The investor who expects the asset price to increase should consider buying call options or writing put options. The investor who expects the price to drop should consider buying put options or writing call options. The certainty of the investor's market view should play a major role in the investment decision. The premium of a bought in-the-money option will react relatively quickly to price changes in the underlying asset. If the future price development is volatile, even the risk of losing the up-front premium is fairly high. Conversely, an option writer who is uncertain of the future price trend should be very careful, because the potential loss of an unfavourable price development is in principle unlimited. It is also important for an option holder that the expected price development occurs within the lifetime of the option, otherwise the option will expire worthless. A fulfilment of an expected trend at the expiry date avails the option buyer little. Conversely, an option writer can take advantage of the expected timing of events before and after the option's expiry.

## 5.5 Option price sensitivity

The option premium is influenced by four essential factors, namely the price of the underlying asset, the time to expiration, the volatility of returns, and the risk free rate. For investors in derivative instruments, it may be relevant to assess the sensitivity in the value of the derivatives portfolio from changes in these influential factors. A number of measures, often referred to as the 'Greek letters' or just the 'Greeks', have been developed to support the analyses of these price sensitivities.

### 5.5.1 Delta

The **delta** ($\Delta$) of an option, also referred to as the **hedge ratio**, indicates the amount by which the option premium changes when the market price of the underlying asset moves by one point. That is, delta is the partial derivative of the option premium with respect to the underlying asset price:

$$\text{Delta } (\Delta) = \delta O / \delta P$$

Using formulas relating to the Black–Scholes framework, this partial derivative can be expressed as:[5]

$$\Delta_c = D_c = N(d_1);$$

$$\Delta_p = D_p = N(d_1) - 1$$

The delta is not a constant but changes as the market price of the underlying asset changes. The call option premium is a function of the market price of the underlying asset and the delta factor is equivalent to the slope of the tangent to the option price curve. The delta corresponds to the differential coefficient of the option price curve with respect to the market price of the asset ($P$). For a sufficiently large market price of the underlying asset, the delta of a call option will be close to 1, that is, when the market price is much higher than the strike price (in-the-money) and the option price curve will be dose to the intrinsic value of the call option. When the strike price is equal to the market price, the delta will be close to 0.5 and will converge toward zero as the strike price increases over the market price (out-of-the-money) (Figure 5.14).

**Figure 5.14 Delta and gamma factors for a call option**

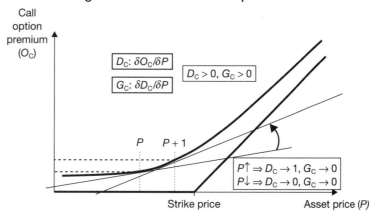

**Figure 5.15** Delta and gamma factors for a put option

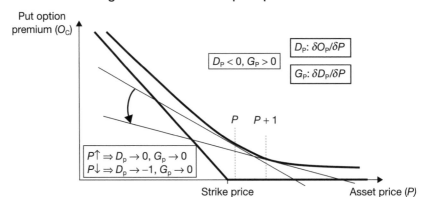

For a sufficiently low market price, the delta of a put option will be close to $-1$, that is, when the market price is much lower than the strike price (in-the-money) because the option price curve will be close to the intrinsic value of the put option. When the strike price is equal to the current market price (at-the-money), the delta is close to $-0.5$ and will converge toward zero as the strike price falls below the market price (out-of-the-money) (Figure 5.15).

*Example*: A call option (42) is quoted a premium of 1.40 at the current asset price of 41, volatility 0.20 (20%) with 90 days to maturity, i.e. $t = 0.25$, and a current interest rate ($r$) of 5%. Hence, the delta ($\Delta$) of the call option is determined as $\Delta_c = N(d_1) = 0.4745$. A put option (40) is quoted a premium of 0.98 at the current asset price of 41, volatility 0.20 (20%) with 90 days to maturity, i.e. $t = 0.25$, and a current interest rate ($r$) of 5%. Hence, the delta ($\Delta$) of the put option is determined as $\Delta_P = N(d_1) - 1 = 0.4745 - 1 = 0.5255$.

Option contracts can be used to establish a delta hedge. The delta, or hedge ratio, indicates the proportion of option contracts to trade to hedge a given asset portfolio. A short call option position and a long put option position both have inverse price relationships to the underlying assets and can, therefore, be used to hedge the asset portfolio.

*Example*: A covered call is created by combining one unit of the underlying asset with $1/\Delta$ short call options each of which provide the right to buy one unit of the asset.

*Example*: A portfolio of 1300 MetPath shares is to be delta-hedged through the purchase of MP Feb. 40 put options with a delta of 0.65. Since each put option is exercisable into 100 shares, the investor buys 20 put option contracts ($= (1300/100) \times 1/0.65$).

### 5.5.2 Gamma

The **gamma** ($\Gamma$) of an option indicates the change of the option's delta when the market price of the underlying asset price moves by one point. The gamma denotes the second differential coefficient of the option premium with respect to the market price of the asset (Figure 5.16):

$$\text{Gamma } (\Gamma) = \delta\Delta/\delta P$$

**Figure 5.16** Delta and gamma values of a call and put option

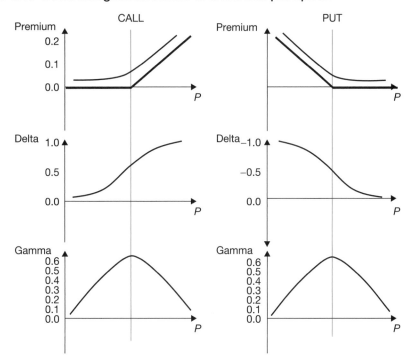

Using formulas derived from the Black–Scholes framework, this partial derivative can be expressed as the change in delta ($\Delta$) for a one point change in the price of the underlying asset:[5]

$$G_c = G_P = \Gamma = N(d_1(P+1)) - N(d_1(P)) \text{ or}$$

$$\Gamma = \frac{N'(d_1)}{(Pv\sqrt{t})}; N'(d_1) = \left(\frac{1}{\sqrt{2\pi}}\right)e^{-(-0.066)2/2}$$

where

$\pi = 3.14159$.

Hence, the gamma is equivalent to the slope of the delta curve and indicates the stability of the delta value. The lower the gamma, the less price sensitive is the delta, and consequently the delta hedge. Since the delta value is a function of the market price of the underlying asset, the delta changes over the course of the option's lifetime. Consequently, a delta hedge must be modified on a current basis to reflect the new delta values. The gamma indicates how stable the delta value of a given option contract is and therefore provides a relative measure of how frequently a delta hedge should be adjusted. The option will typically have the highest gamma value when it is at-the-money, that is, out-of-the-money or in-the-money options provide for more stable delta hedges.

*Example*: A call option (42) is quoted a premium of 1.40 at the current asset price of 41, volatility 0.20 (20%) with 90 days to maturity, i.e. $t = 0.25$, and a current interest rate ($r$) of 5%. Hence, $d_1 = (\ln(41/42) + (0.05 + 0.2^2/2)0.25)/(0.2\sqrt{0.25}) = -0.066$ and $N'(d_1) = (1/\sqrt{2\pi})e^{-(-0.066)2/2} = 0.39894 \times 0.99782 = 0.3981$. The gamma of the option is then calculated as $\Gamma = N'(d_1)/(Pv\sqrt{t}) = 0.3981/(41 \times 0.20 \times 0.5) = 0.0971$.

### 5.5.3 Theta

The **theta** (Θ) of an option, also referred to as **time decay**, indicates how much the option premium changes if and when the time to maturity is reduced by one day with no simultaneous change in the market price of the underlying asset. Hence, theta is the partial derivative of the option premium with respect to the time to maturity (Figure 5.17):

$$\text{Theta } (\Theta) = \delta O / \delta t$$

Using formulas derived from the Black–Scholes framework, this partial derivative can be expressed as:

$$Q_c = \Theta_c = -\frac{PN'(d_1)v}{(2\sqrt{t})} - rSe^{-rt}N(d_2)$$

$$Q_c = \Theta_p = -\frac{PN'(d_1)v}{(2\sqrt{t})} + rSe^{-rt}N(-d_2)$$

The theta value will normally be negative. That is, the time value is reduced toward the option's expiry date, and the relative loss of time value will increase as the time

**Figure 5.17** The time decay of options premium

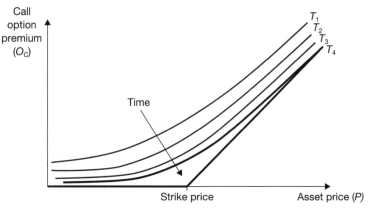

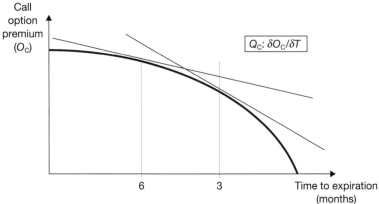

to maturity decreases. Theta tells the investor how quickly the option loses its value over time.

*Example*: Using the same example as above, $d_2 = -0.066^{-0.1} = -0.166$ and $N(d_2) = 0.4351$. The theta ($\Theta$) of the call option is then calculated as $\Theta_c = -PN'(d_1)v/(2\sqrt{t}) - rSe^{-rt}N(d_2) = -(41 \times 0.3981 \times 0.20)/1 - (0.05 \times 42 \times 0.9876 \times 0.4351) = -4.167$. That is, the annual time decay of the call option premium exceeds $4, which, assuming 252 trading days in the year, corresponds to a reduction in the option premium of $0.0165 ($= 4.167/252$) per trading day.

## 5.5.4 Vega

The **vega**, or **eta**, of an option indicates the change in the option premium when the volatility of the underlying asset price changes by one percentage point, i.e. it is the partial derivative of the option premium with respect to the volatility:

$$\text{Vega } (v) = \delta O/\delta v$$

Using formulas related to the Black–Scholes framework, this partial derivative can be expressed as:

$$v = P\sqrt{t}\, N'(d_1); N'(d_1) = \left(\frac{1}{\sqrt{2\pi}}\right)e^{-d_1^2/2}$$

In practise, the vega is mostly positive as suggested by the theoretical value. That is, the higher the volatility of the price development of the underlying asset, the higher is the option premium. Vega can indicate the relative sensitivity of different option contracts and can be used to analyse volatility spreads.

*Example*: Continuing with the example described above, the vega (v) of the call option is determined by $P\sqrt{t}N'(d_1) = 41 \times 0.5 \times 0.3981 = 8.1611$. That is, a 1% point increase in volatility from 20% to 21% would increase the call option premium by $0.0816 ($= 0.01 \times 8.1611$).

## 5.5.5 Rho

The **rho** indicates the marginal change in the option premium when the interest rate is changed by one basis point. It is the partial derivative of the option premium with respect to the risk free rate.

$$\text{rho} = \delta O/\delta r$$

Using formulas relating to the Black–Scholes framework, this partial derivative can be expressed as:

$$\text{rho}_c = Pte^{-rt}N(d_2)$$

$$\text{rho}_p = -Pte^{-rt}N(-d_2)$$

Hence, the value of rho provides a measure for the isolated interest rate sensitivity of a given option contract.

*Example*: Extending the previous example, the rho of the call option is determined by $Pte^{-rt}N(d_2) = 41 \times 0.25 \times 0.9876 \times 0.4351 = 4.4045$. That is, a one basis point increase in the risk-free interest rate will augment the theoretical call option premium by $0.044 ($= 0.01 \times 4.4045$).

## 5.6 Special option structures

There have been a variety of adaptations to the basic call and put option structures over the years. Some of the most characteristic of these are briefly introduced here.[6]

### 5.6.1 Barrier options

A **barrier option** is an ordinary option agreement with the added feature that the development of the market price beyond a second price threshold determines whether the option contract can be exercised by the holder. There are two types of barrier options: **drop-in** and **drop-out**. A **drop-in call** option can be exercised if once before the maturity date the market price has been below the second price level. The second price is lower than the option strike price. A **drop-in put** option can be exercised if once before the maturity date the market price has exceeded the second price level. The second price is above the option strike price. A **drop-out call** option cannot be exercised if once before the maturity date the market rate has been below the second price level. A **drop-out put** option cannot be exercised if once before the maturity date the market price has exceeded the second price level.

### 5.6.2 Look-back options

A **look-back option** is an option agreement that at its final maturity date will be settled at the market price during the life of the option, which is most favourable to the option holder (normal options settle at the prevailing market price at maturity).

### 5.6.3 Average rate options

An **average rate option** agreement, or **arrow**, is settled at final maturity at the average market price during the life of the option agreement. The price average can be based on daily, weekly, or monthly market quotes. This type of option can be useful in hedging an institution's exposure that arises on a current basis, such as overdraft facilities and the like.

## 5.7 Product developments

During the late 1980s and the following decade, the market for currency options was refined further. Some of the product developments catered to clients engaged in competitive bidding situations and provided more applicable option features to these situations. Other product enhancements represent different implicit double option strategies, which through their structure reduced the up-front premium payable on the option hedge. In the competitive market many of the new products had their own peculiarities whose aim was to differentiate the option product from that offered by competitors. In reality the products are to a large extent based on the same core elements.

### 5.7.1 Tender to contract

The **tender to contract** solves a problem for the corporation that wants to hedge a potential currency exposure arising in connection with the submission of commercial bids. As already discussed, currency options are ideal in such situations but the full hedging cost might turn out to be too expensive if the chance of a rejection is high due to the competitive situation. The tender to contract (TTC) option allows the corporate customer to pay a certain percentage of the option premium, such as 10%, the remaining 90% being payable if the tender bid is accepted. The bank offering the TTC option will then have to sell the same option to other corporations involved in the competitive bidding to cover part of the total option premium through risk diversification. At least the bank should be fairly sure that the option has been sold to the corporation that is eventually awarded the contract, in order to be sure to cover the full premium (otherwise the option represents a potential loss to the writer). Conversely, if the TTC option is sold to the corporation that wins the tender then the aggregate premiums from the sale of the option to the other bidders represent an additional and excess profit to the seller.

### 5.7.2 Scout

The **scout** is a variation of the same theme. Here the contract awarder, which could be an overseas government or public entity, buys the option from the bank and re-offers a split option to all the tenderers on the project. Thus the bank is sure that the entity that eventually is awarded the project is among the option buyers, and hence the split premium becomes more competitive for the tenderers. On the contract award date, the successful tenderer is also awarded the option, thereby providing full coverage for the foreign exchange risk. If, for example, the project is being awarded by five firms then each firm will pay 20% of the normal currency option premium.

### 5.7.3 Option-on-an-option

The **option-on-an-option**, often termed a **compound option**, can serve the same purpose. If the underlying currency option is in-the-money, the bank writing the compound option must expect that the holder may want to buy the currency option and exercise it at a profit. Hence, the potential cost of a compound option is lower than or equal to the premium on the underlying currency option. Since there is a chance that the holder might not need or want the currency hedge represented by the currency option, in case the contract is not awarded, the premium is lower than the premium on the underlying option.

## 5.8 Double option products

A range of these modified options products are construed through different combinations of call and put contracts with different strike prices, maturities, etc. The following introduces the most common of these structures.

**Figure 5.18** Profit and loss profile of a cylinder option

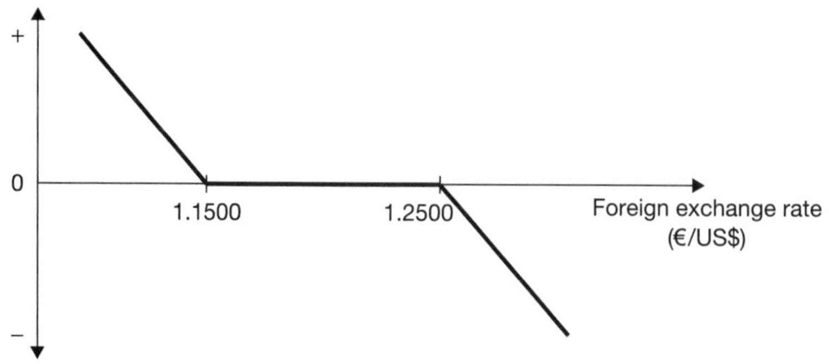

### 5.8.1 Cylinder option

In a **cylinder option**, a receiver of a foreign currency (long position) buys put options on the foreign currency to hedge against a drop in the foreign exchange rate. At the same time the hedger writes call options on the foreign currency at a higher strike price. He pays no premiums on the cylinder because the strike prices on the two underlying option contracts are determined so that the premium paid for the purchase of the put equals the premium received from the sale of the call. In the cylinder, a short currency position is covered by buying call options on the foreign currency and writing put options at a lower strike price.

*Example*: A French company wants to hedge US dollar receivables due in six months (a long currency position). A cylinder option offers rate protection through a US dollar put at 1.1500 €/US$. However, if the US dollar foreign exchange rate increases above 1.1575 €/US$, the hedger must cover a call option. The hedger pays no premium on the cylinder.

If at the expiry date in six months' time the US dollar is below 1.1500 €/US$, the US dollar receivables are converted at 1.1500 €/US$. If the foreign exchange rate is between 1.1500 and 1.2500 €/US$, the US dollar receivables are converted at the prevailing €/US$ spot rate. If the spot foreign exchange rate turns out to be above 1.2500 €/US$, the US dollar receivables are converted at 1.2500 €/US$. The profit and loss profile of the covered position is illustrated in Figure 5.18.

The cylinder option attracts hedgers who cannot be convinced to pay an up-front premium for a single option hedge. Hence, they obtain a downside hedge for free by giving up the upside potential in the underlying currency position over a certain exchange rate.

### 5.8.2 Range forward

The so-called **range forward contract** is a variation of the same option product. The contract specifies two foreign exchange rates determining the top and bottom of a range within which the hedger can take advantage of a positive market movement. That is, the currency amount is exchanged at the current spot foreign exchange rate, while maintaining a minimum (the bottom) and a maximum (the top) foreign exchange rate at which the currency exchange can take place. In practice the hedger will choose either the top or the bottom of the range, while the bank for

**Figure 5.19** Range forward contracts

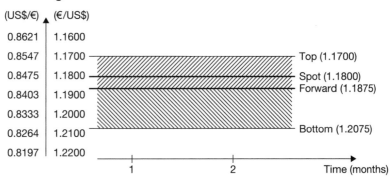

a given contract maturity will specify the range that applies to a no-cost range forward contract.

*Example*: A US company has to purchase euros in two months' time. The current spot rate is 1.1800 €/US$ (0.8475 US$/€) and the two-month forward rate is 1.1875 €/US$ (0.8421 US$/€), which is more favourable than the spot rate. Still, the company is uncertain about the trend and therefore wants a flexible downside cover.

The company wants protection against a low-end dollar foreign exchange rate, say at 1.1700 €/US$ (0.8547 US$/€). The bank then defines the zero-cost price range to be between 1.1700 €/US$ and 1.2075 €/US$ (0.8282 US$/€). In other words, 1.1700 €/US$ is the highest price the hedger will want to pay for the euros. If the spot foreign exchange rate increases above 1.1700 €/US$, the hedger will exchange currency at the spot rate, but never at a rate exceeding 1.1700 €/US$. Therefore, if the foreign exchange rate is above the forward foreign exchange rate of 1.1875 €/US$ at expiry, the hedger will incur a gain as compared to the situation where a full cover at the outright forward rate had been obtained (Figure 5.19).

### 5.8.3 Participating forward

Like the range forward, the **participating forward** contract or **forward plus** contract requires no up-front premium payment. The contract constitutes a forward exchange of currencies at an agreed maximum rate. The buyer of the contract pays for the rate protection by reserving less than 100% of the upside rate potential in the option contract. The level of the guaranteed rate depends on the percentage of participation in the upside rate potential.

*Example*: A Swedish corporation has to buy US dollars in three months' time. The bank offers the following three-month maximum forward rates with a corresponding share of the upside rate potential on the currency option.

| *Forward rate* (SEK/US$) | *Share* (%) |
|---|---|
| 7.2000 | 31 |
| 7.8000 | 53 |
| 7.9000 | 75 |

The corporation chooses the forward rate of 7.8000 (SEK/US$) and obtains a hedge position as illustrated in Figure 5.20.

**Figure 5.20** Participating forward contract

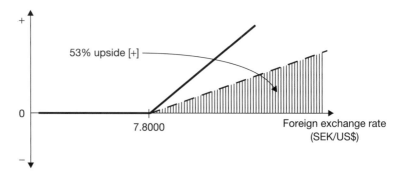

## 5.8.4 Break forward

Another variation is the **break forward** contract, or **fox**, which is a forward foreign exchange agreement that can be unwound at the buyer's choice at a predetermined rate. The buyer of a break forward pays a spread on the outright forward rate, against which the bank determines a break rate. The break rate defines the foreign exchange rate at which the buyer can unwind the forward agreement.

*Example*: A UK-based company is to purchase US dollars in three months' time. The company buys a break forward contract at 1.4250 US$/£ stg. (0.7017 £ stg./US$) from a bank at a break rate of 1.4600 US$/£ stg. (0.6849 £ stg./US$).

The forward foreign exchange rate in the market is 1.4450 US$/£ stg. (0.6920 £ stg./US$), so in this case the break forward rate is about 70 pips below the quoted outright rate and about 170 pips below the current spot rate. If the foreign exchange spot rate at expiry is below the break rate, the US dollars are bought at the fixed rate of 1.4250 US$/£ stg. If the foreign exchange spot rate at expiry is above the break rate of 1.4600 US$/£ stg., the company will buy dollars spot and then sell to the bank at the break rate, thereby scoring a net gain on the foreign exchange rate differential.

## 5.9 Interest rate option agreements

With the emergence of active financial futures markets, e.g. in US Treasuries, eurodollar deposits, pound sterling gilts, etc., the financial intermediaries have been able to provide different types of interest rate hedging services. The financial institutions, in turn, will hedge part of their exposures by taking up corresponding positions in exchange traded financial futures and option contracts. The financial intermediary in effect assumes the basis risk associated with the financial futures and as experienced exchange dealers, they handle the intricacies associated with dealings in financial futures. To many hedgers these are important conveniences. The interest rate hedging services offered by the financial institutions can guarantee a maximum future interest rate for borrowers or a minimum future interest rate for investors. The OTC market also offers double option structures to hedge long and short interest rate gaps.

**Figure 5.21** Hedging with a ceiling rate agreement

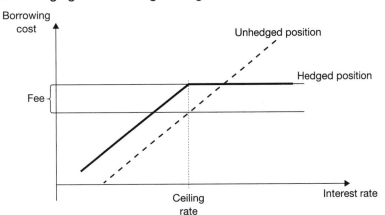

### 5.9.1 Ceiling rate agreements

A **ceiling rate agreement**, or **cap** provides the holder with a hedge against an increase in the interest rate level without actual delivery of funds taking place. This type of agreement will guarantee a maximum borrowing rate for a period of up to ten years. For this type of hedge the institutional client will pay an up-front fee, sometimes payable quarterly in arrears, quoted as a percentage p.a. on the contract amount. The agreement is often settled quarterly, that is, if at the end of each quarter the actual borrowing rate has exceeded the agreed rate, the bank will pay the client the difference in the interest amount. If the actual borrowing rate is below the agreed rate, nothing will happen (Figure 5.21).

Settlement:

$$S = \frac{(MR - CR) \times A \times T}{36\ 000} \quad \text{when } MR > CR$$

$$S = 0 \quad \text{when } MR < CR$$

where

$S$ = interest settlement amount;
$MR$ = market interest rate (reference rate);
$CR$ = ceiling rate (cap);
$A$ = contract amount;
$T$ = number of days in the settlement period.

This type of hedging service is interesting not only to institutions planning to raise funds and thereby wanting to establish an upper limit on the future interest expense. It is also interesting to an institution that fears the effect of an expected increase in interest rates on its already existing floating rate debt.

*Example*: A company has floating rate debt of US$10 000 000 with a final bullet repayment maturing five years down the road. The loan was obtained at a rate of LIBOR + $^{3}/_{4}$% payable quarterly in arrears. Management fears increasing interest rates. So the company buys a US$10 000 000 ceiling rate agreement that guarantees that LIBOR will not exceed a certain level over the next eight quarters.

**Figure 5.22** Hedging with a floor rate agreement

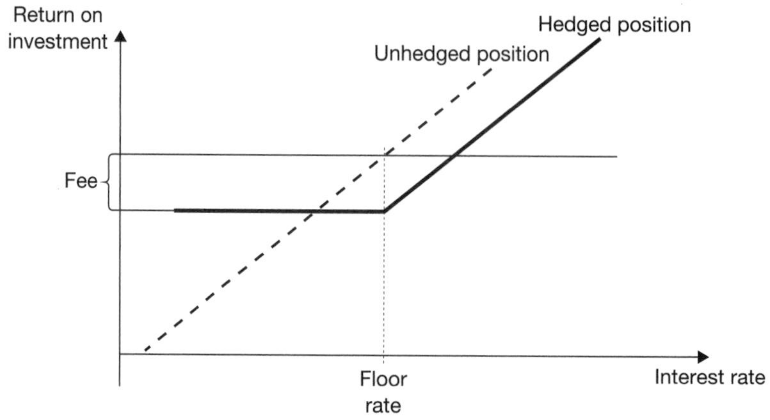

5.9.2 Floor rate agreements

A **floor rate agreement** provides the holder with a hedge against a decrease in the investment rate. That is, the holder can be guaranteed a minimum return on a certain investment portfolio in a period of up to say ten years. The agreement is settled quarterly. If at the end of the quarter the actual investment rate is below the agreed rate, the bank will pay the difference in interest amount. If the actual investment rate is above the agreed rate, nothing happens (Figure 5.22). For this type of interest rate hedge, the holder will pay an up-front fee potentially arranged for payment quarterly in arrears. The fee is usually quoted as a percentage p.a. calculated on the contract amount.

Settlement:

$$S = \frac{(FR - MR) \times A \times T}{36\,000} \quad \text{when } MR < FR$$

$$S = 0 \quad \text{when } MR > FR$$

where

$S$ = interest settlement amount;
$MR$ = market interest rate (reference rate);
$FR$ = floor rate;
$A$ = contract amount;
$T$ = number of days in the settlement period.

The agreement is of interest to any institution that has to periodically place excess liquidity or that maintains a fixed maturity floating rate investment and would like to secure a minimum return on the investment in a falling interest rate environment.

*Example*: A commercial bank is about to extend a two-year floating rate loan of US$15 000 000 at LIBOR + 1% with interest payable quarterly in arrears, and the management board takes the view that the dollar interest rate will continue to decline. The bank then buys a floor rate agreement of US$15 000 000, which guarantees the institution a minimum interest rate on the future loan.

**Figure 5.23** Hedging with a collar rate agreement (borrower)

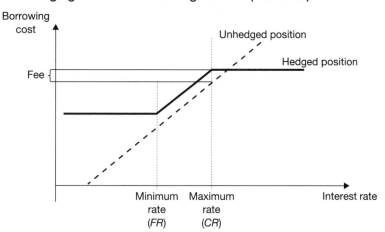

### 5.9.3 Collar rate agreements

While a ceiling rate agreement guarantees a maximum borrowing rate and gives the holder the full benefit of a drop in the interest rate below the maximum rate, the borrower might take the view that the likelihood of a drop in the interest rate is negligible. So, he or she might be inclined to buy a combined ceiling rate and floor rate agreement in the form of a **collar rate agreement**. That is, if the rate exceeds the maximum guaranteed level, such as 6% p.a. for a five-year period, the bank will compensate the holder quarterly for the difference in the interest amount. However, if the interest rate drops below, say 4% p.a. over the same five-year period, the company will compensate the bank quarterly by the difference in the interest amount. Hence the buyer is guaranteed a maximum borrowing rate of 10%. If the interest rate is between 4 and 6% p.a., the buyer will take full advantage of the lower interest rate, but if it drops below 4% p.a., he or she will incur a loss that counter weighs the savings in interest expense (Figure 5.23).

Settlement:

$$S = \frac{(MR - CR) \times A \times T}{36\ 000} \quad \text{when } MR > CR$$

$$S = 0 \quad \text{when } FR < MR < CR$$

$$S = \frac{(FR - MR) \times A \times T}{36\ 000} \quad \text{when } MR < FR$$

where

$S$ = settlement amount;
$MR$ = market interest rate (reference rate);
$CR$ = maximum rate (ceiling);
$FR$ = minimum rate (floor);
$A$ = contract amount;
$T$ = number of days in the settlement period.

While a floor rate agreement guarantees a minimum investment rate and gives the holder the full benefit of an increase in the interest rate above the minimum rate, the investor takes the view that an increase in the interest rate is very unlikely. In that case, he or she might be willing to buy a combination of a floor rate agreement and a ceiling rate agreement in the form of a **collar rate agreement**. That is, if the interest rate is below the minimum rate of, say, 5% p.a. then the bank will compensate the holder quarterly by paying the difference in the interest amount. If the interest rate is between 5 and 7% p.a., the holder will take full advantage of the higher interest rate. If the interest rate exceeds 7% p.a., the holder will compensate the bank quarterly for the difference in the interest amount (Figure 5.24).

Settlement:

$$S = \frac{(FR - MR) \times A \times T}{36\ 000} \quad \text{when } MR < FR$$

$$S = 0 \quad \text{when } FR < MR < CR$$

$$S = \frac{(MR - CR) \times A \times T}{36\ 000} \quad \text{when } MR > CR$$

where

$S$ = settlement amount;
$MR$ = market interest rate (reference rate);
$CR$ = maximum rate (ceiling);
$FR$ = minimum rate (floor);
$A$ = contract amount;
$T$ = number of days in the settlement period.

One advantage of the collar rate agreements is that the front-end fee is lower than the fees on the corresponding ceiling rate and floor rate agreements (this type of interest rate contract corresponds to the cylinder option in the foreign exchange market). Keep in mind, however, that collar rate agreements do not provide full hedges to the holder.

**Figure 5.24** Hedging with a collar rate agreement (investor)

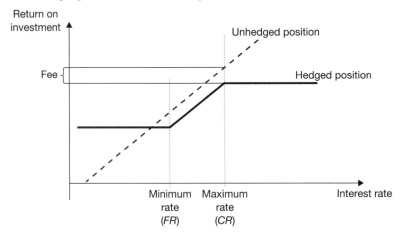

## 5.9.4 Captions

**Captions** are the debt market's parallel to the currency market's option-on-an-option concept. A caption is an option giving the holder the right to acquire or sell a ceiling rate (cap) or a floor rate agreement with a predetermined strike, maturity, interest period, and contract amount.

● A call caption on a ceiling (cap) gives the holder the right to buy a ceiling rate agreement.
● A put caption on a ceiling (cap) gives the holder the right to sell a ceiling rate agreement.
● A call caption on a floor rate gives the holder the right to buy a floor rate agreement.
● A put caption on a floor rate gives the holder the right to sell a floor rate agreement.

Normally captions are European-type options. The contracts are primarily used in connection with public bidding situations, where the submitter of a tender wants to ensure that project funding can be assumed at a guaranteed maximum interest expense in case the project is awarded to them. Consequently, most captions are call captions on a ceiling rate.

## Conclusion

OTC forward and option agreements in many ways provide the hedger a flexibility that cannot be met by engaging in exchange-traded futures and options contracts, notably with regard to maturities and quotes on cross-currencies. On the other hand, OTC agreements are not as easily reversed as the highly liquid exchange traded futures and options. Although a number of financial institutions offer clients the opportunity to write options over-the-counter this element of the market is still under-developed. However, the OTC market for forwards and options provides a useful service to institutional hedgers as reflected in the continued growth of market activities.

## Summary

● Many derivatives linked to foreign exchange rates, interest rates, and other financial prices are offered by financial intermediaries in the over-the-counter market.
● The forward foreign exchange market allows institutions to lock-in the foreign exchange rate on currency receivables and payables due at future dates.
● Institutions can use forward rate agreements to lock-in future interest rates where a borrower buys an FRA and an investor sells an FRA to establish the interest rate hedge.
● The foreign exchange market offers a variety of options based agreements tailored to the requirements of multinational institutions operating across global markets.
● The money market offers a variety of options based interest rate agreements tailored to the specific needs of institutional borrowers and investors.
● Options are typically assessed on the basis of the numerical Black–Scholes formulas or the development of binomial evaluation models.

## Questions

5.1 Explain the major differences between exchange traded contracts and over-the-counter agreements.

5.2 Explain the mechanics of a forward rate agreement (FRA).

5.3 Explain how it is possible to create a synthetic forward rate agreement.

5.4 Mention the factors that influence the value of an option and explain why.

5.5 Explain the rationale underlying the Black–Scholes option valuation technique.

5.6 Discuss the assumptions associated with the Black–Scholes framework.

5.7 Explain the rationale underlying the binomial option valuation model.

5.8 Outline the relationship between call and put option premiums.

5.9 Explain what the delta ($\Delta$) of an option is and what it can be used for.

5.10 Explain what the gamma ($\Gamma$) of an option is and what it can be used for.

5.11 Describe the rationale behind a cylinder option.

5.12 Outline the potential advantages of ceiling and floor rate agreements.

5.13 What is an option-on-an-option?

5.14 What is a caption?

## Exercises

5.1 Assume the following two-way bid and offer prices on the euro/US dollar foreign exchange rate and the spot money market rates.

| | Bid | Offer |
|---|---|---|
| Spot foreign exchange rate (€/US$) | 1.1585 | 1.1595 |
| Three-month euro rate (% p.a.) | 2.75 | 2.85 |
| Three-month US dollar rate (% p.a.) | 4.75 | 4.85 |

(a) Determine the US dollar bid and offer swap against the euro.
(b) Calculate the three-month €/US$ outright rates.

5.2 Assume the following bid and offer rates in the spot money market and consider the forward forward transactions needed to create synthetic forward rate agreements.

| Money market rates | Bid | Offer |
|---|---|---|
| Three months | 2.55 | 2.65 |
| Six months | 2.80 | 2.90 |

(a) Determine the implied bid rate on a three-month forward rate agreement in three months.
(b) Determine the implied offer rate on a three-month forward rate agreement in three months.

5.3 Consider the following market situation for a given asset.

| | |
|---|---|
| Current market price: | 55.0 |
| Volatility of price development: | 30% |
| Risk-free rate: | 3% |

(a) Use the Black–Scholes formula to calculate the option premium on an Asset (56) call option.

(b) Use the Black–Scholes formula to calculate the option premium on an Asset (54) put option.

5.4 Based on the information provided in Exercise 5.3, please do the following.

(a) Use the Black–Scholes framework to calculate the delta ($\Delta$) of the Asset (56) call.

(b) Use the Black–Scholes framework to calculate the delta ($\Delta$) of the Asset (54) put.

## Notes

[1] See, for example, Andersen, T. J. and Hasan, R. (1989), *Interest Rate Risk Management*, IFR Books.

[2] See Black, F. and Scholes, M. (1973), 'The pricing of options and corporate liabilities', *Journal of Political Economy*, **81**, 637–54.

[3] Refer to standard finance textbooks for similar discussions of the call option valuation, e.g. Sharpe, W. F., Alexander, G. J. and Bailey, J. V. (1999), *Investments*, 10th edn, Prentice-Hall.

[4] For a presentation of the binomial option pricing model, see, for example, Cox, J. O. and Rubinstein, M. (1985), *Options Markets*, Prentice-Hall.

[5] See, for example, Hull, J. C. (2000), *Options, Futures and Other Derivatives*, 4th edn, Prentice-Hall.

[6] For a discussion of exotic option structures, see, for example, McDonald, R. L. (2003), *Derivatives Markets*, Addison Wesley, and Jarrow, R. and Turnbull, S. (2000), *Derivative Securities*, 2nd edn, South-Western.

# Chapter 6

# Swap agreements and other derivatives

## Objectives

- Describe the evolution of the swap market
- Discuss common currency and interest rate swaps
- Consider market imperfections that drive swap transactions
- Present second and third generation swap related derivatives
- Outline credit default swaps and hybrid securities
- Introduce alternative risk-transfer instruments

The swap agreement as a derivative instrument has evolved over the past 25 years from predominantly constituting unique bilateral or multiparty transactions to constitute highly liquid markets in standardized transactions for the most common types of interest rate and currency exchanges. The use of financial swap structures has been extended gradually from the exchange of interest rate and currency exposures to comprise other types of risk including investment returns, default risk, credit exposures, and catastrophe-linked risks. The swap agreement provides a relatively flexible legal framework that can be used to organize and structure the exchange of a variety of financial exposures and therefore has become a popular way to formalize these exchanges.

In the early 1980s investment bankers and brokerage houses developed techniques that enabled institutions to switch assets and liabilities from one type of interest rate basis into another and from one currency denomination to another. At first, the market evolved in the form of counter-party transactions where two, three, or more institutional counterparts with different asset and liability profiles were matched to provide each institution with a more suitable exposure. Such arrangements could involve, for example, a Japanese airline, an American shipping company, and an Asian sovereign borrower, just to mention one possible constellation. In general, the more contacts with potential global counterparts, the higher the chance for a successful match of interests in the swaps. This obviously favoured large international financial institutions in the early development of the swap market. As transaction volume increased and the concept has become more familiar to possible benefactors, an active interbank market has evolved for generic swap structures reflecting the most common exchanges of financial exposures.

## 6.1 Interest rate swap agreements

By entering into an **interest rate swap agreement**, an institution can switch an asset or liability from a fixed rate basis to a floating rate basis in the same currency or vice versa. By combining two institutions with opposite interests, a financial intermediary would be able to arrange a swap transaction.

*Example*: A construction company has raised a US$40 000 000 five-year floating rate debt to fund a future project and would like to lock-in the future interest expense related to the project. Conversely, a commercial bank has launched a five-year fixed coupon eurodollar issue of US$40 000 000 to fund its portfolio of floating rate loans. These two counterparts can be combined in an interest rate swap through an intermediary and obtain a type of liability that is more suitable for both of entities.

In principle, this is done by having each of the two institutions service the interest payments of the other party throughout the life of the loans. Since the two liabilities have the same currency denomination, there does not have to be any exchange of principal in the swap. The construction company pays fixed rate interest to the intermediary, and the intermediary pays the floating rate interest to the company to service its floating rate liability. The commercial bank pays floating rate interest to the intermediary, and the intermediary pays fixed interest to the commercial bank to service its fixed rate liability. In this way, the financial institution acts as an intermediary funnelling the interest payments between the two counterparts. In reality, the counterparts will only exchange the difference in interest amounts at each semi-annual settlement period. Nonetheless, the outcome is that the construction company effectively has obtained a fixed rate liability and the commercial bank has obtained a floating rate liability thereby resulting in a better match of the interest rate basis of their assets and liabilities.

The two counterparts, who typically remain unknown to each other, will deal solely with the intermediary, and their contractual obligations regarding the swap transaction are only made against the intermediary. Conversely, the intermediary assumes the counter-party risk of the two parties. The intermediary will sometimes charge a front-end fee, fixed as a percentage of the transaction amount, as compensation for the brokerage function and the counter-party risk associated with the transaction (see Figure 6.1).

**Figure 6.1** Interest rate swaps

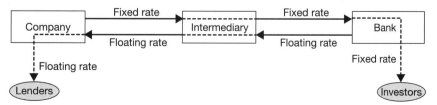

**Table 6.1** US dollar-denominated interest rate swaps (spread over comparable Treasury yield)

| Maturity | Bid | Offer |
|---|---|---|
| Three years | 0.50 | 0.70 |

Often two counterparts with exactly opposing interests cannot be readily found and, therefore, several institutions could be combined to complete a transaction. As the transaction volume has increased, it has also become common practice for the intermediaries to run short-term open positions, which to some extent can be hedged on financial futures exchanges and the FRA market. As this practice expanded, the generic interest rate swaps have developed into active dealer-based interbank markets where the swap transactions are quoted as two-way prices. Today, two-way bid and offer quotes on interest rate swaps are provided by financial intermediaries in the major currency areas. The quotes are normally based on a benchmark fixed-rate indicator in the particular currency area. For example, interest rate swaps in US dollars are typically quoted around the going yield on US treasury bills, notes, and bonds (Table 6.1).[1]

The bid rate indicates the basis point spread over the yield on the US treasury with the corresponding maturity, and indicates the fixed rate interest payment the quoting bank is willing to pay for six-month LIBOR-based interest payments. Similarly, the offer rate indicates the fixed-rate spread over treasuries the quoting bank wants to receive from the counterpart to accept the delivery of LIBOR-based interest payments. Hence, the US dollar swap yield curve is linked to the shape of the yield curve on US treasuries including the swap spread (Figure 6.2).

A three-year US dollar interest rate swap quoted as 0.50–0.70 indicates that the intermediary bids for dollar floating rate interest payments at LIBOR against payment of fixed rate interest payments at the going yield on the three-year US treasury note plus 50 basis points and offers dollar floating rate interest payments at LIBOR against receipt of fixed rate interest payments at the US treasury yield plus 70 basis

**Figure 6.2** Treasury and swap yield curves

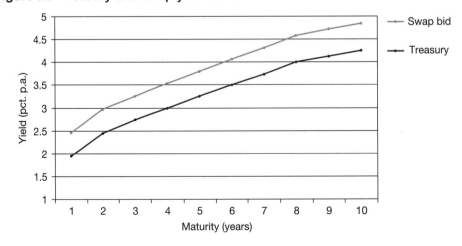

**Figure 6.3** Interest rate swap hedge (institutional investor)

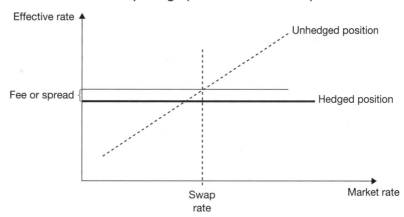

points. Hence, an institutional investor with a portfolio of three-year floating rate notes can lock-in the return on this portfolio over its lifetime through the engagement in an interest rate swap whereby the investor provides the quoting bank with LIBOR payments against receipt of fixed-rate payments tied to the current yield on the three-year benchmark bond. Normally when the intermediating bank provides a swap transaction to a corporate counterpart, it will charge a front-end fee, or subtract a spread from the fixed rate payment, as compensation for the intermediation service and the assumed counter-party risk. The effective hedging position established by an institutional investor is shown in Figure 6.3.

Conversely, a corporate borrower largely funded through a portfolio of floating rate syndicated loans can lock-in the interest rate expense on this debt liability through engagement in an interest rate swap whereby the borrower receives floating rate LIBOR-based interest payments from the quoting bank against payment of fixed-rate interest payments tied to the current yield on the benchmark bond. Again, the bank will often charge a front-end fee or adds a spread to the fixed rate quote when it provides the swap to a commercial counterpart. The hedging position of a corporate borrower is illustrated in Figure 6.4.

**Figure 6.4** Interest rate swap hedge (corporate borrower)

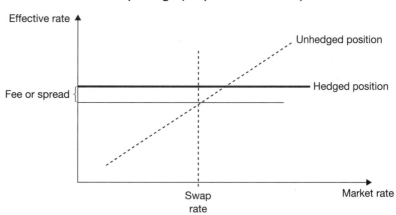

The treasury yield rate indication, such as the resulting fixed rate of 4.375% in the example, is commonly quoted on a semi-annual interest rate basis, because the interest amounts most often are exchanged every six months. To convert this into a comparable annual interest rate basis, the following calculation must be performed: $((1 + 4.375/200)^2 - 1)100 = 4.42\%$ p.a. This rate now corresponds to an annual bond basis, i.e. 360/360 days, like the norm in the corporate bond market. Therefore, if the rate is to be converted into a comparable money market rate, which is based on actual days in a year over 360 days, i.e. 365/360 days, the following rate adjustment must be made: $(4.42 \times 360/365) = 4.36\%$ p.a. The conversion between semi-annual and annual compound interest can be formalized in the following way:

$$i_s = \left( \left( \frac{i_a}{100} + 1 \right)^{1/2} - 1 \right) 200$$

$$i_a = \left( \left( \frac{i_s}{200} + 1 \right)^{2} - 1 \right) 100$$

where

$i_s$ = semi-annual interest rate;
$i_a$ = Annual compound interest rate.

The fixed rate bond basis for most currencies, US dollar, euro, pound sterling, Swiss franc, and so on, is calculated on the basis of a year with 12 months of 30 days each, i.e. 360/360 days per year, whereas rates in the money market are based on actual number of days in a 360 day year, i.e. 365/360 days per year. Hence, the conversion between annual bond basis (*BB*) and money market (*MM*) basis can be formalized in the following way:

$$MM = BB \times \frac{360}{365}$$

$$BB = MM \times \frac{365}{360}$$

Interest rate swaps are quoted for the major currencies, e.g. US dollar, Euro, pound sterling, Swiss franc, Japanese yen, etc., and these prices are published in the principal international business newspapers on a daily basis (Figure 6.5).

As will be observed from the published quotes, there is really no common standard for publicly available quotes. The US dollar interest rate swaps are quoted on an annual money market basis, that is, actual days over 360 days, and against three-month LIBOR. In contrast, the pound sterling and Japanese yen interest rate swaps are quoted as a semi-annual rate based on actual days over 360 days against six-month LIBOR, while the euro and Swiss franc interest rate swaps are quoted on an annual bond basis, i.e. 360 days over 360 days, against six-month LIBOR.[2] This amalgam of quotation bases obviously accentuates the need to convert the prices into comparable formats.

*Example*: Assume that finance departments adopt the annual money market rate as the basis for rate comparisons, which is commonly the case. The US dollar interest rate swaps are

**Figure 6.5** Interest rate swap quotes

## Interest rate swaps — FT

| Jun 17 | Euro-€ | | £ Stlg | | SwFr | | US $ | | Yen | |
|---|---|---|---|---|---|---|---|---|---|---|
| | Bid | Ask | Bid | Ask | Bid | Ask | Bid | Ask | Bid | Ask |
| 1 year | 2.49 | 2.52 | 5.38 | 5.39 | 1.08 | 1.14 | 2.40 | 2.43 | 0.11 | 0.14 |
| 2 year | 2.97 | 3.00 | 5.51 | 5.55 | 1.60 | 1.68 | 3.22 | 3.25 | 0.33 | 0.36 |
| 3 year | 3.33 | 3.36 | 5.59 | 5.63 | 1.94 | 2.02 | 3.75 | 3.78 | 0.58 | 0.61 |
| 4 year | 3.61 | 3.64 | 5.61 | 5.66 | 2.21 | 2.29 | 4.12 | 4.15 | 0.84 | 0.86 |
| 5 year | 3.82 | 3.85 | 5.62 | 5.67 | 2.43 | 2.51 | 4.40 | 4.43 | 1.09 | 1.12 |
| 6 year | 4.00 | 4.03 | 5.62 | 5.66 | 2.61 | 2.69 | 4.63 | 4.66 | 1.33 | 1.36 |
| 7 year | 4.16 | 4.19 | 5.61 | 5.66 | 2.75 | 2.84 | 4.82 | 4.84 | 1.54 | 1.57 |
| 8 year | 4.29 | 4.32 | 5.59 | 5.64 | 2.88 | 2.96 | 4.96 | 5.00 | 1.71 | 1.74 |
| 9 year | 4.39 | 4.42 | 5.58 | 5.63 | 2.98 | 3.06 | 5.09 | 5.12 | 1.84 | 1.88 |
| 10 year | 4.48 | 4.51 | 5.57 | 5.62 | 3.08 | 3.15 | 5.20 | 5.22 | 1.96 | 1.91 |
| 12 year | 4.62 | 4.65 | 5.53 | 5.59 | 3.21 | 3.31 | 5.37 | 5.40 | 2.15 | 2.10 |
| 15 year | 4.78 | 4.81 | 5.46 | 5.55 | 3.38 | 3.48 | 5.56 | 5.59 | 2.35 | 2.31 |
| 20 year | 4.93 | 4.96 | 5.35 | 5.48 | 3.56 | 3.66 | 5.72 | 5.75 | 2.56 | 2.53 |
| 25 year | 5.00 | 5.03 | 5.25 | 5.38 | 3.66 | 3.77 | 5.77 | 5.80 | 2.67 | 2.64 |
| 30 year | 5.02 | 5.05 | 5.17 | 5.29 | 3.71 | 3.81 | 5.78 | 5.81 | 2.71 | 2.69 |

Bid and ask rates as of close of London business. US $ is quoted annual money actual/360 basis against 3 months LIBOR, £ and Yen quoted on a semi-annual actual/365 basis against 6 months LIBOR, Euro/Swiss Franc quoted on annual bond 30/360 basis against 6 month Euribor/LIBOR with the exception of the 1 year rate which is quoted against 3 month Euribor/LIBOR.    Source: ICAP plc.

*Source: Financial Times*, Friday, June 18, 2004.

already quoted on this basis, probably for the very same reason. To convert the pound sterling and Japanese yen interest rate swaps to a comparable basis, however, we must change the semi-annual rate quote to an annual rate. For example, the one-year £ stg. bid quote would become $((1 + 5.38/200)^2 - 1)100 = 5.45\%$ on an annual rate basis. To convert the euro and Swiss franc interest rate swaps to the same basis we must change the annual bond basis to annual money market basis. Hence, for example, the one-year € bid quote would become $(2.49 \times 360/365) = 2.46\%$ p.a., and so forth.

### 6.1.1  Interest rate basis swaps

Institutions that engage in transactions with different interest rate basis on assets and liabilities incur an interest rate basis gap. This could, for example, comprise a commercial bank that makes corporate loans based on the bank's prime rate while funding this loan portfolio on a floating rate LIBOR basis. Usually changes in the prime rate lag somewhat behind changes in the short-term money market rates, and these changes will be less frequent than the day-to-day fluctuations in money market rates. Hence, a bank lending on these terms can get into an interest rate squeeze, e.g. in an increasing interest rate scenario. The bank can eliminate this exposure by

**Figure 6.6** Three-way interest rate basis swap

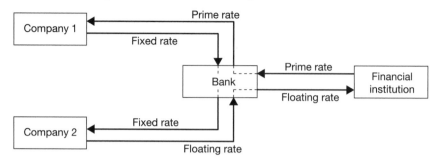

engaging in a prime-LIBOR interest rate swap. The intermediating bank that provides the interest rate basis swap might be in a position where the swap transaction with the corporation can be covered through reverse interest rate flows associated with two other counterparts (Figure 6.6).

## 6.2 Currency swap agreements

By entering into a currency swap agreement an institution can switch an asset or a liability from one currency to another. The swap transaction can be done on the same interest rate basis, that is, fixed into fixed rate or floating into floating rate, or the swap can switch from a fixed interest basis to a floating rate basis in another currency denomination, or switch from a floating rate basis into a fixed rate basis in another foreign currency (Table 6.2).

The currencies are swapped initially through a normal spot foreign exchange transaction, so each of the counterparts has full availability of the currencies they are seeking at the outset. Throughout the life of the swap transaction, each of the counterparts, in effect, act as if they pay the other party's interest obligations,

**Table 6.2** Summary of interest rate and currency swaps

---

**Interest rate swaps**
● Fixed interest payments into floating rate interest payments in the same currency, or
● Floating interest payments into fixed interest payments in the same currency, or
● Interest payments on an interest rate basis into another interest rate basis in the same currency

**Currency swaps**
One currency into another currency, and
● Fixed interest payments into fixed interest payments in the other currency, or
● Floating interest payments into floating interest payments in the other currency, or
● Fixed interest payments into floating interest payments in the other currency, or
● Floating interest payments into fixed interest payments in the other currency, or
● Interest payments on one interest rate basis into another interest rate basis in the other currency

---

although the swap agreement normally outlines a method of exchanging only the difference in the interest amounts. At maturity the currencies are swapped back to the original currencies through a forward foreign exchange transaction, usually at the initial spot exchange rate.

*Example*: A public institution has acquired a seven-year fixed coupon US$40 million loan. It would like to change this loan into a floating rate Swiss franc liability to diversify the loan portfolio across different currencies and take advantage of an expected decrease in the Swiss interest rate level. Concurrently a corporate entity has just issued a seven-year Swiss franc 50 million floating rate note. It seeks to convert this loan into a fixed rate US dollar liability to lock-in the funding cost and also match the company's dollar receivables.

In this situation the currencies are exchanged initially at the spot exchange rate of 1.2500 SFr/US$ (0.8000 US$/SFr). The public institution pays US$40 000 000 to the intermediary against receipt of SFr50 000 000. Conversely, the corporate entity pays SFr50 000 000 to the intermediary against receipt of US$40 000 000. At this point the two counterparts have the currencies they want (Figure 6.7-1).

Throughout the seven years until the final maturity of the two loans, the public institution makes floating rate Swiss franc denominated interest payments to the intermediary against receipt of fixed rate US dollar interest from the intermediary to service the fixed rate dollar loan. The corporate entity will effectively act as if it pays fixed rate dollar interest to the intermediary against receipt of floating rate Swiss franc interest payments from the intermediary to service the floating rate Swiss franc loan (Figure 6.7-2).

### Figure 6.7 Interest rate and currency swap

1. Receiving the proceeds from the initial loan

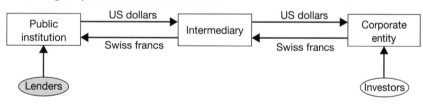

2. Paying interest throughout the life of the loan

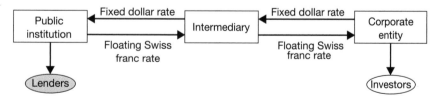

3. Repaying principal at maturity

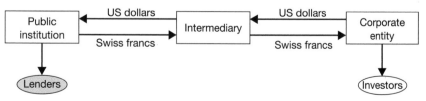

At maturity, the two principal loan amounts in the two currencies are exchanged back at the initial spot exchange rate of 0.8000 US$/SFr. The public institution pays SFr50 000 000 to the intermediary against receipt of US$40 000 000 for repayment of the dollar loan. The corporation pays US$40 000 000 to the intermediary against receipt of SFr50 000 000 for repayment of the Swiss franc note (Figure 6.7-3).

Through this swap, the public institution has serviced debt as if it had assumed a floating rate Swiss franc denominated loan commitment, and the corporate entity has acted as if it had booked a fixed rate dollar loan. However, the public institution, and only the public institution, is fully liable for the dollar loan against the lenders, and only the corporate entity is liable for the Swiss franc note against the investors. Because the two counterparts in all likelihood remain unknown to each other, the intermediary assumes the counter-party risk on them both. The swap arrangement is solely negotiated through the intermediary and each of the counterparts has no obligation to the other. The financial intermediary will normally charge an up-front fee to perform this broker role and assume the counter-party risk associated with the transaction.

The currency swap is a flexible hedging arrangement when an asset or a liability represents a combined interest rate and currency exposure. A corporation's cash flow statements in the major foreign currencies would reveal such exposures. For example, a German institution may have a net outflow of US dollars emanating from a floating rate loan agreement. If it is in the interest of the German institution to lock-in the future cash outflows in terms of euros, it could engage in a combined interest rate and currency swap agreement to bring the floating rate US dollar commitment into a fixed rate euro commitment. As is obvious by now, currency swap agreements may have their particular strength as the means to hedge international financial commitments. Although they can be useful for other hedging purposes, as we will readily see, the vast majority of swap agreements are used to hedge existing financial commitments or to optimize new financial arrangements for borrowers and investors.

The swap markets have other advantages and uses. Swap arrangements can furnish cheaper financing to an institution that is raising new funds because it can approach the cheapest financial market to raise debt and swap the proceeds into the type of liability that is deemed best. The swap technique can also be used to take advantage of expected changes in foreign exchange and interest rates. If the institution's expectation points toward an increasing interest rate level, investors could swap fixed rate assets into floating rate assets and borrowers could swap floating rate liabilities into fixed rate liabilities to take advantage of the expected interest rate movements. Conversely, if the interest rate level is expected to drop, the investors could swap floating rate assets into fixed rate assets, and borrowers could switch fixed rate liabilities into floating rate liabilities. Also, if the market believes that the interest rate will go up, it might indicate a favourable time for a floating rate investor to lock-in the higher future rate. Conversely, if the general market outlook favours an interest rate drop, it could signal an opportune moment for the floating rate borrower to lock-in a lower future rate. Hence the swap technique can be used to take advantage of expected rate movements or to lock-in future rates when the market appears favourable. It goes without saying that the currency swaps can be similarly applied to take advantage of favourable foreign exchange rate expectations.

Currency and interest rate swaps in the major international currencies are also quoted as two-way bid and offer rates provided by active intermediaries in the interbank markets (Table 6.3). The currency and interest rate swap quotes are based on fixed annual rate payments in the currency against six-month US dollar LIBOR

**Table 6.3** Interbank currency and interest rate swaps (quotes on all-in rate bases)

| Currency/maturity | Bid | Offer |
|---|---|---|
| **Euro** | | |
| Three years | 4.86 | 4.95 |
| Five years | 5.29 | 5.42 |
| Seven years | 5.75 | 5.93 |
| **Swiss franc** | | |
| Three years | 4.22 | 4.37 |
| Five years | 4.47 | 4.65 |
| Seven years | 4.62 | 4.85 |
| **Australian dollar** | | |
| Three years | 6.84 | 7.12 |
| Five years | 7.54 | 7.82 |

payments. The swap market has been used frequently by borrowers issuing securities in the Euromarket to convert the currency proceeds and interest rate bases into more applicable terms. If the Eurobonds provide favourable funding to the borrower, the loan can be converted into a currency that is more suitable to the borrower's currency exposure and reflect similarly favourable terms in that currency. Eurobonds denominated in high coupon currencies were for a long time favoured by investors and, thereby, provided good funding opportunities for high-quality borrowers.

*Example*: A corporation obtains a five-year fixed coupon Eurobond loan in Australian dollars at an effective interest cost of 7.40% p.a. A bank offers a five-year A$/US$ currency swap at 7.54–8.02, that is, the corporation receives fixed rate A$ interest payments at 7.54% p.a. against receipt of US$ LIBOR payments.

Hence, a corporation that exploits borrowing opportunities available in, e.g. the Australian dollar market can convert this transaction into a comparable advantage in a more suitable US dollar denominated exposure through engagement in a currency and interest rate swap. In this case, the corporation earns approximately 14 basis points on the A$ payments (= 7.54 – 7.40) and thereby converts this loan commitment into an effective US dollar denominated floating rate cost of LIBOR – 0.14% (Figure 6.8).

The market opportunities in the currency swap market can arise from different sources.[3]

● *Market inefficiencies:* National capital markets can have different appetites for different types of borrowers. Particular types of institutional borrowers might have tapped a regional market extensively, leading to weakening demand for such

**Figure 6.8** US$/A$ currency and interest rate swap

issuers among investors. In this case another type of borrower might get better terms in that market. Hence it might be an advantage for the initial borrower to approach another capital market and swap the proceeds with the new borrower in the initial market.

● *Availability of a certain type of financing:* In situations where market access is restricted, e.g. by queuing arrangements and other regulatory restraints, a potential borrower, which ranks high on the queuing list, might swap loan proceeds with a newcomer to the market, which otherwise might have to wait very long to get financing.

● *Subsidized lending:* For example, national export credit institutions may provide loans in the domestic currency at favourable rates. While the beneficiary might be in a situation where loan proceeds in that currency are impractical it could convert the loan into another currency on similarly favourable terms.

● *Interest rate discrepancies:* When differences between the domestic interest rate level and rates in the Euromarket are sufficiently high, there is a basis for swap-supported arbitrage transactions between domestic markets and the Euromarket.

These are just to mention some of the possible causes leading to the development of a currency swap market.

### 6.2.1 Long-dated forward agreements

In principle a **long-dated forward agreement** works in the same way as a standard forward foreign exchange agreement. The difference, as indicated by the name, is that long-dated forwards exceed the normal maturity of the forward agreements and in some cases offer maturities up to twenty years. The largest transaction volume in the conventional forward foreign exchange market is concentrated around short-term maturities of less than a year while the bulk of the long-dated forward agreements range between two to five years of maturity. Long-dated forward agreements are used by international institutions to hedge long-term assets and liabilities denominated in foreign currencies and thus represent an alternative to currency swap agreements. The main differences are that long-dated forwards, in accordance with the norm in the foreign exchange market, are based on established market practices for individual bilateral currency trades, whereas swap agreements usually are supported by formalized documentation stipulating periodic currency exchanges over a certain contract period.

A major problem associated with the creation and pricing of long-dated forwards is that interbank money markets often may be rather thin, or even nonexistent, in maturities exceeding five-year terms. Consequently, the long-dated forward transactions cannot necessarily be hedged in the traditional way by accessing the money markets in the two currency areas. Hence, the long-dated forward market, like the currency swap market, has developed as counter-party transactions where the financial institution offering long-dated forward agreements tries to match the transactions across counterparts. However, financial institutions increasingly accept open positions in long-dated forwards in the expectation that future transactions may close the gaps. The periodic open positions can be partly hedged in the financial futures in interim periods. As with common forward foreign exchange agreements, long-dated forwards are quoted as a premium or discount on the spot foreign exchange rate where the rate differential is determined by yield indications on benchmark securities in the two currency areas.

*Example*: A Swiss-based trading company is expecting periodic cash inflows of US$10 000 000 every year for the next seven years. The company can get a long-dated forward quote for each of the seven years, which effectively locks-in the future cash inflow in the domestic currency.

*Example*: A US-based institutional borrower has obtained a fifteen-year 5.5% fixed coupon bullet loan of SFr100 000 000 with annual interest payments. The institutional borrower can obtain fourteen long-dated forward foreign exchange quotes for the SFr5 500 000 annual coupon payments and one quote for the principal and interest payment of SFr105 500 000 due in fifteen years and engage into long-dated forward contracts. Hereby the institutional borrower has effectively tied the future cash outflow to the domestic currency.

## 6.2.2　Other swap agreements

Although the currency and interest rate swaps constitute the bulk of the transaction volume in the global swap market, the swap technique has been applied to other types of counter-party exchanges. Just like interest rate swaps constitute periodic exchanges of fixed rate and floating rate interest payments. **Oil swaps** constitute exchanges between oil expenditures determined by fixed and variable prices. Hence, the notional contract amount is determined in terms of barrels of oil and the counterparts exchange the difference in payment amounts at regular intervals during the life of the swap.[4] In principle, this type of fixed versus variable price exchanges can be construed around many different commodities and service charges in **commodity swaps** including natural gas, electricity, orange juice, cement, freight rates, etc. An **equity index swap** exchanges LIBOR based interest payments with interest payments based on an index plus or minus a spread, where the index typically reflects the price development in a particular stock index. However, the index basis may as well reflect many other kinds of price development, e.g. energy expenditures, exploration cost, consumer prices, etc. As an example, a **real estate swap** would exchange LIBOR based interest payments with interest payments indexed around the return on a particular real estate portfolio.

---

**Box 6.1　Swap documentation**

In 1985 the International Swap Dealers Association (ISDA) introduced a code of standard wording in the swap market followed by two standardized master agreements in 1987, the Interest Rate Swap Agreement and the Interest Rate and Currency Exchange Agreement, which were soon established as the predominant swap documentation among international counterparts. This documentation has been adapted in the 1992 ISDA Master Agreements for derivative products designed to comprise all instruments, including interest rate and currency swaps, equity swaps, commodity swaps, caps, collars and floors, equity indexed options, commodity options, etc. Two types of master agreement were introduced for local currency single jurisdiction transactions and multicurrency cross-border transactions respectively. This standard documentation has been reviewed and amended in the subsequent years.

The ISDA Master Agreements were introduced to avoid the nuisance of documenting each and every transaction in completely separate documents. Instead the counterparts agree to the underlying legal and credit relationship terms in the master agreement and provide that all subsequent transactions will be governed by the agreement possibly

▶

documenting the expected types of transactions that would be engaged in. Once the master agreement is signed all following transactions are documented as confirmations that stipulate the economic terms of each transaction and state that it is subject to the master agreement.

These standardized agreements can form the basis for documenting many other forms of risk exchanges and are often incorporated due to its common use and establishment as a universal standard. However, there may be reasonable alternatives to support swap transactions in other established financial fields, For example, risk swaps in the global insurance industry are frequently based on two reinsurance contracts signed by both counterparts and incorporating the standard wording and practices of that industry.

## 6.3 Interest rate swap quotes

As the market for **interest rate swaps** emerged in the early 1980s, banks would typically act as intermediaries to exchange the basis of the interest rate payments between different borrowing clients. For example, one institutional customer might have obtained funds on a fixed rate basis but really preferred to pay interest on a floating rate basis, while another customer might have borrowed money at variable rates but would prefer to pay a fixed interest rate. In such a situation the bank could go between the two parties to 'swap' the interest rate basis of the loans in the wanted direction by paying fixed rate interest to the fixed rate borrower against receipt of floating rate payments, and by making floating rate payments to the variable rate borrower against receipt of fixed rate payments. This way, the bank effectively converted the fixed rate loan into interest payments on a floating rate basis and converted the variable rate loan into fixed rate interest payments. However, as the market for interest rates evolved and matured, interest rate swaps became traded in liquid interbank markets with dealers quoting two-way prices on generic interest rate swaps (Figure 6.9).

**Figure 6.9** US dollar interest rate swap and associated quotes

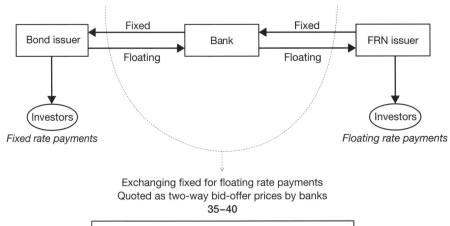

Exchanging fixed for floating rate payments
Quoted as two-way bid-offer prices by banks
**35–40**

- Buy LIBOR for fixed Treasury rate + 35 basis points
- Sell LIBOR for fixed Treasury rate + 40 basis points

Hence, the banks would no longer operate the swap market as pure counter-party exchanges of interest rate payments, but rather trade the floating interest rate against fixed rate payments based on two-way bid and offer prices like in other dealers' markets trading foreign exchanges, securities, etc. The two-way bid-offer rates are typically, but not always, quoted as basis points spread over a benchmark fixed rate indicator in the respective currency, i.e. the treasury yield in the case of US dollar. Assume the following swap quotes:

## Example bank rate sheet

| Maturity | Bid | Offer | Treasuries |
|---|---|---|---|
| Two years | 35 | 40 | 2.70% |
| Three years | 37 | 42 | 2.85% |
| Four years | 40 | 45 | 3.00% |
| Five years | 45 | 50 | 3.10% |

These quotes indicate that the bank providing the quotes is willing to buy floating rate interest payments at LIBOR[5] against payment of fixed rate interest at the two-year treasury rate of 2.70% plus a spread of 35 basis points, i.e. 3.05%. We would have to make adjustments to bring the interest rates into a comparable mode, e.g. the money market convention that calculates interest on a 365/360 days basis. Hence, the rate indication should be converted to an effective annual rate. This implies that the 3.05% bid quote corresponds to 3.0733% effective annual rate $(= ((1 + 3.05/200)^2 - 1)100)$ and further converts into 3.0311% money market basis $(= 3.0733 \times 360/365)$. Conversely, the quoting bank is willing to sell floating rate payments at LIBOR against receipt of fixed rate interest at the two-year treasury rate plus 40 basis points, i.e. 3.10%. The 3.10% offer quote similarly corresponds to 3.1240% effective annual rate $(= ((1 + 3.10/200)^2 - 1)100)$ and further converts into 3.0812% money market basis $(= 3.1240 \times 360/365)$. Hence, assuming the fixed rate borrower in the example above had issued a two-year bond, he would receive fixed rate payments at 3.03% (effective money market basis) semi-annually, against paying floating interest payments at the six-month LIBOR rate. Conversely, the issuer of a two-year FRN would receive floating interest payments at the six-month LIBOR rate from the bank against making fixed rate payments to the bank at 3.08% (effective money market basis).

Similarly, an institutional investor can change the interest payment structure of a given securities portfolio. For example, a portfolio of fixed-income securities can be converted into a stream of floating rate payments if the investor buys LIBOR payments from the bank (bank offer rate), i.e. the investor goes *long* the swap. Conversely, an institutional investor can change the floating rate payments of an FRN portfolio into a stream of fixed coupons if he sells the LIBOR payments to the bank (bank bid rate), i.e. the investor goes *short* the swap.

Since fixed-income securities have higher duration (interest rate sensitivity) than FRNs, the following will apply to any financial or commercial asset manager:

● Buy floating-rate LIBOR (go *long* swap at bank *offer* rate) $\Rightarrow$ Duration $(D) \downarrow$
● Sell floating-rate LIBOR (go *short* swap at bank *bid* rate) $\Rightarrow$ Duration $(D) \uparrow$

In other words, interest rate swaps can be used to manage the duration of investment portfolios, corporate loan portfolios, and business portfolios in specific currencies.

An interest rate swap constitutes an exchange of interest payments between a fixed rate and a floating rate basis, the duration of the swap is equal to the difference between the duration of the two interest payment streams:

$$D_{swap} = D_{fixed} - D_{floating}$$

*Example*: A two-year US dollar-denominated interest rate swap agreement is an exchange between interest payment based on the two-year treasury rate and a six-month floating rate note (FRN), the fixed rate payment stream has a duration of 1.7 and the duration of the FRN is 0.5, so the duration of the swap is 1.2 (= 1.7 − 0.5).

We can use this information to manage the duration of specified portfolios toward a certain duration target.

$$D_{T} = \frac{(D_{P} \times P) + (D_{swap} \times N_{swap})}{P_{S}}$$

$$N_{swap} = \frac{(D_{T} - D_{P})P}{D_{swap}}$$

where

$D_{T}$ = target duration of invested portfolio;
$D_{P}$ = duration of invested portfolio;
$P$ = market value of invested portfolio;
$D_{swap}$ = duration of interest rate swap;
$N_{swap}$ = notional value of the interest rate swap.

*Example*: An investment manager would like to reduce the current duration of 5.0 on an invested portfolio to 3.0 for the coming two-year period. The market value of the securities portfolio is $105 000 000. The duration of the two-year interest rate swap is 1.2. Hence, the duration of the portfolio can be reduced to 3.0 for a two-year period by buying floating rate LIBOR from the bank, i.e. going long a notional swap amount of $175 million (see calculation below):

$$3 = \frac{(5 \times 105\ 000\ 000) + (1.2 \times N_{swap})}{105\ 000\ 000} \Rightarrow$$

$$3 = \frac{525\ 000\ 000 + 1.2 \times N_{swap}}{105\ 000\ 000} \Rightarrow$$

$$N_{swap} = \frac{315\ 000\ 000 - 525\ 000\ 000}{1.2}$$

$$= -175\ 000\ 000$$

A financial institution, e.g. a bank, that trades in interest rate swaps must be able to calculate the value of its current interest rate swap portfolio in order to manage the implied risk exposure. It does that by calculating the net present value of the future cash flows implied in the interest rate swap.

$$PV_{swap} = \sum_{t=1}^{n} \frac{(F_{t} - Y)}{(1 + z_{t})^{t}}$$

**Figure 6.10** Payment structure in interest rate swap

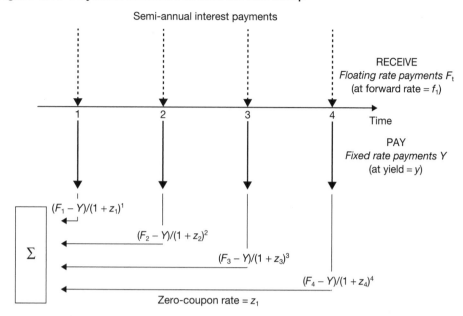

where

$F_t$ = the forward rate payment in period $t$;
$Y$ = the fixed rate payment at the yield;
$z_t$ = the zero-coupon rate for period $t$.

At each six-month period the bank realizes the difference between the fixed interest rate payment determined by the yield on the applicable treasury and the floating rate payment determined by the market's implied forward rate. The present value of these implied future net interest payments is calculated by discounting the related net interest amounts by the appropriate money market spot rates, corresponding to the zero-coupon rates (Figure 6.10).

## 6.4 Currency and interest rate swap structures

A **currency swap** implies that currency amounts corresponding to a given notional contract amount are exchanged at several future dates with six-month intervals, e.g. euros against dollar payments. In reality, this constitutes a series of forward foreign exchange rate contracts (Figure 6.11).

The forward foreign exchange rate is determined by the interest rate parities between the two currencies at the various maturities as discussed in Chapter 1. However, the swap contract might use a single average forward foreign exchange rate for each of the future currency exchanges.

The **currency and interest rate swaps** can be combined to allow for the simultaneous conversion of fixed rate liability (or asset) in one currency, e.g. euros, into a floating rate liability (or asset) in another currency, e.g. US dollars, and vice versa. In

**Figure 6.11** Payment structure in currency swap

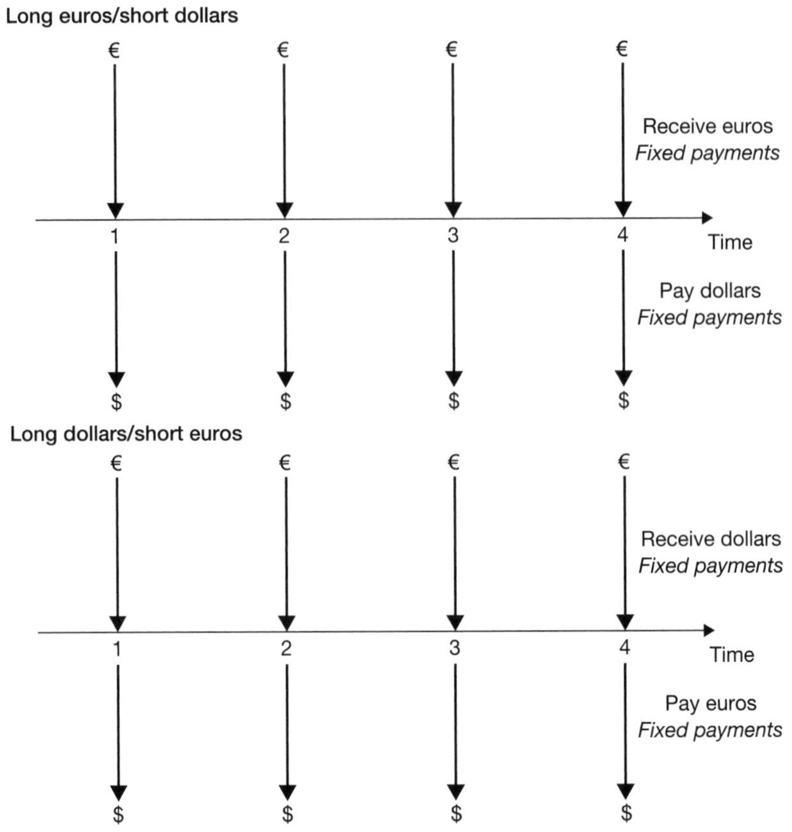

Long euros/short dollars

Long dollars/short euros

order to accomplish this, the bank acting as intermediary would first have to facilitate the exchange of principal currency amounts received as the fixed-coupon bonds and FRNs are placed in the market by the two borrowers. Then the fixed and floating interest amounts are exchanged throughout the lifetime of the loans, which must have the same maturity in this simple example. Finally, the principal currency amounts must be swapped back at the final maturity date of the securities. The fact that the principal amounts of the two currencies must be swapped both at the inception of the swap and at its final maturity increases the implied counter-party credit risk of the combined currency and interest rate swap compared to a pure interest rate swap.

As in the market for interest rate swaps, the combined currency and interest rate swaps are often quoted as two-way prices on the six-month dollar LIBOR rate:

Example euro/dollar currency and interest rate swap
US dollar LIBOR
Bid–Offer
**50–60**
(spread over applicable European government bonds)

This quote indicates that the bank is willing to buy floating rate dollar LIBOR interest payments against fixed rate interest payment at the yield on euro-denominated

**Figure 6.12** Euro/US dollar currency and interest rate swap (bid-rate)

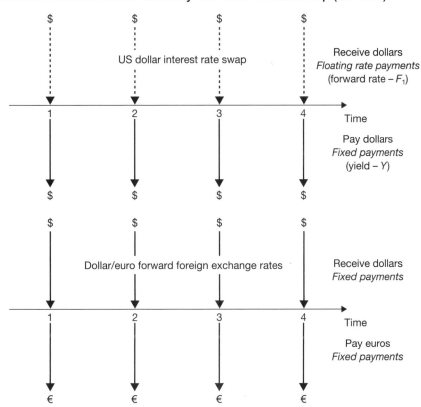

government bonds for the maturity in question plus a spread of 50 basis points. Conversely, the bank is willing to sell floating rate dollar LIBOR interest payments against fixed rate interest payment at the yield on euro-denominated government bonds plus a spread of 60 basis points. As the bank offers the currency and interest rate swap, it effectively combines the underlying cash flows of the currency swap and the interest rate swap. In effect, the bid quote in the dollar/euro currency and interest rate swap, in which the bank buys floating rate US dollar LIBOR payments against delivery of euro-denominated fixed rate payments, combines the bid in a fixed-floating US dollar interest rate swap and a series of forward foreign exchange offers for euros against US dollars (Figure 6.12).

Similarly, the offer quote in the US dollar/euro currency and interest rate swap, in which the bank sells floating rate US dollar LIBOR payments against receipt of euro-denominated fixed rate payments, combines a series of forward foreign exchange bids for euros against US dollars and the offer in a fixed-floating US dollar interest rate swap (Figure 6.13).

By combining elements of the generic forward, option, and swap structures, financial institutions can develop various modified derivatives products. This kind of **financial engineering** activity can serve as the basis for many different instrument adaptations often pursued by the financial intermediaries to accommodate the requirements of specific customer risk profiles.

**Figure 6.13** Euro/US dollar currency and interest rate swap (offer-rate)

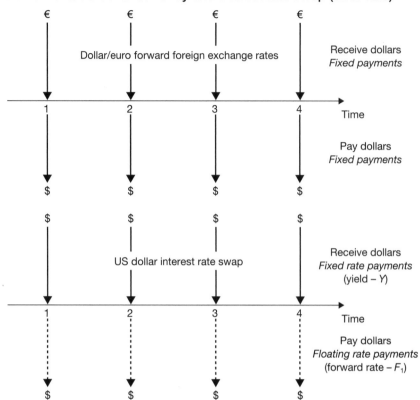

### 6.4.1 Forward swaps

A **forward** or **delayed start swap** allows the holder to engage in a long or short interest rate swap transaction at a later date. This swap transaction constitutes a combination of long and short interest rate swap agreements with different maturities, where a long swap indicates that the counterpart receives LIBOR payments from the financial intermediary (at their offer rate) whereas a short swap indicates that the counterpart provides LIBOR based payments to the intermediary (at their bid rate). Hence, a long one-year interest rate swap with delayed start one year from now can be created by combining a long two-year interest rate swap with a short one-year interest rate swap (Figure 6.14).

Similarly, a short one-year interest rate swap with delayed start one year from now could be created by combining a short two-year interest rate swap with a long one-year interest rate swap. This type of swap agreement could, for example, be useful for a borrower that expects to draw on a floating rate committed credit facility some time in the future and would like to lock-in the future interest expenses. It might also be of potential interest to an institutional investor that expects a cash inflow over a future period and would like to lock-in the return on this liquidity surplus for an extended period of time.

**Figure 6.14** Delayed start swap

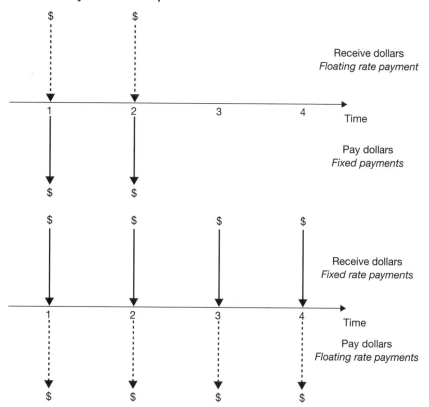

*Example*: A corporation is expecting to draw on a committed credit facility provided by a bank consortium over a twelve-month period approximately a year from today. The credit facility charges overdrafts on a LIBOR plus basis. Since the interest rate outlook indicates a potential for significant increases in interest rates, the corporation might want to engage in a long forward swap agreement to receive LIBOR payments over the twelve-month period on the expected loan amount against payment of fixed-rate interest amounts. This way the corporation has converted a variable rate exposure into a fixed rate exposure and effectively locked-in the interest rate expenses over the twelve month period.

## 6.4.2 Cancellable swaps

A **cancellable** or **collapsible swap** allows the holder of the interest rate swap agreement to cancel out on the swap payments at any of the future semi-annual settlement dates. This type of swap agreement can be obtained by combining a conventional interest rate swap with a series of interest rate options. Hence, a receiver of fixed rate payments has the option to cancel out on the interest exchange if the floating LIBOR interest rate increases above a certain level, which thereby provides an opportunity to take advantage of increases in the interest rate level. Conversely, a payer of fixed rate interest can have the option to cancel out on the interest exchange in case the floating LIBOR interest rate decrease below a certain level and thereby take advantage of a falling interest rate level. The holder of a cancellable

**Figure 6.15** Delayed reset swap

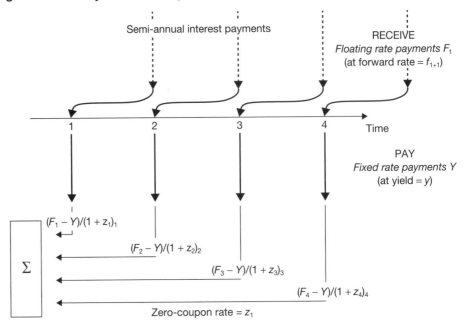

swap agreement pays a premium for this flexibility through an adjustment of the fixed rate basis. That is, the fixed rate payer must make higher fixed rate payments to the counterpart, compared to the market quote on the generic interest rate swap, while the fixed rate receiver receives a lower fixed rate payment from the counterpart as compensation for the underlying interest rate options.

### 6.4.3 Delayed reset swaps

In a **delayed reset swap** the floating rate is not determined by the going LIBOR rate at the beginning of the settlement period, as is the case in a standard interest rate swap, but is fixed at the prevailing LIBOR rate at the end of the settlement period. This type of swap structure is often referred to as an **in-arrears swap** or **back-end set swap**. Hence, the value of this swap is determined by the forward rates extended one period compared to practice in the generic interest rate swap (Figure 6.15).

### 6.4.4 Swaptions

A **swaption** is an option on a swap. The holder of a swaption has the right to engage into a specified swap transaction within a future time period. A **call swaption** provides the holder the right to buy a swap (go long), that is, the right to acquire LIBOR interest payments. This is sometimes referred to as a **payers** since it gives the right to pay fixed interest against receipt of floating rate. A **put swaption** gives the holder the right to sell a swap (go short), that is, the right to sell LIBOR payments. This is sometimes referred to as a **receivers** since it gives the right to receive fixed interest against payment of floating rate.

*Example*: A borrower has issued a floating rate liability to take advantage of an expected drop in the interest rate level. As the interest rate outlook is somewhat uncertain, the borrower would like the opportunity to swap into a fixed interest rate basis after twelve months. This can be achieved by acquiring a twelve-month call swaption. Since the borrower in this case wants to convert the floating rate interest payments to fixed rate payments in a year's time, the relevant swaption for this hedge is a payers.

### 6.4.5 Differential swaps

A **differential swap**, at times simply referred to as a **diff swap** or a **quanto swap**, is an interest rate and currency swap transaction by which one of the interest rate payments can be made in a currency that is different from the currency of the interest rate basis.

*Example*: An institution has a five-year euro-denominated loan and pays interest on a six-month LIBOR basis. The borrower would like to take advantage of an expected decrease in the US dollar interest rate level without changing the present currency exposure. This can be achieved by engaging into a quanto swap with a bank. In the quanto swap, the bank pays six-month euro LIBOR to the borrower. In return, the borrower pays the six-month US dollar LIBOR plus a spread to the bank, where the interest payments are made in euro (Figure 6.16).

The differential swap can be attractive to hedgers because it enables them to take advantage of differences in the interest rate level between two currency areas without imposing additional currency risk on the hedger. The differential swap takes advantage of periodic differences in the yield curves of, for example, the US dollar with an upward-sloping yield curve, and other currencies, such as the euro, with a downward-sloping yield curve. Due to the inversely sloped yield curves, the six-month rate spread can be considerably higher than, for example, the five-year spread or the difference between the five-year fixed interest rate swap quotes in the two currencies (Figure 6.17).

The challenge to the banks offering differential swaps is to hedge the foreign exchange risk arising from the interest payments received in another currency. There is no direct market available in this type of swap and consequently the liquidity in this instrument is constrained and is only offered by banks with a high transaction volume between counterparts in the interest rate swap markets across different currency areas. The differential swap could be construed synthetically through the combination of interest rate swaps in the two currency areas (Figure 6.18).

While the general structure underlying the swap agreement can be adapted to many different types of periodic financial exchanges over time, one of the areas that has seen the highest growth is the markets for credit derivatives and other types of risk-transfer.

**Figure 6.16** US dollar/euro differential or quanto swap

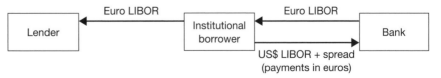

**Figure 6.17** Euro and US dollar yield curves

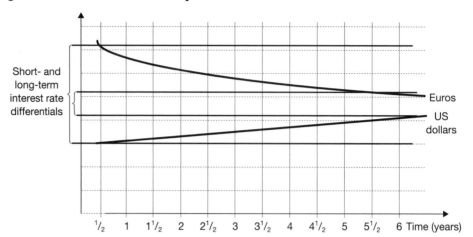

**Figure 6.18** US dollar/euro differential swap

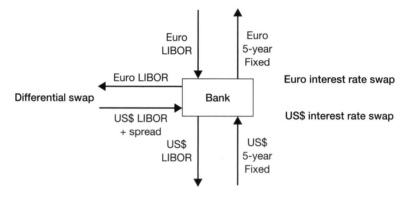

## 6.5 Credit derivatives

Changes in the default risk of borrowers and securities issuers have a significant influence on the market value of financial assets and different commercial receivables in general. To manage the implied credit risk exposures, the market has introduced a number of related derivative instruments. In a **credit swap**, the buyer of the swap (hedger) pays a periodic fee, calculated as a certain percentage of the notional amount of the underlying financial assets. In case of a credit event, e.g. failure to execute a debt service payment in accordance with the loan indenture, the seller of the swap will provide a predetermined compensation payment to the hedger (Figure 6.19).

In effect, a credit swap arrangement constitutes a type of credit insurance contract that can be formalized by the means of a standardized swap agreement. Similarly, a **spread option swap** can also provide protection against the price effects of credit related developments but they are structured slightly differently. It

**Figure 6.19 Credit swap**

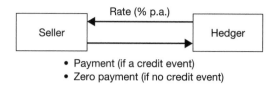

- Payment (if a credit event)
- Zero payment (if no credit event)

can be considered as a combined financial option contract and swap agreement based on the credit spread between two defined classes of risk assets, such as an A-rated or a BB-rated corporate issuer, and the risk free rate, say of the corresponding US treasuries:

$$\text{Credit spread}_1 = c_A - i$$

$$\text{Credit spread}_2 = c_{BB} - i$$

where

$c_A, c_{BB}$ = corporate (risky) rates;
$i$ = the risk free treasury yield.

If the interest rate differential (credit spread) between the two types of assets exceeds a predetermined strike spread, the buyer of the spread option (the hedger) will exercise the option and require the seller to provide an interest compensation payment corresponding to the difference between the new and the agreed interest rate differentials (Figure 6.20).

The hedger pays a premium to the seller for this option structure until the final maturity of the contract. The premium can be paid as a lump-sum front-end fee or as periodic interest payments. In the case of options exercise, the hedger will receive a compensation amount from the seller corresponding to the assumed incremental price effect of the expanded interest rate differential determined by the increase in the rate spread over the strike spread multiplied by a duration factor (remember that the modified duration is a measure of the price sensitivity to marginal changes in the interest rate level). Hence, if the creditworthiness of a corporate borrower in the view of the market deteriorates, the corporate bonds will be priced lower and the credit spread will increase thereby possibly exceeding the strike spread determined in the credit spread swap agreement. As a consequence, this type of credit swap provides the hedger with the possibility for compensation in case the creditworthiness of certain loan assets deteriorates even though no formal credit event might have occurred, i.e. the hedge is based on market pricing as opposed to breach of underlying loan covenant.

**Figure 6.20 Credit spread swap**

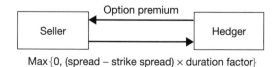

Max{0, (spread – strike spread) × duration factor}

> ## Box 6.2 Credit risk and asset prices
>
> The likelihood that a risky financial asset will be paid back at final maturity will be embedded in the way the market values the risky financial asset compared to the risk free financial asset. Conversely, the yields of the risky financial asset and the risk free asset are a function of the way the market values the two financial assets at a given point in time. In the simple one-period case, the relationship is determined in the following manner:[6]
>
> $$p(1 + k) = (1 + i) \Rightarrow p = (1 + i)/(1 + k)$$
>
> where
>
> $p$ = the likelihood that the loan will be repaid;
> $k$ = yield on risky financial asset;
> $i$ = yield on government bond.
>
> This assumes that the principal is completely lost in case of a credit event (default). However, to the extent that a part of the loan proceeds is recovered after a bankruptcy situation, the relationship should be modified accordingly:
>
> $$(1 - p)\gamma(1 + k) + p(1 + k) = (1 + i)$$
>
> where
>
> $\gamma$ = the part of the principal recovered;
> $(1 - p)$ = the likelihood of default.
>
> As appears, there is a direct relationship between the market yield of a risky financial asset and the likelihood that the underlying financial obligation will be honoured, i.e. the higher the risk of default, the higher the yield required by market participants to compensate for the higher risk level, and the higher the yield, the lower the market price of the financial asset. In other words, there is an inverse relationship between the credit risk associated with a future payment stream and the market value of that financial asset. Hence, the ability to hedge against the price effects caused by changes in the creditworthiness of borrowers and issuers is essential to commercial banks and institutional investors that manage large portfolios of risky financial assets.
>
> Different credit derivatives provide the means for these financial institutions, and other corporate entities as well, to hedge against excessive commitments to risky financial assets by trading and exchanging different types of credit risk exposures across different risk classes. Done appropriately, this process can serve to diversify the credit risk across various types of credit risk, which will reduce the associated price sensitivity of loan portfolios and/or invested portfolios. In a portfolio-theoretical parlance, this corresponds to a situation where the credit derivatives can be used to extend the **efficient frontier** of the invested portfolio in a more favourable north-westerly direction (Figure 6.21).
>
> One way to monitor the overall riskiness of an invested portfolio and/or loan portfolio is through the adoption of the Value-at-Risk (VaR) concept (see Chapter 2 for a discussion of VaR). The VaR is relatively straightforward to calculate for a portfolio of traded securities since the information on daily prices is readily available to calculate the needed variance-covariance relationships of all the securities. When it comes to a portfolio of non-traded loan assets, the trick is to calculate the approximate market value of the loan portfolio and estimate the standard deviation in the value based of historical market changes, a methodology commonly adopted by financial consulting services. Hence, the VaR is determined on the basis of the standard formula:
>
> $$VaR = MV \times Factor \times Standard\ deviation\ of\ portfolio$$

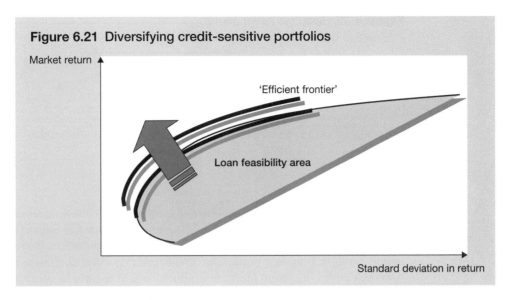

**Figure 6.21** Diversifying credit-sensitive portfolios

The traditional credit default swap is established by a hedger, typically an institutional investor with a relatively large investment commitment in securities issued by a specific institutional borrower or issues belonging to a particular class of risk assets, e.g. BBB-rated corporate bonds. To relieve some of the excessive risk exposures to this risk class, the investor might engage in a credit default swap using a representative bond in the particular asset class as reference asset.[7] In this swap structure, the hedger would pay a periodic interest amount and in turn receive some predetermined compensation in case the reference asset, e.g. a representative BBB-rated issuer, succumbs to a specified credit event, such as a bankruptcy situation or other specified incident (Figure 6.22).

The compensation, or termination payment, in the credit default swap will typically be related to the difference between the par value of the security since the value of the security under normal circumstances should reach parity at final maturity and the actual market value at the time of termination. In case the credit event occurs, the hedger will then obtain a compensation that matches the implied loss in market value caused by the deteriorating credit.

$$\text{Termination payment} = \text{Notional amount} \times (\text{Par} - \text{Market value})$$

**Figure 6.22** Traditional credit default swap

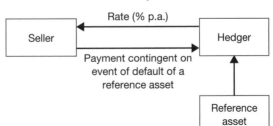

**Figure 6.23** Swap on asset swaps

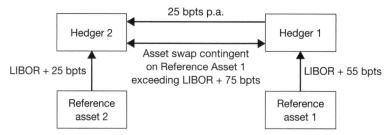

The termination payment is calculated on the basis of the notional amount of the swap agreement. This amount could be smaller than the actual credit exposure assumed by the investor, i.e. the investor might engage in a partial hedge, which would serve to reduce a particular credit risk exposure to a more acceptable level. Conversely, the investor might sell credit default swaps in other reference assets where it is under-invested and thereby receive additional interest income in securities with uncorrelated credit exposures even without making direct investment in those financial assets. These types of transactions can obviously also serve to diversify the invested portfolio.

A more exotic hedge structure is a swap on asset swaps, whereby a hedger has the opportunity to swap one asset swap for another asset swap under certain predetermined market conditions. This type of transaction is sometimes referred to as an **asset swap swap** or a **switch asset swap**. In this structure two hedgers might each engage into credit default swaps based on different reference assets. In case one of the market returns on the reference assets exceeds a certain strike rate, it will trigger a swap, or switch, of the credit swaps on the two reference assets (Figure 6.23).

In this swap transaction, hedger 1 earns a 30 bpts. differential, i.e. he receives LIBOR + 55 bpts. on reference asset 1 and passes on 25 bpts. to hedger 2, the other counterpart to the transaction against the opportunity to receive another, less risky asset swap if the return on the reference asset at some point before final maturity exceeds LIBOR + 75 bpts. That is, hedger 1 gives away, or transfers part of the excess risk on reference asset 1 against the possibility to reduce this risk. Hedger 2 earns LIBOR + 25 bpts. on the less risky reference asset 2 but receives another 25 bpts. from hedger 1 as compensation for assuming the excess risk associated with reference asset 1. Hence, the two hedgers have diversified the risk of their investments in this process and improved the risk-return characteristics of the invested portfolios.

## 6.6 Risk swaps

A **risk swap** is a special application of the financial swap technique to the exchange of insurable risk exposures between two counterparts. These risks could include many different exposures, e.g. car insurance, property insurance, health insurance, mortality risk, etc. The basic criteria for this application are that the risk exposures are clearly specified and documented as is common practice in the insurance industry.

**Figure 6.24 Catastrophe swap**

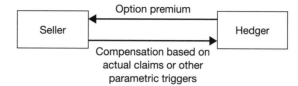

Hence, the swap technique can add flexibility to insurance companies that want to tailor the documentation to their specific needs and requirements. However, this application could also potentially be adopted by corporate entities as one of the counterparts as the means to transfer excess casualty and commercial risk to other insurance companies or the financial market. A particular extension of this type of swap based risk transfer applies to the exchange of catastrophe exposures. Catastrophe exposures relate to interdependent risks, where the exposures relate to low frequency, rapid impact, high potential loss events, such as hurricanes, flooding, earthquake, etc., and man-made disasters comprising industrial accidents as well as terrorism related events. These risks cannot be diversified in ordinary insurance portfolios because the claims are related to each other. Consequently, there is a need to spread these risks among global participants in the reinsurance market and the application of the swap techniques is one way to accomplish this. In a **catastrophe swap**, the cedant of the excess risk exposure (the hedger) pays regular insurance premiums to the reinsurance company (the seller) against coverage in case the specified risk event occurs (Figure 6.24).

The triggers in these risk swaps can comprise actual claims for losses occurred but could also incorporate more readily measurable phenomena such as wind speed, rainfall, catastrophe loss indexes that can be determined rather objectively. The application of the swap technique is most relevant to handle higher risk layers that represent excessive exposures.[8] To the extent excess risk layers are exchanged across the insurance companies through swaps, it serves to diversify risk and improve capital management (Figure 6.25).

In this example, the peak risks of the two insurance companies have been reduced while the loss probability has been reduced through diversification, which in turn reduces the need for risk capital that can be released for other productive enterprise.

**Figure 6.25 Risk diversification and capital management**

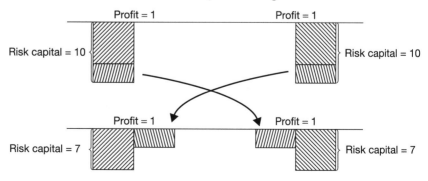

## 6.6.1 Risk securitization

Similarly, the asset securitization technique has been applied to transfer excess risk exposures from the insurance market to the capital market (see Chapter 3 for a discussion of the asset securitization technique). In this context, a **risk-linked security** is a special type of security placed among institutional investors through the capital market where the repayment of the principal is contingent upon underlying insurance triggers. Through issuance of catastrophe risk-linked bonds, **cat-bonds** for short, the issuer, typically an insurance or reinsurance company, can obtain cover for specified catastrophe events. The catastrophe risk-transfer opportunities have primarily been exploited by insurance and reinsurance companies to obtain complementary coverage in the capital market but has also been adopted by corporate entities.[9]

A cat-bond is typically structured around a special purpose vehicle (SPV) established in a tax favourable jurisdiction.[10] The SPV issues the cat-bonds and receives up-front payments from the investors buying the securities. The SPV engages in an insurance contract with the ceding entity, that in turn pays an insurance premium for the entire insurance period up front or on a pro-rata basis. The insurance contract typically provides the cedant with insurance coverage on an excess-of-loss basis corresponding to practice in the catastrophe reinsurance market. Hence, the ceded risk exposure may cover losses associated with particular insurance layers between specified attachment and exhaustion points. The SPV uses the up-front proceeds from the bond issue less the expenses accrued in connection with the placement to buy a liquid securities portfolio of high credit quality and low interest rate sensitivity. The securities portfolio is placed in a trust account as collateral for the debt service payments due on the cat-bonds. The SPV is rated by one of the credit agencies. The SPV often engages into a fixed-floating interest rate swap agreement that converts the interest returns from the invested securities portfolio into monthly LIBOR based floating rate payments. The investors receive a relatively high spread above LIBOR to compensate for the catastrophe risk exposure. The investors only receive the full principal back at maturity if no catastrophe losses materialize in the interim.[11] Hence, the major risk consideration for cat-bond investors is the inherent catastrophe risk exposure.

A critical element of the credit evaluation process is an assessment of the validity and integrity of the supporting catastrophe risk analysis. Such analysis is usually

**Figure 6.26** Securitization of catastrophe risk

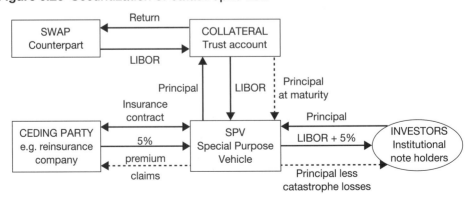

performed by specialized consulting firms on the basis of simulation models that estimate the probabilities of catastrophe events of different magnitudes and the associated losses. The cat-bonds can use different bases to trigger compensation under the reinsurance contract. Compensation can be triggered as a loss indemnity of the actual insurance losses incurred by the ceding party. For the cedant, this solution provides close to perfect coverage of losses. However, for the cat-bond investors the solution is fraught with the issues of moral hazard and adverse selection, because there is no guarantee that the cedant will try to mitigate losses once the cat-bonds are placed, and as an insider, the cedant may actually know more about the catastrophe risk exposure than the investors buying the cat-bonds. The trigger could also be based on a loss index, which eliminates the risks associated with moral hazard and adverse selection, because the index is well defined and cannot be manipulated. However, a standardized index will expose the cedant to basis risk as the index may differ from the actual losses incurred. A final methodology is to adopt a parametric formula as a trigger. This hybrid approach can develop triggers that are closely associated with the cedants exposure, but at the same time are well defined, objectively measurable, and analyzable.

## 6.6.2 Contingent capital

Other instruments provide capital replenishment rather that risk transfer solutions, and therefore establish financial contingencies in the capital market to fund the recuperation of future adverse developments. These instruments can provide committed capital through the issuance of common equity, preferred equity, or senior debt instruments.[12] The contingent capital instruments are effectively put options that give the holders the right to place securities at a predetermined issuance price once a certain indicator has exceeded a predetermined threshold value. These option structures are sometimes referred to as knock-in options, or barrier options, because they are effectuated after an independent trigger has been activated. **Contingent surplus notes** have been issued by a number of insurance companies in a total amount of around $8 billion since the mid-1990s. The contingent surplus notes provide the holder, typically an insurance company, with the right to place notes with investors if certain events occur. Although these instruments were developed initially with the insurance industry in mind they apply equally to use by corporate entities. For regulatory purposes, an insurance company may treat the notes as statutory surplus as it enables the insurance company to finance extreme loss events. Similarly, a corporation could use this type of economic cover in lieu of a general equity base. If medium-term notes are issued through exercise of the contingent surplus notes, they must be repaid in accordance with a predetermined redemption schedule.

## 6.6.3 Hybrid instruments

Many financial derivatives have been issued in the form of hybrid instruments. A **hybrid security** combines a generic bond and a built-in derivative that modifies the underlying payment structure. The issuance of convertible bonds is a prime example of a hybrid security that allows the holder to convert the corporate bond into stock in the company issuing the debt.[13] This conversion right might be attached to the bonds in the form of warrants that can be traded as separate capital market instruments after issuance.[14] There are many examples of hybrid securities where the interest payments are indexed to the price development in different commodities, such as silver, gold, oil, etc. These types of hybrid securities can also be related to the development in price indexes, such as the S&P 500, the inflation rate, etc. They may also be construed as inverse floating rate notes, where the interest payments vary inversely to changes in some interest rate indicator, or as dual currency bonds that are issued in one currency and repaid at maturity in another currency. Hybrids are often issued to counter the borrower's specific exposures to interest rates, foreign currencies, and commodities that provide a natural hedge and thereby allow the corporation to manage firm specific exposures where trading in standardized derivatives constitute a less flexible and more expensive alternative. Investment bankers may also introduce hybrid securities to satisfy specific investor interests where the hybrid securities are created through combinations of generic financial instruments. For example, an inverse floating rate note can be created by combining a fixed-coupon bond structure with a short interest rate swap. Similarly, a dual currency bond can be created by combining a zero-coupon bond with a long dated forward contract that converts the principal repayment at maturity into another currency. Hybrid instruments can be issued opportunistically and placed through the capital market to take advantage of favourable market conditions and thereby satisfy corporate needs for funding as well as providing cover for specific risk exposures. Hence, the advantages of these instruments relate to their idiosyncratic nature adapted to the specific situation of the issuer and potential price advantages gained from favourable market conditions. However, there is also a potential downside associated with the idiosyncratic nature of hybrid instruments caused by lower market liquidity that makes it rather difficult to reverse the embedded hedges should the need arise at a later stage.

## Conclusion

The development of swap agreements provides financial intermediaries, institutional investors, and corporate entities with added possibilities to hedge different financial risk exposures. The swap technique has been extended to many types of risk including basic interest rate and currency exposures as well as credit risk, casualty risk, catastrophe risk, etc. Asset securitization has been used extensively to develop alternative risk-transfer instruments in the capital market including risk-linked securities, cat-bonds, and different types of hybrid securities. Today generic interest rate and currency swaps are traded in fairly standardized forms in international dealer-based markets whereas many other risk swaps remain specific to the needs of individual counterparts and, therefore, are less transparent. The markets for financial swaps provide rich opportunities to manage institutional exposures and serve to diversify the underlying risks among different financial market participants.

## Summary

- Interest rate swaps allow counterparts to periodically exchange fixed-rate and floating-rate interest amounts calculated on agreed notional amounts. The differences between the periodic interest amounts are normally exchanged on semi-annual settlement dates. The swaps are traded in interbank dealer markets and quoted as two-way prices indicating fixed-rate bids and offers for LIBOR-based interest payments.

● Currency swaps allow counterparts to periodically exchange payment in one currency for payments in another currency. In principle, this arrangement constitutes a series of forward foreign exchange contracts with a common forward rate applied to all contracts. The currency payments are normally exchanged on semi-annual settlement dates.

● Combined interest rate and currency swaps allow counterparts to exchange fixed rate payments in one currency for floating rate payments in another currency. The principal amounts in the two currencies are exchanged initially at the spot foreign exchange rate. The interest amounts in the two currencies are normally exchanged on semi-annual settlement dates. The principal amounts in the two currencies are exchanged back at final maturity at the initial spot foreign exchange rate. The swaps are quoted as two-way prices indicating foreign currency fixed rate bids and offers for US dollar LIBOR-based interest payments.

● Credit swaps allow counterparts to exchange credit exposures among them. The credit swaps periodic interest premium against compensation in case of a credit event occurring or the risk premium increasing on a specific reference asset. When counterparts establish credit swaps on their higher excess risk layers, they effectively diversify the credit risk among them.

● Exotic derivatives are developed by combining generic swaps with forwards and options contracts, e.g. to delay execution of the swap or increase flexibility around the execution of periodic interest payments.

● Hybrid instruments extend generic debt structures through combinations with forwards, options, and swaps or by adopting asset securitization techniques that enable risk-transfer to capital market instruments.

## Questions

6.1 Explain the rationale behind the emergence of financial swaps in the form of interest rate swaps and currency swaps.

6.2 Explain how interest rate swaps in US dollars are quoted in the interbank market.

6.3 Explain how a currency and interest rate swap in Australian dollars is quoted.

6.4 Explain how a swap dealer would determine the market value of a US dollar interest rate swap.

6.5 Explain when and how an institutional investor might use an interest rate swap.

6.6 Explain how a potential corporate borrower might use an interest rate and currency swap.

6.7 Explain how interest rate swaps can be used to manage an interest rate gap defined by its duration.

6.8 Explain the mechanics of a credit default swap.

6.9 Explain the difference between a credit default swap and a credit spread swap.

6.10 Provide at least one example of an exotic swap structure created through the combination of a swap and some other derivative instrument.

6.11 Explain the overall risk effects of credit swaps, risk swaps, risk-linked securities, and other types of hybrid instruments.

## Exercises

6.1 An institutional investor has a five-year portfolio of US dollar-denominated FRNs with average returns of LIBOR + $^3/_4$%. The current five-year US dollar interest rate swap quote is 0.65–0.75 and the five-year T-Note currently yields 4.25% p.a. Please determine at what indicative fixed rate the institutional investor can lock-in the returns on the FRN portfolio for the five-year period.

6.2 A corporate borrower has drawn down a US dollar-denominated three-year floating rate credit facility that charges LIBOR + $1^1/_4$%. The three-year US dollar interest rate swap is quoted at 0.70–0.80 and the three-year T-Note yields 3.65% p.a. Please determine the indicative fixed rate at which the corporate borrower can lock-in the interest expense on the credit facility for the three-year period.

6.3 The interest rate swaps in 6.1 and 6.2 are quoted for semi-annual settlement periods and the treasury yields are quoted on semi-annual interest rate bond basis. Please convert the two indicative fixed rates determined above into a comparable money market basis.

6.4 The current spot foreign exchange rate is quoted at 1.1150 US$/€. The ten-year US treasury bond yields 5.35% and the yield on the corresponding German bund is 5.05%. Based on this information, please determine the ten-year long dated forward rate.

6.5 Based on the quotes provided in Figure 6.5, determine at which spread over LIBOR a UK-based borrower can convert the interest expense on a ten-year fixed-coupon corporate bond that currently yields 6.37% (semi-annual actual/365 rate basis).

6.6 A US-based investor has acquired a portfolio of five-year Swiss franc Eurobonds with a nominal value of 50 million and a yield of 4.35% (semi-annual bond basis). Given a five-year Swiss franc swap quote of 4.47–4.65, please determine the spread over LIBOR at which the investor can convert this portfolio into a floating rate US dollar return for the five-year period.

6.7 The fixed-rate leg of a five-year US dollar interest rate swap with semi-annual settlement dates has a duration of 3.7. Please determine the duration of the five-year interest rate swap.

6.8 A bank has engaged into a two-year interest rate swap on a US$10 million notional amount where it receives floating rate US$ interest at LIBOR flat against fixed rate interest payments at a yield of 3.2% with semi-annual settlement. The current six-month forward and zero-coupon rates have been calculated as follows:

| Settlement period | 1 | 2 | 3 | 4 |
|---|---|---|---|---|
| Six-month forward rate | 2.65 | 2.80 | 2.90 | 2.95 |
| Six-month zero-coupon rate | 2.65 | 2.75 | 2.81 | 2.85 |

Please determine the present value of the interest rate swap on the bank's books.

## Notes

1  For example, interest rate swaps in pounds sterling relate to the rates on gilts issued by the Debt Management Office (DMO) on behalf of the UK government, and quotes in euros could relate to rates on German government bonds (Bunds), and so forth.

2  Even here there are complicating exceptions, as the one-year interest rate swaps denominated in euros and Swiss francs are quoted against the three-month LIBOR.

3  See, for example, Andersen, T. J. (1993), *Currency and Interest Rate Hedging*, 2nd edn, Prentice-Hall.

4  See, for example, Smithson, C. W. (1998), *Managing Financial Risk*, 3rd edn, McGraw-Hill.

5  The London Interbank Offered Rate.

6  See, for example, Saunders, A. and Cornett, M. M. (2003), *Financial Institutions Management: A Risk Management Approach*, 4th edn, McGraw-Hill.

7  See, for example, Tavakoli, J. M. (2001), *Credit Derivatives and Synthetic Structures*, Wiley.

8  See, for example, Takeda, Y. (2002), 'Risk swaps', in Lane, M. (ed.), *Alternative Risk Strategies*, Risk Books.

9  See, Andersen, T. J. (2001), *Innovative Financial Instruments for Natural Disaster Risk Management*, Inter-American Development Bank, Washington, DC.

10  There are a number of tax issues related to the establishment of SPVs for catastrophe risk transfer in the USA. Most SPVs have been established in countries such as Bermuda, the Cayman Islands, or Ireland that allow reinsurance companies to establish the SPVs as separate cells with zero or favourable tax status. Without this tax treatment, the securitization technique would not be economical.

11  See Andersen, T. J. (2004), 'International risk transfer and financing solutions for catastrophe exposures', *Financial Market Trends*, No. 87, OECD, Paris, pp. 89–120.

12  See Colarossi, D. (2000), *Capitalizing in Innovation in the Use of Contingent Capital*, Swiss Re New Markets.

13  In special cases, the hybrid instruments may be construed so the bonds can be converted into stocks of other companies than the issuer of the bonds, say an affiliated company, a strategic partner, or the like.

14  A warrant is a type of call options on the firm's stock. The primary difference from stock options is that warrants normally are associated with new capital, i.e. the stockholders' liability increases if the warrants are exercised and the proceeds are added to the paid-in capital of the firm.

# Part 3

# Hedging with financial derivatives

# Chapter 7

# Hedging with financial futures contracts and options on futures

**Objectives**

- Describe the principles of hedging with futures contracts
- Describe the principles of hedging with options on futures
- Provide an overview of different situations where futures contracts can be used for hedging
- Provide an overview of different situations where options on futures can be used for hedging
- Outline documentation, legal, and accounting issues
- Consider regulatory concerns

Chapter 4 provided a general overview of different types of futures contracts traded on exchanges around the globe and introduced options contracts offered on the most frequently traded futures. In this chapter, we will take a closer look at how different types of futures contracts can be used to modify and manage financial exposures. These exposures typically relate to receivables and payables in foreign currencies and interest rate uncertainties related to investment returns and funding costs. However, the same hedging principles apply to futures and options contracts on any other type of financial asset, including precious metals, electricity, catastrophe losses, average temperatures, etc.

## 7.1 Hedging with financial futures

The hedger trades commodity and financial futures contracts to eliminate or modify inherent exposures to erratic price movements of the underlying asset. Buying or selling forward what is needed or is in surplus at some future time, say in nine months, can eliminate or reduce the price uncertainty at the delivery date and provides the hedger with a higher degree of certainty in commercial calculations, at least as far as future prices are concerned.

In the commodity futures market, the contracts may result in physical delivery of the underlying assets that define the contract, but that is rarely the case in the financial futures markets. What is special about financial futures is that the underlying assets can be classified as a type of financial obligation. Due to the daily mark-to-market (the variation margin), the net gain or loss will be fully compensated in cash at the time of delivery, which is what most market participants are looking for. Usually a seller of a futures contract will purchase a similar contract, and a buyer will sell a similar contract no later than the last trading day before expiry. As a result, the position will square out, i.e. there will be no delivery of the underlying financial asset. This procedure, referred to as **closing out**, can be performed at any time during the trading period.[1] However, physical delivery of the underlying asset of a financial futures contract can take place although it is more the exception than the rule.

What drives the financial futures market is the fact that there is a difference between the future contract price agreed to and the contract price around the expiry date. This principle applies to both speculative participants in the market who expect to incur a profit by taking positions in the futures market as well as to hedgers who offset changes in financial price developments, e.g. currency proceeds or interest expenses, by countervailing capital gains or losses on a portfolio of financial futures contracts.

*Example*: A market participant sold a contract at a future price of $110 while the actual contract price on the last trading day before delivery turned out to be $100. Hence, the trader made a profit of $10 by closing out the position on the last trading day.

The contract price at the time of delivery will usually be equal to the going price in the cash market due to **convergence**. That is, any discrepancies between the futures price and the cash market price remaining before maturity could furnish risk-arbitrage and, therefore, the two prices will move closer to each other as the final maturity date approaches (Figure 7.1).[2]

**Figure 7.1 The development in cash market and futures prices**

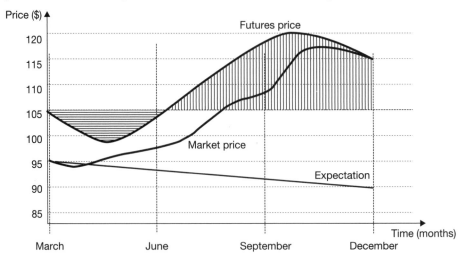

The cash market price in March is $95 and an investor expects the price in nine months to drop to $90 even though the December future trades at $105 (Figure 7.1). If this view of the price development is more correct than the market indication, the investor could sell the December futures contract in the expectation of a profit at delivery, i.e. the futures price of $105 less the expected cost of closing out in December of $90. However, in June the cash market price increases and continues to do so to finish at $115 at the expiration date in December. In this case the investor would incur a loss because the market moved against the initial expectations (the futures price of $105 less the $115 cost of closing out on the last trading day). The futures price initially dropped below $105 and the variation margin, therefore, was positive due to the cash inflow on the settlement account. From June onward, the futures price increased resulting in a negative variation margin and a cash outflow from the settlement account. Note that the price of the December financial futures contract converges towards the contract price in the underlying cash market to finally be equal at delivery date. Hence, the closer we get to the delivery date, the less will be the impact of market expectation. This does not mean, however, that one may assume a stable convergence.

This example is presented from an investor's perspective but could as well be seen from a hedger's point of view. For example, a buyer of the underlying asset who fears that the price will increase would buy a futures contract. In this case, the hedger will close out at the higher cash market price against a purchase at the lower futures price, which was set at the initial purchase of the futures contract. Hence, the hedger will make a profit (the actual price at delivery less the futures price is greater than zero). This profit would offset the increased cost from the actual purchase of the assets in the cash market. The hedger will end up with a positive variation margin and the profit is available in cash on the settlement account at close out. The actual development in the futures price will rarely follow the smooth trend indicated in Figure 7.1. The price development usually follows rather erratic day-to-day movements reflecting the price risk (volatility) of the underlying cash market instrument (Figure 7.2).

**Figure 7.2** The price development of an actively traded futures contract

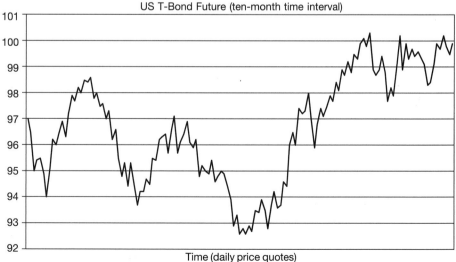

US T-Bond Future (ten-month time interval)

Time (daily price quotes)

### 7.1.1 Interest rate hedging

Consider an institution that has a twelve-month asset of $20 000 000 on its books at a return of 6%. To fund this, the institution has acquired a nine-month liability at a rate of 4% p.a. Looking ahead, a liquidity gap of $20 000 000 will, of course, appear during the three-month period from month 9 to month 12 with funding costs at that time being unknown.

Balance sheet

| Maturity | Assets | Liabilities |
|----------|--------|-------------|
| Three months | $20 000 000 (6.00%) | $20 000 000 (4.00%) |
| Six months | $20 000 000 (6.00%) | $20 000 000 (4.00%) |
| Nine months | $20 000 000 (6.00%) | $20 000 000 (4.00%) |
| Twelve months | $20 000 000 (6.00%) | (funding requirement) |

Assuming that interest is paid at maturity, the institution must provide interest payments in cash at the end of the nine-month period of:

$$\$20\,000\,000 \times 0.04 \times \frac{9}{12} = \$600\,000$$

That is, the funding requirement in the fourth quarter is not $20 000 000 but $20 600 000, namely principal plus interest on the nine-month loan that has just expired. Hence the break-even cost of a three-month loan in the fourth quarter is:

$$\frac{\$20\,000\,000\left((0.06 - 0.04) \times \dfrac{9}{12}\right)}{\$20\,600\,000} \times \frac{12}{3} \times 100 = 5.825\%$$

But who knows what will happen over the next nine months? A less plausible way of closing the interest rate gap would be to obtain a twelve-month liability, preferably at a cost below 6% p.a., and acquire a nine-month asset, preferably at a return above 4% p.a. The asset and liability positions would be fully matched in maturities, but total footings also increased from $20 000 000 to $40 000 000, with whatever impact this has on leverage, profitability ratios, credit standing, etc.

Another possible avenue would be to find a counterpart with exactly the opposite interest rate gapping or an investor who is interested in putting the inverse position on the books and accept a future obligation. This type of search, however, is an arduous process and utterly unnecessary since the financial futures markets deal with financial obligations of this very nature. Hence, the interest gap can be effectively closed by selling three-month eurodollar deposit contracts for delivery in nine months preferably at a rate below 5.825%, i.e. a contract price in excess of 94.175 = (100 – 5.825). The financial futures market thus represents an efficient way of accessing counterparts in futures contracts without affecting the balance sheet.

### 7.1.2 Short interest rate hedges

**Short interest rate hedges** generate a profit when interest rates increase above the market's expected future rate and they are, therefore, used by borrowers to lock-in the future funding cost. The future loan could be an existing loan that is to be rolled over for an extended period or it could be a completely new loan that is intended to cover future cash outflows.

*Example*: In May, a loan of $10 000 000 is to be obtained for a six-month period with three-month rollover periods from September this year to February the following year. If the effective borrowing rate is very close to the domestic certificate of deposit rate, the borrower could lock-in the borrowing cost by selling ten three-month certificate of deposit contracts with nominal values of $1 000 000 for delivery both in September and December.

The interest rate was 5% in May and the borrower is worried that interest rates will increase. The three-month CD contracts for delivery in September and December both trade at a price of 95.00, i.e. implying a future interest rate of 5% p.a. Hence, by selling financial futures contracts at the current price, the future funding cost can be locked-in at the 5% level.

In September the three-month interest rate has increased to 6%, so the three-month CD contract is acquired on the futures exchange at a price of 94.00. For each contract sold at the already settled futures price of 95.00 there will be a price gain of one point. The total capital gain incurred from the sale of futures contracts will count against the increased interest expense incurred on the loan resulting in a net expense on the loan that effectively corresponds to the 5% interest rate.

| *Three-month loan September–December* | |
| --- | --- |
| Price of futures contract | 95.00 |
| Cash price of futures contract | 94.00 |
| Price gain per contract sold | 1.00 |
| Profit per contract sold | $2 500 (= 1.00 × 1 000 000/400) |
| Actual interest expense September–December (6%) US$10 000 000 loan | $150 000 |
| Profit from sale of ten futures contracts | $25 000 |
| Net cash expense on loan | $125 000 |

Corresponding to an effective interest rate of 5.00% p.a.

The three-month interest rate increased to 6.5% by December, i.e. the cash price for the futures contract dropped to 93.50 leading to a price gain of 1.5 points per futures contract sold. Again the net interest expense on the loan will correspond to a 5% effective interest rate.

| *Three-month loan December–February* | |
| --- | --- |
| Price of futures contract | 95.00 |
| Cash price of futures contract | 93.50 |
| Price gain per contract sold | 1.50 |
| Profit per contract sold | $3 750 (= 1.50 × 1 000 000/400) |
| Actual interest expense September–December (6.5%) US$10 000 000 loan | $162 500 |
| Profit from sale of ten futures contracts | $37 500 |
| Net cash expense on loan | $125 000 |

Corresponding to an effective interest rate of 5.00% p.a.

The quotes on the futures exchanges will reflect the average interest rate expectation of the market participants themselves. In this example the market expected a somewhat stable interest rate level since both the September and December contracts were trading at 95 corresponding to the current rate of 5%. However, given the view that rates could increase, the borrower could fix the future funding cost at the market's expected future interest rate, namely 5%, which in this case it turned out to be a wise decision.

In the example, the market expected a flat interest rate development while the actual interest rate level turned out to increase above market expectations. Now, what happens if the interest rate level declines below the expected levels due to same unforeseeable economic developments?

*Example*: The three-month CD rate in September has fallen to 4.5%. The three-month CD futures contract for September delivery would therefore have a cash price of 95.50, and we would be losing 0.5 points on the sale of each contract.

|  |  |
|---|---|
| *Three-month loan September–December* | |
| Price of futures contract | 95.00 |
| Cash price of futures contract | 95.50 |
| Price loss per contract sold | 0.50 |
| Loss per contract sold | $1 250 (= 0.50 × 1 000 000/400) |
| Actual interest expense September–December (6%) US$10 000 000 loan | $112 500 |
| Loss from sale of ten futures contracts | $12 500 |
| Net cash expense on loan | $125 000 |
| Corresponding to an effective interest rate of 5.00% p.a. | |

That is, no matter in which direction the interest rate level moves, the interest rate has been effectively locked-in at a level of 5% p.a.

> A borrower can fix the future cost of funding by selling a suitable number of interest rate futures contracts.

In the preceding example, the funding cost was perfectly correlated with the CD rate and, therefore, it was possible to establish a complete hedge. However, this is not always the case. In the example, the loan periods also correspond to the maturities of the futures contracts, which made the hedging exercise relatively simple. Unfortunately the real world is not always so favourable.

*Example*: In May we foresee a need to draw on a funding source for a six-month period from July to December in the form of a $10 000 000 floating rate loan facility with interest payable at the end of each month at the going one-month CD rate. We would like to hedge the loan against an increase in the interest rate level. As in the previous example, the floating rate loan can be hedged through sale of twenty three-month CD financial futures contracts of which ten are to be delivered in September and ten to be delivered in December.

| | | *Six-month loan July–December* | | | |
| Month | Principal | One-month CD rate | Interest amount | Futures settling account | Net cash outflow |
| --- | --- | --- | --- | --- | --- |
| July | $10 000 000 | 5.50% | $45 835 | – | $45 835 |
| August | $10 045 835 | 6.15% | $51 525 | – | $51 525 |
| September | $10 097 360 | 6.22% | $52 350 | +$24 650 | $27 700 |
| October | $10 149 710 | 6.36% | $53 850 | – | $53 850 |
| November | $10 203 560 | 6.26% | $53 220 | – | $53 220 |
| December | $10 256 708 | 6.37% | $54 500 | +$25 350 | $29 150 |
| | $10 125 529 | 6.15% | $311 280 | | $261 280 |

Corresponding to an effective average interest rate of 5.16% p.a.

These calculations imply that the hedging transactions reduced the average funding cost from 6.15% to 5.16% p.a. However, the example illustrates some of the problems occurring in a more complex situation where we cannot be sure that the three-month CD rate will correspond to the average of the one-month CD rates over the same period. Consequently, the future funding cost cannot be locked in 100% and the timing of the financial futures contracts does not necessarily fit the time schedule of the borrowing program. Nonetheless, the following axiom generally holds true:

> Institutions can hedge against increasing interest rates by selling interest rate futures contracts.

## 7.1.3 Long interest rate hedges

**Long interest rate hedges** generate a profit when interest rates fall below the market's expected future rate. The interest rate futures contracts are, therefore, used by lenders and investors to lock-in the return on future loans and investments.

*Example*: An institution foresees a cash inflow of US$20 000 000 in three months, which it intends to place in one-year US treasury bills for a full twelve-month period. The future return on this investment could be locked-in by buying 80 US treasury bill contracts with nominal value $250 000 for delivery in three months. The return on one-year treasuries is currently 5.75% p.a., but the market expects the rate to fall to 5.00% in three months (as implied by a futures contract price of 95.00). Fearing that rates might move further down, the institution would like to lock-in the future return of 5% p.a. and therefore it buys 80 futures contracts at the quoted price of 95.00.

Three months later, the one-year US T-Bill rate has dropped to 4.75%. Therefore, the futures contracts are now quoted at a price of 95.25, i.e. the futures contracts acquired at a price of 95.00, can be sold at a profit.

| Twelve-month investment | |
|---|---|
| Price on futures contract at close out | 95.25 |
| Price of futures contract bought | 95.00 |
| Price gain per contract bought | 0.25 points |
| Profit per contract bought | $625 (= 0.25 × 250 000/100) |
| | |
| Actual return on investment | $950 000 |
| Twelve months (4.75%) | |
| US$20 000 000 investment | |
| Profit from purchase of 80 futures contracts | $50 000 |
| Net return on investment | $1 000 000 |
| Corresponding to an effective interest rate of 5.00% p.a. | |

If the return on one-year treasury bills instead had remained unchanged at the 5.75% p.a., then the institution would have lost money on the futures contracts because the futures contract bought at a price of 95.00 would sell at 94.25.

| Twelve-month investment | |
|---|---|
| Price on futures contract at close out | 94.25 |
| Price of futures contract bought | 95.00 |
| Price loss per contract bought | 0.75 points |
| Loss per contract bought | $1 875 (= 0.75 × 250 000/100) |
| | |
| Actual return on investment | $1 150 000 |
| Twelve months (5.75%) | |
| US$20 000 000 investment | |
| Loss from purchase of 80 futures contracts | $150 000 |
| Net return on investment | $1 000 000 |
| Corresponding to an effective interest rate of 5.00% p.a. | |

Hence, we see that the return on investment has effectively been fixed at the expected futures rate of 5.00% p.a. Again we know that this 100% locked-in return is obtained because the actual return on the treasury bills was perfectly correlated with the return on the corresponding futures contracts provided that the expiration date matched to the timing of the future cash inflow. Hence, the following statement generally holds true:

> Institutions can hedge against falling interest rates by buying interest rate futures contracts.

### 7.1.4 Hedging investments in long-term securities

So far we have considered interest rate exposures related to short-term cash flow streams. Let us now look at the hedging perspective from the perspective of long-term investors and borrowers.

*Example*: In early January, $10 000 000 has been invested in fifteen-year 6% coupon US treasury bonds. At year end, in twelve months' time, the investor will either sell the securities at market value or record the securities on the balance sheet at the prevailing market price, thereby registering a loss or gain on the income statement. The investor is worried that the initial expectation of an interest rate drop will not hold true, so instead year-end discount values on the securities would incur a loss either because the portfolio is marked-to-market at lower values or because actual securities sales took place at lower market prices.

In this case, the investor decides to hedge against an increase in the interest rate level. According to our rule of thumb the hedge can be completed by selling a suitable number of interest rate futures. The underlying securities portfolio was bought at a market yield of 5.5% p.a. corresponding to a premium price of 105. The market expects the future T-Bond rate to increase to 6%, i.e. the US treasury bond futures contract for December delivery is traded at par. So to hedge, the investor sold 100 treasury bond futures, with a nominal value of US$100 000 each, making up a total market value of US$10 million. If the T-Bond rate increased to 6.5% by the expiry date in December, the investor would incur a capital loss on the portfolio but would gain on the futures contracts sold at the futures price of 100.0 because the price on the fifteen-year T-Bond, and hence the T-Bond futures contract had dropped to 95.3.

| *Twelve-month investment in US treasury bonds* | |
|---|---|
| Price on futures contract sold | 100.0 |
| Price of futures contract at close out | 95.3 |
| Price gain per contract sold | 4.7 points |
| Profit per contract sold | $4 700 (= 4.7 × 100 000/100) |
| Actual return on investment | −$400 000 |
|   6% coupon     $570 000 | |
|   capital loss   −$970 000 | |
| Profit from sale of 100 futures contracts | $470 000 (= 100 × 4700) |
| Net return on investment | $70 000 |
| Corresponding to an effective twelve-month return of 0.7% p.a. | |

If instead the interest rate had dropped to 5.5% in December, the investor would lose on the contracts sold at the futures price of 100.0 because the current price of the contract in that case would increase to 105.0.

| *Twelve-month investment in US treasury bonds* | |
|---|---|
| Price on futures contract sold | 100.0 |
| Price of futures contract at close out | 105.0 |
| Price loss per contract sold | 5.0 points |
| Loss per contract bought | −$5 000 (= 5.0 × 100 000/100) |
| Actual return on investment | $570 000 |
|   6% coupon     $570 000 | |
|   capital gain   $0 | |
| Loss from sale of 100 futures contracts | −$500 000 (= 100 × 5000) |
| Net return on investment | $70 000 |
| Corresponding to an effective twelve-month return of 0.7% p.a. | |

The hedge ensures that the income from the treasury bond investment is aligned to the market's expected future rate of 6%. That is, the hedge cannot provide better terms than implied by the expectations in the futures market but nonetheless ensures that returns will not be worse that those implied by the current expectations. The example also illustrates that a futures hedge covers for the downside risk but excludes profit taking from a more favourable interest rate development. In the end, whether or not the hedge should be pursued, given the economic outlook, depends on how strongly the investor feels that the interest rate level will exceed the expected market rate of 6%.

The hedging situation could also be presented in the context of a different interest rate environment.

*Example*: The futures market expects the treasury bond rate to fall to 5% by December, i.e. the December futures contract trades at 110.4%. Yet, the investor does not agree, thinking rather that a stable or perhaps a slightly increasing interest rate level moving in the range between 5.5–6.0% is more likely over the next twelve months. In this situation the investor could lock-in the potential gain from this market expectation by selling 100 futures contracts. Assuming that the investor was right and the treasury bond yield in December was 6%, i.e. the T-Bond rate increased by a half percent rather than dropped by a half percent as indicated by the futures market, the investor would then be able to lock-in the future rate at 5.0%, despite the adverse rate development in the cash market.

---

#### Twelve-month investment in US treasury bonds

| | |
|---|---|
| Price on futures contract sold | 110.4 |
| Price of futures contract at close out | 100.0 |
| Price gain per contract sold | 10.4 points |
| Profit per contract sold | $10 400 (= 10.4 × 100 000/100) |
| | |
| Actual return on investment | $30 000 |
|   6% coupon     $570 000 | |
|   capital loss    –$540 000 | |
| Profit from sale of 100 futures contracts | $1 040 000 (= 100 × 10 400) |
| Net return on investment | $1 070 000 |

Corresponding to a twelve-month return of 10.7% p.a.

---

The applicability of a financial futures hedge on a long-term securities portfolio, therefore, depends very much on the prevalent interest rate environment, which must be evaluated thoroughly before engaging in a futures position. Another possibility is to perform a partial hedge to reflect management's uncertain outlook on the future interest rate development.

*Example*: The view is that there is a 50% chance that the interest rate level will increase by one percentage point and a 50% chance that the interest rate will drop by one percentage point. The investor could then hedge half the investment portfolio against the effect of an interest rate increase by selling 50 treasury bond futures contracts. In case the interest rate increases, the portfolio will be partially hedged. If the interest rate drops, the investor will incur a fair share of the upside capital gain associated with the increased market value of the securities portfolio.

## 7.1.5 Hedging new issues

In North America and the Euromarkets investment bankers have a long established procedure of underwriting new securities issues, often referred to as **bought deals**. At the closing date of the underwriting agreement, the investment banker commits to forward a fixed amount of money in return for the securities to be sold in the market in connection with the issue. Hence the underwriter carries the full risk of the securities not being sold in the market at the predetermined price. The problem is that the interest rate might increase to a level exceeding what was committed to the borrower at the closing of the underwriting agreement. The securities would then have to be sold in the market at a lower price and would thus impose a loss on the underwriter because he already has committed to a future cash payout to the borrower. Usually the risk will be carried throughout a period of a few days to five or six weeks at the worst. However, adopting the rule of thumb, the risk of increasing interest rates could be hedged through the sale of a suitable number of interest futures contracts.

*Example*: In August the investment banker has committed to underwrite the issuance of an US$20 000 000 fifteen-year 8% coupon Eurobond at an interest rate of 10.75%. That is a committed discount price of 79.74. The treasury bond futures contract for delivery in September is currently trading at 79.7 implying that the market expects the interest rate to remain largely unchanged. The investment banker could lock-in this interest rate by selling 200 treasury bond futures contracts for delivery in September at the going futures price.

It turns out that in September, when the investment banker is ready to sell the Euro securities, the interest rate actually has increased to 11%, i.e. one quarter of a percent up from the August forecast. However, the treasury bond futures contract, for the same reason, trades at a price around 78, and the investment banker, therefore, will make a profit by closing out the treasury bond contracts sold at the future price of 79.7.

| One-month underwriting commitment | |
|---|---|
| Price on futures contract sold | 79.70 |
| Cash price of futures contract | 78.00 |
| Price gain per contract sold | 1.70 points |
| Profit per contract sold | $1 700 ($= 1.7 \times 100\ 000/100$) |
| Underwriting loss on Eurobond issue | −$340 000 |
| Profit from sales of 200 futures contracts | $340 000 ($= 200 \times 1700$) |
| Net effect of hedge | $0 |

As can be seen, the profit from the sale of the treasury bond futures contracts is equivalent to the loss incurred from the Eurobond issue and the interest rate gap has been effectively closed.

## 7.1.6 Cross hedging

As implied by the previous examples, a hedge is performed by trading the number of futures contracts that match up to the face value of the financial obligation to be hedged.

*Example*: Ten US$1 000 000 three-month certificate of deposit contracts were sold with the purpose of hedging the interest expenses associated with a US$10 000 000 three-month loan.

The general hedging principle adhered to when choosing the number of futures contracts is:

> The change in the value of the futures contracts should match the change in the interest income or expense of the cash instrument portfolio to be hedged.

A special problem arises when the maturity of the asset portfolio to be hedged differs from the maturity of the futures contract of the underlying asset.

*Example*: A one-month US dollar investment is hedged by buying three-month interest rate futures contracts. The value of a one-basis-point change in the interest rate on a $1 000 000 one-month investment is $8.33, against the associated value change of $25.00 on a three-month futures contract. Therefore financial futures contracts should be bought to match one-third of the principal investment. Conversely, when three-month futures contracts are used to hedge a six-month investment, interest contracts should be bought to match twice the principal of the underlying investment. The value of a one basis point change in the interest rate on a $1 000 000 six-month investment is $50, against the value change of $25 on the three-month futures contract.

If there is a maturity mismatch between the futures contract and the asset portfolio to be hedged, the number of futures contracts traded should be inversely related to the maturities of the cash instrument and the futures contract:[3]

$$\text{Number of futures contracts traded} = \frac{N}{F} \times \frac{M_c}{M_f}$$

where

$N$ = nominal value of the cash position to be hedged;
$F$ = market value of one futures contract;
$M_c$ = maturity of the underlying cash position to be hedged;
$M_f$ = maturity of the asset specifying the futures contract.

*Example*: To hedge a one-month US dollar investment of $15 000 000 with three-month interest rate futures contracts, buy five contracts: $15 000 000/$1 000 000 × 1/3 = 5.

In previous examples, one was always able to find a financial futures contract that matched the cash position to be hedged because they had the same denominations and maturities and because the pricing of the two financial instruments was fully correlated. Obviously this is far from the case at all times. So a method is called for to tell us, in case no corresponding futures contract exists, how many contracts of an available future to trade in order to obtain a full hedge.

*Example*: An investor wants to hedge a $20 000 000 Eurobond portfolio with a 7% coupon rate and twenty years to maturity by trading in the US treasury bond futures contract.

We can no longer assume that the interest rate movements of the two dollar-denominated securities are fully correlated. They are most likely highly correlated inasmuch as the two instruments in many cases appeal to the same institutional investors and the two types of securities are close substitutes. However, from the investor perspective there is a major difference between the credit risk of the two assets. For a domestic US investor a credit to the US treasury must be considered virtually risk free, whereas a Eurobond represents a loan to an international corporate entity or sovereign institutional borrower and, therefore, represents a higher credit exposure. On top of this, changes in the regulatory environment in the USA and changes in monetary regulations across national jurisdictions may lead to situations in which the yields on the two types of securities do not move in complete unison.

For the hedger, it is interesting to know how the two interest rates have developed and to what extent these time series represent a correlated pattern of price movements. This can be investigated by calculating the **regression coefficient** between periodic price quotes on the two securities. Since the interest rate is inversely related to the price development, it can also be expressed as the correlation between the periodic yields of the two securities. The correlation coefficient then indicates how much a change in the interest rate of one security has 'induced' a change in the interest rate of the other security and vice versa.

For a given period, the daily interest rates of the Eurobond and the cheapest deliverable bond under the US treasury bond futures contract can be plotted (Figure 7.3). In this diagram the development in the Eurobond interest rate is presented as a function of the development in the treasury bond interest rate. The regression analysis assumes that a linear relationship can be applied to describe the covariance between the yields of the two securities where the regression coefficient is calculated by applying the standard formula:[4]

$$b = \frac{\Sigma(E_i \times F_i)}{\Sigma(F_i^2)}$$

where

$i = 1, 2, \ldots n$ is the range of observed datasets plotted into the diagram;
$E_i, F_i = i$th set of observed datasets $(E, F)$;
$E_i$ = yield on Eurobond;
$F_i$ = yield on US treasury bond.

**Figure 7.3 Observed yields on the Eurobond and US treasury bond**

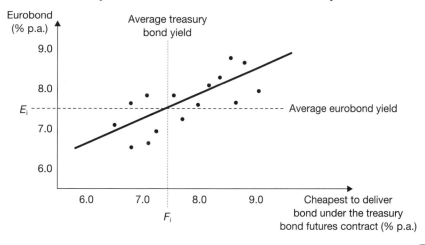

*Example*: Assume that the regression coefficient (*b*) was determined as 1.15 for different reference periods. Hence, for a one basis point change in the treasury bond rate, history suggests that there will be a 1.15 basis point change in the Eurobond interest rate. A one basis point change in the yield corresponds to a $10 250 price change on a $20 000 000 Eurobond portfolio and a price change of $11 200 on the corresponding portfolio of national treasury bonds.

The relative price change of the two asset portfolios is sometimes referred to as the **BPV (basis point value) factor**, because it establishes the relative price sensitivity of the two types of securities measured by the price change per basis point change in the interest rate level:

$$\text{BPV-factor} = \frac{\text{BPV } X}{\text{BPV } Y}$$

where

BVP $X$ = Change in price of $X$ for a one basis point change in the yield;
BVP $Y$ = Change in price of $Y$ for a one basis point change in the yield.

Say the cheapest bond to deliver under the treasury bond futures contract turns out to be the 8% coupon rate bond with twenty years to maturity and the applicable conversion factor to bring this bond into the standard contract is 0.9010. Then the **hedge ratio** is determined by the following formula:

Hedge ratio = Regression coefficient × BPV factor × Conversion factor

*Example*: Extending the previous information, the hedge ratio is calculated as $0.9483 = 115 \times 10\ 250/11\ 200 \times 0.9010$.

With a ratio of 1, we should buy 200 US treasury bond futures contracts to hedge the investment corresponding to the nominal value of $20 000 000 Eurobonds (= 20 000 000/100 000). Adopting the principle that changes in the value of the futures contract should match changes in the value of the cash instruments to be hedged, the number of treasury bond futures contracts to sell is 190 (= $200 \times 0.9483 = 189.66$).

## 7.2 Price relationships

In general, a one basis point change in the cash market price of the underlying financial asset should cause an equivalent one-basis-point change in the price of the futures contract. However, this is not always the case and it becomes less so the further we are from the final delivery date. This is so because the futures price is influenced by carrying costs and foregone dividends while also reflecting the market participants' expectations about the market price of the underlying asset at the contract expiration date, which, of course, can differ from the current market price.

Nevertheless, the futures price will usually follow changes in the cash market price. This relationship is expressed in the **delta value**, which indicates the incremental change in the futures price as a function of a marginal change in the price of the underlying asset:

**Figure 7.4** Profit and loss profile of a futures contract

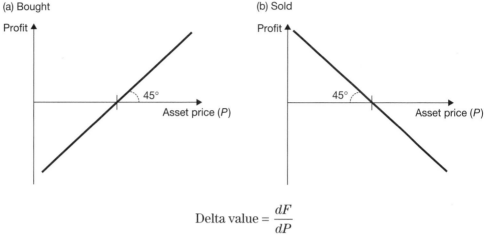

(a) Bought

(b) Sold

$$\text{Delta value} = \frac{dF}{dP}$$

where

$F$ = price of the futures contract;
$P$ = cash price of the underlying asset;
$d$ = derivative (marginal change).

The shorter the period remaining to the delivery date, the more changes in the futures price will correspond to the price movements in the cash market price of the underlying asset, i.e. delta moves toward 1 as we get closer to the expiration date of the futures contract. On the last trading day, delta is usually equal to 1, i.e. the futures price corresponds to the cash market price (Figure 7.4).

## 7.2.1 Spreads

For the astute investor the financial futures market provides a number of investment opportunities. Compared to the cash market, the futures market offers the possibility of investing on a levered basis since the futures position only requires payment of initial and variation margins rather than the full amount. The simple investment opportunity is to take a view on the future price on the underlying cash instrument or on the future asset price itself, thereby establishing a so-called **trend position**. Such positions can be closed out at any time before the delivery date if a favourable market situation should occur or if the price development turns out to go against initial expectations. But there are other ways to establish positions in the futures market. The same futures contract with different delivery dates can react differently to movements in the underlying cash market. In such a situation an investor (speculator) might establish a so-called **spread position** by going long and short in two identical futures contracts with different expiration dates.

*Example*: The June and December contracts are quoted with a higher price difference to the cash market price than the September contract. The investor can establish a spread position, e.g. by buying 200 September contracts and selling 100 June and 100 December contracts.

The spread position technique can be extended from **intramarket spreads**, in the same contract with different maturity dates, to **intercommodity spreads**, involving spread positions between contracts based on the same asset with different maturities in the underlying instruments. For example, a spread position can be established on three-month sterling versus twenty-year gilt contracts. Thereby the investor is taking a view on the development in the structure of interest rates (yield curve).

It is also possible to establish an **intermarket spread** between corresponding contracts traded on different exchanges. In Europe it was quite popular to establish **intercurrency spreads** on different national interest rate instruments to take advantage of changes in interest rate differentials between European currencies. These positions were typically established by selling interest rate futures on high-rate currencies and buying interest rate futures on low-rate currencies. The spread strategy assumes a stable foreign exchange rate development and a strong convergence between the interest rate levels of the currencies.

When such a position is established the investor should apply an appropriate hedge ratio, as discussed previously. This is done to fulfil the general requirement of a spread position that the amount of assets bought must approximately equal the amount of assets sold. An investor that buys $a$ futures contracts in currency A to create a spread position must sell $b$ futures contracts on currency B determined by the following calculation:

$$b = N_A/N_B \times \text{foreign exchange spot rate} \left(\frac{B}{A}\right) \times R_C(A,B) \times \text{BPV-factor} \times a$$

where

A = currency A;
B = currency B;
$a$ = number of futures contracts in currency A;
$b$ = number of futures contracts in currency B;
$N_A$ = contract size on futures contract on currency A;
$N_B$ = contract size on futures contract on currency B;
$R_C(A,B)$ = regression coefficient between the price movement of the futures contract on currency A and the futures contract on currency B;
BPV-factor = (BPV $A$)/(BPV $B$).

### 7.2.2 Portfolio hedging

A portfolio can consist of assets in an investment or funding liabilities. Typically an institution wants to take a longer-term view on its investment and loan portfolios. A net investor, such as a pension fund, can assess the expected timing of payouts to policyholders on the basis of stipulated claims, i.e. they can determine the average life of the liabilities. Similarly, a net borrowing institution can determine the expected average life of its loans. The idea behind portfolio hedging is to safeguard the future return on investment assets established to cover expected liabilities or conversely to secure the funding costs throughout the life of productive assets. The associated interest rate risk can be managed by trying to match the duration of invested assets with the duration of the liabilities. Since duration indicates the time period throughout which the impact of marginal interest rate movements on the portfolio's cash flows is neutralized, the return on the invested portfolio is fixed until payments must be made on existing liabilities. Conversely, the funding costs on a loan portfolio can be fixed for the expected lifetime of the assets. This principle is often referred to as **immunization**. The duration of a given asset (or liability) portfolio is found simply by adding, on a market value weighted basis, the duration of the specific investment (or debt) instruments that make up the portfolio. By buying or selling futures contracts into the portfolio, the hedger can also adjust the duration of the portfolio. Hence, a portfolio manager can adjust the duration of a given portfolio through transactions on the futures market.

An increase in the interest rate will reduce the present value of an asset (or a liability), while the reinvestment rate on the current interest income (or the opportunity cost on current interest payments) will increase. A sold futures contract will incur a capital gain when the position is closed toward the delivery date, but will have no impact on the reinvestment rate (or opportunity cost). The capital gain incurred on the futures contract will further reduce the time required for the higher reinvestment rate to compensate for the capital loss on the portfolio, i.e. the duration is reduced.

A drop in the interest rate will increase the present value of an asset (or a liability), while the reinvestment rate (or the opportunity cost) will decrease. A bought futures contract will incur a capital loss when the position is closed, but will have no impact on reinvestments (or opportunity costs). The capital loss from the futures contract will further increase the time required for the lower reinvestment rate to compensate for the capital gain on the portfolio. In other words, the duration is increased.

> The duration of a portfolio *is* reduced by selling futures contracts.

> The duration of a portfolio *is* increased by buying futures contracts.

The duration of a portfolio including futures contracts is found by calculating the weighted duration of the cash market instruments and the futures contracts:

$$D = \frac{(D_c \times M_c) + (D_f \times M_f \times d)}{M_c}$$

where

$D_f$ = duration of the futures contracts;
$M_f$ = market value of the futures contracts;
$D_c$ = duration of the portfolio of financial instruments;
$M_c$ = market value of the portfolio of financial instrument;
$d$ = delta value of the futures contract (approximately 1).

This formula can be reversed to find the applicable futures position to establish in order to reach a targeted duration for the portfolio in question. This is found by solving the equation for $M_f$:

$$M_f = \frac{(D - D_c)M_c}{D_f \times d}$$

As discussed, the duration measure is a function of the interest rate level. Therefore, a portfolio hedge by means of duration measures should be monitored on a current basis to adjust for periodic changes in the interest rate.

## 7.3 Currency hedging

Transactions involving the exchange of currencies may constitute payments for trade transactions involving delivery of goods and services across national borders, capital transactions involving the extension of cross-border credits, debt service payments on foreign loan commitments, or settlements relating to short-term currency positions. Within these wide categories of foreign exchange transactions one could think of many examples where different institutions would be interested to lock-in the future foreign exchange rate. Here we will focus on a few transactions to show how financial futures can be used to hedge. This hedging technique applies to any situation involving the exchange of foreign currencies.

*Example*: In April an American company has shipped goods for delivery to a corporation in Switzerland and the price has been settled in Swiss francs. The payment of 10 000 000 Swiss francs is expected in mid-June. The present spot foreign exchange rate is quoted at 2.8852 SFr/US$ (0.3466 US$/SF). Given the US dollar exchange rate development the American exporter is worried that the Swiss franc will weaken over the two-month period, so he will receive fewer dollars for the incoming Swiss franc amount at that time.

The Swiss franc futures contract with delivery in June is quoted on the futures exchange at 0.3400 (US$/SFr). The American exporter finds this rate attractive because it is higher than his two-month foreign exchange rate forecast. To lock-in this foreign exchange rate, he sells 80 Swiss franc futures contracts for delivery in June (each Swiss franc futures contract has a nominal value of SFr125 000). In June it turns out that the exporter's worst guess was right, the spot exchange rate has increased to 2.9851 SFr/US$ (0.3350 US$/SFr). Yet, the loss made in the cash exchange market is compensated by the profit gained on the sale of the futures contracts.

| *Two-month foreign currency receivable* | |
|---|---|
| Price of Swiss franc futures contract sold | 0.3400 |
| Cash price of Swiss franc futures contract | 0.3350 |
| Price gain per contract sold | 0.0050 (50 pips) |
| Profit per contract sold | $625 (= 125 000 × 0.0050) |
| Loss on spot sale of Swiss francs | $ (50 000) |
| (= 10 000 000(0.3350 − 0.3400)) | |
| Profit from sale of 80 futures contracts | $50 000 (= 80 × 625) |
| Corresponding to an effective future foreign rate of 0.3400 US$/SF. | |

Now assume, on the other hand, the probable event that the exporter's two-month foreign exchange rate forecast was on the mark as the June spot foreign exchange rate hit 2.8571 SFr/US$ (0.3500 US$/SFr). Then the exporter would gain on the spot exchange of the Swiss francs but would correspondingly lose on the sale of the financial futures contracts.

---

*Two-month foreign currency receivable (US resident)*

| | |
|---|---|
| Price of Swiss franc futures contract sold | 0.3400 |
| Cash price of Swiss franc futures contract | 0.3500 |
| Price loss per contract sold | −0.0100 |
| Loss per contract sold | −$1 250 (= 125 000 × 0.0100) |
| Gain on spot sale of Swiss francs (= 10 000 000(0.3500 − 0.3400)) | $100 000 |
| Loss from sale of 80 futures contracts | −$100 000 (= 80 × 1250) |

Corresponding to an effective future foreign rate of 0.3400 US$/SF.

---

As a consequence, the future foreign exchange rate has been effectively locked-in by trading in the financial futures at the market's expected future exchange rate of 0.3400 US$/SF.

In a similar example, we can show that an American importer who pays for the import in the exporter's currency conversely can lock-in the future exchange rate by buying futures contracts.

*Example*: An American importer is contractually committed to make a payment of 10 000 000 Swiss francs by mid-June. He can hedge this by buying 80 Swiss franc contracts at the market price of 0.3400. In June the Swiss franc spot rate was 0.3500. So, he will have to pay more dollars for the francs on the spot market but will gain from the purchase of the futures contracts.

---

*Two-month foreign currency payable (US resident)*

| | |
|---|---|
| Cash price of Swiss franc futures contract | 0.3500 |
| Price of Swiss franc futures contract bought | 0.3400 |
| Price gain per futures contract bought | 0.0100 |
| Profit per futures contract bought | $1 250 (= 125 000 × 0.0100) |
| Loss on spot purchase of Swiss francs (= 10 000 000(0.3400 − 0.3500)) | −$100 000 |
| Profit from purchase of 80 futures contracts | $100 000 (= 80 × 1250) |

Corresponding to an effective future foreign rate of 0.3400 US$/SF.

---

These examples illustrate the following hedging principles:

> A US resident who receives payments in a foreign currency can hedge by selling futures contracts of that currency against US dollars.

> A US resident who makes payments in a foreign currency can hedge by buying futures contracts of that currency against US dollars.

The following discusses how a comparable hedge will work in the case of a non-US resident.

*Example*: A German exporter is selling to customers in the United States and receives payment in US dollars. In October the exchange rate was quoted at 1.1205 euro/US dollar (0.8925 US$/€). The German exporter is worried that the dollar foreign exchange rate might decrease, i.e. the euro might strengthen so he will get less euros in December when the dollar receivable of US$5 000 000 is due. Since the euro futures contract for December delivery is trading at 0.8925, he is willing to lock-in this rate by buying 56 euro contracts (= 5 000 000 × 1.1205/100 000) for December delivery. In December the exchange rate turned out to be 1.0929 €/US$ (0.9150 US$/€). So, the German exporter received less euros for the dollar receivables when they were exchanged in the spot foreign exchange market in December but this was countered by a gain from the initial purchase of the futures contracts.

| Two-month foreign currency receivables (non-US resident) | |
| --- | --- |
| Cash price of euro futures contract | 0.9150 (1.0929) |
| Price of euro futures contract bought | 0.8925 (1.1205) |
| Price gain per futures contract bought | 0.0225 |
| Profit per futures contract bought | $2 250 (= 100 000 × 0.0225) |
| Loss on spot purchase of euros | −€136 000 |
| (= 5 000 000(1.0929 − 1.1205)) | |
| Profit from purchase of 56 futures contracts | $126 000 (= $2250 × 56) |
| (= 126 000/0.9150) | €137 705 |
| Corresponding to an effective foreign rate close to 1.1205 €/US$ | |

If the German resident instead had been importing goods from suppliers in the United States it might instead make payments in US dollars. The foreign exchange rate associated with the dollar payables could be hedged by selling euro futures contracts against US dollars.

*Example*: Based on the data in the previous example, the German importer would sell euro futures contracts and the following hedging calculations would result.

| Two-month foreign currency payable (non-US resident) | |
| --- | --- |
| Price of euro futures contract sold | 0.8925 (1.1205) |
| Cash price of euro futures contract | 0.9150 (1.0929) |
| Price loss per futures contract sold | −0.0225 |
| Loss per futures contract bought | −$2 250 (= 100 000 × 0.0225) |
| Gain on spot purchase of US dollars | €136 000 |
| (= 5 000 000 (1.1205 − 1.0929)) | |
| Loss from sale of 56 futures contracts | −$126 000 (= $2250 × 56) |
| (= 126 000/0.9150) | −€137 705 |
| Corresponding to an effective foreign rate close to 1.1205 €/US$ | |

This illustrates the following hedging principles for non-US residents.

A non-US resident receiving payments in US dollars can hedge by buying futures contracts on the home currency.

A non-US resident making payments in US dollars can hedge by selling futures contracts on the home currency.

## 7.3.1 Cross-currency hedging

When the US dollar exchange rate is not directly involved in the transaction, i.e. when the receivable (or payable) is denominated in a non-US currency, and the exporter (or importer) is located in a currency area outside the United States, hedging based on currency futures quoted against US dollars, as is the norm in the foreign exchange market, becomes somewhat more complicated.

*Example*: A French producer is exporting to an English importer. In mid-August the producer has shipped the goods and is expecting pound sterling payments of £5 000 000 when the goods have safely arrived in the United Kingdom in mid-September. In mid-August the pound sterling exchange rate is 1.0668 US$/£ stg., and the euro exchange rate is 1.0480 €/US$ (0.9542 US$/€), thus implying a cross rate of 1.1180 €/£ stg. (= 1.0668 × 1.0480). The market expects the pound to strengthen slightly against the dollar because of an improvement in the international spot price on crude oil. The euro is expected to weaken slightly against the US dollar as indicated by the quoted prices on the September futures contracts on pound of 1.0750 US$/£ stg. and euro of 0.9501 US$/€ (= 1/1.0525 €/US$), implying a cross rate of 1.1314 €/£ stg. (= 1.0750 × 1.0525).

The French exporter has experienced the volatility of the foreign exchange market and is worried that the favourable exchange rate development might reverse before the pound sterling denominated payments are received. By selling 200 £ stg. contracts and at the same time buying 225 euro contracts, he can lock-in the value of the foreign currency receivables. If the exporter's worries are justified, i.e. if the spot exchange cross rate in mid-September turns out to be, e.g. 1.1062 €/£ stg., he would receive less euros in the spot foreign exchange market from the pound sterling receivables. However, gains from trading in the euro and sterling futures contracts can compensate for this potential loss.

| One-month cross currency receivable (non-US residents) | |
| --- | --- |
| Price of sterling futures contract sold | 1.0750 |
| Cash price of £ stg. futures contract | 1.0675 |
| Price gain per futures contract sold | 0.0075 |
| Profit per futures contract sold | $187.5 (= 25 000 × 0.0075) |
| Cash price of euro futures contract | 0.9650 |
| Price of euro futures contract bought | 0.9501 |
| Price gain per futures contract bought | 0.0149 |
| Profit per futures contract bought | $372.5 (= 25 000 × 0.0149) |
| Loss on spot purchase of euros (= 5 000 000(1.1062 − 1.1314)) | −€126 500 |
| Gain from sterling futures sold | $37 500    (= $187.5 × 200) |
| Gain from euro futures bought | $83 812.5 (= $372.5 × 225) |
| Total gain (= 121 312.5/0.9650) | €125 715 |

Corresponding to an effective foreign rate very close to 1.1314 €/£

In this example, the hedge was close to being complete. However, the hedge was cumbersome and slightly less advantageous than indicated by the straightforward rates. Due to the standard size of the futures contracts, a 100% hedge is rarely possible in this type of cross-currency hedge. In the preceding example 200 £ stg. contracts were sold, thereby perfectly hedging the £ stg. 5 000 000 conversion into US dollars. However, the purchase of 225 euro contracts does not lock-in the exact amount of US dollars. The cross-currency hedging principles based on futures contracts with US dollar-based foreign exchange quotes can be formalized in the following rules of thumb:

> A non-US resident receiving payments in a foreign currency can hedge by selling futures contracts on the foreign currency against dollars and buying futures contracts on the domestic currency against dollars.

> A non-US resident making payments in a foreign currency can hedge by buying futures contracts on the foreign currency against dollars and selling futures contracts on the domestic currency against dollars.

To circumvent the problems of imperfect hedging in cross-currency exchanges, several futures exchanges now offer futures contracts directly in the major cross-currency quotes.

## 7.3.2 Interest rate hedging in other currencies

Since the interest rate differentials are embedded in the quoted currency futures prices it is in principle possible to use interest rate contracts in foreign currency areas to hedge domestic interest rate exposures by linking trading in these interest rate futures contracts with currency futures between the two currency areas.

*Example*: At the end of April, a German institution is running a short interest rate gap, i.e. it has a six-month fixed-rate euro asset of €10 000 000 on its books maturing in September, which is funded by a three-month fixed-rate euro-denominated CD issued to US investors at a rate of 4.0% p.a. maturing in June. In the expectation of placing another euro-denominated three-month CD in the USA in one month it might be possible to create a euro-denominated interest rate hedge by combined trading in three-month US$ CD contracts and euro currency futures.

The three-month US$ CD contract for June delivery is trading at 96.00, implying that the market expects the three-month dollar CD rate to be 4.00% p.a. by June. The euro futures contract for June delivery is trading at 0.9392 US$/€, implying a future euro exchange rate to be around 1.0647 €/US$ in a month. The euro futures contract for September delivery is trading at 0.9415 US$/€, implying a future spot exchange rate of 1.0621 €/US$. In other words, the market continues to indicate a weakening of the dollar against the euro. In this hedge, we want to accomplish the following:

1. Borrow funds in US dollars at 4% p.a. for three months from June to September.
2. Convert the amount into euros in June at the future exchange rate of 1.0647 €/US$.

3. Convert it back into US dollars in September at the future exchange rate of 1.0623 €/US$.

This hedging strategy effectively creates a future three-month euro-denominated loan. In this context, we want to hedge against an increase in the dollar interest rate, a decrease in the euro foreign exchange rate in June when the dollar loan is converted into euros, and an increase in the euro foreign exchange rate in September when the dollar loan has to be repaid in euros.

*Example*: The first hedge is accomplished by selling ten three-month US$ CD futures contracts (10 000 000/1 000 000). To establish the second and third hedges, we buy 80 euro currency futures contracts for June delivery and sell another 80 for September delivery (10 000 000 000/125 000 = 80).

After this hedge was established the US dollar three-month CD rate increased to 4.5% p.a. by June. The euro spot foreign exchange rate fell to 1.0624 €/US$ by June and increased again to 1.0676 €/US$ by September. The scenario during the entire time period is laid out in the table below.

| | March actual | Financial futures (June) | June actual | Financial futures (Sept.) | Sept. actual |
|---|---|---|---|---|---|
| Foreign exchange rate (euro/US dollar) | 1.0676 | 1.0647 | 1.0624 | 1.0623 | 1.0676 |
| Euro financial futures (US dollar/euro) | 0.9367 | 0.9392 | 0.9413 | 0.9414 | 0.9367 |
| Three-month US$ CD futures | 95.75 | 96.00 | 95.50 | – | – |
| US$ CD interest rate | 3.75% | 4.00% | 4.50% | – | – |

In this scenario, we would have to pay a higher interest rate on the three-month US dollar-denominated loan, get lower proceeds in euros at the June exchange of the loan amount, and have to pay more euros at the September repayment of the dollar loan. However, what is lost in the cash market transactions is counterweighed by the aggregate profits made on the financial futures trades.

*Three-month cross currency interest rate hedge*

| | |
|---|---|
| Price of three-month CD future sold | 96.00 |
| Cash price of three-month CD future | 95.50 |
| Price gain per futures contract sold | 0.50 |
| Profit per futures contract sold | $1 250  (= (1 000 000 × 0.50)/4)* |
| | |
| Cash price of euro futures in June | 0.9413 |
| Price of June euro futures bought | 0.9392 |
| Price gain per euro futures bought | 0.0021 |
| Profit per euro future sold | $262.5 (= 125 000 × 0.0021) |
| | |
| Price of Sept. euro future sold | 0.9414 |
| Cash price of euro future in Sept. | 0.9367 |
| Price gain per euro future sold | 0.0047 |
| Profit per euro future sold | $587.5 (= 125 000 × 0.0047) |

| | |
|---|---|
| Loss on increased funding cost<br>$(= 10\ 000\ 000/1.0624 \times 0.0050/4))$ | −$11 766 |
| Loss on US$/€ exchange in June<br>$(= 10\ 000\ 000(1.00624 − 1.0647)/1.0624)$ | −$21 649 |
| Loss on euro/US$ exchange in Sept.<br>$(= 10\ 000\ 000(1.0623 − 1.0676)/1.0676)$ | <u>−$49 644</u> |
| Total loss in the cash market | −$83 059 |
| Profit from sale of euro futures | $12 500 $(= 1250 \times 10)$ |
| Profit from purchase of June euro futures | $21 000 $(= 262.5 \times 80)$ |
| Profit from sale of Sept. euro futures | <u>$47 000 $(= 587.5 \times 80)$</u> |
| Aggregate profit from futures trades | $80 500 |

\* The settlement amount is converted to a quarterly interest payment, i.e. divided by four.

Like in the case of the cross currency hedge, this hedge is not complete because the standard size of the futures contracts does not allow a perfect match of the involved amounts.

## 7.4 Hedging interest rate gaps

Financial futures contracts on short-term interest rates can be used to hedge the return on periodic placements of excess liquidity as well as the interest expense on periodic funding needs. Consider for example an institution that is expecting to draw on a LIBOR-based overdraft facility to cover an expected funding need of US$60 million during the month of July five months from now. The one-month LIBOR rate is currently 1.80% but the market seems to indicate a potential rate increase in the immediate future. Given the previous interest rate volatility, it is difficult to foresee the interest rate level five months from now, e.g. the rate could increase to say 3.00% or it could drop to 1.00%. A net borrower is influenced by the size of the interest expenses and, therefore, an institution in this position would want protection against a significant increase in the interest rate level. To do this, they may engage in the futures market to settle the one-month interest expense in July by trading a suitable number of short-term interest rate contracts.

The Chicago Mercantile Exchange (CME) trades one-month LIBOR contracts in $3 million denominations with monthly maturities, e.g. April, May, and July. These short-term interest rate contracts are quoted as annual yield discounts. Hence, a 1% market rate corresponds to a quoted futures price of 99 $(= 100 − 1)$, and a 2% rate is quoted as 98, etc. Therefore, if the one-month LIBOR interest rate goes up, the value of the contract goes down correspondingly, and if the interest rate goes down, the contract value goes up, i.e. there is an inverse relationship between contract value and the interest rate as is the case with long-term financial assets. Should a borrower then buy or sell futures contracts to hedge the future short liquidity position? A borrower should sell, because the aim is to hedge against a possible hike in the interest rate level that will increase the interest expense on the loan. If the interest rate goes up, the value of the futures contract will go down. Therefore, an initial sale of futures contracts at a predetermined price can be covered (closed out) as we approach July by buying back the contracts at a lower contract value, which will incur a gain that reverses the higher interest expense associated with the draw down on the credit facility. Conversely, if the interest rate level drops, the short futures position is closed out by buying back futures contracts at a higher contract price, which will incur a loss that countervails the savings from the lower interest cost on the over-draft facility. Hence, the one-month LIBOR-based interest expense has been effectively locked-in at a fixed rate. To demonstrate this, let us assume the following future quotes prevail in the market:

## Futures prices – interest rate
## LIBOR-1 Mo. (CME) – $3 000 000; pts. of 100%

|  | Open | High | Low | Settle | Change | Yield | Change | Open interest |
|---|---|---|---|---|---|---|---|---|
| March | 98.16 | 98.16 | 98.15 | 98.15 | 0 | 1.85 | 0 | 20 900 |
| April | 98.15 | 98.17 | 98.13 | 98.14 | −0.01 | 1.86 | +0.01 | 9 078 |
| May | 98.14 | 98.15 | 98.11 | 98.11 | −0.02 | 1.89 | +0.02 | 2 688 |
| June | 98.04 | 98.06 | 98.00 | 98.00 | −0.05 | 2.00 | +0.05 | 1 164 |
| July | 97.83 | 97.87 | 97.79 | 97.80 | −0.06 | 2.20 | +0.06 | 740 |

If we sell twenty contracts of $3 million each, the interest expense associated with the expected loan amount of US$60 million should be covered. At the current July futures quote of 97.8, we should receive a sales amount at contract settlement that reflects the one-month interest amount based on the implied annual rate quote of 2.2% (= 100 − 97.8), which amounts to $59 890 000 (see scenario 1 below). Let us first see what happens if the interest rate subsequently increases to 3%. Since the interest rate has increased to 3% from March to July, the futures contract will trade around 97 as we get close to July, and therefore can be bought back at a profit where the settlement will reflect the one-month interest based on the annual rate quote of 3% (= 100 − 97), corresponding to US$59 850 000. Hence, we score a profit on the futures position of $40 000 while the interest expense on the overdraft facility during July amounts to $150 000. Together, the interest expense and the profit on the futures position result in a net expense of $110 000, corresponding to an effective borrowing rate of 2.2%.

### Scenario 1: The interest rate increases

| Sold futures | $20 \times \$3\,000\,000 \times 0.99816$* | = | $ | 59 890 000 |
|---|---|---|---|---|
| Bought futures | $20 \times \$3\,000\,000 \times 0.9975^{\dagger}$ | = | $ | −59 850 000 |
| Profit |  |  | $ | 40 000 |
| Interest expense | $\$60\,000\,000 \times 0.03/12$ | = | $ | −150 000 |
| Net |  |  | $ | −110 000 |

$$110\,000/60\,000\,000 \times 12 = 0.022 \ (2.2\% \ \text{locked-in})$$

*$0.99816 = (1 − 0.022/12)$, $^{\dagger}0.9975 = (1 − 0.03/12)$

Then let us see what happens if the interest rate decreases to 1.5%. Since the interest rate has dropped to 1.5%, the futures contract will trade at 98.5 in July and will be bought back at a loss. The settlement reflecting the one-month interest on the annual discount yield of 1.5% (= 100 − 98.5) will correspond to US$59 925 000 (see scenario

2 below). Hence, we incur a loss on the futures position of $35 000 while the interest expense on the overdraft facility amounts to $75 000. Together the interest expense and the loss on the futures position results in a net expense of $110 000 corresponding to an effective rate of 2.2%.

**Scenario 2: The interest rate decreases**

| | | | | |
|---|---|---|---|---|
| Sold futures | $20 \times \$3\ 000\ 000 \times 0.99816$* | = | $ | 59 890 000 |
| Bought futures | $20 \times \$3\ 000\ 000 \times 0.99875^{\dagger}$ | = | $ | −59 925 000 |
| Loss | | | $ | −35 000 |
| Interest expense | $\$60\ 000\ 000 \times 0.03/12$ | = | $ | −75 000 |
| Net | | | $ | −110 000 |
| | 110 000/60 000 000 × 12 = 0.022 (2.2% locked-in) | | | |

* $0.99816 = (1 − 0.022/12)$, $^{\dagger}0.99875 = (1 − 0.015/12)$

The one-month interest rate on the expected funding cost has effectively been locked-in at 2.2%. Whether the rate increases or decreases, the effective net interest expense corresponds to the futures markets expected one-month rate for July, which was quoted at 2.2% at the time. That is, we can use interest rate futures contracts to lock-in a future funding costs at the market's expected future rate.

If an institution instead is faced with a liquidity surplus, say over shorter periods of time, they face opposing concerns. A net investor is influenced by the size of the interest income and, therefore, an institution in this position would want to protect against a decrease in the interest rate level. Say the institution is expecting excess funds during a one-month period, e.g. during July, it may want to place this liquidity in the market at the prevailing LIBOR-based return. To hedge this return, they may engage in the futures market to cover the one-month interest income in July by trading a suitable number of short-term interest rate contracts, i.e. the return can be locked-in by buying short-term July LIBOR interest rate futures. Hence, if the interest rate drops in the interim, the return on the placement is reduced but the value of the futures contracts will increase so the futures position can be closed out at a profit that compensates for the lower return in the money market. If the rate increases, the return on the money market placement will go up, but the futures position is closed out at a comparable loss. So, the future return on the placement of the excess liquidity is effectively locked-in at the market's expected future rate. The principles for using interest rate futures contracts to hedge the interest rate gaps of net borrowers and net investors can be summarized in the following way:

Hedging with interest rate futures contracts

| Liquidity position | Gap position | Hedging position |
|---|---|---|
| NET BORROWER | SHORT | SELL FUTURES |
| NET INVESTOR | LONG | BUY FUTURES |

If the exchange trades options contracts on the interest rate futures as the underlying assets, the hedges can be set up to create added flexibility. Hence, the borrower will buy put options on the futures contracts rather than sell them directly in the market. Thereby, the borrower can make delivery of the futures contracts if the interest rate level has increased and leave them if the interest rate has dropped and take full advantage of the cheaper funding cost. Conversely, the investor will buy call options on the futures contracts and take delivery of the futures contracts if the interest rate has decreased.

## 7.5 Hedging currency gaps

The futures market can be applied in a similar manner to hedge the value of future receivables and payables in foreign currencies. Consider a euro 10 000 000 receivable due in June. The future value of this receivable in US dollar terms can be locked-in by selling a suitable number of euro futures contracts. The Chicago Mercantile Exchange is trading a euro futures contract with a €125 000 denomination. Therefore, if we sell 80 contracts, the full amount of the receivable should be covered (80 × 125 000 = 10 000 000). The current spot foreign exchange rate is quoted at 0.8771 $/€, and the June euro futures contract is quoted at 0.8721 $/€, i.e. the market seems to indicate that the euro will weaken. Obviously, the futures rate, just like the forward foreign exchange rate, is determined by the interest rate differential between the two currency areas. As we approach the month of June, the value of the euro might increase to, say, 0.8800 $/€, or decrease to, say, 0.8700 $/€. As we approach the final maturity date of the futures contract, the futures quotes will converge towards the spot foreign exchange rate.

Let us see what happens in the futures hedge in each of the two situations where the foreign exchange rate appreciates and depreciates respectively. With the sale of 80 euro June futures contracts, we should receive a sales amount at contract settlement of US$8 721 000 (see scenario 1 below). If the euro foreign exchange rate subsequently increases to 0.8800 $/€, the futures position can be closed out by buying the futures contracts back at 0.8800 $/€ corresponding to US$8 880 000. Hence, we incur a loss on the futures position of $79 000, while the euro receivables are converted into US$8 800 000 at the 0.8800 $/€ spot foreign exchange rate. Subtracting the loss on the futures position, the receivable nets $8 721 000, which corresponds to the futures rate of 0.8721 $/€.

**Scenario 1: The euro foreign exchange rate increases**

| | | | |
|---|---|---|---|
| Sold futures | 80 × €125 000 × 0.8721 | = | $  8 721 000 |
| Bought futures | 80 × €125 000 × 0.8800 | = | $ −8 800 000 |
| Loss | | | $    −79 000 |
| Spot market conversion | €10 000 000 × 0.8800 | = | $  8 800 000 |
| Net | | | $  8 721 000 |

0.8721 $/€ foreign exchange rate locked-in

If the euro spot foreign exchange rate decreases to 0.8700 $/€, the futures position is closed out at a profit as the contracts are bought back at 0.8700 $/€, corresponding to US$8 700 000 (see scenario 2 below). Hence, we gain a profit on the futures position of $21 000, while the euro receivables are converted into US$8 700 000 at the 0.8700 $/€ spot foreign exchange rate. Adding the profit on the futures position, the receivables amount to US$8 721 000 corresponding to the futures rate of 0.8721 $/€.

**Scenario 2: The euro foreign exchange rate decreases**

| | | | | |
|---|---|---|---|---|
| Sold futures | 80 × €125 000 × 0.8721 | = | $ | 8 721 000 |
| Bought futures | 80 × €125 000 × 0.8700 | = | $ | −8 700 000 |
| Profit | | | $ | 21 000 |
| Spot market conversion | €10 000 000 × 0.8700 | = | $ | 8 700 000 |
| Net | | | $ | 8 721 000 |

0.8721 $/€ foreign exchange rate locked-in

Hence, we effectively locked-in the future euro foreign exchange rate by engaging into a futures position with an inverse payoff profile of the underlying long euro position of the June receivables (Figure 7.5).

We could establish a similar hedge for a €10 000 000 payable due in June by buying 80 euro June futures contracts at the prevailing futures quote of 0.8721 $/€, which would lock-in the amount to be paid in US dollars (Figure 7.6).

**Figure 7.5** Hedging foreign currency receivables

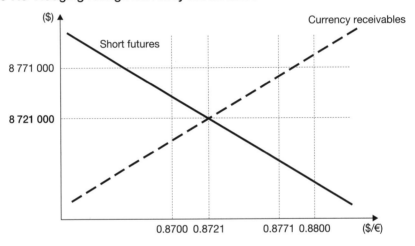

**Figure 7.6** Hedging foreign currency payables

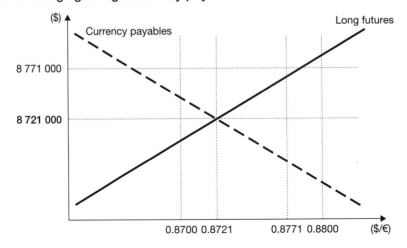

The principles for using currency futures contracts to hedge the foreign exchange gaps of net currency receivables and net currency payables can be summarized in the following way:

Hedging with currency futures contracts

| Foreign exchange position | Gap position | Hedging position |
|---|---|---|
| NET RECEIVABLES | LONG | SELL FUTURES |
| NET PAYABLES | SHORT | BUY FUTURES |

Rather than use futures contracts, we could increase our flexibility by engaging in currency options, e.g. the corresponding option on the futures contract. Hence, in expectation of a €10 000 000 receivable in June, we would buy 80 put option contracts, because the put allows us to sell the underlying futures contracts at a fixed predetermined futures foreign exchange rate if we so wish, but does not oblige us to exercise the option, if the market is in our favor. Assume the CME option on futures contracts are quoted as follows.

**Euro Futures Contract (CME) – 125 000 euros (US cents per euro)**

| Strike price | Calls settle June | Puts settle June |
|---|---|---|
| 0.8700 | 1.98 | 1.77 |
| 0.8800 | 1.53 | 2.31 |

Hence, we could buy a put option at strike price 0.8700 $/€ for a premium of 0.0177$/€, i.e. if we bought 80 put option contracts, the total up-front option premium would amount to US$177 000 (= 80 × 125 000 × 0.0177). In this case, we would only exercise the put options if the spot foreign exchange rate went below the strike price 0.8700 $/€ to hedge the downside risk of a depreciating euro. If the euro spot foreign exchange rate appreciated in the interim, we would let the option lapse and enjoy the full upside potential associated with the higher foreign exchange rate (Figure 7.7).

**Figure 7.7 Hedging currency receivables with option contracts**

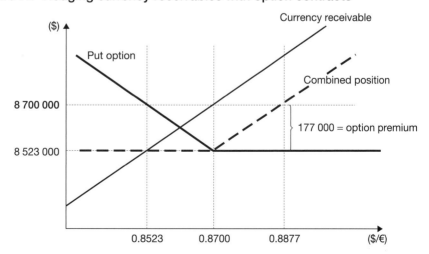

**Figure 7.8** Hedging currency receivables with zero-cost cylinder

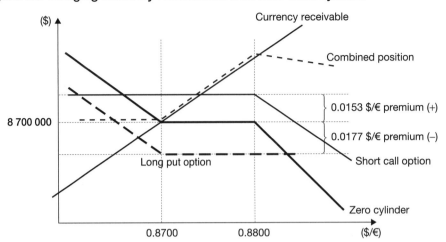

If we have a relatively 'bearish' outlook on the euro, we might be willing to sell (write) a call option and receive some up-front premium income to compensate for the 0.0177$/€ premium we must pay to buy the 0.8700$/€ June put option. To incur less downside risk from the short call option position, we might want to sell a call option with a strike price somewhat above 0.8700, such as 0.8800$/€. This sale would provide premium income at a rate of 0.0153$/€. If we need to buy 80 put option contracts to cover the downside risk associated with the €10 000 000 receivable, we could sell 93 call options to obtain a premium income that was equal to the premium we would have to pay on the put options (80 × 1.77/1.53 = 92.55). This bear spread is sometimes referred to as a zero-cost cylinder (Figure 7.8).

If we are expecting to make a €10 000 000 payable in June, we should buy 80 call option contracts because the call allows us to buy the underlying futures contracts at a fixed predetermined futures foreign exchange rate. Hence, we could buy a call option at strike price 0.8800 $/€ for a premium of 0.0153$/€, i.e. if we bought 80

**Figure 7.9** Hedging currency payable option contracts

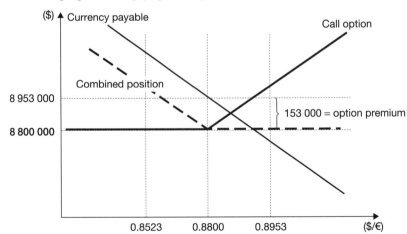

**Figure 7.10** Hedging currency payable with zero-cost cylinder

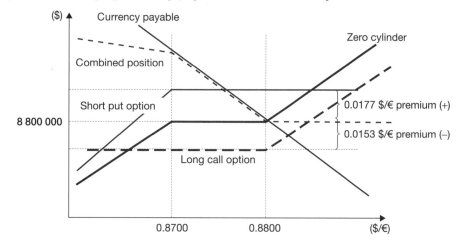

call option contracts the total up-front option premium would amount to US$153 000 (= 80 × 125 000 × 0.0153). In this case, we would only exercise the call options if the spot foreign exchange rate went above the strike price 0.8800 $/€ to hedge the risk of an appreciating euro while enjoying the full upside potential associated with a lower euro foreign exchange rate (Figure 7.9).

If we have a relatively 'bullish' outlook on the euro, we might be willing to sell (write) a put option and receive an up front premium to compensate for the 0.0153$/€ premium we pay for the 0.8800$/€ June call option. We might want to sell the put option at a strike price somewhat below 0.8800, such as 0.8700$/€ to reduce the downside risk associated with the short position. This put option sale would provide premium income of 0.0177$/€. If we need to buy 80 call option contracts to cover the foreign exchange risk associated with the €10 000 000 payable, we could sell 69 put options to obtain a premium income that is equal to the premium we must pay for the call options (80 × 1.53/1.77 = 69.15). This bull spread is another type of zero-cost cylinder (Figure 7.10).

## 7.6 Managing interest rate risk

We can also use long-term interest rate futures contracts to manage the interest rate risk associated with portfolios of longer-term financial assets and liabilities. For example, the Chicago Board of Trade (CBOT) quotes several treasury futures contracts in $100 000 denominations. To hedge a securities portfolio against the negative price effects associated with an interest rate increase, we would sell a suitable number of treasury futures contracts. If the interest rate goes up, the value of the futures contract goes down, so the short futures position can be closed out at a profit that counterweighs the capital loss on the securities portfolio. Conversely, if the interest rate goes down, the futures position will incur a loss that negates the capital gains obtained in the securities portfolio. Hence, you sell futures contracts to reduce the duration of the underlying securities portfolio and buy futures to increase the duration of the underlying securities portfolio, i.e. by going short in futures the price sensitivity of the aggregate securities and futures portfolio is reduced while going long in futures increases the price sensitivity.

- Sell treasury futures contracts ⇒ Duration $(D) \downarrow$
- Buy treasury futures contracts ⇒ Duration $(D) \uparrow$

On this basis, we could manage the duration of our securities portfolio towards more optimally targeted duration levels, often referred to as a **duration hedge**, depending on our view on market developments, i.e. if we expect rates to increase we would reduce the duration and if we expected a rate drop we might want to increase the duration of the portfolio. In other words, we can manage the duration of an asset or liability portfolio without having to modify the underlying asset (or liability) structure.

$$D_{\mathrm{T}} = \frac{(D_{\mathrm{P}} \times P_{\mathrm{S}}) + (D_{\mathrm{F}} \times P_{\mathrm{F}})}{P_{\mathrm{S}}}$$

$$P_{\mathrm{F}} = \frac{(D_{\mathrm{T}} - D_{\mathrm{P}})P_{\mathrm{S}}}{D_{\mathrm{F}}}$$

$$\text{Number of contracts} = \frac{P_{\mathrm{F}}}{\text{Value of the futures contract}}$$

where

$D_{\mathrm{T}}$ = targeted duration of portfolio of securities and futures contracts;
$D_{\mathrm{P}}$ = duration of securities portfolio;
$P_{\mathrm{S}}$ = market value of securities portfolio;
$D_{\mathrm{F}}$ = duration of futures portfolio (duration of the 'cheapest to deliver' bond);
$P_{\mathrm{F}}$ = market value of futures portfolio.

*Example*: An investment manager would like to reduce the duration of the invested portfolio somewhat until the board meeting in June. The nominal securities portfolio is $100 000 000 with an average market price of 105. The portfolio's duration is 5. The June five-year (CBOT) T-Note futures contract is currently settled at 104.3. The duration of the 'cheapest to-deliver' bond amounts to 4.5. The return on the securities portfolio has been highly correlated with the return on treasury notes in the past. Hence, the duration of the portfolio can be reduced to 3.0 until June by selling 447 T-Note futures contracts (see calculation below):

$$3 = \frac{(5 \times 100\ 000\ 000 \times 1.05) + (4.5 \times P_{\mathrm{F}})}{100\ 000\ 000 \times 1.05} \Rightarrow$$

$$3 = \frac{525\ 000\ 000 + 4.5 \times P_{\mathrm{F}}}{105\ 000\ 000} \Rightarrow$$

$$P_{\mathrm{F}} = \frac{315\ 000 - 525\ 000}{4.5}$$

$$= -46\ 666\ 667 \Rightarrow$$

$$\text{Number of contracts} = \frac{46\ 666\ 667}{100\ 000 \times 104.3}$$

$$= -447.43$$

The portfolio could be completely immunized for the time period until June, i.e. $D_{\mathrm{P}} = 0$, by selling more futures contracts or more specifically by selling 1118 (= $5/(5-3) \times 447$) T-Note futures contracts.

The long-term interest rate futures contracts can also be used to manage the implied interest rate risk, **duration gap**, associated with a particular asset and liability structure in a given currency. In this analysis, the financial assets correspond to the institution's different types of cash receivables in the currency and the liabilities correspond to different types of cash payables in the currency.

*Example*: US dollar-denominated assets and liabilities [$1000 (*duration*)]:

| Assets | | Liabilities | |
|---|---|---|---|
| Customer receivables | 30 000 (1) | Overdraft facility | 20 000 (0) |
| Commercial investments | 70 000 (5) | Medium-term notes | 60 000 (4) |
| | | Total liabilities | 80 000 (3) |
| | | Implied equity position | 20 000 |
| Total assets | 100 000 (3.8) | Total liabilities and equity | 100 000 |

$$D_A = 0.3 \times 1 + 0.7 \times 5 \quad = 3.8$$
$$D_L = 0.25 \times 0 + 0.75 \times 4 = 3.0$$
$$D_A - D_L = 3.8 - 3.0 \qquad\qquad = 0.8$$

A positive duration gap indicates that the equity position will incur a loss if the interest rate level increases, and register a gain if the interest rate level decreases.[5]

$$\text{Duration gap: } D_A - D_L$$

The duration of the assets and liabilities indicate how sensitive the firm's implied equity position in a single currency is to changes in the interest rate level of that currency, e.g. US dollars, euros, pound sterling, etc.

$$\Delta E = -\frac{(D_A \times A) - (D_L \times L)}{1 + r} \times \Delta r$$

$$= -\frac{\left(D_A - \left(\frac{L}{A} \times D_L\right)\right) A}{1 + r} \times \Delta r$$

where

$D_A$ = duration of assets;
$D_L$ = duration of liabilities;
$A$ = market value of assets;
$L$ = market value of liabilities;
$E$ = equity position $(A - L)$;
$r$ = interest rate level (yield).

*Example*: What is the expected effect on the implied equity position from a 1% increase in the interest rate level from 5% to 6%?

$$\Delta E = -\frac{(D_A \times A) - (D_L \times L)}{1 + r} \times \Delta r$$

$$= -\frac{\left(D_A - \left(\frac{L}{A} \times D_L\right)\right) A}{1 + r} \times \Delta r$$

$$= -\frac{\left(3.8 - \left(\frac{80}{100} \times 3\right)\right) 100}{1.05} \times 0.01$$

$$= -1.33$$

Is a $1.33 million loss acceptable? Well, it depends. It will not bring the company into bankruptcy with an equity position of $20 million but if annual earnings amount to say $3 million (= 15% ROE), then such a drop in net income might be unwarranted. In this case, the interest rate sensitivity of the equity position could be reduced by selling T-Note futures contracts. For example, if we wanted to reduce the duration from 0.8 to 0.4 then we could sell 213 futures contracts.

$$0.4 = \frac{\left(D_A - \left(\frac{L}{A} \times D_L\right)\right) \times A + (D_F \times P_F)}{A} \qquad \Rightarrow$$

$$P_F = \frac{0.4 - \left(D_A - \left(\frac{L}{A} \times D_L\right)\right)A}{D_F}$$

$$= \frac{0.4 - (3.8 - (0.8 \times 3))100\,000\,000}{4.5}$$

$$= -22\,222\,222 \qquad \Rightarrow$$

$$\text{Number of contracts} = -22\,222\,222/104\,300$$

$$= -213.06$$

The minus (−) indicates that we should sell (i.e. go short) 213 T-Note futures contracts to reduce the duration to 0.4 (the derivation uses an extension of the equation from above $P_F = (D_P - D_S)P_S/D_F$).

## Conclusion

Financial futures contracts can be used to effectively lock-in the price of a financial asset, such as a short-term interest rate, and longer-term security price, a foreign exchange rate, etc., at a later date by buying or selling futures contracts. When the futures position is closed out just before contract expiry, the hedger obtains a capital gain or loss that counteracts losses or gains incurred in the underlying cash market. The hedge can also be made more flexible by acquiring call or put option contracts on the financial futures contracts as the underlying asset. Thereby, the hedger obtains the best of two worlds namely a cover against downside loss from adverse price movements while retaining the upside potential from favourable price developments.

## Summary

● Interest rate futures can be used to hedge the interest rate risk exposures associated with investment positions (long) by buying futures contracts and borrowing positions (short) by selling futures contracts as well as manage short-term interest rate gaps.

● Bond futures can be used to hedge the interest rate exposures associated with investment in long-term securities portfolios and long-term debt portfolios as well as manage duration gaps of the institution's implied equity position.

● Currency futures can be used to hedge the currency exposures associated with foreign exchange receivables (long) by selling futures contracts and foreign exchange payables (short) by buying futures contracts as well as manage net gapping positions in different currencies.

● Engagement in different interest rate and bond futures can be used in cross hedges to provide cover for related financial assets and simultaneous engagement in different currency and interest rate futures can cover interest rate risks in other currencies.

● Interest rate and bond futures can be used to manage the interest rate risk associated with specific portfolios and net interest rate gaps by modifying the duration towards levels targeted in accordance with the current view of the market.

## Questions

7.1 Explain the principle behind short-term interest rate hedges for a borrower and an investor.

7.2 Explain how the interest rate futures are priced and settled.

7.3 Explain the principle behind long-term interest rate hedges for a borrower and an investor.

7.4 Explain how bond futures are priced and settled.

7.5 What determines how many futures contracts should be traded?

7.6 What is the idea behind the concept of immunization?

7.7 Explain the principle behind currency hedges for foreign exchange receivable and payables.

7.8 Explain how zero-cost cylinders can be used to hedge foreign exchange receivables and payables.

7.9 Explain how you could use futures contracts to manage interest rate risk (duration).

7.10 Explain how we can determine the interest rate sensitivity of a institutional equity position.

## Exercises

7.1 You expect a 45-day funding need of $60 500 000 from the beginning of June. The one-month LIBOR futures contract is quoted as follows:

LIBOR-1 MO. (CME) –$3 000 000; points of 100%

| | Open | High | Low | Settle | Change | Discount Settle | Discount Change | Open interest |
|---|---|---|---|---|---|---|---|---|
| June | 93.98 | 94.02 | 93.85 | 94.00 | 0.02 | 6.00 | 0.02 | 11 165 |
| July | 93.87 | 93.93 | 93.74 | 93.90 | 0.01 | 6.10 | 0.01 | 2 163 |

(a) Set up a hedge to protect the funding against an increase in the interest rate level.
(b) What happens if the 1-month LIBOR rate increases to 7%? Show the mechanics of the hedge.
(c) Explain how you would arrange a comparable hedge using a forward rate agreement.

7.2 The (CME) Euro FX Contract is quoted as follows:

Contract size: €125 000
Premium quotes: cents per euro

| Strike price | Calls settle | | | Puts settle | | |
|---|---|---|---|---|---|---|
| | April | May | June | April | May | June |
| 0.8600 | 1.25 | 1.34 | 1.50 | 0.26 | 0.59 | 0.86 |
| 0.8650 | 0.90 | 1.02 | 1.17 | 0.41 | 0.79 | 1.08 |
| 0.8700 | 0.62 | 0.72 | 0.87 | 0.63 | 0.95 | 1.19 |
| 0.8750 | 0.41 | 0.50 | 0.64 | 0.92 | 1.38 | 1.61 |

(a) You are expecting to make payables of €10 000 000 in June. How would you hedge the foreign exchange conversion from dollars into euros using futures option contracts?
(b) You have a somewhat 'bullish' view on the euro right now, so you are willing to establish a double option 'bull spread' to hedge your euro payables. Please explain how you would establish this hedge.
(c) Please explain how you might establish a zero-cost bull spread hedge (zero-cost cylinder).

7.3 You are managing a $94 500 000 nominal bond portfolio with average price of 105.82 and average duration of 4.7. The five-year treasury note contract is quoted as follows:

5 YR TREAS NOTES (CBOT) –$100 000; pts. 32nds of 100%

| | Open | High | Low | Settle | Change | Lifetime High | Low | Open interest |
|---|---|---|---|---|---|---|---|---|
| June | 97–225 | 97–23 | 97–13 | 97–22 | 0.5 | 98–195 | 96–10 | 401 813 |

The duration of the cheapest-to-deliver bond is 4.32

(a) Set up a duration hedge to shield the portfolio against changes in the interest rate level.

(b) How would you reduce the duration of the portfolio from 4.7 to 2.5? Set up the hedge.

7.4 A corporation has the following balance sheet: [market value ($1000), (*duration*)]:

| Assets | | Liabilities and Equity | |
|---|---|---|---|
| Cash | 2 000 *(0)* | Overdraft facility | 3 000 *(0)* |
| Securities | 4 000 *(1)* | Time loans | 5 000 *(2)* |
| Commercial investments | 8 000 *(4)* | Medium term notes | 8 000 *(3)* |
| Real estate and buildings | 8 000 *(9)* | Equity | 6 000 |
| Total assets | 22 000 | Total liabilities and equity | 22 000 |

(a) Please determine the duration gap of the corporate balance sheet.

(b) Please calculate how many $100 000 T-Note futures contracts to trade to completely hedge the duration gap. The duration of the cheapest-to-deliver bond is 3.2 and the T-Note future is quoted at 105.25.

(c) Should we buy or sell the futures contracts?

## Notes

[1] See, for example, Powers, M. J. (1984), *Inside the Financial Futures Market*, 2nd edn, Wiley.

[2] See, for example, Schwager, J. D. (1984), *A Complete Guide to the Futures Markets*, Wiley.

[3] See, for example, Andersen, T. J. (1993), *Currency and Interest Rate Hedging*, (2nd edn), Prentice-Hall.

[4] See any standard statistical text on regression analysis, e.g. Wannacott, R. J. and Wannacott, T. H. (1970), *Econometrics*, Wiley.

[5] See, for example, Saunders, A. and Cornett, M. M. (2003), *Financial Institutions Management: A Risk Management Approach*, McGraw-Hill.

# Chapter 8

# Hedging with forward agreements and options

The previous chapter provided an overview of exchange traded futures and options contracts and their practical uses for hedging purposes. In this chapter, we extend the discussion of derivatives usage with an initial focus on comparable over-the-counter products such as forward and options contracts applied to money market rates, securities prices, foreign exchange rates, and commodities prices. This chapter considers a number of options-based hedging strategies that may apply equally to exchange traded and OTC contracts. The use of financial derivatives for hedging purposes is often considered in connection with single transactions and we will initially adopt the same approach here. However, it is practical to see the hedging efforts in a general asset and liability management perspective as interest rates, foreign exchange rates, and other types of financial pricing gaps expose the entire firm and affect its performance outcomes. Hence, this chapter will also look at possible applications of these instruments in the context of more general corporate risk management situations.

## 8.1 Hedging interest rate risk

Forward agreements, like futures contracts, enable the hedger to lock-in the future prices of underlying assets or liabilities within the maturity spectrum of the contracts offered in the market. Typically, futures contracts are traded for settlement three, six, nine, twelve months hence and sometimes up to 24–36 months. Generally speaking, forward agreements offer the same maturity spectrum and due to their idiosyncratic nature they often provide opportunities to extend maturities beyond the norm for exchange traded contracts as well as other features can be tailored to the specific needs of a corporate counterpart. Hence, disregarding potential basis risk factors, forwards and futures alike make it possible to eliminate uncertainties associated with fluctuations in financial prices in a short- to medium-term time frame.

Forward rate agreements (Chapter 5) provide the means to lock-in the level of short-term interest rates on future dates. A borrower can hedge the future funding cost through the purchase of FRAs while an investor can hedge the future return by selling FRAs. The borrower has, in effect, locked-in the future funding cost against the payment of a front-end fee (Figure 8.1). Conversely, the investor has locked-in the future return against payment of a front-end fee (Figure 8.2).

Hence, the institution buying a forward rate agreement can fix the forward interest rate on any loan or deposit without going through the administrative procedures involved in managing a financial futures hedge. The amount and maturity of forward rate agreements are usually more flexible than financial futures where the contracts are tied to the fixed maturity dates and standard sizes of the futures exchange. On

**Figure 8.1** Bought FRA position (borrower)

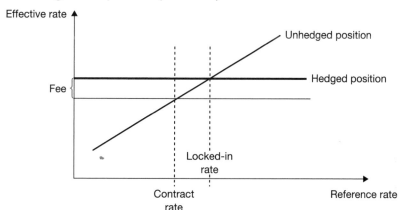

**Figure 8.2** Sold FRA position (investor)

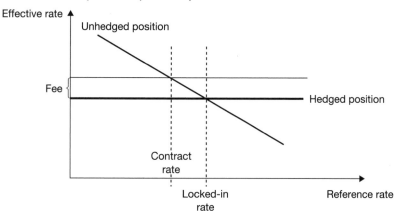

the other hand, users of forward rate agreements must accept the associated counter-party risk, i.e. if the institution providing the FRA goes bankrupt before the contract expires it will not be able to honour the agreement and the risk cover has vanished.

*Example 1*: A construction company needs capital of US$1 million for a six-month period in four months to carry out a project. To lock-in the future cost of funding required to complete the project, the company buys a forward rate agreement, which guarantees that the US$1 000 000 can be borrowed for six months in four months time at a rate of, say, 7.5% p.a. The company pays a fixed fee of perhaps $1/2$% p.a. during the ten months of the forward rate agreement to obtain the forward cover from the bank. Hereby the risk associated with the future financing cost is eliminated and the company can carry out a feasibility study with full certainty, at least as far as funding costs are concerned.

*Example 2*: An international trading company periodically raises funds through issuance of bankers' acceptances (BAs). Traditionally there has been an interest rate advantage of $5/8$% on bankers' acceptance financing as compared to direct bank overdrafts. In one month the company expects a financing requirement of US$3 million for two months but management is worried that interest rates will increase. The company then buys from the bank a forward rate agreement, which secures the borrowing cost on US$3 000 000 in the interbank market for two months in one month's time at a rate of, say, 7% p.a.

At the time of drawdown the interest rate has increased but the $5/8$% advantage remains. The company may, therefore, decide not to fund itself through the bank overdrafts but rather issue banker's acceptances. Hence, the forward rate agreement is used to hedge the bankers' acceptance rate and a cancellation fee is calculated by marking-to-market. Let's say the interbank offer rate has increased to 8% p.a., i.e. the rate has increased by 1% as compared to the forward rate fixed at 7% p.a. The cancellation fee is then calculated as the p.a. interest differential between the forward rate and the new spot rate prevailing at the date of drawdown.

In this case the cancellation fee is in favour of the company, which will be credited the interest amount of 1% p.a. (that is, US$5000) on US$3 000 000 for the two-month loan period. The company will issue bankers' acceptances and raise funds at the new market rate of $7^{3}/8$% p.a. (8% − $5/8$%). The company pays the bank a commission of $1/4$% p.a. during the three-month period of the forward rate agreement and receives a compensation of 1%. Hence, by engaging in the forward rate agreement the company has secured the funding at an all-in cost of $6^{5}/8$% p.a. (= $7^{3}/8$ − 1 + $1/4$), which is $1^{3}/8$% p.a. below the going interbank offered rate.

*Example 3*: An institutional investor periodically places excess US dollar liquidity in short-term commercial paper because this type of investment carries a lower price risk than do, say, US treasury bonds. An investor expects to have idle liquidity of US$5 million during a two-month period in one month's time but fears that the interest rate level might drop in the mean-time. To fix the future investment return, the investor sells a forward rate agreement to a bank and thereby locks-in the future investment rate in the interbank market at $6^{1}/2$% p.a. for the two-month period. At the date of placement, the interbank bid rate has dropped to $5^{1}/2$% p.a. and the commercial paper rate is at the same level. The investor then decides to invest in commercial paper and uses the forward rate agreement to hedge by marking-to-market.

The cancellation fee is the difference between the agreed forward rate of $6^{1}/2$% p.a. and the current spot rate of $5^{1}/2$% p.a., which is in favour of the institutional investor.

The bank therefore pays the interest amount of 1% p.a. on US$5 000 000 for the two-month period to the investor. The investor pays a commission of perhaps $1/4$% p.a. to the bank during the three-month period of the forward agreement but also in this case receives a 1% compensation because the interest rate has dropped. So, through the engagement in FRAs the investment in commercial paper receives an all-in rate of $6^1/4$% p.a. (= $5^1/2$ + 1 − $1/4$). In case the commercial paper rate had dropped more than the interbank bid rate, the investor could choose to deliver the funds directly to the bank to secure a higher return than $5^1/2$% p.a.

The forward rate agreement locks-in the future interest rate, that is, it provides a hedge against the downside interest rate risk. Yet, it does not leave open the upside potential for gains from a favourable development in interest rates.

## 8.1.1 Forward rate agreement

A construction company was awarded a US$15 million contract in December for a major development project as part of a municipal urban development plan to take off in May the following year. The project was a forerunner for several other development projects to commence upon the initial project's completion. To be awarded the first contract meant a 'foot in the door' when future bids should be solicited. The initial construction project was scheduled for completion over an eighteen-month period thus requiring a stepped-up financing scheme throughout the construction period. The municipality would make gradual and partial down payments as the construction work was satisfactorily completed. Hence, a 10% advance payment would be paid as the construction work started in May, around 20% of the total contract price would be paid after six months in November, and another 20% would be due for payment after twelve months in May the subsequent year. The remaining 50% would be paid upon satisfactory completion of the project after eighteen months scheduled for November the subsequent year.

According to the Financial Controller of the construction company they had been awarded the contract in a very competitive bidding process and partially in a situation where they wanted to utilize excess capacity built up in similar works just completed. They made the bid on favourable terms with a view to the potential for future construction contracts that could flow to the company if it was awarded the first construction project. Because the construction company had to invest money in the initial mobilization of equipment and engagement of construction workers, they foresaw some heavy draws on the variable rate overdraft facilities made available by their banks. The interest rate volatility made the future interest expense an unknown factor in the company's calculations. So, the interest rate uncertainty provided them with a bit of a headache when making the cash projections. They were willing to consider the new project at a 'break-even' price or a slight profit but obviously wouldn't like to lose money on it, if they could avoid it. Fortunately, in discussing this issue with one of their banks it was suggested that they engage in interest rate contracts to lock-in the future interest rate.

In mid-December, the short-term interbank offered rate (one to three months) had moved down to around 3% p.a. from a level above 5% earlier in the year. This meant that the company could fund itself presently at a rate of 3.50–3.75% p.a. Looking at the cash flow analysis, a funding rate of 3.75% would result in an overall profit of around US$110 000 on the total construction project. However, assuming instead a funding rate of 5% throughout the construction period until November the

**Table 8.1** Forward rate contracts

| Period | Contracted rate |
| --- | --- |
| 2nd quarter – Year 1 | 3.50% p.a. |
| 3rd quarter – Year 1 | 3.60% p.a. |
| 4th quarter – Year 1 | 3.75% p.a. |
| 1st quarter – Year 2 | 4.00% p.a. |
| 2nd quarter – Year 2 | 4.00% p.a. |
| 3rd quarter – Year 2 | 4.25% p.a. |

subsequent year, this profit figure would turn into a loss of around US$125 000. Given the market outlook toward falling interest rates, the company could lock-in the future rates on rather favourable terms against a fee of ¼% p.a. payable to the bank throughout the period of the forward contracts (Table 8.1).

Forward rate agreements guarantee periodic mark-to-market compensation payments that lock-in the effective short-term interest rates. In contrast, interest rate caps, or options, provide flexibility to the holder. A ceiling rate agreement provides compensation to the holder in periods where the short-term interest rate exceeds a certain predetermined threshold level while there is no counter compensation imposed on the holder when the rate is below the threshold level. Conversely, a floor rate agreement provides compensation to the holder in periods where the short-term interest rate is below the threshold level. Hence, a borrower can exploit a ceiling rate agreement by taking advantage of low interest rate period and receiving compensation in high interest periods. Similarly, an investor can exploit a floor rate agreement by taking advantage of periods with high interest rates and receiving compensation during periods with low interest rates. Hence, the option contracts do not lock-in the future prices of the underlying assets or liabilities but rather establish upper or lower limits on future price developments. Hence, the hedger is protected against potentially adverse price changes but also maintains the full gain if the price development is favourable.

### 8.1.2　Interest rate ceiling

In November a regional building society held a US$14 000 000 portfolio of fifteen-year mortgage loans on its books. The mortgage loans were arranged to match the expected need for commercial building contracts. Repayment of principal and interest on the mortgage portfolio was arranged as 30 equal semi-annual annuities with a fixed rate of 6.50% p.a. The repayment dates were June 1 and December 1 each year until maturity. In accordance with common practice, the building society funded the mortgage portfolio through issuance of medium-term savings bonds. The building society was well aware of the ups and downs in the interbank money market rates, which from year-to-year and even from month-to-month by historical experience could fluctuate widely. They based their intermediate funding strategy on a short-term view of the interest rate development and given the declining interest rate environment the portfolio was funded by rolling over three-month money market loans in the view that the interest rate level at least in the short to medium term would continue to drop (Figure 8.3).

**Figure 8.3** Interest rate structure and money market rates

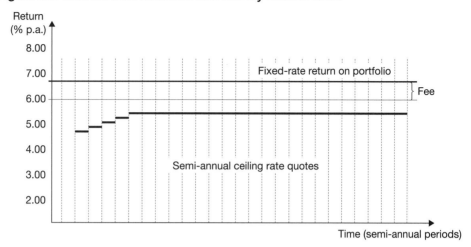

The money market funding strategy provided flexibility to 'play' the market by switching short-term funding maturities according to changes in the interest rate structure. It had led to an overall lower-than-average funding cost over the past year in the falling interest rate environment. However, they were also aware that a fifteen-year fixed rate commitment represents considerable interest rate risk in case the short-term interbank money market rates should increase above the fixed return of 6.50% p.a. on the mortgage portfolio. The interest rate gapping concerned senior management and the issue had been discussed at several board meetings. In the previous month their all-in six-month funding rate was around 3.5% p.a., thus securing a reasonable interest rate differential to the building society in the short to medium term. The prevailing interest rate outlook indicated a continued drop in the interest rate level but with some uncertainties. Hence, the board decided to fund short term for an interim period of two years and then lock-in the interest rate differential for the remaining twelve years to maturity.

They contacted a number of money centre banks to obtain quotes on ceiling rate agreements, which could provide an approximate match to the funding need of the building contract until maturity. The building society signed the ceiling rate agreements and was henceforth guaranteed a maximum funding cost at the quoted rates providing an average maximum funding rate of around 5.25% p.a. In addition, the building society paid a contract fee (option premium) calculated on the total funding need over the life of the contracts amounting to an average around 0.75% p.a. Hence the building society effectively guaranteed a maximum funding rate of around $6\frac{1}{4}$% p.a. well below the fixed rate return on the mortgage portfolio.

## 8.2 Hedging currency risk

Currency gaps can arise from cross-border payables of different sorts completed in connection with international trade and capital transactions. Whether the organization assumes long or short net positions in foreign currencies, they are exposed to the uncertainty of the future foreign exchange rate development and, therefore, may have an interest to hedge these currency gaps. As in the case of interest rate risk, forwards and options contracts can be applied to hedge different foreign exchange positions. A forward agreement locks-in the future foreign exchange rate whereas a currency option provides the holder with the flexibility to only use the forward rate if it is favourable to do so.

## 8.2.1 Short currency position

Currency gaps can arise from import transactions, debt service payments, and various money transfers. These constitute short currency positions where the position holder needs to acquire the foreign currency at some time in the future. This gap can be closed by buying a suitable number of currency futures contracts or by entering into a forward foreign exchange agreement.

*Example*: In April, a US company is expected to make payment of 10 million Swiss francs in two months' time. The current spot foreign exchange rate is 0.7968 US$/SFr and the June futures contract is quoted at 0.7985 US$/SFr. This rate is locked-in by buying 80 futures contracts of SFr125 000 each.

By the end of June, the actual spot foreign exchange rate had increased and turned out to be 0.8035 US$/SFr. Hence, the futures hedge materialized as follows:

| | | | |
|---|---|---|---|
| Revenue from sold futures | $80 \times 125\,000 \times 0.8035$ | = | $ 8 035 000 |
| Payment for bought futures | $10\,000\,000 \times 0.7985$ | = | $ 7 985 000 |
| Gain from futures position | | | 50 000 |
| | | | |
| Purchase of SFr in market | $10\,000\,000 \times 0.8035$ | = | $ 8 035 000 |
| Total $ payment including gain on futures position | | | $ 7 985 000 |

This corresponds to a locked-in exchange rate of 0.7985 US$/SFr. In this case, the futures hedge turned out to be a smart move because the hedger would have lost if it had not bought the futures contracts. On the other hand if the spot foreign exchange rate had dropped in value, the futures position would have resulted in a loss thus effectively locking-in the future foreign exchange rate at 0.7985 US$/SFr. If the spot foreign exchange rate had dropped to 0.7950 US$/SFr, say, the futures hedge would have looked as follows:

| | | | |
|---|---|---|---|
| Revenue from sold futures | $80 \times 125\,000 \times 0.7950$ | = | $ 7 950 000 |
| Payment for bought futures | $10\,000\,000 \times 0.7985$ | = | $ 7 985 000 |
| Loss from futures position | | | (35 000) |
| | | | |
| Purchase of SFr in market | $10\,000\,000 \times 0.7950$ | = | $ 7 750 000 |
| Total $ payment including loss on futures position | | | $ 7 985 000 |

This corresponds to a locked-in exchange rate of 0.7985 US$/SFr. If the company instead had bought a call option of the underlying currency future, it would have been able to take advantage of the favourable market development by cancelling the futures transaction, i.e. the option holder would have the right but no obligation to acquire the underlying futures contract. Call options can also be beneficial to companies engaged in bidding contests where the outcome of the future transactions is uncertain.

*Example*: A US-based company is negotiating an important contract in May to be executed within two months and is committed to give a firm offer. To meet the deadline on the offer, machinery worth 1 million Swiss francs must be bought (imported) from a Swiss manufacturer to be at the production plant in the United States during the month of October. The Swiss manufacturer has promised to ship the machinery in September against cash payment.

To hedge the potential payment of SFr1 000 000 in September, the US company can buy Swiss franc call options up to the contract amount of SFr1 000 000. If the company approaches the Philadelphia Stock Exchange to buy the options, it would purchase sixteen call option contracts of SFr62 500 each. The Swiss franc is quoted at 1.2739 SFr/US$ (0.7850 US$/SFr) and the company wants to hedge against a potential strengthening of the Swiss franc, which would cause them to pay more US dollars for the import in September. The September call options are quoted as follows:

| Strike price (US$/SFr) | Quote (US$/SFr) | Call premium (US$) | |
|---|---|---|---|
| 0.7750 | 0.0248 | 1550.00 | (in-the-money) |
| 0.7950 | 0.0151 | 943.50 | (out-of-the-money) |

The company decides to buy the out-of-the-money call option because the premium is lower than the in-the-money contract and pays up front US$15 100 (16 × 943.50). The company wins the bid for the project and orders the machine from the Swiss manufacturer. In the coming period the expectation of a strengthening franc in general is proven correct but there has been some exchange rate volatility. To assess the potential gain and loss position, calculations are made to get a feel for the sensitivity to the exchange rate movements.

| Exchange rate (US$/SFr) | Profit/(loss) |
|---|---|
| 0.7750 | (15 100) |
| 0.7850 | (15 100) |
| 0.7950 | (15 100) |
| 0.8050 | (5 100) |
| 0.8150 | 4 900 |
| 0.8250 | 14 900 |
| 0.8350 | 24 900 |

A change from the current spot foreign exchange rate to the break-even rate around 0.8100 US$/SFr constitutes a 3.2% change in the foreign exchange rate, the premium of US$15 100 is considered reasonable by the company (Figure 8.4).

The use of currency options is relevant in this situation. The maximum cost of the hedge of US$15 100 is known and if the underlying commercial transaction should be lost in the competitive bidding, the option position does not impose additional cost on the company. At the same time, the option represents a potential gain from a favourable foreign exchange rate development. Had the company instead hedged the currency exposure through the purchase of futures contracts or an engagement

**Figure 8.4** Profit and loss profile (SFr calls)

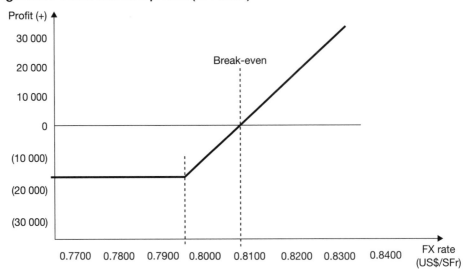

in a forward contract, it would be exposed to a new open position in case the commercial transaction failed to materialize. This new open position would then have to be reversed or covered at an unknown cost.

### 8.2.2 Long currency position

Long currency positions can arise from cross-border receivables related to international commercial transactions, such as export receipts, interest income, etc. Here the position holder must dispose of the foreign currency against the home currency at some time in the future. This gap can be closed by selling a suitable number of currency futures contracts or by engaging in a forward foreign exchange agreement.

*Example*: In April, a US company expects to receive a payment of 10 million Swiss francs in two months' time. The current spot foreign exchange rate is 0.7968 US$/SFr and the June futures contract is quoted at 0.7985 US$/SFr. This rate is locked-in by selling 80 futures contracts of SFr125 000 each.

If the spot foreign exchange rate moves to 0.8035 US$/SFr at the time the Swiss franc receivables materialize then the company incurs an opportunity cost in the form of the foregone windfall gain derived from the positive market development. Had the company instead bought put options on the underlying futures contract, it would retain the flexibility to forego the futures contract if the foreign exchange rate develops favourably. Obviously, the company would have to pay an up-front premium to gain this flexibility. Long currency positions associated with bidding processes make the use of currency put options particularly relevant.

*Example*: During August a German company is bidding for delivery of equipment in December to a US-based manufacturing company. The value of the equipment amounts to US$2 000 000 to be received upon delivery of satisfactory documentation of shipment. The German exporter has potential receivables in US dollars and worries that the dollar will weaken against the euro, because this will reduce earnings measured in the domestic currency.

To hedge the potential receivables of US$2 000 000 in December, the company can buy US dollar put options against euros up to the contract amount of US$2 000 000. This kind of put option provides the holder with the right to sell US dollars against euros at a predetermined exchange rate. This is equivalent to holding a euro call option against US dollars, since it provides the holder with the right to buy € against US$ at a predetermined foreign exchange rate.

A call option of currency ($x$) against currency ($y$) is equivalent to a put option of currency ($y$) against currency ($x$) and vice versa.

Assume the German exporter approaches the Chicago Mercantile Exchange to buy options on currency futures contracts. The euro option contracts have a denomination of €125 000 each. With a spot foreign exchange rate in August around 1.1664 €/US$ (0.8573 US$/€), the number of euro call options to purchase to hedge the contract amount of US$2 000 000 is 19 (18.66 = (2 000 000/0.8573)/125 000). Hence, the German company would have to buy 19 euro call option contracts on the exchange. The company decided to buy the out-of-the-money call option with strike price 0.8600 and a call premium of 1.25 ¢/€. The premium paid by the company for the purchase of 19 euro call option contracts was US$29 687.50 (19 × 1.25 × 125 000) or €34 629.07 (29 687.50/0.8573). To assess the option position the company made a profit and loss analysis reflecting the consequences of different developments in the foreign exchange rate.

| Exchange rate (US$/€) | Profit/(loss) |
| --- | --- |
| 0.8400 | (29 687) |
| 0.8500 | (29 687) |
| 0.8600 | (29 687) |
| 0.8700 | (5 937) |
| 0.8800 | 17 813 |
| 0.8900 | 41 563 |
| 0.9000 | 65 313 |

The profit and loss profile of the (0.8600) call option as a function of US$/€ exchange rate is shown below (Figure 8.5).

### 8.2.3 Cross-currency hedge

Most exchange traded currency option contracts are traded against US$ as a primary international currency although the number of contracts based on cross-currency quotes is increasing. In the absence of a specific cross-currency contract, it is possible to construe an options based cross-currency hedge by combining two conventional currency options.

*Example*: A French company is exporting goods to a UK-based sales company. Receivables of £ stg. 1 500 000 are expected in six months. To hedge the euro value of the future pound sterling receivables, the French exporter wants to buy pound put options against euros in an amount equivalent to the face value of the export order.

**Figure 8.5** Profit and loss profile (euro call options)

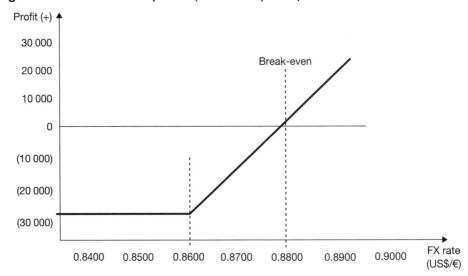

Hence, the French exporter could buy pound put options against US dollars and euro call options against US dollars. Thus the exporter (the option holder) would have the right to sell pound sterling against US dollars at a predetermined foreign exchange rate and concurrently maintain the right to buy euros against US dollars at a predetermined rate.

The six-month pound sterling put option with strike price 1.4550 US$/£ is quoted at 2.20¢/£ and the six-month euro call option with strike price 0.8800 US$/€ is quoted as 0.75¢/€. The French exporter decides to purchase 24 £ stg. (1.4550) put options (1 500 000/62 500) and to buy 20 euro (0.8800) call options (((1 500 000 × 1.4550)/0.8800)/125 000). This corresponds more or less to the purchase of pound sterling put options against euros with a strike price of 1.6534 €/£ (1.4550/0.8800) at a total up-front premium of US$51 750 ((24 × 1375) + (20 × 937.50)). A profit and loss analysis of the combined put option position of pound sterling against euro was carried out.

| Exchange rate (US$/£) | Exchange rate (US$/€) | Cross rate (€/£) | Profit/(loss) (US$) |
|---|---|---|---|
| 1.4150 | 0.9000 | 1.5722 | 108 750 |
| 1.4250 | 0.9100 | 1.5659 | 68 750 |
| 1.4350 | 0.9000 | 1.5944 | 28 250 |
| 1.4450 | 0.8900 | 1.6236 | (11 750) |
| **1.4550** | **0.8800** | **1.6534** | **(51 750)** |
| 1.4650 | 0.8700 | 1.6639 | (51 750) |
| 1.4750 | 0.8600 | 1.7151 | (51 750) |

The profit and loss profile of this €/£ hedge combining pound sterling put options and euro call option is illustrated below (Figure 8.6).

**Figure 8.6** Profit and loss profile (£ puts and € calls)

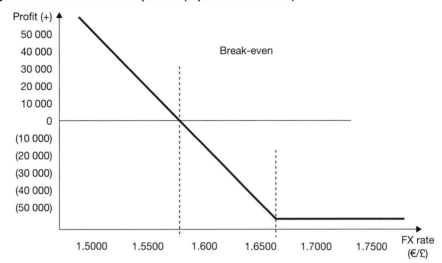

The profit and loss profile illustrated here is based on an assumption that the euro will strengthen against the US dollar when the pound sterling weakens against the US dollar. Keep in mind, however, that the €/£ exchange rate can represent a wide range of foreign exchange rate combinations of euro and pound against the US dollar. In many cases the price relationships may be the other way around, i.e. when the value of the dollar changes it happens against all other currencies at the same time. In this case the profit and loss profile could be recalculated as follows.

| Exchange rate (US$/£) | Exchange rate (US$/€) | Cross rate (€/£) | Profit/(loss) (US$) |
|---|---|---|---|
| 1.3850 | 0.8100 | 1.7099 | 63 250 |
| 1.3950 | 0.8200 | 1.7012 | 48 250 |
| 1.4050 | 0.8300 | 1.6928 | 33 250 |
| 1.4150 | 0.8400 | 1.6845 | 18 250 |
| 1.4250 | 0.8500 | 1.6765 | 3 250 |
| 1.4350 | 0.8600 | 1.6686 | (11 750) |
| 1.4450 | 0.8700 | 1.6609 | (36 750) |
| **1.4550** | **0.8800** | **1.6534** | (51 750) |
| 1.4650 | 0.8900 | 1.6461 | (26 750) |
| 1.4750 | 0.9000 | 1.6389 | (1 750) |
| 1.4850 | 0.9100 | 1.6319 | 23 250 |
| 1.4950 | 0.9200 | 1.6250 | 48 250 |
| 1.5050 | 0.9300 | 1.6183 | 73 250 |

Consequently, the hedge is more complicated to analyze because the two currency options must be assessed in the context of all the possible future cross-currency exchange rate scenarios. It is interesting to look at how the 'locked-in' cross rate of

1.6534 €/£ is made up of the combined strike prices of the pound put option and the euro call option. In this analysis, let $y$ represent the US$/£ stg. exchange rate and $x$, the US$/€ rate. At the combined strike price, the relationship could be expressed in the simple linear relationship $y/x = 1.6534$ or $y = 1.6534x$.

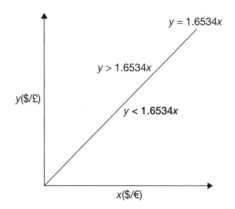

All combinations of the US$/£ stg. and the US$/€ rates that correspond to a cross-currency rate of 1.6534 €/£ are contained on the straight line ($y = 1.6534x$). Exchange rate combinations leading to a cross-currency rate in excess of 1.6534 €/£ will fall above this line and exchange rate combinations leading to a cross currency rate below 1.6534 €/£ fall below the line. The foreign exchange rate development can then be classified within the following scenarios: (a) €/£ = 1.6534, (b) €/£ > 1.6534, and (c) €/£ < 1.6534. In this example we are particularly interested to hedge against situations occurring under scenario (c) where $y < 1.6534x$, i.e. we get less euros for our sterling receivables. The problem is that we can only expect a complete hedge under this scenario if the two foreign exchange rates move in opposite directions against the US dollar, which will rarely be the case. In other words, the hedge is imperfect and illustrates the complexity of cross-currency hedges using traditional currency options against the US dollar. Today the Chicago Mercantile Exchange (CME), for example, offers cross-currency futures on the major currencies against the euro as well as other contracts, such as pound sterling against Swiss francs, Swiss francs against Japanese yen, etc.

## 8.3 Double option strategies

Before discussing the use of double option strategies for hedging purposes we will take a closer look at the 'brokers' language' for various types of hedging strategies. A bullish option strategy is based on the expectation of an increase in the price of the underlying asset. Conversely, a bearish option strategy assumes a decrease in the price of the underlying asset. In a vertical option strategy, the option contracts have the same expiration dates but different strike prices. Conversely, in a horizontal option strategy (often termed a **calendar spread**) the option contracts have the same strike price but different expiration dates where the option trader tries to take advantage of the development in the option's time value.

**Figure 8.7** Vertical bull spread

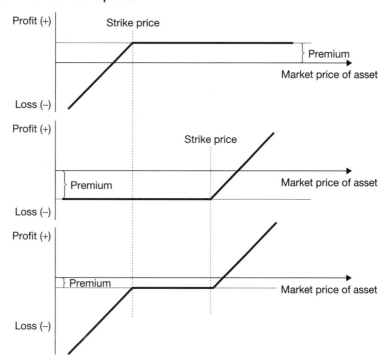

### 8.3.1　Vertical bull spread

A **vertical bull spread** can be established to hedge a short position in the underlying asset. In the single option strategy, a short exposure can be hedged by buying a call option. If an increase in the price of the underlying asset is expected (a bullish market), the likelihood that a put with a lower strike price will be exercised is relatively low. So the hedger may concurrently write a put option contract against receipt of the option premium. The profit and loss profile of a vertical bull spread combines the profiles of the put option and the call option (Figure 8.7).

### 8.3.2　Vertical bear spread

A **vertical bear spread** can be established to hedge a long exposure of the underlying asset. In the single option strategy, a long exposure is hedged by buying a put option. However, since expectations point to a decrease in the price of the underlying asset (a bearish market), the likelihood that a call option with a higher strike price will be exercised is limited. So, the hedger may concurrently write a call option against receipt of the option premium. The profit and loss profile of a vertical bear spread can be illustrated graphically by combining the profit and loss profiles of the put and call options (Figure 8.8).

### 8.3.3　Straddle

A **straddle** position is established by buying a call option and a put option with the same strike price. This option position gives the holder the right to buy the underlying

**Figure 8.8** Vertical bear spread

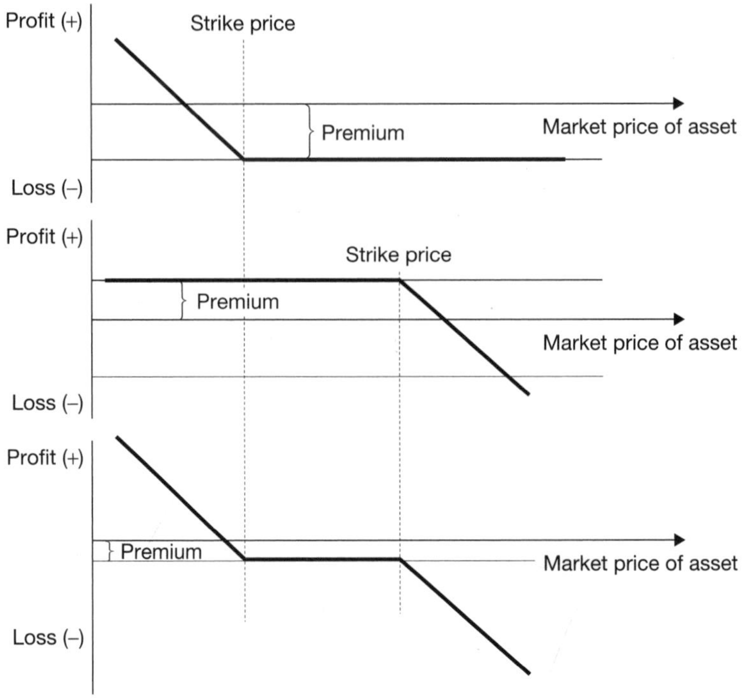

asset at a predetermined price, which is an advantage if the asset price escalates. At the same time, the holder has the right to sell the asset at a predetermined price, which is an advantage if the asset price collapses. Hence establishing a straddle position will be advantageous when the price development of the underlying asset is very volatile but shows no distinct trend. The profit and loss profile of the straddle position can be obtained by combining the profit and loss profiles of the call and put options (Figure 8.9).

### 8.3.4 Strangle

A **strangle** position is similar to the straddle position in that it entails the simultaneous purchase of a call and a put option but the two options have different strike prices. The two option contracts would be bought at out-of-the-money strike prices to reduce the double premium cost, so the strike price of the put option will be less than the strike price of the call option (Figure 8.10).

### 8.3.5 Butterfly

A **butterfly spread** position entails three strike prices. It can be conceived as a combination of a bull spread and a bear spread in which the bull spread assumes the lower two strike prices and the bear spread the two higher strike prices. The underlying bull and the bear spreads are established as discussed previously (Figure 8.11). The long butterfly spread is pertinent in situations where the hedger has a view of volatile asset prices. Compared to the straddle, this position has lower risk and limited profit potential.

**Figure 8.9  Straddle position**

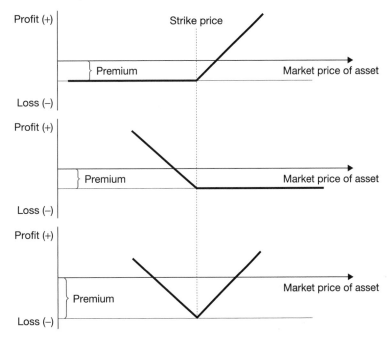

**Figure 8.10  Strangle position**

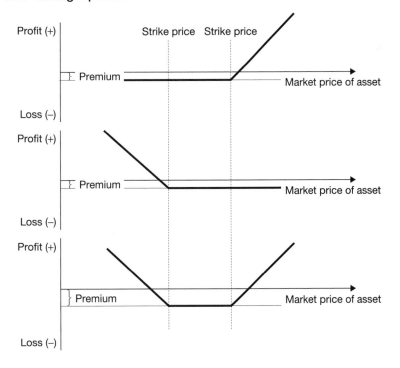

**Figure 8.11** A butterfly spread

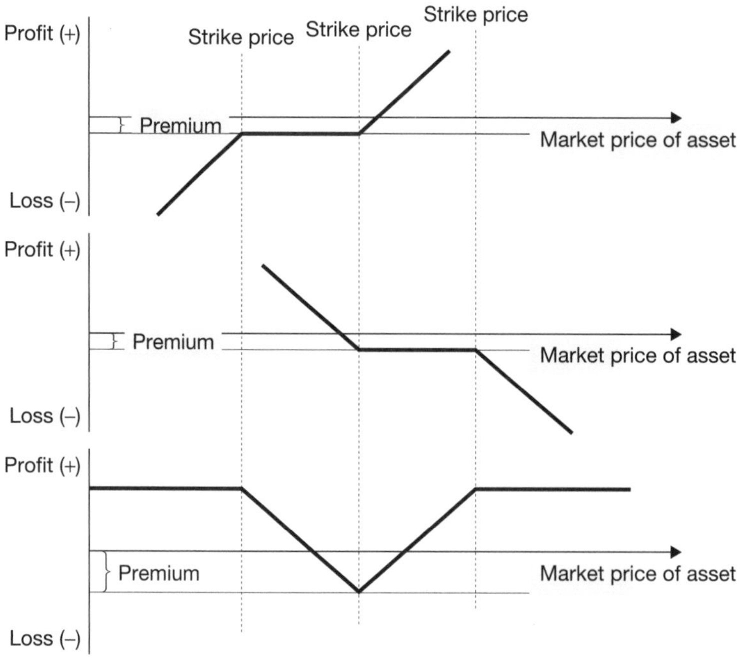

## 8.4 Ratio spreads

Ratio spreads are established by trading the underlying options contracts in different quantities, that is, in different ratios to each other.

### 8.4.1 Ratio call spread

A **ratio call spread** position is established through the purchase of one call option and simultaneous sale of two call options (ratio = 2) at a higher strike price. This position is relevant for hedgers with a view that while asset prices may rise they will not increase to extreme heights in the near term (Figure 8.12).

### 8.4.2 Ratio put spread

A **ratio put spread** position is established by purchasing a put option and selling two put options (ratio = 2) at a lower strike price. This position can be relevant for institutions that expect falling asset prices but not immediately and not by a large amount (Figure 8.13).

The option positions described above can be inverted to establish straddle write positions, reverse butterflies, and reverse ratio spreads (Figure 8.14). The positions can also be 'ratio-ed' and geared in different ways to the particular view of the hedger as the ratio takes any positive number to suit a given hedging situation. A ratio of 1 in these spreads will correspond to a **call bull spread** and a **put bear spread** position respectively (Figure 8.15).

**Figure 8.12** Ratio call spread

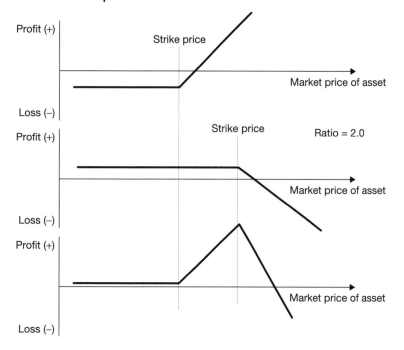

**Figure 8.13** Ratio put spread

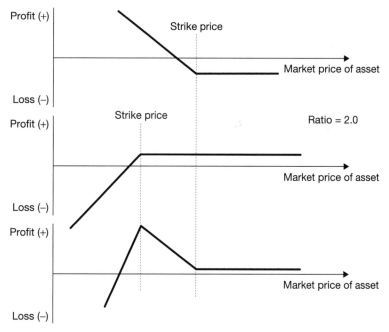

**Figure 8.14** Straddle write, reverse butterfly, and reverse ratio back spread

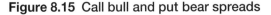

**Figure 8.15** Call bull and put bear spreads

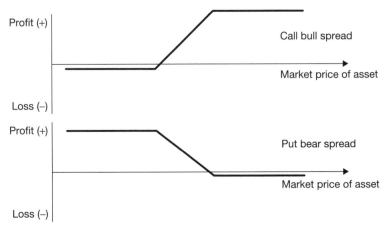

The option positions discussed above are summarized in Table 8.2. These option positions can represent hedged investment transactions pursued by professional market participants who use the markets for futures and option contracts to establish investment positions.[1] However, the option positions can also be established by commercial hedgers while using an underlying transaction exposure as one of the elements of the hedge.

**Table 8.2** Some double option positions

| | |
|---|---|
| Straddle (one strike price): | Buy a call option and buy a put option at same strike price |
| Straddle write (one strike price): | Write a call option and write a put option at the same strike price |
| Strangle (two strike prices): | Buy a call option and buy a put option at a lower strike price |
| Vertical bull spread (two strike prices): | Buy a call option and write a put at a lower strike price |
| Vertical bear spread (two strike prices): | Buy a put option and write a call at a higher strike price |
| Call bull spread (two strike prices): | Buy a call option and sell a call option at a higher strike price |
| Ratio call spread (two strike prices):[†] | Buy a call option and sell two call options at a higher strike price |
| Put bear spread (two strike process): | Buy a put option and sell a put option at a lower strike price |
| Ratio put spread (two strike prices):[†] | Buy a put option and sell two put options at a lower strike price |
| Butterfly spread (three strike prices):[*] | Write a put at a lower strike price, buy a call and put at a middle strike price, and write a call at a higher strike price |
| Reverse butterfly (three strike prices):[*] | Buy a put at a lower strike price, write a call and put at a middle strike price, and buy a call at a higher strike price |

[†] These ratio spreads correspond to a ratio of 2, but the ratio can take any other number.
[*] This formula corresponds to the examples discussed – a butterfly spread can be established in several other ways.

*Example*: A US-based exporter is expecting payments in euro and, therefore, has a natural underlying long position in euros represented by a straight upward-sloping profit and loss line. By buying at-the-money put option contracts, the position is converted to a synthetic call option position – the dotted line in Figure 8.16.

**Figure 8.16** Hedged long position – bought call

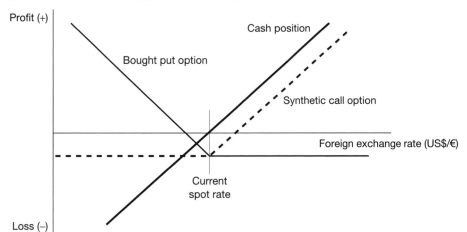

*Example*: The US-based exporter wants to establish a strangle position based on the underlying long currency position. This can be done by buying out-of-the-money put options, which combined with the bought call option position establishes a strangle position (Figure 8.17).

**Figure 8.17** Hedged long position – strangle

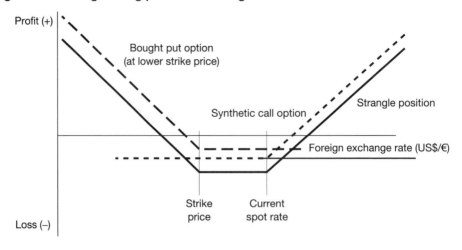

( 8.4.3 ) ## Hedging a short currency position

Assume that a Scandinavian institutional investor holds a US dollar-denominated securities portfolio with a total market value of US$10 000 000. The institution takes the view that the euro will strengthen against the US dollar over the next year and therefore finds it opportune to switch the portfolio from a dollar exposure to a euro exposure. For various reasons the investor cannot switch the portfolio for three months. Adopting a single option strategy to hedge the foreign exchange gap, the institution could buy euro call options, i.e. US dollar put options against euros, in an amount equivalent to the total value of the portfolio. However, due to a strong view that the euro will strengthen against the US dollar, it simultaneously sells an equivalent number of euro put options against US dollars at a lower strike price. The premium income from the sale of the euro put options counts against the premium to be paid for the purchase of the call options, thereby reducing the net premium due to establish the hedge. At the same time, the likelihood that the put holder will exercise the options is considered very small, and so the downside risk is deemed marginal.

*Example*: The current spot foreign exchange rate is 1.1061 (US$/€) and the three-month euro call and put options are quoted as follows:

| Strike (US$/€) | Calls (¢/€) | Puts (¢/€) |
| --- | --- | --- |
| 1.0900 | 2.57 | 0.26 |
| 1.1000 | 1.34 | 0.54 |
| 1.1100 | 0.86 | 1.00 |
| 1.1200 | 0.46 | 1.70 |
| 1.1300 | 0.26 | 2.50 |
| 1.1400 | 0.13 | 3.30 |

The institution chooses the euro (1.0900) put option because it is sufficiently out-of-the-money that the chance of exercise seems reasonably small. The euro (1.1200) call option is chosen because it gives a reasonable hedge in the bullish market.

Hence the institution decides to buy 72 euro (1.1200) call options ((10 000 000/ 1.1061)/125 000) and to write 72 euro (1.0900) put options. Thus the institution will pay an up-front premium for the call options of US$41 400 (72 × 125 000 × 0.46/100) and will receive a premium from writing the put options of US$23 400 (72 × 125 000 × 0.26/100). The net premium of US$18 000 is less than half the cost of the single option strategy. To assess the sensitivity of the hedge to changes in the foreign exchange rate development the profit and loss as a function of the foreign exchange rate was calculated:

| Exchange rate (US$/€) | Profit/(loss) (US$) |
|---|---|
| 1.0800 | (108 000) |
| 1.0900 | (18 000) |
| 1.1000 | (18 000) |
| 1.1100 | (18 000) |
| 1.1200 | (18 000) |
| 1.1300 | 72 000 |
| 1.1400 | 162 000 |
| 1.1500 | 252 000 |

This allows us to graph the profit and loss profile of the double option position – a vertical bull spread (Figure 8.18). As shown, the institution has obtained a hedge against a strengthening of the euro against the US dollar for a limited fee. There is, nonetheless, a sizeable downside loss potential even though the likelihood that it will materialize might be small.

### 8.4.4 Hedging a long currency position

An international trading company is expecting payment of Swiss franc receivables in three months. The company intends to use the proceeds to make a US$2 000 000

**Figure 8.18** Profit and loss profile – vertical bull spread

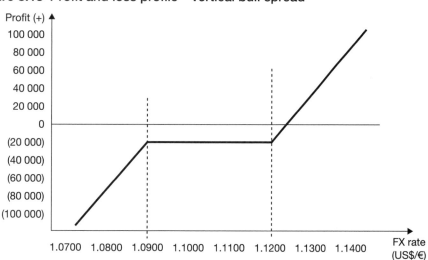

payment due at this time. The company has a strong belief that the Swiss franc will
weaken against the US dollar in the interim and, therefore, would like to hedge this
currency exposure. Adopting a single option strategy, the company could buy a
number of Swiss franc put options corresponding to the total amount of the dollar
payment. However, since they have a very strong view that the Swiss franc will
weaken against the US dollar, the company decides to write an equivalent number of
Swiss franc call options at the same time.

*Example*: The current spot foreign exchange rate is 0.8296 (US$/SFr) and the three-month
Swiss franc call and put options are quoted as follows:

| Strike (US$/SFr) | Puts (¢/SFr) | Calls (¢/SFr) |
| --- | --- | --- |
| 0.8300 | 0.31 | 1.17 |
| 0.8400 | 0.54 | 0.72 |
| 0.8500 | 0.88 | 0.48 |
| 0.8600 | 1.55 | 0.19 |
| 0.8700 | 2.26 | 1.12 |

The company decides to buy the at-the-money SFr (0.8300) put options and write the
out-of-the-money SFr (0.8600) call options. Hence, the company buys 19 puts
((2 000 000/0.8296)/125 000)) at a premium of $7362.50 (19 × 125 000 × 0.31/100), and
it writes 19 calls against receipt of a premium of $4512.50 (19 × 125 000 × 0.19/100).
The net cost of this double option position, a vertical bear spread, thus amounts to
$2850 (7362.50 – 4512.50). The sensitivity of the combined option position to changes
in the foreign exchange rate was analyzed and the associated profit and loss profile
was determined (Figure 8.19).

**Figure 8.19 Profit and loss profile – vertical bear spread**

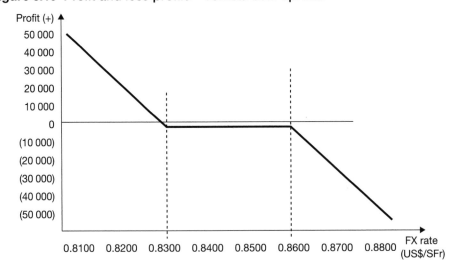

| Exchange rate (US$/SFr) | Profit/(loss) (US$) |
|---|---|
| 0.8100 | 44 650 |
| 0.8200 | 20 900 |
| 0.8300 | (2 850) |
| 0.8400 | (2 850) |
| 0.8500 | (2 850) |
| 0.8600 | (2 850) |
| 0.8700 | (26 600) |
| 0.8800 | (50 350) |

## 8.4.5 Hedging a short interest rate position

In August a US corporation is planning to raise funding in US dollars some time over the coming months. However, the financing cost is not known at this point and, therefore, the corporation is interested in hedging against an interim increase in the interest rate level. The issue is how this can be done through trading in options contracts. For example, the three-month eurodollar deposit options offered on various international futures and options exchanges could provide a basis to hedge against moves in the short-term US dollar interest rate. Alternatively, the options contracts on the treasury bond futures could provide the corporation with the opportunity to hedge against an increase in the long-term interest rate.

If the loan is expected to take place in the form of a domestic corporate bond or Eurobond issue, the treasury bond contract provides a reasonable hedging vehicle. Suppose the US dollar loan is expected to materialize in December, that is, in four months, then the corporation can buy a suitable number of December put options giving the right to sell treasury bond futures at a predetermined price. If the interest rate level increases, that is, if the Treasury bond price drops by more than the market expectation then the option holder will gain from exercising the Treasury bond put options, a gain which will compensate for the increased interest expense on the loan. The number of put option contracts to buy will depend on the correlation between the bond prices and the interest rate of the type of loan to be obtained. By adopting a double option strategy to this hedging situation, it is readily seen that a vertical bull spread can be established through the write of a call option at a higher strike price, i.e. a lower interest rate, which will hedge the interest rate level within a band determined by the strike prices of the long put and short call. If the borrowing instead is planned to take place in the eurodollar market, e.g. in the form of a LIBOR-based syndicated term-loan, the eurodollar contracts represent a better hedging alternative than the treasury bond contracts.

Just like the potential corporate borrower will have an exposure to the future interest rate level so would an institutional investor that expects to place a future cash inflow. For example, an investor who is expecting a positive net liquidity position in US dollars, e.g. in December four months hence can hedge against a decrease in the interest rate by buying call options on the December interest rate futures contracts. The hedge could also pursue a double option strategy through the simultaneous sale of put option contracts at a lower exercise price, i.e. a higher interest rate level. In this case the minimum interest rate will be guaranteed whereas there is an open loss position if the interest rate level increases dramatically. Therefore, this double option position, a vertical bull spread, should only be assumed when there is a strong view that securities prices in general will increase, i.e. the interest rate is very likely to drop.

*Example*: The following option quotes on US$1 000 000 three-month eurodollar deposit futures contracts are prevailing for the December delivery with the current three month LIBOR rate quoted at 2.75% p.a.:

| Strike (price) | Implied rate (% p.a.) | Calls (%) | Puts (%) |
|---|---|---|---|
| 96.00 | 4.00 | 1.37 | 0.01 |
| 96.50 | 3.50 | 0.91 | 0.05 |
| 97.00 | 3.00 | 0.50 | 0.14 |
| 97.50 | 2.50 | 0.22 | 0.36 |
| 98.00 | 2.00 | 0.06 | 0.70 |

Say the institutional investor is expecting to make a US$10 000 000 three-month eurodollar deposit in December the return of which should be hedged. The investor could then buy ten call option contracts at a strike price of, for example, 97.50, which is slightly out-of-the-money and hence carries a slightly lower premium. This would effectively lock-in the future placement return at 2.50% p.a. for the three-month period commencing in December. That is, if the interest rate level drops during the interim period until December then the value of the three-month eurodollar futures contract will correspondingly increase and the long futures position implied in the call option can be closed at a profit that counterweighs the lower return incurred in the cash market. A double options strategy could then, for example, entail the simultaneous sale of ten put option contracts with a strike price of 97.00, which represents an interest rate scenario that is deemed rather unlikely to happen.

The sensitivity of this hedging position to changes in the interest rate level was analyzed and the associated profit and loss profile determined (Figure 8.20). The total premium to be paid on the long call (97.00) position amounts to US$22 000 ($10 \times 1\,000\,000 \times 0.22/100$) and the total premium received on the short put (97.50) position will be US$14 000 ($10 \times 1\,000\,000 \times 0.14/100$) thus resulting on a net premium for the combined position of US$8000 (22 000 − 14 000).

| Interest rate (% p.a.) | Future (price) | Profit/(loss) (US$) |
|---|---|---|
| 1.50 | 98.50 | 92 000 |
| 2.00 | 98.00 | 42 000 |
| 2.50 | 97.50 | (8 000) |
| 3.00 | 97.00 | (8 000) |
| 3.50 | 96.50 | (58 000) |
| 4.00 | 96.00 | (108 000) |

Returning to a corporate borrower's situation where funding of US$10 000 000 fixed to the three-month LIBOR is to be effectuated in December. A hedge against an

**Figure 8.20** Profit and loss profile – vertical bull spread

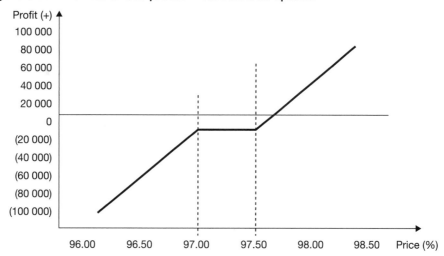

increase in the interest rate level could then be established by buying a put option contract at a strike price of, say 97.00, which is slightly out-of-the-money and hence carries a lower premium. By engaging in this hedge, the borrower has guaranteed a maximum funding rate of 3.00% p.a. for the three-month period commencing in December while retaining the potential gains if the interest rate level decreases rather than increases. The borrower could also pursue a double option strategy by combining the long put position with a short call position at a higher strike price, i.e. a lower interest rate. That is, if the borrower has a strong view that the interest rate will increase while the likelihood of a drop is remote, it might be willing to write calls at a high strike price against receipt of the front-end premium, i.e. establish a vertical bear spread.

In the concrete situation, the corporate borrower could then, for example, sell ten call option contracts with a strike price of 97.50, which may represent an interest rate scenario that is deemed fairly remote. The sensitivity of this double option hedge to changes in the interest rate level was analyzed and the profit and loss profile calculated (Figure 8.21). The total premium to be paid on the long put (97.00) position amounts to US$14 000 ($10 \times 1\ 000\ 000 \times 0.14/100$) and the premium received on the short call (97.50) position is US$22 000 ($10 \times 1\ 000\ 000 \times 0.22/100$), resulting in an overall premium income on the combined position of US$8000 (22 000 – 14 000).

| Interest rate (% p.a.) | Future (price) | Profit/(loss) (US$) |
|---|---|---|
| 1.50 | 98.50 | (92 000) |
| 2.00 | 98.00 | (42 000) |
| 2.50 | 97.50 | 8 000 |
| 3.00 | 97.00 | 8 000 |
| 3.50 | 96.50 | 58 000 |
| 4.00 | 96.00 | 108 000 |

**Figure 8.21** Profit and loss profile – vertical bear spread

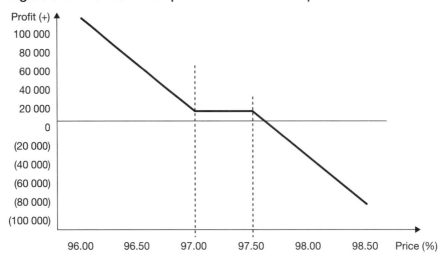

The double option position established above only hedges the interest expenses of the borrower for the first three-month period. Say, the borrower decided to engage into a five-year LIBOR based syndicated loan facility, then there would be a need to make comparable hedges for all the subsequent three-month time intervals throughout the lifetime of the loan, i.e. twenty three-month periods in total. Since LIBOR based syndications often are based on six-month Eurocurrency rates, the corresponding interest rate hedge in this situation would entail hedges for ten six-month periods throughout a five-year loan.

### 8.4.6 Scale-down floor

A **scale-down floor** agreement is made up by a combination of floor rate agreements (over-the-counter put options) with different strike prices and contract amounts thus effectively establishing a ratio put spread (Figure 8.22). The position can be relevant when the market expects a gradual drop in the interest rate level. The scale-down floor can be construed in such a way that the premium paid on the bought floor corresponds to the premium received on the sold floor at a higher contract amount thereby making it a zero cost position.

*Example*: A scale-down floor agreement could offer a zero cost two-year agreement on the following payment terms: Receive 0.50% when LIBOR > 8.0%, receive 0.50% + (8.0 − LIBOR) × 1.5 when 7.5% < LIBOR < 8.0%, receive LIBOR − 6.3% when 6.3% < LIBOR < 7.5%, and pay 6.3% − LIBOR when LIBOR < 6.3% (Figure 8.23).

### 8.4.7 Hedging a short stock position

Assuming that an investor as a long-term fund manager is benchmarked against the return on equity investments as opposed to the three-month eurodollar rate, another hedging approach must be adopted.

**Figure 8.22** Profit and loss profile of a scale-down floor agreement

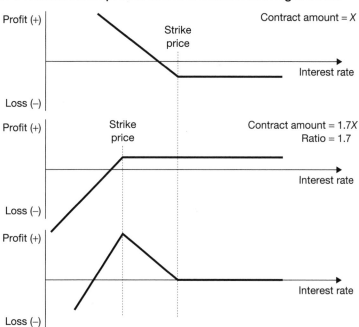

**Figure 8.23** Profit and loss profile of a scale-down floor agreement

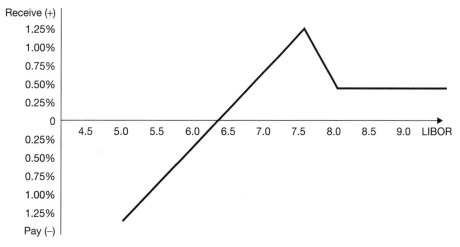

*Example*: A portfolio manager expects to receive an inflow of funds of US$10 000 000 in three months. The funds are intended for investment in a diversified stock portfolio. However, the investor fears that stock prices are bound for a significant rise in the near future before they have the time to invest the cash inflow.

Such a potential shortfall in stock returns can be hedged by buying a suitable number of stock index call options for the three-month period against payment of an

**Figure 8.24** Profit and loss profile – stock index

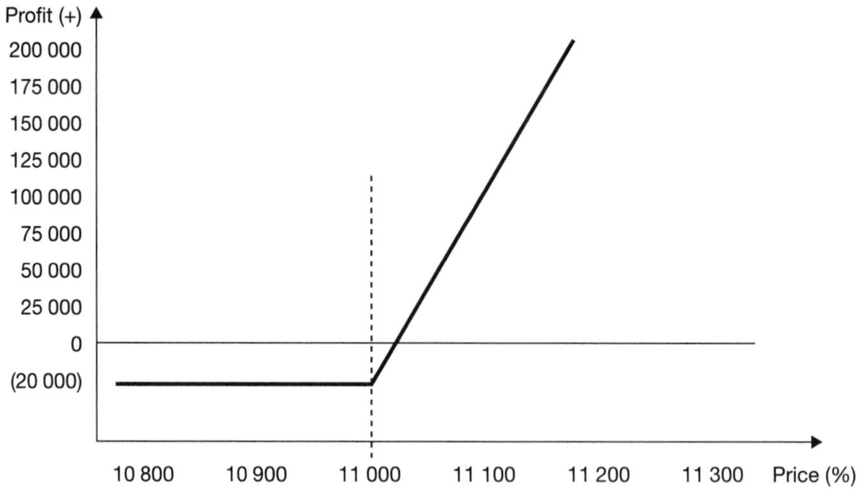

up-front option premium. Assume that the S&P 500 index option contract is quoted as follows:

| Strike (index) | Calls (index points) |
| --- | --- |
| 10 800 | 38.20 |
| 10 900 | 27.60 |
| 11 000 | 23.00 |
| 11 100 | 17.10 |
| 11 200 | 14.70 |

The portfolio manager decides to purchase at-the-money call option contracts with a strike price of 11 000. Since each index point corresponds to a US$10 value, the investor decides buy 91 (10 000 000/(11 000 × 10)) call contracts to match the market value of the expected cash inflow. The premium to pay up front amounts to $20 930 (91 × 23 × 10). The profit and loss profile of this single option hedge can be determined as a function of changes in the underlying stock index (Figure 8.24).

## 8.5 Portfolio hedge

Portfolio hedging often attempts to modify the interest rate sensitivity of the invested portfolio and possibly 'immunize' the effect of changes in the interest rate for the expected investment horizon, e.g. by making the duration of the invested portfolio match the duration of the institution's financial obligations. Assuming that options on futures contracts are used in the portfolio hedging, the analysis will be focused on the option's underlying asset, i.e. the futures contract. Using the principle of market value weighted determination of the portfolio's duration the number of options on futures contracts to trade to adjust the duration of the portfolio is determined by the following formula (see duration hedge in Chapter 7):

$$N = (D_T - D_P)/D_F \times P/F$$

where

$N$ = number of futures contracts;
$D_T$ = targeted duration of the invested portfolio;
$D_P$ = duration of the invested portfolio;
$D_F$ = duration of the futures contract;
$P$ = market value of the invested portfolio;
$F$ = market price of the underlying futures contract.

Hence, the $N$ indicates the number of futures or options on the futures contract to be traded to modify the duration of the invested portfolio to the targeted duration of the invested portfolio. A positive $N$ indicates the number of futures or call option contracts to buy, while a negative $N$ indicates the number of futures contracts to sell or put option contracts to buy. The indicated number of futures or option contracts to trade applies to a hedge of the return characteristics of the invested portfolio over the period until the derivative contracts expire. Once the futures and option contracts expire, a new set of derivatives must be engaged into again to modify the contours of the portfolio returns. Since the duration of the portfolio is sensitive to changes in the portfolio combination and changes in the interest rate structure, the portfolio hedge should be reconsidered and adjusted on an ongoing basis.

## 8.5.1 Delta hedging

The previous hedges using futures and option contracts are based on the idea of obtaining compensation gains (or losses) on the underlying futures contracts that more or less match the cash effects from changes in market prices and thereby lock-in or guarantee a future asset price. However, a hedge can also be established to take advantage of the price sensitivity of the option premium to changes in the market value of the underlying asset and thereby the interest rate level. The option's delta value ($\Delta$) indicates the number of units of the underlying asset that is hedged by one option contract. For example, if an at-the-money put option has a delta of $-0.5$ the hedger should acquire two put options to hedge the underlying asset against changes in the interest rate level. When the asset price drops by one point, the two put options will incur a price gain of one point since there is a negative relationship between the put option premium and a change in the value of the underlying asset ($\delta O_P/\delta P < 0$). In effect such a **delta hedge** establishes a long straddle position, which can be illustrated by the profit and loss profile of the position at the expiration dates of the option contracts (Figure 8.25).

When buying put option contracts in quantities that differ from the delta values, the hedged positions represent *ratio-ed*, or *skewed*, straddle positions (Figure 8.26).

The characteristic feature of a straddle position, as discussed, is that it generates a profit if the price of the underlying asset is volatile. If the asset price increases, the hedger can buy more put options that are cheaper because the put is more out-of-the-money. Conversely, the hedger can sell the more expensive puts when the asset price decreases. If a delta hedge is maintained on an ongoing basis, the hedger can

**Figure 8.25** Profit and loss profile – long straddle

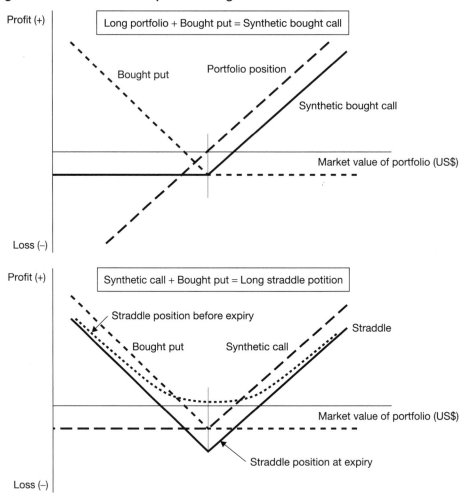

**Figure 8.26** Profit and loss profile – skewed straddle

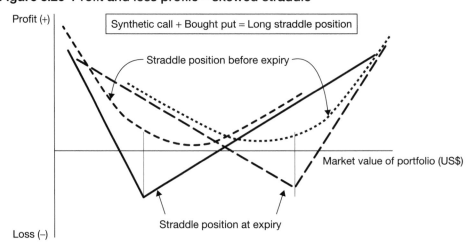

generate income by buying cheaper puts and selling more expensive puts. This hedging principle is sometimes referred to as **gamma scalping**.

*Example*: A hedger has bought twenty MP February 40 put options at a premium of US$3.85 per option contract. The price of the MetPath share increases and the delta of the MP February 40 put option increases from −0.65 to −0.35. Hence, the portfolio of 1300 MetPath shares is no longer delta neutral. The delta value of the position has increased by 6 ((0.65 − 0.35) × 20) from 0. To adjust the portfolio to a delta neutral position, the hedger buys another seventeen MP February 40 put option contracts (1300/(100 × 0.35) − 20) at a premium of US$2.15 per option contract.

Subsequently the share price drops and the delta of the put option decreases to −0.85. The delta value of the position has consequently dropped by 18.5 ((0.85 − 0.35)37). As a consequence, the hedger sells 22 MP February 40 put option contracts (37 − 1300/(100 × 0.85)) at a premium of US$4.87 per option contract.

The hedging transactions are:

- bought 20 contracts at US$3.85;
- bought 17 contracts at US$2.15;
- sold 22 contracts at US$4.87.

A hedger that wants to manage and maintain a delta hedge on a current basis must be sufficiently professional to take advantage of current premium changes on the put contracts and thereby generate a profit before the option contract loses time value. A hedger who only wants to establish an initial delta hedge without maintaining it thereafter must have a strong view of high price volatility for it to pay off.

## 8.6 Using options to establish a delta hedge

The sensitivity of the option premium from a marginal change in the underlying asset price is expressed by the option's delta ($\Delta$) value, which expresses the linear relationship between the option premium and the price of option's underlying asset:

$$\text{Delta } (\Delta) = \frac{\delta O}{\delta P}$$

where

$O$ = option premium;
$P$ = price of underlying asset.

The delta of a call option is positive, i.e. it displays a positively sloping tangent to the call option price curve, while the delta of a put option is negative, i.e. it displays a negative sloping tangent to the put option price curve (Figure 8.27).

Recall that the duration measure indicates the linear relationship between the asset price and marginal changes in the interest rate:

$$\text{Duration } (D) = \frac{\delta P}{\delta r}$$

where

$P$ = price of asset;
$r$ = interest rate.

**Figure 8.27** Deltas of call and put options

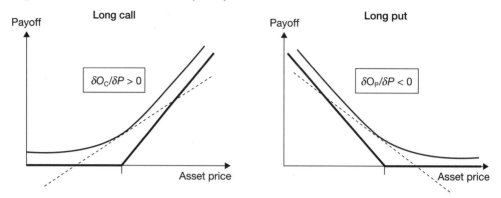

Then the delta ($\Delta$) multiplied by the duration ($D$) indicates the relationship between the option price and changes in the interest rate:

$$\Delta \times D = \frac{\delta O}{\delta P} \times \frac{\delta P}{\delta r} = \frac{\delta O}{\delta r}$$

The delta of a put contract is negative ($\Delta_P < 0$), which means that an increase in the interest rate level that causes the asset price to drop will result in a higher put option premium. This change in the option price is inverse to the change in the asset price. So, the price sensitivity of the put option contract can be used for hedging purposes aimed at neutralizing the effect of changes in the interest rate level. By buying a suitable number of put options on a long-term interest rate futures contracts, such as the CBoT five-year treasury note futures, we can hedge the price sensitivity of a securities portfolio or any other positive duration gap. We can determine the resulting duration of the combined securities and futures portfolio in the following manner:

$$D_T = \frac{(D_P \times P_S) + (\Delta \times D_F \times P_F)}{P_S}$$

$$P_F = \frac{(D_T - D_P)P_S}{\Delta \times D_F}$$

where

$P_F$ = market value of futures portfolio;
$D_T$ = targeted duration of invested portfolio;
$D_P$ = current duration of invested portfolio;
$P_S$ = market value of invested portfolio;
$\Delta$ = delta value of put option on futures contract;
$D_F$ = duration of the future (cheapest to deliver T-Note).

$$\text{Number of put option contracts} = \frac{P_F}{\text{Market price of futures contract}}$$

*Example*: An investment manager would like to use June put option contracts to reduce the duration of the invested portfolio of nominal $100 000 000 securities with average market price of 105 and duration of 5. Hence, the duration of the portfolio can be reduced to 3.0 by buying 895 put option contracts on the five-year T-Note future, currently trading at 104.3 and where the 'cheapest-to-deliver' bond has duration of 4.5. The duration of the put option is −0.5.

$$3 = \frac{(5 \times 100\ 000\ 000 \times 1.05) + (\Delta \times 4.5 \times P_F)}{100\ 000\ 000 \times 1.05} \Rightarrow$$

$$3 = \frac{525\ 000\ 000 + (-0.5 \times 4.5 \times P_F)}{105\ 000\ 000} \Rightarrow$$

$$P_F = \frac{315\ 000\ 000 - 525\ 000\ 000}{(-0.5) \times 4.5}$$

$$= 93\ 333\ 333 \Rightarrow$$

$$\text{Number of put option contracts} = \frac{93\ 333\ 333}{100\ 000 \times 104.3/100}$$

$$= 894.85$$

Note that we need precisely twice as many put contracts to make the delta hedge as we need in a pure futures hedge ($895 = 2 \times 447$) because the $\Delta$ of the put option is $-0.5$. Furthermore, the portfolio could be completely immunized for the time period until June, i.e. $D_T = 0$, by buying more put options on the T-Note futures contract or more specifically $2237$ ($= 5/(5-3) \times 895$) put option contracts.

The principle behind the delta hedge could be used in a similar manner to manage the duration gap of the asset and liability structure in a given financial institution or corporation as expressed by the duration of the institution's equity position determined by the duration of total assets minus the duration of total liabilities ($D_E = D_A - D_L$).

*Example*: The interest rate sensitivity of equity position of an institution with total assets of 100 million and total liabilities of 80 million that establish a positive duration gap with duration of assets equal to 3.8 and duration of liabilities equal to 3.0 could be reduced by buying put option contracts on the T-Note future. To reduce the duration from 0.8 to 0.4, the institution could buy 426 put options on the futures contract.

$$0.4 = \frac{\left(D_A - \frac{L}{A} \times D_L\right) \times A + (\Delta \times D_F \times P_F)}{A} \Rightarrow$$

$$P_F = \frac{0.4 - \left(D_A - \frac{L}{A} \times D_L\right) A}{\Delta \times D_F}$$

$$= \frac{(0.4 - (3.8 - 0.8 \times 3))100\ 000\ 000}{(-0.5) \times 4.5}$$

$$= 44\ 444\ 444 \Rightarrow$$

$$\text{Number of put option contracts} = \frac{44\ 444\ 444}{104\ 300}$$

$$= 426.12$$

In case the institution wanted to reduce the duration of certain liabilities, e.g. a loan portfolio, it would have to buy call options on the T-Note futures contract as opposed to put option contracts. Similarly, a negative duration gap could be reduced by buying a suitable number of call option contracts.

## Conclusion

Financial futures and options on futures contracts traded on formal exchanges as well as forward and option agreements offered in the over-the-counter market can be used to hedge a variety of financial gaps. The option exchanges provide the financial world with liquid and efficient markets for a wide range of option positions with a wealth of hedging applications. A disadvantage of exchange-traded options is that they are traded in standard sizes, which will not always completely match the requirements of the hedger's position. Also, the limited maturity of options contracts sometimes restricts their usage. Nevertheless, a vast number of participants on the options exchanges are investors who through relatively small initial capital investments can position themselves to earn a profit and thereby they become indispensable counterparts to the hedgers. The many financial derivatives can be combined in different ways to establish unique hedging positions adapted to specific institutional gaps geared to management's particular market views. Options contracts are interesting because, unlike financial futures, they offset or minimize the downside risk while leaving open the upside potential for gains. Double option strategies all take a view on price movements and therefore carry an element of downside risk, which should be carefully scrutinized. Single option strategies, however, provide holders with complete hedges. This chapter initially discussed the use of these derivatives in the context of single financial transactions, such as currency receivables and payables, specific funding requirements, and situations of excess liquidity. However, the derivatives can also be used to manage portfolio and equity positions pointing to more managerial uses of derivatives.

## Summary

- Forward rate agreements (FRAs) offer compensation to buyers and sellers according to developments in short-term interest rates and thereby provide opportunities to lock-in interest rate amounts. Ceiling and floor rate agreements offer compensation when interest rates increase and drop respectively and thereby provide protection against directional changes in short-term interest rates.

- Forward foreign exchange rates traded in the interbank market provide the means to lock-in future foreign exchange rates. Call and put options on different currencies provide cover against directional changes in foreign exchange rates while the upside potential for currency gains on the underlying position is retained by the option holders.

- Using options for hedging purposes can add flexibility as they provide cover against downside risks and leave the upside potential for gain from favourable price movements open. Trading in options contracts provides additional hedging possibilities against adverse price movements through the establishment of delta hedges.

- Options can establish various 'bull' and 'bear' positions to reflect the specific views assumed on price developments in the financial markets and may serve as building blocks in different hybrid instruments.

## Questions

8.1 Explain how a borrower and an investor respectively can use forward rate agreements (FRAs) to hedge the interest rate risk.

8.2 What are ceiling rate agreements and floor rate agreements and how are they used?

8.3 Explain the advantages associated with the use of currency option contracts as opposed to currency futures contracts to hedge currency positions.

8.4 Explain the rationales behind the double option positions called a vertical bull spread and a vertical bear spread and propose situation where they might be appropriate.

8.5 What is the difference between a straddle and a strangle position and a straddle and an inverse straddle?

8.6 How can we establish a butterfly spread and an inverse butterfly spread?

8.7 When might it be interesting to engage in a ratio call spread and a ratio put spread?

8.8 Explain the underlying rationale of a delta hedge.

8.9 Why might anyone want to establish a ratio-ed straddle position?

## Exercises

8.1 A US company will have to pay €50 000 000 in six months. It wants to buy euro call options to cover the currency exposure. The euro is trading at 1.1275 US$/€ and the six-month call option contract are quoted as follows:

| Strike price (US$/€) | Quote (US$/€) | |
|---|---|---|
| 1.1270 | 0.0300 | (in-the-money) |
| 1.1290 | 0.0160 | (out-of-the-money) |

Outline the profit and loss profile of the two options and decide which one of the contracts to buy.

8.2 The US company expects the euro to strengthen and therefore considers a vertical bull spread. The six-month euro call and put option contracts are quoted as follows:

▶

| Strike (US$/€) | Calls (¢/€) | Puts (¢/€) |
|---|---|---|
| 1.1230 | 12.2 | 0.9 |
| 1.1250 | 8.4 | 1.4 |
| 1.1270 | 3.0 | 2.7 |
| 1.1290 | 1.6 | 3.7 |
| 1.1310 | 1.1 | 8.5 |
| 1.1330 | 0.7 | 13.0 |

(a) Choose one call option and one put option contract and outline the profit and loss profile of the vertical bull spread established by the two contracts.

(b) Discus whether it is a good choice of contracts.

8.3 A US company will receive 100 million Swiss francs in three months and expects the currency to weaken. Therefore, the company decides to establish a vertical bear spread. The foreign exchange rate is currently trading at 0.8345 (US$/SFr) and the three-month Swiss franc call and put options are quoted as follows:

| Strike (US$/SFr) | Puts (¢/SFr) | Calls (¢/SFr) |
|---|---|---|
| 0.8200 | 0.23 | 1.67 |
| 0.8300 | 0.42 | 1.15 |
| 0.8400 | 0.65 | 0.75 |
| 0.8500 | 0.96 | 0.44 |
| 0.8600 | 1.65 | 0.35 |
| 0.8700 | 1.96 | 0.21 |

(a) Choose one put option and one call option contract and outline the profit and loss profile of the vertical bear spread established by the two contracts.

(b) Discuss whether it is a good choice of contracts.

8.4 A corporation has the following balance sheet [market value $1000 (duration)]:

| Assets | | Liabilities and equity | |
|---|---|---|---|
| Cash | 5 000 (0) | Overdraft facility | 4 000 (0) |
| Securities | 5 000 (1) | Bank loans | 8 000 (2) |
| Commercial investments | 10 000 (3) | Corporate bonds | 8 000 (3) |
| Productive assets | 10 000 (8) | Equity | 10 000 |
| Total assets | 30 000 | Total liabilities and equity | 30 000 |

(a) Determine the duration gap of the corporate balance sheet.
(b) Calculate how many $100 000 put option contracts on T-Note futures to trade to completely hedge the duration gap (assuming we are hedging the interest rate gap during a period well ahead of the option's final maturity date). The delta of the put option contract is −0.6, the duration of the cheapest-to-deliver bond is 3.2 and the current market value of the bonds underlying the options contract is $105 250.
(c) Should we buy or write the put options?

## Note

[1] See, for example, McMillan, L. G. (1992), *Options as a Strategic Investment*, 3rd edn, New York Institute of Finance.

# Chapter 9

# Hedging with swap agreements and other derivatives

So far, we have looked at different uses of futures and options contracts as well as various over-the-counter derivatives for general hedging purposes. In this chapter the application of derivatives is rounded off with a look at a number of hedging scenarios using different types of swap agreements and other derivatives. As in previous chapters, there is an initial focus on hedging of individual transactions. However, there is also a discussion of more general applications aiming to manage and hedge overall corporate exposures. This chapter also considers instruments used to hedge other types risk including credit risk, insurance risk, and related commercial exposures.

## 9.1 Hedging with interest rate and currency swaps

Futures contracts and forward agreements can be used to match single transactions as well as more complex term exposures. However, the maturity for these types of instruments is often of a relatively short-term nature, say within a year or at most a two-year horizon. Options on futures contracts and comparable over-the-counter options obviously share the same limitations. In contrast, the swap agreements constitute vehicles for regular medium to longer-term exchanges of payment structures. Hence, the swaps can be useful instruments to convert bond payments across different interest rate and currency bases while maintaining inherent advantages of the underlying financing or investment opportunities.

### 9.1.1  Short interest rate

Corporate borrowers may be in a position where they have obtained favourable funding on one rate basis in a particular currency. Yet, due to the aggregate interest rate and currency gaps across the corporation and senior management's view on future rates, it might be better to modify these exposures through the use of interest rate and currency swap agreements. Hence, a borrower with predominantly floating rate based funding might want to convert this into fixed-rate funding in situations where they expect future interest rates to increase. Conversely, predominantly fixed-rate funded institutions might want to convert these debt obligations into floating rate commitments when they have strong expectations that interest rates will fall over the coming years. In either case, the corporation can easily convert the interest rate basis of the loans by acting on either side of the bid and offer quotes on the interest rate swap.

A fixed-rate borrower that wants to convert the debt into floating rate obligations will react to the bank's bid rate, which indicates the basis point spread over the yield on the US treasury with the corresponding maturity the bank is willing to pay to receive LIBOR-based interest payments from the counterpart. Hence, in this transaction the borrower receives fixed-rate interest payments from the bank to cover its current loan obligations while paying floating rates interest to the bank thereby effectively converting the fixed-rate payments into floating rate LIBOR payments. Similarly, a floating rate borrower that wants to convert the debt into fixed-rate obligations would react to the bank's offer rate, which indicates the fixed-rate spread over treasuries the quoting bank requires from the counterpart to deliver LIBOR-based interest payments. If the borrowers go long the swap, they receive floating rate interest payment to cover the debt servicing of the existing debt obligations while they pay fixed-rate interest amounts to the bank, thereby effectively converting the floating rate debt into fixed-rate debt obligations. Assume the interest rate swaps in US dollars are quoted as follows around the yield on US T-Bills, Notes, and Bonds (Table 9.1).

The five-year US dollar interest rate swap is quoted as 0.55–0.75. This indicates that the quoting bank is willing to make regular interest payments at the yield of the five-year T-Note plus 55 basis points against receiving floating rate LIBOR-based interest payments regularly throughout the five-year period. It further indicates that

**Table 9.1** US dollar-denominated interest rate swaps spread over comparable treasury yield

| Maturity | Bid | Offer |
| --- | --- | --- |
| One year | 0.52 | 0.72 |
| Two years | 0.53 | 0.73 |
| Three years | 0.50 | 0.70 |
| Five years | 0.55 | 0.75 |
| Seven years | 0.58 | 0.78 |
| Ten years | 0.60 | 0.80 |

**Figure 9.1** Short interest rate hedge

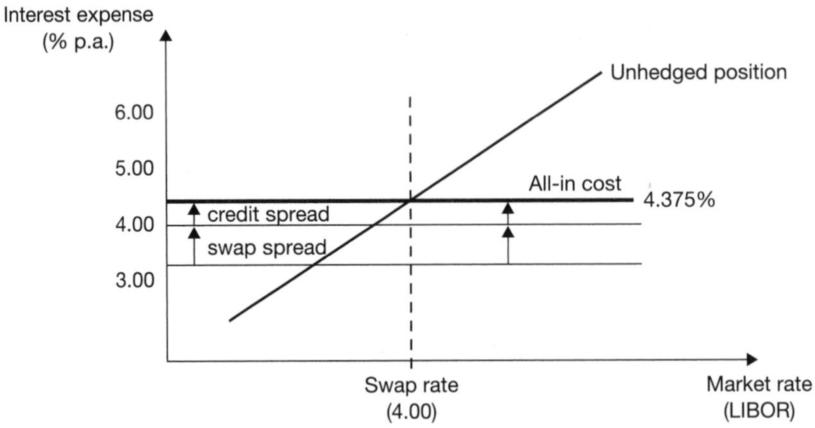

the intermediary is willing to make regular LIBOR-based floating rate payments against receipt of regular fixed rate payments at the yield of the five-year T-Note plus 75 basis points throughout the five years.

*Example*: A corporation has obtained in a five-year LIBOR-based US dollar loan. Interest payments are made at six-month LIBOR plus a spread of $^3/_8$% p.a. The corporation fears that the interest rate level will increase in the future and, therefore, wants to engage in a fixed-floating interest rate swap to convert the floating rate interest payments to fixed-rate interest payments. The five-year swap quote is 0.55–0.75, that is, the bank will make LIBOR payments against receipt of interest payments at the US Treasury rate plus 75 basis points. With a yield on the five-year treasury note of 3.25%, the total fixed rate interest rate expenses on the loan amounts to 4.375% (3.25 + 0.75 + 0.375) (Figure 9.1).

The treasury yield indication, reflected in the fixed rate of 4.375% in the example, is quoted here on a quarterly interest rate basis, i.e. it is changing every three months. This rate indication should be converted into a comparable annual interest rate basis of 4.45% p.a. $(= ((1 + 4.375/400)^4 - 1)100)$ corresponding to the rate calculated on an annual bond basis. This rate is further converted into a comparable money market rate basis of 4.39% p.a. $(= 4.45 \times 360/365)$.

As a consequence of engaging in a short interest rate swap position, the borrower has been able to lock-in the interest rate expense through the five-year life of the loan.

### 9.1.2 Long interest rate

Institutional investors may be faced with comparable interest rate gaps that could be hedged through engagement in interest rate swaps. An investor might be in a position where an otherwise favourable investment contributed to an adverse interest rate gap. That is, the aggregate interest rate and currency gaps across the invested portfolio and management's view on future rate developments might encourage a modification of the exposure through engagement in interest rate and currency swap agreements. Consequently, an institutional investor with a portfolio of floating rate notes might want to convert this into an investment in fixed-rate bond instruments if they expect future interest rates to drop. Conversely, institutions predominantly invested in fixed-rate bonds might want to convert these assets into floating rate investments if they expect that interest rates are likely to increase over the coming years. In either case, the institutional investor would easily be able to convert the interest rate basis of the assets by acting on either side of the interest rate swap bid and offer quotes.

A floating rate note investor that wants to convert the investment into fixed-rate bonds will react to the bank's bid rate, which indicates the basis point spread over the yield on the US Treasury with the corresponding maturity the bank is willing to pay to receive LIBOR-based interest payments from the counterpart. When investors go short the swap in these transactions, they pay floating rates interest to the bank passed on from the floating rate notes and in turn receives fixed-rate interest payments from the bank thereby effectively converting the floating rate LIBOR-based returns into fixed rate returns. Similarly, a fixed-rate bond investor that wants to convert the investment into floating rate notes will react to the bank's offer rate, which indicates the fixed-rate spread over treasuries the quoting bank requires from the counterpart to deliver LIBOR-based interest payments. Hence, in this transaction the investor will pay fixed-rate interest amounts to the bank passed on from the invested bonds and in turn receive floating rate interest payment thereby effectively converting the fixed rate bond investment into floating rate returns.

*Example*: An institutional investor has a three-year money market portfolio receiving floating rate dollar interest payments at LIBOR + $^1/_4$% and would like to fix the return on the investment over the three years. The investor has received the swap quote 0.50–0.70 for a fixed-floating US dollar interest rate swap. The investor can then provide the financial intermediary with interest payments at LIBOR and will in return receive fixed interest payments based on the US treasury rate at the time of signing the swap agreement plus 50 basis points. To reach the total fixed rate payment, the investor should add the 25 basis points spread over LIBOR. If the three-year US treasury rate at the time of signing is 2.75%, the return on the investment has been locked-in at a rate of 3.50% p.a. (2.75 + 0.50 + 0.25) over the three-year period (Figure 9.2).

Again, the Treasury yield rate reflected in the fixed rate of 3.50% in the example is quoted on a quarterly interest rate basis. This rate indication is converted into a comparable annual interest rate basis of 3.55% p.a. $(= ((1 + 3.50/400)^4 - 1)100)$

**Figure 9.2** Long interest rate hedge

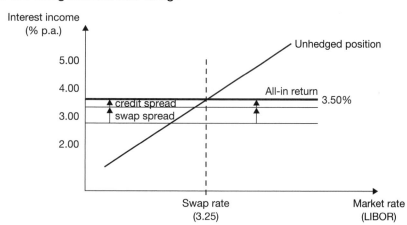

corresponding to annual bond basis. This rate is then converted into a comparable money market rate basis of 3.50% p.a. $(= 3.55 \times 360/365)$, which in this particular case turns out to be the same as the three-month bond basis rate.

Through the engagement in a long interest rate swap, the investor has been able to lock-in the return on the investment throughout the three-year life of the invested portfolio.

### 9.1.3 Interest rate basis swap

A US headquartered financial institution acquired a stake in a London-based bank conglomerate and used this as a platform for potential funding sources in the Euromarket. Therefore, a substantial part of the institution's short-term financing had become interbank related largely arranged through the London affiliate. This was reflected in the bank's official balance sheet and constituted publicly available information (Table 9.2). The funding was primarily obtained on a floating rate basis with rates varying in accordance with movements in short-term money market rates indicated by LIBOR. Per convention, the medium- and longer-term loan commitments made by the financial institution were usually tied to the bank's official prime rate. Whereas the prime rate could be adjusted it was rarely done in complete tandem with the day-to-day fluctuations in short-term money market rates and changes in the interest rate structure. The financial institution was aware that the prime rate also is influenced by competitive forces in the banking market, which in itself could impose restrictions on the ability to adapt loan rates to immediate changes in short- to medium-term market rates. Since the institution to a large extent funded its loan portfolio through money market placements obtained in the interbank market, the interest rate margin could get squeezed in periods where the money market experienced an upward trend in interest rates. This development in market rates might only gradually be reflected in the institution's prime rate, possibly after a considerable time lag, and then only if the upward move in interest rates was persistent and reflected a general industry policy.

Two months ago, in November, the financial institution booked a four-year committed loan structure to a major corporate client totalling US$25 000 000 with annual repayments of principal and interest. The interest calculation on the loan was based on the bank's going prime rate plus 7/8%. The funding for the loan was obtained through the London affiliate at six-month LIBOR flat. After the loan was booked LIBOR had seen both upward and downward moves and the current market carried

**Table 9.2** Bank balance sheet (US$ million)

| Assets | | Liabilities and equity | |
|---|---|---|---|
| Cash | 214.5 | Deposits | 2249.6 |
| Interbank placements | 259.7 | Interbank loans (foreign) | 1442.5 |
| Securities | 466.0 | Interbank loans (domestic) | 289.9 |
| Loans and advances | 3529.8 | Other liabilities | 219.9 |
| Other assets | 150.3 | Net worth | 418.4 |
| Total assets | 4620.3 | Total liabilities and equity | 4620.3 |

**Figure 9.3** Interest rate development

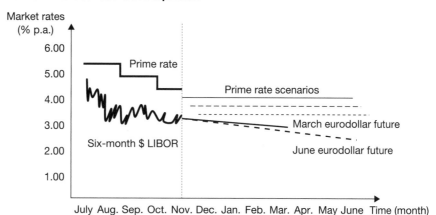

a bullish sentiment expecting a drop in the interest rate level. With the prime rate strongly influenced by domestic competition, management had envisaged the risk of a squeeze on the interest rate margin if the LIBOR rates were to bounce back up again. Therefore, they found the continued drop in the interest rate level as a good opportunity to hedge the interest rate gap (Figure 9.3).

Senior management in the financial institution voiced concern about the potentially unfavourable interest rate development. Even if there were a strong link between domestic interest rates and the Euromarket rates, the institutional prime rate could also be influenced by other factors than movements in short-term rates, such as competitive moves. As funding was increasingly obtained on a LIBOR basis for the expanding domestic loan portfolio based on the prime rate, the interest rate differential would be vulnerable to different movements in the two interest rates. The solution to this basis risk gap was found to be an engagement into an interest rate basis swap with one of the money centre banks. Quotes were obtained from several banks on interest rate swaps converting prime rate into a LIBOR-based rate. In this specific case the institution accepted a quote to exchange LIBOR for prime-$1\frac{1}{4}$%. The swap agreement was adapted to the payment structure of the four-year loan. Under the swap agreement the financial institution would pay the interest amount on the principal outstanding at each due date based on prime-$1\frac{1}{4}$%. In turn they would receive an equivalent interest amount based on LIBOR from the money center bank (Figure 9.4).

**Figure 9.4** Interest rate basis swap

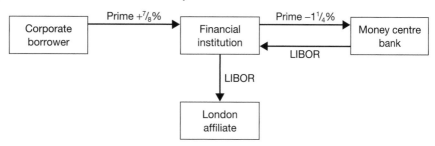

By engaging in this interest basis swap the financial institution effectively locked-in an interest rate spread of $2^1/8\%$ on the $25 million loan, thus securing lifetime earnings of more than $2 million on the loan during the four years until final maturity.

### 9.1.4 Short currency position

It is also possible to convert floating rate payments in one currency denomination into fixed rate payments in another currency denomination, and vice versa, by engaging in combined interest rate and currency swaps. Like in the case of pure interest rate swaps, the bid and offer quotes on the combined interest rate and currency swap is fixed rate payments in one currency against LIBOR payments in another currency (Table 9.3). The price indications show that, e.g. the quoting bank is willing to accept US dollar LIBOR-based interest payments over a two-year period by paying fixed interest amounts of 4.72% in euros (bid rate) and conversely, the bank is willing to provide US dollar LIBOR-based interest payments against receiving fixed interest amounts of 4.81% in euros (offer rate).

The quotes would typically relate to semi-annual interest rate fixing periods,[1] i.e. every six months the two counterparts will exchange fixed rate euro-denominated interest payments with six-month US dollar LIBOR-based payments. Since the two interest amounts have different currency denominations they cannot be netted against each other, that is, both payments must be made in full and, therefore, the transaction entails a larger counter-party risk than conventional interest rate swaps where only the net difference in interest amounts is paid by one of the two parties each period.

The combined interest rate and currency swap can be convenient for an international borrower to manage inherent currency exposures and interest rate gaps in different currencies. For example, a borrower with variable rate funding that wants to convert the loan portfolio into fixed rate loans in a different currency will react to the bank's offer rate, e.g. fixed euro against US dollar LIBOR, indicated either as the basis point spread over the yield, e.g. on German Bunds with the corresponding maturity or as all in fixed rates as indicated in Table 9.3. When the borrower goes long the interest rate and currency swap in this transaction, he will receive floating rate interest payments in US$ LIBOR terms from the bank and will in turn pay fixed rate euro-denominated interest payments to the bank thereby effectively converting the floating rate US$ LIBOR-based interest expenses into fixed rate euro-denominated

**Table 9.3** Euro currency and interest rate swap (all-in euro fixed rate for US$ LIBOR)

| Maturity | Bid | Offer |
| --- | --- | --- |
| Two years | 4.72 | 4.81 |
| Three years | 4.86 | 4.95 |
| Four years | 5.04 | 5.16 |
| Five years | 5.29 | 5.42 |
| Six years | 5.53 | 5.66 |
| Seven years | 5.75 | 5.93 |

interest payments. Similarly, a fixed-rate euro-denominated borrower that wants to convert the interest rate expense into floating rate US dollar terms will react to the bank's bid rate, which may indicate a fixed rate spread over German Bunds or an all-in euro-denominated fixed rate the quoting bank will pay to the counterpart against receipt of US$ LIBOR-based interest payments. Hence, in this transaction the borrower pays floating rate US$ interest amounts to the bank and in turn receives fixed-rate euro-denominated interest payments to pass on as payment for the existing loans thereby effectively converting the floating rate US dollar-denominated loan into a fixed rate euro-denominated debt obligation.

*Example*: A German corporate borrower has a three-year US dollar denominated loan portfolio paying floating rate dollar interest payments at LIBOR + $^3/_4$% and would like to fix the rate on the loans in euro terms over the three-year period. The borrower has received the swap quote 4.86–4.95 for a fixed euro–floating US dollar interest rate swap. In accordance with the quotes, the borrower can then receive US dollar-denominated interest payments at six-month LIBOR from the financial intermediary against payment of euro-denominated fixed interest payments at 4.95% semi-annually over the three-year period. Hence, the borrower receives US$ LIBOR payments to cover the floating rate loan commitments and pay fixed rate interest in euros to the bank thus effectively imposing the exposure of a euro-denominated fixed rate loan over the three years.

## 9.1.5 Long currency position

An international institutional investor can similarly use combined interest and currency swaps to modify the interest rate and currency exposures of the invested portfolio. For example, an institution with investments in US dollar-denominated variable rate returns may want to convert the portfolio into fixed rate euro-denominated returns to modify the interest rate risk in accordance with prevailing market views and manage the currency gaps. A floating rate note investor that wants to convert the investment into fixed rate bond payment will react to the swap bid rate, which indicates the basis point spread over the Bund yield, or an all-in euro interest rate like in Table 9.1, the quoting bank is willing to pay to receive US dollar LIBOR-based interest payments from the counterpart. Hence, when the investor goes short the swap in this transaction, he will pass on the floating rate interest payments in US$ from the FRN portfolio to the bank and will in turn receive fixed rate interest payments in euros from the bank thereby effectively converting the floating rate LIBOR-based returns into fixed rate returns. Conversely, when a Euro-based fixed-rate bond investor that wants to convert the portfolio into a US$-denominated floating rate note investment will react to the swap offer rate, which indicates the fixed rate spread over the Bund yield, or an all-in euro interest rate, the quoting bank requires from the counterpart to deliver US$ LIBOR-based interest payments. Hence, in this transaction the investor will pay fixed-rate interest amounts to the bank passed on from the invested coupon bonds and will in turn receive floating rate interest payments thereby effectively converting the fixed-rate bond investment into floating rate returns.

*Example*: A French institutional investor has a five-year US$-denominated portfolio of floating rate notes paying US dollar interest at LIBOR + $^1/_2$% and would like to fix the return on this investment in euro-denominated coupon payments until final maturity in five years. The investor has received a two-way swap quote of 5.29–5.42 on a fixed euro–floating US dollar interest rate swap. According to this, the institutional investor can provide US$-denominated interest payments at LIBOR to the financial intermediary and in return receive euro-denominated fixed interest payments at a rate of 5.29%. To reach the total fixed rate return the investor receives on the modified portfolio, he should add the 50 basis points spread over LIBOR earned on the floating rate notes, i.e. the return on the investment has been locked-in at a rate of 5.79% p.a. (5.29 + 0.50) over the three years.

## 9.1.6 Interest rate and currency swap

A US-based manufacturing company had just signed a contract with a major German supplier in August for delivery of tools and equipment with a total value of €14 000 000 approximately equal to US$12 500 000 at the going foreign exchange rate. The German exporter had made a favourable three-year euro-denominated loan available on the total amount of the purchase price to commence upon delivery. However, if the US manufacturing company accepted this financing offer, the loan would have to be repaid in euros and hence the loan repayments would represent a currency exposure. The current spot foreign exchange rate was quoted around 1.1200 €/US$ but there was considerable uncertainty as to the future movement of the €/US$ foreign exchange rate and senior management expressed its concerns about this prospect. Whereas the US manufacturing company received a very attractive loan offer from its German supplier, interest on the loan would have to be repaid semi-annually at an interest rate equivalent to the euro interbank offered rate (Euribor), which at the time hovered around 3.5% p.a. and was slightly lower than the equivalent US interest rate. However, a euro-denominated loan at the same time presented a dilemma because the foreign exchange exposure from this loan was extremely difficult to evaluate. The US dollar had been rather stable for some time but had shown recent signs of weakness coupled with increasing political pressure to deflate the dollar exchange rate (Figure 9.5). Hence, they feared that the dollar might weaken over the coming years, which would make a loan in euros potentially unattractive despite the favourable financial terms.

**Figure 9.5** Foreign exchange rate development

**Figure 9.6** Currency and interest rate swap

The manufacturing company ideally wanted to know the exact cost of the equipment in order to refine the cost–benefit evaluation of a plant facility and to create certainty at least as far as the financial charges were concerned. In this situation the company contacted their major bank to get a comparative offer for a three-year fixed rate loan in US dollars to fund the import purchase. It turned out that a fixed rate dollar loan would cost around 5.75% p.a. based on the same repayment structure as made available by the German exporter. At the same time an equivalent dollar variable rate offer could be done at a rate of around 4.50% p.a. for the first six-month period, that is, a rate somewhat above the euro-denominated alternative. As they engaged in discussions with the bank on the matter, the idea emerged that the company could take advantage of the favourable € financing offer from the German exporter and instead swap the variable payments in euros into a favourable fixed-rate payment structure in US dollars. By engaging in a €/US$ fixed-floating rate swap, it turned out that the manufacturing company could get away with paying a fixed dollar rate of $4\frac{1}{8}$% p.a., i.e. considerably lower than the alternative fixed-rate proposal and even lower than the variable rate offer. Under this currency and interest rate swap agreement the manufacturing company accepted the euro loan and exchanged the euro principal into US dollars at the current €/US$ spot foreign exchange rate. Throughout the life of the loan, the company would pay fixed-rate dollar interest to the bank, which in turn would pass variable rate euro payments to the manufacturing company to use for the debt servicing to the German exporter (Figure 9.6). The principal amounts of the loan would be exchanged back at the initial spot foreign exchange rate at the final maturity of the loan.

By engaging in a fixed-rate US dollar for floating rate euro swap, the manufacturing company obtained the best of two worlds. It eliminated the uncertainty of the €/US$ exchange rate and it managed to lock-in and convert the favourable euro-denominated floating interest rate payments into equivalently favourable US dollar fixed interest rate payments.

## 9.1.7 Interest rate and currency swap

An investment bank was in a position to arrange an international bond issue for a major institutional borrower. The bank offered a unique ten-year fixed-rate issue of €500 million at an all-in rate of 4.60% p.a. Given the reputation of the borrower, the funding rate was rather favourable compared to the going market rate. The investment bank was able to attract investors to this issue through its domestic associates in the financial industry and thereby could offer slightly better terms than the norm for this type of issue. However, the borrower maintained a major part of its cash flows in US dollar and hence would prefer to obtain the funding in dollars to eliminate the currency exposure associated with the loan. The view of the borrower was that US interest rates would decline over the coming 1–2-year period (Figure 9.7) and, therefore, favoured a floating rate funding arrangement.

**Figure 9.7** Interest rate development

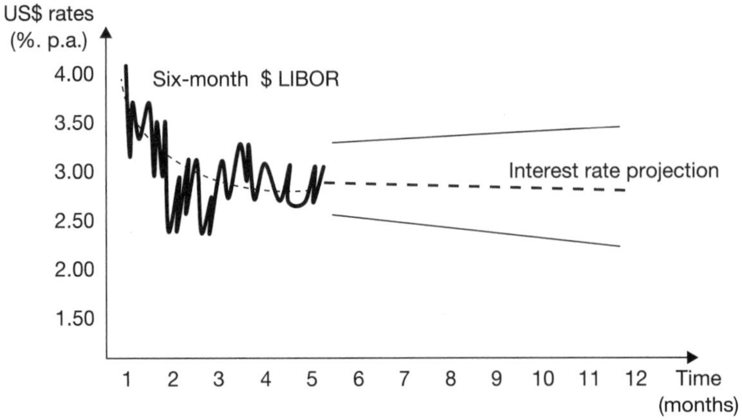

US$ rates
(%. p.a.)

4.00     Six-month $ LIBOR

3.50

3.00                           Interest rate projection

2.50

2.00

1.50

1   2   3   4   5   6   7   8   9   10   11   12   Time
(months)

**Figure 9.8** Currency and interest rate swap

The investment bank was in a situation where it could arrange fixed rate long-term funding in euros to a major international issuer on very favourable terms with the fixed funding rate being almost $\frac{1}{4}$ percentage point below the current market rate for comparable issues. As the institutional borrower was likely to give preference to a floating rate US dollar proposal in the current foreign exchange and interest rate scenario, they proceeded to arrange a combined currency and interest rate swap to convert the fixed-rate euro funding opportunity into a floating rate US dollar transaction. The investment bank approached international financial institutions in competitive bidding to obtain quotes for a € fixed rate for US$ floating rate swap. The most favourable swap quote was obtained from a London-based merchant bank proposing to provide euro payments at the Bund yield plus 0.45% corresponding to 4.70% against receipt of US dollar payments at three-month LIBOR. This meant that the 4.60% fixed-rate euro-denominated interest payments could be converted into LIBOR – 0.10% = LIBID, which constitutes a very favourable variable funding rate in US dollar terms (Figure 9.8). The investment bank was, therefore, able to offer a ten-year US$450 million funding proposal (approximate dollar value at the prevailing €/US$ foreign exchange rate) at a rate of three-month LIBID. The borrower considered this a very interesting proposal and accepted the offer.

### 9.1.8 Portfolio hedging

Interest rate swaps can be used to manage the duration of investment portfolios, corporate loan portfolios, and the implied equity duration gaps in a specific currency. Since an interest rate swap can be considered an exchange of interest payments between a fixed income security and a floating rate note, the duration of the swap must be equal to the difference between the duration of the two interest payment streams, e.g. in the two-year swap, the fixed-rate payment stream has a duration of 1.7 and the duration of the FRN is 0.5, so the duration of the swap is 1.2 (= 1.7 − 0.5).

$$D_{swap} = D_{fixed} - D_{floating}$$

We can use this information to manage the duration of an invested securities portfolio toward a specific duration target:

$$D_T = \frac{(D_S \times P_S) + (D_{swap} \times N_{swap})}{P_S}$$

$$N_{swap} = \frac{(D_T - D_S)P_S}{D_{swap}}$$

where

$D_T$ = targeted duration of portfolio of securities and futures contracts;
$D_S$ = duration of securities portfolio;
$P_S$ = market value of securities portfolio;
$D_{swap}$ = duration of interest rate swap;
$N_{swap}$ = notional value of the interest rate swap.

As discussed previously (Chapter 2), the duration measure indicates the price sensitivity of the asset or liability portfolio to incremental changes around the current interest rate level. Therefore, adaptations to the duration of different interest rate positions can be used as a tool to manage interest rate exposures maintained in different currency areas. The interest rate swap quotes available in the major currency areas provide for efficient opportunities to modify inherent interest rate gaps.[2] While the quoted rates obviously have importance for locked-in rate levels, the general principle of fixed–floating interest rate and currency swaps will suffice in a generic discussion of interest rate risk management.

*Example*: An institutional investor wants to reduce the duration of its invested portfolio from 6.5 to 5.0 over the next three years. The market value of the invested portfolio is around US$500 000 000. The duration of the three-year interest rate swap is 2.6. Hence, the duration of the invested portfolio can be reduced by buying floating rate LIBOR from the bank, i.e. going long the interest rate swap. The notional amount of the interest rate swap then amounts to US$288.5 million:

$$5 = \frac{(6.5 \times 500) + (2.6 \times N_{swap})}{500}$$

$$= \frac{3250 + 2.6 \times N_{swap}}{500} \qquad \Rightarrow$$

$$N_{swap} = \frac{2500 - 3250}{2.6}$$

$$= -288.5$$

*Example*: The portfolio could be completely immunized, i.e. $D_T = 0$, by buying even more floating rate payments, or more specifically, by going long a larger notional swap amount, in this case with an amount corresponding to $1250 million:

$$0 = \frac{(6.5 \times 500) + (2.6 \times N_{swap})}{500}$$

$$= \frac{3250 + 2.6 \times N_{swap}}{500} \qquad \Rightarrow$$

$$N_{swap} = \frac{-3250}{2.6}$$

$$= -1250$$

The minus in front of the calculated nominal amount indicates that we must go long the swap to reduce the duration of the securities portfolio.

Conversely, the duration could be increased by selling floating rate payment against fixed-rate payments, for example, to take advantage of windfall gains related to an expected drop in interest rates. That is, by increasing the duration of an invested portfolio the rate sensitivity of the portfolio's market value is increased so the capital gains and losses associated with changes in the interest rate level are higher.

*Example*: An institutional investor wants to increase the duration of the investment portfolio from 3.5 to 6.0 over the next three years. The market value of the invested portfolio is around US$450 000 000. The duration of the three-year interest rate swap is 2.6. Hence, the duration of the portfolio can be increased by selling floating rate LIBOR to the bank, i.e. going short the interest rate swap. The notional amount of the interest rate swap amounts to US$432.7 million:

$$6 = \frac{(3.5 \times 450) + (2.6 \times N_{swap})}{450}$$

$$= \frac{1575 + 2.6 \times N_{swap}}{450} \qquad \Rightarrow$$

$$N_{swap} = \frac{2700 - 1575}{2.6}$$

$$= 432.7$$

Just like an investor has an interest in the active management of the interest rate sensitivity of the portfolio's market value, a borrower might see similar advantages related to the active management of the loan portfolio's interest rate sensitivity. For example, if the interest rate level is expected to increase in the near future it might be an advantage to increase the duration of the loan portfolio. That is, if the yields increase the market value of the debt will go down so less will be owed, or to express it differently, the cheaper it becomes to buy back the debt obligations in the market. The duration of liabilities can be increased by engaging in a fixed–floating interest rate swap and thereby converting the variable rate commitments into fixed-rate commitments. In practical terms, this also means that the loan rates are fixed and thereby made insensitive to potential rate increases until the maturity of the loans.

*Example*: A corporate borrower wants to increase the duration of its loan portfolio from 2.5 to 4.0 over the next four years. The market value of the loan portfolio is around $350 000 000. The duration of the four-year interest rate swap is 3.5. Hence, the duration of the loan portfolio can be increased by buying floating rate LIBOR from the bank, i.e. going short the interest rate swap. The notional amount of the swap amounts to $150 million (see calculation below):

$$4 = \frac{(2.5 \times 350) + (3.5 \times N_{swap})}{350}$$

$$= \frac{875 + 3.5 \times N_{swap}}{350} \qquad \Rightarrow$$

$$N_{swap} = \frac{1400 - 875}{3.5}$$

$$= 150$$

Conversely, the interest rate sensitivity of the liabilities could also be reduced. For example, if the interest rate level is expected to decrease it might be advantageous to reduce the duration of the loan portfolio. The duration of liabilities can be decreased by engaging in a fixed–floating interest rate swap that converts the fixed rate commitments into variable rate commitments, which means that loan rates change more frequently thus allowing the borrower to take advantage of potential drops in interest rates until the loans mature.

*Example*: A corporate borrower wants to reduce the duration of its loan portfolio from 4.5 to 3.0 over the next two years. The market value of the loan portfolio is around $300 000 000. The duration of the two-year interest rate swap is 1.7. The duration of the loan portfolio can be reduced by selling floating rate LIBOR to the bank, i.e. going short the interest rate swap. The notional amount of the swap amounts to $264.7 million:

$$3 = \frac{(4.5 \times 350) + (1.7 \times N_{swap})}{300}$$

$$= \frac{1350 + 1.7 \times N_{swap}}{300} \qquad \Rightarrow$$

$$N_{swap} = \frac{900 - 1350}{1.7}$$

$$= -264.7$$

When combining the interest rate risk management views of assets and liabilities, we notice that an expectation of increased market yields should urge investors to reduce the duration of the invested portfolio and borrowers to increase the duration of the loan portfolio. Conversely, an expectation of falling market yields should encourage investors to increase the duration of the invested portfolio and borrowers to reduce the duration of the loan portfolio. All organizations have assets as well as liabilities. In principle, the assets reflect the future cash flows from business activities and the liabilities reflect the cash flows associated with the funding of these activities. The overall interest rate sensitivity of the organization constitutes a combination of these asset and liability effects weighted at their respective market values, which can be expressed in the duration of the equity position (assets minus liabilities):

$$D_E = D_A - D_L$$

Hence, we can use fixed–floating interest rate swaps to manage the interest rate sensitivity of the organization's implied equity position in the major currencies in which the organization is engaged, e.g. US dollars, euros, etc. Together, the interest rate gaps in different currencies constitute the aggregate interest rate exposure of the corporation:

US dollar-denominated assets and liabilities [$1000 (*duration*)]

| Total assets | 100 000 (*3.8*) | Total liabilities | 80 000 (*3.0*) |
|---|---|---|---|

$$D_A - D_L = 3.8 - 3.0 = 0.8$$

Euro-denominated assets and liabilities [€1000 (*duration*)]

| Total assets | 125 000 (*3.3*) | Total liabilities | 97 000 (*2.4*) |
|---|---|---|---|

$$D_A - D_L = 3.3 - 2.4 = 0.9$$

etc. . . .

It is possible to reduce the duration gap on the implied equity position in US dollar from 0.8 to, e.g. 0.4 for, say, a two-year period just like was done in the previous examples, that is, by going long a nominal two-year interest swap at an amount of US$58.8 million the duration of the equity position has been halved:

$$0.4 = \frac{\left(D_A - \frac{L}{A} \times D_L\right) \times A + (D_{swap} \times N_{swap})}{A} \Rightarrow$$

$$N_{swap} = \frac{\left(0.4 - \left(D_A - \frac{L}{A} \times D_L\right)\right) A}{D_{swap}}$$

$$= \frac{(0.4 - (3.8 - 0.8 \times 3))100}{1.7}$$

$$= -58.8$$

Note that the duration of the liabilities ($D_L$) is multiplied by the ratio between the market values of total liabilities over total assets (L/A) since assets usually exceed liabilities.[3] The same gap calculations could be performed for all the other major currencies in which the organization has material activities and the total interest rate exposures is reflected in the aggregate interest rate gaps measured in the currency of accounting.

Whereas the interest rate sensitivity of assets and liabilities is discussed here as two rather distinct elements of the firm's risk management exposure, it is of course much more complex when considered in a real corporate setting possibly spanning several business areas and commercial activities crossing multiple currency areas. In that case, the balance sheet will include many different postings and not all of them relate strictly to future cash flows but often emerge as a consequence of depreciation and special accounting treatment of long-term balance sheet items. Therefore, for the purposes of interest risk management it is necessary to go behind the economics of the assets and liabilities to stipulate the true expected cash flows regarding business activities on the asset side and future financial and commercial obligations on the liability side. Assuming that such an exercise has been performed with reasonable care regarding all US dollar-denominated business engagements, i.e. stipulating all material future cash flows and assessing their actual market value based on appropriate discounting procedures, then we can apply the same interest rate management approach to the interest rate gaps on corporate equity positions as well (see below).

## US dollar-denominated assets and liabilities [$1000 (*duration*)]

| Assets | | Liabilities | |
| --- | --- | --- | --- |
| Transactional accts | 25 000 (*1*) | Overdraft facility | 30 000 (*0*) |
| Receivables | 20 000 (*1*) | Payables | 25 000 (*1*) |
| Plant and machinery | 65 000 (*5*) | Medium-term notes | 30 000 (*4*) |
| Real estate | 50 000 (*5*) | Corporate bonds | 25 000 (*4*) |
| | | Total liabilities | 110 000 |
| | | Implied equity position | 50 000 |
| Total assets | 160 000 (*3.8*) | Total liabilities and equity | 160 000 (*3*) |

Assuming that all future cash flows have been reaffirmed and discounted to find appropriate market values for all asset and liabilities categories, we can determine the implied equity position in market value terms as the difference between total assets and total liabilities:

$$\text{Implied equity position} = \text{Total assets} - \text{Total liabilities}$$

*Example*: Based on the data given above, total assets amount to US$160 000 and total liabilities to US$110 000, and hence the implied equity position is calculated as US$50 000 (= 160 000 – 110 000).

Given that all balance sheet items are assessed on a market value basis we can determine the weighted average duration of both assets and liabilities weighted by market values, i.e. net present value of future cash flows.

*Example*: Based on the data given above, the average duration of total assets is determined as 3.88 (= (25 + 20)/160 × 1 + (65 + 50)/160 × 5) and average duration of liabilities as 2.23 (= (30/110 × 0) + (25/110 × 1) + ((30 + 25)/110 × 4) and, therefore, the interest rate gap of the implied equity position is positive and amounts to 1.65 (= 3.88 – 2.23). Hence, if the interest rate increases the firms will lose market value and if the interest rate decreases it will gain value.

As observed previously, the duration gap determined this way on the implied equity position can be managed over longer time periods through engagements in fixed–floating interest rate swaps. For example, if the corporation wanted to increase the interest rate sensitivity of the equity position due to bullish market sentiments, it could be done by going short the interest rate swap for, e.g. a three-year period as was done in the previous examples. Say we want to increase the duration of the equity position to 3.0, then we must go short a nominal three-year interest swap at an amount of US$40.2 million:

$$3.0 = \frac{\left(D_A - \frac{L}{A} \times D_L\right) \times A + (D_{swap} \times N_{swap})}{A} \Rightarrow$$

$$N_{swap} = \frac{\left(3.0 - \left(D_A - \frac{L}{A} \times D_L\right)\right) A}{D_{swap}}$$

$$= \frac{(3.0 - (3.88 - \frac{110}{160} \times 2.23))160}{2.6}$$

$$= 40.2$$

## 9.2 Hedging with credit derivatives

The use of duration to assess the interest rate gap of an institutional equity position relates to the sensitivity of market values to changes in interest rates and yield curve structures. However, as discussed previously the interest rate level is also influenced by macroeconomic conditions and the default risk associated with the future cash flows of assets and liabilities. That is, a credit margin should be added to the risk free rate as compensation to the holder for the expected loss of principal. When corporate defaults emerge due to mismanagement or general repayment conditions get worse due to adverse economic conditions a common outcome is that the maturity of cash flows is extended. For example, rather than making payment in 30 days it might now be done in 60 days and projected revenues from new ventures are postponed to later periods. Similarly, as loan covenants are broken and default situations develop it usually triggers renegotiations whereby credit terms are extended and final repayment postponed. In extreme cases this may develop into a bankruptcy situation where part of or possibly the entire principal is lost. Hence, the potential for maturity extensions and loss of principal is related to commercial exposures and credit risks. The maturity extension effects can be partially assessed and managed through the duration gapping method discussed above. In addition, various credit derivatives are traded among counterparts whereby one party provides cover to the other party in case of bankruptcy against receipt of periodic interest payments and thereby represent instruments that serve to distribute risk among market participants and manage institutional risk exposures through diversification.

### 9.2.1 Credit default swaps

A conventional credit default swap is a bilateral agreement whereby failure to honour debt service payments determined in the loan indenture of a predefined loan, or loan portfolio, triggers a predetermined compensation payment to one counterpart, the hedger, by the other, the seller. The hedger that obtained the risk cover has in turn committed to make periodic interest payments to the other party as compensation for the associated default risk. For example, a European bank (Euro Bank) has

**Figure 9.9** Credit default swap

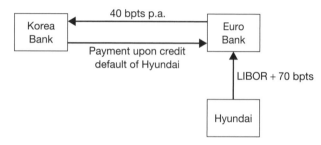

participated in a syndicated loan facility issued to Hyundai, the Korea-based global car manufacturer to assume commercial exposure on the buoyant Korean economy. However, the bank might not feel it has sufficient knowledge about the commercial activities of the borrower nor is sufficiently familiar with its top management team to assume an extensive credit exposure. In this situation, Euro Bank could engage into a credit default swap with a regional bank, e.g. Korea Bank, that is closer to the local operations and headquarters of the firm. The regional bank might be willing to acquire more credit risk due to it superior insights and thereby assume part of the excess credit exposure held by the European bank. Hence, Euro Bank makes quarterly interest payments of 40 basis points (0.40% p.a.) calculated on the loan principal to Korea Bank until final maturity, and Korea Bank in turn promises to pay the principal loan amount at maturity if the borrower, i.e. Hyundai, should default in the interim (Figure 9.9). Since the Euro Bank receives LIBOR plus 70 basis point on the syndicated loan and passes on 40 basis points as payment for the credit cover, it has obtained a commercial loan exposure on the Korean economy with limited credit risk exposure at an all-in interest rate spread of 30 basis points above LIBOR (= 70 – 40).

The compensation, or termination payment, in the credit default swap could be related to the difference between the par value of a specified bond (since the bond price under normal circumstances should reach parity at final maturity) and the actual market value at termination. In case a credit event occurs, the hedger will then obtain a compensation that matches the implied loss in market value caused by the deteriorating creditworthiness.

$$\text{Termination payment} = \text{Notional amount} \times (\text{Par} - \text{Market value})$$

The termination payment is calculated on the basis of the notional amount of the swap agreement. This amount could be smaller than the actual credit exposure assumed by the investor, i.e. the investor might engage in a partial hedge, which would serve to reduce a particular credit risk exposure to a more acceptable level. Conversely, the investor might sell credit default swaps in other reference assets where it is under invested and thereby receive additional interest income in securities with uncorrelated credit exposures even without making direct investment in those financial assets. These types of transactions can obviously serve to diversify the invested portfolios.

Assume that a corporate bank has established a loan portfolio that it deems has excess weighting on specific industrial sector risks or geographical exposures and, therefore, would like to dispose of part of these credit exposures, it could do so on that very portfolio or basket of corporate loans. It might also relate to an institutional investor with engagements in corporate bonds that possibly feel it has

**Figure 9.10** Basket credit default swap

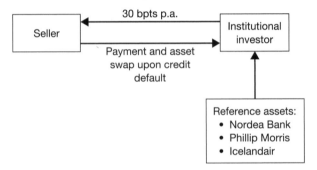

established overweight within certain industries and regional issuers. For example, the institutional investor might have a basket of corporate bonds issued by, say, Nordea Bank, Phillip Morris, and Icelandair, where they would like to reduce their credit exposure. The basket of corporate issuers represents actors operating in different industrial sectors and headquartered in different national economies and, therefore, represents a degree of portfolio diversification. However, since the institutional investor feels overexposed he is interested to cover the credit risk associated with a certain share of this corporate bond portfolio. This can be achieved through engagement in a basket credit default swap whereby a counterpart, the seller of the credit risk cover, is willing to acquire the portfolio of corporate bonds at a predetermined price if either of the three borrowers default on their debt obligations before final maturity. The institutional investor in turn pays an interest rate amount of 30 basis points (0.30% p.a.) calculated on the nominal value of the bond portfolio quarterly as compensation for the associated credit risk assumed by the seller (Figure 9.10). Such baskets of corporate bonds or commercial loans can combine many different assets and as a general principle, the more diversified the credit portfolio, the lower the interest rate compensation required by the seller. Again, the overarching idea behind these types of credit swaps is to spread the credit risks across a larger number of internationally engaged banks and global institutional investors.

### 9.2.2 Credit spread swap

Since changes in the credit quality, and hence the repayment capacity of institutional borrowers, will be reflected in the credit spread charged on those credit facilities, the swap arrangements can be structured around relevant threshold rates on specific benchmark credits, e.g. A-rated issuers, BB-rated issuers, etc. Significant changes in the underlying creditworthiness of these types of issuers would be reflected in the credit spread over the risk free rate, i.e. the benchmark government bond with corresponding payments and maturity structure. In a credit spread swap agreement, the seller would promise to provide a predetermined compensation amount to be paid in case the reference credit spread exceeds a certain threshold level either at final maturity or some time during the life of the swap agreement while the hedger would pay a quarterly interest amount calculated on the notional amount of the swap (Figure 9.11). Hence, this type of hedging arrangement can be organized within a swap format but in reality constitutes an option contract construed as a European or American option.

**Figure 9.11** Credit spread swap

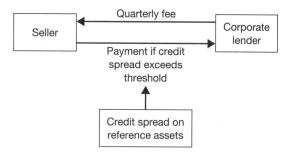

A more complex version of a credit spread swap arrangement can be construed as options on differential credit spreads between asset classes, e.g. between A-rated issuers and BB-rated issuers. For example, an institutional investor with an over-weight in corporate bonds by A-rated issuers might want to engage into a spread option swap that provides the right to compensation if the credit spread differential between A-rated issuers and BB-rated issuers exceeds a certain threshold level. Conversely, an institutional investor with an overweight in corporate bonds by BB-rated issuers might want to engage into a spread option swap that provides the right to compensation if the credit spread differential between BB-rated issuers and A-rated issuers exceeds a certain threshold level. Investors typically engage in credit spread swaps to diversify the invested portfolios but they might also engage in these swap arrangements to take a view on the credit spread differentials between specified asset classes. Focusing on two specific classes of risk assets, e.g. A-rated and BB-rated corporate issuers, then the credit spread is determined by the difference between the corporate yield and the risk-free rate indicated by the corresponding government bond:

$$\text{Credit spread}_1 = c_A - i$$

$$\text{Credit spread}_2 = c_{BB} - i$$

where

$c_A, c_{BB}$ = yield on risk classes;
$i$ = risk free rate (government bond).

The difference between the two credit spreads is then expressed as (credit spread$_1$ − credit spread$_2$) = $(c_{BB} - i) - (c_A - i) = (c_{BB} - c_A)$. That is, the credit spread differential simply corresponds to the difference between the yields on the two risk asset classes (Figure 9.12). If the interest rate differential between the two types of assets exceeds a predetermined threshold level, the institutional investor will exercise the option and require the seller to provide a compensation payment corresponding to the difference between the interest amounts based on the new and the agreed interest rate differentials calculated on the notional amount of the swap.

### 9.2.3 Asset swap swap

Swaps on asset swaps allow the hedger to convert one asset swap for another asset swap under certain predetermined conditions. For example, assume that an institutional investor and a commercial bank have established credit default swaps based

**Figure 9.12 Spread option swap**

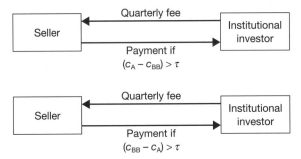

on different reference assets. Say, the institutional investor has engaged into a credit default swap on an Italian debt portfolio and the commercial bank has engaged into a credit default swap on a Korean debt portfolio. In this case, the two holders of credit default swaps can engage into an asset swap swap whereby the bank obtains the right to switch its credit default swap on Korean debt into a credit default swap on Italian debt if the market return on the Korean debt portfolio exceeds a threshold level of LIBOR plus 65 basis points (Figure 9.13). The bank in turn compensates the investor with quarterly interest payments at 20 basis points (0.20% p.a.) to assume this cover against a deterioration of creditworthiness of the Korean credit exposure. On the other hand, by engaging in this swap agreement the investor obtains an all-in spread of 40 basis points from its investment in Italian debt because it is willing to assume the excess credit risk on the Korean debt portfolio.

In this swap transaction, the bank earns 25 bpts, i.e. he receives LIBOR + 45 bpts on the Korean debt portfolio and passes on 20 bpts to the investor, the other counterpart to the transaction, against the opportunity to received another, less risky, asset swap based on an Italian debt portfolio, if the return on the Korean debt at some point exceeds LIBOR + 65 bpts before final maturity. That is, the bank gives away, or transfers, part of the excess credit risk on the Korean debt portfolio against the possibility to reduce this risk. The investor earns LIBOR + 20 bpts on the less risky Italian debt portfolio but receives another 20 bpts from the bank as compensation for assuming the excess risk associated with the Korean debt portfolio. Hence, the two hedgers have diversified the risk of their debt portfolios in this process and improved the risk-return characteristics of the invested assets.

**Figure 9.13 Asset swap swap**

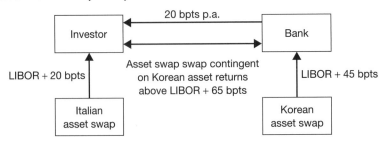

# 9.3 Hedging with risk swaps

The swap structure can also be adapted to handle insurance-related risk covers where the hedger pays an insurance premium to the insurer against compensation for losses incurred in connection with predefined adverse events. Such a risk swap could, for example, provide cover to a corporation against a specific industrial risk factor, such as, operational disruption, plant closures, or other firm specific incidents. Under the risk swap the corporation would make regular premium payments, e.g. quarterly, semi-annually, or annually, to the insurer throughout the duration of the swap agreement between the two parties. The insurer in turn commits to provide compensation for the documented costs associated with predefined events specified in the swap agreement (Figure 9.14). The risk swap agreement could also use predefined events to trigger payment under the swap agreement rather than pursue an actual claims process. Since event triggers often can be structured around independent environmental indicators that cannot be manipulated by any of the two counterparts to the swap agreement, such as, official economic, market, and financial data, the potential for moral hazard and adverse selection is vastly reduced.[4] The application of risk swaps may be particularly relevant to handle the higher risk layers of firm specific risk exposures that are less prone to standardized insurance contracts.[5] When higher risk layers are exchanged between insurers it serves to diversify the exposures in their risk portfolios.

## 9.3.1 Casualty risk

Independent risk events that may occur in everyday activities can be assessed on the basis of actuarial principles. That is, the risk profile of, for example, auto accidents, mechanical failures, property fires, etc., can be determined reasonably accurately based on data registers of historical events. Given the law of large numbers it is possible to assess the likelihood of occurrence under given pre-defined circumstances. The insurance industry bases its core activities on actuarial calculations since they can diversify many of the underlying risks by aggregating as many insurance takers as possible into their customer portfolios. However, large corporations can do the same thing and manage their own insurance business if they possess sufficiently large portfolios of exposed entities, e.g. a company with a large auto fleet might as well use the law of large numbers to self-insure their automobiles. Similarly, a multinational company with production facilities spread out in different locations around the globe might as well self-insure these property investments since they are likely to represent a diverse set of real estate assets where environmental impacts are unrelated. In many cases, the multinational company may establish their own insurance entities in cost effective locations, often referred to as captive insurance companies,

**Figure 9.14 Risk swap**

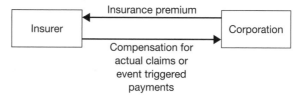

**Figure 9.15 Casualty risk swap**

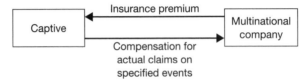

captives for short. Hence, the multinational company formally pays insurance premiums on a regular basis to the captive and will in turn receive coverage for certain specified casualty type risk events (Figure 9.15).

## 9.3.2 Catastrophe risk

When corporate assets and resources are prone to environmental rapid onset events like severe winter storms, hurricanes, floods, avalanches, etc., we are dealing with catastrophe exposures, i.e. low frequency high impact incidents. These types of exposures constitute interdependent risk events because the natural phenomena usually hit commercial entities throughout an entire region and thereby expose all economic assets within a larger geographical area. In this case the law of large numbers no longer applies and actuarial risk assessment methodologies fall short. Therefore, other risk transfer opportunities are needed to cope with these exposures. One way to deal with these risks is to diversify them through the international reinsurance industry, which in effect will serve to diversify exposures to natural catastrophes across larger global portfolios. This has conventionally been done through reinsurance contracts but this type of risk cover can also be effectuated in the form of catastrophe risk swaps. In the catastrophe risk swap, the hedger that cedes the excess risk exposure to the reinsurance company pays regular insurance premiums to the reinsurance company (the seller). The reinsurance company, in turn, provides compensating payments to cover actual claims for losses arising from specified natural events (Figure 9.16). The swap agreement could also use objective measures, such as wind speed and rainfall intensity, as triggers for payment.

The swapped catastrophe risk exposure could, for example, constitute a specified risk layer defined by predetermined attachment and exhaustion levels and as such could be used to 'fine tune' overall institutional exposures to different natural phenomena. The swap techniques could also be used to effectively exchange excess catastrophe exposures between reinsurance companies to further diversify their global catastrophe risk portfolios. The determination of appropriate attachment and exhaustion points is dependent on the quality of the supporting catastrophe risk analysis and therefore requires professional expertise often supported by external consulting firms specialized in advanced risk simulation techniques. The compensating payments can be triggered by actual catastrophe loss indemnities or through

**Figure 9.16 Catastrophe risk swap**

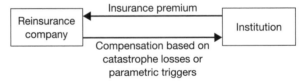

adoption of parametric formulas that incorporate objective measures of the potential catastrophe exposures. In either case, the determination of reasonable triggers for payments must be supported by detailed analysis of the underlying natural phenomena.

## 9.4 Alternative risk transfer

Asset securitization has increasingly been used as a technique to transfer a variety of risk exposures to the capital market (Chapter 3). This is frequently accomplished through the issuance of risk-linked securities where repayment of principal at maturity is contingent on payouts to cover specified risk events over the term of the securities. The associated risks can take many forms from general financial exposures to foreign exchange rates, interest rates, and commodity prices to more firm specific risks related to credit portfolios, commercial exposures, etc. In the latter case, the exposures are often transferred from coverage through conventional insurance contracts to engagements by professional institutional investors.

### 9.4.1 Risk-linked securities

The risk-linked securities are typically structured around a special purpose vehicle (SPV) that assumes the implied risk exposures by engaging in a conventional insurance contract, or a risk swap, as the seller and in return receives regular premium payments from the hedger. The SPV issues securities and uses the insurance premium payments, or option premiums, to enhance the spread offered on the regular coupon payments of the risk-linked securities. The proceeds from issuance of the risk-linked securities are invested in liquid high quality securities held in a trust account and interest payments from this portfolio are passed on to the holders of the risk-linked securities as regular debt service payments including the additional insurance or option premium payments. For example, a ceded risk exposure might receive semi-annual premiums corresponding to 4% p.a. of the notional risk cover as agreed in an insurance contract. The SPV might have placed the proceeds in high quality floating rate notes providing regular interest payments at LIBOR. Then the risk-linked securities may provide the securities holders with an excess return of LIBOR plus 4% (Figure 9.17). This premium return might attract additional investors particularly if the underlying risk exposure is unrelated to the returns on the existing invested portfolio. However, the investor runs the risk of course that part of the principal will not be repaid at maturity if the predefined risk event occurs in the interim. The investors will only receive the full principal back at maturity if there are no insurance losses.[6] For the hedger, issuance of risk-linked securities constitutes an alternative way to obtain cover for inherent risk exposures and thereby provide risk managers with added flexibility and more hedging opportunities.

When the risk factors ceded through issuance of risk-linked securities relate to extreme natural phenomena or man-made events we talk about catastrophe exposures and hence refer to these securities as catastrophe bonds or cat-bonds for short. The bulk of hedgers in this market has so far been insurance or reinsurance companies that seek alternative market venues for catastrophe risk covers although the same technique has been adopted by a few corporate entities.[7] Hence, the major risk consideration for cat-bond investors is the inherent catastrophe risk exposure.

**Figure 9.17** Risk-linked security

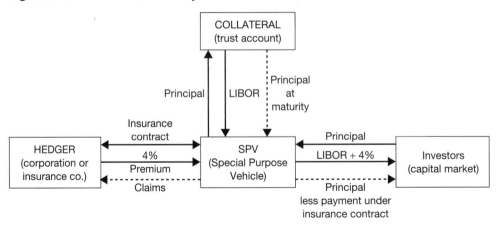

## 9.5 Hybrid instruments

Many financial derivatives are issued as hybrid instruments combining a generic fixed-income security with an attached or built-in derivative structure that modifies the underlying payment structure. There are many types of hybrid securities linking the effective return on investment to price developments in other financial markets including foreign exchange rates and commodities prices, such as silver, gold, oil, etc. An international US-based company with overseas currency exposures might be interested to make a US dollar-denominated securities issue where the redemption of principal depends on the development in a foreign exchange rate for a currency where the company holds significant exposures. For example, if the company has large exposures in euros, the company could issue a US$ bond where the repayment depends on the US$/€ foreign exchange rate, i.e. the bond redemption in US dollar terms could be inversely related to the strength of the US dollar vis-à-vis the euro. Hence, if the US dollar strengthens, i.e. the euro gets weaker, the issuer would lose on its euro-denominated assets but would repay a smaller US dollar amount of the loan, which would counterweigh the loss from the currency exposure. Conversely, if the US dollar weakens, i.e. the euro gets stronger, the issuer would gain on the euro-denominated assets but would provide part of that windfall to the bond holders (Figure 9.18). Investors interested in such a currency-linked securities issue would

**Figure 9.18** Structured securities

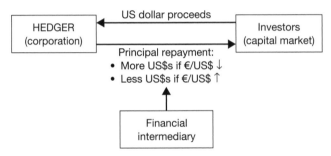

be institutions with the inverse position, e.g. European investors with US dollar-denominated exposures.

*Example*: An institution issues US dollar-denominated securities where the final redemption is a function of the development in a foreign exchange rate of Japanese yen in the following way:[8]

| Foreign exchange rate (¥/US$) | Redemption amount (US$) |
| --- | --- |
| > 109.0 | 1000 |
| < 109.0 | $1000 - \max[0, 1000(109/Y_t) - 1)]$ |
| < 64.5 | 0 |

Hence, the highest loan redemption is made when the yen exchange rate is high and the lowest when the yen exchange rate is low. This might be interesting to an issuer with commercial investment in Japan, where future revenues will be realized in yen, i.e. there is a natural long yen position. Conversely, the security might be interesting to a Japanese investor with US$-denominated financial investment, because a lower ¥ foreign exchange rate will result in compensation from the appreciation in the US$-denominated asset investment, which therefore constitutes a natural hedge against fluctuations in the $ foreign exchange rate.

These types of hybrid instruments could be construed in a myriad of ways and may incorporate any kind of firm specific risk exposure, e.g. related to individual currency and commodity prices or price indexes that describe the underlying risk exposure. The ability to place such issues will depend the existence of institutional investors that hold opposing positions or have an interest in new securities that can diversify an existing portfolio and enhance the risk-return profile of the investment.

## Conclusion

The application of swap agreements offers additional flexibility to institutional hedgers. Interest rate and currency swaps are traded in well-established interbank markets and provide many opportunities to hedge individual transactions as well as managing overall institutional interest rate and currency exposures. The swap technique has also been applied in the rapid development of markets for credit risk and other hazards that expose financial institutions and corporations alike.

## Summary

- Interest rate swaps provide the opportunity to exchange fixed for floating interest rate payments on longer-term financial commitments in different currencies and thereby offer the means to modify and manage inherent interest rate exposures.

- Combined currency and interest rate swaps provide the opportunity to exchange fixed for floating interest rate payments between different currencies and thereby offer the means to manage interest rate and currency gaps at the same time.

- The liquid generic interest rate swap markets in the major currencies constitute effective tools to adjust institutional risk exposures for longer time periods as complementary interim approaches to needed balance sheet adjustments.

- The swap technique has been extended to include many additional risk factors, such as credit risk, commercial risk, casualty risk, and catastrophe risk, which enhance the ability to manage other relevant risks beyond a narrow focus on financial exposures.

- A range of hybrid instruments combining elements of conventional financial assets and derivative structures have evolved over time to deal with firm specific risk exposures and exploit temporary needs in the investor community.

## Questions

9.1 Explain how interest rate swaps can help manage the interest rate risk of a borrower.

9.2 Explain how interest rate swaps can help manage the interest rate risk of an investor.

9.3 What is the idea behind an interest rate basis swap?

9.4 Explain the mechanics of a combined currency and interest rate swap.

9.5 When can a currency and interest rate swap be useful to a hedger?

9.6 Explain how interest rate swaps can help in fine-tuning the duration of an invested portfolio.

9.7 Explain how interest rate swaps can help in fine-tuning the duration of a loan portfolio.

9.8 Explain how interest rate swaps can help manage a corporate interest rate risk exposure.

9.9 Explain the underlying rationale behind the formation of credit swaps.

9.10 How does a credit spread swap work and how can it help manage credit exposures?

9.11 How does an asset swap swap work and how can it help manage credit exposures?

9.12 How does a generic risk swap work and how can it help manage risk exposures?

## Exercises

9.1 A company has a three-year US dollar-denominated loan at six-month LIBOR plus $\frac{1}{2}$% p.a. The three-year fixed-floating interest rate swap is quoted at 0.70–0.80 and the yield on the three-year treasury note is 3.50%. Determine the total fixed rate interest rate expenses to be paid on the loan if the company engages in an interest rate swap.

9.2 An investor has a five-year portfolio of US dollar-denominated floating rate notes paying six-month LIBOR + $\frac{7}{8}$%. The five-year fixed–floating interest rate swap is quoted at 0.45–0.55 and the five-year US treasury rate is 3.85%. Determine the total fixed rate interest rate payments received on the portfolio if the company engages in an interest rate swap.

9.3 A German institution has a four-year US dollar-denominated bank loan paying six-month LIBOR + $1\frac{1}{8}$%. The fixed euro–floating rate US dollar interest rate and currency swap is quoted at 4.55–4.67. Determine the total fixed rate interest rate expenses in euros to be paid on the loan if the institution engages in a currency and interest rate swap.

9.4 You are managing a US$243 500 000 nominal bond portfolio with average price of 106.34 and average duration of 5.2. The five-year swap is quoted as 6.10–6.20 and has a duration of 3.6.

(a) Use the swap market to set up a hedge that reduces the duration of the portfolio from 5.2 to 2.6, and determine the notional principal of the swap.
(b) Should we go long or short the swap?

9.5 A company has the following balance sheet [market value $1000, (duration)]:

| Assets | | Liabilities and equity | |
|---|---|---|---|
| Cash | 1 000 (0) | Overdraft facility | 7 000 (0) |
| Securities | 7 000 (1) | Syndicated loan | 15 000 ($\frac{1}{2}$) |
| Commercial investments | 8 000 (3) | Medium term notes | 8 000 (3) |
| Project portfolio | 19 000 (9) | Equity | 5 000 |
| Total assets | 35 000 | Total liabilities and equity | 35 000 |

(a) Determine the duration gap of the corporate balance sheet and calculate the nominal value of the fixed–floating interest rate swap we should trade to completely hedge the duration gap. The two-year swap is quoted at 3.15–3.25 and has a duration of 1.6.
(b) Should we go long or short the swap?
(c) Do you think the engagement in a swap is the best way to manage the interest rate risk?
(d) What could be some alternative risk management actions for the company?

## Notes

1. Alternatively, the interest rate fixing periods could be quarterly.
2. See, for example, Andersen, T. J. and Hasan, R. (1989), *Interest Rate Risk Management*, IFR Books.
3. If that is not the case, the firm would be bankrupt.
4. A moral hazard can arise if the hedger, or insured party, tries to manipulate reported losses in the claims report to the insurer. Adverse selection can happen, e.g. if the insurer tries to manipulate the hedger because it has more information about the true exposures of the insured risk.
5. See, for example, Takeda, Y. (2002), 'Risk swaps', in Lane, M. (ed.), *Alternative Risk Strategies*, Risk Books.
6. See Andersen, T. J. (2004), 'International risk transfer and financing solutions for catastrophe exposures', *Financial Market Trends*, No. 87, 91–120, OECD, Paris.
7. These include, e.g. Tokyo Disney Sea, Disney Hotels, and Disney Resort Line (Oriental Land Co.) obtaining securitized cover against Japanese earthquake risk and Universal Studio's (Vivendi) covering for California earthquake risk.
8. These so-called index currency option notes (ICONs) were commonly issued through the intermediation of Bankers Trust in 1980s.

# Strategic risk management

# Chapter 10

# Strategic exposures and real options

## Objectives

● Review different types of risk
● Discuss aggregate risk exposures
● Revisit the issue of firm specific risk
● Introduce common real option structures
● Consider risk management using real options
● Present general risk management issues

International markets for goods, services, and financial resources have become more intertwined as trade barriers and foreign exchange regulations have eased. The associated increase in market dynamics requires that corporations respond more effectively to changes in their competitive environment.[1] Corporations are challenged in their ability to satisfy customer demands around the globe to increase economic efficiencies through internationalization of business activities and operating assets structured in flexible global networks that facilitate adaptability. The globalization of markets increases cost pressures while ongoing innovation forces corporations to mobilize creative minds across the organization and integrate specialized expertise to retain competitive advantage often furnished by use of information and communication technologies.[2] The new technologies allow flexible exchange of tacit information between managers located in different parts of the corporation including observations, insights, ideas, reflections, etc., and enable broadband transmission of data intensive sources, such as customer profiles, technical specifications, design formulas, production schedules, etc. These technological capabilities have reduced the meaning of geographical distance and made it possible to coordinate planning, manufacturing, sourcing, distribution, etc., across corporate entities dispersed throughout the world. While corporations dealing with physical goods must take global logistics systems and transportation opportunities into consideration, other aspects of corporate activities, such as technological research, design programs, software development, administrative tasks, customer services, etc., may be located more freely. Such a globally networked organization can exploit factor cost advantages and obtain access to diverse human resources and organizational competencies. The ability to source inputs, organize production, and structure distribution on a global scale can improve economic efficiencies and provide the corporation with operational flexibilities that increase responsiveness to changing conditions.

The continued internationalization of corporate business activities has enforced financial risks associated with interest and foreign exchange rate developments as well as exposures to political, economic, and strategic risk factors have intensified in the wake of market globalization. For example, operational risk exposures are extended in global sourcing networks that link functional entities together in intricate webs of suppliers, partners, and customers. Locating operational platforms in different overseas markets will obviously create new sovereign risk exposures and as demand conditions, competitive moves, technology changes, etc., evolve across connected national markets they will influence corporate economic performance. In other words, there are a variety of risk factors at play in the global marketplace and corporations that operate in this contemporary environmental setting must learn to cope effectively with all the associated risks. Where previous chapters have focused primarily on market related risk factors, this chapter extends the perspective to comprise other relevant types of risk and seeks to develop an integrative framework for dealing with the aggregate corporate exposures.

## 10.1 The importance of a risk management focus

Focusing attention around essential risk factors that may expose the corporation can have a significant effect on corporate performance outcomes while a lack of risk management can be detrimental to corporate survival. Examples of firms getting into trouble due to neglect of potential risk exposures abound and a representative sample of cases from the past decade illustrates the issue.

In the early 1990s Metallgesellschaft Refining and Marketing, the American subsidiary of Metallgesellschaft, engaged in long-term forward contracts of up to ten years to sell petroleum products at prices above current spot prices. They hedged these open positions by buying comparable numbers of short-term energy futures contracts on an ongoing basis. That is, the short long-term position was covered by long short-term positions in the futures market. However, as energy prices continued to drop, the futures contracts had to be closed out at significant losses, i.e. the futures contracts were sold at lower settlement prices before final maturity. So, even though the value of the long-term fixed price forward contracts in principle were valuable, the corporation was exposed to an immediate liquidity squeeze because the loses incurred from closing out on the short-term futures contracts had to be paid in cash. As corporate headquarters for various reasons refused to make the needed cash available to the subsidiary, the entire position had to be liquidated incurring total losses in excess of US$1 billion.

In the mid-1990s Bankers Trust, which has since been acquired by Deutsche Bank, was very active in the market for over-the-counter derivatives and solicited corporate clients actively as counterparts to these transactions. They were successful in promoting a derivatives product referred to as a leveraged interest-rate swap, which basically provided the corporate clients with bets on stable or falling interest rates with positions in some cases leveraged by a ratio of twenty-to-one. However, as the Federal Reserve Bank increased interest rates repeatedly during 1994, the unfortunate corporations incurred significant losses at three-digit US dollar million levels. Some of the corporate counterparts, e.g. Procter & Gamble, sued Bankers Trust for misleading sales tactics and unfair exploitation of their financial sophistication. Hence, even though Bankers Trust established fairly stringent contractual relations, they were accused of breaking the trust of their customers. Eventually, these law suits were settled at significant cost to the bank, e.g. Procter & Gamble achieved a net gain of US$78 million and Air Products and Chemicals, another counterpart, received a compensation of US$67 million during 1996. These events damaged the market reputation of Bankers Trust and thereby provided further ammunition to the subsequent take-over of the institution.

In 1994, Orange County in California, was declared bankrupt due to losses incurred from its investments in leveraged interest-linked securities, inverse floating rate notes, and leverage interest derivatives. The overall investment position engaged the county in a large bet on a positive yield curve with short-term interest rates remaining lower than medium-term rates. However, as the Federal Reserve Bank increased the FED funds rate the county's positions got under water. The bankruptcy was triggered by increasing calls for cash collateral from its brokers in the wake of reported investment losses and it eventually brought Orange County into a liquidity crunch where positions had to be liquidated at losses in excess of US$1.5 billion. Subsequently, Merrill Lynch, which had been an active broker and counterpart to these derivative transactions were sued by the county for their role in establishing the unfortunate investment position and a settlement of US$400 million was reached in 1998.

In February 1995 Baring Brothers, the oldest merchant bank in the UK, went bankrupt because a derivatives trader in their Singapore division went over limits. Nick Leeson, who was later immortalized in the movie 'Rogue Trader' took unauthorized positions in futures contracts linked to the Nikkei 225, Japanese government bonds, and options on the Nikkei stock index. Leeson was able to book his trades on an unused error account and was, therefore, able to keep the mounting losses hidden from senior management for a long period of time. Eventually, he left an accumulated deficit of pound sterling 827 million on the account, which brought the venerable bank to its knees. It was later sold to ING, the Dutch financial conglomerate, for the neat amount of £1.

Long Term Capital Management (LTCM), was established as a so-called 'hedge fund' in 1994 by John Meriweather – a highly regarded bond trader from Salomon Brothers. The fund tried to combine trader savvy with state-of-the-art quantitative financial analysis in their investment strategies and was able to engage the Nobel price-winning economists Myron Scholes and Robert Merton in the venture. The fund mainly engaged in convergence trades whereby it would take long positions in undervalued and short positions in overvalued government-backed securities. These convergence positions were established between sovereign issuers in the USA, Japan, and Europe, within Europe, and against selective emerging markets. To make money on the small margins involved, the positions were leveraged manifold. These international market positions worked well until August 1998 when Russia declared a debt moratorium on some of its government issues and devalued the ruble. This event caused international investors to revert funds to safe havens, i.e. benchmark government bonds within the OECD area, which fundamentally changed previous interest rate relationships. These unexpected market events shattered the interest rate relationships that underpinned the convergence strategy and imposed tremendous losses on the fund. Eventually, the LTCM was bailed out through a rescue package orchestrated by the Federal Reserve Bank of New York whereby a consortium of leading investment and commercial banks injected US$3.5 billion into the fund against a 90% share of the fund equity.

---

### Box10.1 The tale of a successful energy company[3]

In late 1998 KN Energy was ranked the second largest natural gas pipeline operator in the USA with over 27 000 miles of pipe and the sixth largest integrated energy company with total assets exceeding US$9 billion. The company had developed into a super-regional gas pipeline and distribution company operating in the centre of United States. The company's overarching goals were to be the No. 1 or No. 2 regional player as a value-added energy product and services provider and to optimize value creation through internal growth, strategic acquisitions, and alliances. The organization was in aggressive pursuit of these goals throughout the 1990s and the company accomplished its ambition for growth in many ingenious ways. Top management had instilled a corporate culture emphasizing action and increased shareholder value. The company was favoured by a strong management team, and maintained a relatively flat organization ensuring speed and flexibility. Together company directors and employees held around 15% of the company's stock and aligned them with general shareholder interests.[a] The company's core activities were concentrated around so-called 'midstream' energy businesses comprising interstate and intrastate transportation and storage of natural gas. An acquisition of MidCon Corp. for US$3.5 billion in early 1998, financed through issuance of securities and equity, more than doubled the miles of pipeline operated by the company and quadrupled the consolidated balance sheet. After the acquisition KN Energy transported around 17% of all natural gas delivered in the United States. At the same time KN Energy was engaged in three other major pipeline projects expanding the gas transportation capacity out of the Rocky Mountain region. The company began construction of the TransColorado pipeline, which would move 300 million cubic feet of natural gas per day through the Rocky Mountain area. In addition the company was pursuing gathering, processing, and transmission projects in Wyoming, which would increase reserve access by 5 trillion cubic feet and add 300 million cubic feet per day of pipeline capacity.

The growth outlook for the natural gas industry was bright predicting a 36% increase in annual consumption by the year 2010. Nuclear plant shutdowns, increased emphasis on distributed power after market deregulation, and environmental concerns would increase demand for natural gas for years to come.[b] Hence, it was natural to widen the operating base in various 'upstream' gas development activities to secure the supply of natural gas. This comprised engagement in natural gas well development, processing plants, and gas pipelines in nine states connecting a supply basin stretching from Canada to Mexico. KN Energy acquired important natural gas supply assets to support the corporate earnings development. It also seemed clear that expansion into 'downstream' activities in energy marketing, services, and retail distribution would extend the growth potential. This led to the acquisition of Thermo Cos. providing the first electric generation assets and capabilities to develop power plant projects. KN Energy planned to build 5000 megawatts of gas-fired power stations

[a] KN Energy, *Annual Report*, 1997.
[b] KN Energy, *Third Quarter Report*, 1998.

along its pipeline system over the next years. The company acquired an interest in Igasamex to extend natural gas distribution in Mexico. All in all the company expanded its reach across the natural gas value chain by completing more than 25 acquisitions of other energy outfits within the decade.

The company expanded through internal growth as well. KN Energy introduced SimpleChoice as the first national brand for bundled energy related home services consolidated on one bill and the en•able affiliate was fairly successful at selling the bundling concept to other utilities on a franchising basis. The company developed telecom opportunities in partnership with PathNet to sell upgraded digital communication services to local and inter-exchange carriers. As a consequence of this prolonged growth trajectory, operating revenues increased by 30–40% per annum in recent years and net income increased by more than 20% on a year-by-year basis. EBITDA (Earnings Before Interest, Taxes, Depreciation and Amortization) increased 14% over the last fiscal year and the long-term debt of US$554 million represented 44% of total capital, only slightly above the company target. As a consequence the stock price (NYSE: KNE) had developed favourably in recent years and shareholders had received in excess of 40% return on their investment over the past year thus outperforming the stock indices.[c]

**Figure 10.1** KN energy stock price development (1996–8)

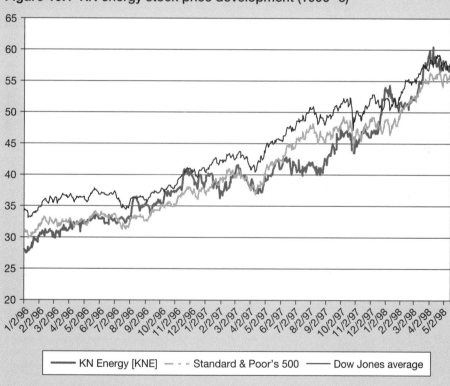

*Source*: Yahoo Finance

[c] News release, February 4, 1998.

KN Energy, Inc. reported a 104% increase in operating revenues to nearly US$4.4 billion and a 136% increase in operating income to $345 million during 1998. Net income totalled $60.0 million or $0.92 per diluted share.[d] For the fourth quarter, the company reported – after taking $27.8 million in charges – a net loss of $3.7 million or $0.05 per diluted share on 68.8 million weighted average shares outstanding compared to net income of $28.5 million or $0.59 per diluted share in 1997, based on 47.3 million weighted average shares outstanding. The fourth quarter charges included the recognition of a loss on the sale of certain unprofitable gas processing facilities; recognition of the outcome of the arbitration of certain environmental claims and reductions of the carrying value of natural gas liquids (NGL) inventories and certain natural gas in storage and due from third parties to reflect their current realizable values. Consistent with the industry experience, KN Energy's results reflected the record warm weather that year, low NGL prices, natural gas processing margins at historic lows, and compressed pipeline basis differentials. The company achieved increased volumes but market conditions changed dramatically during the year and challenged margins on every front. As a consequence the immediate outlook in the natural gas market, the price of KN stock dropped.

**Figure 10.2** The natural gas and stock price development (1998–9)

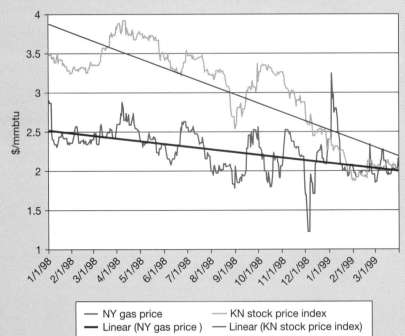

— NY gas price      — KN stock price index
— Linear (NY gas price )      — Linear (KN stock price index)

*Source*: Yahoo Finance

[d] News release, February 2, 1999.

In February 1998 the boards of Sempra Energy and KN Energy announced unanimous agreement to combine in a stock-and-cash transaction valued at US$6 billion. Under the agreement Sempra would acquire each KN share at a ratio of 1.115 Sempra shares or $25.00 in cash representing a 24% premium on the market price of KN Energy common stock based on the average closing prices over the previous week. The media tried to get to grips with the anticlimactic outcome of KN Energy's successful expansion in the past and the dramatic events of offers and counteroffers that followed the company's poor stock performance. KN Energy was hit by the mild winter weather, which was 38% warmer than average. Liquid gas prices dropped, along with KN Energy's profits and cash flows. The company was caught in a liquidity squeeze. KN Energy needed capital badly and Sempra with its strong balance sheet became a victorious bidder for the firm. Whereas the realization of the grand plan to extend the commercial reach along the natural gas energy value chain was proceeding, the company got caught up by short-term adverse fluctuations in the natural gas prices that completely surprised top management. With hindsight the company should have been conscious about the heavy exposure to natural gas prices that should have been hedged. But who knew?

In June 1999 the companies terminated the agreement to combine Sempra and KN Energy due to unsatisfactory negotiations. Hence, KN Energy had to sell assets and seek partnerships to fund operations and reduce its financial leverage. In October 1999 Kinder Morgan, Inc. announced its merger with KN Energy and KN ceased to exist as an independent company.

**Figure 10.3** Stock price development (1998–9)

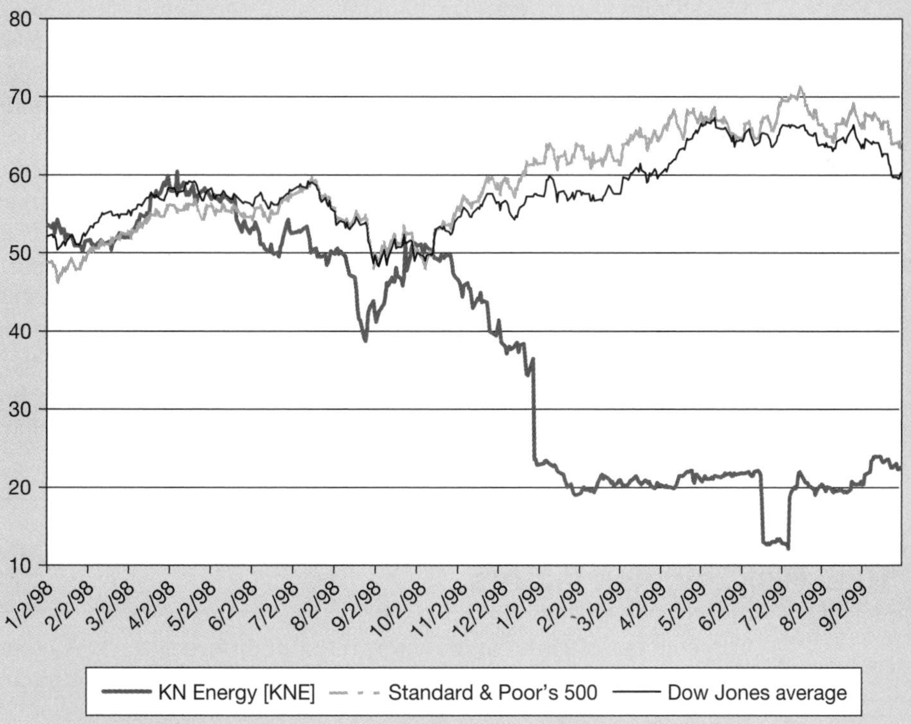

Legend: KN Energy [KNE] — – – Standard & Poor's 500 — Dow Jones average

*Source*: Yahoo Finance

The list of unfortunate corporate risk exposure events continues. Enron filed for bankruptcy in December 2001 after disclosing a non-recurring loss of US$1 billion and a US$1.2 billion write-off against shareholders' equity. Part of Enron's problems was related to the use of partially owned special purpose entities (SPEs) used to 'park' losses from various business activities outside the official corporate accounts. Some of these entities also seemed to provide handsome compensation to some of the Enron executives outside the corporation's commercial activities. Other transactions were devised to take financial exposures off the corporate balance sheet. This was sometimes accomplished through derivatives related arrangements transferring asset ownership between different accounting periods. The revelation of those accounting practices provided a blow to the confidence in the accounting profession, and the incident triggered the demise of the venerable auditing outfit Arthur Andersen, which at the time figured as one of the world's leading auditing firms. It is truly amazing how Enron, which was generally recognized for its employment of financial engineers with widespread expertise in derivative instruments, could fail so utterly to adapt their insights in managing the organization's own corporate exposures. Part of the explanation must be found in senior management's flawed belief that off-balance-sheet risk can be discarded or maybe it was bounded in utter ignorance of the true risk exposures.

In July 2002 WorldCom filed for bankruptcy after a US$11 billion accounting fraud was discovered. Whereas this could be attributed to the ability of senior managers to falsify the accounting treatment of corporate expenses, it also had severe repercussions for WorldCom's bankers. Citigroup, through its investment banking outfit Citigroup Global Markets, formerly Salomon Smith Barney, had been house bank for WorldCom. The investment banking outfit, through its lead analyst Jack Grubman, had continued to provide positive investment recommendations on WorldCom stock and, therefore, the bank was litigated in the Southern District of New York for providing misleading financial advise. The case led to a US$2.65 billion settlement with Citigroup in May 2004. Incidentally, Arthur Andersen was the auditor for WorldCom. Other investment banks faced similar litigations, e.g. Credit Suisse First Boston settled an amount of US$100 million in connection with investment advice provided in its dual capacity as lead manager of initial public offerings (IPOs). Accounting irregularities caused similar havoc on the other side of the Atlantic. Royal Ahold, the Dutch-based global retailer, announced a US$500 million overstatement of earnings in February 2003. While this amount dwarfs somewhat in relation to the WorldCom case, the incidence did lead to the resignation of both the Chief Executive Officer and the Chief Financial Officer of Royal Ahold. The list of risk-inflicted corporate misfortunes could go on but the sample presented here is symptomatic for some of the flawed risk management practices (Figure 10.4).

## 10.2 Risk and risk factors

The concept of **risk** can be interpreted in different ways. A common interpretation in finance is variability, which renders the construct susceptible to measurement, i.e. risk is typically indicated by the standard deviation in returns.[4] Another interpretation reflects the outlook for adverse economic effects, which is a common perspective among insurance companies as providers of cover for potential losses caused by

**Figure 10.4** Commonly reported risk factors

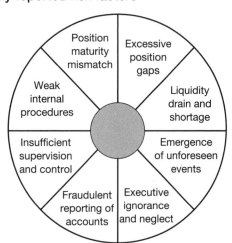

factors outside the insurer's direct influence. This view is akin to the concept of downside risk, which might be measured as the propensity to reach below average performance.[5] A variation of this perspective considers the failure to reach the upside potential as equally important and interprets this as an opportunity cost, i.e. risk also relates to the ability to achieve stipulated potentials. Risk can also be seen as the difference between expectations and actual outcomes and thereby approaches an interpretation of risk as uncertainty,[6] i.e. the inability to foresee outcomes and events in advance. Incorporating these views, we define **risk factors** as the environmental conditions that give rise to and cause risk exposures to arise, i.e. the chance that some identifiable things can happen that may inflict economic damage or impose opportunity cost on the corporation. We can discern influences from a number of different risk factors in the examples described above. The identification of these risk factors can be pursued along the confines of specific types of risk categorized according to the origin of influences and their term effects. The most commonly recognized risk factors relate to changes in financial market prices and constitute a significant element of the discussions pursued in previous chapters. A central characteristic of these risks is that the underlying price developments typically are determined in actively traded markets with rather comprehensive and accessible databases on historical price developments.

### 10.2.1  Financial and market risks

When corporations engage in commercial interactions, effectuate payments to complete these, and manage the associated cash flows streams they get exposed to different kinds of financial and market related risk factors:

● *Foreign exchange risk* – when a corporation has commercial and financial cash flows denominated in foreign currencies, the economic performance depends on changes in foreign exchange rates.
● *Interest rate risk* – when interest payments associated with financial assets and liabilities have different bases, the corporation is exposed to changes in the yield curves of the currency areas where it has invested funds and obtained funding.

- *Liquidity risk* – when the term structure of assets and liabilities differs the corporation is exposed to future liquidity gaps where periodic funding needs may represent tight market conditions.
- *Default risk* – whenever an institution interacts with commercial and financial counterparts they depend on that party's ability to honor future obligations.
- *Stock price risk* – investments in stock portfolios are exposed to general price movements in the equity market and funding through issuance of stocks depends on prevailing market conditions.
- *Commodity price risk* – manufacturing companies are exposed to changes in input prices including basic raw materials such as agricultural products, metals, energy, etc. In the case of bulk producers of industrial commodities they have similar exposures to changing prices of their outputs.

As the corporation performs commercial transactions in the real economy, e.g. buys physical input factors, sells finished products and services, finances long-term investments in the capital markets, etc., there will be a variety of associated cash flows. These cash flow streams are typically exposed to different price risks that could have a significant influence on the corporation's economic performance. The derivative instruments dealt with in the previous chapters have been developed to allow institutions to counteract and manage these inherent exposures (Figure 10.5).

These markets for financial derivatives work best when they relate to many institutional and corporate entities that constitute natural counterparts. For example, buyers and sellers across national borders in the foreign exchange markets or institutions with counteracting currency positions and market views. Similarly, borrowers and investors may serve as counterparts in markets for interest rate derivatives as well as institutions with different market outlooks. In the commodity markets we see natural counterparts in agricultural and metal derivatives among farmers and miners that grow and extract the raw materials and industrial manufacturers that use them as inputs in the production of consumers goods, and so forth.

While a range of financial derivatives can facilitate the hedging of specific financial and market related risk exposures, there are many other environmental factors that could influence corporate performance. A relatively simple way to assess the associated economic exposure to corporate performance is partially captured in the measure of the duration gap on the implied equity positions. Whereas the duration gap primarily is used to assess the potential effect of changes in the interest rate level, the underlying duration measure is itself a function of the future cash flow

**Figure 10.5** Financial and real exposures of corporate cash flows

patterns of the assets and liabilities. All balance sheet items posted at their market values whether they figure as assets or liabilities in principle relate to stipulations of their underlying cash flows, i.e. the market value is the net present value of the discounted future cash flows. Consequently, we can adopt duration measures not only to financial assets and liabilities but also to receivables, inventories, commercial assets, machinery, etc. Hence is, the duration concept provides a corporation with the means to determine its overall sensitivity to changes in the interest rate, which in turn depends on the maturity of the cash flows of assets and liabilities. The duration gap of the implied equity position corresponds to the weighted average duration of the assets minus the weighted average duration of the liabilities:

$$D_{\text{equity}} = D_{\text{assets}} - D_{\text{liabilities}}$$

The effect on the implied equity position for a given change in the interest rate level is then determined by the following equation (see Chapter 6):

$$\Delta E = -\frac{\left(D_A - \dfrac{L}{A} \times D_L\right)}{(1 + r)} \times A \times \Delta r$$

where

$D_A$ = duration of assets;
$D_L$ = duration of liabilities;
$A$ = market value of assets;
$L$ = market value of liabilities;
$E$ = equity position (A–L);
$r$ = interest rate level (yield).

This implies that we can extend the duration analysis on financial assets and liabilities to comprise all types of material assets and liabilities on the corporate balance sheet. The only condition is that we should determine the expected future cash flows that characterize the assets and liabilities. This means that in some instances there is a need to adjust the accounting items included on the balance sheet and modify them to reflect the true underlying cash flows. This exercise may take some pondering but once completed it is relatively straightforward to apply the duration calculations to determine the implied duration gap of the equity position. Whereas the determination of the underlying cash flows could be demanding, it arguably provides a better measure of the net exposures imposed by commercial engagements and the way they are financed. Some of the commercial assets will relate to the expected future cash flows from projects, market initiatives, and current business activities. It should be no harder to determine these cash flows than in other project related present value analyses applied in capital budgeting exercises. However, there are some interesting artifacts associated with the commercial cash flows on the balance sheet that differ from the cash flows related to financial assets. While the cash flows of financial instruments normally are contractually determined, the commercial cash flows depend on other economic factors, such as general demand conditions, the overall business outlook, etc. Hence, if the business outlook takes a turn for the worse, the underlying cash flows tend to be prolonged, i.e. future revenues will materialize later than stipulated initially, which in turn will increase the duration of that asset class. Conversely, if the business outlook improves, the inverse will happen and the duration will contract. To some extent this is similar to the reality of loans gone sour where the final maturity date of the loan eventually is prolonged as a result of renegotiations between debtor and creditor. Banks, for example, do not take this into consideration in interest rate gapping analyses but build up reserve positions to cover for this as a default risk. While corporations might take the same approach, they could also try to assess the perceived sensitivity of the underlying cash flows to changes in general economic conditions. Hence, if an adverse business scenario is expected to lead to significant extensions in the realization of future cash inflows the associated duration effects should be taken into consideration in the implied equity duration gap. This way the gapping analysis can be used as the means to assess the potential risk exposure of the business portfolio and the appropriateness of the capital structure established to fund these activities. If, say, Enron had performed this type of relatively simple analysis, even on a 'back of an envelope' format, all the underlying cash flows of their projects and business ventures would have been made transparent and, in all likelihood, the analysis would indicate a relatively high engagement in risky ventures with future cash flows highly sensitive to adverse economic conditions and the existing balance sheet insufficiently capitalized.

*Example*: A successful corporate entity in the retailing business is reconsidering its current funding sources. The composition of assets, liabilities, and earnings flows has developed steadily over the past years. The finance office has estimated that the duration of short-term assets ($D_{STA}$) is around 0.35, the duration of long-term assets ($D_{LTA}$) around 10.5, the duration of short term debt ($D_{STL}$) around 0.5, and the duration of long-term debt ($D_{LTL}$) around 4.5. The balance sheet with assets and liabilities assessed at market value and associated income statement look as follows:

### Consolidated balance sheets

| Years ended December 31 (US$ million) | 2005 | 2004 | 2003 |
|---|---|---|---|
| **Assets** | | | |
| Short-term assets | 250 000 | 200 000 | 175 000 |
| Property and plants | 120 000 | 110 000 | 100 000 |
| Machinery and equipment | 30 000 | 30 000 | 20 000 |
| Plants under construction | 115 000 | 85 000 | 50 000 |
| Fixed assets | 265 000 | 225 000 | 170 000 |
| Total assets | 515 000 | 425 000 | 345 000 |
| **Liabilities and stockholders' equity** | | | |
| Short-term debt | 90 000 | 55 000 | 25 000 |
| Banks and mortgage institutions | 80 000 | 60 000 | 50 000 |
| Other long-term debt | 160 000 | 150 000 | 130 000 |
| Long-term debt | 240 000 | 210 000 | 180 000 |
| Stockholders' equity | 185 000 | 160 000 | 140 000 |
| Total liabilities and stockholders' equity | 515 000 | 425 000 | 345 000 |
| **Consolidated statements of income** | | | |
| Operating income | 42 000 | 37 000 | 27 000 |
| Interest income | 18 000 | 10 000 | 8 000 |
| Interest expenses | (20 000) | (15 000) | (10 000) |
| Income before income tax | 40 000 | 32 000 | 25 000 |
| Income tax | (15 000) | (12 000) | (10 000) |
| Net income | 25 000 | 20 000 | 15 000 |

Assuming that all future cash flows have been reaffirmed and discounted to find appropriate market values for the short and long-term assets and liabilities, we can determine the implied equity position as the difference between total assets and total liabilities:

$$\text{Implied equity position } (E) = \text{Total assets } (A) - \text{Total liabilities } (L)$$

Based on the data total assets amount to US\$515 000 and total liabilities to US\$330 000, and hence the implied equity position is calculated as US\$175 000 (= 515 000 − 330 000).

Provided that all balance sheet items have been assessed on a market value basis we can determine the weighted average duration of total assets and liabilities weighted by their market values. Based on the data the average duration of total assets is determined as 5.57 (= 250/515 × 0.35 + 265/515 × 10.5) and the average duration of liabilities as 3.41 (= 90/330 × 0.5 + 240/330 × 4.5). The interest rate gap of the implied equity position is, therefore, positive and amounts to 2.16 (= 5.57 − 3.41). That is, if the interest rate increases the firm will lose market value and if the interest rate decreases it will gain value.

The expected value effect on the implied equity position from a 1% increase in the interest rate level from the indicative current yield of 4.25% on medium-term treasury notes can then be determined as follows:

$$\Delta E = -\frac{\left(D_A - \dfrac{L}{A} \times D_L\right)}{(1 + r)} \times A \times \Delta r$$

$$= -\frac{\left(5.57 - \dfrac{330}{515} \times 3.41\right)}{1.0425} \times 515\,000 \times 0.01$$

$$= -16\,738.61$$

That is, if the interest rate level increases by one percentage point the corporation will incur a total loss amounting to around US\$16.7 billion. Compared to an annual net income level of US\$20−25 billion this level of losses is sizeable and should cause some reconsideration among senior management.

Whereas the current business outlook is quite favourable, it is not inconceivable that this might change. In connection with a scenario analysis considering the not inconceivable possibility of a reversal of business conditions, it is estimated that the duration of long-term assets that constitute various business projects might increase from 10.5 to 15.75. In this case, the interest rate sensitivity of the equity position would increase and the corresponding loss associated with a percentage increase in the interest rate level would increase to US\$30.1 billion. Since this is not an unlikely outcome, senior management might use this analysis to reduce its engagement in long-term projects and try to obtain more long-term funding arrangements.

In principle, the interest gapping analysis should be completed for each of currencies in which the corporation holds assets and liabilities of material size. If we add the implied equity duration gaps together per currency, converted at the prevailing spot foreign exchange rates, it will tend to overestimate the actual exposure because interest rate movements are unlikely to be completely correlated across currencies even though there may be a strong relationship between changes in the interest rates of freely convertible currencies. However, it will provide a good first estimate. One way to deal with this issue is to use the aggregate duration gap as an upper risk measure. Conversely, one could try to estimate the correlation between the interest rate levels in different currencies and use a variance-covariance approach to determine a more accurate risk level. One could use data on historical interest rates to calculate aggregate exposures or adopt computerized simulation techniques to determine exposure measures and extreme scenario effects (see Chapter 2). Since the common duration measure only takes changes in the general interest rate level into account, a duration gap analysis is quite appropriate for 'back-of-the-envelope' risk assessments. Whereas this might suffice for all intensive purposes, the calculations can obviously be refined in simulations that take potential shifts in the interest rate structure into account in the relevant currency areas to support further risk assessments.

## 10.3 Other types of risk

The possible risk exposures are numerous and corporations can be exposed to many other factors than market risks the relative importance of which can vary from one organization to another. A systematic search for relevant risk factors could be pursued in accordance with a formalized risk management framework. There are a string of factors beyond the relatively narrow scope of financial risks (Figure 10.6).

Other risk factors can have their origin in a variety of exogenous influences that are beyond the control of corporate management. Whereas the adverse effects of risk events cannot be managed directly, the sources of the risk exposures might be addressed and the vulnerability of corporate exposures reduced through active involvement.[7] In many cases it might even be possible to observe new emerging risk factors although it typically is difficult to influence them directly because they are environmentally imposed. However, it may be possible to adapt the organization in response to new risk conditions and take actions that mitigate potentially adverse effects and at the same time possibly exploit opportunities arising from the new situation. A good first approach to this task is to identify all the relevant risk factors and subsequently consider how to handle them. To make the risk identification process more effective, we may use a systematic classification scheme considering, e.g. overall environmental risks, industry-related risks, and company-related risk.[8] The idea

**Figure 10.6 Exogenous factors influencing performance**

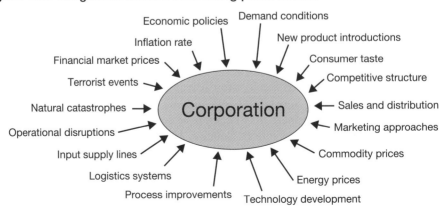

**Figure 10.7** Layers of exogenous risk factors

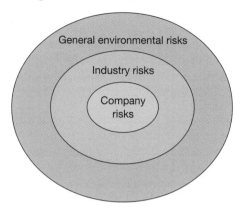

behind this framework is to first analyze general conditions and then gradually narrow the scope to more firm specific concerns (Figure 10.7).

## 10.3.1 Environmental risks

The environmental risks comprise factors that characterize the physical context for business operations and trends in the overall socio-economic system. The physical context includes influences from natural phenomena, accidents, and uncontrolled man-made interferences. The socio-economic developments include evolving political sentiments, macroeconomic conditions, regulatory intervention, etc.

- *Natural hazards* – productive assets in the corporation may be exposed to destruction in connection with extreme natural events, such as, storm, hurricane, flood, earthquake, landslide, forest fire, etc., that may cause operational disruption and foregone business.
- *Man-made disasters* – productive assets can also be damaged and disrupted by inadvertent human interference or negligence that cause major explosions, operational malfunctions, technological breakdowns, building collapses, etc.
- *Terrorist events* – the economic damage inflicted by intentional human actions is a common concern in international business that may cause harm to both tangible and intangible assets as well as affect the general business outlook.
- *Economic risk* – fiscal and monetary policy measures affect economic conditions within and across currency areas and ultimately influence demand conditions and price developments across national markets with different currency denominations.
- *Political risk* – political turmoil is associated with erratic price developments in financial markets and will eventually affect demand conditions and credit quality. International political crisis can influence supply and demand conditions and hence affect the price development of global commodities.
- *Regulatory risk* – the likelihood of disruptive bankruptcies and economic restructurings is influenced by regulatory effectiveness. Major trends of industry deregulation and ongoing trade liberalizations can have wide repercussions for competitive conditions.

### 10.3.2 Industry-related risks

Once we go beneath general environmental and socio-economic conditions, there are a number of factors that influence the competitive situation of the specific industry context in which the corporation operates. This comprises elements that are peculiar to the industry, such as modifications in customer needs, actions of close competitors, new business initiatives, etc.

- *Consumer taste* – corporate performance can be affected by changes in customer preferences, modifications in required product characteristics, introduction of new product standards, new ways to use products, etc.
- *Competitive moves* – when major competitors change their pricing policies and introduce new market features or when new business entities enter the industry with product concepts, the long-term corporate performance is potentially jeopardized.
- *Input factor markets* – development of new sourcing networks, changes in the bargaining power of conventional suppliers, introduction of new inputs and resources, and so forth, can influence future corporate performance.
- *New technologies* – invention of new approaches to the input–output conversion and the introduction of new production capabilities can revolutionize manufacturing as well as related sourcing and distribution channels.
- *Product innovation* – the development of new product configurations, product containment characteristics, and customer support systems can influence the competitive position and hence affect corporate performance.
- *Process innovation* – the emergence of new more effective procurement, production, logistics, promotion, and customer servicing processes can have corporate performance effects.

### 10.3.3 Company-related risks

Finally a series of risk factors relate to internal conditions prevailing within the organization itself as they are manifested, e.g. through the ways work flows are organized, people are motivated, decisions are made, actions controlled, and so forth.

- *Operational risk* – corporate procedures might break down and impose temporary costs as well as expose the company to collateral damage of its brand image. Such events can be caused by human negligence, accidents, fraudulent behavior, technological breakdowns, power failures, etc.
- *Documentation risk* – in all engagements, client relationships, supplier relationships, cooperative partnerships, subcontracting arrangements, financial transactions, etc., the corporation has entered into contractual obligations. If contractual obligations are broken, the corporation will have to litigate and legally apprehend potential offenders. This is a time consuming, costly, and potentially uncertain process with unknown outcomes.
- *Commercial risk* – whenever the corporation has honoured financial or real commitments before receipt of cash payments, it is exposed to the future economic well being of its customers and the long-term economic viability of business partners.

## Box 10.2  Classifying risk factors

There is no single way to approach the classification of risk factors, which differs substantially among different authors. Although there is no consensus on a formal risk classification standard, the risk discussions usually comprise all the most common types of risk. In view of this, corporate management should use the classification scheme that seems most appropriate for their specific purposes. In some cases risk management is seen to require differentiation between primary exposures including credit risk, market risk, stock price risk, investment risk, and hedging risk, and secondary exposures, such as operational risk, insurable risk, catastrophe risk, business risk, cultural risk, and reputation risk. The primary risk exposures are seen as direct price and market effects whereas secondary risk exposures are imposed effects on revenue and cost developments.[9] Others distinguish between market risk, counterparty risk, operational risk, and event risk (Figure 10.8).[10] Market risk includes conventional price related factors, such as interest rate risk, foreign exchange risk, equity price risk, liquidity risk, concentration and correlation risks. Counter-party risk comprises credit risk and supply chain disruptions. Operational risk includes breakdown of internal systems, errors associated with transaction execution, misjudgement in project evaluations, failures in accounting and controls. Event risk comprises exogenous environmental factors related to natural phenomena, political, legal, regulatory, and reputation risks.

Realizing the importance of corporate risk management, several associations have attempted to establish comprehensive analytical frameworks for risk assessment. For example, the Institute of Financial Services analyzes different sources of risk and classifies these as business risk and non-business risk.[11] Business risk comprises product risk, macroeconomic risk, and technology risk. Non-business risk includes several sub-categories, such as financial risk, operational risk, and event risk. Financial risk, in turn comprises credit risk, foreign exchange risk, interest rate risk, market risk,

### Figure 10.8  Major areas of risk

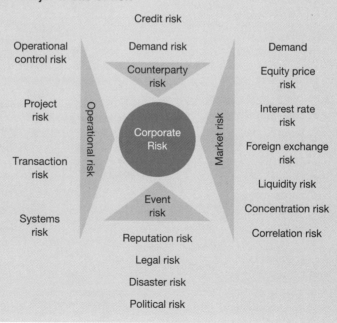

and liquidity risk. Operational risk includes potential errors arising from human or technological breakdowns. Event risk includes disaster risk, political risk, regulatory risk, and litigation risk. The Risk Management Institute (RMI) has attempted to establish a risk management standard together with the Association of Insurance and Risk Managers (AIRMIC), and the National Forum for Risk Management in the Public Sector (ALARM).[12] In this framework they distinguish between risk exposures driven by external factors and risk exposures driven by factors internal to the organization (Figure 10.9). External factors include financial risks, operational risks, hazard risks, and strategic risks. Financial risks comprise interest rate, foreign exchange, and credit risk. Operational risks comprise the regulatory environment, cultural artifacts, and corporate governance practices. Hazard risks comprise natural phenomena and contractual relationships to suppliers and partners. Strategic risks comprise changes in tastes, demand conditions, industry structure, and competitor moves. The internally driven factors comprise human resources, research and development, organizational processes, accounting systems, and controls.

An alternative perspective looks upon strategic risk as events or conditions that reduce the ability to implement an intended business strategy.[13] Such events can include operational risk relating to breakdown of internal processes. They could also relate to asset impairment risk whereby the likelihood of receiving the future cash flow deriving from the asset is reduced, e.g. due to credit risk, sovereign risk, or counterparty risk as well as physical asset disruption caused by natural phenomena, terrorism events, etc. Competitive risk is caused by changes in the competitive environment ascribed to competitor moves, changes in customer demand, supplier behaviour, and

**Figure 10.9** Key drivers of risk

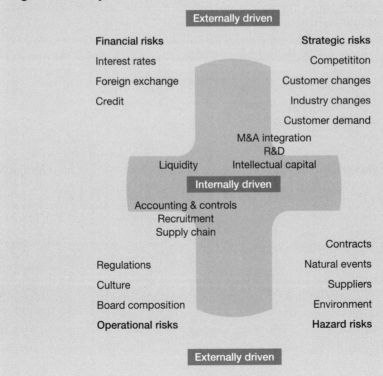

regulatory conditions. When all of these risks reach a level that might impair the survival of the organization, it can be considered a franchise risk. In the end the strategic risk is synonymous with business risk (Figure 10.10).

**Figure 10.10** Overview of business risk

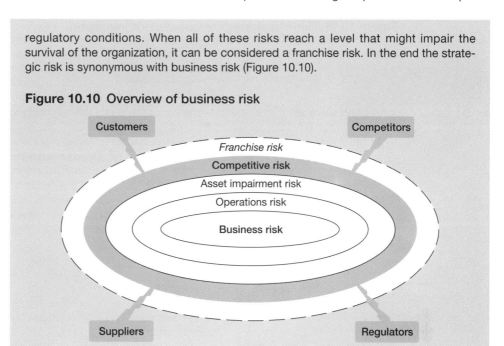

## 10.4 Dealing with the risks

Many financial exposures can be covered by trading in financial futures, options on futures, and various over-the-counter (OTC) derivatives. This kind of hedging can lock-in the future price and shield against market volatility for intermediate time intervals covering a current accounting period, i.e. typically 3–12 months and in some cases even longer. When hedging this way, the corporation will fix price relationships at the market's expected future prices as reflected in the financial futures prices. Therefore, to gain abnormal returns a company must take a view on future price developments that differ from market expectations – and be right about it. Nonetheless, by fixing future price levels the corporation can diminish unpleasant fluctuations in corporate earnings. However, in the increasingly dynamic business environment, corporations will be exposed to many real market factors that are not traded in financial markets and hence are not prone to conventional hedging techniques. Many risk factors are even idiosyncratic to the individual corporation and its specific resource endowment and consequently cannot be hedged through use of conventional derivative instruments.

To assess all the potential risks that expose the corporation, senior management might want to perform a comprehensive risk review of businesses entities focused on the conditions that permeate their external competitive environment as well as internal organizational traits including asset structure, resource base, operational infrastructure, processes, etc. Such a focused review can identify potential risks that could inhibit the ability to achieve longer-term corporate objectives but could also drive the development of new responsive initiatives. The identification of essential risk factors can be ordered by placing the most crucial exposures at the top of the list.

**Figure 10.11** Generic strategic management framework

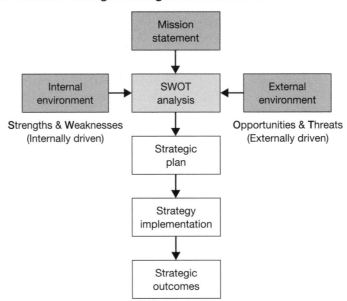

This exercise creates awareness around important environmental changes that could affect corporate performance. Some of these changes may not require immediate action but are brought to the attention of corporate management while other developments might need more immediate courses of action.[14] In many ways, this is exactly what is supposed to take place in a formal strategic planning process (Figure 10.11).

The mission statement should provide general inspiration and direction by stating the overarching purpose of the corporation, the core values that drive business activities, and the long-term aspirations that motivate corporate actions. In an uncertain world, the mission statement can give solace and guidance to decision makers navigating 'uncharted waters'. It can also direct their considerations about external market conditions and internal organization. Formally, the analysis of the external environment should identify opportunities, e.g. those offered by changes in customer demands, and threats, e.g. those imposed by new competitive moves. Similarly, the internal analysis should identify areas where the corporation has strengths that can be exploited and weaknesses to be counteracted. Ideally, the two analytical perspectives should point toward a superior strategic position where internal capabilities can be employed effectively to match essential market needs. This synthesis is often referred to as SWOT analysis, the acronym reflecting the areas of **S**trengths, **W**eaknesses, **O**pportunities, and **T**hreats.[15]

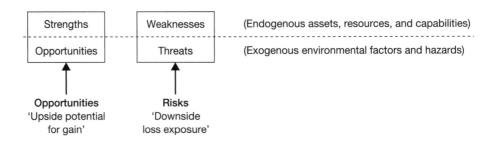

In effect, the generic strategic management framework embraces risk assessment as an integral part of the strategy analysis and is therefore consistent with the risk management approach in the attempt to determine essential risk factors. That is, strategic risk factors are taken into account in the planning process. This analytical exercise may result in the completion of a strategic plan stipulating actions needed to reach the identified superior strategic position. While this can prove illusive under turbulent market conditions, the analytical process could consider contingency plans and extreme environmental scenarios that prepare decision makers for the unexpected and increase general risk awareness. Formalized risk control systems can monitor identified risk factors and initiate responses to mounting exposures but it cannot address completely unexpected risks that arise from exogenous events. To cope with these challenges, the corporation must nurture a corporate culture that thrives on risk awareness where all managers are attentive to environmental changes that could affect the corporation. Engaging all thinking minds in the corporation and making them observant of potential risks increases the likelihood of early recognition of warning signals and effective initiatives to mitigate those potential risks. The risk management process can also comprise a type of quality control that encourages managers to analyze internal processes, procedures, and practices to assess inherent risks and improve efficiencies. This way risk management is extended from the one-sided view of avoiding downside effects from imposed events to proactively considering what can be done to exploit new opportunities.[16] Hence, the true risk management paradigm can embrace the underlying ideas of strategic analysis, namely to foresee environmental threats and exploit emerging strategic opportunities.

## 10.5 An integrative perspective on strategic risk

Conventional views on corporate risk exposures primarily consider the impact from variations in foreign currency markets and longer-term effects from developments in macroeconomic conditions. Multinational financial management typically considers three categories of risk exposures (see Chapter 2).[17] Transaction exposures relate to the effects of changes in foreign exchange rates on foreseeable future cash flows denominated in foreign currencies. The foreign currency-denominated cash flows in the transaction exposure can relate to receivables from goods sold overseas, returns from foreign financial assets or direct investments, payables on internationally sourced inputs, and service payments on global debt commitments. Translation exposures refer to the official net income effects that foreign exchange fluctuations impose on reported foreign currency-denominated assets and liabilities. The foreign currency denominated assets can relate to short-term receivables, investment in manufacturing plants, company acquisitions, goodwill, etc. while foreign currency-denominated liabilities typically relate to short-term payables and medium-term debt engagements. Economic exposures refer to longer-term effects on the corporation's future cash flows from changes in foreign exchange rates and macroeconomic conditions. The effects on corporate cash flows can emanate from advantages and disadvantages associated with different overseas production locations, internationally sourced inputs, and competitive sales in overseas markets with different currency denominations.

The exact distinction between transaction and translation exposures, however, can be difficult to discern, because some of the longer-term assets might give rise to future cash flow transactions although one cannot be sure that they will. It can also be difficult to distinguish between translation exposures like goodwill, brand equity, and longer-term economic exposures. Similarly, it can be demanding to draw an exact line between accounted cash flows included in the transaction exposure and recognized future cash flows that partially coincide with economic exposure effects. To circumvent these potential ambiguities it has been suggested that all potential future cash flow effects should be considered in conjunction with the assessment of financial risk exposures.[18] This means that all accounted transactions definitely should be considered and that all other not yet reported but realistically expected future cash flows should be taken into consideration either as interim recognized transaction flows or longer-term economic effects. However, it also implies that translation exposures only should be considered to the extent they represent true potential transactions, e.g. a foreign subsidiary, product licence, or brand that could be sold for cash. Translation exposures that are virtually illiquid must be considered 'sunk cost' and prudent depreciation policies should write off these assets within a reasonable time frame.

It is important to consider the interrelationship between different financial and economic risk factors and not just assess short-term foreign exchange market risks in isolation. Over time, changes in foreign exchange rates are most likely related to comparable moves in interest rate structures between currency areas as well as differences in inflationary expectations across national economies (see Chapter 2). Similarly, input supply, product demand, and competitive risks can be related to fluctuations in real exchange rates. In other words, different types of financial and economic risk exposures are often interrelated.[19] Therefore, it is important to consider interactions across the full range of risk factors that may affect future corporate performance including political, economic, competitive, and technological risks.[20] The interrelatedness may possibly extend across several other risk factors, such as hazards like natural catastrophes and terrorist events could be related to macroeconomic and financial market variables. Hence, the challenge is to consider all the relevant risk factors rather than adopting simple one-to-one mapping of risk exposures; hedging practices should consider the entire corporate risk profile and deal with the risk factors in an integrated manner considering how they might interact.[21]

Hence, the assessment of risk effects on the corporation's future cash flows is typically performed within different time horizons. In conventional analyses of potential effects from market volatility discussed in the finance field is typically performed within an anticipated future based on rather short-term accounting exposures. However, the less quantifiable medium and longer-term exposures can be just as important. Whereas this is generally recognized, it is rarely addressed in practice. The significance of medium and longer-term exposures of, say political, competitive, and technology risks is further accentuated by the changing nature of the external business environment where change is the order of the day. In many cases the true risk factors cannot even be known in advance and may arise without prior warning. Such factors can include operational risk where corporations are exposed to a number of internal vulnerabilities related to process quality, control systems, etc. From a risk perspective both external and internal risk factors are important and should be considered in the risk management process.

**Figure 10.12** The US$/€ foreign exchange rate development (1999–2005)

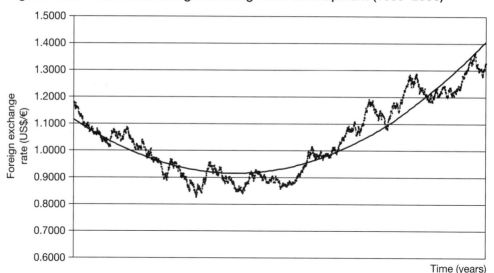

Whereas it is possible to use different derivative instruments to hedge and adjust financial risk exposures, it might not always be a viable route. For example, it might not be reasonable to use short-term interest rate futures and medium-term interest rate swaps to modify the duration gap of the corporation's implied equity position, which can be significantly influenced by long-term assets and liabilities (see the example of Metalgesellschaft). In such a situation, it would be more realistic to modify the maturity structure of assets and liabilities, i.e. if the duration gap is considered to be too large, it makes sense to reduce the leverage of the corporation and modify the corporation's engagement in projects with long-term prospective revenue streams. In other words, traded derivative instruments can provide meaningful ways to modify short- to medium-term financial risk exposures but if these exposures relate to longer-term economic exposures the corporation should adjust the underlying asset and liability structure. For example, in situations where a central foreign exchange rate seems to be developing in time cycles that exceed the normal maturities offered in the market for financial derivatives other hedging approaches are required to do the job. The development in the euro–US dollar foreign exchange rate displays such a situation (Figure 10.12).

The US dollar posted strong gains after the inauguration of the common European currency, the euro, in 1999/2000. However, the euro then gained close to 50% in value against the dollar from a low point in July 2001 until early 2005. Such persistent trends over prolonged time periods go beyond the reach of most currency futures contracts and forward foreign exchange agreements. As a consequence a number of European based exporters with significant sales in the US market felt the heat during 2004 as the value of their US dollar receivables fell sharply. The European corporations that fared best during this period were companies with overseas manufacturing facilities, including the US market which, therefore, could take advantage of the weaker dollar by reducing the cost base. Hence, in the global automobile industry a number of manufacturers have built 'natural' hedges by spreading production across several overseas locations.

*Example*: DaimlerChrysler produces its M-class Mercedes in Alabama, USA, and Volkswagen has some production in Mexico but BMW and other Mercedes models had to post higher prices in the US market during 2004. In contrast, the US automakers generally have established production facilities in different currency areas and, therefore, posted limited gains from the slide in the dollar foreign exchange rate.

Risk exposures are often firm specific particularly with respect to economic, competitive, and operational risks that depend on the corporate resource base and the ability to engage them in effective proactive actions. As a consequence, these risks and the responses to them must be considered and managed in view of the specific corporate environment. The identification of essential risk factors will differ from one organization to another partly because business portfolios rarely are completely comparable but also because risk perceptions are influenced by the capabilities and knowledge imbedded in the organization. The handling of emerging risks and unexpected situations depends on the ability to sense environmental change and mobilize internal resources to respond in an appropriate and timely manner. In short, the perception of uncertainty and responsiveness to risk constitute idiosyncratic corporate phenomena.

Financial hedging techniques often disregard longer-term economic, competitive, and technology risks simply because these risks are more diffuse and go beyond the maturity horizon of traded derivative instruments. In effect, they are not suited to deal with the longer-term effects of economic exposures. However, the ability to handle economic risk exposures is essential to the strategic endurance of the corporation and, therefore, should be considered in the corporation's strategic planning process and related risk management programme. One of the fundamental contributions of the risk management perspective is to extend the scope of risk analysis from short-term trading exposures to incorporate longer-term economic effects. To accomplish this, the scope of risk management instruments must be extended from conventional traded derivatives to consider real asset structures and internal competences that could provide the foundation for strategic flexibilities reflected in essential real options structures and corporate response capabilities.

Adopting a real options perspective can facilitate the identification of firm specific flexibilities that increase the corporation's ability to avoid downside risk and exploit upside potential. It can also provide an analytical framework to support resource committing strategic decisions under conditions of environmental uncertainty. It has been argued that a structure of flexible manufacturing facilities located conveniently within major currency areas constitutes options to switch production to the most cost effective locations within the multinational network and there does seem to be evidence that it has a positive effect on equity valuation.[22] The markets for derivative instruments provide multiple risk transfer opportunities to cover all conceivable market related risk exposures as discussed in previous chapters. However, the introduction of real option structures provides an entirely new perspective to the handling of strategic and economic risk exposures and thereby has the potential to extend strategic risk management beyond a focus on market exposures (Figure 10.13).

**Figure 10.13** An integrated risk exposure perspective

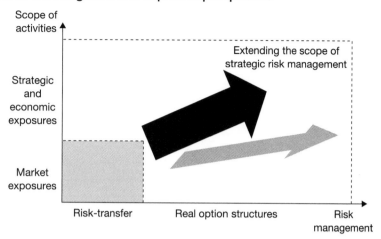

## 10.6 Real option structures

The focus on real options was inspired by the identification of growth options in association with capital budgeting exercises prescribed by corporate finance. There was a growing realization that conventional investment analysis ignored potential follow-up investments as projects could develop competencies to support future strategic initiatives. The discounted cash flow (DCF) methodology adopted to calculate the net present value (NPV) of investment proposals usually conceived investment alternatives as predetermined paths implying either-or investment decisions. Hence, the DCF approach ignores potential value associated with embedded flexibilities related to the timing of investments and alternative uses of assets. Another consequence of the DCF methodology is that uncertainty has a negative connotation, i.e. the higher the uncertainty of future cash flows, the higher the discount rate, and the lower the present value of the investment. Hence, there is a value discount ascribed to uncertain market conditions, which is contrary to option valuation theory where a prime determinant of the option premium is the price volatility of the underlying asset. Asset flexibility and the ability to re-deploy corporate resources in the face new competitive realities is an essential element of effective risk management although many corporations ignore the value of it. Hence, a basic tenet of the real options approach is to consider the value of embedded flexibilities in investment projects and use option valuation techniques to take them into consideration. A **real option structure** constitutes a right, but not an obligation, to carry out particular actions at some point into the future. All resource committing decisions in an organization can be construed within such a real option structure and when they exert significant influence on the future business activities of the corporation they may be referred to as **strategic options**.[23] The real option structures represent incremental value to the corporation because they can be exercised under favourable conditions and left alone if conditions turn out to be unfavorable. Hence, the more environmental change envisaged around the payoff from a resource committing action, the higher the incremental value of the associated option structure, because it represents an

### Figure 10.14 Key elements of financial and real options

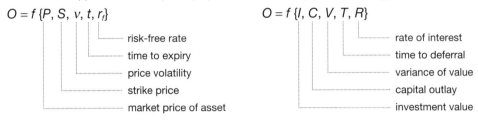

*A real options perspective extends the conventional DCF
approach and transposes project terms onto the options terminology*

$O = f\{P, S, v, t, r_f\}$                    $O = f\{I, C, V, T, R\}$

- risk-free rate
- time to expiry
- price volatility
- strike price
- market price of asset

- rate of interest
- time to deferral
- variance of value
- capital outlay
- investment value

The 'intrinsic value' of the option corresponds to the NPV of the underlying project, i.e. (I – C).

opportunity to execute the investment under extraordinarily favourable conditions. Evaluating a real option structure entails an assessment of the value potential associated with the environmental dynamics surrounding the new business opportunity. Where financial options valuation is based on the price development of an underlying asset, real options valuation is typically based on the investment value of the underlying project (Figure 10.14).

Hence, a major difference between financial options and real options is that financial options are based on assets that are traded and priced in active and transparent markets while real options are based on investment opportunities that are idiosyncratic to the corporation itself and usually remain undisclosed to the market until the time of implementation. A number of formal differences can be identified between the two types of options (Table 10.1). Financial options are

### Table 10.1 Comparing financial options and real options

| Characteristic | Financial option | Real option |
|---|---|---|
| Writing | Formal contract based on legal terms | Identifying, creating, or acquiring an investment opportunity to act or change |
| Exercising | The decision to act under the terms of the formal contract | The decision to act or change in accordance with the planned opportunity |
| Strike price | The trigger price that allows the holder to act on the contract | The initial investment required to act or change in accordance with the opportunity |
| Call option | The right to acquire an underlying asset at a given price | The ability to execute an underlying opportunity to act or change |
| Put option | The right to dispose of an underlying asset at a given price | The ability to forego, contract, or defer an underlying opportunity to act or change |
| Liquidity | Typically standardized instruments that are actively traded in formal markets with transparent prices | Usually unique structures supported by firm specific assets and competencies and hence rarely traded in transparent markets |
| Underlying asset | Usually a publicly traded financial instruments or commodity | Typically projects, investments, and switching opportunities planned by the firm that can be readily executed |

written into legally binding contracts while real options relate to the identification and planning of investment opportunities. Hence, the strike price of a financial option is the predetermined price level of the underlying asset specified in the contract while the strike price of a real option corresponds to the investment required to effectuate the investment opportunity and realize the underlying investment value.

The adherence to a real options perspective can furnish a more disciplined approach to identify and evaluate strategic opportunities available to the corporation that otherwise might be overlooked. It can also provide a systematic framework to evaluate alternative option structures and assess the dependencies between strategic opportunities that draw on assets and resources across the corporation.

---

**Box 10.3 The potential value of real options**

Consider an investment opportunity whereby you invest US$800 million now and can expect an investment value of US$1000 million, i.e. the investment represents a net present value of US$200 million (Figure 10.15). However, the investment value is subject to uncertainty as the economic outcomes depend on the actual market conditions that might prevail when the project is implemented and these conditions could change considerably over the life of the project. That is, the net present value might turn out to be substantially higher or lower than the suggested mean value of US$200 million. Nonetheless, in this situation you have to make a decision up front whether or not to go ahead with the investment and commit all resources now.

**Figure 10.15 Real options in strategic investment decisions**

1. Commitment to the full investment now

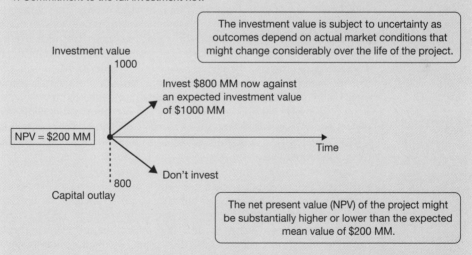

Consider another investment opportunity based on the same business proposition but structured slightly differently. Hence, you have the opportunity to invest half of the needed funds immediately whereas the remaining half can be invested later (Figure 10.16). Due to the loss of scale economies in this delayed investment structure, the required investment amount is US$450 million now and US$450 million later. In either case there is an expected investment value of US$500 million. The net present

## Figure 10.16 Invest half now and defer the other half

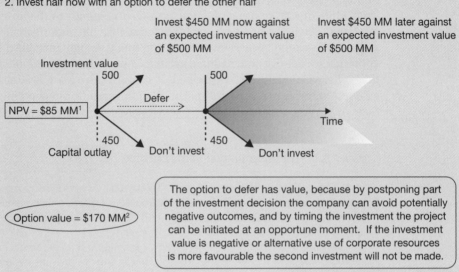

2. Invest half now with an option to defer the other half

Invest $450 MM now against an expected investment value of $500 MM

Invest $450 MM later against an expected investment value of $500 MM

Investment value

NPV = $85 MM[1]

Defer

Capital outlay

Don't invest

Don't invest

Time

Option value = $170 MM[2]

The option to defer has value, because by postponing part of the investment decision the company can avoid potentially negative outcomes, and by timing the investment the project can be initiated at an opportune moment. If the investment value is negative or alternative use of corporate resources is more favourable the second investment will not be made.

value of the first investment is US$50 million and the net present value of the second investment is determined as US$35 million because the future investment value of US$50 million is discounted to the present value. That is, the total net present value of the entire investment is US$85 million.

However, the investor is not obliged to make the second investment if the first investment turns out to be a bad idea. In other words, the structure constitutes an option to defer, i.e. rather than investing the entire amount initially, we can defer half of it to some time later. This option to defer has value because the initial investment develops further insight about the project and its economic viability and therefore the ability to avoid making the second investment under unfavourable conditions means that the investor can avoid potentially negative future outcomes. Hence, if the investment value turns out to be negative, or alternative uses of the resources turn out to be more favourable, the second investment will not be made and the investor will avoid losses and possibly gain opportunity cost. The value of this option is determined at US$170 million. That is, the net present value of the project and the embedded deferral option represents an aggregate value of US$255 million.

Consider a third investment opportunity based on the same business proposition but structured so you can make a relatively small probing investment of US$50 million initially to test out the viability of the project while retaining the possibility of making a full investment later with a total investment outlay of US$900 million against an expected investment value of US$1000 million (Figure 10.17). The later investment has a net investment value of US$100 million, which discounted corresponds to a net present value of US$70 million. Hence, the net present value of the initial investment is US$ 20 million after subtracting the initial investment outlay.

However, again the investor is not obliged to complete the full investment later, if market conditions turn out to be unfavourable. That is, the investor has an option to abandon the entire project if conditions turn out to be unfavourable. This option to abandon has value because the initial investment provides further insight about the project and the ability to skip subsequent investment allows the investor to avoid

## Figure 10.17 Small investment now and option to abandon

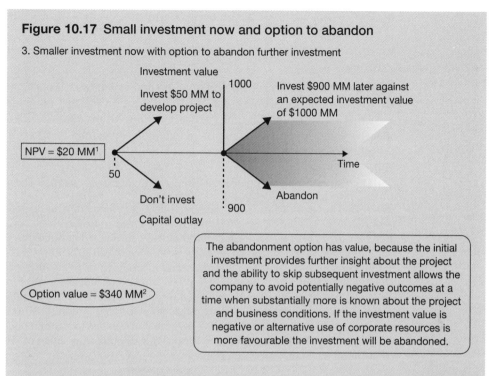

3. Smaller investment now with option to abandon further investment

Investment value

Invest $50 MM to develop project

1000

Invest $900 MM later against an expected investment value of $1000 MM

NPV = $20 MM[1]

50

Time

Don't invest

Abandon

900

Capital outlay

Option value = $340 MM[2]

The abandonment option has value, because the initial investment provides further insight about the project and the ability to skip subsequent investment allows the company to avoid potentially negative outcomes at a time when substantially more is known about the project and business conditions. If the investment value is negative or alternative use of corporate resources is more favourable the investment will be abandoned.

potentially negative outcomes at a time when substantially more is known about the viability of the project. If the investment value is negative, or alternative uses of corporate resources are more favourable, the investment will be abandoned. The value of this option is determined at US$340 million. That is, the net present value of the probing investment and the associated abandonment option represents an aggregate value of US$360 million.

The three examples constitute three alternative ways of structuring the project financing of the same underlying business proposition. Now the issue is which one of the three is most beneficial to the investor and which one of the alternatives we should choose. The net present value of the first investment structure is the highest but it is also associated with the largest downside risk if the project fails. The two other alternatives have lower net present values but the associated options structures represent increasing values, which together with the net present values of those alternatives exceed the net present value of the first alternative.

The real option structures can be construed around a variety of alternative forms and different types of options provide incremental flexibility to the corporation's strategic investment decisions. Real option structures can comprise elements of different option types:

● *Expansion option* – the opportunity to expand the scale and scope of a strategic investment.
● *Deferral option* – the ability to defer a strategic investment decision to a later point in time.
● *Abandonment option* – the possibility to abandon further commitments to a strategic investment.

- *Contracting option* – the ability to terminate, dispose of or subcontract business activities.
- *Switching options* – the ability to change the use of corporate assets and resources.

**Expansion** and **deferral options** can be construed as call options that provide the holder with the opportunity but not the obligation to start or extend new business activities at some point in time before a certain future date. The deferral option perspective can be applied to major irreversible investments when it is beneficial to postpone the investment decision until a point in time where market conditions are understood and known with a higher degree of certainty. The value of these call options can often be sufficiently estimated by relatively 'simple' analytic solutions.

*Example*: (Refer to Table 1 on website www.pearsoned.co.uk/andersen.) An irreversible investment in a major business venture is determined to be €1 000 000 million (strike price) and the current investment value of the venture is currently determined as €1 050 000 (market price) thus representing a positive net present value of €50 000. However, the development of the investment value is highly uncertain and is assumed to follow a log-normal distribution with a volatility of 35%. The underlying investment opportunity is expected to be valid for some time but probably must be executed within the next two years to utilize a superior technological capability. Hence, this project has an embedded option to defer the investment for two years (time to maturity). Since the deferral corresponds to a future opportunity to exploit the project it can be formalized as a European call option the value of which can be determined using the Black–Scholes formula:

$$O_c = P(N(d_1)) - S(N(d_2))e^{-rt}$$

$$d_1 = \frac{\ln\left(\frac{P}{S}\right) + \left(r + \frac{v^2}{2}\right)t}{v\sqrt{t}}$$

$$d_2 = \frac{\ln\left(\frac{P}{S}\right) + \left(r - \frac{v^2}{2}\right)t}{v\sqrt{t}} = d_1 - v\sqrt{t}$$

where

$O_c$ = call option price;
$P$ = market price;
$N(\bullet)$ = cumulative normal density function;
$S$ = strike or exercise price;
e = 2.71828;
$r$ = risk free rate;
$t$ = time to maturity (days/360);
$v$ = volatility – annualized standard deviation of returns.

The theoretical real option premium of the deferral call ($O_c$) can be determined on the basis of a strike price of 1000 corresponding to the initial investment, two years to final maturity, i.e. $t = 2.00$, an assumed volatility of the underlying investment value of 35% (= 0.35), and a risk-free rate of 5%. We first calculate $d_1$ = (ln(1050/1000) + (0.05 + 0.35²/2)2)/(0.35 × $\sqrt{2}$) = (0.0488 + 0.1113 × 2)/0.495 = 0.5481 and then determine $d_2$ = 0.5481 – 0.4950 = 0.0531. Thereafter, we determine $N(d_1) = N(0.5481) = 0.7082$ and $N(d_2) = N(0.0531) = 0.5211$. Then $O_c = P(N(d_1)) - S(N(d_2))e^{-rt}$ = 1050 × 0.7082 – 1000 × 0.5211 × $e^{-0.05(2.00)}$ = (743.61 – 471.51) = 272.1. Hence, the deferral option is worth approximately US$272 100 under the given assumptions. In this case, the investment should not be pursued because the net present value derived from the project does not exceed the value of the deferral option that is foregone if the investment is made.

**Figure 10.18** Perpetual deferral option

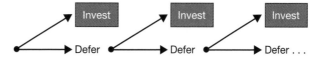

The option to defer may apply to all future times as well as it can be meaningless to assign a final date to the project. Hence, the deferral option can be construed as a continuous series of deferral or call options. In many cases deferral can take place over long time horizons, in principle in perpetuity. Hence, a continuous deferral option perspective can be adopted to describe long-term American-type call options where each deferral is considered to take place within small time intervals (Figure 10.18). The **perpetual deferral options** invite the application of an analytical valuation methodology based on a derivation through dynamic programming.[24]

*Example*: Assume the same project as before the only difference being that in this example the project can be deferred and executed at any time. So, there is really no final maturity date, i.e. the project can in principle be pursued forever into the future. The option value of this perpetual continuous deferral option can be determined on the basis of the following formula:[25]

$$O_{PDC} = AP^\beta$$

$$A = (\beta - 1)^{\beta-1}/[(\beta)^\beta S^{\beta-1}]$$

$$\beta = 0.5 - \frac{(\rho - \sigma)}{v^2} + \sqrt{\left(\frac{\rho - \delta}{v} - 0.5\right)^2 + \frac{2\rho}{v^2}}$$

where

$O_{PCD}$ = perpetual continuous deferral call option price;
$S$ = the investment outlay (strike price);
$P$ = the investment value of the project (market value);
$\rho$ = the discount rate applied to the project;
$\delta$ = the opportunity cost associated with a deferral of the project;
$v$ = volatility – annualized standard deviation of returns.

Assuming a discount rate ($\rho$) of 10% and an opportunity cost ($\delta$) of 5%, $\beta$ is determined as $0.5 - (0.10 - 0.05)/0.35^2 + \sqrt{\{[(0.10 - 0.05)/0.35 - 0.5]^2 + 2 \times 0.10/0.35^2\}} = 0.5 - 0.4082 + \sqrt{(0.1276 + 1.6326)} = 1.4186$. Thereafter, $A$ is calculated as $(0.4186)^{0.4186}/[1.4186^{1.4186} \ 1000^{0.4186}] = 0.6945/(1.6421 \times 18.0174) = 0.0235$ and $O_{PCD}$ is finally determined as $0.02385 \times 1050^{1.4186} = 453.245$. Hence, the perpetual deferral option is worth approximately US$453 245 under the given assumptions. As could be expected this value is significantly higher than the two-year European deferral option because it is associated with a higher degree of flexibility. As a consequence, the decision to pursue the investment must pass a higher hurdle since the value of the deferral option to be foregone through the investment is higher.

**Abandonment** and **contracting options** can be construed as put options that provide the holder with the opportunity but not the obligation to withdraw from or scale down on current business activities. The abandonment option perspective applies to initial retractable development investments with no cash flows and where future commitments can be staged to allow for premature project withdrawal. The value of these put options can often be sufficiently estimated by relatively 'simple' analytic solutions.

*Example*: (Refer to Table 1 on website www.pearsoned.co.uk/andersen.) A product development investment of €50 000 may provide the basis for a subsequent product introduction expectedly after two years at an investment of €100 000 and an investment value estimated around €165 000. Adopting a discount rate of 15% the NPV of this proposition is negative −€850 (= (165 000 − 100 000)/1.15² − 50 000). However, the development of the investment value is quite uncertain and is assumed to follow a log-normal distribution with a volatility of 45%, i.e. there is substantial downside risk and upside potential for gain. The project structure constitutes an abandonment option because the full project can be abandoned after a year if the product development process has a negative outcome. The value of this flexibility can be determined as a European put option on the basis of the Black–Scholes formula:

$$O_p = S(N(-d_2))e^{-rt} - P(N(-d_1))$$

$$(d_1) = \frac{\ln\left(\dfrac{P}{S}\right) + \left(r + \dfrac{v^2}{2}\right)t}{v\sqrt{t}}$$

$$d_2 = d_1 - v\sqrt{t}$$

where

$O_p$ = put option price;
$P$ = market price;
$N(\bullet)$ = cumulative normal density function;
$S$ = strike or exercise price;
e = 2.71828;
$r$ = risk-free rate;
$t$ = time to maturity (days/360);
$v$ = volatility – annualized standard deviation of returns.

At a risk-free rate of 5% we first calculate $d_1 = (\ln(165/100) + (0.05 + 0.45^2/2)2)/(0.45\sqrt{2}) = (0.5008 + 0.3025)/0.636\,4 = 1.2622$ and then determine $d_2 = 1.2622 - 0.6364 = 0.6258$. Thereafter, we determine $N(-d_1) = N(-1.2622) = 0.1034$ and $N(-d_2) = N(-0.6258) = 0.2657$. Then $O_P$ is calculated as $100 \times 0.2657 \times e^{-0.05 \times 2} - 165 \times 0.1034 = (24.04 - 17.06) = 6.98$. Hence, the abandonment option has a theoretical value of €6980 with the given assumptions. Therefore, if we take the option structure into account the product development project could be interesting, i.e. the value of the abandonment option exceeds the negative NPV.

Abandonment options can be combined as options-on-options to expand future activities, i.e. an integrated call option structure. Accordingly, development investments can be arranged in sequential stages where initial investments are made to gain insights that inform subsequent investment decisions. Arranging sequential abandonment options in a two-stage option-on-option approach, e.g. including an initial and an interim investment stage often provides sufficient analytical rigour. A **two-stage abandonment option** perspective allows the application of an analytical valuation methodology (Figure 10.19).

**Figure 10.19** Two-stage abandonment option

*Example*: (Refer to Table 2 on website www.pearsoned.co.uk/andersen.) The previous project could be structured differently, e.g. by first pursuing a smaller exploratory investment of say €10 000 into a new technology that underpins the product development investment of €50 000 (first strike price) that can be attempted after one year if the exploratory venture has positive outcomes and that, in turn, may provide the basis for a subsequent product introduction in year 2 at an estimated investment of €100 000 (second strike price) and an investment value around €165 000 (market price). This setup constitutes a two-stage abandonment option made up by the product development investment in year 1 and a subsequent product market investment in year 2. The option value of this two-stage abandonment option can be determined on the basis of the following formula:[26]

$$O_{TSA} = PM(h + v\sqrt{t_1}, k + v\sqrt{t_2}, \gamma) - S_2 e^{-rt_2} M(h, k, \gamma) - S_1 e^{-rt_1} N(h)$$

$$h = \frac{\ln\left(\dfrac{P}{S_1}\right) + (r - 0.5v^2)t_1}{v\sqrt{t_1}}$$

$$k = \frac{\ln\left(\dfrac{P}{S_2}\right) + (r - 0.5v^2)t_2}{v\sqrt{t_2}}$$

where

$O_{TSA}$ = two-stage abandonment option price;
$P$ = the investment value of the project (market value);
$S_1$ = the initial investment outlay (first strike price);
$S_2$ = the subsequent investment outlay (second strike price);
$N(\bullet)$ = univariate cumulative normal density function;
$M(\bullet)$ = bivariate cumulative normal density function;
$r$ = the risk free rate;
$v$ = volatility – annualized standard deviation of returns;
$\gamma = \sqrt{t_1/t_2}$.

Assuming a risk-free rate of 5% we first calculate $h = (\ln(165/50) + (0.05 - 0.5 \times 0.45^2)1)/(0.45\sqrt{1}) = (1.1939 - 0.0513)/0.45 = 2.5391$ and $k = (\ln(165/100) + (0.05 - 0.5 \times 0.45^2)2)/(0.45\sqrt{2}) = (0.5008 - 0.0513)2/0.6364 = 1.4126$. Then $O_{TSA}$ is determined as $165 \times M(2.5391 + 0.45\sqrt{1}, 1.412 6 + 0.45\sqrt{2}, \sqrt{1/2}) - 100e^{-0.05 \times 2} M(2.5391, 1.4126, \sqrt{1/2}) - 50e^{-0.05} N(2.5391) = 165 \times M(2.99, 2.05, 0.71) - 100 \times 0.9048 \times M(2.54, 1.41, 0.71) - 50 \times 0.9513 \times 0.9945 = (161.20 - 83.06 - 47.30) = 30.84$. Hence, the two-stage abandonment option has a theoretical value of around €30 840, which is significantly higher than the value of the simple one-stage abandonment option illustrating the value derived from the added flexibility of staging the investments.

The deferral and abandonment perspectives can have major applications in the analysis of strategic investment decisions:

● Deferral options apply to exercise of strategic options.
● Abandonment options apply to the creation of strategic options.

The deferral and abandonment options, in effect, can be adapted to analyze different stages of the strategic option life cycle. The abandonment options relate to initial resource commitments to create, test, and develop promising strategic opportunities, whereas the deferral options relate to the eventual full-fledged implementation of a new strategic opportunity that requires major irreversible resource commitments (Figure 10.20).

## Figure 10.20 Creating and exploiting strategic options ('the options life cycle')

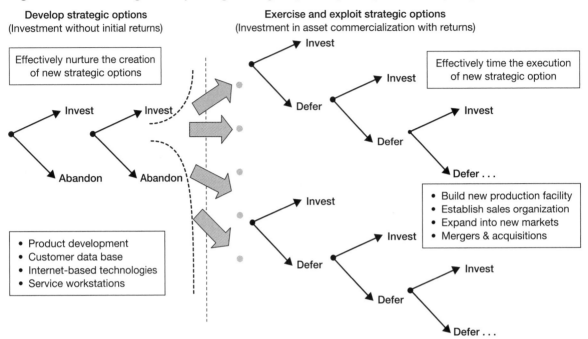

Applications of options theory have so far primarily been adopted in strategic investment analysis as the value of different option structures, such as growth, contractions, and switching options, are taken into account.[27] Two major insights seem to spring from the consideration of options in investment decisions. The first is to arrange committed resources in ways that give the corporation more flexibility to adjust the operational structure when environmental conditions change. The second is to avoid over-commitment of resources when large irreversible investments are made to introduce new business initiatives. One way to operationalize such advice is to differentiate between investments at different stages of the options life cycle from the initial creation of the investment opportunities, or options, to their final execution.[28] From this perspective, it is advantageous to make relatively small initial development investments and stage them so additional resources are committed only if interim outcomes prove satisfactory. Conversely, the large resource commitments typically needed in the final implementation of strategic opportunities should only be made when there is sufficient clarity about the expected investment outcomes.

Real options are shaped by capabilities and knowledge embedded in corporate resources including assets, processes, and intellectual capital. The option structures can, for example, provide the corporation with opportunities to implement new technologies and procedures, offer new products and services, approach new customer segments, geographical markets, etc. These opportunities can be conceived as strategic opportunities that establish unique choices between alternative actions and thereby allow the corporation to change market position under turbulent environmental conditions. Since the choice to exploit these opportunities is under discretionary corporate control, they have value above and beyond their stipulated net present values because management can choose to implement the opportunities

## Figure 10.21 Creating and managing real options over time

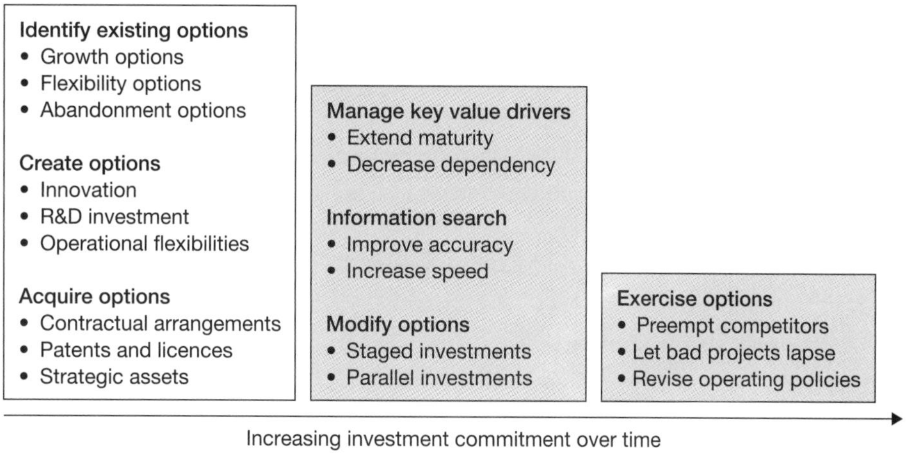

**Identify existing options**
- Growth options
- Flexibility options
- Abandonment options

**Create options**
- Innovation
- R&D investment
- Operational flexibilities

**Acquire options**
- Contractual arrangements
- Patents and licences
- Strategic assets

**Manage key value drivers**
- Extend maturity
- Decrease dependency

**Information search**
- Improve accuracy
- Increase speed

**Modify options**
- Staged investments
- Parallel investments

**Exercise options**
- Preempt competitors
- Let bad projects lapse
- Revise operating policies

Increasing investment commitment over time

when circumstances are beneficial but have no obligations to do so in unfavourable situations.

Some strategic opportunities are framed already within the firm's existing resource base and constitute so-called latent options that are waiting to be discovered. Therefore, it is necessary to recognize the existence of particular option structures and potential business opportunities before they can be developed and eventually utilized. This process of internal recognizance and information gathering has been described as sense making and organizational learning to identify useful competences.[29] However, the latent options are not necessarily visible to everyone and may actually require further development before they constitute viable opportunities to the firm (Figure 10.21). In contrast to financial options, new business opportunities constitute real options based on assets and capabilities that are idiosyncratic to the firm and for which no official market prices exist. These strategic options are unique and hence the volatility of expected returns from the underlying opportunities are to a large extent firm specific because uncertainty depends on the level of collective insight and environmental knowledge that reside among managers and key individuals in the corporation. It is in this context that probing initiatives may provide valuable insights that help reduce the level of uncertainty circumscribing the execution of alternative business opportunities.

Investing to gain knowledge about new markets and subsequent entry into them can create growth options that allow the company to enter other related markets at later points in time. Initial investment in new business activities can also allow the company to exit and reenter related markets as conditions change. However, determining the appropriate timing of the underlying investment decisions requires a lot of judgement based on diverse insights from different constituents (Figure 10.22). The utilization of identified option structures for risk management purposes is, therefore, highly dependent on the corporate strategy process where the engagement and ongoing interaction among organizational members can improve market insights in support of options exercise decisions.

When operating in a highly uncertain environment the probability that something can go wrong is significant and choosing an appropriate strategic management framework, risk management process, and managerial decision structure to address

**Figure 10.22** Timing the execution of strategic options

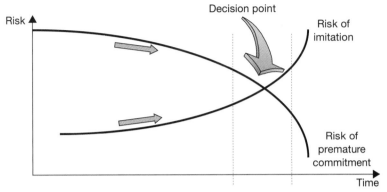

these risk issue constitutes a major challenge. In the past, many of the inherent risks that exposed the corporation were analyzed and handled by different corporate functions but this is not the most effective approach because it disregards inter-actions between the key risk factors. Instead management should identify all the essential risks, assess the associated exposures, determine the extent to which the corporation can tolerate different risk levels, and manage the exposures through hedging, risk transfer, and financing arrangements within a tolerable risk profile. One way to accomplish this is to integrate the risk management into the strategic man-agement process. Assuming a real options perspective may provide a complement-ary analytical framework to identify and evaluate alternative strategic opportunities available to the corporation. Identifying and quantifying all corporate risk exposures on a comparable basis despite its deceptive simplicity might reveal new valuable insights and support the management of financial and economic exposures to enhance corporate profitability and avoid major downside losses that otherwise could jeopardize the survival of the firm.

## Conclusion

Risk management is an important discipline and entails many types of risk extending from financial exposures to competitive factors that are harder to quantify and requires integration with the strategic management process. A real options perspec-tive can provide a useful framework for identifying and assessing embedded busi-ness opportunities and operational flexibilities that may increase the corporation's strategic response capabilities and support corporate strategy considerations.

## Summary

● Recent corporate history is replete with examples of organizations that incurred significant losses or ceased to exist as independent entities due to their negligence of significant underlying exposures and failure to manage the associated risks.

● Corporate exposures extend well beyond financial risk factors and also comprise other types of risk including company related risks, industry related risks, and environmental risks that are increasingly difficult to identify and quantify.

● General interest rate gapping measures on the corporation's implied equity position can be adopted as a useful 'back-of-the-envelope' methodology to assess overall risk exposures but can also form the basis for more sophisticated corporate risk simulations.

● The analytical strategic management process incorporates considerations about corporate risk exposures in the form of conventional SWOT analysis that can be supported by formal risk management processes.

● The real options perspective can be a useful approach to deal with harder-to-quantify strategic risk exposures by identifying embedded flexibilities that can increase corporate maneuverability in response to changing environmental conditions.

## Questions

10.1 List different types of exposure and discuss how associated risk factors may affect corporate performance.

10.2 Explain how the duration gap of the corporation's implied equity position can be determined.

10.3 What is the potential significance of the duration gap of corporate equity?

10.4 Explain how the strategic management process implicitly deals with risk exposures.

10.5 Outline the major differences between financial and real options.

10.6 Outline major types of real options structures in a corporate context.

## Exercises

10.1 Consider a corporation in early 2002 with the following financial statements that follow a general principle of booking assets and liabilities at their true market value.

Consolidated statements of income

| Years ended December 31 | 2001 | 2000 | 1999 |
|---|---|---|---|
| (US$ million) | | | |
| Total operating revenue | 2 576 161 | 2 097 218 | 1 883 269 |
| Change in inventory stocks | 323 440 | 122 299 | 108 385 |
| Cost of goods sold | (1 512 380) | (1 061 075) | (1 070 112) |
| Other expenditures | (482 699) | (353 802) | (269 554) |
| Salaries | (481 543) | (366 221) | (343 733) |
| Depreciation | (106 383) | (76 100) | (66 763) |
| Operating income | 316 596 | 362 319 | 241 492 |

▶

| | | | |
|---|---|---|---|
| Interest income | 58 010 | 9 387 | 25 522 |
| Interest expenses | (84 114) | (92 158) | (71 418) |
| Other, net | – | – | – |
| Income before income tax | 290 492 | 279 548 | 195 596 |
| Income tax | (82 069) | (68 516) | (60 799) |
| Consolidated result | 208 423 | 211 032 | 134 797 |
| Minority interests | (11 381) | (3 249) | (11 435) |
| Net income | 197 042 | 207 783 | 123 362 |

### Consolidated balance sheets

| Years ended December 31 (US$ million) | 2001 | 2000 | 1999 |
|---|---|---|---|
| **Assets** | | | |
| Cash and cash equivalents | 178 960 | 93 009 | 132 465 |
| Securities | 169 | 22 597 | 16 539 |
| Accounts receivable | 281 733 | 219 647 | 185 465 |
| Other receivables | 135 542 | 59 534 | 76 604 |
| Materials and supplies | 103 735 | 148 100 | 121 706 |
| Goods in process | 96 898 | 43 407 | 40 858 |
| Finished goods | 768 446 | 498 497 | 378 747 |
| Deferred charges | 57 840 | 71 997 | 9 892 |
| Short-term assets | 1 623 323 | 1 156 788 | 962 276 |
| Goodwill | 15 486 | 8 743 | – |
| Property and plants | 248 141 | 135 500 | 119 437 |
| Machinery and equipment | 218 819 | 98 670 | 70 959 |
| Other equipment | 167 061 | 117 560 | 84 848 |
| Plants under construction | 42 712 | 80 172 | 31 046 |
| Fixed assets | 692 219 | 440 645 | 306 290 |
| Deferred tax | 57 618 | 46 077 | 34 228 |
| Total assets | 2 373 160 | 1 643 510 | 1 302 794 |
| **Liabilities and stockholders' equity** | | | |
| Current maturities of long-term debt | 53 300 | 39 917 | 50 673 |
| Banks and mortgage institutions | 417 027 | 310 016 | 204 428 |
| Accounts payable | 218 328 | 159 481 | 134 578 |
| Other debt | 148 519 | 98 801 | 108 646 |
| Accrued taxes | 21 378 | – | 1 758 |
| Other deferrals | – | 6 | 111 |
| Dividends payable | 24 750 | 24 750 | 24 750 |
| Short-term debt | 883 302 | 632 971 | 524 944 |
| Banks and mortgage institutions | 269 352 | 183 365 | 115 012 |
| Other long-term debt | 474 598 | 275 898 | 228 002 |
| Long-term debt | 743 950 | 459 263 | 343 014 |
| Common stock | 5 500 | 5 500 | 5 500 |
| Additional capital | 5 580 | 5 789 | 5 544 |
| Retained earnings | 721 278 | 535 135 | 405 354 |
| Total stockholders' equity | 732 358 | 546 424 | 416 398 |
| Minority interests | 13 550 | 4 852 | 18 438 |
| Total liabilities and stockholders' equity | 2 373 160 | 1 643 510 | 1 302 794 |

It has been estimated that the duration of short-term assets $(D_{STA})$ is around 0.25, the duration of long-term assets $(D_{LTA})$ around 7.5, the duration of short-term debt $(D_{STL})$ around 0.25, and the duration of long-term debt $(D_{LTL})$ around 3.5.

(a) Determine the duration gap of the implied equity position.
(b) Assess whether this represents a reasonable risk position.
(c) Discuss ways in which the corporation might modify the risk position.

10.2 A business opportunity has a total investment need of €450 000 million and the expected investment value associated with the project is expected to be around €550 000. The business project is considered promising but rather risky expressed by an assumed volatility of the investment value around 50%. This investment opportunity is deemed to have longer-term potential but probably should be executed within five years.

(a) Determine the value of the embedded deferral option.
(b) Determine the value of the perpetual deferral option.
(c) What are the implications of these option valuations?

10.3 A product development investment of €100 000 can lead to a product introduction after three years that will require an investment of €500 000 with an estimated investment value of €600 000. The outcome of the new product market entry is considered rather uncertain reflected in an assumed volatility of the investment value of around 50%.

(a) Determine a net present value of the product development investment.
(b) Determine the value of the abandonment option and discuss the implications of this valuation.
(c) Consider alternative ways of structuring the development investment and discuss the implications.

## Notes

1 For example, Roth, K. (1995), 'Managing international interdependence: CEO characteristics in a resource-based Framework', *Academy of Management Journal*, **38**, pp. 200–31.

2 Andersen, T. J. (2005), 'The performance effects of computer-mediated communication and decentralized strategic decision making', *Journal of Business Research*, **58**, in press.

3 This case was prepared to stimulate risk analysis and strategic management discussion not to illustrate effective or ineffective corporate management situations.

4 Volatility is a standardized measure indicating the annualized standard deviation.

5 Miller, R. D. and Reuer, J. J. (1996), 'Measuring organizational downside risk', *Strategic Management Journal*, **17**, pp. 671–91.

6 Knight, F. (1921), *Risk, Uncertainty, and Profit*, Houghton Mifflin.

7 See Berry, A. and Phillips, J. (1998), 'Enterprise risk management: pulling it together', *Risk Management*, **45**(9), pp. 53–8.

8 See Miller, K. D. and Waller, H. G. (2003), 'Scenarios, real options and integrated risk management', *Long Range Planning*, **36**, pp. 93–107.

9 See, for example, Lam, E. (203), *Enterprise Risk Management: From Incentives to Controls*, Wiley.

[10] See, for example, Clarke, C. J. and Varma, S. (1999), 'Strategic risk management: the new competitive edge', *Long Range Planning*, **32**, pp. 414–24.

[11] See Coyle, B. (2002), *Risk Awareness and Corporate Governance*, Institute of Financial Services.

[12] See, *A Risk Management Standard* (2002), AIRMIC, ALARM, IRM.

[13] Simons, R. (2000), *Performance Measurement and Control Systems for Implementing Strategy*, Prentice Hall.

[14] See, for example, Schneier, R. and Miccolis, J. (1998), 'Enterprise risk management', *Strategy & Leadership*, March/April.

[15] For some of the original work developing this approach see, for example, Andrews, K. R. (1980), *The Concept of Corporate Strategy*, Irwin.

[16] Britton Harris, T. and DeMarco, M. (1998), 'A new paradigm for risk management', *Derivatives Quarterly*, Summer.

[17] See, for example, Eiteman, D. K. and Stonehill, A. I. (1998), *Multinational Business Finance*, Addison-Wesley.

[18] Andersen, T. J. (1993), *Currency and Interest Rate Hedging*, 2nd edn, Prentice-Hall.

[19] Oxelheim, L. and Wihlborg, C. G. (1987), *Macroeconomic Uncertainty: International Risks and Opportunities for the Corporation*, Wiley.

[20] Miller, K. D. (1998), 'Economic exposure and integrated risk management', *Strategic Management Journal*, **19**, pp. 497–514.

[21] See, for example, Micalizzi, A. and Trigeorgis, L. (1999), 'Project evaluation, strategy and real options', in Trigeorgis, L. (ed.), *Real Options and Business Strategy: Applications to Decision Making*, Risk Books.

[22] Kogut, B. (1985), 'Designing global strategies: profiting from operating flexibility', *Sloan Management Review*, **27**(1), pp. 39–48; Kogut, B. and Kulatilaka, N. (1994), 'Operating flexibility, global manufacturing, and option value of a multinational network', *Management Science*, **40**, pp. 123–39; Tang, C. Y. and Tikoo, S. (1999), 'Operational flexibility and market valuation of earnings', *Strategic Management Journal*, **20**, pp. 749–61.

[23] This is consistent with the view of strategy as a pattern of resource committing actions over time. See, for example, Mintzberg, H. (1978), 'Patterns in strategy formation', *Management Science*, **24**, pp. 934–48.

[24] The dynamic programming derivation may be relevant when it is difficult to find a market portfolio that exactly matches the risk–return characteristics of the project. However, the dynamic programming approach reaches comparable solutions to the contingent claims approach. See Dixit, A. and Pindyck, R. S. (1994), *Investment Under Uncertainty*, Princeton University Press.

[25] This formula is similar to the solution derived through contingent claims analysis. The only difference is that the discount rate ($\rho$) has replaced the risk-free rate ($r$) in the derivation of $\beta$.

[26] See, for example, Geske, R. (1979), 'The valuation of compound options', *Journal of Financial Economics*, **7**, pp. 63–81.

[27] For a comprehensive exposition of options analysis in capital budgeting, see Trigeorgis, L. (1996), *Real Options: Managerial Flexibility and Strategy in Resource Allocation*, MIT Press.

[28] See Andersen, T. J. (2000), 'Real options analysis in strategic decision making: an applied approach in a dual options framework', *Journal of Applied Management Studies*, **9**, pp. 235–55.

[29] See, for example, Bowman, E. H. and Hurry, D. (1993), 'Strategy through the options lens: an integrated view of resource investments and the incremental-choice process', *Academy of Management Review*, **18**, pp. 760–82.

# Chapter 11

# Managing strategic risk

As competition intensifies in increasingly turbulent environments risk management becomes essential. Input cost, energy prices, capital cost, demand conditions, output prices, currency conversions, etc., are influenced by international market dynamics and expose global enterprises to price volatilities in financial markets and general socio-economic developments. At the same time industries across the board are increasingly exposed to **hypercompetition** where ongoing innovation intensifies competitive behaviours.[1] Products and services continue to change character as market participants and entrants introduce new product features and technologies that make talks about standard outputs irrelevant. The contours of dynamic industry environments are becoming blurred making it difficult to determine the potential competitors as companies enter and exit specific product markets in conjunction with the realization of new business initiatives. Frequent, rapid, and abrupt changes are becoming the norm rather than the exception in many industries. Under this competitive reality corporations need to stay observant about changing conditions and develop internal processes that enable the organization to react effectively under environmental change. Corporations must sense changing conditions in an ongoing and timely manner and improve their ability to re-deploy corporate resources in view of changing competitive realities.

The pursuit of risk management is often described as a three-phased process. The first step is to recognize all the relevant risk factors, the second is to measure the size of potential exposures arising from these risks, and the third step is to determine how to handle the exposures, i.e. whether they should be ignored, modified, or hedged. We will argue that these steps should constitute an ingrained part of the formal strategic management process. However, an important precursor to effective risk management is to create a general atmosphere of risk awareness in the organization. In a turbulent environment where competitive changes are frequent and unexpected in nature effective responses require a certain level of involvement among the corporation's core constituents. The ability to observe and interpret market events is enhanced through the engagement of key people who communicate actively to assess circumstances as they evolve. There is a similar need for formal risk management to provide a general overview of the diverse risks that exposure the corporation, assess potential interactions between them, and outline the contours of the aggregate risk profile as an integral element of the corporation's strategic considerations.

## 11.1 Getting to grips with uncertainty

Risk is associated with environmental uncertainties that may have both adverse and favourable economic effects on the corporation. Whereas conventional views may tend to focus on the downside loss exposures associated with uncertainty, the subsequent discussions also consider the significance of upside potentials for gain to organizations that have effective response capabilities. However, the underlying concept of uncertainty is not universally defined. In finance, uncertainty constitutes a measurable property usually captured by the standard deviation in returns. Since finance typically deals with instruments that are traded in transparent markets there are rich databases on historical price developments available for analyses. The fact that uncertainty and the associated risk can be specified and measured has led to many advances in the finance field. For example, modern portfolio theory is based on the ability to assess variability and covariance of returns across different types of invested assets and financial options pricing models depend on volatility calculations to determine the theoretical options prices. However, another interpretation of uncertainty associates the phenomenon to events that cannot be foreseen with any exactitude and which, therefore, in effect leaves the construct unmeasurable.[2] From this perspective, **uncertainty** constitutes the unknowable parts of the future that inevitably may hit the organization from time to time. Many competitive moves, technological innovations, political crisis, market collapses, etc., may comprise this type of uncertainty. The high degree of uncertainty associated with different types of natural and man-made catastrophes also has connotations of unknowability. However, even in the data rich financial industry, the observant follower will notice that some of the most devastating events derived from unexpected market developments where price relationships, due to one-time exogenous events, might take a differential path from previous patterns analyzed on the basis of historical price developments (see the example of Long Term Capital Management in Chapter 10).

The organization literature has addressed the uncertainty phenomenon from both an external and an internal perspective. The external perspective has tried to characterize different dimensions of the external environment as they may apply to different types of industries. **Dynamism** reflects the variability caused by external risk factors, such as demand conditions, employment levels, operational profitability, etc. For example, a firm that experiences a high variance in total sales could be operating in a dynamic industrial environment. **Complexity** refers to the diversity of issues management has to consider and handle on an ongoing basis. As organizations employ an increasing number of specialists and differentiate operations across larger numbers of specialized departments, the level of complexity increases. **Turbulence** reflects environments comprising both dynamism and complexity, which exacerbate the managerial challenges of dealing with frequent changes across a wide range of specialized areas. **Munificence** is an environmental characteristic used from time to describe industrial settings with relatively favourable profitability conditions. For example, public utilities have long been used to capture an industry displaying steady positive returns. However, as the electricity markets in the USA and EU are being liberalized this type of business environment is threatened by extinction.

The internal perspective has tried to pinpoint essential organizational conditions as firms respond to the uncertainties imposed from the external environment. One perspective looks at how managers are influenced by the situational framing of the corporation, e.g. **prospect theory** suggests that decision makers are risk averse when business prospects are positive and risk seeking when business prospects are negative.[3] An extension of this perspective looks at managerial risk behaviours in the context of their past experiences, management homogeneity, organizational culture, etc. Another perspective addresses the amount of **information processing** organizations have to perform arguing that firms operating in turbulent environments need to process more information to carry out essential business activities compared to firms operating under stable conditions.[4] Hence, uncertainty can be described as the difference between the amount of information available and the amount of information required to accomplish organizational tasks. The information processing perspective has implications for how organizations can be assumed to deal more effectively with uncertain conditions, e.g. by being better at information search, collection, processing, dissemination, and interpretation. By incorporating behavioural perspectives it is readily seen that if managers have cognitive biases they may blur environmental assessments and hence obscure the development of effective organizational responses. Similarly, if managers are ignorant about the need to take responsive actions, it will exacerbate the effects of environmental uncertainty.[5] Managerial ignorance could be a partial cause for organizational uncertainty although it can be genuinely difficult to determine the precise outcome effects of ongoing organizational actions, which obviously augments the challenge of devising effective responses to changing conditions.

Risk management as an approach to deal with effects from different types of uncertainty has traditionally focused on coverage of the downside economic impact of risk events, including casualty risks such as automobile accidents, property fire, etc. This is very much the focus assumed by insurance companies serving as mechanisms to pool the risks and provide cover to households and business entities against up-front premium payments. These risks can typically be actuarially determined based on historical loss profiles and customer characteristics. Corporations with large portfolios of economic assets could use the same pooling technique and might be better off self-insuring the exposures using the pooling principles on their own asset portfolio. To the extent that the corporations are incurring excess exposures these higher risk layers could be covered in the reinsurance market on an excess of loss basis. Other financial institutions such as banks have a natural tendency to think about downside risk primarily because the return on a conventional loan portfolio still depends on the ability to get the entire principal paid back from the borrower. To a commercial banker the principal task is to perform a decent credit evaluation and price the credit extension appropriately to cover the associated default risk on economically viable terms. For the institutional investor default risk also matters, so downside risk is an important consideration but scoring a higher return in opportunistic investment strategies obviously cannot be ignored. Nonetheless, modern portfolio theory will argue that investors should aim for a return in line with the total market, which reflects the systematic risk that cannot be avoided through portfolio diversification and the common use of index benchmarks to assess portfolio returns is testament to this.

Even though the unsystematic risk associated with investment in individual publicly traded firms in principle can be diversified away by investors, the firm specific uncertainties are still a reality for the management of those individual corporations. Whereas the portfolio perspective might argue that risk management is irrelevant for their purposes because they can diversify the invested portfolios, it may still be very relevant to the individual firms for a number of reasons. First of all, not all corporations are publicly traded and private owners presumably are not interested in excessive risk exposures that might jeopardize the long-term viability of the firm. In addition, with the continued globalization of business activities the cyclical swings in foreign exchange rates can have a significant impact on the relative profitability of firms operating in the same industries, e.g. automobiles. In addition, it can be argued that firms with excessive levels of bankruptcy risk will have to pay substantial premiums for any debt they incur and may eventually be confronted with reduced credit facilities to the detriment of their ability to engage in positive net present value projects. This under-investment dilemma could be used an argument for the hedging of risk exposures.[6] Furthermore, a number of stakeholders, including suppliers, customers, partners, employees, etc., (Figure 11.1) may be forced to charge a price premium on commercial interactions with the corporation if it is perceived as being too risky and eventually the corporation may have difficulty attracting the necessary business relationships to carry out their business effectively. In other words, excessive risk exposures could be associated with mounting adverse cost effects.[7] The close ties established in selective supplier and distributor relationships might be jeopardized if the corporation is perceived as an excessively risky counterpart. That is, to remain a reliable partner that induces counterparts to invest selectively in firm specific assets to enhance business flows and value creation among them the corporation needs to manage its risk exposures within reasonable limits. Hence, risk management is arguably a necessity for corporations that want to reap the economic benefits associated with firm specific investments required in knowledge intensive industries.

To some extent operational risks, e.g. interpreted as operational disruptions, can be considered a downside risk exposure to the corporation. However, an attentive focus on operational risk factors can also be associated with upside potential for gains in terms of efficiency improvements deriving from quality control and continuous process improvements. Hence, some would argue that risk management processes could instil better work practices and thereby lead to better and more efficient internal processing capabilities. Financial risks are typically associated with price variability, which entails both downside risk and upside potential, while strategic risks are more related to the type of uncertainties that border on unknowability. However, these risks can also be perceived as representing both a downside risk as well as an upside potential for gain. This is reflected in the analysis of threats and opportunities in the formal strategic management process (Chapter 10). Hence,

**Figure 11.1 Major stakeholder groups**

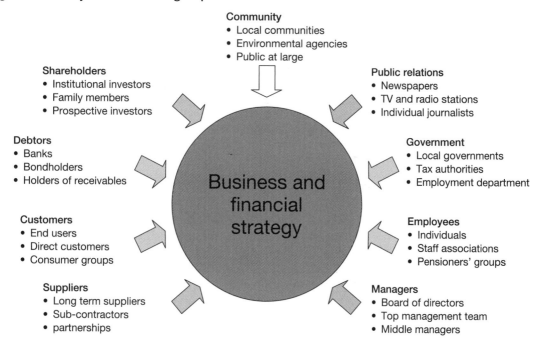

every threat that is identified can also be considered a potential opportunity if the corporation is able to respond effectively to the identified risk.

A major caveat in risk management is the handling of the relatively rare disastrous events that may happen but are hard to forecast. Such events could relate to financial risks, e.g. when price structures change abruptly in unexpected ways or business confidence collapses as witnessed in global stock markets at the beginning of the century. They could also relate to political crisis such as sovereign default events, mounting military actions, or civil unrest. They may also relate to major technology shifts or extreme disaster events of different kinds. It is a challenge for corporate management to deal with these types of low-probability high-impact risk factors some of which are very hard to measure or even discern in advance. The potential effects from natural and man-made disasters and terrorism events can be assessed through the use of model simulations based on risk scenarios, risk intensity patterns, and identified asset vulnerabilities. Many strategic risks might employ comparable assessment techniques but in some cases are harder to identify, quantify, and assess. Therefore they could pose a real challenge to the organization's ability to sense ongoing change and analyze it when something significant seems to be emerging. The real options perspective may be useful in this context as an analytical and practical approach to manage underlying flexibilities is response to risk events. The ability to create options is an essential feature of an organization's responsiveness, whether the options are established on an *ex ante* basis and are pending exercise at an opportune moment or are recognized only after certain unforeseeable events have occurred. In either case, a real options perspective may help outline possible responses in strategic choice situations and thereby improve the corporation's ability to respond to unexpected situations. In this regard, the existence of an inherent set of options related flexibilities seems important but it is equally important to have a level of preparedness in the organization to identify relevant skills and competencies that allow managers to recognize new options when they are needed.

*Example*: When Southwest Airlines was rejected as a subscriber to UAL, the joint flight reservation system of Continental and Delta Airline's, the company was faced with an unpleasant strategic reality that had to be resolved quickly to ensure the continued survival of the firm. In this situation, it turned out that employees in the company already had taken initiatives to develop the basis for a ticket-less booking system in an attempt to make the airline more competitive. In effect, they had created a strategic option that could be executed at a time when the firm had an acute need to deal with a strategic risk. The ticket-less system eventually turned out to have a true upside potential as on-line ticket-less sales soared and provided significant cost savings and became a distinctive competitive advantage for Southwest Airlines.

To probe the effect of uncertainty in essential business decisions risk has been conceived from two different perspectives.[8] Uncertain outcomes associated with managerial decision making is a type of risk that all practising managers have been faced with. This **managerial risk** concept reflects the *ex ante* uncertainty that surrounds important resource committing decisions at the time they have to be made. The future is unknown and as a consequence decision outcomes are surrounded by uncertainty. This type of risk is obviously important, because ultimately a firm's strategic development path is determined by the characteristics of those resource committing decisions made over time. However, this type of *ex ante* risk is difficult to measure with any sort of precision because it relates to future expectations and the individual organization's ability to cope with the risks that circumscribe a particular commercial situation. On the other hand, the volatility of historical income streams that result from these decisions over time can be measured with high statistical precision. Consequently, this type of **organizational risk** represents the typical risk measure considered in management research. This risk concept reflects *ex post* organizational outcomes and as such represents the aggregate effects of a number of managerial decisions made over time as well as environmental influences from economic and competitive developments. Both concepts of risk are important but there is not necessarily a direct relationship between the two. For executives faced with major strategic decisions the ability to assess *ex ante* risk factors is essential. There is a general understanding among managers that higher future return is associated with the acceptance of high *ex ante* risks and that the assessment of these risks entails some evaluation of the organization's ability to cope with uncertain and unforeseeable circumstances. However, the *ex ante* risk for a given commercial proposition is not the same for two different organizations because each firm manages unexpected events on the basis of their specific endowment of tangible and intangible assets, capabilities, human expertise, information processing and communication skills.

*Ex post* risk can be an important guiding measure but it enters into the managerial equation as a consequence of the organization's ability to manage through uncertain and unknown events as they emerge over time, which might entail competitive threats as well as opportunities to exploit the corporation's unique resources. To the extent organizations show a strong ability to manage through the turmoil of turbulent environments *ex post* risks tend to be relatively low. In other words, some firms can assume large *ex ante* risks and excel profit growth while the realized *ex post* risk turns out on the low side. This is consistent with the risk–return relationships observed across industries (Figure 11.2). Furthermore, investors do seem to attach a

**Figure 11.2 Risk–return relationships in select industries (1991–2000)**

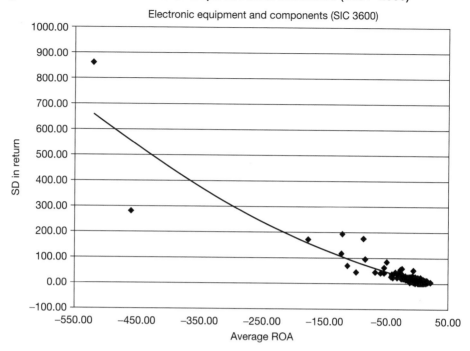

Electronic equipment and components (SIC 3600)

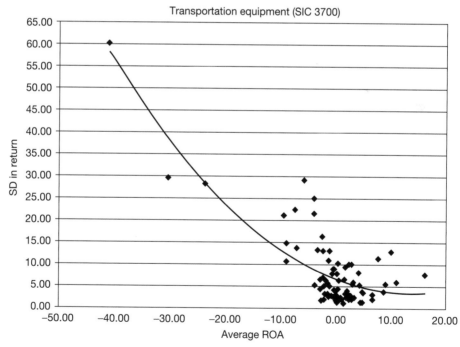

Transportation equipment (SIC 3700)

*Source*: Compustat data

premium to non-financial information such as corporate management's ability to execute against a credible strategy, handle unforeseen events, and engage human resource talent with prospective innovativeness that allow the organization to adapt through market turmoil.[9]

Instituting a general awareness about environmental risks is a way to sharpen an organization's ability to manage *ex ante* risk more effectively. To the extent that management can feel comfortable that key people across the organization are trained to observe changing environmental conditions and ponder their possible consequences for the firm, there is a higher likelihood that the firm will be able to react to emerging environmental changes in a timely manner. Whereas the engagement in formal risk assessment exercises can provide a better understanding of the risk exposures and enhance corporate risk awareness it obviously does not constitute a universal provision to avoid all unfortunate consequences of environmental uncertainties. The fact that some of the major components in contemporary risk scenarios are made up of elements that cannot be known in advance accentuates this point. However, formal risk management can sharpen recognition around identified elements of risk. It is equally important to establish an organizational ability to sense and react to the emergence of hitherto unknown environmental threats and opportunities.

Different types of risk factors represent differences in data availability, measurability, and knowability. Financial and market risks intermediated through financial institutions and hazards, such as casualty and life insurance risk covered by insurance companies constitute data rich exposures that are relatively easy to describe and quantify. Natural and man-made catastrophes, operational risks, and strategic risks, such as general economic conditions, demographic trends, competitive moves, etc., are more difficult to describe because information on these phenomena is vague and incomplete, and consequently they are more difficult to discern. Other strategic risk factors, such as sovereign risks, market reputation, supplier relationships, customer relationships, political trends, social trends, technology developments and innovations, are only very loosely described with few hard data available and, therefore, true insights depend on qualified experts and information networks the organization maintains with external entities. Hence, as we move from financial risks towards strategic risks we see a descending order of data availability and an associated increase in the difficulty to quantify the exposures (Figure 11.3).

Underlying all of these risk factors, however, is an element of unknowability. For example, financial risk exposures are particularly dangerous when markets behave in abnormal and unexpected ways that are hard to forecast. The prevalence of unknowability is more obvious in the case of low-frequency high-risk events like catastrophes, operational disruption, and technology shifts. This does not mean that it is impossible to quantify the potential impact of these risk factors but other techniques may be adopted in this process, such as, stress testing, scenario analysis, and computerized simulations. The divergence in data availability and quantifiability constitutes a dilemma when we want to integrate the risk exposures into a single exposure measure like Value-at-Risk (VaR). A major idea behind the VaR construct is that it takes the interaction between the various risk factors into account and thereby provides a better overview of the corporation's true aggregate exposure. However, it is difficult to pursue the complete quantification route in practice and the integrative analysis must be conceptual rather than quantitative as it incorporates some of the more unknowable types of risk. The further one moves toward strategic risk factors

**Figure 11.3** Risk categories, data availability, and uncertainty

| Risk categories | Quantifiable data | Type of risk |
|---|---|---|
| **Financial risks**<br>• Interest rate risk<br>• Currency risk<br>• Market risk | Rich price data | Uncertainty |
| **Hazards**<br>• Casualty risk<br>• Natural disasters<br>• Terrorist events | Data on certain risks | |
| **Operational risks**<br>• Operational disruptions<br>• Technology breakdowns<br>• Errors and fraud | Selective data | |
| **Strategic risks**<br>• Economic risks<br>• Competitor risks<br>• Political risks<br>• Social trends<br>• New technologies<br>• Innovations | Few concrete data | Unknowability |

that are unknowable, the harder it is to quantify and thereby integrate the risk exposures into an overarching VaR measure. Nonetheless, it is still useful to recognize potential risk factors and emerging risk areas for continued scrutiny and encourage awareness about significant exposures however vague.

---

**Box 11.1  Risk assessment, mitigation, and transfer**

Risk management can be framed around a rational analytical process, which first identifies the major risk factors and hazards that might affect the corporation, determines the resulting risk exposures, evaluates opportunities for hedging, risk-transfer, and financing solutions, and then arranges various covers for residual risks that are deemed to go beyond a prudent corporate risk profile. A general risk management model is shown in Figure 11.4.

- *Identify major risk factors*. The first step in the risk management process is the identification of risk factors and hazards that expose economic assets, tangible and intangible, in the corporation. Trends, patterns, and changing frequencies of events, etc. are essential elements of this analysis while remaining aware that certain phenomena may be rather vaguely defined and difficult to describe and predict.
- *Outline the contours of economic exposures*. Based on the identification of the major risk factors and hazards and predicted event frequencies and intensities, vulnerability models can transpose the risk analyses into probabilistic estimates of likely direct economic effects associated with major risk events. These analyses can use model specifications with different levels of sophistication.
- *Analyze cost/benefits of risk mitigation initiatives*. Better quality control processes, information systems, decision structures as well as better physical construction and operational flexibilities, etc. can reduce the economic vulnerability to various phenomena but there is a trade-off between up-front investments needed for

**Figure 11.4** Risk mitigation and risk-transfer

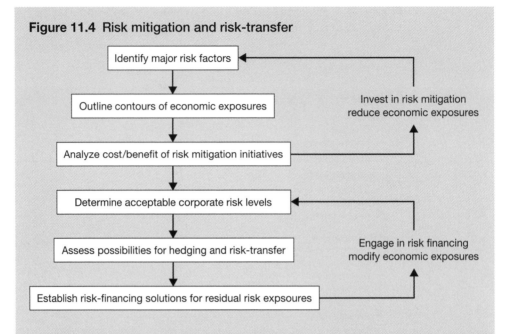

these purposes and the expected positive economic effects. Risk mitigation should be pursued as long as the future benefits are expected to exceed the associated costs.

● *Determine acceptable corporate risk.* Once there is a sense of the potential corporate economic effects associated with major risk factors and related events, there is a need to determine the tangible and intangible assets, with associate future cash flow streams, and the corporation should obtain cover for in case of adverse risk events. In practice this exercise must be divided according to the major risk categories that expose the corporation.

● *Assess possibilities for hedging and risk-transfer.* Whereas active risk mitigation efforts can serve to reduce exposures there are limits, therefore, there is a need to search for ways to hedge and transfer parts of the remaining risk exposures that are deemed excessive. In this process, the corporation should monitor global derivatives markets, insurance contracts, and alternative risk-transfer solutions available in the international financial markets.

● *Establish risk-financing solutions for residual risk exposures.* Based on the vulnerability analyses, assessments of the corporate economic exposures, and market opportunities for hedging and risk-transfer solutions, hedging programmes should be established to cover for specific exposures and engage in up-front financing arrangements. All the while internal decision structures, communication systems, and strategic management processes should be adapted for optimal responsiveness to un-expected events.

Hence, it is worthwhile to assess whether different risk mitigation efforts can serve to materially reduce the risk exposures before actual hedging and risk-transfer exercises are considered, e.g. leading and lagging currency payments, changing international sourcing patterns, pooling multinational cash flows, exploiting operational flexibilities, etc. Obviously the risk mitigation assessments should be based on prudent cost–benefit analyses to ensure that relevant risk mitigation initiatives provide exposure reductions that justify any associated cost. Under all circumstances the resulting cost

**Figure 11.5 Risk simulation model**

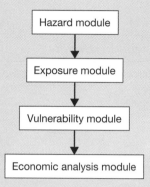

of risk-transfer solutions will become cheaper the more the economic exposures can be modified in advance.

The technical calculation of economic exposures can be completed in sequential modules. Whereas this approach is particularly associated with simulations of hazards it may also inspire the analyses of other types of risk exposures (Figure 11.5). The hazard module determines the potential intensity of different risk factors or hazards across the exposed parts of the corporate business portfolio. The exposure module specifies exposed economic assets and associated cash flow streams and determines the corporate value exposed. The vulnerability module determines the potential damage ascribed to different business assets. Finally, the economic analysis module calculates the total economic performance effects of the simulated risk events. The analytical framework can also be assumed as a basis for determining the potential economic effects of extreme risk situations and perform stress testing.

The determination of the economic performance effects (*EP*), can be formalized as follows:

$$EP = p \times v \times h \times VE$$

where

$p$ = probability of the risk event;
$v$ = vulnerability factor of economic assets;
$h$ = intensity of risk factor;
$d = v \times h$ = impact ratio;
$VE$ = value exposed.

The key objective in the risk assessments is to quantify the economic risk exposures of different parts of the corporate business portfolio and the enterprise as a whole. For this purpose the model simulations can develop a number of essential insights for use in ongoing risk exposure assessments.

Based on the contours of the corporate risk exposures revealed from preceding risk analyses management must decide whether these exposures are acceptable or not. If the exposures are deemed to be excessive, efforts must be invoked to reduce them. In practice, financial exposures that represent high frequency transactions may not necessarily be handled on a deal by deal basis. For example, financial institutions typically implement systems of aggregate limits for different types of financial risks

**Figure 11.6** Risk ranking framework

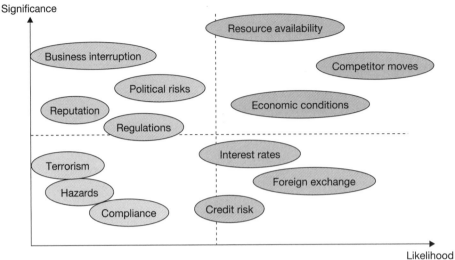

and impose effective controls systems around them and corporations may impose general policies concerning insurance against hazards. Nonetheless, the acceptable aggregate exposures and the associated risk limits should fit the overall risk profile determined by the executive board. When it comes to operational and strategic risks the task is slightly different since these exposures relate to longer-term business positions. There is still a need to list the significant risk factors and prioritize them but it is harder to reach a single number for the aggregate exposure because it is difficult to quantify these risks. Management should perform a ranking of the identified risk factors including financial prices, natural hazards, terrorism, business interruption, competitive moves, political developments, etc. The ranking can be based on a simple mapping of the risk exposures in terms of their economic significance and their likelihood of occurring (Figure 11.6).

The overall assessment of the aggregate risk exposure and the targeted risk profile might reveal a need to curb some of the risk exposures using various financial instruments and risk management approaches alike to modify the risk profile:

● hedging (financial derivatives);
● risk-transfer (insurance, risk-linked securities);
● risk-financing (committed credit facilities, contingent capital);
● quality management (process improvement and control);
● real options perspective (create and execute strategic opportunities).

This is the very idea behind **enterprise risk management**, namely to address all risk factors that could affect the corporation's ability to achieve its strategic objectives.[10] While the extended risk perspective might have evolved from an insurance perspective rather than a financial derivatives perspective the insurance contracts and derivative instruments constitute two sides of the same coin. That is, insurance in essence constitutes a type of option and vice versa. Hence, the ability to cover risk exposures comprises many alternative instruments available in the financial markets as well as complementary risk management approaches to handle more firm specific exposures deriving from hard to quantify risk factors (Figure 11.7).

**Figure 11.7** Integrated risk management

Risk factors

| | | | | |
|---|---|---|---|---|
| Currency rates | Workman's compensation | Terrorist attacks | Operational flows | Competitive risk |
| Interest rates | Property risk | Flooding incidents | Accounting & control | Technology risk |
| Commodity prices | Casualty risk | Windstorm risk | Fiduciary risk | Economic risk |
| Financial derivatives | Insurance contracts | Alternative risk-transfer | Internal control | Real options |

Risk Management Approach

In general the corporation will assume a certain level of acceptable risk retention across all risk categories but will employ various hedging, risk-transfer, and management techniques to cope with excessive risk exposures. The higher-level commodity and financial market risks are relatively easy to cover in the derivatives markets at least for short to medium-term time periods. Casualty risks may be covered through general policies obtained from the insurance industry, which may be construed as multi-line insurance arrangements. Higher layer exposures related to hazards may be ceded in the reinsurance market on an excess of loss basis and possibly through issuance of risk-linked securities. For hard to quantify risk exposures hedging and risk-transfer may not be a viable route but could instead be covered through committed credit facilities of different kinds as general liquidity buffers. For general insurance exposures and specific commercial risks it might also be possible to issue different types contingent capital instruments (Figure 11.8).

**Figure 11.8** Corporate risk coverage

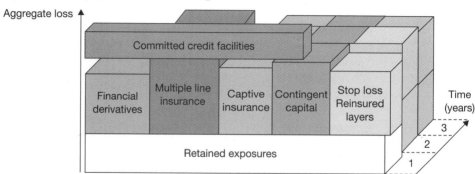

There is a limit to the availability of cover for very firm specific risks. Therefore, corporate management should consider natural internal hedges that could reduce the exposures. For example, in the case of long-term movements in foreign exchange rates the associated economic exposures might be reduced if production facilities are distributed across major currency areas. If globally distributed manufacturing plants represent operational flexibility it might even be possible to exploit favourable currency trends by shifting production volume between currency areas. This constitutes a real option structure and the establishment of other relevant options-related flexibilities could prove tremendously valuable, for example, by establishing flexible sourcing channels that allow for periodic shifts in input supplies from different currency areas, etc.

The ultimate shield against excessive risk exposures is the firm's equity position. The shareholders' paid in capital and retained earnings constitute the ultimate cover if economic performance fails. This is obviously why financial institutions are highly regulated on this important risk-buffer but the debt–equity ratio also affects the perceived riskiness of corporate entities depending on the volatility of their earnings flows. However, the better the corporation is at managing its risk exposures either through financial hedging, risk-transfer, and risk financing or through response capabilities and adaptive management skills, the lower the need for a large capital buffer to maintain credibility as a reliable commercial counterpart. As an added benefit, the better the firm is able to manage its inherent risk exposures and reduce the *ex post* volatility of its earnings flows, the lower will be its cost of capital. Hence, the pursuit of effective enterprise risk management efforts requires an integrated approach to business management and financial management, where financial management is focused on the possibilities for risk management solutions in the financial markets while business management is focused on internal resource development and external market positioning (Figure 11.9). This also illustrates why risk management should be considered an integral part of the strategic management process rather than a specialized functional task.

**Figure 11.9** Integrating business and financial management

- Strategic positioning
- Product and process innovation
- Establish flexible resources
- Create business opportunities

- Execute business opportunities
  - opportunistic market initiatives
  - operational improvements
- Switching business activities

- Capital structure
- Financing alternatives
- Project evaluation
- Capital budgeting

- Financial hedging
- Risk-transfer arrangements
- Risk-financing arrangements

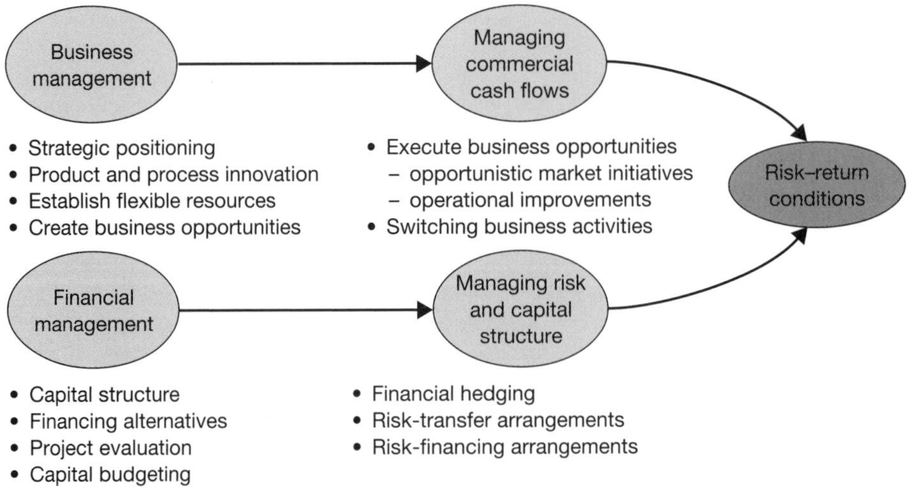

## 11.2 Risk awareness

The more difficult it is to foresee, quantify, and assess the risk exposure in advance the higher the need for risk awareness among organizational members and a general preparedness to act if the unexpected should happen. Hence, a fundamental first step to manage inherent risk exposures is to instil corporate awareness among senior management, middle managers and employees alike. Organizational inertia is a prevalent phenomenon among groups of human agents.[11] As companies grow successful the agents that operate in them tend to become complacent, self-sufficient, and self-contained in their own success criteria. Managers tend to develop a common cognitive understanding based on similar experiences incurred through the development of the organization. It could be argued that managers assume a **dominant logic**,[12] which is characterized by the experiences gained within a specific environmental setting. This corresponds to the conceptualization of the **competency trap**, where successful firms overemphasize past success criteria and continue to refine their distinctive competencies to the point where they become obsolete.[13] However, at this point it is too late to develop other competencies that may be needed to compete on the new terms dictated by competitive developments. It could also mean that potential risk elements are neglected either out of ignorance or simply due to inconceivability on behalf of the managers. Nevertheless, new threats may arise that could fundamentally change and disrupt the competitive advantage on which the corporate success was built in the first place. These types of development abound as new business models have challenged and outpaced previous ways of doing business.

*Example*: Nucor took the unusual step of refining steel out of metal scrap based on new technologies developed in post-war Europe that provided the basis for highly efficient mini-mills operating in rural areas of the United States using a minimal administration. This approach was in complete contrast to the labour- and capital-intensive processes surrounding conventional high ovens managed through vast layers of bureaucracy.

*Example*: Southwest Airlines introduced cost efficient point-to-point flights between regional airports based on use of standardized planes and quick turn-around times at the gates that challenged the conventional way of routing flights through complex networks structured around central hubs.

*Example*: Wal-Mart implemented a more cost-efficient way of distributing consumer goods to ordinary Americans through large outlets placed in accessible locations and supported by an information technology driven logistics system.

These are just a few examples of new successful business approaches that have revolutionized the way business can be done and the earnings track record of these firms operating in highly competitive industries is legendary. General awareness among people in the organization that environmental conditions can change and that some things evolving might have the potential to disrupt the favourable corporate position is a necessary initial requirement for the responsive organization. It does not help to have a sophisticated exposure measurement system if people in the organization are unaware of its implications. Often the collection and interpretation of subtle observations of changing conditions is more important than a large formal system that nobody pays attention to. Hence, some of the most successful companies are able to sustain organizational awareness and incur a sense of tension and urgency that keep people on their toes.

*Example*: Managers in Microsoft often seem to underplay corporate achievements and emphasize the potential competitive threats that surround the company's business activities. Similar organizational climates can be found in other successful organizations, such as, Dell, Sharp, Honda, etc.

It is argued that creativity and innovative behaviour can thrive on environmental uncertainty and the tension of high organizational aspirations where creative chaos arises out of the ambiguity of the challenge.[14] Therefore, the demands imposed from a turbulent industrial environment can improve performance in organizations where management is able to develop effective response capabilities through the right combination of strategic intension and individual autonomy to act.

## 11.3 Risk management culture

Imposing a risk awareness culture on an organization starts with the unconditional commitment of senior management. Management must recognize that external change can have a significant effect on the corporation's financial performance. Risk exposures can impose financial losses on the corporation. These losses are not just related to avoidable expenses but also refer to opportunity costs arising from negligence in identifying strategic opportunities that leave the initiative in the hands of major competitors. This realization is a necessary prerequisite for effective implementation of organization-wide risk management practices. From this perspective risk management is not only a way to recognize potential losses but also a way to encourage employees to be proactive and sensitive to new business opportunities that may enhance the corporation's competitive position and reduce its vulnerability to environmental uncertainty. If senior managers adhere to the stringency of a formal risk management approach, then there is a reasonable chance that middle management and the people working under their supervision will pay attention. However, the risk management practices must be visible as an ingrained element of the strategic thinking process in the organization rather than constituting something handled by specialists in the back office. It must become part and parcel of the corporate culture and the way the organization performs business.

For a risk management system to be truly effective, employees should be recognized for effective adherence to the risk management considerations. If new opportunities are ignored they represent opportunity costs as the corporation fails to develop valuable product offerings and efficient process improvements thereby providing competitors with an edge in the market. The more turbulent the industrial environment the higher the need to stay attentive to environmental changes in technology shifts, customer needs, competitive moves, regulatory requirements, etc. Such attentiveness encourages organizational members to reconsider the appropriateness of internal processes and product offerings with an aim of adapting these to align the corporation better to prevailing environmental conditions.

**Figure 11.10** The relative emphasis on risk factors

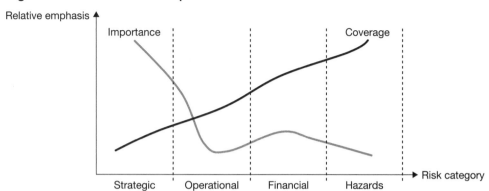

The foundation for the corporate risk management approach lies in top management's imposition of an internal risk awareness culture and request for internal reporting to register exposures that represent potential effects on corporate performance. Nevertheless, investigations seem to indicate an increasing managerial realization that risk management matters but also reveals somewhat rudimentary reporting of underlying risk exposures.[15] Corporate management pays more attention to conventional risk areas covered by the insurance market. Hence, close to half of the firms obtain cover for identified hazard risks while the remaining companies have reasonable covers. Financial risks receive full coverage in around 40% of the firms while other 40% are resonably attentive to these exposures. However, when it comes to operational and strategic risk factors, there is little awareness as only about 10% of the firms try to manage these exposures actively while close to a third have some awareness of these exposures (Figure 11.10). As appears, the risk factors that are hardest to measure and quantify and represent the highest elements of unknowability receive the least attention. However, this does not mean that they constitute the least important risk exposures. The good news is that management seems to recognize this. In their evaluation operational risks, insurable hazards, and financial risks are relevant but strategic risk factors are considered the most important influencers of corporate performance. This finding pinpoints a need to improve our way of dealing with these risk exposures in conjunction with the overall strategic management process.

*Example*: The most important risk factor for a soft drinks producer, e.g. the Coca Cola Corporation, is not financial exposures, natural hazards, terrorist acts, or public relations failures but rather the availability of continuous flows of clean high quality water at accessible locations. This input sourcing issue emerges as the most important corporate concern, i.e. a strategic risk of central importance for the long-term viability of the business but also a risk factor that is hard to quantify through simple measures.

## 11.4 Risk management as quality control

The risk management perspective should be moved from an out-of-pocket loss avoidance mindset to a consideration of economic and strategic opportunity costs where the risk considerations can help improve overall corporate performance.

Conceptually, risk management could assume a sort of quality control function that permeates the organization so it eventually constitutes an instinctive concern that guides the corporate actions. To obtain this status management might do a number of things:

- Incorporate a risk perspective into the mission statement and instil risk awareness as an element of the corporate culture.
- Impose a risk management perspective on all business practices and incorporate it in education, training and planning exercises.
- Make essential risk management principles visible and incorporate them in recognition and reward systems.
- Emphasize process improvements as responses to environmental change in corporate communication and internal business reviews.
- Use a risk management framework to further internal reviews and revisions to existing business processes.
- Make risk management part of the strategic thinking and consider responses to strategic exposures including economic, competitive, technology, and regulatory risks.
- Develop expertise to handle specific risk exposures, e.g. operational, credit, commercial, legal, compliance, and regulatory risks.
- Adopt an integrative diagnostic risk reporting system without letting technocratic sophistication cloud the overall strategic objectives.

To achieve strategic responsiveness from the quality process it is important to distinguish between the control and learning aspects of the associated total quality management process.[16] Quality control can be important to ensure that customer needs and product durability requirements are fulfilled but it is often more important that the fulfillment is achieved in a manner that enhances organizational learning so new business opportunities are explored and better internal processes developed. Whereas an overarching aim is to ensure that processes are performed as perfectly as they possibly can be to ensure economic efficiencies it is equally important to engage in process renewal to modify and improve existing ways of doing things. In many ways the dual emphasis on operational quality and continuous improvement reflects the fundamental balance requirement between exploitation and exploration.[17]

Whereas total quality management is more focused on internal operational and process oriented issues the general perspective of enterprise risk management is focused on the ability to achieve strategic objectives. This perspective is also built into the formal strategic management framework as **strategic control** as a mechanism providing periodic follow-ups on strategic goals. In its generic form, strategic control aims to monitor how well the organization has achieved the intended goals as stated in the formal missions and expressed in the strategic plan (Figure 11.11). However, it can also be construed as a strategic learning process whereby management can reassess the competitive situation and modify strategic initiatives accordingly. As such it can be an instrument to continuously assess the environment for potential significant change indicators. These approaches are often supported by a so-called **balanced scorecard** approach monitoring essential parameters for business performance, customer satisfaction, operational efficiency, and supportive capabilities.[18] However, to use the balanced scorecard effectively as a dynamic strategy tool requires a certain flexibility to furnish new environmental observations and creative organizational initiatives of potential future importance that may arise

**Figure 11.11 Strategic control and performance evaluation**

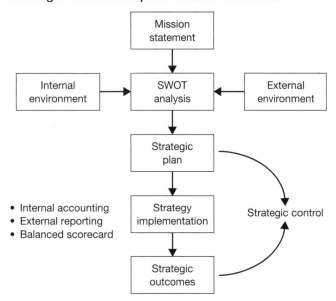

- Internal accounting
- External reporting
- Balanced scorecard

from engaged employees. Hence, the formal strategic control process might be able to fulfil a central monitoring mechanism as well as act as a source for identifying emerging threats and opportunities that could affect the future risk profile of the corporation.

Financial derivatives are typically based upon financial assets traded in transparent markets with wide price dissemination. The price volatilities of the underlying assets represent both downside risks and upside potentials but hedgers use these instruments to protect themselves against downside financial losses whereas the potentials for upside gains are left to active investors and speculators. When it comes to the more esoteric strategic risks things are less clear-cut because the risk exposures usually are highly firm specific and, therefore, the potential hedging opportunities are equally dependent on internal capabilities that may be construed as real option structures. The very recognition of the related strategic options available to the corporation is to a large extent dependent on self-imposed abilities.

## 11.5 Strategizing through real options

Real option structures are shaped by skills, capabilities, and knowledge embedded in a firm's resources including assets, processes, and human-based insights embedded in the firm's intellectual capital. The real options can provide the firm with opportunities to implement new technologies and procedures, offer product features, introduce service offerings, cater to new customer segments, etc. These opportunities can be conceived as strategic options that furnish competitive advantage by providing unique choices between alternative actions and allow the firm to change market position under turbulent environmental circumstances. Since the choice to exploit these opportunities is under management's discretionary control, they have value above and beyond their stipulated net present values because the firm can choose to implement the opportunities when circumstances are beneficial but have no obligations to do so in unfavourable situations. Therefore, if the firm is able to develop unique strategic options and utilize them wisely it should be possible to create excess returns. These options can influence the strategic path of the firm by expanding market coverage and switching business scope in new directions, while other opportunities may constitute simpler flexibility options that allow the firm to adapt business volume and resource utilization. Flexibility options can be advantageous by improving operational efficiencies while growth and switching options can have more profound influences on the firm's strategic positioning.

---

### Box 11.2 Using a real options logic

The performance of integrated circuits in computer chips and semi-conductors in wireless communication equipment, data switchers, Internet routers, etc., improved exponentially for more than 25 years. 'Moore's law' had fairly accurately projected that the number of transistors included on integrated circuits would double every eighteen months. However, the continued improvement in the existing so-called bulk CMOS technology required the development of new materials and processes. An alternative approach based on a silicon-on-insulator (SOI) technique was under development and appeared a promising new technology. As electronic gadgets continued to get smaller while capacity and performance capabilities increased, competitors in the global semi-conductor industry had to consider whether to adopt the CMOS-SOI technology or choose other alternatives. The choice of technology platform is an essential strategic issue. An industry participant was considering these developments and had to assess the possibilities of the CMOS-SOI technology. Several competing companies had already, or were about to, embark on the new technology. On the other hand, the success of the technology was not given, i.e. there was significant uncertainty with a real chance that the technology could fail.[19]

In this situation the company realized it had three basic choices: (1) adopt CMOS-SOI only, (2) pursue bulk-CMOS only, or (3) incorporate both technologies. The first option was not realistic given an estimated 30% technology success rate. The second option was not acceptable either given the competitive market situation. Hence, the third option was considered the only realistic choice (Figure 11.12). One possibility would be to immediately start building the new technology either through internal development, through outsourcing, or through a technology partnership. These possibilities would be reflected in typical NPV project evaluations. However, the company reasoned that it did not have to invest right away but had flexibility to postpone the final investment decision. This deferral option would be valuable if the uncertainty about the commercial viability of the technology could be reduced over time and thereby help the company avoid potential downsides associated with failed investment outcomes. However, the company could also engage in a probing research project on the new technology possibly together with an industry partner and then decide later whether or not to pursue the technology. This abandonment option would allow the company to engage with a relatively low-cost probe to develop internal technology capabilities and more accurately determine the applicability of the new technology. This option would be valuable because it could improve the company's ability to exploit the new technology if it turned out to be viable while constituting a considerably scaled down investment commitment.

**Figure 11.12 Setting the decision framework for new technology choice**

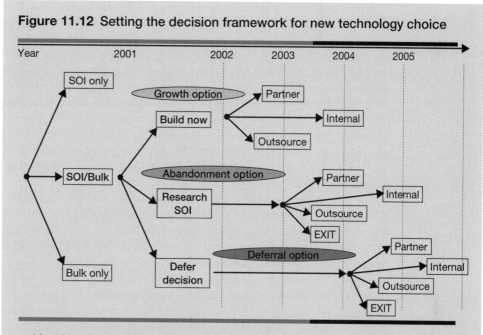

After identifying these realistic strategic options available to the corporation the company analyzed the expected values of each of the proposed solutions taking the implied real option structures into account. This approach demonstrated that the research project abandonment option was the most attractive of the three viable alternatives. The real options approach combined with a good ability to present the framework as a hands-on analytical process provided a strong basis for management discussions about the consequences of different base assumptions and scenarios and eventually helped reach a better strategic decision under highly uncertain circumstances.

## 11.5.1 Latent options

Some strategic options are arguably framed already within the firm's existing resource-base and constitute so-called **latent options** that are waiting to be discovered, i.e. it is necessary to recognize the existence of option structures and potential business opportunities before they can be developed and utilized. This process of internal recognizance and information gathering has been described as sense making and organizational learning to identify useful competencies.[20] However, the latent options are not necessarily visible to everyone and may require further development before they constitute viable opportunities that can be exploited by the firm. Hence, the options development process is likely to involve a form of creative awareness among managers and key people in the corporation nurtured by an organizational environment that values idea generation and displays a willingness to support new ways of doing things. In this case, organizational learning extends beyond the mere identification of existing options. Rather, it constitutes a dynamic knowledge creation process where elements of the current resource-base are recombined through the active engagement of organizational members to develop new operational process and market offerings.

A firm that is able to develop a series of alternative actionable opportunities, i.e. strategic options, will be better off than a firm that has no such alternatives particularly in rapidly changing environments. From an options perspective environmental uncertainty, therefore, constitutes a higher value potential because the strategic options represent different ways to exploit alternative opportunities under changing circumstances. The presence of a strategic options portfolio can provide competitive advantage by allowing the firm to reposition itself in the market and take advantage of more suitable products, distribution systems, technologies, etc. This outcome contrasts the lower present value normally associated with a riskier investment environment. However, a high level of uncertainty can arguably be a strategic advantage for an organization that is able to respond to and exploit the implied environmental turbulence.

The real options perspective extends the formal strategic management framework, and has the potential to improve management's view of the **strategic action space** that is available to the corporation. Some opportunities and threats can be identified and stipulated through strategic planning exercises that engage the organization's minds in strategic thinking and the corporation can consider various steps to exploit interesting opportunities and hedge against environmental risk factors. However, in a dynamic industrial environment many events are relatively unpredictable and therefore difficult to plan for. So, to be strategically responsive an organization must commit resources and build capabilities within flexible structures that avoid premature commitments to invest in fixed assets.

Strategic options give the corporation the ability to commit resources and take strategic actions with a view to changing market conditions. The availability of strategic options can provide the corporation with the ability to pursue important alternative uses of resources and capabilities, which increases the strategic action space available to the corporation. However, acquiring options at market prices can be costly and, therefore, may not necessarily enhance corporate value. Therefore, it is key to institute strategic decision processes that facilitate options creation at low or no marginal cost. Furthermore, optimizing the value of existing strategic options may furnish little economic benefit unless the organization subsequently is able to exploit them in an optimal manner. Consequently, it is equally important that the strategic decision processes enhance effective execution of the corporation's strategic options portfolio (Figure 11.13).

To facilitate the corporation's ability to navigate in an available strategic action space, management must try to identify the important strategic options that circumscribe the organization's competitive environment. The conscious awareness of the

**Figure 11.13** Managing strategic options

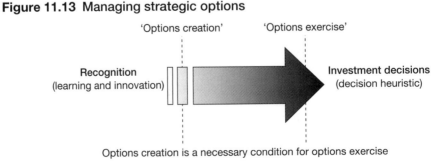

Options creation is a necessary condition for options exercise

strategic options concept can encourage managers across the organization to think about actions and opportunities that can provide future strategic value. The real options approach should not just enable management to identify and create import-ant strategic options but should also help to structure and time organizational resource commitments in a more optimal manner. Once strategic options have been identified, e.g. in connection with a strategic planning discussions or analysis of emergent strategy issues, potential interdependencies between the option structures should be considered. By mapping related strategic options, management can form a view of the corporation's ability to act and obtain a more nuanced view of available options. Too often corporations are merely imitating the actions of major compet-itors because it seems more safe and right when certain activities, product traits, technology platforms, etc., are gaining momentum. However, alternative strategic flexibilities are often ignored due to simple inattention to the organization's inherent real option structures. By maintaining awareness about the corporation's strategic options portfolio, senior management may respond more effectively to market opportunities, competitive moves, technology trends, etc.

Autonomy and dispersed decision power can facilitate creativity and options development. Often it takes an effective informal communication network to identify and create options that are based on new combinations of corporate knowledge and skill sets developed through trial and error learning processes throughout the organ-ization. However, real options can also be developed through conscious R&D invest-ments and incorporated into formal real asset investment schedules to enhance the corporation's flexibilities. The abandonment option perspective allows the corpora-tion to structure development investment in a more effective manner. However, establishing a wide portfolio of strategic and real options is not an end in itself – it must be used appropriately to create value. Particularly if the portfolio is acquired at something that resembles a 'market price', mismanaging the execution of the real options can impose losses on the corporation. Exploiting the full value embedded in real options requires that the options are executed optimally, i.e. the timing must be right so execution takes place at the most opportune moment in time.

The organization can do a number of things to improve the likelihood that timely execution will take place:

● Informal communication links provide instantaneous and less biased market information, which is a prerequisite for effective market recognizance.
● Information technology enhanced communication links among dispersed man-agers provide quick interfaces to sound out information and a basis for interpreta-tion and synthesis.
● Involving key people in the strategic planning discussions can help the identification of critical circumstances that drive the options execution.
● Involving key people in major strategic decisions can ensure that all aspects are considered before a decision is made and facilitates better decision outcomes.

The volatility or uncertainty pertaining to a corporation's real options is firm specific, that is, it depends on the idiosyncratic experiences and insights of organiza-tional members and the ability to effectively mobilize the relevant environmental knowledge is central to effective decision making. Formal option theoretical valua-tions can provide helpful guidance to the execution of strategic options. Execution typically relates to significant irreversible investments to commercialize fully de-veloped strategic options. In this process, the deferral option perspective ensures

**Figure 11.14** Managing the value of flexibility

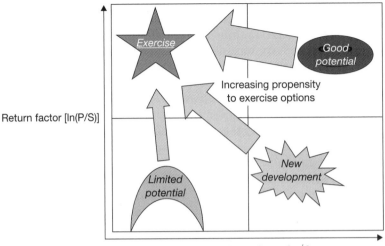

that the corporation only invests if the potential return is sufficiently high and the uncertainty surrounding the investment is reasonable.

Once the portfolio of real options or strategic opportunities has been identified and described, the portfolio can be assessed on the basis of the relative return from exercise and remaining time value of the embedded option structures. The options can be characterized by their 'return' and 'time-variance' factors. The **return factor** is determined as the natural logarithm of the investment value over the cash outlay $[\ln(P/S)]$ and indicates the relative return associated with options exercise. The **time-variance factor** is the square root of the time remaining to exercise multiplied by the volatility of the investment value $[v\sqrt{t}\,]$ indicating the relative value potential of the option (compare the two option characteristics to the call option pricing formula in Chapter 5). Best estimates of the two strategic option factors can be plotted into a two-by-two table for further analysis (Figure 11.14).[21]

Strategic options with high return and low time-variance factors are prone to be exercised because returns are relatively high and there is little uncertainty associated with exercise. Options with high return and high time-variance factors are good potential candidates for future exercise because return is high and there are strong time value prospects. Options with low return and high time-variance are typically development options that might represent strong but uncertain future earnings potentials. Options with low return and low time-variance factors have a limited potential for exercise because returns are low and there is little time value.

## 11.5.2 A real options perspective

The creation of real options is obviously necessary for the firm's subsequent exploitation of different strategic opportunities. However, options creation is not a sufficient condition for superior performance. First of all, the costs associated with the options creation process matter. It is not a question of establishing as much organizational flexibility as possible because the cost of creating this flexibility can in some cases be prohibitive to achieve economic returns. Also, some flexibilities are more meaningful and important to the firm than others, i.e. optimal options creation processes are cost efficient and effective in reaching relevant option structures. Furthermore, to create excess returns on an *ex post* basis, the firm's strategic options must be exercised in an optimal manner throughout their lifetime. Therefore, the creation of as many real options as possible and optimizing their aggregate theoretical value has little merit if the subsequent utilization of the strategic options is ineffective. The challenge is extended to devise processes that allow the firm to better optimize strategic options execution that result in superior returns. An important step towards effective strategic options management practices is to recognize that firms must be able to create and identify new relevant real options in a relatively costless manner and then effectively exploit them in the turbulent market environment. The development of relevant optionalities depends on capabilities that can assess the potential value of the strategic options under the prevailing external market conditions even though they may represent emerging opportunities many of which only have vague contours. Options exercise, in turn, depends on abilities to effectively scan the environment and assess current and prospective business conditions based on financial and organizational as well as strategic risks. The underlying organizational capabilities are highly complex and imprecise in nature but are all driven by informal knowledge networks and effective communication links between the corporate decision makers.

Once option structures have been identified and formally recognized it is essential to execute the options portfolio as close to the optimal path as possible to reap *ex post* benefits from the underlying options based flexibilities. The ensuing process of monitoring and exercising the firm's real options portfolio is conceivably a function of appropriate strategic decision making processes, e.g. that allow relevant 'ears and eyes' throughout the organization to reveal what is going on in the environment and contribute with views and perspectives. Optimal exercise of options depends both on an accurate assessment of the firm's internal ability to effectuate the strategic project that underpin the real options and a fairly accurate assessment of the options' applicability under prevailing market conditions. This may correspond to an organizational information processing capability that scans, collects, monitors, and reacts to current impressions from ongoing market developments. However, it probably cannot follow a predetermined stringent heuristic or formalized processing rule. Rather, it must be based on a high degree of managerial autonomy, rich cross-functional communication capabilities, and the flexibility of mutual adjustment processes that allow internal capabilities to be reorganized in response to changing environmental conditions.

The execution of real options largely depends on an ability to correctly assess external market preparedness for a new strategic initiative and the alleged competitive responses to it. The formal process of assessing the external market environment relates to the part of the SWOT-analysis where the firm's strategic opportunities and threats are recognized and described (Chapter 10). In a sense it reflects a need to integrate market oriented perspectives into the strategy process to ensure that the strategic opportunities are properly exercised. In other words, the dual consideration of internal real options identification and the application of those options in view of external market opportunities constitute the essential aspects of the strategic considerations.

## 11.6 Risk in the strategic management process

To furnish a higher degree of corporate responsiveness it is necessary to instil a managerial mindset that is sensitive to new environmental developments, displays openness to change, and a willingness to challenge prevailing mental models. This mindset can have its origins in the corporate mission statement, which formally should indicate the overall purpose of the organization, interim goals and long-term objectives, and the values that should prevail throughout the organization. The value statements will serve to clarify the relationships with the corporation's major stakeholders and express the importance of maintaining strong credibility with major stakeholders to reduce relationship risks. Hence, the underlying risk management concerns can be tied to the mission statement and enhance awareness about the importance of reducing volatility in these counterparty relationships. The risk responsiveness of the entire organization is also related to the way the organization carries out its strategy process, i.e. the way planning is enacted throughout the organization. This also entails a general alignment of decision structures, information systems, compensation schemes, reporting requirement, etc. Hence, the initial steps in the risk management process, identification of major risk factors and collecting supportive data should be an integral part of the corporate strategy analysis (Figure 11.15). The resulting risk gapping measures, value-at-risk indicators, stress tests, and scenario simulations would provide useful information to evaluate how the overall risk exposure should be curbed. Finally, the ongoing process of managing the identified risk exposures and monitor the risk environment should be part and parcel of the strategic control process, which not only monitors exposures but also observes indicators of emerging environmental change.

The corporation should maintain an organizational structure and instil a corporate culture that facilitates and nurtures an urge to change and adapt organizational processes and respond when significant environmental changes are observed. This capability builds on the inherent resource base and human insights and can be enhanced by an institutionalized risk management approach. It is by convention assumed that higher return is associated with higher risk features. This relationship arises out of analyses of financial market statistics that reflect investor behaviours but managerial common sense also associates good business opportunities with the

**Figure 11.15** Aligning risk management and strategic planning

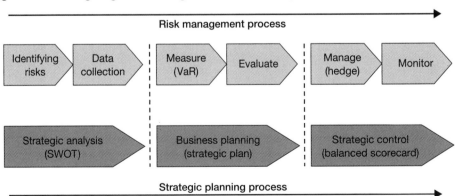

**Figure 11.16** The risk management cycle

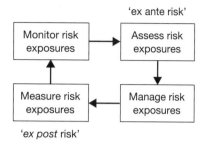

'ex ante risk'

assumption of *ex ante* risk. However, managers also assume that risk can be tamed over the course of events, i.e. *ex post* risk can be reduced and may conceivably be lower than the anticipated risk level at the time the investment decision was made. The interaction between *ex ante* risk assessments and monitoring of realized *ex post* risk levels is captured in the basics of the risk management cycle where risk managers learn from the discrepancies observed between *ex ante* and *ex post* evaluations (Figure 11.16).[22]

The underlying learning cycle is quite comparable to the strategic planning process and the implied role of strategic control and the risk management cycle can readily be imposed on the strategic learning cycle as an integral element of the corporation's strategy process (Figure 11.17).

Whereas this integrated perspective is primarily imposed on a formal planning framework it also depends on the more complex informal process elements that take place within a responsive organization. A responsive mindset will normally require a certain emphasis on supporting organizational structures and capabilities. Organizations that are able to effectively coordinate work tasks across flexible networks of functional entities and individual specialists have a better chance to interpret information about environmental changes and convert them into relevant organizational responses. Such networks are supported by informal communication capabilities and can be enhanced by use of advanced information technologies. Open

**Figure 11.17** The strategic learning cycle

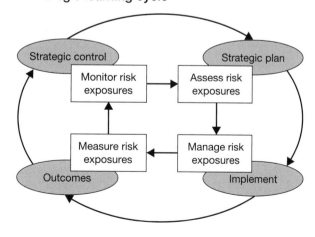

and informal communication capabilities among managers throughout the organization reduce information distortion and enable coordination of organizational tasks. Richer and more detailed information can be processed because it is registered and exchanged closer to the original sources without distortions caused by formalized interpretations up and down a hierarchical chain of command. The fact that the information can be exchanged, reviewed, and commented on by managers from different functional areas representing other perspectives can facilitate the interpretive process of the information and could lead to more innovative responses. When informal communication and cooperative practices are combined with a degree of power dispersion that allows managers to take certain responsive actions, the speed of sensing, interpreting, and reacting to environmental changes is enhanced. Hence, providing managers with some dispersed decision power that allows them to take initiatives can enhance both the speed of actions as well as the quality of outcomes from those actions, because the responsive decisions are made close to all the relevant information and market understanding located in the field.[23]

Information technology enhanced communication capabilities among decentralized decision nodes can improve the managers' ability to involve functional specialists in other parts of the organization in the decision process and coordinate organizational actions. This can provide more reflective assessments of environmental trends, impose better coordination of possible corporate actions taken on the basis of the available information, and thereby improve the quality of decision outcomes. Cooperative agreements and alliances with external organizations that might possess specialized skills and knowledge can also help the corporation's ability to enrich the supportive information flows and take more appropriate and effective actions in response to changing conditions. The development of external networks of specialized institutions and individual specialists facilitates the dispersed decision makers' ability to interpret change and develop effective responses, because they can absorb relevant information and learn things that are crucial to develop successful responses.

One of the major challenges for the responsive corporation is to integrate the strategic thinking, centralized coordination, performance and exposure reporting that constitute the essential parts of the strategic planning process with a decentralized organizational structure based on management involvement and dispersed decision making capabilities. Embracing risk management in this integrative strategic planning approach may entail the following elements:

● Perform regular strategic analyses to gather environmental information and business ideas from the field and assess them in a 'grand' strategy perspective.
● Involve key managers in the regular strategic planning discussions and have them participate selectively in decisions of strategic importance.
● Establish flat non-hierarchical organizational structures with some dispersion of decision power to middle managers that allow them to take new initiatives.
● Maintain regular vertical communication channels up and down the hierarchy as well as lateral communication networks across functional managers and specialists.
● Instil an organizational climate that encourages informal communication to reduce information distortion and increase speed.
● Develop integrative information and data communication systems and support their implementation and use throughout the organization.

## Conclusion

Competitive environments are becoming increasingly dynamic across industries and impose new demands on corporate risk management capabilities. The new risk factors extend well beyond conventional financial and market related exposures and confront management with risk factors that are more difficult to measure, such as economic, competitive, and strategic risks. These diverse risks should be considered in an integrated manner to assess the overall performance effects on the enterprise. A real options approach can facilitate strategic considerations under these uncertain circumstances but must be supported by an effective strategy process that involves key constituents in environmental scanning and interpretive activities.

## Summary

- The risks associated with contemporary competitive environments are increasingly characterized by uncertainty in the form of unknowability and management will have to find ways to deal effectively with this reality.

- Strategic resource commitments are characterized by managers' *ex ante* risk assessment in preparation for decision-making under uncertainty but the methodologies applied in these analyses are based on measures of *ex post* risk phenomena.

- General risk awareness at the managerial echelons and among organizational members at large is a prerequisite for the development of strategic response capabilities and dealing more effectively with environmental uncertainty.

- Operational risk management can be considered within a total quality control perspective and real options management can be adapted in the strategy process to deal with competitive and strategic risk exposures that are harder to measure.

- The risk management process and the strategic management process are compatible organizational functions and risk management should be an ingrained part of strategic management.

### Questions

11.1  Explain how the external competitive environment is changing.

11.2  What can corporate management do in response to the new competitive environment?

11.3  Outline the formal risk management process and list approaches to deal with the diverse risk exposures.

11.4  Explain the underlying idea behind the real options perspective.

11.5  How can a real options approach support corporate risk management?

11.6  Explain the rationale behind the return factor and the time-variance factor.

## Exercises

11.1 Corporate management has identified the following strategic options available to them through engaged discussions among key constituents throughout the organization and have developed best estimates for their related value characteristics:

(i) Introduction of a new consumer electronics product based on a tested technology.

$P = €145$ million; $S = €105$ million; $t = 2$ years; $v = 25\%$

(ii) A joint venture with a leading technology firm to develop a new technology with many promising market applications.

$P = €55$ million; $S = €5$ million; $t = 5$ years; $v = 65\%$

(iii) Entry into a new geographical market with an existing successful product.

$P = €75$ million; $S = €60$ million; $t = 180$ days; $v = 25\%$

(iv) Improving internal production and procurement processes on existing product lines.

$P = €45$ million; $S = €20$ million; $t = 1$ year; $v = 15\%$

(v) Research and development project to extend an existing technology to new product uses.

$P = €100$ million; $S = €10$ million; $t = 8$ years; $v = 50\%$

(a) Plot the projects into a return/time-variance map.
(b) What you think should be done with each of the five strategic options?
(c) Do you think the options are interrelated and what are some potential implications of this?

## Notes

[1] See, for example, D'Aveni, R. A. (1994), *Hypercompetition*, Free Press.
[2] See, Knight, F. (1921), *Risk, Uncertainty, and Profit*, Houghton Mifflin.
[3] See, for example, Kahneman, D. and Tversky, A. (1979), 'Prospect theory: an analysis of decisions under risk', *Econometrica*, **47**, pp. 263–92.
[4] See, Galbraith, J. R. (1977), *Organization Design*, Addison-Wesley.
[5] See, Burns, T. and Stalker, G. M. (1961), *The Management of Innovation*, Tavistock.
[6] See, Froot, K. A., Scharfstein, D. S. and Stein, J. C. (1994), 'A framework for risk management', *Harvard Business Review*, **72**(6), pp. 91–110.
[7] See, Miller, K. D. and Chen, W. (2003), 'Risk and firms' costs', *Strategic Organization*, **1**, pp. 355–82.
[8] Palmer, T. B. and Wiseman, R. M. (1999), 'Decoupling risk taking from income stream uncertainty: a holistic model of risk', *Strategic Management Journal*, **20**, pp. 1037–62.
[9] Low, J. and Siesfeld, T. (1998), 'Measures that matter', *Strategy & Leadership*, March/April.
[10] See, for example, Lam, J. (2003), *Enterprise Risk Management*, Wiley.

[11] See, for example, Aldrich, H. E. and Auster, E. (1986), 'Even dwarfs started small: liabilities of age and size and their strategic implications', *Research in Organizational Behaviour*, **VIII**, pp. 165–98.

[12] See Bettis, R. and Prahalad, C. K. (1995), 'The dominant logic: retrospective and extension', *Strategic Management Journal*, **16**, pp. 5–14.

[13] Levinthal, D. A. and March, J. G. (1991), 'The myopia of learning', *Strategic Management Journal*, **14**, pp. 95–112.

[14] See, for example, Nonaka, I. (1994), 'A dynamic theory of organizational knowledge creation', *Organization Science*, **5**, pp. 14–37.

[15] Schrøder, P. W. (2004), 'Barriers to effective enterprise risk management programs', unpublished dissertation, Henley Management College.

[16] Sitkin, S. B., Sutcliffe, K. M. and Schroeder, R. G. (1994), 'Distinguishing control from learning in total quality management: a contingency perspective', *Academy of Management Review*, **16**, pp. 537–64.

[17] March, J. G. (1991), 'Exploration and exploitation in organizational learning', *Organization Science*, **1**, pp. 71–87.

[18] See, for example, Kaplan, R. S. and Norton, D. P. (1996), 'Strategic learning and the balanced scorecard', *Strategy & Leadership*, **24**(5), pp. 18–24.

[19] This example is extracted from Andersen, T. J., Carroll, T. A., Shierstadt, P. and Tromholdt, N. (2001), 'A real options approach to strategy making', Strategic Management Society Annual International Conference, San Francisco, October 2001.

[20] See, for example, Bowman, E. H. and Hurry, D. (1993), 'Strategy through the options lens: an integrated view of resource investments and the incremental-choice process', *Academy of Management Review*, **18**, pp. 760–82.

[21] See, Luehrman, T. A. (1998), 'Strategy as a portfolio of real options', *Harvard Business Review*, **76**(5), pp. 89–99.

[22] See, for example, DeLoach, J. W. (2000), *Enterprise-Wide Risk Management*, Financial Times-Prentice Hall.

[23] Andersen, T. J. (2004), 'Integrating decentralized strategy making and strategic planning processes in dynamic environments', *Journal of Management Studies*, **41**, pp. 1271–99.

# Glossary

**Abandonment option** – an opportunity but not an obligation to withdraw from a business activity.

**American option** – an option that can be exercised at any time before the expiration date.

**Arbitrageur** – agents trading assets across different markets to earn a risk free return from price differentials on the same assets.

**Arrow** – an option settled at the average market price during the life of the option.

**Asset swap** – an agreement stipulating a future exchange of two financial assets if a predefined credit default event occurs.

**Asset swap swap** – an agreement stipulating a future exchange of two credit swaps if a predefined credit default event occurs.

**Attachment point** – the lower loss level defining a layer of a specific risk phenomenon.

**At-the-money** – when the market price of the underlying asset is equal to the option's strike price.

**Average rate option** – an option settled at the average market price during the life of the option.

**Back-end set swap** – an interest rate swap where the floating rate is determined by the LIBOR rate at the end of the settlement period (see **delayed reset swap** and **in-arrears swap**).

**Backwardation** – when commodities are traded lower in the future than in the spot market (see **inverted market**).

**Balanced scorecard** – an internal reporting system focused on essential measures of economic performance, customer satisfaction, operational efficiency, and supportive capabilities.

**Bankruptcy risk** – the chance that a firm will be unable to fulfil its commercial and financial obligations and as a consequence must go into bankruptcy.

**Barrier option** – an option contract where exercise is triggered by the market price crossing a second threshold before final maturity.

**Basel accords** – agreements sponsored by the Bank for International Settlement proposing a global standard for minimum capital requirements and other regulatory conditions in the banking industry.

**Bid limit** – all market participants want to buy (see **limit up**).

**Bid rate** – the price at which a participant in the interbank market is willing to buy the financial asset or instrument.

**Bond future** – a contract formalizing an exchange of a longer-term interest-bearing financial asset in a standardized amount at a given future date.

**Bought deals** – new securities issues where underwriters guarantee placement at a minimum price.

**BPV (basis point value) factor** – the relative price change of two financial assets.

**Break forward** – a forward foreign exchange rate that can be unwound at a predetermined rate.

**Brownian motion with drift** – an ongoing process where incremental changes in outcomes are a function of time. Influenced by a stochastic element (noise) along a longer-term trend (**drift rate**).

**Butterfly** – an option position combining a vertical bull spread and vertical bear spread.

**Calendar spread** – a position in options contracts with the same strike price but different expiration dates.

**Call bull spread** – an option position established by a long call and a short call at a higher strike price.

**Call option** – a right but not an obligation to buy an asset at a given price at a future date.

**Call swaption** – an agreement that provides the holder with the right to buy a swap, i.e. pay fixed rate against floating rate, on predetermined conditions (see **payers**).

**Call writer** – the provider or seller of a call option.

**Cancellable swap** – interest rate swap with a right, but no obligation, to exchange periodic fixed rate payments against floating rate payments.

**Cap** – an interest rate agreement that compensates the holder if the interest rate increases over a certain threshold level.

**Caption** – an option on a ceiling rate agreement or cap.

**Capital accounts** – the parts of the official balance of payment accounts that register capital transactions, such as bank lending and depositing, securities placement and investment.

**Capital market line** – indicates the exchange of consumption between different time periods as determined by the applicable term interest rate.

**Capital requirement** – a minimum required ratio between shareholders' equity and total assets.

**Carrying charge** – when short-term futures prices are lower than longer-term futures prices (see **contango** and **normal market**).

**Cash market** – the day-to-day market for an asset.

**Catastrophe swap** – an agreement stipulating exchanges of regular premiums against a future compensation if a predefined catastrophe event occurs.

**Cat-bond** – corporate bond whose return is influenced by the occurrence of a catastrophe event.

**Ceiling rate agreement** – an interest rate agreement that compensates the holder if the interest rate increases over a certain threshold level.

**Closing out** – reversing a futures position by buying or selling a similar amount of contracts before the contract maturity date.

**Closing transaction** – a futures trade or delivery under contracts terms that offsets an open position.

**Collar rate agreement** – a combined ceiling rate and floor rate agreement.

**Collateralized mortgage obligations** – securities issued on the basis of cash flows received on a portfolio of mortgage loans that are structured in tranches with different payment structures.

**Committed backstop facility** – a commitment to provide short-term funding typically to support a commercial paper or medium-term note issuer in case the conventional market is dried up.

**Commitment fee** – a fee paid by a potential borrower to a financial institution for making a credit facility available on fixed terms.

**Commodity swap** – periodic exchanges of fixed oil commodity and variable commodity price amounts.

**Competency trap** – overemphasis on existing success criteria to the detriment of developing capabilities to compete in the future.

**Complexity** – the level of issue diversity management must deal with.

**Compound option** – the right but not the obligation to acquire another option on predetermined conditions at a future date (see **option-on-option**).

**Contango** – when commodities are traded higher in the future than in the spot market because future delivery saves storage costs (see **carrying charge** and **normal market**).

**Contingent surplus notes** – put options that provide the holder with the right to place securities, e.g. common equity, preferred equity, and senior debt instruments, on predetermined conditions once a certain indicator has exceeded a certain threshold level.

**Contracting option** – an opportunity but not an obligation to scale down on a business activity.

**Convergence** – the movement of the futures price towards the cash market price of the underlying asset as the contract maturity date gets closer.

**Conversion** – the creation of a risk free position by going long the asset, long a put on the asset, and short a call on the asset.

**Conversion factor** – the par value multiplier that converts the value of a given cash flow structure into a standardized bond.

**Covered call** – writing a call option while holding a corresponding portfolio of the underlying asset.

**Credit default swap** – exchange of periodic interest amounts, premiums, against compensation if a credit event takes place before maturity.

**Credit spread swap** – exchange of periodic interest amounts, premiums, against compensation if the yield on a reference asset exceeds a predetermined level or a predefined credit spread is exceeded.

**Credit swap** – an agreement that provides the holder (buyer or hedger) with the right to received compensation (from the seller) in case a credit event occurs before maturity.

**Cross-currency hedge** – trade in interest rate and foreign exchange derivatives denominated in one currency to reduce an exposure in another currency.

**Cross hedging** – using a derivative with one underlying asset to hedge a position in another asset.

**Cross rates** – foreign exchange rate quotes denominated as the amount of one foreign currency per unit of another foreign currency.

**Currency and interest rate swap** – periodic exchanged of fixed-rate interest amounts in one currency for floating rate interest amounts in another currency.

**Currency exposure** – arises from a mismatch between assets and liabilities denominated in different currencies whereby the conversion of those futures cash flows into the currency of accounting provides an exposure to changes in the foreign exchange rates.

**Currency forwards** – an agreement between two parties to exchange one currency for another at a predetermined foreign exchange rate at a future point in time.

**Currency future** – a contract formalizing an exchange of one currency for another in a standardized amount at a given future date.

**Currency hedge** – trade in derivatives or other risk-transfer instruments to reduce a currency exposure.

**Currency swap** – periodic exchanges of payments in one currency for another currency.

**Current accounts** – the parts of the official balance of payment accounts that register trade transactions, earnings flows, such as interest payments and dividends, and one-way transfers.

**Cylinder option** – an option structure combining a long call with a short call at a lower strike price or a long put with a short put at a higher strike price thus reducing overall premium costs.

**Day trader** – a speculator taking positions during the trading day.

**Debt-equity swaps** – the exchange of debtor exposures for ownership exposures between two counterparts.

**Deferral option** – an opportunity but not an obligation to postpone a business activity.

**Delayed reset swap** – interest rate swap where the floating rate is determined by the LIBOR rate at the end of the settlement period (see **back-end swap** and **in-arrears swap**).

**Delayed start swap** – interest rate swap executed at a future date (see **forward swap**).

**Delivering** – the commitment to provide the standardized asset specified in the futures contract at expiry.

**Delta** – the amount by which the option premium changes when the market price of the underlying asset changes.

**Delta hedge** – using the sensitivity of options contracts to the market price of the underlying asset to create a hedge against price changes in that asset.

**Delta value** – the incremental change in the futures price for a marginal change in the price of the underlying asset.

**Derivatives** – financial instruments whose value is based on (derived from) the price of a financial asset, a commodity, or other defined construct (the underlying asset).

**Differential swap** – interest rate and currency swap where the interest amount can be paid in a currency that is different from the rate basis.

**Direct insurance** – the sale of insurance contracts directly to customers.

**Direct quote** – a foreign exchange rate quote denominated as the amount of domestic currency per foreign currency unit.

**Discount market** – see **inverted market**.

**Dominant logic** – a common mindset developed by managers as they gain experiences from operating in a specific business environment over longer periods of time.

**Drift rate** – the change per time unit in the Brownian motion as an idicator of a longer-term trend.

**Drop-in option** – a call or a put option structured as a barrier option.

**Drop-in call** – a barrier option where the call can be exercised if the market price has been below the second threshold level.

**Drop-in put** – a barrier option where the call can be exercised if the market price has been above the second threshold level.

**Drop-out option** – a call or a put option structured as a barrier option.

**Drop-out call** – a barrier option where the call cannot be exercised if the market price has been below the second threshold level.

**Drop-out put** – a barrier option where the call cannot be exercised if the market price has been above the second threshold level.

**Duration** – the weighted average maturity of future cash flow streams using the present value of each of the future cash flows as the weight.

**Duration gap** – the difference between the duration of assets and liabilities.

**Duration hedge** – trade in derivatives or other risk-transfer instruments to reduce a duration gap.

**Dynamism** – the variability of issues management must deal with.

**Economic exposure** – all cash flow effects imposed by changes in foreign exchange rates on registered as well as expected future business activities.

**Efficient frontier** – the combinations of possible investment alternatives that will provide the highest expected returns for a given level of risk.

**Enterprise risk management** – an integrative approach to manage all the risks that expose the corporation and influence the ability to achieve intended outcomes.

**Equity index swap** – periodic exchanges of equity index determined and floating rate interest amounts.

**Eta** – the amount by which the option premium changes when the volatility of the option is changed.

**Euro market** – extension of credit in a national economy denominated in other currencies than the currency of that nation.

**European option** – an option that can be exercised only on the expiration date.

**Exchange delivery settlement price** – the quoted price of a bond future.

**Exercise** – the option holder's use of the right to buy or sell the underlying asset.

**Exercise price** – the price at which the option holder can use the right to buy or sell the underlying asset.

**Exhaustion point** – the upper loss level defining a layer of a specific risk phenomenon.

**Expansion option** – an opportunity but not an obligation to extend or expand a business activity.

**Expectations theory** – the proposition that interest rates are determined by the expectation of borrowers and lenders in the capital market about the future interest rate structure.

**Expiration date** – the final date on which a futures contract can be traded and an option can be exercised.

**Financial engineering** – creating more complex derivatives through combinations of generic derivatives.

**Flat rate forward** – a series of forward foreign exchange agreements settled at the same forward foreign exchange rate.

**Floor rate agreement** – an interest rate agreement that compensates the holder if the interest rate decreases below a certain threshold level.

**Foreign market** – extension of credit to non-residents of a national economy denominated in the national currency.

**Forward foreign exchange rate** – the foreign exchange rate applicable to a currency exchange at some future date.

**Forward plus** – an option contract where the buyer pays no premium but shares part of the potential gain at maturity.

**Forward rate agreement** – an agreement between two parties to fix a future interest rate.

**Forward rates** – the implied return during a future time period.

**Forward swap** – interest rate swap executed at a future date (see **delayed start swap**).

**Fox** – a forward foreign exchange rate that can be unwound at a predetermined rate.

**Futures contract** – a legal commitment to exchange a standardized form of an asset at a quoted price on a specific future date.

**Gamma** – the amount by which the delta of an option changes when the market price of the underlying asset changes.

**Gamma scalping** – a delta hedge on a straddle position that allows the hedger to generate income when the price of the underlying asset varies.

**Global capital market** – the stage for credit intermediation across all national markets and funds exchanges between them.

**Go long swap** – buy floating rate LIBOR based interest payments against fixed rate payments.

**Go short swap** – sell floating rate LIBOR based interest payments against fixed rate payments.

**Hedge accounting** – offset of gains and losses on derivatives against losses and gains incurred on hedged positions.

**Hedger** – an entity acting to eliminate, reduce, or modify an underlying risk exposure.

**Hedge ratio** – the amount by which the option premium changes when the market price of the underlying asset changes.

**Historical simulation** – is used when the actual market prices of all the assets included in the invested portfolio provide the basis to assess the expected risk-return profile of the portfolio.

**Hybrid security** – corporate bond where the return is influenced by one ore more exogenous factors.

**Hypercompetition** – a state of ongoing innovation where product markets continuously change character and companies engage in relentless competition by disrupting the status quo.

**Immunization** – trade in derivatives or other risk-transfer instruments to eliminate an interest rate exposure.

**Implied volatility** – the volatility corresponding to the market price quoted on an option based on the Black and Scholes theoretical valuation model.

**In-arrears swap** – an interest rate swap where the floating rate is determined by the LIBOR rate at the end of the settlement period (see **back-end set swap** and **delayed reset swap**).

**Information processing** – an organizing perspective suggesting that organizational structure is influenced by the environmental requirements to process information.

**Initial margin** – the money paid when a futures contract is traded on the exchange.

**Interbank market** – a dealer based market structure where participants trade on the basis of freely quoted two-way prices on financial assets and instruments.

**Intercommodity spread** – a position in futures contracts with underlying assets of different maturities.

**Intercurrency spread** – a position in comparable interest rate futures contract in different currencies.

**Intermarket spread** – a position in comparable futures contracts traded on different exchanges.

**Interest only** – securities issued on the basis of cash flows received on a portfolio of mortgage loans where payments constitute the interest amounts.

**Interest rate basis swap** – periodic exchanges of basis rate and floating rate interest amounts.

**Interest rate exposure** – arises from a mismatch between the maturity of assets and liabilities whereby the pricing of investment and funding takes place at different points in time thereby creating an exposure to changes in interest rates over time.

**Interest rate hedge** – trade in derivatives or other risk-transfer instruments to reduce an interest rate exposure.

**Interest rate swap** – periodic exchanges of fixed-rate and floating-rate interest amounts between two counterparts.

**Interest rate basis swap** – an agreement stipulating regular future exchanges of interest rate amounts between two counterparts based on two different interest rate bases.

**Interest rate future** – a contract formalizing an exchange of a short-term interest-bearing financial asset in a standardized amount at a given future date.

**In-the-money** – when an option contract can be exercised at a profit.

**Intramarket spread** – a spread position assumed within the same futures market.

**Intrinsic value** – the value of an asset determined by the individual investor or the profit made from exercise of an option at expiration.

**Inverted market** – when short-term futures prices are higher than longer-term futures prices.

**Investment opportunity set** – the maximum possible productive output (consumption) under a given resource endowment.

**Investor** – an agent acquiring derivative instruments with the purpose of obtaining future returns on the capital used to acquire and trade the derivatives until they expire.

**Itô process** – a Brownian motion with drift where the drift rate and the noise element are functions of the outcome variable and time.

**Latent options** – real options framed by the firm's existing resources but not yet recognized.

**Layer** – the loss levels between which the reinsurance company has assumed an exposure to a specified risk phenomenon.

**Lead-manager** – the leading institution in the management group of investment banks that complete a new securities issue or other major financial transaction.

**Limit down** – all market participants want to sell.

**Limit up** – all market participants want to buy (see **bid limit**).

**Limited option** – an option contract where the premium is paid on the expiration date.

**Liquidity hypothesis** – the proposition that interest rates are determined by the liquidity preferences of borrowers and lenders in the capital market.

**Loan participation** – the ability to buy into a share of a larger syndicated loan facility whether in connection with the initial loan arrangement or at a later time before maturity.

**Long-dated forward** – exchange of one currency for another currency on future dates that are beyond common maturities in the spot money markets, e.g. 10–20 years.

**Long interest rate hedge** – trade in derivatives or other risk-transfer instruments to reduce the interest rate exposure of an investor.

**Long position** – a spot or future purchase of, or a current investment in, an asset.

**Look-back option** – an option settled at the market price during the life of the option that is most favourable to the holder.

**Macro hedging** – offsetting gains and losses on all derivatives against losses and gains incurred on interest rate and currency exposures.

**Maintenance margin** – an additional margin required throughout the life of a future or options contract if the value of contract position declines.

**Management group** – the investment banks that work together to structure and complete a new securities issue or other major financial transaction.

**Managerial risk** – the *ex ante* risk assumed by decision makers that are confronted with an uncertain future.

**Market segmentation theory** – the proposition that interest rates are determined by the institutional behaviours of borrowers and lenders in specific parts of the capital market.

**Mark-to-market** – valuing and posting an asset at its current market value on the official balance sheet.

**Medium-term note issuance facility** – an arrangement whereby a group of financial institutions commit to support a borrower with the issuance and placement of securities with medium-term maturities.

**Modified duration** – the duration measure divided by one plus the interest rate. It indicates the absolute change in asset value for a given change in the interest rate.

**Mortgage-backed securities** – securities issued on the basis of cash flows received on a portfolio of mortgage loans typically through a special purpose vehicle.

**Monte Carlo simulation** – is used when the variance-covariance calculations of returns on all assets in the invested portfolio are used to generate random market events that provide the basis to assess the expected risk-return profile of the portfolio.

**Multiplier** – the link between the price of an index future and the value of the underlying index.

**Munificence** – a setting enjoying relatively favourable performance conditions.

**Naked call** – writing a call option without holding the underlying asset.

**Net present value** – the resulting valuation of cash flow streams that aggregate the future cash flows discounted to their present values with inflows counted positive and outflows negative.

**Noise** – the stochastic or random element of a Brownian motion.

**Normal market** – when short-term futures prices are lower than longer-term futures prices (see **carrying charge** and **contango**).

**NVP factor** – the relative return on options exercise expressed as the investment value over the cash outlay.

**Offer rate** – the price at which a participant in the interbank market is willing to sell the financial asset or instrument.

**Offsetting transaction** – buying or selling a futures contract to close an open short or long futures position.

**Oil swap** – periodic exchanges of fixed oil price and variable oil price amounts.

**Open interest** – the total number of a given future or options contract that are outstanding on the exchange.

**Open position** – the sale or purchase of a futures contract that commits the holder to deliver or take delivery of an asset without a countervailing long or short position in the asset.

**Operating exposure** – the effects imposed by changes in foreign exchange rates on the cash flows deriving from longer-term changes in economic conditions.

**Option-on-an-option** – the right but not the obligation to acquire another option on predetermined conditions at a future date (see **compound option**).

**Option premium** – the market price of an option agreement.

**Organizational risk** – the *ex post* risk reflecting the organization's ability to moderate its income stream.

**Original margin** – the money paid when a futures contract is traded on the exchange.

**Out-of-the-money** – when exercise of an option has no profit.

**Outright rate** – the forward foreign exchange rate determined in practice in the interbank market based on the interest rate differential between the two currencies.

**Par forward** – a series of forward foreign exchange agreements settled at the same forward foreign exchange rate.

**Participating forward** – an option contract where the buyer pays no premium but shares part of the potential gain at maturity.

**Payers** – an agreement that provides the holder with the right to buy a swap, i.e. pay fixed rate against floating rate, on predetermined conditions (see **call swaption**).

**Perpetual deferral option** – an opportunity but not an obligation to postpone a business activity in perpetuity.

**Portfolio hedging** – adapting the interest rate risk associated with an invested portfolio or a debt portfolio.

**Position limit** – the maximum uncovered position in an underlying asset.

**Position trader** – a speculator taking short-term positions.

**Price limit** – the maximum allowable change in the market price during a trading day.

**Principal only** – securities issued on the basis of cash flows received on a portfolio of mortgage loans where payments constitute the principal repayment.

**Prospect theory** – a perspective suggesting that risk behaviour is influenced by situational circumstances, i.e. decision makers become risk averse when performance prospects are positive and risk seeking when performance prospects are negative.

**Purchasing power parity** – the proposition that global market prices and interest rates will remain unchanged in real terms.

**Put bear spread** – an option position established by a long put and a short put at a lower strike price.

**Put option** – a right but not an obligation to sell an asset at a given price at a future date.

**Put swaption** – an agreement that provides the holder with the right to sell a swap, i.e. receive fixed rate against floating rate, on predetermined conditions (see **receivers**).

**Put writer** – the provider or seller of a put option.

**Range forward** – a cylinder option determined by two strike prices that results in zero premium cost.

**Ratio call spread** – an option position established by a long call and a number of short calls at a higher strike price.

**Ratio put spread** – an option position established by one long put and a number of short puts at a lower strike price.

**Real estate mortgage investment conduit (REMIC)** – a defined legal entity engaged in pass-through securitization of mortgage loans and therefore are tax exempt from US federal tax.

**Real estate swap** – periodic exchanges of real estate price index determined and floating rate interest amounts.

**Real option structure** – an opportunity but not an obligation to carry out particular actions at some future time.

**Receivers** – an agreement that provides the holder with the right to sell a swap, i.e. receive fixed rate against floating rate, on predetermined conditions (see **put swaption**).

**Receiving** – the right to receive (acquire) the standardized asset specified in the futures contract at expiry.

**Reference rate** – the agreed interest rate basis in a forward rate agreement.

**Regression coefficient** – the linear relationship between two variables expressed in a regression equation.

**Reinsurance** – the sale of insurance exposures to market professionals specialized in buying parts of insurance portfolios or special exposures from primary insurers.

**Reinvestment risk** – a mismatch situation where there is a need to replace investment arrangements that create an exposure to changes in investment returns.

**Reportable limit** – the minimum number of contracts above which a trader must report total positions.

**Re-pricing gap** – a mismatch situation where there is a need to renew funding arrangements that create an exposure to changes in the funding rates.

**Required rate of return** – the yield required by investors in general to acquire all outstanding financial assets of a specific class.

**Reserve position** – the part of the official balance of payment accounts that register the country's official reserve deposits in foreign currency usually held by the Central Bank.

**Return factor** – the natural logarithm of the investment value divided by the cash outlay needed to complete the investment.

**Revolving term facility** – a credit arrangement where funding is provided over longer periods of time through periodic execution of short-term funding instruments.

**Rho** – the amount by which the option premium changes when the interest rate is changed.

**Risk** – the potential for downside loss and/or failure to capture upside potential often measured by the standard deviation of returns.

**Risk factor** – an environmental condition that may give rise to a risk exposure.

**Risk-linked security** – corporate bond where the return is influenced by the development of an exogenous risk factor.

**Risk swap** – an agreement stipulating exchanges of regular premiums against a future compensation if a predefined risk event occurs.

**Sales consortium** – a group of securities firms engaged by a manager typically in connection with a new securities issue to support the placement of securities to end-investors.

**Scale-down floor** – a hybrid derivative combining floor rate agreements with different strike prices in a ratio put spread.

**Scalper** – speculators taking extremely short-term positions, e.g. measured in minutes.

**Scout** – a tender to contract option bought by a contract awarder who buys the option and offers it to participating tenderers at reduced premiums (see **tender to contract**).

**Settlement amount** – the differential interest amounts exchanged between two parties to forward rate agreement.

**Sharpe ratio** – the relationship between the expected return of an invested portfolio and the risk associated with that investment.

**Short interest rate hedge** – trade in derivatives or other risk-transfer instruments to reduce the interest rate exposure of a borrower.

**Short position** – a spot or future sale of an asset or existing liability.

**Short-term commercial paper** – a promissory note issued by institutional borrowers typically with maturities of less than 6 months.

**Smile curve** – plots of the implied volatility of option contracts against their strike prices.

**Special drawing rights** – facilities that allow countries to draw additional funds from the IMF on predetermined conditions as an incremental component of international liquidity.

**Special purpose vehicle** – a separate legal entity established solely for the purpose of completing a specific financial transaction, such as, securities issuance based on asset receivables.

**Speculator** – agents taking a position on an asset in the expectation of a future gain.

**Spot market** – the day-to-day market for an asset.

**Spread option swap** – an agreement stipulating exchanges of regular premiums against a future compensation if the difference between two predefined credit spreads exceeds a predetermined level.

**Spread position** – a position in the same futures contract with different maturity dates.

**Stock index future** – a contract formalizing an exchange of a given index in a standardized amount at a given future date.

**Stock option** – a contract providing the holder with the right but not the obligation to acquire a specific stock at a predetermined price at a given future date.

**Straddle** – a double option position established by a long call and put at the same strike price.

**Strangle** – a double option position established by a long call and a long put at a lower strike price.

**Strategic action space** – the alternative strategic opportunities available that may allow an organization to shift the use of its resources and reposition itself in the market.

**Strategic control** – a follow-up process monitoring the organization's ability to reach intended strategic objectives.

**Strategic option** – a real option structure that may influence the future strategic direction of the corporation.

**Strike price** – the price at which the option holder can use the right to buy or sell the underlying asset.

**Structured security** – a coupon-bearing or zero-coupon bond combined with one or more risk derivatives reflecting an exposure specific to the issuer.

**Swap** – the difference between the spot foreign exchange rate and the forward foreign exchange rate.

**Swaption** – option on a swap.

**Switching option** – an opportunity but not an obligation to switch a business activity from one part of the organization to another thereby changing the use of corporate assets.

**Synthetic** – a determination of a future foreign exchange rate or interest rate through transactions in the spot money and foreign exchange markets.

**Tender to contract** – an option where the full premium is payable only on predetermined conditions, e.g. fulfillment of bidding contract (see **scout**).

**Term structure of interest rates** – the relationship between the risk free yields for different maturities often illustrated by graphically.

**Theta** – the amount by which the option premium changes when the time to maturity is reduced.

**Three-way arbitrage** – the ability to earn a risk free return by engaging in foreign exchange trades across three currency areas.

**Time decay** – the amount by which the option premium changes when the time to maturity is reduced.

**Time value** – the difference between the option premium and the intrinsic value.

**Time-variance factor** – the relative value potential in the option expressed by the square root of the time to exercise multiplied by the volatility of the investment value.

**Trading limit** – the maximum price movements allowed by a futures and options exchange.

**Transaction exposure** – the effects imposed by changes in foreign exchange rates on the cash flows deriving from registered future transactions.

**Translation exposure** – the bookkeeping effects imposed by changes in foreign exchange rates on the income statement from assets and liabilities accounted for in the official balance sheet.

**Traynor ratio** – the relationship between the expected return of an invested portfolio and the return of the total market portfolio.

**Trend position** – a position based on an expected future price development in the futures contract or the underlying asset.

**Turbulence** – the combined influence of issue diversity and variability.

**Two-stage abandonment option** – an abandonment option where the opportunity to withdraw from a business activity is structured into two subsequent stages at different future times.

**Utility curves** – the maximum level of general 'satisfaction' an agent, an organization, or a society can obtain from a given productive output (consumption).

**Unbundling** – the separation of a financial transaction into its smaller components.

**Uncertainty** – the elements of the future that cannot be known in advance exemplified by the emergence of unexpected events.

**Uncovered call** – writing a call option without holding the underlying asset.

**Under investment problem** – arises when managers are unwilling to assume incremental risk and thereby avoid committing to positive net present value projects.

**Underwriting** – a commitment to acquire securities from an issuer at a minimum price typically provided by an investment bank in connection with a new securities issue.

**Value-at-risk** – an indication of the expected potential loss incurred on an invested portfolio at a specified level of statistical confidence.

**Variance–covariance approach** – is used when the risk-return profile of the invested portfolio is assessed from variance and covariance of returns across all the assets included in the portfolio.

**Variation margin** – an additional margin required throughout the life of a future or options contract if the value of contract position declines.

**Vega** – the amount by which the option premium changes when the volatility of the option is changed.

**Vertical bear spread** – a double option position established by a long put and short call at a higher strike price.

**Vertical bull spread** – a double option position established by a long call and short put at a lower strike price.

**Volatility** – the annualized standard deviation in returns.

**Volatility spreads** – positions in options contracts with different levels of implied volatility.

**Yield-to-maturity** – the implied return on a financial asset at its current market price.

**Zero-coupon rate** – the implied return on a single future cash flow at a specific maturity.

# Index

Notes:
1. Page numbers in **bold** indicate definitions in **glossary** and **text**
2. Page numbers in *italics* indicate chapters